'You know it makes sense.'

THE COMPLETE A–Z OF

BY RICHARD WEBBER
WITH JOHN SULLIVAN

ORION

Contents

First published in 2002
by Orion Books Ltd.
Orion House, 5 Upper St. Martin's Lane
London WC2H 9EA

Text Copyright © Richard Webber 2002

Personal photos were provided by the following:
Eric Walmsley; Sue Bishop; Phoebe De Gaye;
Saul Hunnaball; Adrian Pegg; Denis Lill;
Duncan Cooper; Janet Bone; Terry Dite;
Sandy Ross-Brown; Perry Aghajanoff;
Fred Mossman; Faye McCallum; Ian Nixon;
Bobby Bragg; Chris Wadsworth; Nigel Woodford
and David Hitchcock.

Other pictures supplied by: Radio Times

Sketch of Del's costume © Phoebe De Gaye

Sketches in 'The Return of the Trotters'
© David Hitchcock

A CIP catalogue record for this book
is available from the British Library.

ISBN 0-75284-731-7

Printed and bound in Italy by Printer Trento S.r.l.

Only Fools and Horses Television Episodes

Original transmission dates shown in brackets

Series 1
Big Brother (8/9/81)
Go West Young Man (15/9/81)
Cash and Curry (22/9/81)
The Second Time Around (29/9/81)
A Slow Bus to Chingford (6/10/81)
The Russians are Coming (13/10/81)

Christmas Special 1981
Christmas Crackers (28/12/81)

Series 2
The Long Legs of the Law (21/10/82)
Ashes to Ashes (28/10/82)
A Losing Streak (4/11/82)
No Greater Love… (11/11/82)
The Yellow Peril (18/11/82)
It Never Rains… (25/11/82)
A Touch of Glass (2/12/82)

Christmas Sketch 1982
The Funny Side of Christmas: Christmas Trees (27/12/82)

Christmas Special 1982
Diamonds are for Heather (30/12/82)

Series 3
Homesick (10/11/83)
Healthy Competition (17/11/83)
Friday the 14th (24/11/83)
Yesterday Never Comes (1/12/83)
May the Force be with You (8/12/83)
Wanted (15/12/83)
Who's a Pretty Boy? (22/12/83)

Christmas Special 1983
Thicker Than Water (25/12/83)

Series 4
Happy Returns (21/2/85)
Strained Relations (28/2/85)
Hole in One (7/3/85)
It's Only Rock and Roll (14/3/85)
Sleeping Dogs Lie (21/3/85)
Watching the Girls Go By (28/3/85)
As One Door Closes (4/4/85)

Christmas Special 1985
To Hull and Back (25/12/85)

Series 5
From Prussia with Love (31/8/86)
The Miracle of Peckham (7/9/86)
The Longest Night (14/9/86)
Tea for Three (21/9/86)
Video Nasty (28/9/86)
Who Wants to be a Millionaire? (5/10/86)

Christmas Special 1986
A Royal Flush (25/12/86)

Christmas Special 1987
The Frog's Legacy (25/12/87)

Christmas Special 1988
Dates (25/12/88)

Series 6
Yuppy Love (8/1/89)
Danger UXD (15/1/89)
Chain Gang (22/1/89)
The Unlucky Winner is… (29/1/89)
Sickness and Wealth (5/2/89)
Little Problems (12/2/89)

Christmas Special 1989
The Jolly Boys' Outing (25/12/89)

Christmas Special 1990
Rodney Come Home (25/12/90)

Series 7
The Sky's the Limit (30/12/90)
The Chance of a Lunchtime (6/1/91)
Stage Fright (13/1/91)
The Class of '62 (20/1/91)
He Ain't Heavy, He's My Uncle (27/1/91)
Three Men, a Woman and a Baby (3/2/91)

Christmas Special 1991
Miami Twice – Part 1: The American Dream (24/12/91)
Miami Twice – Part 2: Oh to be in England (25/12/91)

Christmas Special 1992
Mother Nature's Son (25/12/92)

Christmas Special 1993
Fatal Extraction (25/12/93)

Christmas Trilogy 1996
1 Heroes and Villains (25/12/96)
2 Modern Men (27/12/96)
3 Time On Our Hands (29/12/96)

Comic Relief Special (14/3/97)

Christmas Special 2001
If They Could See Us Now…! (25/12/01)

Remaining episodes yet to be seen as at date of writing
Strangers on the Shore
Sleepless in Peckham

'Lovely jubbly.'

Acknowledgements

So many people have helped in the production of the book. First and foremost I would like to thank John Sullivan for allowing me the opportunity to compile an A–Z on his award-winning series, and for giving up so much of his time during an incredibly busy period to talk about his creation.

Thanks, also, to screen legends Ray Galton and Alan Simpson for writing the foreword, and to Perry Aghajanoff, the president of the Only Fools and Horses Appreciation Society, for all his expertise and help.

I'm also grateful to all the actors, relatives and friends of deceased cast members and everyone in the production team over the years who were willing to complete questionnaires, chat on the phone, supply photos or drawings, or write about their memories of helping bring the sitcom alive. Thanks to David Jason for taking time out of his busy schedule to chat about *Only Fools*. Special thanks also to John Challis, Sue Holderness, Roger Lloyd Pack, Tessa Peake-Jones, Gwyneth Strong, Paul Barber, Roy Heather, Sheila MacDonald, Gareth Gwenlan, Ray Butt, Susan Belbin, Johnny Shier, Janet Bone, Penny Thompson, Graham Brown, Eric Walmsley, Michael Spencer, Adrian Pegg, Chris Wadsworth, Sandy Ross-Brown, Denis Lill, David Hitchcock, Jacky Levy, Angela Bruce, Chris Booth, Peta Bernard, Michèle Winstanley, Mark Sevant, Bill Morton, Don Babbage, Gareth Hunt, Jo Austin, Martin Shardlow, Doremy Vernon, Richard Greenough, Anne Bruzac, Alec Curtis, John Jarvis, Malcolm Rougvie, Tony Snoaden, Harold Snoad, Duncan Cooper, Colin Lavers, Chris Seager, Philip Pope, Simon Price, Andy Dimond, Peter Clayton, Steven Woodcock, Faye McCallum, Bernard Lloyd-Jones, Pheobe De Gaye, Sue Bishop, Angie De Chastelai Smith, Chris Ferriday, Chris Barker, Fred Mossman, Thelma Thomson, Nick Harding and everyone else who gave so much of their time – thank you all.

Among the other people I'd like to acknowledge are Neil Somerville and Simon Hall at the BBC, David Hamilton, Jacki Hastings at Lifeline, Ian Abraham, Iain Wilson, Ian Nixon, Saul Hunnaball, Bobby Bragg, Charlie Smith, Jim Trowers, Jan Francis, Jonathan Betts, Mona Adams, Terry Dite, Michael Ward, Peter Durrent, Hilary Johnson, Paula for helping with the overwhelming research, my agent Jeffrey Simmons, Don Smith (who not only helped supply most of the photos used in the book but took them as well), Keith Turley for allowing me to reproduce his excellent painting, Harry Green for his design expertise and last, but certainly not least, Trevor and Pandora at Orion.

Incidentally, anyone interested in contacting Keith Turley about his painting should call 01384 270143 or email him at showbizart@aol.com

Foreword
by Ray Galton and Alan Simpson

What a great pleasure to be asked to write the foreword to this splendid celebration of *Only Fools and Horses* and thus the genius of John Sullivan. This A–Z (or for those dyslexics amongst you P–C) is an invaluable compendium to those of you whose curiosity knows no bounds. It includes all those things you wanted to know about *Fools and Horses* but were afraid to ask.

In careers spanning over 50 years this is the first time we have been approached to write a tribute to a fellow writer. We tell a lie, we were once asked to provide a reference for Barry Cryer when he applied for his minicab licence. We didn't hear any more so we assume he got it. But that is a horse of a different feather. We don't have to perjure ourselves in extolling the talent of John Sullivan. It's not often one says 'I wish I'd written that' but with John's work this happens far too often. It doesn't help when next morning sadistic friends ask you if you enjoyed the show. You really shouldn't be expected to go through life with gritted teeth and a rictus smile. We have found the easiest way to avoid discomfort when a Sullivan series is on is not to watch television and avoid awards ceremonies altogether. It is very difficult to applaud with tightly clenched fists.

But seriously, folks, as Arthur Askey used to say (aah, those were the days), it really is a pleasure to salute John. He is a wonderful writer. Beautiful plotting; great characterisation; tight, crisp dialogue; a master of the art of comedy writing. He has reached the pinnacle of his craft. It doesn't come much better than Sullivan. The ability to make millions laugh is not given to many. As the great actor said on his deathbed when asked what it was like to die, 'Dying is easy, comedy is hard'. You take *Crime and Punishment*. A good book granted, but not a laugh in it. Most people cry at the same thing but they don't laugh at the same thing. But most people laugh at John Sullivan. Not that there isn't great drama in *Only Fools and Horses*, there is, that's what makes it so special.

In recent years many critics have written about the superiority of American sitcoms over the home grown variety. Be assured that *Fools and Horses* does not come into this category. Our American counterparts are written by teams of writers. At the date of writing this, 62 episodes of *Only Fools and Horses* are the product of just one man's mind. So now read on and take with you this picture of a lonely figure in a cold garret in South London, huddled over a flickering candle, quill in hand, crumpled paper strewn round his feet as he shakily lights his fresh Cohiba with a fifty pound note. John Sullivan, good luck to you. From two of your greatest admirers.

N.B. No money changed hands during the writing of this eulogy.

Interview with David Jason

'I was working on *Open All Hours* when Syd Lotterby, the director, handed me a script. He wanted me to read it and let him know my opinion. Ray Butt, who was having problems finding someone for Derek Trotter, had sent it to Syd, asking him to let me take a look at it. I read it overnight, passed it back to Syd and said: "I think it's fantastic." He asked, out of interest, what part I would have liked if it had been offered. At that time I was doing a lot of character parts, playing old men and all sorts of people, so I might well have been interested in Grandad. I told him it was one of the best scripts I'd read for a long time and I thought the central character of Del Boy was fantastic. And that was the end of it, or so I thought.

'A few days later I got a call to come in and read with Nick Lyndhurst, and that's how it all came about. Of course, there were a number of people before me that were considered for the part, and I was like the tail-end Charlie! John Sullivan will admit that he didn't think I would be right because I'd always played losers, and that was fair comment, but Ray Butt had seen my work and knew I could do a perfect London accent, so when I came in and read with Nick, John changed his mind.

'I'd never worked with Nick before, but our relationship formed quite quickly; when our names were put together, though, John Howard Davies, at the BBC, didn't think it would work because we didn't look like brothers. It was true, we weren't similar at all: Nick's about six foot six and I'm about four foot eleven! But we all thought that sometimes kids are completely different from their brothers and sisters. Eventually, of course, John Sullivan being John Sullivan used this to his advantage, developing the idea that maybe Del and Rodney are so different because they had different fathers.

'John is a brilliant writer who goes all-out for truth. He's one of the few people I know who's honest and true, and always gives credit where credit is due. That's an admirable trait. He's got a heart of gold and is as soft as putty.

'Nick, Lennard and I completed a few readings together before we were told they wanted us to play the parts. At that point, the three of us went up to the BBC bar for a celebratory drink. I remember saying to the others that there was something different about the script, something I hadn't seen before. I didn't believe it was a sitcom, I felt it was a sitcom drama, and as time went on John gradually started exploring more serious themes in the show.

'As you all probably know, the first series was only watched by about three people, and one of them was me! When it went out no one took us particularly seriously – after all, who'd ever heard of cockney people being in a successful situation comedy? It had always been middle-class families. I don't think a lot of people felt it had much of a future, and we got some disappointing viewing figures. One of the good things about the BBC at that time, was that the powers that be felt it was only fair to give it another outing because it shouldn't be judged on first airing. That attitude is is why so much of BBC comedy has been successful; they're prepared to wait,

whereas with ITV comedies, if you don't hit the ratings on the first time out, it's the axe.

'Nick and Lennard were great to work with. Although he was very young, Nick had spent his entire life, more or less, in the business because he'd been a child actor. Lennard Pearce, meanwhile, had been a stage actor for all his life – I'd even worked with him much earlier in rep. So we were dealing with actors who I had a healthy respect for because they had served their apprenticeship. Both of them were tremendously easy to get on with, but I think a lot of that was because we'd all worked a lot of time in the theatre, travelling the country, working every night with a live audience, learning our trade. That is hugely beneficial when you work in television. So with John Sullivan's scripts, and the experience of the cast, I knew we had the essential ingredients.

'The cast changed, of course, when dear Lennard died. We were filming when he was taken ill. We re-scheduled the filming, which meant we could carry on shooting the scenes without him, but then one morning we heard that he'd passed away. Obviously we just packed up and went home. Eventually we had to organise a meeting because the show had to go on. John, Ray, some other BBC executives and I discussed the way forward, and one of the suggestions was to get a look-a-like and just carry on. Both John and I were horrified at that suggestion, and both said we wouldn't do it. John felt that attitude was so disrespectful to Lennard, who'd served *Fools and Horses* so well.

'Then someone suggested we brought in an aunt. Everyone started warming to the idea except me. I said: "If you think we're going to have a success with me telling a little old lady to "Shut up, you stupid old cow", and bundling and pushing her into the back of a van, you're mistaken – we'd be off the air in a fortnight. Even if you didn't want to be politically correct, having Del Boy treat an older woman like he did others just wouldn't work.

'A day or two later, Ray Butt told us about a letter and photo he'd received. He showed us, and somebody said the sender looked like a little, old sailor. That got everyone thinking; we realised we didn't want to lose all those old war stories, which were so funny. Whether you believed them or not didn't matter because they were endearing, although there was always a sting in the tail. So John suggested introducing Grandad's brother, who was in the war in some capacity, and that's how Buster's part came about.

'Dealing with Lennard's death was difficult for all of us, but John Sullivan had the added pressure of having to rewrite the scripts, and deal with Grandad's funeral in "Strained Relations". I knew John had such a range as a writer, and I tried encouraging him to use it, particularly as he wanted to start writing about more serious themes in the programme; but he was a bit tentative at the beginning because it didn't seem to be the "done thing" in sitcoms; in fact, as far as I can recall, no one had dared do a funeral of a main character. I remember John telling me that he wanted to write the episode because he felt nobody wants anyone to die, and when you see it happening to a family it's as cruel and as hurtful as if it were your own family. He wanted the Trotters to go through the pain of missing Grandad, which was a brilliant concept. As soon as we read the script we knew he'd done a brilliant job.

'After a few series, John was really beginning to get the bit between his teeth – he was amazingly on song. He was producing some of the funniest material I'd ever read, and I said to him one day: "John, I'm really getting fed up with this." He asked why, and I replied: "Because you're over writing, we're having to cut, and we're throwing away more funny lines than most situation comedies have in their whole 30 minutes." We'd often had to cut John's work, but it was becoming a hatchet job. It was like chopping off bits of your own body: you'd cut your hand off, then up to your elbow, then off at the shoulder. I phoned him one day to discuss this. He too was desperately unhappy because he felt that some of his best material was ending up on the cutting-room floor. We had a long chat and decided to stand our ground. While the BBC felt that situation comedy was all about 30 minutes, we wanted to go to 40, even if that meant inventing a new 40-minute slot. After much furore, as well as John and I threatening not to work on the series any more, we were given the opportunity. But then it ended up as bloody 50 minutes!

'But I'm so glad that John and I stuck to our guns because it broke the mould, and gave John a much better chance to breathe. He could actually flesh out his characters more, and had extra time to develop his storylines.

'There are too many episodes I love to actually pick out a favourite, but I'm particularly fond of "The Russians are Coming", and I love the blow-up dolls scenes in "Danger UXD", as well as the Batman and Robin scenes in "Heroes and Villains". Tony Dow, the director, had a magic touch on this in particular, especially the filming in and around the streets of Bristol where Del and Rodney are seen emerging from the mist. There are so many happy moments.

'One of the reasons I think the show has been successful is because we never had a bad moment with anyone in the cast – I wouldn't have allowed it. The main reason, however, for the show's success is John's writing, followed by the huge team of wonderful people who enjoyed working on the series. It was a joy, and has to be my favourite job.

'When I was working with Ronnie Barker and we were filming a particularly funny bit of business in *Open All Hours,* and we were laughing in the rehearsal room, Ronnie eventually stopped, turned to me and remarked: "Isn't that wonderful, we're being paid awfully well to make ourselves laugh." I never forgot that, and it's something I often said to Nick.

'When the show came to an end – or so we thought – in 1996 with the Trilogy, it seemed the right time to stop, and I didn't think we'd get back together again. Things had moved on: Nick and I were doing different types of work. I'd been doing, amongst other things, *Frost,* a heavy detective series, and we'd had such a fantastic time with *Fools and Horses* over the years that I wondered whether we should leave it alone; I also dragged my heels about returning to the character, not because I wondered if John could do it, that wasn't a problem, it was whether Nick and I could as older characters. But it's worked out well. Now we still have two episodes to come out and they're great scripts.

'Everyone on *Fools and Horses* is just like one big family, but we miss terribly those who weren't around to film the current episodes. Ken MacDonald was just wonderful; he was a real joker, and we'd always be taking the mickey out of each other. In every episode, as we were all getting ready to record or something, he'd take a lump out of a beer mat, stick it on his nose, turn around and ask: "Who threw that? Who threw that?" It looked like someone had thrown it and the mat was stuck. It was a silly, silly moment, but Ken loved it – then again, we all laughed the first time, but after the 56th time we got a bit used to it! Out of tradition and respect for him, though, I did it in the last two episodes on the night of recording. It was something I did in memory of Ken. It was one of those lovely moments, and if I hadn't done it, it just wouldn't have been *Fools and Horses.*

'As for even more episodes, we need to wait and see how the people in the business, and the viewers, review the two still to be shown. But I would say, if they're successful and people love them, then who knows. My job is being an entertainer, and if the audience really want more *Only Fools,* that's what I'll do.' DAVID JASON

Introduction

Long before the Trotters marched off into the sunset back in 1996, loveable wide-boy Del, his gormless brother Rodney and the rest of the motley crew back at The Nag's Head were firmly enshrined as national icons. Such was the show's popularity, it had occasioned the formation of its very own appreciation society, the launch of a myriad of websites dedicated to the sitcom and a cornucopia of merchandise items, from videos and model cars to key rings and phone covers.

When we were first invited to visit the hapless Trotter family at Nelson Mandela House in 1981, the inaugural episode, 'Big Brother', was watched by just over nine million inquisitive people, many doubtless wondering what a sitcom with an elongated title spotlighting a family of market traders had to offer.

Scriptwriters and television companies are well aware that the viewing public is notoriously mercurial; audiences can be merciless, able to determine a fledgling programme's future with a quick flick of the remote control. The fact that the final instalment in the 1996 Christmas Trilogy was watched by over 24 million, figures that had steadily increased over the sitcom's 15 years on the box, is irrefutable evidence of how John Sullivan's masterpiece has been ingrained into the British psyche.

When examining why the dysfunctional Trotters have won a place in the hearts of the viewers while other sitcoms are discarded as swiftly as the blink of an eye, one has no alternative but to point towards a bunch of hoary old clichés which appear to apply to all the 'classic' sitcoms whose longevity is centred on a good solid foundation, allowing the programme to flourish. John Sullivan harnessed all the components needed for a sitcom to thrive.

One aspect of John Sullivan's success as a scriptwriter is his ability to evince a degree of realism in his work, carefully interwoven with humorous lines and magical situations. Although each page of script glitters with an array of quips and its fair share of uproarious moments, the work is enriched with a sense of reality, an astute study of people's foibles and life's issues. Sullivan's adeptness at writing scenes full of hilarity, penning lines which focus on his characters' vulnerability and being able to turn his mind to producing moments which are (as is often the case with the most outstanding sitcoms) tear-jerking, are just some of the many reasons why *Only Fools* rockets to the top of the viewing figures chart whenever we're lucky enough to be treated to another dose of John Sullivan's magic formula. Who can

studying people's behaviour and mannerisms, something which has nearly got him in hot water. 'I'm fascinated by people and can't help watching them, but a couple of times guys have looked at me as if they want to punch my lights out because I've been staring too much,' he explained. 'I'm intrigued in watching how people act and

individuals and in today's cut-throat television industry, the product will be labelled a failure and assigned to the dusty shelves of the archive before it's had time to draw breath. The thespians recruited for *Only Fools and Horses* were spot-on: the chemistry which quickly formed between the actors, particularly David Jason and Nicholas Lyndhurst, meant the production glided along like a well-oiled machine. But one must never underestimate the value brought to the show by the likes of Lennard Pearce, John Challis, Sue Holderness, Roger Lloyd Pack, Buster Merryfield, Gwyneth Strong, Tessa Peake-Jones, Kenneth MacDonald, Roy Heather and Paul Barber.

forget the side-splitting scene in 'The Yellow Peril' when the Trotters discover to their dismay that the paint they're using to decorate the Chinese restaurant is luminous? Then there is the time when Del suffers the miseries of unrequited love in 'Diamonds are for Heather', and the trauma endured by Rodney and Cassandra as they lose their baby in 'Modern Men'. Brilliant vignettes likes these are the norm in a Sullivan script, and are executed by well-rounded characters who are as close to real-life as you're ever likely to see on the little box in the corner of your room.

In one of the many conversations I had with John during the research period for this book, we discussed his ability to create in depth characterisations. Although he's too modest to acknowledge openly the efficacy of his scriptwriting, he did admit that perhaps it's due to his predilection for

move; I even find myself making notes all the time.'

Through his scripts, John has focused on subjects less accomplished writers might regard as 'dangerous' subjects for comedy, including miscarriage, impotence, violence, fraud, thievery and death. His ability to confront such matters with wonderful aplomb, while underpinning the scenes with truth, subtlety and delicacy, make for perfect viewing, something which is sadly lacking in today's television schedules. His study of the intricacies of family life is fascinating, with Del usually subjugating his own desires and beliefs to those of his kid brother, but always remaining a true family man. To Del, family always comes first.

Equally crucial to any show's success is the cast assembled to bring the writer's words and characters alive. Pick the wrong

It seems Trigger only has to stroll on to the set to receive a laugh, while everyone knows a Boycie and Marlene, who are as common as muck once you strip away the ostentatious façade. Then there's Raquel and Cassandra, both thoughtful, career-minded women, who simply want to lead a 'normal' life with their respective partners, which isn't always easy considering they've got themselves tangled up with the Trotter boys. In fact, the rest of the regulars are true gems as well, such is the calibre of the scripts and the actors who have brought them to life.

Now, fans of the sitcom – which examines so beautifully the plight of the underdog who's always aspiring to greater things – are being treated to more doses of *Only Fools and Horses*, keeping their spirits up during these uninspiring days of television sitcom. The first episode for five years, 'If They Could See Us Now…!', became the most-watched programme during Christmas 2001, and – at the time of writing – another two episodes are waiting to be transmitted later this year. But when the curtain drops at the end of the final scene, one fears that might be the end of Del Boy, Rodney et al. If this is the case, at least we can rest easy at night knowing there are over 46 hours' worth of episodes just waiting to entertain the millions of fans for many years to come.

RICHARD WEBBER
Clevedon, March 2002

The Inspiration Behind the Episodes

MANY WRITERS REGARD THE TASK OF FORMULATING A STORY-LINE AS ONE OF THE
MOST DIFFICULT ELEMENTS IN SCRIPTWRITING, SO HOW DID JOHN SULLIVAN
COME UP WITH ENOUGH CRACKING IDEAS TO SUPPORT SEVEN SERIES AND ENDLESS
CHRISTMAS SPECIALS? WHAT INCIDENT INSPIRED HIM TO WRITE THE FAMOUS
CHANDELIER SCENE IN 'A TOUCH OF GLASS'? WHY DID WE SEE DEL'S PATERNAL
INSTINCTS SURFACING IN 'DIAMONDS ARE FOR HEATHER', EVEN THOUGH HE WAS
YEARS AWAY FROM HAVING HIS OWN SON? WHO WAS THE INSPIRATION BEHIND
THE COLOURFUL CHARACTER BLOSSOM IN 'WANTED'? ALL THESE QUESTIONS AND
MORE ARE ANSWERED BY JOHN SULLIVAN IN THIS CHAPTER.

'A Losing Streak'

'We kicked off with "Big Brother" which was all about establishing the main characters, something we were still doing to a certain extent in "Go West Young Man". But when it came to "Cash and Curry", I wrote a story based on a title I liked. I had this friend who always called cash-and-carry retailing outlets cash-and-curry. I just thought it would make such a lovely title, and if I could think of a story-line involving some Asian guys, I'd have an episode; so for that one I invented a story from the title.

'I'm not sure where I got the idea for "The Second Time Around", but there are no doubts about "A Slow Bus to Chingford". I remember visiting a pub called The Duke of Devonshire, which was one of my father's favourite pubs; it hadn't changed at all, and the guy who ran it was called Boycie, which is where the name came from. It was so ancient inside, almost unbelievable. The floor was a kind of sticky carpet or lino, I can't remember, but it obviously hadn't altered since the war. To be honest, I didn't really want to drink in there; by then I'd got used to a better class of dive. I remember going to the toilet and there was a young bloke there, he looked like a hippy, and I told him what I thought of the place. He turned to me and said: "This is ethnic English." I'd never thought of that: I didn't think the English could be ethnic, but the idea stuck in my mind.

'The first series came to an end with "The Russians are Coming". I'd read about some people who'd actually bought this lead-lined shelter and suddenly found that the council wouldn't give them permission to erect it, so they were stuck with an air-raid shelter.

'There's no particular story behind "Christmas Crackers", it was just a last-minute script for a Special, and I wrote "The Long Legs of the Law", partly because my niece became a policewoman. I don't know where the idea for "Ashes to Ashes" came from, and although I never gambled myself, my father did, which helped when it came to writing "A Losing Streak". I used to go along to gambling sessions with my

friends and I usually ended up asleep, only to be woken up by some trouble of one kind or another.

'"No Greater Love …" was written to show how far Del would go to help his brother. In fact, Del would go right to the end for his kid brother – he'd even have his head kicked in to save Rodney. It was

'Friday the 14th'

something I wanted the audience to know, but not Rodney. I'm not sure about "The Yellow Peril" and in "It Never Rains…". I just wanted to explore Grandad's history a little. I'd hoped we could film the episode in Spain, but when I was told the budget wouldn't run to it I wasn't surprised, so we all went down to Dorset. Actually, we had a great time: it was Nick's 21st birthday during the filming, and I took my wife, Sharon, and our two kids with me and it was wonderful.

'There's certainly a story about "A Touch of Glass". My father told me a tale on which I based the episode; strangely enough, I wrote the final scene first and then thought: "Now, how did Del, Rodney and Grandad get themselves there? Who would invite the Trotters inside their manor house?" So I had to work backwards on this one.

'My father had been shop steward on building sites. He was a strong union man and a great fighter for the working man's rights. When I was an apprentice plumber, he was always telling me to be careful, to double-check things, don't just assume other people are going to do things, and always to be wary of other people's feelings or shortcomings. He told me about the time he was serving his apprenticeship and there was an incident at this manor house. Central heating was being installed in the property. There were two very expensive chandeliers hanging in the house, so for safety's sake they had to take them down. While one chap nipped upstairs to undo the bolts from underneath the floorboards in the room above, the others were up this ladder holding one of the chandeliers. They all shouted, "Yeah, we're ready!" The trouble was, the man upstairs undid the wrong chandelier and it crashed to the ground.

'Imagining the scene, I started to laugh when my old man told me, but he wasn't too pleased. He said: "We all got the sack for that. It was the 1920s and they were hard times without work: without money, you could starve or freeze to death." He couldn't see the funny side to the incident but I knew I had to use it in an episode.

'After "A Touch of Glass" was transmitted I waited with trepidation for my dad to call. He was always the first person to ring after an episode had been shown;

kids – he adores children; the episode reveals that if he met a woman who already had a kid he would bring the child up as his own. I thought the episode was a nice way of showing that he desperately loves children and would like to be a dad.

was a charlady at an art gallery. I suddenly thought, "What if you had a Trotter working in an art gallery as a cleaner?" The old girl could have lifted something years ago and then lived in fear of being discovered. Then it was passed down to Del, who knew of the

'Yesterday Never Comes'

when the phone rang that evening I thought: "Oh God!" because I hadn't told him what I was going to do. I picked up the receiver and he didn't say a word – not even hello. Then he uttered: "Yeah, all right, it *was* funny!"

'I did a couple of things for Christmas 1982: first there was "Christmas Trees", a short sketch. I was asked to do the scene so I just decided to knock something out about Christmas trees. Then there was "Diamonds are for Heather" in which I wanted to show Del in a reflective mood. He would love to have married and had

'There wasn't any particular motivation behind "Homesick", and in "Healthy Competition" I wanted to show that Rodney had reached the age at which he was ready to break free a little, to stand on his own two feet. In "Friday the 14th" the ending works well with Del knowing the police are on their way but deciding that in the meantime he'll try to win some money from the axeman, even though he could lose his life at any moment. And "Yesterday Never Comes" showed Del getting conned. Part of the idea stemmed from a friend's mum who

item's origins; a woman pretends to befriend Del and ends up conning him out of the item, but in fact she's ended up lumbering herself with stolen property after registering it in her name and trying to auction it off. It was a nice twist at the end of the story.

'"May the Force be with You" was a vehicle for introducing Slater. It seemed to me that in every little gang of boys there was always one who became a police cadet; I thought it would be fun showing one of the old boys from Del's school coming back and seeking revenge for all the tricks they had played on him. Some people at the time misinterpreted this episode. I remember one critic wrote that he now had a completely different view of Del because he was simply a common thief. There's a scene in the episode where Del admits to stealing the

name was Blossom and she was well known around the area: she was always drunk and a bit disturbed. She'd obviously opened the back door and kipped all night in his car. When my friend saw her he almost went off the road, but there was something there that told me

thought I'd bring their father into the series, but then began thinking it might be an interesting idea to see the difference between the two boys with their father around, especially when it came to all the family loyalties highlighted at Christmas time.

'Strained Relations'

microwaves, but this was the only way to ensure that everyone else caught up in the problem could walk free; he wasn't actually admitting he'd taken the machines, he was giving the only answer possible in the circumstances.

"Wanted" was based loosely on a true story and it was an episode I enjoyed. A friend of mine came out of his house one day and got in his car. The windows were all misted up so he put on the demisters and started driving down the road. He glanced in his mirror and suddenly saw this woman staring back at him; her

that if you came across a Blossom, she could terrify you, especially if you were a little naïve like Rodney; whereas my mate would simply have stopped the car and told her to get out, Rodney wouldn't know what to do. And then it begged the question, "What would Del do?" I always thought he'd take a joke too far because we've all met people who don't know when to stop.

"Who's a Pretty Boy?" introduced Denzil and Mike, while the Christmas Special "Thicker Than Water" saw Del and Rodney's father appear. I never

'Series 4 started with "Happy Returns", the first which I had to write without Grandad. I'd already written the series when we heard about Lennard's death, so had to rewrite the episodes quickly; I ended up writing a couple of new episodes and this was one of them; we also pushed two episodes – "From Prussia with Love" was one of them – on to the next series. "Happy Returns" was the most difficult episode I ever had to write, purely because it was straight after Lennard's death; ironically it won our first BAFTA!

'The next in the series, "Strained Relations", contained the funeral scene; it also introduced us to the new character, Uncle Albert. It showed how Del and Rodney dealt with grief in their own ways: Del goes on a guilt trip, which now having suffered bereavements in my own family,

pensation – that was until he got found out. "It's Only Rock and Roll" just showed Rodney trying to hit the big time, while "Sleeping Dogs Lie" was all about a gag I'd heard, and as for "Watching the Girls Go By", I don't recall what inspired me to write that one.

'The fifth series started with "From Prussia with Love" although I'm not entirely sure where the story-line came from. It was to do with the sale of a baby – so it had rather Dickensian overtones. Another influence could have been the idea that Boycie couldn't father a child.

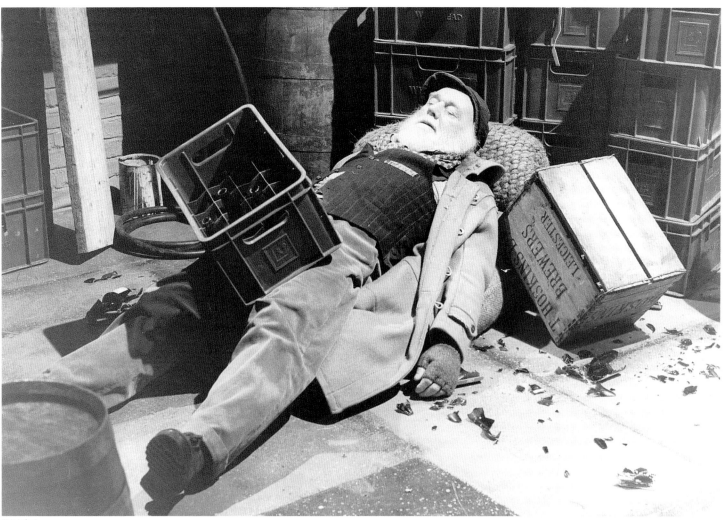

'Hole in One'

I'm fully aware of, although I wasn't when I wrote the script. In hindsight, had I known what it was like to experience grief, I might have explored the guilt aspect more; I decided to play it that Del doesn't know how to deal with emotion: he's the hard man who has to bottle everything up inside; for so-called tough men there is a problem when it comes to grief or love; all they can express is anger or joy.

'"Hole in One" was based on a true story. My grandfather, who was called Dickie, was a coalman who fell down things a few times in order to claim com-

'I'd actually read about a rare butterfly that a collector was looking for and was offering a reward, although it wasn't the sort of money referred to in "As One Door Closes". "To Hull and Back" was the first episode we did without an audience. It was fun filming the episode up in Hull. I love living by the sea and watching the water, but I'm not fond of being out on it, so I never went out when they filmed the scenes on the boat. I remember going around looking for the right boat and when I spotted the *Inge*, I said: "That's it, but *I'm* not going out on it!"

Boycie always regarded himself as such a man but he couldn't do the one thing that he wants the most: to produce a child, particularly a son.

'"The Miracle of Peckham" shows Del's good heart even though he nicked the lead from the church roof in the first place, while "The Longest Night" was based on a true story about a robber who went into a supermarket and was blatantly shoplifting. He was arrested and dragged up to the office, where he immediately pulled out a gun because he knew that was where the safe was. He got the

money and cleared off. I thought it was a great con but wanted to develop the idea further by involving the Trotters, so had to think of a way of getting Del, Rodney and Uncle Albert into the office; of course, it turned out to be a con between the shoplifter, the security manager and the store manager. But the actual premise was based on a true event.

'"Tea for Three" was just about rivalry, what a woman can do to two men, and what they'll do to each other in order to win the favours of the lady. The penultimate episode in Series 5, "Video Nasty", came about after reading an article in a newspaper about a youth club which had been given some money by the local council to make a film of their area; they were given the cameras and all the other equipment, but nothing was ever made, the cameras went missing and the money vanished. So I started wondering what they would do if it happened in Peckham?

'I finished off the series with "Who Wants to be a Millionaire", which was written because I had dinner with David Jason one night and he kind of announced that he didn't want to do any more *Fools*. He wanted to concentrate on more plays and dramas so it was possible that this episode was going to be the last. At that point I hadn't written the script, so I went to see Gareth Gwenlan who was then Head of Comedy and told him about it; he asked if I could write a final episode but to leave it open just in case we ever came back to it at a later date. So I wrote the script with Del going off to Australia and leaving Rodney at Heathrow. There was a chance we might have had a spin-off series called *Hot Rod*, where Rodney and Mickey Pearce took over the trading company. Before completing the script – or I might have just finished it, I can't remember – Gareth phoned and said David's agent had been in touch and he was happy to continue with the show. I don't know what had happened, I never discussed it with him, but I just altered the ending. However, it was originally written as the final episode.

'We then had a run of three Christmas Specials before the next series. In 1986 we had "A Royal Flush", which never quite worked, in my opinion. It was supposed to be filmed in front of an audience but we never had the time, partly because I was also doing a *Just Good Friends* episode in Paris, so everyone was rushing around here, there and everywhere. Then I was told they'd get the episode finished and show it to me over in Paris and that way we could also get an audience reaction, but it never worked out; in fact, we were finishing the final scene on Christmas Eve; if you

'Tea for Three'

watch it you'll notice there are no outside sounds, no dogs barking or police cars going by, it's just cold and blank because we didn't even have time to dub it. We've often talked about doing a remix, perhaps by showing bits and pieces of it to an audience and recording their response, but we've never got round to it.

'The next year we did "The Frog's Legacy", and a part of this was about trying to suggest the Trotter boys might have had different fathers. It gave me the opportunity to mention this man, Freddie Robdal, a character from

the past who was an art connoisseur, who was everything Rodney is; it was a chance to give another background note about one of the central characters.

'In 1988 I wrote "Dates", my favourite episode. It's one I love. As a writer, it was one of those stories that just fell into place all the way. 'The story-line shows a bit of desperation creeping into Del when he visits a dating agency because he's not pulling the girls himself anymore; it was also an opportunity to show him falling in love again and then ruining it because he finds out Raquel works as a stripagram. There's such a hypocrisy when it comes to lap dancers, stripagrams and that sort of thing: guys cheer and shout but if they find out the girl they're in love with is doing it, there's trouble. In many ways, the episode reveals the hypocrisy of men.

'I wrote another series in 1989, beginning with "Yuppy Love". The episode concentrated on Rodney falling in love, which is something I wanted him to do, to show that he was capable of more than just pulling a bird somewhere; now he was capable of having a heavy relationship.

'The scene in which Cassandra gives Rodney a lift home and he directs her to the wrong house, because he's embarrassed to let her know where he really lives, was something that happened to me years ago. This girl, who was an airline stewardess, offered me a lift home one evening. I knew she lived in a very nice house somewhere, whereas I lived in a hell-hole. As we drove along I wondered what I was going to do, then I remembered a house I'd seen when I used to be at school, a big white place, so I directed her there. I never saw her again; that was my reverse snobbery. I thought Rodney would be like that.

'I'm not sure where the idea for "Danger UXD" came from; I know that when we were celebrating Nick's 21st birthday whilst away filming in Dorset, someone, as a joke, gave him some inflatable dolls as a present and he was very embarrassed, so whether something came from that, I'm not sure. And I'm unsure about the origins of "Chain Gang", whereas the inspiration behind "The Unlucky Winner is…" came from having a drink with David and Nick one night. We had a laugh about exploiting Rodney's boyish charm and looks, doing something where Del makes out his younger brother is a teenager, then Rodney has to go along with it.

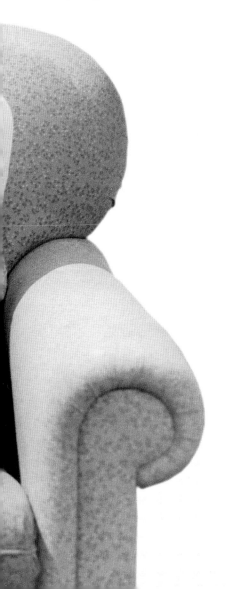

'In "Sickness and Wealth" I wanted Del to encounter illness for the first time in his life, whereby he would be facing his own mortality, and in "Little Problems" we had Rodney's wedding. There were some sad moments in that one and I received letters from two or three mothers asking me to write to their young sons or daughters and assure them that Del wasn't lonely even though he was on his own. So I wrote to them saying things like: "No, Del is out with his friends a lot, and Rodney keeps coming round and they all have a lovely time."

'For Christmas 1989 we had another Special, "The Jolly Boys' Outing". The idea for this was influenced by my sister-in-law Penny whose dad worked in the print. They used to have an event called the Jolly Boys' Outing; it seemed a silly name for a beano, but I just loved it. I also remember going on outings when I was younger but I'd never written about them, so I thought it would be good to do something about Southend or Margate. The setting started off as Southend but I opted for Margate because by then I'd got to know the singers Chas and Dave, who'd written that great song "Margate", and I hoped they could record the closing music for it.

'Preceding the final series was another Special, "Rodney Come Home", which showed Rodney's despair as his marriage hit the rocks, and then "The Sky's the Limit" began Series 7 on 30 December 1990. This one came about because of my family's holiday in Portugal. There were eight of us and we booked well in advance, but when we got to the airport we discovered to our horror that we weren't booked on the plane! There had been a terrible cock-up and the guy who took the booking had been fired. The holiday officials were saying that they might be able to send *some* of us to Barcelona and get a flight from there to Lisbon.

'In the end they managed to get us all on, but asked if I minded sitting in the jump-seat; I didn't even know what it was but assumed it was where the stewardess sat. I replied: "Yeah, I'll go anywhere. I'll sit in the hold if you give me a warm coat." But my seat was actually up with the pilot! We got talking and one of the topics of conversation was the landing beacons they use on runways, and I suddenly thought it would be interesting if Del got hold of one. Of course, I doubt if we'll ever see this episode again, bearing in mind the tragic events in America last year, and the fact that the final scene shows the jumbo heading towards Nelson Mandela House.

'In "The Chance of a Lunchtime" we see how Del handles the thought of Raquel going back to work as an actress, and then hearing that he's going to be a dad after all these years. I'm not sure about the inspirations behind "Stage Fright", but I wrote the next instalment, "The Class of '62", because I'd had a football team reunion. All the guys came back and I can remember walking into the room and not recognising some of my old team mates. Everybody had changed so much, including our blond-haired centre-forward who all the girls used to fancy, and who was now bald. I just knew I had to do something like that for *Only Fools*, so I opted for a school reunion. I thought about what could happen and the idea of bringing Slater back came to me, then everything evolved from there. Raquel had mentioned before that she had been married, and of course, her ex-husband turned out to be the reviled Slater.

'"He Ain't Heavy, He's My Uncle" was an opportunity to show the vulnerability of Uncle Albert, while the closing episode, "Three Men, a Woman and a Baby", needs little explanation.

'We then had a series of Christmas Specials, beginning with "Miami Twice" in 1991. In fact, it was only ever supposed to be one episode but the story went along so well it became obvious it would need to be spread over two parts, hence the title.

'The following year we had "Mother Nature's Son". I remember hearing about people who had their water supply closed down because something had been dumped in a nearby resevoir. Somebody also told me about a shop which had opened in Knightsbridge selling nothing but different kinds of water. It seemed that water was becoming the new champagne. I thought, "If only Del could get in on the act." We'd often mentioned Grandad's allotment but had never used it, so this seemed the ideal opportunity to visit the site.

'I'm not sure of the reasons behind "Fatal Extraction", but when it came to 1996's Christmas Trilogy I thought we'd reached the end of the run, which is why you see them walking off into the sunset. I wanted them to become cartoon figures as they walked away, thinking that once they'd become cartoons they would no longer be real and, therefore, couldn't come back; but the director Tony Dow fought against it and persuaded me to change my mind. I certainly had fun writing the three episodes – in fact, I enjoyed every single second of writing *Only Fools and Horses*.'

About this Book

Writing this book has been a mammoth task. One of the biggest problems faced by anyone contemplating penning an A–Z of any description is knowing where to draw the line. A manageable task can quickly become an uncontrollable monster; usually time constraints provide the final discipline, but it's no easy feat deciding what qualifies for inclusion in an A–Z of any TV show. Since setting out to compile a definitive reference book exploring, hopefully, every aspect of *Only Fools and Horses* I have been faced with just such issues.

One of the most difficult and time-consuming tasks has been tracking down some of the actors, actresses and crew members associated with the sitcom, some of whom have long since left the profession or died. Often, agents held no contact address or records, which made it virtually impossible, in some cases, to obtain enough material to write a sufficient profile for the book. I have included as many profiles as possible, which I hope will help fans of the sitcom to know a little more about the careers of thespians who appeared in supporting or minor roles, or those who helped behind the scenes. Inevitably, given the enormity of the task, it's not been possible to include career details on everyone. If I had another two years to write the book, no doubt I could cover more, but many searches finally drew a blank after exhaustive research, particularly when it came to some of the children who were seen in the show.

I've tried making the book as comprehensive as possible, cramming in as much information as time and the final word count would allow, but there are bound to be some details, or areas that do not appear. However, I hope you find what is included informative, entertaining and helpful in answering all those nagging questions you have about the sitcom. As well as actor profiles I've included character profiles, too. Even those unseen characters who were mentioned in the scripts have been given their rightful place in this publication, together with details of who mentioned them, in which episode and the context in which their names were used. If during my research I have been unsure about the spelling of a particular place or character, I have referred to Sullivan's original scripts.

Enjoy your read.

Abdul

Played by Tony Anholt

A mate of Del's who's initially mentioned in 'Diamonds are for Heather'. He receives discount at Hatton Gardens, and buys the ring that Del later offers Heather as an engagement ring. Luckily, Del's got the symbol of love on a week's approval, thus saving his money when he returns the item after she declines his proposal.

Abdul is later seen in 'To Hull and Back', conducting business with Boycie. They try interesting Del in their fifty grand deal, which involves Mr Van Kleefe from Amsterdam. At first, Del doesn't want any involvement in the caper but the thought of a £15,000 slice of the pie is eventually too much to resist.

Although he's never seen again, Abdul is mentioned once more by Del in 'Video Nasty'.

Abrahams, Steve

Location manager on three episodes: 'Heroes and Villains', 'Modern Men' and 'Time On Our Hands'

Born in London in 1966, Steve gained valuable experience working as a student assistant stage manager at The Royal Court Theatre during a summer break from university. Upon graduating, he joined the BBC in 1990, employed initially as a runner on *EastEnders*. He then became an assistant floor manager, working on shows such as *Bottom* and *French and Saunders*, followed by a spell as a locations manager before taking up the role of production manager on, among others, *Last of the Summer Wine*, *2 Point 4 Children*, *Parkinson* and *League of Gentlemen*.

Steve, who's worked in TV for 12 years, was made redundant in 2001 and now works as a freelance line producer/production manager/1st assistant director. Recent work assignments include *Rocking the Blind* for BBC and *Doubletake* for an independent production company.

Abroad

Fans of *Only Fools and Horses* span the world. In Holland, TV executives liked the format of John Sullivan's show so much that they decided to make their own version: *Wat Schuift Het?* which translates to *What's It Worth?* Its cast consisted of Johnny Kraaykamp Jnr playing Stef (based on Del),

Sacco Van Der Made as Grandpa (based on Grandad) and Kasper Van Kooten as Robbie (based on Rodney).

Another country to embrace the concept of Sullivan's sitcom was Portugal, who made *O Fura-Vidas*, an indigenous expression describing someone who makes a living with suspect deals. Adaptations of episodes from series one to five were first aired during 1999, and it quickly became one of the year's most successful shows. A further series (covering episodes from series six and seven) was made in 2000.

The big market that every scriptwriter wants to conquer is America; John Sullivan tried his luck by adapting one of his scripts, but the idea never got off the ground. Based on 'No Greater Love…', the programme was to be titled 'This Time Next Year'. It was never recorded, but the idea for an American version of the sitcom is still being considered by another production company.

'The first company wanted an actor from *M*A*S*H* to play the grandfather and to make him the lead,' recalls John Sullivan. 'But it wouldn't have worked; you've got to have Del as the energy because he's the dynamo keeping everything going. I couldn't see it working out with the grandfather as the lead character.'

Then another production company became interested but also wanted to make some changes to the premise of the series, including amending the family name to the Flanagans because the producer believed it would work better if the family were either a black family or Irish-Americans. The 45-minute show would also have seen Rodney's name altered to Marlon. Again, nothing materialised, but John is happy with the show's success abroad. 'It's sold around the Commonwealth particularly well, so it's been a pretty good investment for the BBC.'

Ackland-Snow, Vivien

Floor manager on four episodes: 'Heroes and Villains', 'Modern Men', 'Time On Our Hands' and 'If They Could See Us Now…!'

Born in Folkestone, Kent, Vivien worked as a production assistant for a small production company after gaining a degree in English and Drama at university. She then joined *Good Morning Britain* as an assistant floor manager. By the time she left TV-AM, she had been promoted to floor manager. After freelancing for a while, she joined the BBC and worked as a floor manager for seven years; she was made redundant in 2001.

Among the shows Vivien, who's once again working as a freelance floor manager, has particularly enjoyed working on are entertainment shows such as *Never Mind the Buzzcocks*, *National Lottery*, *They Think It's All Over*, *Night Fever* and *Top of the Pops*, which she still currently works on.

MEMORIES OF ONLY FOOLS

★ ★ ★ ★ ★ ★

'The then Head of Production in Entertainment scheduled me on to *Only Fools and Horses* because there was a lot of work to do, which gave the show a freelance location manager – Lisa McArthur – and a BBC one – me. I was determined to work on the show, so delayed other plans and holiday leave to make sure I was available.

'I remember we had a film sequence with the three-wheeler chugging along an open road. To tie in with another location, I managed to get permission to use the A40 into London by the Perivale turning and bridge.

'As the Reliant was going to be firing smoke and appearing to be almost falling apart as it went along, I arranged for a police escort to tail the van, keeping other traffic at a safe distance. One of the police cars was called on to an emergency as we set up, leaving just one other, with the promise that another vehicle would join us shortly. When that car arrived, as we began the filming sequence, one of the policemen in the car called a colleague in the other vehicle and asked: "Are we chasing that heap of junk or going to tow it?"

'I have to add that no sequence on the roads of London is possible without booking the police, and them showing a great sense of humour. That was a good enough line to include in the script.'

STEVE ABRAHAMS

Action News

Two employees of the American television station, Action News, are seen filming over the wall at Victor Occhetti's home in 'Miami Twice'.

Ada, Aunt

Ada is Uncle Albert's estranged wife. They never saw eye to eye and didn't speak to each other for years. She even threatened to kill him if she ever set eyes on him again. Although we never see Ada in the sitcom, Albert discusses her in 'Strained Relations' and 'Tea for Three'. Despite the ill-feeling that existed between them, Albert must have retained an ounce of love for the woman because upon hearing she's been taken ill, he dedicates a song to her during the local talent contest at The Nag's Head.

When Albert first met her, at the local Palais, he regarded her a deadringer for Ginger Rogers. Such was his determination to get his girl, he even fought his own brother for her affections. A classic example of the fickleness of the heart, perhaps their relationship was founded on infatuation rather than true love.

Adams, Charmian

Art director on one episode: 'Fatal Extraction'

Canadian-born Charmian Adams, who's a freelance art director, assisted designer Donal Woods on the 1993 Christmas Special, but she originally trained as an architect at the Brighton College of Art and Craft. However, she decided not to pursue a career in that field and joined the BBC instead, working initially as a design assistant.

After a few years she left and raised a family, and didn't work in television for the next 17 years, except for a period as a freelance researcher on *The Money Programme*. She was also successful in gaining another degree before returning to work as an art director, initially with BBC Bristol.

Among her numerous TV credits are *Goodbye Mr Steadman*, *The Woman in White*, *The Shell Seekers*, *Take A Girl Like You*, *Great Expectations* and films such as *Sid and Nancy*, *Global Heresy* and her first feature, *Hilary and Jackie*.

Adams, Mona

Researcher on one episode: 'Time On Our Hands'

Mona, who was born in Belfast, worked for the city's *Telegraph* newspaper before joining the newsroom of Ulster TV. By 1964 she was working as a researcher in London for BBC Schools' Television, followed by moves into news and current affairs and, finally, documentaries, during which time she helped produce such acclaimed series as *The Road to War*, *News '44* and *Cuban Missile Crisis*.

In 1992 Mona turned freelance and has been working as an historical consultant ever since, with recent projects including *A Lonely War* and *Mary, Queen of Scots* for BBC Films and script development for John Malkovich's company, Mr Mudd. She also wrote and produced a CD-ROM titled, *Sound On: Vision On*, celebrating 75 years of the BBC, which was presented to staff, public libraries and Colleges of Further Education to mark the anniversary.

Adrian

Played by Ian Redford

During 'The Chance of a Lunchtime', Adrian directs the Shakespearian play *As You like It*, for which Raquel auditions.

Adrian

Played by Michael Shallard

A 'yuppy' estate agent, Adrian eats boeuf bourguignon in The Nag's Head, while his girlfriend, Chloe, tucks into a salad. Seen in 'Danger UXD', this smartly dressed gentleman pays £2.75 for his meal, even though an identical dish had just been sold to Denzil for a pound, under the guise of stew. Adrian and his friends regard The Nag's Head as a place of solace and are only frequenting the pub because Del has started drinking in their usual haunts whilst going through his irritating 'yuppy' phase.

Adult Education (Business And Commercial Studies) Centre, The

This grand, pre-war building is seen in 'Yuppy Love' and it's where Rodney attends evening classes, studying for a computer diploma. It holds a special place in his heart because it's where he first sets eyes on his wife-to-be, Cassandra Parry.

Advanced Electronics Research and Development Centre, The

Formerly Ron's Cash and Carry, the Research and Development Centre is mentioned by Del in 'Danger UXD'. Del has a drink with the Centre's managing director, Ronnie Nelson, and believes it's where the 'big business opportunities occur'.

Ahern, Kevin

Dubbing editor on two episodes: 'Miami Twice (Parts 1 & 2)'

Kevin's work covers both television and cinema. As a dubbing editor he's worked on productions such as *The Clandestine Marriage* and *Just a Little Harmless Sex*, while as a visual effects editor his credits include the 1998 film, *Lost in Space* and the 2001 TV series, *Band of Brothers*.

Ahmed

Played by Raj Patel

Ahmed appears briefly in 'No Greater Love…' as a young Indian who talks to Del in a London back street and is cajoled into buying one of the overcoats Del is selling for £25. He pays for the coat in weekly instalments.

Ailes-Stevenson, Ann

Make-up designer on one episode: 'The Frog's Legacy'

Ann, who was born in Ipswich, trained as a hairdresser while working for Fortnum and Mason's. Talking to someone who worked in Australian TV fanned her ambition to move into television make-up, something she achieved by joining the BBC in 1964, at the age of 19. After completing three months' training at the Beeb's make-up school she became a trainee make-up artist, assisting on shows including *The Black and White Minstrels*. After eight years with the BBC she was promoted to make-up designer and went on to work on some popular shows, such as *Softly, Softly*; *Barlow at Large*; *The Liver Birds*; *Steptoe and Son*; *The Day of the Triffids*; *Dear John*; *Lorna Doone*; *Last of the Summer Wine*; *Bergerac*; *Grange Hill*; *That's Life*; *Anna Karenina*; *EastEnders*; *Blankety Blank* and four series of *Keeping Up Appearances*.

Ann left the BBC in 1992 and now works freelance.

Aitchison, Kennedy

Musical director on one episode: 'Stage Fright'

Kennedy acted as musical director for the songs, 'I'll Never Fall in Love' and 'Delilah' sung by Philip Pope, and for 'Crying' sung by Pope and Tessa Peake-Jones during the episode, 'Stage Fright'.

Alan

(See 'Parry, Alan')

Albert, Uncle

(See 'Trotter, Albert')

Alder, Steve

Role: Eddie Chambers

Appeared in 'The Jolly Boys' Outing'

Steve, who died in 1997, aged 47, appeared in a number of dramas and sitcoms during the 1980s and '90s, including two series of *The Other 'Arf*, as Brian Sweeney; an episode of *Minder*; an episode of *The Gentle Touch*; *Constant Hot Water*, as Frank Osborne; an episode of *Spender*; *The Bill*, as Trevor Jackson; an episode of *The Upper Hand*, as Eddie Sullivan and several episodes of *The Professionals* as Murphy.

On the big screen, one of his roles was as Terry in *Scrubbers*, while his stage work included appearances in *Grease*, *Hair* and *Jesus Christ Superstar*.

Aldridge, Ron

Role: Bronco

Appeared in S7, episode 1

As well as being an actor, Ron is an accomplished director and writer, who directed and appeared in a recent Middle and Far East tour of *Funny Money*. In this capacity, he's also been involved in *Hovering*, which he also wrote, and for which he was nominated for an award at the 1994 Edinburgh Festival.

His career started in repertory theatre before television parts came his way. He's since appeared in shows such as *Minder*, *London's Burning*, *2 Point 4 Children*, *Expert Witness*, *Robin's Nest*, *The Knock* and *Nelson's Column*. On the stage, meanwhile, he's toured nationally with a range of productions, including *Heartbreak House*, *Living Together* and *Absent Friends*.

Alex (The Travel Agent)

Played by Jim McManus

Appeared in S2, episode 6

Alex is seen in 'It Never Rains…', buying a drink for Del at The Nag's Head. His travel business isn't fairing too well: just when he thought he would earn bucket loads of money selling World Cup tickets, his plan falls flat because he can't get his hands on any. With thousands of pounds worth of holidays unsold, Alex is deeply depressed, but Del claims to have the answer to all his woes: an 80 per cent discount on a trip anywhere in the world for the next customer in the shop. What Alex doesn't realise is that Del's motives are purely selfish because he fancies a break in the sun.

The travel agent is mentioned again, although not seen, in 'Miami Twice'. Del tells Rodney that Alex is offering return tickets to Miami for £250, and with a 'two for the price of one' offer, he should take Cassandra away on holiday. Del, however, knows that Cassandra is attending a banking conference; it's all a devious plan to accompany his little brother on a two-week jolly.

Alice

Del, Rodney and Grandad attend Alice's funeral in 'Ashes to Ashes'. Alice was Trigger's grandmother, but it's clear there's no love lost between the Peckham roadsweeper and his late grandparent when he describes her as a 'miserable old cow'; Grandad Trotter, meanwhile, holds a different view of Alice, remembering her as an ebullient woman, always the life and soul of the party. She is never seen in the sitcom.

Alice was married to Arthur, who's also dead, but she didn't speak to her hubby for the last 15 years of his life because he discovered she'd been entertaining a man in the house while he was serving in the army. Although Trigger hasn't a clue who it was, Grandad Trotter admits to Del and Rodney that it was him, but is quick to point out it was a platonic relationship, they were just two lonely people keeping each other company.

Alldridge, Rita

Although she lives in the same block of flats as the Trotters, Rita is never seen in the sitcom, although Del mentions her in 'Homesick'. When Rodney is collecting data regarding crime in the area, Rita tells him she was indecently assaulted beside the adventure playground. However, when Del adds that she didn't report the matter to the police until the man's cheque bounced, we can only assume she's a local prostitute. She's mentioned again later in the episode, when Del blackmails the reluctant Dr Becker into visiting Grandad by claiming he'll inform the doctor's wife about his supposed involvement with Alldridge.

Allen, Carolyn

Role: Yvonne
Appeared in S4, episode 6

Carolyn, who was born in 1952, trained at London's Royal Academy of Music and spent the early years of her career as a singer, before making her acting debut as a maid in a 1983 Ray Cooney production, *Two into One*, at the Shaftesbury Theatre.

After a spell in repertory theatre, her television break was in *Slinger's Day*, playing an angry housewife, before popping up in other shows, including three episodes of *The Upper Hand*.

The lion's share of her time in the acting world has been spent on the stage. At the Redgrave Theatre, Farnham, she was seen as Eliza Doolittle in *My Fair Lady*, while in *The Mikado* at London's Westminster Theatre, she played Pitti Sing. She's also worked extensively in musical theatre, including *Les Miserables*, *Pirates of Penzance*, *See How They Run*, *Robinson Crusoe* and *The Rogers and Hammerstein Story*.

Amanda

Played by Dawn Perllman

Appearing in 'Video Nasty', Amanda is a punkette who's first spotted with Mickey Pearce in The Nag's Head. She's later seen at Rodney's flat, dressed in a nurse's uniform, stockings and suspenders, starring in Mickey's attempt at home movies.

American reporter

(See 'Fox, Sandra')

Amor, Jay

Role: Tony
Appeared in 'Miami Twice' (Part 2)

American-based actor/stuntman, Jay Amor has worked on a number of productions: as an actor, his credits include playing a punk in *Master*

Blaster; Bernardo in the 1988 production *Clinton and Nadine* and Tito in *The Last Marshall* (1999). His work as a stuntman has seen him appear in a host of shows, such as *Spring Break*, *The Heavenly Kid*, *Black Rain*, *La Florida*, *Bad Boys*, *Striptease*, *There's Something About Mary* and *Holy Man*. He recently worked as stunt coordinator on *Donzi: The Legend*.

Amro Bank

Seen in 'To Hull and Back', the Dutch bank is where Mr Van Kleefe finds out that the notes he's been given by Boycie and Abdul in exchange for smuggled diamonds are counterfeit.

Anderson, Gill

Production manager on three episodes: S6, episodes 1 & 3 and 'Dates'

Anderson, John

Designer on one episode: 'The Jolly Boys' Outing'

Born in the Worcestershire town of Stourport-on-Severn, John worked in the drawing office of a Birmingham engineering company before emigrating to Australia in 1968. Two weeks after an unsuccessful application for a design assistant's job with the Australian Broadcasting Commission, he was offered a temporary contract by the chief designer. He stayed with the Commission for three years.

John returned to the UK in 1971 and joined the Beeb two years later as a holiday relief design assistant. He was promoted to designer status in the early 1980s, working mainly in light entertainment, with credits including shows with Russ Abbot, Val Doonican and Les Dennis, as well as *Doctor Who* and *Dear John*.

In 1997 John left the BBC and has worked freelance ever since. Recent projects include *Joking Apart* and *Holding the Baby*.

Andrews, Caroline

Production assistant on six episodes: S4, episodes 1–5 & 7

Andy

Played by Mark Colleano

A hang-gliding enthusiast who lends Del his equipment in 'Tea for Three', Andy also turns out to be Trigger's niece's fiancé. He's seen again in 'The Frog's Legacy', when he finally marries Lisa.

Angelino, Tony

Played by Philip Pope

After working on the dustcarts by day, The Singing Dustman entertains (or tries to) during the evening. With a memorable stage name, Tony Angelino – whom Trigg believes has a terrific voice – is first seen at The Down By The Riverside Club in 'Stage Fright'.

Sporting a fake tan, Tony sings along wearing a black, curly Tom Jones wig, sunglasses, open shirt, tight trousers and the obligatory medallion. He goes down well with the middle-aged women who swoon around him after the performance, clammering for his autograph.

'Stage Fright'

A friend of Trigger's, he's been singing at the club for six years before the Trotter International Star Agency snaps him up for a special performance at The Starlight Rooms. Del offers him £100 to sing with Raquel the following evening. Angelino accepts, mainly because the most he's ever earned for a gig before is £50. His repertoire of songs is small because he can't pronounce his Rs, thereby restricting the songs he can sing without becoming a laughing stock.

Anholt, Tony

Role: Abdul
Appeared in 'To Hull and Back'

Tony, who was born in Singapore in 1941, trained at The Royal Court before embarking on a busy and successful career spanning every strand of the business. He's spent many years working as a continuity announcer on BBC World Service radio, while his extensive list of television credits include *Jason King*, *The Sweeney*, *Terry and June*, *Minder*, *Angels*, *Juliet Bravo* and *A Family at War*. He also played Paul Buchet in *The Protectors*, David Law in *Coronation Street*, Tony Verdeschi in two series of *Space 1999* and, arguably, his most famous role, Charles Frere in six series of *Howards' Way*.

Anita

Played by Nora Connolly
(Also known as 'First plain girl')

Anita is seen at The Monte Carlo Club when Del and Rodney turn up in 'Christmas Crackers'. A real Plain Jane, she thinks Del and Rodney want to drive her and her friend home, but when the girls give up their chairs to collect their coats, Del – who's been looking for a table all night – jumps into their places.

Anna

Played by Erika Hoffman

An attractive 19-year-old German language student who appears in 'From Prussia with Love', Anna has virtually mastered the English language but struggles to understand The Nag's Head lingo. Sitting alone in the pub, she's vulnerable and sad; she's been in England for a year working as an au-pair whilst studying; but, the family employing her have kicked her out and she's now homeless. To make matters worse, Anna is also pregnant, so Rodney takes pity and offers her a bed at the flat, which leads to a potential business opportunity for Del in illegal baby adoption.

Antha Chime

Seen in 'The Chance of a Lunchtime', the Antha Chime is Del's latest line in rejected goods, but the doorbells which play 36 different national anthems are never going to make him a millionaire. He tries selling them for £13.50 each, claiming they normally retail at £36.

Aqua Nibbo

Although we never hear anything about these underwater pens, the Trotter flat is piled high with them in 'Heroes and Villains'.

Arndale Centre

The Trotters conduct a lot of business at the Centre.

Arnie

Played by Philip McGough

In his late forties, Arnie – who's seen in 'Chain Gang' and drives a Jaguar XJ6 – appears to have a gentle and generous nature. He's a new arrival to the area, having moved from Lambeth with his wife, Pat, and two sons, Gary and Steven. Although he claims to have retired from his job as a jewellery dealer due to ill health (he suffered heart problems, collapsed and was given six months to live unless he altered his lifestyle) he still partakes of a little private business on the quiet.

It turns out that Arnie is a conman and, together with his two sons, sets up a con trick involving gold chains. His so-called heart problems are all part of the scam.

Arnold Road

Mentioned by Albert in 'Three Men, a Woman and a Baby', the street is the setting for the local Hare Krishna temple, where Albert suggests Del tries flogging his reject wigs.

Arthur

Not seen in the programme, Arthur – a lifelong member of Peckham Bowling Club – was Trigger's grandfather and is mentioned in 'Ashes to Ashes'. He was married to Alice, whose funeral is spotlighted in the episode. It appears his wife was a real live-wire when younger, and Trigger believes that's what helped finish his grandfather

'As One Door Closes'

off. For the last 15 years of his life, he didn't speak to Alice after discovering she had entertained another man in the house whilst he was away in the army. During the episode, Grandad Trotter admits that he was the man. The Trotters try scattering Arthur's ashes in various places around the locale, but end up losing them inside a road sweeper.

Arthur

Played by Derek Martin

Arthur – who's seen in 'Fatal Extraction' – is one of Del's neighbours who lives on the estate. Del wakes him up one night when he returns home drunk after yet another visit to the local casino.

Arturo

Louis Lombardi's pet canary is seen in 'Who's a Pretty Boy?'. When the Trotters are in desperate need of a bird to replace Denzil and Corinnes', which died after breathing in paint fumes, they send Grandad down to Lombardi's pet shop to buy a replacement. There aren't any canaries in stock, and Louis is reluctant to sell his own pet canary, until he is offered £45.

'As One Door Closes'

Original transmission: Thursday 4 April 1985, 8.00 pm

Production date: 3 March 1985

Original viewing figures: 14.2 million

Duration: 30 minutes

First repeat: Saturday 21 December 1985, 8.50 pm

Subsequent repeats: 30/11/91, 31/5/96, 23/9/97, 15/12/98, 7/10/00

CAST

Del Trotter	David Jason
Rodney Trotter	Nicholas Lyndhurst
Uncle Albert	Buster Merryfield
Denzil	Paul Barber
Man in crowd	Doug Rowe
Walk on	Patrick Wright (in market scene)

PRODUCTION TEAM

Written by John Sullivan

Title music arranged and conducted by Ronnie Hazlehurst, composed and sung by John Sullivan

Audience Warm-Up: Jeff Stevenson

Make-up Designer: Linda McInnes

Costume Designer: Richard Winter

Properties Buyer: Chris Ferriday

Location Video:

　　Lighting: Len Stephens, Sound: Mike Johnstone,

　　Cameraman: Mike Winser, Vision Supervisor: George Wagland

Film Cameraman: Chris Seager

Film Sound: Dennis Panchen

Film Editor: John Jarvis

Camera Supervisor: Ken Major

Studio Lighting Director: Don Babbage

Studio Sound: Dave Thompson

Technical Coordinator: Tony Mutimer

Videotape Editor: Chris Wadsworth

Production Assistants: Caroline Andrews and Lesley Bywater

Assistant Floor Manager: Gavin Clarke

Vision Mixer: Shirley Coward

Production Manager: Andy Smith

Designer: Eric Walmsley

Directed by Susan Belbin

Produced by Ray Butt

'As One Door Closes'

River policeman . . . . .John D Collins
Council cleansing lorry driver . .Terry Duggan
Captain . . . . .Victor Reynolds
Woman at window . . . . .Christina Michaels
Walk ons . . . .(Vicar – edited out before transmission) Peter Roy. (Builder's labourer) Roy Brent. (Middle-aged woman passer-by) Margot Abbott. (People at bowling club) Christina Michaels, Victor Reynolds, Peter Whitaker, Jay McGrath, Dennis Jennings, Vie Delmar-Emerson, Winifred Davies and Joan Ware. (People in street market) Chris Breeze, Myra Morris, Nancy Gabrielle, Jean Taylor, Olwyn Atkinson, Bobby James, Harry Klein, Tony Starr and Charles Finch.

PRODUCTION TEAM
Written by John Sullivan
Title music arranged and conducted by Ronnie Hazlehurst composed and sung by John Sullivan
Audience Warm-up: . . . . .Felix Bowness
Make-up Designer: . . . . .Shaunna Harrison
Costume Designer: . . . . .Anushia Nieradzik
Properties Buyer: . . . . .Roger Williams
Film Cameraman: . . . . .John Walker
Film Sound: . . . . .Dennis Panchen and
 Nigel Woodford
Film Editor: . . . . .Mike Jackson
Camera Supervisor: . . . . .Ron Peverall
Studio Lighting Director: . . . . .Henry Barber
Studio Sound: . . . . .Dave Thompson
Technical Coordinator: . . . . . .Derek Martin
Videotape Editor: . . . . .Chris Wadsworth
Production Assistant: . . . . .Penny Thompson
Assistant Floor Manager: . . . . .Tony Dow
Graphic Designers: . . . . .Peter Clayton and Fen Symonds
Vision Mixer: . . . . .Bill Morton
Production Managers: . . . . .Janet Bone and Sue Bysh
Designers: . . . . .Derek Evans and Andy Dimond
Produced by Ray Butt

Del's investing in louvre doors and intends selling them to painter and decorator Brendan O'Shaughnessy, who's just secured a contract to refit and decorate a new housing estate at Nunhead. The trouble is, Del's supplier, Teddy Cummings, will only deal in bulk and Del's got to stump up two grand by tomorrow afternoon or the deal is off. The Trotters spot Denzil at the market *en route* to the Job Centre and persuade him – after chasing him for over a mile – to invest his £2000 redundancy money into the louvre door scheme.

But when Del hears from O'Shaughnessy that his supply of 165 doors is no longer required, he's gobsmacked. The Trotters head for their mother's monument in the cemetery – Del's retreat in moments of contemplation – to mull over their predicament. They're short of ideas, until Rodney spots a rare butterfly worth £3000 to lepidopterists. After finally netting their valuable find, Denzil arrives on the scene and tragedy strikes!

'Ashes to Ashes'

Original transmission: Thursday 28 October 1982, 8.30 pm

Production date: Sunday 20 June 1982

Original viewing figures: 9.8 million

Duration: 30 minutes

First repeat: Tuesday 12 July 1983, 8.30 pm

Subsequent repeats: 26/10/90, 27/1/95, 10/6/97, 21/1/00

CAST

Del Trotter . . . . .David Jason
Rodney Trotter . . . . .Nicholas Lyndhurst
Grandad Trotter . . . . .Lennard Pearce
Trigger . . . . .Roger Lloyd Pack

Del takes pity on Trigger, who's going alone to his gran's funeral and offers to come along with Rodney and Grandad. Never one to miss a business opportunity, even at funerals, Del promises Trigger that he'll take some of Alice's possessions off his hands, claiming Trigger will be ripped off if he lets any old person dispose of her belongings. He takes particular interest in a couple of urns, but Grandad later discovers that they contain ashes, which they decide must be those of Trigger's late grandfather.

Keen to dispose of the ashes while Trigger's away on holiday, they consider the most appropriate place to dump them. As Trigger's grandfather was an avid bowler, they try scattering his remains over the local bowling green, but the plan fails. When their scheme to drop the ashes in the River Thames is thwarted too, Del becomes frustrated and considers throwing them in a cement mixer. Eventually, the ashes are accidentally sucked up by a passing road sweeping lorry, much to the disgust of the driver. But there's a shock in store for the Trotters when they open the remaining urn.

Ashley, Lorraine

Role: Receptionist

Appeared in 'Modern Men'

Attwell, Michael

Role: Ray

Appeared in S2, episode 6

Born in Watford in 1943, Michael graduated from RADA and made his acting debut in a 1965 musical at Stratford East. His early years as an actor were largely spent in musicals, but he made his television debut as St John in the 1967 production, *The First Churchills*. His favourite small-screen roles are Razor Eddie in *Turtle's Progress* and Bill Sikes in *Oliver Twist*, while others credits include *Bergerac, Inspector Morse, Casualty, Boon, Roll Over Beethoven, Poldark* and *EastEnders* (as Kenny Beale). Recent credits include the guest lead in *My Family* and *The Bill*.

Michael has also appeared in a handful of films, such as *Buster* and *Tom and Viv*.

Attwell, Solly

Played by Colin Jeavons

In 'Hole in One', Rodney calls the solicitor when Albert falls through the cellar trapdoor – even if it was on purpose. But Rodney is dubious about Attwell and remarks that he's no better than the villains he represents.

'Hole in One'

Auctioneer

Played by Garard Green

The auctioneer works at Huddleston's auction rooms in Chelsea, where Del arrives to find Miranda Davenport bidding. The auctioneer is in charge of proceedings for the day's auction in 'Yesterday Never Comes'.

Auctioneer

Played by Glynn Sweet

The auctioneer in charge of events in 'Healthy Competition', attended by Del, Rodney and his new business partner, Mickey Pearce.

Auctioneer

Played by Seymour Matthews

In 'Time On Our Hands', the auctioneer is in charge of proceedings at Sotherby's when the famous Harrison watch is auctioned, making the Trotters millionaires in the process.

Audio cassettes

BBC Audio released an audio cassette (ISBN: 0563557044) on 12 October 1998, price £9.99. It contained four episodes from 1982, taken from the original TV soundtrack and edited for audio purposes. The episodes were: 'The Long Legs of the Law', 'The Yellow Peril', 'A Losing Streak' and 'No Greater Love…'. It was reissued in October 2000 (ISBN: 056355214X).

Audrey (Cousin)

In 'Strained Relations' Uncle Albert tells Del and Rodney that he lived with Audrey and her husband, Kevin, for a year, until one day they sent him down to Sainsbury's and emigrated whilst he was away. Audrey is never seen in the sitcom.

Audrey

(See 'Turner, Audrey')

Aussie Man

Played by Nick Stringer

The Aussie, who's in his thirties, arrives on the scene in 'Go West Young Man', and ends up buying the black Cortina convertible that Del and Rodney acquired from Boycie. An outspoken customer, who calls Del a 'cockney villain', it's a wonder he's fooled into buying the overpriced heap. He's seen again at the end of the episode when he smashes into the back of Del and Rodney's car, thanks to the Cortina's faulty brakes. To make matters worse, Del was driving Boycie's E-type Jag at the time.

Austin, Jo

Production Manager on 'Christmas Crackers'

Born in Wolverhampton, Jo studied at a business college in London before returning to her home town and working in an estate agents. She eventually moved back to London and, after temping for a while, joined a market research company.

Always interested in working within the television industry, she applied to the Beeb when BBC2 was launched, and was offered a position in 1962. After working as Bill Cotton's secretary for a time, she completed a production course and transferred to the production department at the end of 1963, initially as a production assistant on shows like *It's A Square World*, *The Beat Room* (an early music show), *The Likely Lads*, *'Till Death Us Do Part* and *Top of the Pops*. While working for David Croft, she also helped on *Are You Being Served?* and *It Ain't Half Hot, Mum*.

Jo took early retirement in 1989 after 27 years' service with the Beeb.

Australian Reporter

Played by Peter Wickham

A member of the Australian broadcasting camera crew that arrives at the church to watch the statue of the Virgin Mary and Baby weep during 'The Miracle of Peckham'. He's shocked when he discovers how much Del is charging for photos of the weeping statue.

Audience Figures

The viewing figures are testament to the dedicated following the sitcom has attracted during its long run on our television screens. Between the time the first episode, 'Big Brother', was transmitted on 8 September 1981, and the 2001 Christmas Special, 'If They Could See Us Now…!', which was the most popular show over that festive period, the viewing figures trebled. The pinnacle of the series' popularity came in 1996, when over 24 million people tuned in to wave goodbye to Del, Rodney and the rest of the crowd, and to celebrate the Trotters' long-overdue piece of luck in finding a timepiece which made them millionaires.

Average Viewing Figures Per Series

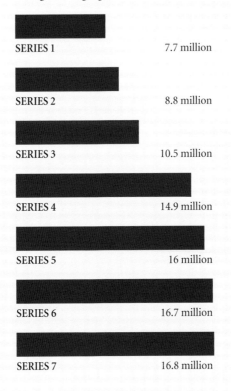

SERIES 1	7.7 million
SERIES 2	8.8 million
SERIES 3	10.5 million
SERIES 4	14.9 million
SERIES 5	16 million
SERIES 6	16.7 million
SERIES 7	16.8 million

Viewing Figures for Christmas Specials

'Christmas Crackers' (1981)	7.5 million
'Christmas Trees' (1982)	7.2 million
'Diamonds are for Heather' (1982)	9.3 million
'Thicker Than Water' (1983)	10.8 million
'To Hull and Back' (1985)	16.9 million
'A Royal Flush' (1986)	18.8 million
'The Frog's Legacy' (1987)	14.5 million
'Dates' (1988)	16.6 million
'The Jolly Boys' Outing' (1989)	20.1 million
'Rodney Come Home' (1990)	18 million
'Miami Twice' – Part 1 (1991)	17.7 million
'Miami Twice' – Part 2 (1991)	14.9 million
'Mother Nature's Son' (1992)	20.1 million
'Fatal Extraction' (1993)	19.6 million
'Heroes and Villains' (1996)	21.3 million
'Modern Men' (1996)	21.3 million
'Time On Our Hands' (1996)	24.3 million
'If They Could See Us Now…!' (2001)	20.3 million

Source: BBC Written Archive Centre, Caversham

Babbage, Don

Lighting director on 34 episodes: S1; S3; S4, episodes 3, 5, 6 & 7; S6, episodes 1, 3, 4, 5, 6; S7, episodes 1–4; 'Christmas Crackers'; 'Diamonds are for Heather'; 'Thicker Than Water'; 'The Frog's Legacy'; 'Dates'; 'The Jolly Boys' Outing'; 'Rodney Come Home'; 'Mother Nature's Son'

London-born Don Babbage gained considerable knowledge of working with transmitters while doing his his national service in the RAF. He then put this to good use whilst working in the same field at the BBC. He transferred to television in 1957, moved into the lighting section three years later, and was lighting in a junior capacity by 1964. Promoted to lighting director in 1975, he worked on numerous shows during his 37 years with the Beeb, including *Play School, Jackanory, Top of the Pops, Citizen Smith, Doctor Who, Just Good Friends, As Time Goes By* and many of the Les Dawson and Mike Yarwood shows.

Don retired from the Corporation in 1994 and has since travelled extensively.

Baby

Played by Michael Peters

The baby is seen in the closing scenes of 'From Prussia with Love'. When Anna, the German student, falls pregnant, the father and his parents (the Wainwrights) dismiss the situation, call Anna a liar and throw her out on the street. Del tries arranging an adoption with the help of the then childless Boycie and Marlene, but the plans fall through, which is for the best because Anna changes her mind about giving up her baby.

Baby Damien

(See 'Trotter, Damien')

Baby Tyler

(see 'Boyce, Tyler')

Baker, Del

Role: Policeman
Appeared in 'The Jolly Boys' Outing'

London-born Del Baker worked in engineering before enrolling at the Actors' Workshop and subsequently making his acting debut in a 1966 instalment of *Danger Man*, playing a 'heavy'. Del, who has never worked in the theatre, has appeared regu-

larly on the screen, either as an actor – credits include *Willow, The Living Daylights, Magnum P. I., Treasure Island, A View to a Kill* – or as a stuntman/coordinator. An active member of the Stunt Coordinators' Guild, he's organised the action on a number of productions, such as *Hope and Glory, Dracula, My Life So Far* and Disney's *Count of Monte Cristo*.

Baker, Jill

Role: Pauline Harris
Appeared in S1, episode 4

After training at the Bristol Old Vic Theatre School, Jill made her professional debut at the city's theatre in a 1972 production of *Charley's Aunt*. She gained valuable experience in repertory theatre around the country from Sheffield to Salisbury, before working with the Royal Shakespeare Company and the National Theatre.

Jill – whose film credits include *Hope and Glory* and *Shakespeare in Love*, in which she played Lady Margaret de Lessops – has also worked extensively on television. Her credits include Esther in BBC's *Perfect Strangers*, Sarah in *Fish*, Lady MacDuff in *Macbeth*, Jennifer in *Inspector Morse* and Mrs Haines in *Boon*. She also teamed up with David Jason again in *March in Windy City*, a 1998 production in which she played Dr Prudence Cox.

Baker, Mr

Not seen in the sitcom, Mr Baker, an American, is mentioned in 'The Second Time Around' by Del's ex-fiancée, Pauline Harris, who's back in Peckham after 12 years. She married Baker whilst working as an air hostess in the States.

Baker, Mrs

Played by Katharine Page

Mrs Baker, who's seen in 'The Jolly Boys' Outing', owns the Sunny Sea guest house in Margate. A kind-hearted woman, she suggests alternative accomodation when the Trotters are struggling to find a room for the night.

Banana Daiquiri

The drink Del orders at The Nag's Head when he's out drinking with Jumbo Mills in 'Who Wants to be a Millionaire'.

Barber, Henry

Lighting director on 13 episodes: S2 & S5

Born in Battersea, London, Henry worked in a bank for three years before completing his national service. Upon returning to civvy street he enrolled at a college and completed an electronics degree. He was employed by Decca's marine and airfield radar division before joining the BBC in 1962 as an assistant studio engineer. After completing a course in studio lighting, he transferred departments and became a TM2 (technical manager 2) in the early 1970s, then a lighting director by the mid-1970s, working on shows like *Z Cars*, *Butterflies*, *Top of the Pops*, *To the Manor Born*, *Doctor Who* and *Blackadder*.

Henry retired from the Beeb in 1993, and is enjoying his retirement in Southern Ireland.

Barber, Paul

Role: Denzil
Appeared in 16 episodes: S3, episode 7; S4, episode 7; S6, episodes 2, 3 & 6; S7, episode 4; 'To Hull and Back'; 'The Jolly Boys' Outing'; 'Miami Twice' (Parts 1 & 2); 'Mother Nature's Son'; 'Fatal Extraction'; 'Heroes and Villains'; 'Modern Men'; 'Time On Our Hands' and 'If They Could See Us Now...!'

When Paul first started playing Denzil, he was unprepared for the impact it would have on the public. 'I certainly wasn't expecting people to shout his name out in the street,' he admits. 'I'd be walking along the road in the early days and hear people shouting: "Denzil! Denzil!", and I'd carry on walking because I'd never known a Denzil, especially a black Denzil and didn't think for one moment that it was me they were calling. So it took time before I got used to being recognised for playing the character.'

Such success and adulation hasn't gone to Paul's head though, which is something he attributes to his tough upbringing, dominated by years spent in children's homes. When his mother died of tuberculosis in 1958, by which time his father had already left the family to live in Manchester, he was taken into care. But in hindsight, the experience helped shape his outlook on life, as he explains. 'Being brought up in care kept my feet firmly on the ground: I grew up never expecting too much from life.'

Years of being shipped between foster parents also affected his views on the career path he wished to take. Desperately wanting to experience a sense of belonging, he set his heart on joining the forces. 'I wanted to go into the army, then the navy, but I was too thick basically,' he says with a smile. 'Now, it all sounds mad, but the only reasons I wanted to join-up were to get out of Liverpool and to have a uniform.'

When he walked out of the school gates for the last time, though, Paul didn't head for the recruitment office. Instead, he moved between a series of manual jobs, working in factories, until he got the sack. 'I hated doing overtime; it was the summer and I wanted to be out in the sun rather than couped up inside the factory. This didn't go down too well with the bosses.'

Next stop was Lewis' department store in Liverpool. Aged 18, Paul worked in the basement, stocking shelves. One day his friend Alvin paid him a visit and unknowingly helped direct Paul's future. The local rag carried an advert inviting prospective thespians along to audition for the forthcoming musical *Hair*. 'Alvin had seen the advert, came running over to Lewis' and asked if I could get the afternoon off so that I could go to The Empire with

him because he wanted to try his luck. I don't think I even knew what the word "audition" meant, but agreed to go along to keep him company.'

Although by this stage in his life Paul was an integral part of an a cappella band, he didn't harbour serious dreams of working in the showbiz world. 'We always hung around together and practised our harmonies, but did it for fun; other friends had bands, too, and some of them formed The Real Thing and went on to have chart success.'

At The Empire, it looked as if Alvin's chance of stardom had vanished when they arrived late and bumped into the director and producer rushing out of the theatre door. The auditions had finished and they were heading to Manchester to see the next batch of hopefuls. 'We didn't know what to do,' explains Paul, 'then the director said: "Oh let's go back in again and sort you two out."' After hearing Alvin sing, it was Paul's turn. 'They asked if I wanted to have a go, but I told them I didn't know what to do, so they suggested singing "Yesterday".'

Although he'd only accompanied his pal to the auditions, it was Paul who was offered a part in *Hair*. But when Alvin didn't make the grade, Paul turned the chance down, until he was persuaded by Alvin's mother to rethink his decision. 'When she heard why I'd turned it down, she almost dragged me by the ear to the telephone and said: "You get on that phone and tell them you made a mistake and want the job."' Luckily, the part hadn't been recast and Paul embarked on a two-year tour with the production, marking the beginning of a fruitful career.

From *Hair*, Paul joined the cast of *Jesus Christ Superstar* in 1971; it was during his spell with the production that he made his small-screen debut, in *Lucky*, an instalment from the *Play for Today* season. Paul has a friend – Angela Bruce, who played Councillor Murray in 'Heroes and Villains' – to thank for this opportunity. 'She'd been in *The Rocky Horror Show* and had already been cast in the play,' explains Paul. 'When she heard the director saying they were looking for the leading man, she asked what type of lead they wanted. The director explained he wanted a tall scouser of mixed race, so she suggested me.'

A string of television appearances followed, including roles in *The Brothers McGregor*, *Gangsters* and, one of Paul's favourites jobs, playing Malcolm in BBC's sitcom *The Front Line*. While Alan Igbon played Sheldon, a Rastafarian, Paul played his brother who joined the police force.

Paul continues to work on the stage, with recent assignments including *High Life*, a play at the Bush Theatre, where he appeared alongside Nigel Planer and David Schofield. 'It was about four morphine addicts who intended robbing a bank, which was quite comical, even though it contained serious themes.'

On the movie front, he was part of the record-breaking home-grown triumph, *The Full Monty*. 'Whenever people speak to me it's either about *Only Fools* or *The Full Monty*; after all the years I've been in the profession, it's these two which stick in people's minds. Although occasionally I receive fan

mail and people refer to jobs I can't even remember doing, which is quite refreshing.'

Bardon, John

Role: Tom Clarke (the Security Officer)
Appeared in S5, episode 3

John, who was born in London in 1939, trained as an industrial designer before turning to acting. His theatrical career includes many West End performances, such as *The Good Companions* and *Kiss Me Kate*, for which he won a Laurence Olivier Award. He toured with his one-man show, *Here's a Funny Thing*, dedicated to Max Miller, and has worked in rep at Exeter and Oxford, with the Royal Shakespeare Company and at the National Theatre.

He's appeared regularly on TV, earlier in his career in *General Hospital*, *The Sweeney* as Doc Boyd, *Anthony and Cleopatra* and BBC2's *Joey*. More recent credits include *Seconds Out*, Ron Armitage in *Hi-De-Hi!*, *After Henry*, *Birds of a Feather*, *The Paradise Club*, Jack Morris in *Casualty*, *The Bill*, Eric Lumsden in *Coronation Street*, *The Darling Buds of May*, *Goodnight Sweetheart* and two series of the sitcom *Get Back*. Currently he's appearing as Jim Branning in *EastEnders*.

John has also appeared in several films, such as *S.P.Y.S.* with Donald Sutherland, *Khaki Doesn't Suit Me*, *One of Our Dinosaurs is Missing*, *The Keeper*, *84 Charing Cross Road*, *Ordeal by Innocence* and *Clockwise*, playing a ticket collector.

Barker, Ken

Role: Stuntman/Double for Del
Appeared in S5, episode 4

Actor/stuntman Ken Barker, who was born in London, began acting in 1949 and for 15 years appeared in such shows as *Z Cars*, *Dixon of Dock Green* and *New Scotland Yard*, before concentrating on stunt work. He worked as a stuntman in many films, including *Superman*, *Indiana Jones* and *Octopussy*, as well as TV shows including *Last of the Summer Wine*, *Are You Being Served?* and *The Fall and Rise of Reginald Perrin* (he's the swimmer who appeared in each episode's opening credits). Ken died of prostate cancer in 1998.

Barmaids at The Nag's Head

The transitory nature of the British barmaid is reflected in *Only Fools*, where various incumbents are seen over the years. It seemed each series was blessed with a new face behind the bar at The Nag's Head, beginning with **Peta Bernard**, as Joyce, whom Del classes as an 'old dog', even though he has a soft spot for her.

Appearing at ease behind the bar was easy for Peta because her friends owned a pub in Kent. 'I used to go behind the bar if they were rushed, so I never felt uncomfortable when it came to recording the scenes at The Nag's Head.' Joyce was the first barmaid she had played on television. 'I've played a lot of tarts and expensive call girls, but never a barmaid, so that was a first.'

When she was auditioned for the part of Joyce, Peta took her agent's advice and adopted a cockney

'Peta Bernard'

accent. 'My agent told me that the director [Ray Butt] had hurt his back, which had caused a little upheaval on the production; as my part was still to be cast, my agent suggested I adopted the accent they were looking for because if I went along using my normal voice, they might not want to take the risk – especially with so much else going on – on me being able to adopt the accent well enough.'

'Michèle Winstanley'

One memory which will remain with Peta is having to wear skin-tight leather trousers. 'I don't know how I got them on, they must have poured me into them,' she says, smiling. 'They were just right for Joyce, who – as Del said – was a bit of dog really. I had to take a deep breath, while someone held the trousers together using their full strength and another person zipped them up. They were tighter than any corset I've worn in period dramas – I could just about walk in them.' Popping to the loo posed serious problems! 'A dresser had to come along to help me get out of them, and then someone else had to be around to help put them back on.'

Although her appearances were brief, her presence was sufficient to generate fan mail. 'I had lots of letters, probably because of the low-cut blouse with a lot of cleavage showing.' Peta remembers the reaction the letters caused from her husband. 'The

people would say things like: "Can I have a photo because I think you're the most beautiful thing on TV." He would look at them and remark: "What's the matter with them all, are they mad or something?" Not much of a confidence boost.'

In series three **Michèle Winstanley**, who was 19, played Karen. 'It was a long time ago that I played Karen, but I remember I auditioned originally for just one episode but ended up staying for four; they also asked me back for the next series, but I was contractually obliged to another job so couldn't return, much to my unending disgruntlement.'

Michèle recalls her audition. 'Ray Butt was directing then. I walked in and there he sat, in a swivel chair, a chain-smoking, straight-talking mini dynamo of a man. He briefly described the character and her storyline to me, then said: "You can do that, can't you?", more as a statement than a question. I was delighted to get the part, but also scared; I'd seen the show and was a little star-struck.'

She has happy memories of working with the main cast, albeit briefly. 'In those days, dear old Lennard Pearce was still alive. He was a lovely fellow, just how he appears on the telly: slightly doddery with that hesitant, husky speech. But what I remember most clearly is that David Jason and Nicholas Lyndhurst were funnier in real life than they appeared on the screen.

'When it came to the first day of rehearsals, I took in some knitting (it was the '80s, knitwear was big). The part of Karen wasn't exactly challenging – a few lines per episode – so I spent quite a lot of time sitting about in the rehearsal hall at White City. Like you do, I got quite absorbed with my knit-one-pearl-one, and when I looked up I found the whole rehearsal room had stopped working and was looking at me; David Jason and Nicholas Lyndhurst were in the middle of a quite lascivious appraisal of my appearance: "Just giving you some sexual harassment at work," David explained; a sexual harassment lawsuit had been in the news that day and they didn't want me to feel left out. Thanks boys. Everyone was laughing and I blushed beetroot – naturally it was repeated throughout the day, and several days to follow.'

At the end of the week Michèle popped down the pub with the cast and crew one lunchtime. 'Nicholas Lyndhurst was quite private even then, so it was nice to have him around for lunch. The pub was virtually empty, and the pool table free, so Nicholas offered me a game. This was my chance to get my own back; unbeknown to him I was a pool wizard and had recently won a cue at a local tournament, beating the mostly male competitors hands down. Naturally, I won, much to his surprise – I laughed like a drain, and David declined me a further game. Such happy memories.'

Other barmaids that were employed by Mike included Nervous Nerys (Andrée Bernard); Maureen (Nula Conwell); Julie (Julie La Rousse) and Vicky (Kim Clifford). Several others were seen from time to time but didn't stay on the scene for long, perhaps not making the grade or, perhaps, unable to work for Mike, the landlord.

Barman

Played by William Thomas

In 'Yuppy Love' the barman takes Del's order for a bottle of Beaujolais Nouveau, when he's trying to impress two attractive girls, Marsha and Dale.

Barman

The bespectacled barman works at The Monte Carlo Club and serves Del and Rodney when they arrive at the establishment in 'Christmas Crackers'.

Baron, Denise

Make-up designer on eight episodes: S3 and 'Thicker Than Water'

During Denise's career with the BBC, she worked on numerous programmes, such as *Doctor Who*, the Harold Pinter play *Old Times*, and the *Chronicles of Narnia – The Silver Chair*. She now teaches at the London School of Fashion.

Barr, Linda

Role: Dog owner
Appeared in S4, episode 5

Sadly, Linda was forced to give up her career when she developed M.E.. However, she has since recovered and retrained as a clinical nutritionist, a profession she currently practises in. After 15 years in complementary medicine – including a period at the Institute of Optimum Nutrition, where she gained her diploma – she established the Nutrition and Health Company in 1990.

Barritt, Ian

Role: Man in the pub
Appeared in S7, episode 2

Born in Burnley in 1944, Ian worked as a teacher before deciding to opt for an actor's life. He made his debut in a 1967 production of *The Entertainer*, at Lincoln Theatre Royal, before gaining more stage experience at Leeds and York.

His first taste of television came in the late sixties, playing a policeman in *Coronation Street*, and over the years work in this area has included appearances in *Secret Army*, *The Russ Abbot Show* and *Office Gossip*.

Ian continues to work in theatre and recent assignments include *Coriolanus* and *Richard II*, in London, New York and Tokyo.

Barry

Played by Walter Sparrow

Seen in 'Danger UXD', Dirty Barry is a Cockney who owns a sex shop (Ecstasy) in Walworth Road. When Del finds he's lumbered with 50 inflatable sex dolls, he tries selling them to Barry, but doesn't have any luck because the council has just revoked his trading licence, forcing the shop's closure. Barry is a dishevelled character who's well suited to his backstreet life.

Bartlett, Susannah

Location manager on one episode: 'Mother Nature's Son'

Susannah was born in Hong Kong and came to England at the age of nine. When she left school she intended joining RADA, but her mother fell ill, and she postponed plans of joining drama school.

Susannah began her working life with the Beeb at the age of 21, working as a secretary on *Songs of Praise,* before moving into studio management as a floor assistant, concentrating mainly on drama. She worked through the ranks and was 1st assistant director when she agreed to help Tony Dow as locations manager on the 1992 Christmas Special.

She left the BBC in 1994 to raise a family and now lives in Wiltshire. When her children are older, she intends forming her own locations company.

Bass, Jacqui

Film editor on one episode: S7, episode 6

Born in London in 1965, Jacqui joined the BBC in 1987, working as secretary to the editor of *That's Life!* Other programmes she's worked on include *Hearts of Gold, Holiday* and the *Sydney Olympics 2000.* After working in other roles with the Corporation, including researcher, film editor and PA to Head of Television Features, she left in 1994 and worked for a communications company. After taking a year out travelling, she returned to the BBC in 1998, and currently works as PA to the controller of *Five Live.*

Bass Player

Played by Dave Richmond

The bass player is part of the group entertaining at the Mardi Gras Club in Margate during 'The Jolly Boys' Outing'.

Bates, Brigid Erin

Role: Inga
Appeared in 'The Jolly Boys' Outing'

Baz

Played by Ron Pember

The cigarette-puffing Baz (real name Basil) is chairman of the tenants' committee at the start of 'Homesick', and is relieved when he's able to dump the responsibility on the unsuspecting Rodney.

Bazalgette, Olivia

Production manager on one episode: 'A Royal Flush'

Olivia, who's married to actor Daniel Hill, was born in Newtown, Hampshire, in 1957. She joined the BBC as a secretary in 1977, working initially in radio before transferring to TV drama and then light entertainment. Nowadays she works as a freelance producer and is a reader for a film company.

Only Fools was Olivia's first job as a production manager, but other shows she worked on during her 16-year career at the Beeb include *Doctor Who, Blackadder the Third* and a series of *Victoria Wood.*

Becker, Dr

Played by John Bryans

The doctor's sole appearance is in 'Homesick'. When he's reluctant to visit Grandad, who collapses in the flat, Del reminds the doc that he knows about his peccadillo with the local good-time girl, Rita Alldridge. When Del adds that he often sees the doctor's wife at his market stall, he agrees immediately to make a house call.

After examining Grandad, he tells Del they should seriously consider moving to one of the new council bungalows in nearby Herrington Road, because Grandad's legs won't take much more clambering up 12 flights of stairs.

Becker, who's been the Trotters' doctor for years, is mentioned again in 'Thicker Than Water', when Rodney suggests Del visits him when they're querying their blood groups.

Belbin, Susie

Director on seven episodes: S4

Born in Glasgow, Susie wanted to work in the theatre from childhood. At nine, she attended part-time drama classes, but by the time she left school she knew that stage management was where her true interest lay, and enrolled on a full-time course for a year. Upon graduating she worked at Glasgow's Citizens' Theatre for 12 months before turning freelance and working at several venues, including the Opera House in Harrogate.

When the opportunity to help at BBC Scotland came along, she snapped it up, and before long was offered a permanent contract and was promoted to assistant floor manager. During her 28-year career in the Beeb, she spent four years based at Television Centre in Scotland, and the rest in London, beginning a three-year spell on the *Morecambe and Wise Show* in 1973.

By 1976 she was working for David Croft, and during the seven years she was assigned to his office, she worked on shows like *Come Back, Mrs Noah; It Ain't Half Hot, Mum; Are You Being Served?; Hi-De-Hi!; 'Allo 'Allo!,* which she helped direct; and *Dad's Army.* During her career she's directed *Bread* as well as *Only Fools and Horses,* and produced and directed *One Foot in the Grave, Life Without George* and *Sitting Pretty.* She also produced *Jonathan Creek* and was the BBC comedy department's executive producer for a time. During her time with the Beeb she won two BAFTAs, for *One Foot in the Grave* and *Jonathan Creek.*

Susie has now retired from the television industry.

Baxter, Joan

Role: Singer
Appeared in S5, episode 4

'Homesick'

MEMORIES OF DIRECTING SERIES 4

★ ★ ★ ★ ★ ★

'I'd just completed a director's training course when Ray Butt called me in to direct the fourth series. This was the series, of course, when we lost Lennard Pearce. In many respects it was probably fortunate that I was new to the programme because when news of Lennard's death broke, it really hit everyone hard, including Ray Butt and John Sullivan, whereas I could remain objective because I wasn't so emotionally involved. Sure, I was upset as well, but not to the level of the rest of them who'd known him from day one.

'It was certainly a job in which I learnt on my feet. I remember standing outside a courthouse for one scene – we were doing rewrites – and it was freezing cold. There I was standing on the pavement with Del, Rodney and the new character, Uncle Albert, waiting for the pages of the script for the scene we had to shoot to arrive! So I had no idea what the shots were or what my characters were going to be doing. Duly John Sullivan placed three or four pages of script in our respective hands and we had to get on with it. It was tragic for the others who had to go on and be jolly, but good experience for me as a new director.

'When we filmed the funeral scenes there was one lovely moment when Mother Nature took a hand: everybody was dressed in black but because it had snowed the night before there was a covering in the graveyard, creating this wonderful black and white effect, which gave the scene an added dimension.

'The idea to throw the hat down on to the coffin was excellent; John Sullivan's approach to maintaining the comedy, albeit just with little touches, was a good thing because it blended in beautifully with the sad occasion.

'I enjoyed working with John Sullivan and went on to work with him on other series. He's well known for being a bit last minute, with everything being pushed to the edge in terms of scripts, but I believe he has to work that way to get the best out of himself.

'I don't know how he turns out script after script of pure quality. It was always exciting when he delivered a script: I remember we met at a pub once and he handed over the latest script; it was almost like passing over an envelope full of national secrets, and you open it and read the script, while John buys himself a pint and sits there in silence. Of course, it was rare that I was able to sit in silence because I was laughing out loud as I turned the pages.

'One of John's huge talents is being able to take you to the point where tears are about to fall and then suddenly pulling the rug away and you find yourself laughing. That's exactly what happened with "Strained Relations". There was the up and down, the light and dark and the audience just went with it. At appropriate moments you could hear a pin drop; for example, the argument between Del Boy and Rodney back at the flat was really moving and the audience reacted to that.

'One of the other major events during the series was the appearance of Marlene, played beautifully by Sue Holderness. It's very daunting for actors coming in to a successful series, but Sue did well from the start; I liked her as an actress and she had the full measure of the character from day one. It would have been so easy for Sue to have turned the part into an over-the-top caricature, but she remained on the side of believability.

'Everyone was very welcoming to me being a new director, including David and Nick. I remember filming this scene in a market and I was nervous about not covering the scene sufficiently and that we'd return to the editing suite and I'd be asked where the close-up shot of something was. I was a bit over eager and shot more bits than I actually needed. I can remember David coming up to me when I told him I wanted to do another close-up and asking whether I had a couple of minutes. He took me aside and said: "Susie, I really think you've covered this scene enough, and if Ray Butt says anything afterwards I'll have a word with him, but I do believe you've done enough." He was absolutely right, of course.

'I remember another time we were at rehearsals when David and Nick thought it would be a wheeze to make out that there had been a dreadful row between the three of us. I said: "God, no, I'll get the sack!" Anyway, they did it and their timing was perfect. They were having a row when Ray walked into the room, going at it hammer and tongs before storming out.

'Ray turned to me and shouted: "What the **** is going on?" I told him I didn't know but there had been a terrible row. He had a go at me, saying: "These are my leading ******* actors and I can't leave you for ten minutes!" At that point, I think David and Nick realised I was succumbing and going under rapidly so they came back in to the room and explained. It was quite sweet, really, and again it was their way of bringing me into the fold.

'I learnt a lot from working on the series, especially about comedy and timing. There is no question about it, David is a master. Nick, in my view, though, is the ultimate master; I don't think he gets enough recognition for his role as Rodney. I have never seen anybody do stillness the way he does: where another actor would feel it necessary to pull a face, Nick doesn't move. His reactions are superb.'   **SUSAN BELBIN – Director**

Belcher, Joe

Role: Boatman

Appeared in 'To Hull and Back'

Joseph, born in 1928, was a greengrocer before changing direction and becoming an actor. He made his professional debut playing a father in *Spend, Spend, Spend* at the age of 39, just two weeks after throwing in his greengrocer's apron.

He's appeared in several films, such as *Dracula, The Link* and *An American Werewolf in London*, and various television shows, including *Coronation Street* and *Dalziel and Pascoe* in 1999.

Bell, Rachel

Role: Lil

Appeared in 'To Hull and Back'

Rachel, who's just celebrated 30 years in the profession, graduated in drama from Hull University (1968–71) and immediately secured employment at the Hull Arts Centre. In 1972, she left to become a founder member of the Hull Track Theatre Company, where she remained until 1976.

Her television debut was in a play for the BBC, back in 1975, and she has since gone on to become a familiar face to viewers thanks to her energetic performance as the highly strung Louise in two series of John Sullivan's *Dear John*, Edith Pilchester in three series of *The Darling Buds of May* and six series as Mrs Holmes in *Grange Hill*.

Rachel, who was born in 1950, has built up an extensive list of credits, predominantly in theatre and television. On stage she's been involved in a national tour of *Absent Friends*, and performed at the Royal National Theatre in *Yerma* and *Under Milk Wood*. Other screen appearances include a *One Foot in the Grave* Christmas Special, *The Upper Hand*, *Last of the Summer Wine*, *Home to Roost*, *Doctor Who*, *Shoestring* and *Crown Court*.

Bellman, Gina

Role: Carmen

Appeared in S6, episode 4

Born in New Zealand in 1966, Gina made her debut playing Tamar in the 1985 movie *King David*. Small parts on television followed, but her big break came in the title role of BBC's mini-series, *Blackeyes*, written and directed by Dennis Potter.

While her favourite small-screen role is Jane in two series of *Coupling*, she's been seen playing characters such as Samantha in *Jonathan Creek*, Henrietta Spain in *Ted and Ralph* and Gina Mussolini in *Mussolini*, for NBC in America. On the big screen she's appeared in *Pressure Points*, *Seven Days to Live*, *Silent Trigger* and *Everything I Like*.

Gina is also a busy stage actress and recent roles include Karen in *Speed-the-Plow* at the Duke of York's Theatre, Ophelia in *Hamlet* and Imogen in *Cleo, Camping* and *Emmanuelle and Dick*, at the Royal National Theatre.

Benfield, Derek

Role: Registrar

Appeared in S6, episode 6

Derek made his professional stage debut in 1948

whilst on vacation from RADA: he played Abner in *Wishing Well*, for Brian Rix, at the King's Hall Theatre, Ilkley.

After graduating, he plied his trade at various repertory companies around the country, including Preston, Hull, Croydon, Worthing and Salisbury. He then made his first television appearance as Professor Bergman in BBC's 1955 production *Return to the Lost Planet*. In this medium, Derek is probably best known for playing Bill Riley in nearly 100 episodes of *The Brothers*, and Robert Wainthropp – opposite Patricia Routledge – in *Hetty Wainthropp Investigates* between 1995–99, two of his favourite jobs.

Derek, who's also appeared in several films, remains busy in the industry; he's also a playwright, whose writing includes *Touch and Go, Caught on the Hop, Beyond a Joke* and *Bedside Manners*.

Benson

Nicknamed 'Bend-over Benson', the old headmaster at the Martin Luther King Comprehensive is discussed in 'The Class of '62'. Boycie, Trigger and Del completed their education at the school, and attend a mystery school reunion at The Nag's Head. When they start worrying about who organised the event, it's even suggested that Benson's the man behind it, even though some incident (the nature of which we never discover) has seen him institutionalised for years, with doctors recommending that he shouldn't be allowed back into society. Although we never see him, he wouldn't be easy to miss: he's tall, has a scar running down from the bridge of his nose, and his right ear is missing!

Benson, Elizabeth

Role: Lady Ridgemere
Appeared in S2, episode 7

Bolton-born Elizabeth Benson trained at LAMDA and began her foray into the acting world in the 1946 film *The Shop at Sly Corner*. Her early career was spent largely in theatres around the country, including a spell at the Old Vic. Her television debut was in a 1956 episode of *Dixon of Dock Green*, while other credits include two appearances in *Fawlty Towers* (Mrs White in 'The Kipper and the Corpse' and Mrs Heath in 'Gourmet Night'); Geraldine in *Shelley*; a secretary in the 1978 miniseries *Love for Lydia*; Mrs Wallis in a 1985 production of *Sense and Sensibility*; Doris Proctor in *Cover Her Face* and, more recently, *London's Burning*.

Beringer, Paul

Role: Policeman
Appeared in 'Dates'

Paul has worked in all areas of the industry, including appearances as a sales assistant in *The Nanny*, a policeman in *Minder* and Paul O'Donnell in the 1985 soap *Albion Market*. On the big screen, meanwhile, he's been seen in *Letter to Brezhnev* and *Project Redlight*, as Jon Gordon. He's also written his own short film, *The Silencing*, which he also directed in 2000.

Bernard, Andrée

Role: Nerys (the barmaid)
Appeared in S6, episode 5 and 'Dates'

Andrée started her career in repertory theatre, performing at venues such as Birmingham, Coventry, Derby and the Chichester Festival Theatre. Other work on the stage has seen her appear in *The Sweet Smell of Success* and *Side by Side by Sondheim* in Toronto, *Hair* and *Kiss Me Kate* at the Old Vic and *A Chorus Line*.

She's also been busy on the screen. Her film credits include *The Sea Change, Chaplin, Bernard and the Genie, The Crying Game* and her first movie, *Absolute Beginners*. On television, meanwhile, she's played many roles in *The Bill* and has been seen in *Anne of Green Gables, Baddiel's Syndrome, Poirot, Silent Witness, Dalziel and Pascoe* and *The Brittas Empire*.

Andrée remains busy in the profession and is appearing in *We Will Rock You*, the new Ben Elton/Queen musical.

Bernard, Peta

Role: Joyce (the Barmaid)
Appeared in S1, episodes 1 & 4

Although she was born in Swansea, Peta was brought up in Ireland. She returned to England at the age of 13, attending a boarding school in Bournemouth. She wanted to become an actress but parental pressure caused her to change her plans, opting for a career in photographic modelling instead.

Eventually she was offered the chance of theatre work, and began appearing in provincial theatre, pantomime and summer seasons around the country. Later in her career she appeared on television in *Grange Hill, Sorry!, The Professionals* and, on the big screen, playing Mabel in the 1978 picture *The Class of Miss MacMichael*.

In 1989, Peta started working as an astrologer, and she's now a full-time astrological consultant (a subject in which she has a degree) and counsellor. She also works as a counsellor outside astrology, teaches, lectures and runs workshops.

Bernice

Rodney talks about Bernice to Trigger – who's paying little attention – in The Nag's Head during 'May the Force be with You'. He claims he had to put his foot down when she started getting too serious, so we can only assume that she's another of Rodney's exes – though we never actually see her.

Bernie

Referred to in 'Thicker Than Water', although not seen in the episode. Bernie worked at the local market and was married to Maisie Turner until they divorced when she started seeing someone else.

Betatime

In 'Heroes and Villains', the Trotter home is packed with Betatime boxes, containing the 150 Latvian quartz radio alarm clocks with everlasting solar batteries; their only fault is that they have a mind of their own and go off whenever they feel like it.

Bevan, Graham

Dubbing editor on one episode: 'Mother Nature's Son'

Beveridge, Angela

Vision mixer on three episodes: S2, episodes 5, 6 & 7

Angela, who was born in London, trained and worked as a ballet dancer for 20 years before joining the BBC in the mid-1960s. She worked in the costume department for six months before moving into vision mixing, a job she remained in until leaving the BBC in 1989.

Among the numerous shows Angela worked on are classic comedies like *Are You Being Served?*; *It Ain't Half Hot, Mum*; *Hi-De-Hi!*; *'Allo 'Allo!*; *Terry and June*; *Sorry!*; *Blackadder*; *No Place Like Home*; *Yes, Prime Minister; Ever Decreasing Circles* and *Three Up, Two Down*.

Nowadays she runs a company with her husband, John Beveridge, marketing and managing television and film studios.

Beverley

Played by Mel Martin

Beverley is a medical receptionist who appears in 'Fatal Extraction' intially to inform Mr Ellis, the dentist, who's treating Del at the time, that Mrs Patel has cancelled her four o'clock appointment. Del takes a fancy to her attractive smile, especially when he discovers that the blonde-haired receptionist – who has a daughter and a grandson called Damien – has been divorced for nine years. He plucks up the courage and invites her on a date, which he feels justified to do considering Raquel has walked out on him.

But when he later hears from Rodney that Raquel is very upset about their split, the guilt pangs begin and he cancels the date. From that moment, Del can't seem to rid himself of the pretty Beverley and spots her wherever he goes; when she turns up at the flat in response to an advert concerning the sale of Damien's old high chair, it's the final straw. He confronts her at the hospital but gets his ear chewed off in return.

Bhatti, Babar

Role: Indian restaurant manager
Appeared in S1, episode 3

For many, Babar is best remembered for playing Punkah-Wallah Rumzan in six series of Jimmy Perry and David Croft's *It Ain't Half Hot, Mum*, but over the years he's appeared in numerous shows, particularly comedies, including *The Tommy Cooper Show, Some Mothers Do 'Ave 'Em* and *Shelley*.

Biffo

Played by John Pierce Jones

Seen in the closing scene of 'The Miracle of Peckham', Biffo's band is playing at The Nag's Head disco. He's also the owner of the trumpet Rodney wakes Uncle Albert up with when he brings it back to the flat. In a moment of madness, Rodney went on stage, snatched the trumpet from Biffo, blew down the wrong end, gave him the V-sign and walked out with it. Biffo, who's nicknamed 'The Bear', was fuming. To make matters worse, Albert threw the trumpet down the dust chute, buckling it in the process. In the end, Biffo catches up with Rodney, who's lost for words before scarpering, with Biffo in pursuit.

Big Brenda

In 'Watching the Girls Go By' Del sets up a blind date for Rodney, with none other than Big Brenda, Southern Area Shot-put Champion. Later, when Rodney is desperate to find a female companion to accompany him to a do at The Nag's Head, Del suggests resuming contact with Brenda, whom we never see.

'Big Brother'

Original transmission: Tuesday 8 September 1981, 8.30 pm

Production date: Sunday 7 June 1981

Original viewing figures: 9.2 million

Running time: 30 minutes

First repeat: Wednesday 13 June 1984, 9.30 pm

Subsequent repeats: 12/4/87, 7/9/90, 8/9/97, 23/4/99

CAST

Del Trotter . . . . .David Jason
Rodney Trotter . . . . .Nicholas Lyndhurst
Grandad Trotter . . . . .Lennard Pearce
Joyce, the barmaid . . . . .Peta Bernard
Trigger . . . . .Roger Lloyd Pack
Walk-ons: . . . .(People in pub) Ridgewell Hawkes, Alan Talbot, Dave Ould, Danny Lyons, Kenneth Lawrie, Pat Butler, Jean Taylor, Linda French, Penny Lambirth and six extras. (Market stallholder) Chris Breeze. (Woman in market) Patsy Peters.

PRODUCTION TEAM

Written by John Sullivan
Title music arranged and conducted by Ronnie Hazlehurst composed and sung by John Sullivan
Audience Warm-Up: . . . . .Felix Bowness
Make-up Designer: . . . . .Pauline Cox
Costume Designer: . . . . .Phoebe De Gaye
Properties Buyer: . . . . .Chris Ferriday
Film Cameraman: . . . . .Bill Matthews
Film Sound: . . . . .Dennis Panchen
Film Editor: . . . . .John Jarvis
Camera Supervisor: . . . . .Ron Peverall
Studio Lighting Director: . . . . .Don Babbage
Studio Sound: . . . . .Mike Felton
Technical Coordinator: . . . . . .Robert Hignett
Videotape Editor: . . . . .Mike Taylor
Production Assistant: . . . . . . .Penny Thompson
Assistant Floor Manager: . . . .Mandie Fletcher
Graphic Designer: . . . . .Peter Clayton
Vision Mixer: . . . . .Hilary West
Production Manager: . . . . .Janet Bone
Designer: . . . . .Tony Snoaden
Directed by Martin Shardlow
Produced by Ray Butt

Against the advice of business acquaintances, Del has made Rodney a partner in the family business, Trotter's Independent Traders, although he has second thoughts when he finds Rodney, who fancies himself as the company's new financial adviser, keeping accounts. Fearing the books could be used as ammunition by the tax man, he berates Rodney, who claims it's the only way he can keep Del in check, especially as he thinks he's cheating him in some way.

Rodney's claim for the position of financial adviser is further weakened when he sticks his oar in and spoils a deal Del makes with Trigger; however, it transpires that if Del had listened to Rodney's initial advice, they wouldn't have been lumbered with 25 useless briefcases no one can open because the combination is locked up inside!

Before the day is out, Rodney and Del have another row. Fed up and desperate to prove he can stand on his own two feet, Rodney leaves home and heads for Hong Kong – trouble is, he forgets his passport and fails to make his big escape.

Bigden, Alf

Role: Drummer
Appeared in 'The Jolly Boys' Outing'

London-born Alf Bigden was a watchmaker's apprentice, worked on the stock exchange and joined the RAF before forging a career for himself as a professional musician. Although he had played instruments from childhood, it wasn't until the 1950s that he turned professional, concentrating on drums and Latin America percussion.

Work opportunities soon came his way, including studio work, radio broadcasts and productions for both small and big screen. His extensive television credits include shows with Tom Jones and Engelbert Humperdinck, while among the film scores he's worked on are *The Dirty Dozen*, *The Dam Busters*, *The Eagle Has Landed* and *The Bridge on the River Kwai*.

Biggastaff, Mr

Played by Norman Kay
In 'To Hull and Back' the middle-aged Mr Biggastaff

is seen but not heard, when he and his wife listen to Boycie's sales patter concerning one of his cars. One of Boycie's employees, Colin, interrupts to informs his boss that Del is on the phone, but Mr Biggastaff eventually buys the car only to discover just how poor Boycie's customer service is. When he breaks down on the A1 and calls Peckham's infamous car salesman for help, he is brushed aside.

Biggastaff, Mrs

Played by Brenda Mortine
Mrs Biggastaff is seen in Boycie's showroom with her husband during 'To Hull and Back'.

Bill

Played by Victor Reynolds
Captain of the Peckham Bowling Club, Bill appears briefly in 'Ashes to Ashes', when he's called over to the clubhouse window by a female club member, who thinks she's spotted an urn standing in the middle of the green. The urn is quickly retrieved by the Trotters, however, and by the time the Captain looks out, it's nowhere to be seen and he remarks that she's been drinking too much.

Bingley-Hall, Paul

Dubbing editor on three episodes: 'Heroes and Villains', 'Modern Men' and 'Time On Our Hands'

MEMORIES OF 'MIAMI TWICE'

★ ★ ★ ★ ★ ★

'The programme was a personal favourite of mine, and I was immensely proud to be associated with it. That my enjoyment was shared with over 20 million other people, still gives me a buzz of excitement, even today. I remember being in the gallery whilst the final scenes were shot in the studio at Television Centre, with a tear in my eye and a lump in the throat at what was then to be the "last" episode.

'I also remember the tight security surrounding the shooting and how the single image that got to the press was one of Del Boy and his Rolls Royce with the number "Del 1", leading them all to believe, incorrectly, that the Trotters had won the lottery. When Del and Rodney appeared as Batman and Robin, I laughed as if for the first time, although I had seen it many times before in the course of my work. And when the watch was discovered and auctioned I felt a huge sigh of relief that the secret was out.

'With the wealth of talent both in front of and behind the camera, it remains the one programme that I was, and still am, overawed by, and think myself very lucky to have been part of.'

PAUL BINGLEY-HALL – Dubbing editor

Bird, Ted

Lighting gaffer on one episode: 'The Jolly Boys' Outing'
Ted has worked in both the film and television industry, with credits including *Prisoner of Honour* and *Bright Hair* for the small screen, and the 1996 thriller, *Crimetime*, directed by George Sluizer, for the big screen.

Bishop, Graham

Properties buyer on four episodes: 'Fatal Extraction', 'Heroes and Villains', 'Modern Men' and 'Time On Our Hands'
Graham worked in stage management for ten years before joining the BBC in Cardiff in 1983. After working as a TV operative, he moved to London's Television Centre in 1987 and joined the props department. The first show he worked on was *Sorry!*, though since then he has concentrated mainly on dramas, such as *Lovejoy*, *Secret Agent* and *Bergerac*. He was made redundant in 1997, since when he's worked freelance. One of his recent projects has been *Man and Boy*, for the BBC.

Bishop, Sue

Assistant floor manager on three episodes: S6, episodes 5 & 6 and 'The Frog's Legacy'
Sue, who was born in Carshalton, completed a drama degree at Hull University and worked in fringe theatre before joining the BBC as a floor assistant in 1984. Whilst working as an assistant floor manager she was given a nine-month attach-

ment to Belfast working on *Foreign Bodies* for BBC Drama; she grew to like the area so much that she opted to leave the Beeb in 1990 when the attachment came to a close, and started to work freelance.

After a while she decided to change career, and upon completing a one-year postgraduate course in 1991, qualified as a primary teacher, a job she still does today. Some of the programmes she worked on whilst employed by the BBC include *Top of the Pops*, *Saturday Superstore* and *Dear John*.

Bisset, Donald

Role: Wallace (the butler)
Appeared in S2, episode 7
Donald, who was born in London in 1911, was a veteran of stage and screen. His television work included appearances in *Crane*, *Doctor Who*, *Doctor*

in the House, *The Professionals*, *Pollyanna*, *Love for Lydia* and *The Old Curiosity Shop* during the 1960s and '70s. By this time, he'd already cut his teeth in films, having been cast in productions such as *Murder in the Cathedral*, *Little Red Monkey*, *The Brain Machine*, *Up the Creek*, *The Headless Ghost* and *Carry On Again, Doctor*.

He remained busy in the profession until his death in 1995, with later assignments seeing him play Mr Morgan in 1993's *The Black Velvet Gown*, a manservant in *The Hound of the Baskervilles* and Trafford Simcox in *Paradise Postponed*. Donald was also a published children's writer.

Black Man

Played by Lewis St Juste
In 'To Hull and Back', this character buys one of Del's Japanese watches for ten quid.

Blackshaw Road

In 'The Second Time Around', we learn that the cemetery where Pauline Harris' first hubby, Bobby Finch, is buried can be found in Blackshaw Road.

Blackwood, Vas

Role: Lennox Gilbey
Appeared in S5, episode 3
Vas, whose recent credits include playing Rory Breaker in the film *Lock, Stock and Two Smoking Barrels*, trained at the ALRA Drama School before clocking up an extensive list of credits on stage and screen. In the theatre he's worked on productions such as *Robin Hood* at the Lewisham Theatre, *The Ghost of Riddle-Me-Heights* at Birmingham Rep and *Barbarians* at the Young Vic.

On television he's appeared in, amongst others, *Casualty*, *Girls on Top*, *Angels*, *French and Saunders*, *The Brief*, *Right About Now* and *Fun at the Funeral Parlour*, while his film work includes *Mean Machine*, *The Escapist*, *Romeo Error* and *By Far*.

Blaine, Philip

Role: Frank
Appeared in 'Rodney Come Home'
Born in Pontypool in 1934, Philip graduated from RADA and began his career in 1953's *Out of the Whirlwind*, a coronation play performed in Westminster Abbey. Work in various repertory the-

atres, including Derby and Perth, followed before he made his television debut in an early BBC2 play, *The Physicists*, in 1964.

Other television work includes *The Sandbaggers*; *Hale and Pace*; *Yes, Prime Minister*; *To Be the Best*; *The Professionals* and his favourite, 'The Nesbitts are Back', a two-episode story in *Z Cars*, from which the spin-off series *The Nesbitts Are Coming* originated.

Philip has appeared in a handful of films, such as *Oliver!*, *The Amorous Adventures of Moll Flanders*, *Georgie Girl* and *The Magnificent Two*, while his various spells on the West End stage have included appearances in *Salad Days* and *Canterbury Tales*. Philip, however, no longer works in the theatre.

Blake, Roger

Role: Eugene Macarthy
Appeared in S7, episode 3
Born in 1957, Roger trained at the Central School of Speech and Drama, with Tessa Peake-Jones as a contemporary. Upon graduating, he headed west and, in 1978, appeared in *Pygmalion* at the Theatre Clwyd, before moving on to other reps up and down the British Isles, as well as fringe theatre.

He was given his induction to television in 1980, playing a Welshman in *Dear John*. His favourite roles in the medium are Sir Geoffrey Piddle in *Blackadder*, and Wing Commander Campbell-Stokes in *All Along the Watchtower*, but his list of credits extends to shows such as *Alistair McGowan's Big Impression*, *The Professionals*, *Berkeley Square*, *Casualty*, *Ellington*, *Red Dwarf* and *Class Act*. He also does a great deal of voice work and was a regular on *Spitting Image*.

Roger, who hasn't worked in the theatre for some years, has also been seen in minor roles on the big screen in films including *Buddy's Song* and *Young Winston*.

Bland, Paula-Ann

Role: Michelle
Appeared in 'Rodney Come Home'
Paula-Ann, who was born in Blyth, Northumberland, in 1968, trained at Italia Conti before making her professional debut in *Grange Hill*, back in 1980 – she went on to play Claire Scott for seven years. Other television roles include Betsy Horrocks in the 1987 mini-series, *Vanity Fair*, Sylvie in *Waiting for God*, a jilted bride in *The Bill* and Mrs London in *Health and Efficiency*.

No longer an actress, Paula-Ann is now a director of Paola Tregemini, a designer shoe shop in London's fashionable Kings Road, which supplies shoes to the stars, including Madonna, Geri Halliwell, Minnie Driver and Victoria Beckham.

Blizard, Helen

Role: Trudy
Appeared in S7, episode 2
Helen, who was born in 1956, worked as an auxiliary nurse at the Queen Mary's children's ward, Roehampton, before turning to acting. She finished

her training at the Bristol Old Vic Theatre School, and made her professional acting debut in Manchester, playing Anna in *The Prisoner of Zenda*, while her first part on television was in LWT's *Metal Mickey*. However, it was a medium she was already familiar with, having made numerous appearances with the doo-wop band, Rocky Sharpe and the Replays, who enjoyed seven hit singles between 1978 and 1983.

On stage, Helen's early work took her from Hornchurch Rep to the West End's Fortune Theatre, as well as on a tour with the New Vic Theatre Company. On the small screen, meanwhile, Helen regards her roles in *Only Fools and Horses* and Yorkshire TV's play, *Glorious Day* – in which she played the lead, Gloria – as her favourite jobs, though she's also been seen in programmes such as *EastEnders*, *The Bill*, *London's Burning* and *Kid in the Corner*.

Nowadays, as well as various roles on TV, much of Helen's time is spent writing for the small screen; she's contributed to shows including *EastEnders* and *Heartbeat*.

Blossom

Played by Toni Palmer

Blossom – who's aged around 45, has peroxide hair, purple fingernails and piles on the make-up – appears in 'Wanted'. She's drunk and slumped on a garden wall when Rodney passes one evening. When he realises she's unstable on her feet, due to alcohol, he prevents her collapsing, only for her to accuse him of molesting her. As she cries for help, Rodney makes a dash for it. Blossom, who wears an identity necklace, is well known in the area and, as Del explains, she's as nutty as a fruit cake, lives in the 'happy home' and is only let out at weekends. The occasion with Rodney isn't the first time she's tried such an act: once she even accused Marilyn (Trigger's tomboy cousin) of touching her, and had the nerve to claim that the wheelchair-bound Old Man Corby assaulted her.

Blythe, Debbi

Role: Receptionist
Appeared in S4, episode 5

Debbi sold men's shirts in Harrods before winning a scholarship to the Guildhall School of Music and Drama. She made her professional debut in 1976 in weekly rep at Frinton, and spent the early years of her career in repertory around the country, including York and Coventry.

She made her television debut in *By The Sea*, a silent film with The Two Ronnies, but her extensive list of small-screen credits include *The Mad Death*, playing a rabies victim for BBC Scotland; *Just Good Friends*; *Waiting for God*; *Bergerac*; *Dear John*; *Emmerdale Farm*; *Alas Smith and Jones*; *Blake's 7* and *General Hospital*.

Boatman

Played by Joe Belcher

In 'To Hull and Back', Del asks the boatman where he can hire a vessel. His boat (the Inge) is worth ten grand, as far as the insurance papers are concerned, so he's not too worried about leaving it in the incapable hands of the Trotters.

Boatman's friend

Played by Johnnie Allen

Seen in 'To Hull and Back', the boatman's friend is surprised when his colleague agrees to hire out his boat to Del and Rodney, whom he refers to as 'Southern Nancies'.

Bob

Not seen in the sitcom, Rodney claims Bob – who's mentioned in 'Go West Young Man' – is a friend from his evening class with whom he supposedly socialises on his trips to West End clubs. It's likely that Bob is a figment of Rodney's imagination.

'Body Language: The Lost Art'

Rodney enjoys reading this book whilst lounging around on the sofa in 'Christmas Crackers'. He tells Grandad that it teaches you 'how to say filthy things to women from great distances without actually speaking'. He's borrowed the book from Mickey Pearce.

Bond, Philip

Role: Mr Van Kleefe
Appeared in 'To Hull and Back'

Philip, who was born in Burton-on-Trent, Staffordshire, has worked in all strands of the industry. On the stage, his many appearances include Blake in *Shooting Star*, Anselme in *The Miser*, Frank in *Educating Rita* and West End runs in *The Good Sailor*, *The Rivals* and *All My Sons*.

On the small screen he's been seen in *The Onedin Line*, *The Champions*, *Doctor Who*, *Warship*, *General Hospital*, *Bergerac*, *Brookside*, *The Scott Enquiry* and *The Life and Adventures of Nicholas Nickleby*. His film work, meanwhile, includes *Fever Pitch*, *Hell Is A City* and *Foxhole in Cairo*.

Bone, Janet

Production manager on 13 episodes: S1 and S2

Born in London, Janet joined the BBC as a junior secretary in 1955 and worked in the engineering department and sound archive before transferring to television in 1962 as a trainee production secretary (later retitled production assistant). The first programme she worked on in this capacity was *This Is Your Life*.

Her first assignment as a trained production assistant was *An Evening with Nat King Cole* in 1963. For a while she worked with Yvonne Littlewood, who produced some successful music programmes for light entertainment, including shows with many of the top musicians, such as Duke Ellington, Percy Faith, Henry Mancini and Mantovani.

Janet also worked in comedy, and among her credits are five series of *Dave Allen at Large*, *Terry and June* and the pilot episode of *Citizen Smith*. Her first job as production manager was on the final series of the same show.

She took early retirement from the Beeb in 1993, but returned six months later in a PR role, conducting tours of Television Centre. She continued the job, periodically, over a four-year period. Now she's fully retired from the industry and carries out voluntary work.

Books

To date, several books have been published about *Only Fools and Horses*:

Only Fools and Horses – The Trotter Way to Millions was published in hardback by Guild Publishing in 1990, price £8.99. The book was republished a year later by BBC Books, and in 1994 was issued in paperback through Penguin (ISBN 0140239561).

Only Fools and Horses – The Trotter Way to Romance was published in hardback by Weidenfeld and Nicholson in 1991, price £9.99 (ISBN 0297812270).

ONLY FOOLS AND HORSES – THE NOVEL OR TROTTER: EARLY YEARS

A project which has been on the backburner for some time is a novel about the Trotters' life pre-1981, when the sitcom began. But now it looks as if the project is close to coming to fruition with John Sullivan already in the process of writing the book.

John says: 'We'd be going back to 1962 and concentrating much more on the Trotter boys' mother and father and various other relationships. Del would be going through his Mod days, riding a scooter and going to Who concerts.

The Only Fools and Horses Story by Steve Clark was published by BBC Books in October 1998, price £12.99 (ISBN 056338445X).

Only Fools and Horses: The Bible of Peckham (Volume 1) by John Sullivan was published in hardback by BBC Books in October 1999, price £15.99 (ISBN 056355150X). It contains all the scripts from Series 1 to 5, including the Christmas Specials. It was published in paperback during October 2000, price £9.99 (ISBN 056353818X).

Only Fools and Horses: The Bible of Peckham (Volume 2) by John Sullivan was published in hardback by BBC Books in October 2000, price £15.99 (ISBN 0563551771). It contains the scripts from Series 6 and 7, as well as Peckham's Who's Who.

Only Fools and Horses: The Bible of Peckham (Volume 3) by John Sullivan was published in hardback by BBC Books in October 2001, price £15.99 (ISBN 0563537450). It contains all the scripts for the feature-lengths episodes from 1986 to 1996, the 'Christmas Trees' sketch, the Royal Variety Performance scene, the Gulf War sketch and the script for the special short episode broadcast during Comic Relief in 1997. The book also contains The Nag's Head Pub Quiz and Del's Cocktail List.

The BBC had intended publishing the scripts from the entire seven series, plus all the Christmas Specials, barring 'If They Could See Us Now…!', as a compendium in a box set. *Only Fools and Horses: The Scripts* was due for publication in paperback during November 2001, price £29.99 (ISBN 0563534559). This idea was later dropped by BBC Books.

Other books with an *Only Fools and Horses* link

During the War – and other encounters, the autobiography by Buster Merryfield, was published by Summersdale in 1996 price £4.99 (ISBN 1873475543).

The David Jason Story – A Perfect Life, written by Stafford Hildred and Tim Ewbank, was published by Blake in 1991 (ISBN 09058494X).

David Jason – The Biography, written by Stafford Hildred and Tim Ewbank, was published by Blake Publishing, price £16.99, in October 1997 (ISBN 1857821874). The publisher issued a paperback in September 1998, price £5.99 (ISBN 1857823109).

Hildred and Ewbank's work on Jason has also seen the publication of *David Jason – A Life in Pictures*. Again published by Blake Publishing, the book sold for £14.99 and was published in hardback during October 1999 (ISBN 1857823923).

The Dream Team, a book about the working partnership of Lyndhurst and Jason was also written by Hildred and Ewbank. Blake Publishing issued the hardback in October 2000, price £16.99 (ISBN 1857823893). The paperback arrived in the bookshops in November 2001, price £6.99 (ISBN 1857824326).

Another biography on Jason titled, *David Jason – The People's Man*, was written by Ross Clarke and published by Kingsfleet Publications in 1991, price £4.99.

Two books by Steve Clark feature a section about some of the locations used in *Only Fools and Horses*. *The Location Guide*, which is now out of print, was published by Seaspite Publishing back in 1993, for £5.99 (ISBN 0952196204). Blake Publishing later issued the paperback, *On Set!* in 1999, for £6.99 (ISBN 1857823915).

Booth, Chris

Videotape editor on four episodes: S3, episode 5; S4, episodes 3, 4 & 6

Chris – who was born in Esher, Surrey, in 1945 – joined the BBC straight from school in 1963 as a technical assistant; recruited in preparation for the launch of BBC2, he completed his training and was allocated a position in Television Recording and Videotape at TV Centre. In his early days as an engineer, he worked on a multitude of programmes, including *Tonight* and *Steptoe*, but by the time of the 1966 World Cup, Chris had progressed to editing programmes, although he wasn't officially appointed as an editor until 1973.

After 34 years with the Beeb, Chris took early retirement in 1993, by which time he'd built up an extensive list of credits, from sports programmes such as *Grandstand,* the 1992 Barcelona Olympics and *Match of the Day* to *Monty Python, Z Cars, Jim'll Fix It, Horizon, Butterflies* and *Seconds Out.*

He returned to the BBC as a freelance videotape editor in 1995, staying a further two years. Nowadays he works as a consultant for a company producing business videos for software houses.

Bowles, Dominic

2nd assistant director on three episodes: 'Heroes and Villains', 'Modern Men' and 'Time On Our Hands'

Other programmes Dominic has worked on include John Sullivan's 1996 wartime comedy drama, *Over Here*, as 3rd assistant director.

Boyce Auto Sales And Car Accessories

Boycie's premises are seen in 'To Hull and Back', 'He Ain't Heavy, He's My Uncle' and 'Time On Our Hands'. Behind the façade of this run-of-the mill car showroom lies a business run by an unscrupulous character who wouldn't think twice about dumping one of his so-called 'quality' cars on his own mother. His brash manner, insolence and total disregard for after-care is enough to put off any potential customer.

Boyce, Marlene

Played by Sue Holderness

Marlene – who's married to the inimitable Boycie – is first mentioned in 'A Losing Streak', but not seen until the fourth series, in 'Sleeping Dogs Lie'. Unbeknown to her husband, Marlene has something of a reputation amongst the male population

of Peckham; even the disliked Detective Inspector Roy Slater knows of Marlene's reputation: as Boycie departs The Nag's Head in 'May the Force be with You', Slater comments sarcastically: 'Give my love to Marlene, everyone else used to.'

For some years, Marlene Boyce and her husband have been trying, with no success, to start a family. To help ease the pain and frustration over the predicament, Boycie splashes out £600 on a puppy, believing it will take her mind off the matter and give her someone to love. Just when it looks like they will never be blessed with the patter of tiny feet running around their mock-Georgian abode, Marlene announces in 'Sickness and Wealth' that she's pregnant.

Marlene – whose father was a tattooist, which probably explains the heart and dagger she has tattooed on her thigh – worked in a betting shop in Lewisham Grove when Boycie first cast eyes on her. In her younger days, she had a predilection for acting – people even told her she had a promising acting career but she never pursued this line of work.

Although she's dippy and, perhaps, a little brazen, Marlene is a kindhearted individual; the antithesis of her po-faced hubby, she frequently partakes in a little frivolity and enjoys a laugh, especially if Del, for whom she has a soft spot, is on the scene. This probably stems from the time, before marrying Boycie, when she dated Del for a month: she dumped him just as he had saved the money to take her away on a holiday.

MEMORIES OF PLAYING MARLENE

★ ★ ★ ★ ★ ★

'Marlene was an old slapper who'd slept with everybody in Peckham. All the boys remembered her and she had this glorious reputation of being the girl who couldn't say no.

'As soon as the script arrived I knew the part was going to be bliss. The first scene I appeared in was short but very funny. After saying hello to Del, I ask him if he had had a nice Christmas, to which he says "'triffic". Marlene then adds: "I had a dog!", to which Rodney replies: "Yeah, we had a turkey same as every other year."

'I was thrilled to pieces to be there for what amounted to only three hours' filming. I hadn't met any of these people before and was jolly nervous because I was a bit in awe of them, but I was made very welcome and had a lovely day.

'In the script, John Sullivan had given a clear description of how the character should look, and I liked the idea of this big, fuzzy mane of hair, long, painted nails and far too much make-up; she has more time on her hands than she knows what to do with to make herself look gorgeous, as well as lots of money, but not a lot ot taste.

'The shopping sprees for Marlene's outfits are always huge fun because you go into these dress shops and try on outfits that are completely outrageous, with shop assistants commenting: "Oh madam looks wonderful", although you know you're purposely going out of your way to make her look extremely over the top.

'It's certainly the happiest and luckiest job I could possibly have wished for. When you think how many actresses there are in the profession, very few get a lucky break like this, with wonderful writing and a glorious character you immediately associate with.

'A lot of people recognise me in the street now. Some think that they know me intimately from Tesco's, while others refer to me as Marlene. I occasionally get my bottom pinched but, on the whole, I get treated very nicely because people are very fond of Marlene. And, of course, Del is too. They have a special relationship. On Rodney's wedding day when everybody had left the party in the pub, there's that moment when Del, with "Holding Back the Years" playing in the background and feeling at his lowest, confides in Marlene.

'She's got a heart of gold, and although she's not the brightest girl in the world, she's streetwise and pretty manwise, and Del and Marlene, who fancied each other rotten, are now good mates – there's certainly a lot of history between them!'

SUE HOLDERNESS

Boyce, Tyler

Played by Elliott Russell (S7, episodes 1 & 2); Danny Rix ('Miami Twice' – for UK scenes) and Joshua Rosen ('Miami Twice' – US scenes)

First seen in 'The Sky is the Limit', Tyler is Boycie and Marlene's son. Sadly for Boycie, he can't get too close to the boy because his face scares him! His only other appearance as a baby is in 'The Chance of a Lunchtime', although he's mentioned again in 'He Ain't Heavy, He's My Uncle'. By the time we see him at the christening of Del and Raquel's baby in 'Miami Twice', the blond-haired boy has really shot up.

Boyce Video And Leisure Arts Company, The

Boycie's video company, which is mentioned in 'Video Nasty', is short-lived. His one and only film – as far as we know – is a rather blue offering: *Night Nurse*.

Boycie

Played by John Challis

Although he mellows somewhat during the sitcom's life, Boycie's cold, unamiable, ostentatious mien attracts few friends. He swanks around with delusions of grandeur although in many respects he's cut from the same cloth as Del Boy. Rodney even claims he'd scalp you if dandruff had a going rate.

A self-centred character who has little sympathy for others, Del once remarked that he's the man who 'cheered when Bambi's mother died'. Boycie owns a second-hand car firm in Lewisham and is first seen in 'Go West Young Man'. He specialises in vehicles that have been crudely patched up in an attempt to mask their obvious inadequacies, but is a strong advocate of diversification and from time to time tries branching out into other areas of business, such as selling pirate videos.

The first bit of business we see him conduct involves selling an old clapped-out black convertible to Del for £25, in return for the Trotters looking after an E-type Jag he's bought for his 'bit on the side'. It must be a fleeting affair because we never hear of her again.

Married to Marlene – who's well known by all the lads around town – the rapacious Boycie, or Mr Boyce, is an ardent cigar smoker with extravagant tastes: while smoked salmon is regularly on the table at home, he claims in 'A Losing Streak' that selling a recent car for £850 won't even provide enough money to heat his swimming pool for a week. We first see the interior of his plush home, which is next door to a Chief Inspector, in Kings' Avenue, in 'From Prussia with Love'; any visitors who are unsure of the address only need to look out for the Jolly Roger flying from the chimney.

MEMORIES OF 'MIAMI TWICE'

★ ★ ★ ★ ★ ★

'We had three different boys playing Tyler over the years, including Elliott Russell who appeared as a baby. We never had any problems with any of them, they've always been absolutely sweet. I was never very good with babies but now that I've had my own I've become rather devoted to all of them.

'One of the memories that sticks in my mind of recording "Miami Twice" in Florida is the length of time it took to complete the first bit of filming. The boy who'd been hired as a Tyler lookalike out there was very lively, bouncy and noisy, and we didn't get everything we'd planned in the can. As a result, we had to stay a few days to reshoot bits that hadn't worked first time around, but the boy became terribly sick and had to be nursed through the filming by paramedics; he'd featured in some close-ups so we had to use the same boy, and although he wasn't ever in danger, it just highlights one of the hazards of filming.'

SUE HOLDERNESS

Boycie's opulent lifestyle extends to a weekend cottage, which is seen in 'Friday the 14th', in Tregower, Cornwall, sited in woodland, near one of the best salmon fishing streams in England.

Boycie – who's a Mason – and Marlene have been married for over 20 years but struggled to start a family, which has led to much jesting in The Nag's Head. When desperation sets in, Boycie tries placating Marlene by splashing out £600 for Duke, a puppy, in 'Sleeping Dogs Lie'. He even considers buying Anna's baby in 'From Prussia with Love'. Just when it looks as if the couple will remain childless, Baby Tyler appears on the horizon, with Marlene announcing her pregnacy in 'Sickness and Wealth'.

A contempoary of Del, Trigger and the rest of the gang at the Martin Luther King Comprehensive, he left school in 1962. Although we learn little about his early background, we do discover that he did a bit of porridge when he was younger, which is why the couple were declined at the adoption agency when they investigated the possibilty of adopting a child. He was sent to prison for perjury, embezzlement, conspiring to pervert the course of justice, fraudulent conversion of travellers' cheques and trying to bribe the Mayor of Lambeth.

'Boys Will Be Boys'

Heard briefly in 'It's Only Rock and Roll', the song is the debut single for the rock band A Bunch of Wallies. Rodney used to belong to the group, so is

---

MEMORIES OF PLAYING BOYCIE

★ ★ ★ ★ ★ ★

'I'd appeared in an episode of *Citizen Smith* which, of course, John Sullivan had written. He told me he liked the character, and thought of putting him into a series one day. I didn't think anything more of it until the offer to play Boycie came along. Knowing John's feelings about the character I'd played previously, I invested the same sort of qualities into Boycie but adjusted them a bit because this time he was a second-hand car dealer. I did a further series the following year and the character caught on.

'Boycie became a larger-than-life character, but I started off by simply basing him on this guy I knew from a local pub I frequented. He had this supercilious voice and was a dreadful snob, a man who knew a little about everything. He drove everyone mad. I just lifted a few of his characteristics when it came to playing Boycie: the character grew and John Sullivan began writing more scenes involving him. I don't really know how Boycie's famous laugh started, but John liked it and the next script contained a reference to "Boycie does one of his laughs". Now I'm asked to do it wherever I go.

'Boycie was married to Marlene, of course, but she started off as a sort of "her indoors" character. There was the running joke with Boycie frequently reminded that all the lads remembered Marlene; she had this reputation for

getting around a bit, but Boycie wasn't fully aware of her past. I remember having conversations with John about whether she should appear or not, and when she did, Sue Holderness created this wonderful character.

'The Boyces' life, with their mock-Georgian mansion, gravel drive, baby and, of course, the dog, developed as the series moved along. I remember in "The Sky's the Limit" Boycie shouts at Duke, who's in the garden. He was supposed to be racing about, trampling over the flowerbeds, barking furiously. But the animal, who was brought to the location by a handler, wouldn't move – it just sat looking soppy in the middle of the lawn. The handler kept on saying: "Come on, boy, come on", trying to get it to move, but it wouldn't budge. Suddenly it went berserk, started barking and dived on something; we couldn't work it out but eventually realised it was one of the furry microphone covers! Thinking it was some sort of animal, he'd grabbed the cover and savaged it. Of course, the sound man went berserk, too, trying to rescue it – it was hilarious.

'Another of my favourite episodes is "From Prussia with Love". I love it because it's politically incorrect, with the baby being coloured. I remember everybody talking about it, saying: "Christ, can we get away with this?" The whole episode worked well because it was just on the edge. John Sullivan is so good at those sort of scenes: he's a sensitive man and

tackles such scenarios in a manner that means you end up smiling about them, rather than being annoyed.

'The success of *Only Fools and Horses* is largely down to the scripts, which are about people's lives, issues that affect people, not just a string of jokes. The fact that *he's* written all the scripts helps, too. Sometimes writers of long-running shows farm out the episodes for other people to write, which rarely works, but with this one John didn't do that. Another key to the show's success is having the right actors, where a certain chemistry exists between the cast. Of course, David Jason and Nicholas Lyndhurst are one of the greatest double-acts of all time: they're very different but their styles complement each other superbly.

'As each series passed, Boycie matured, losing a little of the villainous streak evident at the beginning. He became the Peckham version of landed gentry, or that was how he saw himself. He always smoked a cigar, but while Del opted for a big, fat type, Boycie chose a long thin version, which I think was a bit more sinister. In many ways, he was a conflict character: superior, slightly evil, very successful and always looking down on Del, making him puff his chest out, look up and want to be up there, too. He's a great character.'

JOHN CHALLIS

devastated when he discovers that the single has reached 26 in the charts and they're appearing on *Top of the Pops*. The song was written for the show by John Sullivan and arranged by Steve Jeffries.

Brabants, Dave

Film sound recordist on four episodes: S5, episodes 1–4

London-born Dave Brabants joined the BBC in 1971, aged 19. Among the early shows he worked on are *Fanny by Gaslight, Shoestring* and *Bergerac*. After 28 years' service with the Corporation he left and became a freelance production sound mixer. Nowadays, his work takes him around the world: recent assignments have seen him film surfing in Hawaii, anniversary celebrations in Korea and a programme featuring Rostrapovich in Russia.

à la Del

★ ★ ★ ★ ★ ★

'Oh very mal de mer!'

('Big Brother')

Brabbins, Anna

3rd assistant director on three episodes: 'Heroes and Villains', 'Modern Men' and 'Time On Our Hands'. 2nd assistant director on 'If They Could See Us Now…!'

After graduating with a degree in media and communications, Anna entered the television industry six years ago as a runner on John Sullivan's sitcom *Roger, Roger*. Anna, who was born in Kingston-upon-Thames, has also worked as a freelancer on shows such as *League of Gentlemen* and *Happiness*.

Bradford, Andy

Stunt coordinator on one episode: 'Fatal Extraction'

Andy was born in Cambridge but spent most of his childhood years in London. Just when it looked as if a career in the police force beckoned, he changed direction and was offered a place at the Webber Douglas Academy of Dramatic Art, from which he graduated in 1964.

After a season at Glasgow's Citizens' Theatre, plenty of stage work followed, including spells at Bristol's Old Vic, Edinburgh and London, where he starred in the original production of *The Rocky Horror Show*. Andy made his small-screen debut in a 1966 episode of *Dixon of Dock Green*, but his most significant piece of television work was a play titled, *Robin Red Breast*.

When he reached his mid-thirties, Andy's career veered more towards stunt work. He's since worked on numerous films and television shows in this capacity, namely the original *Star Wars, Superman, Flash Gordon, Highlander* and several Bond movies. He now coordinates stunt work and has recently completed an assignment in Romania.

Braine, Richard

Role: Producer of Goldrush
Appeared in 'If They Could See Us Now…!'

In recent years, Richard has worked in the theatre and on screen. On stage he's played roles such as Peter Sellers in *Being There With Peter Sellers*, while on the big screen he was cast as Reverend Tweeb in *Stiff Upper Lips*. His television work includes playing Reverend Stoop in *Murder Most Horrid*, Squiffy in *Polterguests*, St John Featherstone in *My Uncle Silas*, Head Teacher in *Bernard's Watch* and Spencer in *Without Motive*.

★ ★ ★ ★ ★ ★

'**M**y involvement in "Fatal Extraction" was minuscule because I was just asked to choreograph the riot in the episode. I arranged with the producer to have a certain number of stuntmen involved within the crowd, primarily as watchers to make sure it didn't get out of control. When you organise a riot, especially if you're employing a lot of people locally, all of whom you know nothing about, you can sometimes attract the wrong types.

'As choreographer I also had to woo the crowd, which isn't easy. All you have is a loudhailer, you've never met them before and you've got to tell everyone what you're trying to achieve. A lot of students from the Bristol Old Vic Drama School were brought in to make up the crowd.

'I was amazed at how smoothly it went because they are the nightmare of all things to do; if anybody asks me what the most difficult job a stunt coordinator has to do is, it would be to choreograph a riot.'

ANDY BRADFORD – Stunt coordinator

Branson, Richard

Role: Himself
Appeared in 'Miami Twice' (Part 1)

Richard Branson, seen at the boarding gate when Del and Rodney head off to Miami, needs little introduction. Born in 1950, the British entrepreneur steered his Virgin company to success in a broad range of fields, from retail to airlines. His first real taste of success came in 1968, with the launch of *Student* magazine.

Brenda

Not seen in the sitcom, Brenda is mentioned by Grandad in 'Christmas Crackers'. She's married to Terry and has three children: Shirley, Shaun and Shane. Their Christmas card is accidentally dropped into the Trotters' flat, who have never heard of the family.

Brendan

(See 'O'Shaughnessy, Brendan')

Brett, Terry

Technical coordinator on one episode: S3, episode 5

Other shows Terry has worked on over the years include *Are You Being Served?, Terry and June* and the 1983 series of *The Black Adder*.

Brian

Played by Roger Brierley

Brian, who appears briefly in 'Diamonds are for Heather', babysits for Heather while she attends the Spanish evening at The Nag's Head. He lives in the flat below Heather's in Brixton, and will shortly be attending university as a mature student.

Bridge attendant

Played by Alan Hulse

The bridge attendant is working on the Humber Bridge in 'To Hull and Back' when Rodney arrives at the toll booth, hot on the heels of Del, who's stuck inside Denzil's articulated lorry.

Bridie

Del has a chat with Bridie on the phone during 'As One Door Closes'. She is never seen in the sitcom but, although it's unclear, we can assume that she is Brendan O'Shaughnessy's partner.

Briegel, Hilary

Vision mixer on two episodes: 'Dates' and 'Modern Men'

Whilst Hilary – who was born in Haywards Heath in 1952 – was completing a business course and her A-levels at college, a speaker from the BBC visited and talked to the students about careers with the Beeb. Hilary took an application form, applied and was offered a job in 1971, by which time she'd also completed a drama course at the Guildhall School of Speech and Drama.

Initially she worked as a production secretary for schools' radio but was promoted to studio manager in 1974, widening the scope of programmes she worked on.

Hilary transferred to television in 1978 as a trainee vision mixer and worked on shows from *Jackanory, Grandstand* and *Nationwide* to the Eurovision Song Contest, *Absolutely Fabulous* and the Commonwealth Games.

Brierley, Roger

Role: Brian
Appeared in 'Diamonds are for Heather'

Roger Brierley, who was born in Stockport, has made over 200 TV appearances. He appeared in amateur dramatics from the age of 14, but didn't pursue an acting career immediately after leaving school; instead, he qualified as a chartered accountant. It wasn't until he was completing his national service that he decided to make acting his future. Returning to civvy street he joined Bristol's Old Vic Theatre School, a decision which didn't please his father, also an accountant.

Four years of repertory work followed, before he

ventured to London with the aim of breaking into television. Roger achieved his goal, appearing as Julian in an episode of *The Likely Lads*. Other TV parts quickly followed, including appearances in *Doctor Who*, *Telford's Change*, *The Politician's Wife*, *Jeeves and Wooster*, *Rising Damp* and *Pennies from Heaven*. Roger has also been seen in a handful of films, such as *Superman II* and *Young Sherlock Holmes*.

Brill, Francesca

Role: Emma
Appeared in S6, episode 1

Francesca, who's also a successful writer and director, has worked in all areas of the profession. As well as many stage appearances, she's built up a list of credits on television and the big screen, including *Tales of the Unexpected*, *Bergerac*, *Alas Smith and Jones*, *Boogie Outlaws*, *First Born*, *As Time Goes By*, *A Very Peculiar Practice*, and films such as *Bullshot* and *Champions*.

Bristow, Ron

Lighting director on four episodes: S7, episodes 5 & 6 and 'Miami Twice' (Parts 1 & 2)

After completing national service, Ron – who was born in Reading in 1933 – applied for a job in radio at the BBC, but as his chief hobby was photography, it was suggested he worked in television instead.

He started his BBC career at Lime Grove in 1955, transferring to Television Centre a year later. By the time he'd reached the position of lighting director, he had gained experience in all categories of programmes, from sports shows and documentaries to comedies and dramas. But his latter years were dominated by work in light entertainment. He worked regularly with director/producer Sydney Lotterby on shows such as *Butterflies*, *Open All Hours*, *Ever Decreasing Circles* and *As Time Goes By*, but also lit programmes like *Fawlty Towers*, *Terry and June*, *The Two Ronnies* and *Blackadder the Third*.

Ron – who received a Royal Television Society nomination for his work on the 1988 drama, *Shadow of the Noose* – was still working for the Beeb when he died of cancer in 1993.

Brittain, Bryan

Role: Texo
Appeared in 'Fatal Extraction'

Britton, Corinne

Role: Nurse
Appeared in 'Modern Men'

Corinne, who was born in Bristol in 1969, trained at the Birmingham School of Speech and Drama and made her professional debut in the 1992/3 national tour of *Elektra*. In the same year she made her first appearance on television playing Lorraine, a receptionist, in Channel 4's *Family Pride*.

She's also appeared in a couple of short films, such as *Shopping for Love*, plus the feature-length *Goodbye and Hello*, based on Rosamund Pilcher's book, in which she played Emily.

More recent television appearances include playing Meena in BBC's *Lenny Goes Wild*, a shop owner in *Casualty* and Mercury in *First Frontier*. Other work includes various commercials and corporate videos.

Broadbent, Jim

Role: Detective Inspector Roy Slater
Appeared in S3, episode 5; S7, episode 4 and 'To Hull and Back'

Winner of a Golden Globe Award in 2002 for his supporting role in *Iris*, Jim Broadbent has established himself as one of the most popular character actors around. Born in Lincoln in 1949, he graduated from the London Academy of Music

Jim Broadbent (right) as Roy Slater

and Dramatic Art in 1972 and began working in the theatre, before television and film work came his way.

On the big screen, his extensive list of credits includes appearances in productions such as *Time Bandits*, *The Crying Game*, *Little Voice*, *The Avengers*, *The Borrowers*, *Moulin Rouge* and *Bridget Jones's Diary*, while on television he's been seen in, amongst others, *Blackadder*, *Happy Families*, *Murder Most Horrid*, *Inspector Morse*, *The Comic Strip Presents* and *Victoria Wood As Seen on TV*.

Bronco

(See 'Lane, Bronco')

Brown, Gaye

Role: Irene Mackay
Appeared in S2, episode 4

Born in 1941, Gaye graduated from the Guildford

School of Music and Drama, by which time she had already made her professional debut: in 1945, she appeared at the Royal Albert Hall playing a snowflake in *The Snow Queen*.

Once out of drama school, a great deal of her early career was spent at Joan Littlewood's Theatre Workshop, while her first experience of television was in a 1962 episode of *No Hiding Place*. Other TV credits include *Warship*, *Z Cars*, *Shelley*, *Tickets for the Titanic*, *When the Boat Comes In*, *Last of the Summer Wine* and *The House of Eliott*.

Her film work includes *A Touch of Class*, *Relative Values* and *The Golden Bowl*, while on stage she's worked with the Royal Shakespeare Company and in a host of other productions, from *Once in a Lifetime* at the Piccadilly Theatre to *An Ideal Husband* with the English Speaking Theatre of Frankfurt.

Brown, Graham

Visual effects on two episodes: 'Dates' and S6, episode 6
Note: Although only credited on two episodes of *Only Fools and Horses*, Graham worked on several other instalments, including 'As One Door Closes'

Born in 1956, Graham worked as a legal executive at a solicitor's for five years, during which time he became a member of the Law Society. His interest, however, had always been in art, and when someone saw some of his work at an art exhibition, he was offered the chance to join the BBC visual effects department.

Graham has worked for the Beeb for 25 years on a host of programmes, including *Doctor Who* (he's worked with all the doctors, except Hartnell), *Blake's 7*, *Crackerjack*, *Dad's Army*, *Howards' Way*, *Poldark* and *Pride and Prejudice*. He's now a

MEMORIES OF ONLY FOOLS

★ ★ ★ ★ ★ ★

'I moved house recently and came across the butterfly I made for "As One Door Closes". It was made out of painted tissue paper and I fluttered it around on the end of a pole with the help of some fine conjuring nylon; it's funny how things change – nowadays you'd be asked to put some thick orange string on it because it's easy to take out in post-production whereas for years we'd always try and find the finest material imaginable.

'I remember standing in the pond in London's Ravenscourt Park waggling this butterfly around. The first time we turned up to film, the pond was frozen over. Filming was postponed and we returned later to complete the shoot.

right by the bar, about 30 sex dolls popped out all over the floor! There was much riotous laughter that night.

'Being visual effects, we tend to be called to the set a bit early and often end up standing around for hours. Because for a lot of the time you're not doing anything but can't, of course, leave the set, you end up frozen. I always keep a 12-volt television and a couple of hot water bottles in the back of the car, which I fill from the tea urn. It means my assistant and I can skulk in my car, with hot water bottles on our lap, watching the tele until we're needed.

'Another job that comes to mind was making it look as if the engine of the Trotters' van had packed in at a pub car

ONLY FOOLS AND HORSES	VISUAL EFFECTS REQUIREMENTS	

PLEASE ATTACH MARKED-UP SCRIPT

29/30
12.88   Please supply us with the following visual effects for our filming on 29th and 30th December '88.
1. 3X 3" round Balsa tables for an artist to fall on in a stunt fight, in a restaurant.
2. 6 wine bottles all identical in sugar glass to dress the table before the fall.
3. 6 plates to match restaurant plates to break easily and safely.
4. 8 sugar glass wine glasses to match restaurant type.
5. 4 sets of knives, forks and spoons, dummy type to save any accidents.
All to be discussed with the designer.

'As the Trotters dived for the butterfly I had to make it flutter off by lifting the fishing pole it was fixed to. Everything was okay until the wind picked up and then it was a bit of a nightmare.

'I also remember working on "Danger UXD" with the sex dolls. I had to go and look at some proper dolls and knew immediately that we couldn't show them before the watershed, so we got some specially built. I tracked down a guy who had workshops in London, gave him the sex dolls and asked him to modify them so they were more acceptable for filming. We had about a dozen dolls converted to suitable models, including an ethnic selection – it was at the time when political correctness was crucial, hence making one of each colour! The Prop Buyer, meanwhile, bought a load of genuine sex dolls for filling the back of the Trotters' van, and these made their way into the hotel at which we were staying after a night shoot.

'After a few drinks back at the hotel, someone came up with the idea of filling Nicholas Lyndhurst's room with all the dolls. Loads were stuffed in through the door, but when he saw them he pushed them back into the lift. When the lift came down from the sixth floor and the doors opened,

park in "Dates". It was a last-minute request, so I used a technique I'd developed whilst working on *Crackerjack* where I hung a bucket underneath the bonnet. The director wanted something visual as well as the sound of the engine playing up, so I bought some gravy browning, which was the only thing I could get hold of at the time, and put it into a bucket, together with some nuts and bolts. The bucket stood underneath the bonnet and was connected to a piece of metal which came through into the cab, so when it was pulled, the bucket tipped and poured all the material out on to the floor.

'My assistant, John Vanderpool, broke his hand for this scene. I asked him to punch a hole through the fibreglass of the car, to allow the metal rod to come through into the cab. He was making the hole with a screwdriver and went too hard and smashed his hand. He thought he'd just bruised himself, or dislocated a finger. Later that day, he asked me to try and click his finger back in position, so I was there heaving on it. The following day his hand looked like a bunch of bananas so I took him to hospital where we found it was broken.'

GRAHAM BROWN – Visual effects

Managing Senior Designer of the BBC visual effects department, still working on current shows such as *EastEnders*, *Waking The Dead* and *Judge John Deed*. He's also a producer on various game shows such as *Pump It Up* and *Petswap*.

Brown, Linford
Role: Policeman
Appeared in 'Fatal Extraction'
Linford was also seen as a policeman (PC Liam Walsh) in a 1997 episode of BBC1's *Dangerfield*, while his other credits include playing Jeff in C S Leigh's 2001 movie, *Far From China*, and touring with the play *Game, Set and Match*.

Brown, Ron
Film sound recordist on one episode: S1, episode 3
Born in Greenock, Scotland, in 1939, Ron gained his first experience in broadcasting whilst living in Africa. His work on the radio was advantageous when he returned to the UK and joined the Beeb at the age of 25.

His 40-year career began as a trainee sound recordist, and he's gone on to work on numerous shows, like *Around the World in 80 Days* and *Fourteen Days in May*.

Ron took redundancy and left the BBC in 1995. He's since been working freelance, with recent projects including *One Very Big Adventure*, his inaugural excursion into producing.

à la Del

★ ★ ★ ★ ★ ★

'Mon dieu ...'
('Go West Young Man')

'"Son et lumière", wouldn't you say?'
('Go West Young Man')

Bruce, Angela
Role: Councillor Murray
Appeared in 'Heroes and Villains'
Born in Leeds in 1951, Angela was adopted at a young age and grew up in Craghead, County Durham. Upon leaving school she studied catering at technical college, but after working in the industry for just a few months decided it wasn't the career for her. Watching a performance of the musical *Hair* led her into the acting world: when the audience were invited to dance on stage at the end of the show, Angela joined the crowds, was spotted and offered an audition. She joined the production in 1970 and stayed three years, touring the country before entering London at the Shaftesbury Theatre.

MEMORIES OF PLAYING COUNCILLOR MURRAY

★ ★ ★ ★ ★ ★

'One thing I remember about filming "Heroes and Villians" was the newspaper photographer. It was about five in the morning, we'd all moved from a day shoot to a night shoot, so were very tired and cold. Then this photographer arrived on the scene; I don't know which paper he worked for, but he decided to hang out at the location to try and get a shot of the lads and work out what the storyline was. If he'd managed to get a photo of them in their Batman and Robin costumes it would have killed the entire joke. The crew set up huge arc lights and shined them towards him, preventing him from taking his photos, by which time everyone's patience was wearing thin because we'd been hanging around a long time.

'The first time I saw the Batman and Robin scene in rehearsals I couldn't stop laughing. The guys were great to work with; often if you come into a long-running series and are only guesting, you can feel lonely, but everyone was friendly and made me feel welcome. Tony Dow, the director, has a way of making it very relaxing on the shoot, too.

'I went away to Boston and didn't watch the original transmission, so never realised just how many people tuned in to see it. But as soon as I returned home, people were telling me that over 21 million people watched – I couldn't believe it.

'One of the other things I remember about my scenes in the episode was having my foot trod on by one of the blokes who was trying to steal my handbag. He must have been over enthusiastic because he kept stamping on me every time he tried pulling the bag away – my foot was bruised all over!'   **ANGELA BRUCE**

She left *Hair*, joined the *Rocky Horror Show* and spent the early part of her career in theatre before earning her big break in television as Sandra Ling in three series of *Angels*. The 1970s was a busy period for Angela on the small screen, with other roles including Janice Stubbs, who broke up Deirdre and Ray Langton's marriage in *Coronation Street*, and Gloria in *Rock Follies*.

Nowadays, although she contines working in theatre, television dominates her career, with credits including *Doctor Who*, *Red Dwarf*, *Van der Valk*, *Up Line*, *Prime Suspect*, *Silent Witness*, *The Bill* and *Holby City*. She's also made several films, the most recent being *Mrs Caldicot's Cabbage War*, with Pauline Collins and John Alderton.

Bruns, Gail

Location manager on two episodes: 'Miami Twice' (Parts 1 & 2)

Gail is based in the States and was responsible for finding all the locations used in and around Miami.

Bruns, Ken

1st assistant director on two episodes: 'Miami Twice' (Parts 1 & 2)

Based in the States, Ken helped direct the filming sequences in Miami.

Bruzac, Anne

Role: French girl
Appeared in S2, episode 6

Although Anne, who was born in France, has numerous film and television credits to her name, she'll always be remembered by many people as one of the sexy Benny Hill Babes, appearing alongside the comic throughout his long-running television shows.

Anne made her mark in modelling before concentrating on acting, with her first assignment being a 1977 edition of BBC's *Omnibus*, titled 'Anatomies', and based on the poems of John Donne; she was chosen to depict the perfect face and body for Donne's poems, as well as playing several cameo parts.

She's worked for all the major television stations, with one of her favourite roles being a zany French girl in 24 instalments of *What's on Next?*

Bryans, John

Role: Dr Becker
Appeared in S3, episode 1

John has enjoyed a busy career in all strands of the profession. His television work has seen him in many of the ITC classics from the 1960s, including *The Baron*, *Danger Man* and *The Champions*. The '70s and '80s were equally busy, with him clocking up appearances as Bercol in *Blake's 7*, Al Fiegleman in *Rock Follies*, Dr Elder in *Nanny*, Timothy's head-master in *Sorry!* and Chief Superintendant Mercer in *Death of an Expert Witness*.

His film credits include *The House That Dripped Blood*, *Henry VIII and His Six Wives* and *Duel*.

Bryson, Ann

Role: Nurse
Appeared in S6, episode 5

In recent years, Ann's work has mainly been on the stage and small screen. On television she has appeared in three series of *Space Vets*, *Sometime Never*, *Days Like These*, *A Lump in My Throat*, *Lord of the Dance* and *Inspector Morse*, while her various stints on the stage include playing Beverly in *Abigail's Party*, Dorine in *Tartuffe*, Mari in *The Rise and Fall of Little Voice* and Mrs Brindman in *Blithe Spirit*.

'Bunch of Wallies, A'

Seen in 'It's Only Rock and Roll', the rock band is fronted by the lead singer, Mental Mickey, with Rodney on drums, while Charlie and Stew play guitar. Del gets them a gig at The Shamrock Club, which turns into a disaster. After a disagreement, Rodney quits the band, but soon regrets his decision when he spots them singing their debut hit, 'Boys Will Be Boys' – which reaches 26 in the charts – on *Top of the Pops*.

Burdis, Mark

Role: Colin
Appeared in 'To Hull and Back'

Mark began acting as a child, with appearances in *Bless Me, Father* and *Grange Hill*, in which he played Christopher 'Stewpot' Stewart. Other television roles include Kevin Watts in *This Is David Lander*, Joe Riley in *The Bill* and PC Naylor in *A Touch of Frost*. His film work, meanwhile, has seen him appear in productions such as *Never Never Land*, *Clockwise*, *The Krays*, *The Runner*, *Final Cut* and *Mike Bassett: England Manager*.

MEMORIES OF PLAYING THE FRENCH GIRL

★ ★ ★ ★ ★ ★

'My agent explained that Ray Butt wanted me to do a guest appearance in *Only Fools and Horses*, and I subsequently had a friendly meeting with Ray and John Sullivan at the BBC. They told me there was no script and I was to improvise in French with Del chatting me up in one scene, and me seducing Rodney in another!

'It was when they told me that we'd all be on holiday in Spain that I agreed, since I spent a lot of time in the South of France as a child and love the warmth of the sun. I seized the opportunity of being transported away from cold, wet London, and had already packed my bikinis and sombrero when, a few days before the shoot, I was told it was to be filmed near Poole, Dorset, instead. As it turned out, the location and weather were brilliant, almost like the Côte d'Azur. Before travelling I met up at the Routier Bistro in Camden Lock with my dear late friend Arthur Mullard, for a crash course in cockney slang. It was great fun and I was looking forward to surprising Del and Rodney.

'I hadn't met David or Nicholas before. David was what I expected him to be: very confident, gregarious and funny off set. I also found him very supportive. Nicholas was incredibly shy.

'In between takes on the set, David enjoyed practising his pidgin French with me and at the same time playing to the cast and crew, for example: "Excusez moi, avez vous le bidet in zee hotel room?" I promptly answered: "Yes, Del, I have two." David thought, and replied: "Cor blimey… I must have the wrong room."

'I enjoyed working on *Only Fools and Horses* but didn't realise then what a cult it would become.' **ANNE BRUZAC**

Burton, Keith

Film cameraman on one episode: 'A Royal Flush'

Born in Birmingham in 1940, Keith worked as a camera mechanic for Rank before joining the BBC in 1960 as a trainee dubbing projectionist. For two years (1965–67) he worked as an assistant film editor before becoming an assistant film cameraman. By 1976 he was a fully fledged film cameraman and when he left in 1992 to develop a freelance career, had been promoted to Director of Photography. During his time at the Beeb, Keith worked on a host of programmes including *Arena, Airline, Birds of a Feather, Bread, Clarence, Little and Large, One Foot in the Grave* and *Jim'll Fix It*.

Nowadays, he divides his time between homes in France and London.

Buson, Tommy

Role: Clayton

Appeared in S6, episode 2

Tommy's other screen roles include playing the medicine man in the 1958 film *Diamond Safari* and Tami in 1987's *Cry Freedom*.

Butt, Ray

Producer on 38 episodes: S1–S5, 'Diamonds are for Heather', 'Thicker Than Water', 'To Hull and Back', 'A Royal Flush' and 'The Frog's Legacy'. Director on 14 episodes: S3; S5, episodes 5 & 6; 'Diamonds are for Heather', 'Thicker Than Water', 'To Hull and Back', 'A Royal Flush' and 'The Frog's Legacy'

Ray, who was born in London, couldn't wait to leave school. He was 15 when he walked through the school gates for the last time, and it wasn't long before he was earning his first wage packet as a student laboratory technician at the University of London. Whilst he was employed at the university, he studied for a City and Guilds' qualification in chemistry and history, and attended evening classes at a polytechnic in Kentish Town to try and pass his O-levels.

By 1953 he was completing national service in the RAF, gaining experience in electronics via his job in Coastal Command. Approaching demob, Ray – who had reached the rank of sergeant – started contemplating where his future lay: he considered briefly the idea of a career in civil aviation, but was put off by an official at the Ministry of Civil Aviation. 'I went along for an interview, and when I told him I had experience in sonar and radar, he replied: "Son, I wouldn't go into that because in five years' time they won't have radio officers; with all the new technology they won't need them because pilots will be using satellites and all that sort of technology."'

Ray was unsure where his future lay until a friend spotted a newspaper advert for technical staff to join the BBC. Ray applied and was successful in his application. 'This was 1955 and commercial television had just started in London with the likes of ATV and Associated Rediffusion. A lot of staff left the BBC to join the new stations which meant there were a lot of vacancies at the BBC.'

Ray Butt (right) gets ready for another shoot.

His career with the Beeb began as a probationary technical assistant in 1955, mending cameras and monitors, but he knew he wanted to be operating the cameras. He switched to become a probationary technical operator, the beginning of a long period working as a cameraman, including spells on classic shows like *Hancock's Half Hour*. By 1968 he was working as an acting senior cameraman when he applied to become a production manager in light entertainment. After a six-month attachment to the department, he returned briefly to his duties behind the camera, before he secured a permanent posting as a production manager. For four years he worked on *Dixon of Dock Green* and got his first taste of directing on *The Liver Birds*, working with Sydney Lotterby. 'Syd became my mentor in many ways because he was the first senior cameraman I reported to; I followed the same route as him to become a director/producer.'

The first production he directed in his own right was *Seconds Out*, with Robert Lindsay in 1981, although he'd taken over the last series of *Citizen Smith* from Dennis Main Wilson the previous year, the first time he received producer and director credits. Working with John Sullivan on his sitcom about Tooting's Popular Front led to their long association through *Only Fools, Just Good Friends* and *Dear John….*

After 32 years working with the BBC, Ray took early retirement and moved on to pastures new, accepting the position of Head of Comedy at Central Television, a decision he later regretted, leaving the company 18 months later. 'It was a very interesting experience, but their way of working was so different to the method I was used to at the BBC, and I wasn't comfortable.'

An offer of a short-term contract back at the Beeb saw Ray complete a further year's service before finally calling it a day. A number of freelance projects followed before he reached the decision that he was 'sick to death of television'. He then gave up the profession and decided to enjoy his retirement.

Nowadays, Ray divides his time between properties in Suffolk and France.

Byfield, Trevor

Role: Eric

Appeared in S7, episode 3

Trevor, who was born in 1943, initially earned a living in display and advertising during the day, while performing as a rock'n'roll singer and cabaret artist in the evening. Known as Ziggy Byfield at this point, he decided to forge a career for himself in the entertainment world, and in 1969 achieved a breakthrough as George Berger in *Hair* in the West End and the first UK tour. Other productions he worked on around this time include *Jesus Christ Superstar, Mother Earth* and *The Rocky Horror Show*.

It was 1970 when he made his television debut in BBC's *The Lotus Eaters*, since when he has made a myriad of appearances, including Harry Field in *Inspector Morse*, Bob Rosen in *Taggart*, Gifford in *Back Up*, George English in *A Touch of Frost*, Bloody Bill in *Coral Island* and roles in *Yesterday's Dreams* and *Rides*.

Although television has dominated his career, Trevor has appeared in several films, such as *Who Dares Wins, Shock Treatment, Crime in the City* and *Golden Eye*.

Bysh, Sue

Production manager on eight episodes: S2 and 'Diamonds are for Heather'

Sue was a trainee production manager when first assigned to the series and is responsible for finding Claesmore School, formerly Wolverton Manor, which was used as Ridgemere Hall in 'A Touch of Glass'.

She was soon directing and producing her own shows. Among her credits as a director are seven episodes of *Dear John* and *Just Good Friends*, two episodes of *Birds of a Feather*, three of the sitcom *Late Expectations* and five of *Waiting for God*. As a director/producer, she worked on several shows including the 1989 sitcom *A Touch of Spice* and 1992's *Side By Side*,

Bywater, Lesley

Production assistant on nine episodes: S4, 'To Hull and Back' and 'A Royal Flush'. Production manager on one episode: 'The Frog's Legacy'

Lesley, who was born in Doncaster, started her career as a production secretary in radio, working on shows such as *Kaleidoscope*. She switched to television when she was offered a post as production assistant and among the programmes she worked on are *Dear John* and *Just Good Friends*. Lesley left the Beeb in 1997 to work as a freelance production manager.

Calvin

Played by Dennis Conlon

A Rastafarian who's seen briefly in The Nag's Head during 'To Hull and Back', Calvin accidentally spills lager on the bar, which Del then puts his sleeve in.

Camilla

When Del fools Grandad into thinking he's won half a million on the pools, Grandad celebrates his win with a girl called Camilla in the West End, until, that is, he remembers that he doesn't even do the pools. Grandad reminds Del of this in 'Wanted'. Camilla is never seen in the sitcom.

Captain

(See 'Bill')

Carey, Richenda

Role: Lady at opera
Appeared in 'A Royal Flush'

After graduating from drama school, Richenda made her acting debut in 1970 at Derby Repertory Theatre, before working all over the country in rep. Her first appearance on the screen came in an early 1970s production, *Country Matters*. She's since worked extensively on television, including roles as Diana Curry in *Nanny*; Mrs Hale in *Lace* and *Lace II*; Nanny in the mini-series *A Perfect Spy*; Lady Bradshaw in *Mrs Dalloway*; Miss Culper in *Dear John*; the Head Nurse in *Upstairs, Downstairs*; Lady Penelope in *Dinnerladies*; Lady Ingram in *Jane Eyre* and her favourite role, Bridget Cavendish, the Dean's wife in *The Choir*. On the big screen her credits include the 1999 picture *Whatever Happened to Harold Smith?* and, in 2001, *Vacuum*, as Mrs Cartwright.

Carey, Ron

In 'The Chance of a Lunchtime', Ron is mentioned by Alan Parry in a discussion with Rodney. They had lunch with him a few months ago and the Harvey's mail order employee gives Parry's company a three-year contract to print junk mail, catalogues and office stationery. Ron is never seen in the series.

Caribbean Stallion

An exotic cocktail Del Boy orders while nightclubbing with Rodney in 'Go West Young Man'. An uncertain waiter is instructed in the drink's composition by Del. It contains a shot of tequila, coconut rum and crème de menthe, a smidgin of Campari, with the merest suggestion of Angostura bitters. It's then topped with fresh grapefruit juice, shaken and poured over broken ice. Finally, it's garnished with slices of orange, lime and occasional seasonal fruits. The drink is topped off with a decorative plastic umbrella and two translucent straws. Del claims it's a cocktail 'specially created for the discerning palates of the international jet set.'

Carl

Actor not named on the cast list

Carl, who lives in Bethnal Green, is Denzil's brother. He's seen in 'Chain Gang' and, together with his brothers, plans to buy the gold chains from Arnie, the conman.

Carlotti

Played by Roger Pretto

In 'Miami Twice', Carlotti owns the waterside restaurant Del and Rodney dine at with Rico and the boys. Mistaking Del for Occhetti, Carlotti approaches the Peckham trader with respect and fear.

Carmen

Played by Gina Bellman

Seen in 'The Unlucky Winner is…', Carmen works as a rep on the Mallorcan holiday the winners of the Mega Flakes painting competition enjoy. When Rodney, who's pretending to be 14, is embarrassed to join the other children, Carmen tries coaxing him on to the Fun Bus.

Carnell, Mike

Role: Young towser
Appeared in S3, episode 2

Mike's busy career has covered all areas of the profession, but he's been busiest in television in recent years. His roles on the small screen include playing a goblin salesman in *You Rang, M'Lord?*; a taxi driver in *The Magician*; a choir master in *The Brittas Empire*; a newspaper editor in *Life School*; a betting shop manager in *In Sickness and In Health*; an irate father in *Hi-De-Hi!* and Lennie in *Big Deal*.

Recent stage credits include Crawshay in *Raffles*, Purdue in *Habeus Corpus* and an ugly sister in *Cinderella*.

Carol Singers, The

Played by The Fred Tomlinson Singers

The Fred Tomlinson Singers are seen singing carols

à la Del

'Pas de Basque'
('Cash and Curry')

in the street during 'Diamonds are for Heather'. A disconsolate Del, who's just split up with Heather, gives the leading carol singer some cash in return for them singing 'Old Shep', one of Del's favourite songs.

Carroll, Andy

Graphic designer on two episodes: 'Miami Twice' (Parts 1 & 2)

Andy studied illustration at art school before working as a freelance illustrator for BBC Wales for a time; when his wife, who also works in television, secured a job at TV-AM, Andy – who was born in London – followed her to London and began working for Thames TV, concentrating on news graphics.

'I was responsible for designing the big portrait of David Jason dressed in all the gangster attire which was used in the programme. I got David into the studio and took some photographs, then blew one up and had it mounted on to a canvas-textured material. It was then varnished, which added brush strokes to the picture and made it appear as if it was a proper painting.'

ANDY CARROLL – Graphic designer

In 1985, Andy was given the opportunity to work on the last series of *The Two Ronnies*, before he returned to Thames for a further two years. Still freelance, other shows he's worked on include *Are You Being Served?*, *In Sickness and In Health* and *The Fast Show*, as well as working with the likes of Russ Abbot, Les Dennis, Jasper Carrott, Frank Skinner and Alistair McGowen.

Carron, Ali Bryer

Assistant floor manager on one episode: 'Fatal Extraction'

Born in Essex, Ali worked on a voluntary basis in the theatre before studying stage management at the Guildhall School of Music and Drama. Upon graduating she worked in theatres up and down the country, including spells in the West End. She joined the BBC in 1990 and worked initially as an assistant floor manager. Nowadays she's a line producer on sketch shows, including *TV to Go*, but during her 12 years in the industry has worked on a host of programmes, including *Waiting for God; Honey for Tea; Roger, Roger* and *Heartburn Hotel*.

Carter

Played by Ifor Gwynne-Davies

Seen in 'A Royal Flush', Carter is a footman at Covington House, the home of the Duke of Maylebury, who's bored rigid when Albert starts telling him one of his naval tales.

'Cash and Curry'

Original transmission: Tuesday 22 September 1981, 8.30 pm

Production date: Sunday 21 June 1981

Original viewing figures: 7.3 million

Duration: 30 minutes

First repeat: Friday 21 September 1990, 7.35 pm

Subsequent repeats: 10/4/97, 7/5/99

CAST

Del Trotter	David Jason
Rodney Trotter	Nicholas Lyndhurst
Grandad Trotter	Lennard Pearce
Mr Ram	Renu Setna
Vimmal	Ahmed Khalil
Indian restaurant manager	Babar Bhatti
The heavy	Roy Questel

Walk-ons: (Men with deep-freeze) Leslie Bates and John Cannon. (Car trader) Richard Graham-Clare. (Trader at garage block) Derek Suthern. (Men with TV set) Kelly Garfield and Harry Fielder. (Jeweller) Albert Welch. (Indian waiter) Tapan Ghosh. (People at town hall) Michael Leader, Reg Lloyd, Terry Rendle, Sheila West, Christina Michaels, Lee Richards, Roy Seeley, Colin Thomas, Martin Clarke, Leslie Adams, Liz Adams, Alison McGuire, Rosina Stewart, Juliet Hunt. (People in Indian restaurant) Ten extras.

PRODUCTION TEAM

Written by John Sullivan

Title music arranged and conducted by Ronnie Hazlehurst composed and sung by John Sullivan

Audience Warm-Up:	Felix Bowness
Make-up Designer:	Pauline Cox
Costume Designer:	Phoebe De Gaye
Properties Buyer:	Chris Ferriday
Film Cameraman:	Bill Matthews
Film Sound:	Dennis Panchen and Ron Brown
Film Editor:	John Jarvis
Camera Supervisor:	Ron Peverall
Studio Lighting Director:	Don Babbage
Studio Sound:	Mike Felton
Technical Coordinator:	Robert Hignett
Videotape Editor:	Chris Wadsworth
Stills Photographer:	John Jefford
Production Assistant:	Penny Thompson
Assistant Floor Manager:	Mandie Fletcher
Graphic Designer:	Peter Clayton
Vision Mixer:	Hilary West
Production Manager:	Janet Bone
Designer:	Cynthia Kljuco

Directed by Martin Shardlow

Produced by Ray Butt

Del is out to forge new business contacts at the Peckham and Camberwell Chamber of Trade Dinner/Dance and chats to a new man around town, Vimmal Malik, whom Del believes to be rich and willing to throw some business the way of Trotters' Independent Traders.

Walking back to their cars after the do, Malik is confronted by Mr Ram and a bit of muscle he's brought along for effect. Miraculously, Del settles the argument by flooring the heavy with a quick blow in the groin, and as Rodney ushers Vimmal away and takes off in his car, he leaves Del all alone. Mr Ram wants to discuss the matter, and over a meal at one of the restaurants he claims to own, he explains to Del that Vimmal has a porcelain statuette which rightfully belongs to his family. A long-running family feud between the Rams and Maliks came to a head when Vimmal's family destroyed the Rams' home, sold their land and built up a business empire from the proceeds. The only item that remains from his birthright, the simple statuette, is with Vimmal. Mr Ram wants it back, and he'll pay four grand to retrieve it.

Del plays straight into Mr Rams' hands when he offers to adopt the role of mediator between the two parties. He doesn't realise until it's too late, and he's lost a mint of money in the process, that Malik and Ram are fraudsters and in partnership, touring the country preying on gullible fools like Del Boy with their fictitious tales of family feuds.

Casino waitress

Played by Lorraine Parsloe

The waitress works in Ronnie Nelson's 121 Club and informs Del in 'Fatal Extraction' that Ronnie won't be turning up that evening, which is disappointing because Del was hoping to finalise a business deal.

Cassandra

(See 'Trotter, Cassandra (née Parry')

Cathles House

During a conversation in 'The Long Legs of the Law', Del asks Grandad if he remembers Tommy Razzle who used to live in Cathles House. We never hear about the place again.

'Chain Gang'

Original transmission: Sunday 22 January 1989, 7.15 pm

Production dates: Saturday 14 and Sunday 15 January 1989

Original viewing figures: 16.3 million

Duration: 50 minutes

First repeat: Friday 22 September 1989, 7.30 pm

Subsequent repeats: 29/1/92, 14/1/94, 21/8/96, 25/7/97, 7/7/99, 16/2/01

CAST

Del Trotter	David Jason
Rodney Trotter	Nicholas Lyndhurst
Uncle Albert	Buster Merryfield
Cassandra	Gwyneth Strong
Mike	Kenneth MacDonald
Denzil	Paul Barber
Arnie	Philip McGough
Boycie	John Challis
Trigger	Roger Lloyd Pack
Otto	Mick Oliver
Grayson	Peter Rutherford
Mario	Frank Coda
Woman in crowd	Marie Lorraine
Steven	Sam Howard
Gary	Steve Fortune

Walk-ons: Luke Anthony, Stuart Myers, Ivan Santon, Harjit Singh, Simon Crook, Chris Andrews, Joanna D'Eathe, Seva Dhalivaal, Christian Fletcher, April Ford, Peter Gates Fleming, Penny Lambirth, Ray Martin, Ranjit Nakara, Robert Pearson, Steve Rome, Patrick Ford, Lee Richards, Trisha Clarke, Terry Dacey, Avril Kay, Felicity Lee, Bryan Jacobs.

PRODUCTION TEAM

Written by John Sullivan

Title music arranged and conducted by Ronnie Hazlehurst composed and sung by John Sullivan

Make-up Designers:	Jean Steward and Sylvia Thornton
Costume Designer:	Richard Winter
Properties Buyer:	Malcolm Rougvie
Film Cameramen:	Alec Curtis and Alan Stevens
Film Sound:	Michael Spencer and Peter Hobbs
Film Editor:	John Jarvis
Camera Supervisor:	Ken Major
Studio Lighting Director:	Don Babbage
Studio Sound:	Alan Machin
Technical Coordinator:	Reg Poulter
Videotape Editor:	Chris Wadsworth
Production Assistant:	Amita Lochab
Assistant Floor Manager:	Kerry Waddell
Graphic Designer:	Peter Clayton
Vision Mixer:	Helen Gilder
Production Managers:	Adrian Pegg and Gill Anderson
Designer:	Graham Lough

Directed by Tony Dow

Produced by Gareth Gwenlan

Del strikes up a conversation with Arnie – a retired jewellery dealer – at The One Eleven Club, and agrees to meet him back in his car to see if they can do business together. When Arnie shows him a case full of 18-carat gold chains, he agrees to buy them for £12,500, much to Rodney's amazement. When Rodney queries how he'll be able to cough up twelve grand, Del explains his idea for a consortium involving Mike and Boycie. Before long Trigger, Albert and Rodney have also signed up.

Then Arnie hears from his wife that Mr Stavros, who originally intended buying the chains, has arrived in London and wishes to meet Arnie for lunch. He wants to buy the jewellery and won't take no for an answer. Del sees an opportunity to make a profit so suggests Arnie keeps the lunch appointment.

At the rendezvous Arnie collapses with a suspected heart attack and is rushed to hospital, together with his briefcase containing the gold chains and the consortium's £12,500. Later, an unnamed doctor calls to break the sad news that Arnie has died and that his widow, Pat, has been given his possessions.

But when Rodney spots Arnie leaving another restaurant on a stretcher, he realises that the consortium has been taken for a ride. With the help of Denzil and his brothers, Arnie soon gets his comeuppance.

Challis, Jean

Role: Mrs Sansom
Appeared in 'Dates'

Jean, who was born in Cheadle Hulme in 1934, graduated from the Rose Bruford College and made her acting debut at Tynemouth Rep, in a 1954 production of *On Monday Next*. A long spell in repertory theatre followed, working in places such as Norwich, Buxton, Cheltenham. Westcliff, Ipswich and Farnham.

Her break into television was in a 1960 episode of *Dixon of Dock Green*, but her favourite roles are Mrs Arnott in John Sullivan's *Dear John* and Mum Matheson in 20 episodes of *She-Wolf of London*. Other small-screen credits include Mildred in *One Foot in the Grave*, Matron in *Goodnight Sweetheart*, Mrs Winterton in *Babara* and Mrs Gogarty in *The Lake of Darkness*.

On stage, more recent appearances have been in *Animal Crackers*, playing Mrs Rittenhouse; *Fortune's Fool* as Ivanova and Widow Corney in *Oliver!*.

She's also worked extensively on the radio, including time as a continuity announcer (1962–66), programme compiler and presenter for the British Forces Broadcasting Service in Cyprus. Now, nearly four decades later, Jean has returned to the island, where she's been living since January 2001.

Challis, John

Role: Boycie
Appeared in 31 episodes: S1, episode 2; S2, episode 3; S3, episodes 5, 6, & 7; S4, episodes 5 & 6; S5, episodes 1, 5 & 6; S6, episodes 2, 3, 5 & 6; S7, episodes 1–5; 'To Hull and Back'; 'The Frog's Legacy'; 'Dates'; 'The Jolly Boys' Outing'; 'Miami Twice' (Parts 1 & 2); 'Mother Nature's Son'; 'Fatal Extraction'; 'Heroes and Villains'; 'Modern Men'; 'Time On Our Hands' and 'If They Could See Us Now…!'

A failed romance led John Challis to a crucial juncture. Just when it looked as if he was heading for a life on the other side of the Atlantic, a letter arrived. 'I'd been working in America with a theatre company and got seduced by the country: it was so different and very exciting; it was a voyage of discovery and I knew it was where I wanted to be. I'd also met someone, who I thought I was in love with, and planned to sell up in the UK, marry her and live in the States. Then I received a phone call offering me a job in England, which left me undecided. But my mind was made up when she wrote me a "Dear John" letter. So that was that. Shortly after, I was offered the part of Boycie.'

Playing the second-hand car dealer has brought some security and, perhaps, recognition within the profession, but it's just a single element of a career spanning all strands of the entertainment world. Although he'd always wanted to be an actor, it looked as if his future was heading in a different direction upon leaving school. 'Everybody kept putting me off, saying how insecure it was as a profession, so I joined a firm of estate agents instead.' The job only lasted six months. 'I got so bored and we came to a mutual understanding; my

boss thought it best if I left and I agreed.' Of course, John's prospects hadn't been helped by the fact he was constantly imitating the voices of his superiors. 'I'd practised doing voices since I was a kid; I was always more fascinated by other people than myself. I got bored sitting in the office, so started inventing these deals and impersonating one of the partners in the process. It was a bit cheeky really because I'd phone people pretending to be him; in the end I got found out and that was the end of that.'

Although he was born in Bristol in 1942, he spent little time in the city. His father worked for the Admiralty in nearby Bath, but when the offices were relocated to the capital, the family moved to southeast London, where he grew up and was educated. After the brief excursion into the world of estate agents, John 'rebelled against society' and drove a grocer's van for six months, whilst contemplating where his future lay. 'At the time I was living in Epsom, Surrey, which was a bit of a closed society, and I began realising that I wanted to get out of the area, so I found a job with a touring children's theatre. I didn't need any qualifications, and was given the chance to play lots of different roles, which I loved doing. We'd charge around the country in a van giving performances of stories like *Pinocchio* and *The Emperor's Nightingale* at schools – I had a great time.'

The experience made John realise he wanted to act. 'I just loved mucking about and showing off, but I didn't have any great plan; I met someone who introduced me to an agent, and because there was a theatre in almost every town, I was soon offered work.' John moved from one repertory theatre to the next, gaining vital experience, and didn't stop working for four years. 'I started off acting and

doing stage management, which I dropped eventually, but whereas people had been constantly warning me about how much time I'd spend out of work, I thought life as an actor was easy, going from job to job.'

Soon, John had made his West End debut and worked with the Royal Shakespeare Company. 'I auditioned for the RSC and also for the West End play at the same time. I was lucky enough to be offered both jobs, but as I'd already agreed to the West End role, even though it was only a tiny part and understudying, I took that one. I thought I'd lost my chance of working with the RSC, but as soon as the West End play (*Portrait of a Queen*) came off, there was an opening with the Royal Shakespeare and I joined the company, which meant I'd been working for about six years non-stop. Although it was only a small part in the West End – I was playing a gentleman of the press, which was cut after about a week, leaving me to simply understudy one of the major parts – it gave me much-needed experience.

A change of agent in the late 1960s brought new opportunities in the world of television, beginning with six episodes of the early BBC soap *The Newcomers*. Although he enjoyed the job, his memories of this period are tinged with disappointment. 'At the time, the Beatles made the *Magical Mystery Tour* and were looking for someone to be the courier on their coach. My agent had heard about this so put my name forward. I met three of the Beatles (George wasn't there) and was over the moon when they offered me the part. I thought it was the greatest thing in the world, so you can imagine my disappointment when my agent called later that day and said: "I've got some bad news for you: the BBC won't release you because it clashes by one day with your work on *The Newcomers*." You go through a lot of despondency in this business, but that was, perhaps, the biggest disappointment I've ever had.'

Other television appearances include two roles in *Coronation* Street: playing a football hooligan in one episode, and a policeman in over a dozen. 'It was terrific fun. Len Fairclough was accused of murdering his fancy woman, but it turned out to be her husband, although by then we'd given him a grilling and pushed him about a bit.' In *Doctor Who*, meanwhile, he appeared opposite Tom Baker in a six-part story called 'The Seeds of Doom'. He's also been seen in *Softly, Softly*; *The Sweeney*; *Z Cars* and *Citizen Smith*, a programme for which John has very fond memories, not least because it led to him being offered the role of Boycie in *Only Fools and Horses*. More recently, he's appeared in *The Bill*, *Heartbeat*, *Casualty* and *Soldier, Soldier*.

He's also just finished a radio series, *Getting Nowhere Fast*, and, during the mid-1990s, presented his own show on Radio 2. 'It was more difficult than I thought it would be, but was something I'd always wanted to do. I'd been a frequent guest on other people's shows and thought talking and playing music for a couple of hours must be the greatest thing. Then one day, I was working in a studio and got talking to a producer and he told me they were looking for new presenters for an early morning slot. He suggested I cobbled something together and sent it off.' So he recorded a five-minute tape and submitted it. A month later he was offered a job.

John completed eight shows, during which time he was also working in open air theatre at Regent's Park, but he felt he approached the job in the wrong way. 'Being an actor, I did my version of what I thought a DJ sounded like, instead of being myself. It took two or three shows for me to unravel this.'

In many respects, assignments John undertakes will always be overshadowed by the huge success he's had with Boycie in *Only Fools*, but he doesn't worry in the slightest, and is grateful for the opportunity to play the second-hand car shark. Thousands of fans regularly attend conventions organised by the Only Fools and Horses Appreciation Society, clammering to see the stars of the show, and John is a regular guest. 'It's remarkable to see all the fans. I remember at one convention the queues were massive; all the guests were signing copies of books and memorabilia as quickly as possible, as well as having a chat with the fans, which I think is important. After all, if they don't turn on their teles, you're out of a job, so we owe the fans a lot. Towards the end of the queue, someone had been waiting four and a half hours to get our autographs. I apologised to him, and he replied: "No, it's worth it." Getting us to sign our names on his goods meant so much to him.'

Chambers, Eddie

Played by Steve Alder

A friend of Mike Fisher, Eddie is seen at the pub the boys stop at *en route* to Margate in 'The Jolly Boys' Outing'. Mike bumps into him, they get chatting and we discover Eddie used to own a rival pub in the East End before selling up and buying another property on the Isle of Wight. He's since moved on to a club in Margate called the Mardi Gras.

'Chance of a Lunchtime, The'

Original transmission: Sunday 6 January 1991, 7.15 pm

Production dates: Saturday 1 and Sunday 2 December 1990

Original viewing figures: 16.6 million

Duration: 50 minutes

First repeat: Wednesday 25 March 1992, 8.00 pm

Subsequent repeats: 25/2/94, 8/8/97, 20/4/01

CAST

Del Trotter . . . . .David Jason
Rodney Trotter . . . . .Nicholas Lyndhurst
Uncle Albert . . . . .Buster Merryfield
Raquel . . . . .Tessa Peake-Jones
Cassandra . . . . .Gwyneth Strong
Alan .Denis Lill
Boycie . . . . .John Challis
Mike .Kenneth MacDonald
Trigger . . . . .Roger Lloyd Pack
Marlene . . . . .Sue Holderness
Man in the pub . . . . .Ian Barritt
Trudy . . . . .Helen Blizard
Jules .Paul Opacic
Adrian . . . . .Ian Redford
Baby Tyler . . . . .Elliot Russell
Walk-ons: . . . .(Diners) Charley Hart, Gary Rich, Adrian Fletcher, Keith Allington, Richard Allenson, Tony Field, Clive Bryan, Darren Harrison, Kayla Miller, Verona Chard, Karen Ashley, Shirley Day, Nicki Stevens, Wendy Dewar, Andy Turvey, Glen Finnick, Bill Chapman, Andrew O'Leary, Elvis Williams, Jason Marrett, Roland Kitchen, Barnabas Spender, Giancarla, Shaye Lewton, Brigitte Coombes, Alison Williams, Lozeena Rees, Lyn Thomson, Carol Luke and Tina Duskey. (Waiters) Wayne Maclean and Kevin Barber. (Waitresses) Susie Barton and Sandra Forbes. (Cab driver) Dav Owen. (Pub customers) Patrick Small, Barbara Allen, John Christopher-Wood, Alan Crisp, Nick Sanquest, Michelle Grand, Jacqui Docker, Elaina le Grand, Christine Firth, Graham Russell, Terry Duggan, Bob Heath, Ashley Daly, Charles Rayford, Jay McGrath, Gary Ridley, Bob Terson, Christopher Paul, Andrew Karl, Jimmy Morris, Graham Brooks, Martin Kennedy, Laura Dixon, Beverley Jennings, Joann Allchin and Helena Clayton. (Barmaid) Alptha Anthony.

PRODUCTION TEAM

Written by John Sullivan

Title music arranged and conducted by Ronnie Hazlehurst composed and sung by John Sullivan

Audience Warm-up: . . . . .Jeff Stevenson
Make-up Designer: . . . . .Christine Greenwood
Costume Designer: . . . . .Robin Stubbs
Properties Buyer: . . . . .Malcolm Rougvie
Film Cameraman: . . . . .Alec Curtis
Film Sound: . . . . .Michael Spencer
Film Editor: . . . . .John Jarvis
Dubbing Mixer: . . . . .Michael Narduzzo
Camera Supervisor: . . . . .Ken Major
Studio Lighting Director: . . . . .Don Babbage
Studio Sound: . . . . .Alan Machin
Technical Coordinator: . . . . . . .Peter Manuel
Videotape Editor: . . . . .Chris Wadsworth
Production Assistant: . . . . .Teresa Powick
Assistant Floor Managers: . . . . .Debbie Crofts and Miles Cherry
Graphic Designer: . . . . .Andrew Smee
Vision Mixer: . . . . .Sue Collins
Production Managers: . . . . .Angela de Chastelai Smith and Adrian Pegg
Production Secretary: . . . . .Amanda Church
Designer: . . . . .Richard McManan-Smith
Casting Adviser: . . . . .Judy Loe
Directed by Tony Dow
Produced by Gareth Gwenlan

Raquel is getting nervous about her audition for a part in Shakespeare's *As You Like It*, and Rodney still hasn't patched things up with Cassandra, so Del tries playing reconciler: while fixing a new front door to Cassandra's flat, he tells her that Rodney wants to meet for a meal. Back home, he informs his brother that Cassandra would like to meet at 7.30pm. The tryst goes well; they even laugh when they realise that the devious Del is behind the rendezvous. They make up and agree to meet at their flat in half an hour.

En route, Rodney pops in to the pub to thank Del, only to find him trying desperately to get rid of an old fiancée, Trudy. When a taxi arrives to take her home, Rodney helps the inebriated blonde outside and into the cab. Just at that moment, Cassandra drives by, spots them together and jumps to all the wrong conclusions; more bad news follows when Rodney finds himself out of a job, but there is one scrap of good news: Raquel turns down the chance of a nine-week school tour of Shakespeare's plays because she's pregnant – much to Del's delight.

Chapman, Constance

Role: Elsie Partridge

Appeared in S6, episode 5

Born in Weston-super-Mare in 1912, Constance trained at Bristol and made her professional debut in a BBC production in Cardiff in 1929. Her early years were spent largely around the Bristol area, and it was from the city, in 1953, that she first appeared on television.

Although Constance has now retired from the stage, over the years she has performed around the country. Repertory seasons at Nottingham, Birmingham and Manchester have been intermingled with spells at the Royal Court, in the Lindsay Anderson productions of *In Celebration* and *The Contractor*, and at the National Theatre in *The March on Russia*.

On screen, her occasional sojourns into films have included roles in *Clockwise* and *Raging Moon*, while on television an extensive list of credits include *Casualty*, Miss Bates in *Emma*, *A Kind of Loving*, *Bergerac*, Mrs Jones in *Run for the Lifeboat*, five episodes as Connie in Channel 4's *Never Say Die*, and Old Margaret in *Shadowy Third* for the BBC.

Charles

Played by Nicholas Courtney

Charles is a waiter at the Hilton Hotel in Park Lane. When Del takes Raquel there on their first date, he is out to impress, and arranges for Charles to interrupt their tête-à-tête and announce that Del's New York office is on the phone.

Charles

Played by Peter Tuddenham

Charles is a guest at the Duke of Maylebury's shoot at his country house in Berkshire.

Charleson, Andrew

Role: The dentist (Mr Ellis)

Appeared in 'Fatal Extraction'

Andrew, who was born in London in 1962, trained at the Guildhall School of Music and Drama. He made his professional stage debut in *Twelfth Night* at the St George's Theatre, London, while his first appearance on the small screen was in *No Place Like Home*, taking over from Martin Clunes for the last two series of the sitcom as Nigel Crabtree.

Other television credits include *Stay Lucky, The House of Eliott, Seekers, Next of Kin, This Life, Rough Treatment, Family Affairs, Best of Both Worlds* and, more recently, *A Line in the Sand* for Anglia TV. On the big screen he's been seen in *Before I Die Forever, Edward II* and *Being Human.*

Andrew remains busy on screen and stage, with recent theatre outings including an international tour of *Harvey*, playing in Malaysia, Thailand, Sri Lanka, Bahrain, Oman and Hong Kong.

Charlie

Played by Marcus Francis

Charlie plays acoustic guitar in 'A Bunch of Wallies', the band Rodney quits in 'It's Only Rock and Roll'.

Chas

In 'Video Nasty', Del speaks to Chas on the phone whilst waiting for a Chinese takeaway. Del's doing a bit of business with him, but has to cancel the rhino he'd planned to hire because Rodney – who's making a local community film – wasn't impressed with Del's idea for a film plot. Chas is not seen in the series.

Checkout girl

(See 'Sheila')

Cherry, Miles

Assistant floor manager on four episodes: S7, episodes 1–3 and 'Rodney Come Home'

Born in Radlett, Hertfordshire, Miles completed a film and drama degree at Reading's Bulmershe College before joining the BBC in 1988, initially as a video enquiry clerk. He moved over to become a floor assistant and progressed to the position of assistant floor manager but left the Corporation in 1991 to travel the world for a year and a half.

Upon his return he became an actor for a while before launching his own company, React – Acting for Business, in 1993, supplying actors for corporate work. Nowadays he rarely acts himself, spending all his time running the business.

Chief of Security

(See 'Robson, Chief')

Chin, Mr

Played by Rex Wei

In 'The Yellow Peril', Mr Chin owns The Golden Lotus, a Chinese takeaway. When he's tipped off about an impending visit from a health inspector, he does some business with Del, recruiting the services of Rodney and Grandad for £150 to paint the restaurant's kitchen. What he doesn't realise is that the anonymous caller was none other than Del, trying to conjure up some trade.

China Gardens Takeaway, The

In 'Danger UXD', Denzil spends £5.54 on his dish at this Chinese takeaway, but whilst he's waiting he hears a TV news report about some highly dangerous inflatable dolls, items he's been involved with.

Chinese takeaway owner

(See 'Tony')

Chinese takeaway owner

Played by Takashi Kawahara

The owner of the China Gardens Takeaway is seen briefly in 'Danger UXD' when he serves Denzil.

Chloe

Seen in 'Danger UXD', Chloe eats a salad at The Nag's Head. She's there with her boyfriend, Adrian, who's an estate agent. Their presence in the pub is unusual: normally they would be seen in the wine bars and bistros, but since Del has adopted his 'yuppy' image and has begun drinking there himself, they've reverted to The Nag's Head to avoid him. They can't believe it when he arrives on the scene.

Chris

Played by Tony Marshall

Chris, who appears briefly for the first time at The Nag's Head in 'Dates', is a ladies' hairstylist. He's a friend of Mickey Pearce and Jevon, and finds it hilarious that Rodney has a date with Nerys, the barmaid, whom he refers to as 'Nervous Nerys'. The next time we see Chris is at a nightclub in 'Rodney Come Home'; he's there with Mickey Pearce and Rodney, who's started drinking heavily since his split from Cassandra. His final appearance in the show is back at The Nag's Head in 'Mother Nature's Son', where we see him enjoying the biggest party in the world during the dream sequence.

'Christmas Crackers'

(Christmas Special 1981)

Original transmission: Monday 28 December 1981, 9.55 pm

Production date: Wednesday 23 December 1981

Original viewing figures: 7.5 million

Duration: 35 minutes

First repeat: Friday 24 December 1999, 5.30 pm

CAST

Del Trotter . . . . .David Jason
Rodney Trotter . . . . .Nicholas Lyndhurst
Grandad Trotter . . . . .Lennard Pearce
Earl . . . . .Desmond McNamara
Anita/First plain girl . . . . .Nora Connolly
Walk-ons: . . . .(Second plain girl) Antonia Moss. (Two pretty girls) Melinda Ashford and Jean Havilland. (Man to leave bar) Malcolm Ross. (Girl walking past) Beverley Andrews. (Boys asking girls to dance) Nick Kidd and Brian Jacobs. (Two people to vacate chairs for girls) Michael Leader and Jeanette Lampshire. (Disc jockey) George Agard. Other walk-on: . . . . .Chris Breeze
Extras: . . . . .Debbie Baker, Lynne Brotchie, Charlotte Corbert, Ros Kendall, Elaine Payne, Roy Brent, Barney Lawrence, Dennis Shore, Gwynne Sullivan, Clemmie Cowl, Isolde Dawes, Linda French, Shirley Sinclair, Sue Tarry, Barbara Hampshire, Ridgewell Hawkes, Ray Lavender, Harriet Keevil, Bridget Lynch-Blosse

PRODUCTION TEAM

Written by John Sullivan

Title music arranged and conducted by Ronnie Hazlehurst composed and sung by John Sullivan

---

MEMORIES OF CHRISTMAS CRACKERS

★ ★ ★ ★ ★ ★

'I only did one episode of *Only Fools and Horses* and that was "Christmas Crackers", which was put into the schedules at the last minute following the success of the first series. None of the regular production team were available, so David, Nick and Lennard were confronted with a bunch of people they'd never set eyes on before!

'It was difficult for them as they had enjoyed a good rapport with their regular team during the series and with no pre-filming, and only one week to rehearse and record the show, we didn't have much time to get in tune. It wasn't the best show by their standards but still very good entertainment for the viewers and, as far as I was concerned, it was great fun to work with them.

'I have to confess that as I didn't know any of the cockney phrases and East End patois I spent the first couple of rehearsals pointing out what I thought were mistakes or mistypes in the script – at least the cast and John (Sullivan) thoroughly enjoyed sending me up rotten for the entire week!'

JO AUSTIN – Production manager

Make-up Designer: . . . . .Jean Speak
Costume Designer: . . . . .Alan Hughes
Properties Buyer: . . . . .Chris Ferriday
Camera Supervisor: . . . . . . .Peter Hills
Studio Lighting Director: . . . . . .Don Babbage
Studio Sound: . . . . .Mike Felton
Technical Coordinator: . . . . . .Robert Hignett
Videotape Editor: . . . . .Graham Sisson
Production Assistant: . . . . .Jane Garcia
Assistant Floor Manager: . . . . .Clare Graham
Graphic Designer: . . . . .Peter Clayton
Vision Mixer: . . . . .Hilary West
Production Manager: . . . . .Jo Austin
Designer: . . . . .Cynthia Kljuco
Produced by Bernard Thompson

It's Christmas time at the Trotters', and Rodney is fed up with the familiarity of the occasion: burnt turkey, even blacker Christmas pud and nothing but circuses on the box. The only thing of interest this festive period is the book he borrowed from his mate, Mickey Pearce, titled: 'Body Language: The Lost Art'.

By evening, Rodney is so depressed he suggests to Del that they venture out somewhere, but Del isn't interested, pointing out that Christmas is to be spent with family. But when Grandad opts for the OAPs' do at the local community centre instead of enduring Del and Rodney's company, it's The Monte Carlo Club for the brothers. Fancying his chances with the girls, spurred on by what he's read in the body language book, Rodney plucks up enough courage to cross the dance floor and ask a couple of attractive girls for a dance. But before he's more than halfway, Del stops him in his tracks with some embarrassing comments, shattering his delicate confidence in one blow. By the time the boys finally decide who's best-suited for chatting up the girls, they're pipped to the post.

'Christmas Trees'

(For information about the 1982 Christmas sketch, see 'Funny Side of Christmas: Christmas Trees, The')

Church, Amanda

Production secretary on five episodes: S7, episodes 1–4 and 'Rodney Come Home'. Production assistant on two episodes: S7, episodes 5 & 6

Clark, Dan

Role: Scott
Appeared in 'Heroes and Villains'
After leaving school, Dan – who was born in Beckenham, Kent – completed a BTec course in performing arts, before writing and acting in a play at the Edinburgh Festival.

Nowadays, Dan concentrates on live comedy and is part of the act, Electric Eel. However, other television credits include playing Jerry Zachery in the act's own sitcom for Channel 4, *Roy Dance is Dead*, and various roles in *Comedy Nation* and *The Stand-up Show*.

MEMORIES OF ONLY FOOLS

★ ★ ★ ★ ★ ★

'The night before I was offered a part in *Only Fools and Horses* I was with some friends at the flat we shared. One of the guys had bought a tape of the sitcom and we watched it until the early hours. We all remarked on how good the series was, but at that time didn't have any knowledge that they were making the Christmas Trilogy. You can imagine my surprise when the following day I received a call from my agent asking if I wanted to audition for the part of Scott!'

DAN CLARK

Clarke, Catherine

Role: Sheila (Checkout girl)
Appeared in S5, episode 3
Catherine has now left the acting profession, but during her time as an actress she appeared on television – including playing the Night Nurse in *Bramwell* – and in the occasional film, such as *Made in Britain*, as a girl in the Job Centre.

Clarke, Gavin

Assistant floor manager on eight episodes: S4 and 'To Hull and Back'

Clarke, Nobby

Grandad talks about his old friend Nobby in 'It Never Rains…'. They had both tried joining the Foreign Legion at the same time, and had both failed in their attempt. Stuck in Tangiers, Nobby and Grandad bumped into an Arab who offered them a job, taking his motor launch over to Spain to deliver some cargo: a pile of guns. In the end they made seven similar trips before being arrested and imprisoned outside a town called Tarifa. Nobby, who had previously worked as a caretaker at a seaman's mission in Grimsby, was tortured.

Clarke, Tom

Played by John Bardon
Tom is Top-Buy supermarket's Head of Security at the branch the Trotters visit in 'The Longest Night'. When he was younger, Tom served five years with the Kenyan Police Force, but has turned to a life of crime with his involvement in the safe job at the supermarket.

Clarke, Tracy

Role: Girl in disco
Appeared in S6, episode 1
Tracy is no longer in the acting business and it's believed that she's living abroad.

'Class Of '62, The'

Original transmission: Sunday 20 January 1991, 7.15 pm
Production dates: 20 and 21 December 1990
Original viewing figures: 16.2 million
Duration: 50 minutes
First repeat: Wednesday 8 April 1992, 8.00 pm
Subsequent repeats: 11/3/94, 6/12/96, 31/3/99, 11/5/01

CAST
Del Trotter . . . . .David Jason
Rodney Trotter . . . . .Nicholas Lyndhurst
Uncle Albert . . . . .Buster Merryfield
Raquel . . . . .Tessa Peake-Jones
Boycie . . . . .John Challis
Trigger . . . . .Roger Lloyd Pack
Mike . . . . .Kenneth MacDonald
Denzil . . . . .Paul Barber
Roy Slater . . . . .Jim Broadbent

'The Class of '62'

(The scene involving the following actors was edited out before final transmission)

Club owner . . . . Roger McKern
Singer . . . . Mitch Basketfield
Rehearsal pianist . . . . Kenneth Mobbs
Walk-ons: . . . . Susie Whitmarsh, Patrick Edwards, Elaine le Grand, Julie Lawrence, Michelle Grand, Susan Goode, Beverley Jennings, Christopher Paul, Jimmy Morris, Graham Brooks, Derek Southern, Richard Baron, Pat Shepherd and Dave Leggett

PRODUCTION TEAM
Written by John Sullivan
Title music arranged and conducted by Ronnie Hazlehurst composed and sung by John Sullivan
Make-up Designer: . . . . Christine Greenwood
Costume Designer: . . . . Robin Stubbs
Properties Buyer: . . . . Malcolm Rougvie
Casting Adviser: . . . . Judy Loe
Camera Supervisor: . . . . Ken Major
Studio Lighting Director: . . . . . Don Babbage
Studio Sound: . . . . Alan Machin
Resources Coordinator: . . . . . . Peter Manuel
Videotape Editor: . . . . Chris Wadsworth
Production Assistant: . . . . Amanda Church
Assistant Floor Manager: . . . . . Debbie Crofts
Graphic Designer: . . . . Andrew Smee
Vision Mixer: . . . . Sue Collins
Production Manager: . . . . Angela de Chastelai Smith
Designer: . . . . Richard McManan-Smith
Directed by Tony Dow
Produced by Gareth Gwenlan

Del's latest craze is selling 'Futafax, the fax machines of tomorrow, today'. His only purchaser to date has been Mike, at The Nag's Head, who paid £45 for the machine and it's already playing up. While Del receives an invite to a school reunion, Raquel is the recipient of a letter from her solicitor, confirming they've traced her estranged husband who's considering his response to her starting divorce proceedings. Momentary depression is soon forgotten when Del boosts her spirits by stating that she and the impending baby are the best thing that's ever happened to him. He claims he'd do anything for her, but flatly refuses not to get plastered when he meets up with his old school chums at the reunion.

At The Nag's Head, Boycie, Del, Denzil, Trigger and Rodney (who's accompanying his brother) await the host of the reunion. He finally arrives in the shape of Roy Slater, who's supposedly a born-again Christian since being kicked out of the police force and sentenced to a five-year prison sentence in Parkhurst for diamond smuggling. Claiming he's a changed person, he wants to wipe the slate clean. Everyone finds his wish hard to swallow but after much deliberation they accept his offer of a drink, and before the night is out are flipping through old photo albums at Del's flat. Worming his way into the flat is one of Slater's devious plans. After establishing via the poll tax register at the town hall that Raquel is now living with Del, he's arrived back on the scene to force his

CUT FROM 'THE CLASS OF '62'

A NIGHTCLUB
A SIGN READS 'AUDITIONS. PLEASE REPORT TO BACK DOOR.' THE OWNER AND MANAGER OF THE CLUB (BOTH TOUGH-LOOKING CHARACTERS OF 45) ARE SEATED FACING THE STAGE, ON WHICH A 20-YEAR-OLD GIRL IS SINGING, ACCOMPANIED BY THE CLUB'S PIANIST. SEATED AT THE BAR ARE DEL, EXCITED AND POWER-DRESSED, AND RODNEY, BORED AND CASUALLY DRESSED. THE GIRL IS SINGING 'FEELINGS'.

DEL (QUIETLY TO RODNEY) She ain't a lot of cop, is she?
RODNEY I honestly ain't got a clue, Del. I don't even know why you brought me here.
DEL Well, you're out of work, Rodney, so what else would you be doing at 10 o'clock in the morning? Laying in your pit, playing tents! I thought you'd like to come along here and give Raquel a bit of encouragement.
RODNEY Encouragement? Have you heard the song she's chosen for her audition? I mean, it's ridiculous, stupid!
DEL I chose that song.
RODNEY Did you? Well, that explains it!
DEL It's a beautiful song.
RODNEY It's hardly appropriate.
DEL Of course it's appropriate. The old numbers are coming back.
OWNER (CALLS TO GIRL SINGER) Yes, thank you, love, thank you. Next. (CALLS) Raquel Turner.
RAQUEL ENTERS THE STAGE AND SMILES NERVOUSLY TO DEL AND RODNEY. DEL SMILES PROUDLY. RODNEY RETURNS A NERVOUS SMILE.
OWNER (TO DEL) Are you her agent?
DEL Yes, I am. (HANDS OWNER HIS INTRODUCTION CARD) Derek Trotter of the Trotter International Star

Agency, Peckham. You want 'em; we've got 'em. That's our motto. Do you know Shirley Bassey?
OWNER Well, not personally.
DEL (WINKS AND CROSSES HIS FINGERS) Like that, like that!
THE PIANIST PLAYS THE OPENING BARS TO 'CHAPEL OF LOVE'
RAQUEL (SINGS) I'm going to the chapel and I'm gonna get married. Going to the chapel and I'm gonna get married.
SHE NOW TURNS SLIGHTLY AND WE SEE SHE IS FIVE MONTHS PREGNANT. WE SEE THE SHOCKED REACTIONS OF THE OWNER. HE LOOKS TO RODNEY AND DEL.
OWNER (CALLS TO RAQUEL – LOUD) Next! (DEL IS BEMUSED, RODNEY EMBARRASSED)

THE TROTTER'S LOUNGE. DAY
ALBERT IS LYING ASLEEP IN THE ARMCHAIR. THERE ARE TWO LARGE CARDBOARD BOXES, ONE ON TOP OF THE OTHER. LARGE PRINTING ON THE BOX READS 'FUTUAFAX. THE FAX MACHINE OF TOMORROW – TODAY!' STENCILLED ACROSS THE BOXES IS THE WORD 'REJECT'. BENEATH THIS IS A WHITE SQUARE OF GLUED ON PAPER UPON WHICH IS PRINTED 'LOT 41'. ON THE BAR IS ONE OF THE FAX MACHINES. THE MACHINE BEGINS PRINTING OUT A MESSAGE. NOW ALL THE LIGHTS GO OUT, ACCOMPANIED BY AN ELECTRONIC BEEP WHICH SLOWLY DIES. THE FRONT DOOR OPENS. ALBERT IMMEDIATELY WAKES UP, IS OUT OF THE CHAIR AND IS RUNNING A CARPET SWEEPER OVER THE RUG. RODNEY AND RAQUEL ENTER FROM THE HALL.
RODNEY All right, Unc?
ALB Phew, I haven't stopped since you went out. How'd the audition go?

wife, Raquel, to sign a post-nuptial agreement. But realising that Del's reputation – what there is of it – as a trader would be permanently tarnished if people heard he was living with an ex-copper's girl, Slater decides to take advantage of the situation. The Trotters, however, are having none of it and have a shock in store for Slater.

Classic Curtains

When Rodney is employed by Alan Parry in 'Rodney Come Home', his secretary, Michelle, mentions that Mr Coleman of Classic Curtains is due in for a meeting.

Clayton

(See 'Cooper, Mr')

Clayton, Peter

Graphic designer on 15 episodes: S1; S2; S6, episode 3 and 'Christmas Crackers'
After studying graphic design and photography at Maidstone Art School, Peter joined the BBC as an

assistant graphic designer in 1973. He gained experience working on a host of shows, from *Horizon* to *Three Of A Kind*. By the time he designed the titles for *Only Fools*, Peter had been promoted to designer.

Peter was a senior designer on sports programmes when he left the BBC in 1989 to join the sports' channel, BSB, as Head of Graphics. In 1991, however, he was made redundant and worked freelance for ten years for various clients including Channel 4, Eurosport and TWI, by whom he's now employed, as a producer on Premier League football coverage.

Clerk

Played by Les Rawlings
The Clerk of the Court appears in 'Hole in One' when Uncle Albert's compensation claim is heard.

Cleveland, Carol

Role: American reporter (Sandra Fox)
Appeared in S5, episode 2
London-born Carol Cleveland's parents met on a

film set so it's no surprise their daughter wanted to act. She grew up in California, returning to England to attend RADA. After graduating she worked in theatre and television, including *Randall and Hopkirk (Deceased), The Saint, The Lotus Eaters, Are You Being Served?* and *About Face* with Maureen Lipman.

She also worked as a 'glamour stooge' for Ronnie Corbett, Roy Hudd and Spike Milligan, but she's best known for appearances in every series of *Monty Python*, as well as the films and stage spin-offs. Recent work has mainly been in the theatre.

Clifford, Kim

Role: Vicky
Appeared in 'To Hull and Back'

Kim, who was born in 1961, began acting as a teenager, appearing in two productions for the Children's Film Foundation: Becky in 1974's *Where's Johnny?* and Barbara Evans in *Copter Kids,* two years later. Before she was 20 she'd played Joyce in an episode of *Juliet Bravo,* Rose Holloway in an instalment from *Agatha Christie's Partners in Crime* and Denise in *Bar Mitzvah Boy,* in the *Play for Today* series. She also made an early film appearance as a maid in *Chariots of Fire.*

The 1980s was a busy time for Kim. She was a regular in *Alas Smith and Jones* and played Mandy in *Colin's Sandwich.* In 1988 she started a nine-year association with the drama series, *London's Burning,* in which she played Sandra Hallam.

Coach And Horses, The

In 'Dates', Rodney mentions that a stripper is entertaining at The Coach and Horses, and asks Del if he's intending to pop along.

Cochrane, Martin

Role: Naval officer
Appeared in 'Dates'

Martin, who was born in London in 1946, trained at Glasgow's Royal Scottish Academy of Music and Dramatic Art. As well as working in Canada he was also a partner in a Edinburgh hotel before starting in showbusiness as a guitarist and singer.

He made his acting debut at the Horseshoe Wharf Club (part of the Mermaid Theatre) in the 1966 production *Times are Getting Hard, Boys.* Rep work followed at various theatres, including Glasgow, Perth, Harrogate and Newcastle, and television work started coming his way, such as *Sutherland's Law* for the BBC, and *High Living,* Scottish Television's first soap opera.

Although he rarely works in the theatre these days, he's still busy on screen. His film credits include two pictures for the Children's Film Foundation, as well as the Harrison Ford movie, *Patriot Games,* and *War and Remembrance.* On the small screen, recent appearances include playing Clive Thomson in *Heartbeat,* Macduff in *Sharpe,* Jackson in *The Knock* and Chief Inspector Winter in *The Bill.* However, his most recent assignment has seen him planning a series of television shows for ABC in Australia.

Cockney man

Played by Michael Roberts

Seen briefly at The Nag's Head during 'Hole in One', the Cockney man complains to Maureen, the barmaid, about how long he's been waiting for his chicken meal. Maureen explains that the delay is because the deep-fat fryer, which Del supplied, is on the blink.

Cocktails

When it came to organising the props required for a particular scene, any cocktails to be used by Del were classed as 'action props' and were ordered by the assistant floor manager (AFM) on a props list, which would include the soft drink substitutes they were made of, glasses and decorations for the glass.

In the early days of television, cold tea was always used as a substitute for whisky, but when programme budgets improved, ginger ale or apple juice was used instead. Blackcurrant juice was a replacement for red wine and a specially bottled non-alcoholic fizz with an authentic label was available as champagne.

Coda, Frank

Role: Mario
Appeared in S6, episode 3

Frank, who was born in 1931, was part of a song and dance act in variety, continental nightclubs and theatre, before trying his luck as an actor. He made his debut in 1961 at the famous Joan Littlewood's Theatre Workshop at Stratford East.

A year later, he'd chalked up his first pay cheque in television, in *Falling in Love* for Associated Rediffusion. Then, in 1963, Frank was seen in his longest TV engagement, as Mario Bonetti, the café owner in *Coronation Street.*

Frank's big screen appearances to date include roles in *The Sweeney*, *Queen of Hearts* and *Omen III*, while his television list extends from *Minder* and *Rumpole of the Bailey* to *The Love Boat* and *Ever Decreasing Circles.*

Cody, Alan

Role: Ticket collector

Appeared in 'A Royal Flush'

Alan, who was born in London in 1946, worked in sales before training to become an actor at the Webber Douglas Academy of Dramatic Art. Upon graduating he embarked on a busy acting career which has covered stage and screen.

Among his numerous television appearances are roles such as Sergeant Goodwin in *Juliet Bravo*, Ralph in *Relative Strangers*, Pip in *Drummonds*, Jack Bayliss in *First Among Equals*, Ted Fisher in *Wycliffe* and Hal Swift in *The Gentle Touch*, his small screen debut.

Although he no longer works in the theatre, his previous credits in this field include three years with the Royal Shakespeare Company, a UK tour of *Bare Necessities* and playing Macduff in *Macbeth* and Antonio in *Twelfth Night* for the English Shakespeare Company on a national and international tour.

Coed, Jez

Music producer on two episodes: 'Miami Twice' (Parts 1 & 2)

Coleman, Mr

A non-speaking character from Classic Curtains, Mr Coleman arrives to see Rodney at work in 'Rodney Come Home'. Unfortunately he arrives in the office at the wrong moment and catches Rodney foraging through the rubbish bin.

Colin

Played by Mark Burdis

Colin works for Boycie as a car cleaner, and is seen in 'To Hull and Back' informing his boss that someone (Del) is on the phone wanting to talk about diamonds.

Colleano, Mark

Role: Andy

Appeared in S5, episode 4 and 'The Frog's Legacy'

Born in London in 1955, Mark – who trained at the Corona Academy – made his television debut in a 1965 episode of *Court Martial*. Two years later, he was playing the lead in *Mystery Hall*, but his favourite role on the box was El Macho in Eric Chappell's *Duty Free*.

Mark soon gained experience working in Europe as well as the UK in all mediums, including films like *Hornets' Nest* with Rock Hudson, and *The Horsemen* starring Omar Sharif.

Recent work assignments have seen him spending a great deal of time on the stage in Los Angeles.

Collin, Dinah

Costume designer on eight episodes: S3 and 'Thicker Than Water'

Dinah, who was born in Barnsley, graduated in graphic design from London's Central School of Arts and Crafts. She painted sets in theatre and ran her own stall at Kensington Market, selling period costumes, until she applied for a job as a costume designer at the BBC in 1968.

She worked for the Beeb for just over two years before leaving and establishing her own business, selling costumes and designing her own clothes, many of which sold around the world. Dinah returned to the BBC as a freelance costume designer in 1979 and has since worked on a myriad of shows, especially dramas. Credits include *Pride and Prejudice*, *Portrait of a Marriage*, *Tale of Two Cities* and a recently completed feature film in Malaysia.

Collins, Sue

Vision mixer on eight episodes: S7, 'The Jolly Boys' Outing' and 'Rodney Come Home'

Sue graduated from university and joined the BBC, initially working as a production secretary in current affairs. After applying for an attachment to the vision mixing department, she began her career in that field, which saw her work on numerous shows, including *Tanya*, *One Foot in the Grave*, *As Time Goes By*, *A Prince Among Men*, *Top of the Pops*, *Chambers* and *Big Break*. Sue died in 2001.

Collins, Georgie

Del mentions Georgie in 'Chain Gang'. He was given six months to live, but then doctors realised they had mixed up his records with those of another man. Unfortunately, the other man only had three months to live!

Collins, John D

Roles: River policeman and Vet

Appeared as River policeman in S2, episode 2 and as Vet in S4, episode 5

Educated at Harrow, John – who was born in 1942 – worked as a shop assistant for a year before joining RADA after winning Ivor Novello and Robert Donat scholarships. A busy career has included a ten-year association with Spike Milligan as assistant director and actor, and running his own theatre company at Frinton-on-Sea between 1963 and 1964.

Among his TV credits are *Get Some In!*; *A Family at War*; *Some Mothers Do 'Ave 'Em*; *Yes, Minister*; *Peak Practice* (playing David Cornish) and several shows produced by David Croft, such as the Q series; *Hi-De-Hi!*; Fairfax in *'Allo 'Allo!*; Jerry in *You Rang, M'Lord?*; *Dad's Army* and *Oh, Doctor Beeching!*

Collis, Mr

(See 'Vet')

Combe, Dominique

Role: Concierge

Appeared in 'If They Could See Us Now…!'

Dominique, who appeared as the concierge at the Hotel De Paris in Monaco, worked with Gareth Gwenlan's production team on 'If They Could See Us Now…!'. With experience of acting in France, as well as working on more than 40 television and film productions, he was the contact point when it came to organising filming in Monte Carlo. He works as an assistant director and line producer.

Comedian

Played by Jeff Stevenson

Seen in The Nag's Head during 'Little Problems', the comic entertains at Rodney's stag night.

Comic Relief Special

Original transmission: Friday 14 March 1997, 7.40 pm

Original viewing figures: 10.6 million

Duration of sketch: approx. 15 mins

First repeat: Friday 23 January 1998, 8.00 pm

CAST

Del Trotter . . . . .David Jason
Rodney Trotter . . . . .Nicholas Lyndhurst
Uncle Albert . . . . .Buster Merryfield
Raquel . . . . .Tessa Peake-Jones
Damien . . . . .Jamie Smith

While Rodney browses through some holiday brochures getting more and more depressed because his wages won't stretch to the kind of sun-drenched break he yearns for, Del considers earning extra cash by putting Damien forward for modelling assignments. But their lot in life is put into context by Uncle Albert, who suggests they spare a thought for the millions of starving people in Africa. In turn, Del and Rodney appeal to the viewers to part with their dosh because they might even be able to establish Trotter Relief!

Community Centre

The local centre organises an old folks' Christmas do in 'Christmas Crackers'. Grandad pops over there because he thinks it will be more fun than sitting in front of the televisions, whilst Del and Rodney argue all night.

Concierge

Played by Dominique Combe

The concierge, who was called Dominique, greets Del upon his arrival at Monaco's Hotel De Paris in 'If They Could See Us Now…!'.

Connolly, Nora

Role: Anita

Appeared in 'Christmas Crackers'

Nora studied Fine Art at art school before training to become an actress at The Abbey Theatre, Dublin. It was here that she made her professional debut in *Oedipus*, before moving on to London's Lyric and National Theatres.

She clocked up her first television part as Maureen, selling raffle tickets at a church fête during an episode of the comedy *Bless Me, Father*, alongside Arthur Lowe. Her favourite roles on the small screen are Brenda in *Agony* and Glenda in *The Bill*.

Nora, who was born in 1949, has also been seen in several films such as *The Fool*, playing Audrey, *The Witches* (Beatrice), *Incognito* (barmaid) and *Scarlett* (Mrs Scanlon).

Today, she continues to work in all areas of the profession, and recently played the title role in *Moll Flanders*, which toured around the country.

Convey, Colum

Role: Roland
Appeared in 'If They Could See Us Now…!'

Colum's busy career has included a range of stage and screen appearances. On television his recent roles include playing Clive Bremner in *Dangerfield*; Walter in *Where the Heart Is*; Sergeant Freddie Lewis in *Soldier, Soldier*; Tony Farrington in *Seconds Out*; Ceefax in *Roughnecks*; Hawley in *Middlemarch*; DS Nies in *The Inspector Lynley Mysteries – A Great Deliverance* and Larry in *As the Beast Sleeps*.

On stage, he's performed with the Royal Shakespeare Company, while his many other appearances have seen him working at venues such as Dublin's Abbey Theatre and the Royal Court.

Conwell, Nula

Role: Maureen
Appeared in S4, episodes 1, 2, 3 & 6; S5, episode 1

Nula, who was born in London in 1959, has worked in all areas of the profession. On the big screen her roles include a gang member in *Red Saturday* and Nurse Kathleen in *Elephant Man*, while on the small screen she's been seen as a counter girl in *Shoestring*, Viv Martella in *The Bill*, a role she played for nine years, Tina Bennett in *The Upper Hand*, Michelle Newman in *Holby City* and Mrs Charles in *Bad Blood*.

On the stage, her work includes appearances in *Obsession*, *Misery* and *Maria Marten – The Red Barn Murder*.

Cooke, Beryl

Role: 'Auntie Rose'
Appeared in S1, episode 4

The late Beryl Cooke's career spanned almost six decades, and she's probably best remembered for her television roles as Aunt Lucy in *Happy Ever After* and Mrs Vance in the drama series, *Tenko*.

Born in London, Beryl initially worked as an English and drama teacher, before joining The London Theatre of Drama, followed by a seven-year stint with Harry Hanson's repertory company. She left repertory theatre in 1953 and joined the cast of *The Boyfriend*, followed a year later by her film debut in *Knave of Hearts*, then *Conflict of Wings*, with John Gregson and Muriel Pavlow, and *The Crooked Sky*.

The 1960s saw her appear in several films in the *Hammer House of Horror* series, and various TV roles, including a receptionist in the show *Public Eye*, *The Troubleshooters*, *Compact*, *The Newcomers* and *Z Cars*. But her first love was the theatre, and she continued her work in the medium, including a 1984 European tour of *My Fair Lady*.

A keen writer, Beryl saw one of her short stories commissioned by the organisers of the Festival of Britain, wrote a children's book and produced several plays around the country.

In the years before her death, aged 94, she was seen on television, in shows such as *Casualty*, *A Perfect Hero*, *Waiting for God* and, her final job, in the thriller *Century Falls*, in 1993.

Cooper, Duncan

Location manager on one episode: 'The Jolly Boys' Outing'

Duncan – who was born in Tonbridge, Kent – graduated with honours in English and Drama from the University of Kent at Canterbury. He earned a diploma in stage management from RADA (winning the stage management prize) and got his Equity card as an assistant stage manager touring with Wayne Sleep's company, Dash, as well as constructing scenery for trade shows on a freelance basis.

A summer season as ASM on *Paul Daniels' Magic Show* at Blackpool's Opera House, and a year with *Little Me* (starring Russ Abbot) at the Prince of Wales Theatre followed before joining the BBC in 1986 as a relief assistant floor manager assigned to *Play School*.

In this capacity, he worked on various shows from *Little and Large* and *Jasper Carrott* to *Blankety Blank* and *Opportunity Knocks*. He was subsequently promoted to production manager and, then, 1st assistant director, and has been involved in countless productions, such as *Noel's House Party*, two series of *Blackadder*, *One Foot in the Grave*, *Last of the Summer Wine*, *Top of the Pops* and the launch of the *National Lottery*. As a director, his assignments have included two series of *Jim Davidson's Generation Game*, over 60 live *National Lottery* programmes and *The Laurence Olivier Awards*.

Duncan is now working with BBC Worldwide for a year as Editorial Adviser and Series Producer on all programmes in development for the Indian market. This follows on the success of last year's project, *Ji Mantra Ji* (*Yes, Minister* adapted and remade in Hindi), which won Best Sitcom and Best Comedy Actor at the Indian TV Academy Awards.

Cooper, Mr

Played by Tommy Buson

An elderly black man, we see Clayton Cooper briefly in 'Danger UXD'. Whilst Del and Rodney try desperately to load two inflatable dolls into the back of their van without being spotted by any of the neighbours, Clayton walks by and strikes up a conversation.

Cooper, Paul

Role: Waiter
Appeared in S6, episode 2

Paul's work in television includes playing Ron in *Minder*, Tailor in *'Allo 'Allo!*, Truman in *The Piglet Files*, a car salesman in *The Bill* and a chauffeur in *EastEnders*. He's also made a handful of film appearances, such as a night guard in *Lifeforce* and a cook in *Britannia Hospital*. His busy stage career, meanwhile, has covered such productions as *An Inspector Calls* and *The Actor's Nightmare* for the Hong Kong Actors' Rep Theatre.

Corey, Dave

Role: Lurch
Appeared in 'Miami Twice' (Part 2)

American actor Dave Corey's recent work includes playing Cellmate Dwight in the 2002 film *Big Trouble*. Other credits range from Goodwin in 1995's *New Adventures of Flipper* and a hospital security guard in *The Truman Show*, to an announcer in 1998's *Holy Man* and a Miami Hall guard in *Analyze This*.

Corinne

Played by Eva Mottley

Denzil's wife, Corinne, is seen in 'Who's a Pretty Boy?'. Candid and strong-willed she can't stand the sight of Del, and claims that whenever her husband mixes with Trotter Snr he ends up drunk or out of

Eva Mottley (left) played Denzil's wife, Corinne.

pocket. Further incidents that have tainted her view of the man include the time Del sold Denzil an overcoat which suited the Hunchback of Notre Dame more than her hubby. The disaster that will forever irk her, however, is when he messed up the catering at their wedding: instead of lobster vol-au-vents, game pie, kidney with saffron rice, beef and anchovy savouries and Philadelphia truffles, they ended up with pie and chips. And to top it all, the fridge went on the blink, the icing on the cake melted and they were probably the only couple to be photographed cutting a jam sponge on their wedding day!

Corinne is again mentioned in 'As One Door Closes' and 'Fatal Extraction', by which time Denzil explains they've been separated seven years, but she's never seen again.

Cornwell, Phil

Role: Man in hospital
Appeared in 'Modern Men'

Born in Rochford, Essex, 1957, Phil worked in the motor trade in Southend between 1974 and 1978, as well as various other jobs (waiter, barman, selling advertising space, etc.) before training at the E15 Acting School. His professional debut was as a stand-up/impressionist at Paddock's Club, Canvey Island, in 1974. He won £1 prize money in the talent show.

He worked the pubs and clubs around Essex and London's East End, then made his television debut in *Something Else*, in 1980. Other credits in this medium include *Sunburn*, *Lovejoy* and *The Comic Strip Presents*, but his favourite small-screen roles are Robert in *Clocking Off*, transmitted by BBC in February 2002, and playing Michael Caine and DJ Dave Clifton in *Stella Street* and *I'm Alan Partridge* respectively. Phil has also appeared in a handful of films, such as playing Ed in *Out of Depth*, Doug in *Blood* and Barry Mousley in *Large*.

MEMORIES OF 'MIAMI TWICE'

★ ★ ★ ★ ★ ★

'I'll always remember playing the drunken man at the hospital in "Modern Men". Just as I was punched and knocked to the floor by Del Boy, I inadvertently broke wind! It was hilarious as far as everyone else was concerned, especially for David Jason, who had to say the line: "Are you feeling better, sir?".'

PHIL CORNWELL

Corone, Antoni

Role: Rico
Appeared in 'Miami Twice' (Part 2)

Antoni's long list of credits include appearing in *Miami Vice*, *Superboy*, *The Fugitive* for the small screen, as well as films such as *Cape Fear*, *Fair Game*, *Striptease*, *Plato's Run* and *Landfall*. He's currently appearing in the American television series, *Oz*, playing Frances Urbano. Antoni is based in America.

Corrie

In 'To Hull and Back' Del shouts across The Nag's Head to Corrie, enquiring about her well-being.

Costumes

The original costume designer on *Only Fools and Horses* was Phoebe De Gaye, who remembers the day she was allocated the job. 'I was a young designer; in fact, I might have been an acting designer, and the job was given to me as a way of trying me out before deciding whether to appoint me as a full-blown designer. I can't remember exactly, but I do know inexperienced designers were often tested out on sitcom pilots.'

Phoebe took the opportunity seriously and proceeded to research the styles and costumes required for Sullivan's sitcom of life in Peckham. 'I took lots of photos of blokes in used-car showrooms and things like that, which came in useful when picking costumes for Boycie in particular. I also remember taking David Jason out shopping in a terrible old white mini I had at that time. It used to smoke and rattle so much he must have thought it was going to fall apart at any moment!

'We used to pop down to places like Oxford Street and to a warehouse off the North Circular Road which stocked all these horrible brightly coloured shirts – they were vile. We visited a shop near Marble Arch, which sold terrible cut-price suits; they creased as soon as you touched them. I thought they were perfect but David wasn't convinced. However, we were successful that day because we managed to find the patchy sheepskin coat that Del wore quite often.'

Phoebe was keen for Del Boy to have a perm. 'At that time, a lot of blokes – especially used-car salesmen – seemed to have them. Sadly, David didn't want to pursue that idea. If I was doing it today, I would have pushed harder for that style because it would have worked well. But you have to respect that the actors need to consider what kind of image they want the character to project. It just wasn't the direction David Jason wanted.'

When it came to kitting out Rodney and Grandad, Phoebe relied on local markets. 'I just bought clothes from places like Shepherd's Bush market and mixed them up with items from the BBC's stockroom. To age the clothes Grandad wore, we rubbed Vaseline into them, which gave them a greasy, grubby look. We also used cheese graters, soap and sandpaper for a worn, threadbare look.

'It was an enjoyable show to work on and one I will always have fond memories of.'

Council cleansing lorry driver

Played by Terry Duggan

The driver of the road sweeper which sucks up the ashes of Trigger's grandad is seen in 'Ashes to Ashes'.

RESEARCH PHOTOS 'only Fools and Horses'

KODAK SAFETY FILM 500

dyed hair

neck jewellery

pneumatic
grey sheepskin
car coat
or full
length coat

wrist jewellery
flashy watch
etc.

trousers
tight over
bum -
beer belly
problems
in four.

teeny
fashion
concious feet
- lattice work
etc.
BUILT UP HEELS

flashy
rings

unpleasant
colour
combinations

Courtney, Nicholas

Role: Charles
Appeared in 'Dates'

Nicholas, who was born in Egypt in 1929, has built up a lengthy list of credits over the years, particularly in theatre and television. During the sixties, his was a regular face in much of ITC's output, appearing as Dr Strayman in *Jason King*, Max in *Randall and Hopkirk (Deceased)* and Dr Farley in *The Champions*. He was also seen in a few episodes of *The Avengers* and *Doctor Who*. Other appearances include Paul Cotterell in a 1978 instalment of *All Creatures Great and Small*, Superintendent Austin in *Juliet Bravo*, the Marquis in the 1989 series *French Fields*, and, more recently, English Stan in BBC Wales' production, *Satellite City*, and a brigadier in the *Harry Hill Show*.

Recent excursions onto the stage include playing the President in a 1992 production of *The Nineteenth Hole*, Ambassador Toulon in *M Butterfly* and Judge Hawthorn in *The Crucible* at Birmingham.

Cousin Audrey

(See 'Audrey (Cousin)')

Cousin Jean

(See 'Jean (Cousin)')

Cousin Stan

(See 'Stan (Cousin)')

Covington House

This is the family home of Vicky (Lady Victoria Marsham-Hales) and her father, the 14th Duke of Maylebury. The house is set in the Berkshire countryside and is seen in 'A Royal Flush'.

Coward, Shirley

Vision mixer on two episodes: S2, episode 3 and S4, episode 7

Shirley, who was born in Watford, joined the BBC in 1954, working initially as a production secretary in children's television. She moved on to religious programmes, followed by a spell in the drama department before becoming a vision mixer in 1965, a job she retained until retiring from the Beeb in 1989, after 35 years' service. She worked on a multitude of shows, including *The Six Wives of Henry VIII*, *Blue Peter*, *The Onedin Line*, *Doctor Who*, *The Pallisers* and, latterly, *Going Live*.

Shirley is now enjoying her retirement in the south of England and works on a voluntary basis as a guide at Portsmouth Cathedral and a steward at Windsor Castle.

Cowper, Gerry

Role: Lisa
Appeared in S5, episode 4 and 'The Frog's Legacy'

Gerry, who was born in London and has two sisters who also act, has made many appearances on television in programmes including *The Bill*, *S.W.A.L.K.*, *Little Lord Fauntleroy* and *Yes, Minister*.

'Strained Relations'

Cox, Pauline

Make-up designer on six episodes: S1

Pauline, who was born in Bristol, trained in graphic design at Kingston School of Art before spending a year in the United States in 1965–66. She worked as an au-pair and taught at a local art school before returning to the UK and joining the BBC's make-up department in 1969.

During 27 years' service with the Beeb (25 as a make-up designer) she worked on a full range of shows, including *Butterflies*, *The Liver Birds*, *Are You Being Served?*, *Grace and Favour*, *Bread* and *Sense and Sensibility*. She left in 1996 and has worked freelance ever since, with a recent project being the children's television series, *I Was a Rat*, a co-production between the BBC and Catalyst of Canada.

MEMORIES OF ONLY FOOLS

★ ★ ★ ★ ★

'One thing I remember more than anything else was just how funny the read-throughs were. I've worked on quite a few comedies where you go along to the read-throughs and the actors have to work so hard to get some laughs out of it, but reading the scripts of the first series was just a riot, they were so funny.

'I was make-up designer for the first series and remember meeting to talk about the characters. I wanted Del Boy to have long sideboards, but the idea wasn't picked up; I did have to put his hair in a style that resembled a quiff, though. We also had to age Lennard Pearce somewhat, partly by having some veins drawn in on his cheeks to make him look a bit weather-beaten. I used a very fine brush and a little greasepaint to create the effect. I also used greasepaint to enhance the look of the skin under his eyes, giving the appearance of bags. The rest of the characters didn't really pose any particular challenges. It was certainly a happy show to work on.'

PAULINE COX – Make-up designer

Cox, Sandra

Played by Carol Cleveland

Seen in 'The Miracle of Peckham', Sandra is an American reporter representing NBC in New York, who's over in the country to broadcast on the so-called miracle of the Virgin Mary statue.

Craig, Leigh

Properties buyer on one episode: 'The Jolly Boys' Outing'

Born in Radcliffe, near Manchester, Leigh spent 14 years working for the John Lewis department store before accepting a short-term contract as a holiday relief in the props deparment at the BBC. He was offered a permanent contract in 1971 and, after eight years, was supervising the department .

After 25 years' service with the Beeb he retired in 2000, by which time he'd worked on everything

'The Jolly Boys' Outing'

from dramas to children's programmes. He now lives near the New Forest.

Creswell, Mrs

Played by Rosalind Knight

The peculiar, greasy-haired owner of the Villa Bella guest house in Margate is seen in 'The Jolly Boys' Outing'. As a last resort, the Trotters have to stay at the dingy property when they struggle to find accommodation elsewhere.

Crofts, Debbie

Assistant floor manager on nine episodes: S7, 'Rodney Come Home' and 'Miami Twice' (Parts 1 & 2)

Debbie, who was born in Cleethorpes in 1960, worked in the theatre before joining the BBC in 1987. Initially she worked on children's television and shows like

Open Air, but favourite work assignments during her 14-year career in the industry have been on *Waiting for God, The Russ Abbot Show* and *Only Fools.*

Nowadays Debbie works as a programme finance coordinator, monitoring programme budgets on Music Entertainment shows.

Croupier

The croupier works at The One Eleven Club and is seen in 'Chain Gang'.

Crowning Glory

In 'Three Men, a Woman and a Baby', Del has acquired a few boxes of 'Crowning Glory – Wigs of Distinction' from Mustapha's nephew, who works for a top West End wigmaker; unfortunately they're men's wigs and Del's intended customers are all female.

Crowther, Graeme

Stunt artist on one episode: 'Dates'

In 'Dates', Graeme sits in the back of the American car that chases Rodney and his date, Nervous Nerys, in their Reliant van. Now living in France, his first job was in *The Prince and the Pauper* at the age of 23. After working as a stunt artist for many years, he began concentrating on coordinating work around ten years ago.

His lengthy list of credits as a stunt performer include *The Medusa Touch, For Your Eyes Only, A View to a Kill, The Living Daylights, Henry V, Hamlet, Golden Eye, Braveheart* and *Mission Impossible.* As a coordinator, he's worked on *Dungeons and Dragons, Ever After 'A Cinderella Story', Anna Karenina* and *Some Mother's Son.*

Cummings, Teddy

Not seen in the sitcom, Teddy is mentioned in 'As One Door Closes'. He manages a joinery works and is Del's supplier of louvre doors.

Curtis

In 'Miami Twice', Curtis is a non-speaking ranger who works at the Everglades National Park.

Curtis, Alec

Film cameraman on 14 episodes: 'Diamonds are for Heather'; 'Dates'; S6, episodes 1–3; 'The Jolly Boys' Outing'; 'Rodney Come Home'; S7, episodes 1–3, 5 & 6; 'Miami Twice' (Parts 1 & 2)

Born in Loughborough in 1943, Alec worked as a lab technician and stills photographer at the Anti-Locust Research Centre in Kensington, London. When the Centre wanted to make a film of their work overseas, Alec was sent on a month's course at BBC Bristol, which ultimately led to him changing career direction and joining the Beeb as a trainee cameraman in 1966.

As an operator, he worked on numerous programmes, including *War and Peace, Churchill* and a series of Somerset Maugham plays, while as a film cameraman he filmed a wide range of productions, from *Blue Peter, Horizon* and *Chronicle* to *The Fall and Rise of Reginald Perrin, Alas Smith and Jones* and *To the Manor Born.* He was also allocated various music shows and dramas, including *Bergerac* and *Fame is the Spur.*

After 36 years in the business, Alec now works as a director of photography. He left the BBC back in 1997, just after filming *Rhodes* in South Africa. Recent assignments have seen him working on *Harbour Lights, Hostile Waters* and *Roger, Roger,* as well as filming in Portugal and Berlin.

Cyril

Cyril is not seen in the sitcom, but Del and Trigger use his story in an attempt to stop Rodney (who's just been given the elbow by Cassandra) giving up on people. Cyril – who's Trigger's cousin – owed £500 on his mortgage and was due to be evicted. In desperation, he drove to Beachy Head and was considering ending it all by driving over the cliff. But he was driving a bus at the time and, not wanting to end his passenger's lives in the same fashion, he decided against such drastic action. Taking pity on Cyril, the passengers organised a whip round and raised the cash to clear his debt.

à la Del

★ ★ ★ ★ ★ ★

'Bouilla baise, mon ami'

('Cash and Curry')

Daker, David

Role: Tommy Mackay

Appeared in S2, episode 4; S4, episode 6

Busy character actor David Daker has an extensive list of credits to his name. His television career includes playing PC Owen Culshaw in *Z Cars*; Ben Campbell in *Crown Prosecutor*; Roy Stevens in *Strangers*; *Doctor Who*; *UFO*; *Juliet Bravo*; *Sorry!*; *Casualty*; *The Bill*; *Porridge*; *Midsomer Murders*; *The Fallen Curtain*; *Boon* and *The Woman in Black*.

Dale

Played by Diana Katis

First seen getting out of a Porsche – together with her friend Marsha – Dale appears in 'Yuppy Love'. She enters a wine bar, followed quickly by Del, who tries, unsuccessfully, to pour on the charm. We never discover anything about the character's background.

Dale, Paul

Assistant floor manager on one episode: 'Dates'

Paul, who was born in London, trained to become an actor at the Webber Douglas Academy of Dramatic Art, but when he became house manager at London's Donmar Warehouse he gave up acting.

He joined the BBC in 1986 when he was offered a 16-week contract helping on the broadcast of the Commonwealth Games; periods in Birmingham and London followed, during which time he particularly enjoyed working on *Only Fools*, *Casualty*, *EastEnders* and *Berkeley Square*.

Paul, who has been working freelance for four years, is now a 1st assistant director and has recently worked on BBC's factual series, *Walking with Cavemen*.

Damien

(See 'Trotter, Damien')

Dando, Harry

In 'Who Wants to be a Millionaire', Rodney moans to Del about Harry because he had to clear up rubbish from his fruit and veg stall. He's a veteran trader who's suffering from rheumatism and arthritis. Although we never see Harry, Del does a little business with him, agreeing to clear up his mess for £5; inevitably, Rodney gets landed with the task.

'Danger UXD'

Original transmission: Sunday 15 January 1989, 7.15 pm

Production date: Sunday 8 January 1989

Original viewing figures: 16.1 million

Duration: 50 minutes

First repeat: Friday 15 September 1989, 7.30 pm

Subsequent repeats: 22/1/92, 7/1/94, 14/8/96, 30/6/99, 9/2/01

CAST

Del Trotter . . . . .David Jason
Rodney Trotter . . . . .Nicholas Lyndhurst
Uncle Albert . . . . .Buster Merryfield
Cassandra . . . . .Gwyneth Strong
Mike .Kenneth MacDonald
Denzil . . . . .Paul Barber
Barry .Walter Sparrow
Boycie . . . . .John Challis
Trigger . . . . .Roger Lloyd Pack
Waiter . . . . .Paul Cooper
Adrian . . . . .Michael Shallard
Chinese takeaway owner . . . . .Takashi Kawahara
TV presenter . . . . .David Warwick
Clayton . . . . .Tommy Buson
Walk-ons: . . . .(Chinese takeaway) Mark Irwin, Jason Beazley, Pat Shepherd, Shirley Chantrell. (Pub) Kelly Murray, Kerry Barrett, Darryl Brook, Bert Crome, John Baker, James Delaney, Ella Cerri, Della McRae, Bertie Green, Jack Street, Maggie Mitchell, Gregory Ball, Teddy Massiah and Jean Dean.

PRODUCTION TEAM

Written by John Sullivan

Title music arranged and conducted by Ronnie Hazlehurst composed and sung by John Sullivan

Costume Designer: . . . . .Richard Winter
Make-Up Designer: . . . . .Sylvia Thornton
Film Editor: . . . . .John Jarvis
Film Cameraman: . . . . .Alec Curtis
Film Sound: . . . . .Michael Spencer
Camera Supervisor: . . . . .Ken Major
Studio Lighting Director: . . . . .Don Babbage
Studio Sound: . . . . .Alan Machin
Videotape Editor: . . . . .Chris Wadsworth
Properties Buyer: . . . . .Malcolm Rougvie
Production Assistant: . . . . .Amita Lochab
Assistant Floor Manager: . . . .Kerry Waddell
Vision Mixer: . . . . .Heather Gilder
Technical Manager: . . . . .Reg Poulter
Production Manager: . . . . .Adrian Pegg
Designer: . . . . .Graham Lough
Produced by Gareth Gwenlan
Directed by Tony Dow

Del thinks that one of the keys to success is having the right image, so he tells Rodney to wear a suit, thinking it will help sell 50 video recorders he's acquired from Ronnie Nelson, who runs the Advanced Electronics Research and Development Centre. Del's still going through his 'yuppy' stage and continues drinking at select bistros and wine bars, even though the clientele he desperately tries mingling with avoids him like the plague.

Always on the prowl for business opportunities, Del helps Denzil out by taking 50 dolls off his hands; what he doesn't realise until the deal is sealed is that he's just acquired 50 inflatable sex dolls!

When Dirty Barry – who owns a local sex shop – doesn't want the goods, Del decides to hang on to them for a while, until Rodney discovers from Cassandra that a batch of dangerous inflatable dolls are on the loose – the manufacturer has inadvertently inflated them with propane.

Dar, Fuman

Role: Kevin

Appeared in 'Heroes and Villains'

Fuman, who's been playing Ronnie Silva, a regular character in *London's Burning* since 2000, has made many appearances on television, from Denzel in *Grange Hill* and Wayne Cotterall in *The Bill* to a homeless man in *Staying Alive* and Tutankhamun in the *Landmark* series. On stage, meanwhile, his range of roles has included appearing as Caliban in *The Tempest* and Paris in *Romeo and Juliet*.

Darren

Played by Daniel Jones

Darren is the son of Heather and her estranged husband, Vic. In 'Diamonds are for Heather' Del has a brief fling with Heather, and takes a shine to the boy, who is nearly three and a half at the time.

'Diamonds are for Heather'

'Dates'

'Dates'

(Christmas Special 1988)

Original transmission: Sunday 25 December 1988, 5.05 pm

Production dates: Friday 9 December – Sunday 11 December 1988

Original viewing figures: 16.6 million

Duration: 80 minutes

First repeat: Sunday 2 April 1989, 7.15 pm

Subsequent repeats: 22/12/89, 29/11/92, 17/3/02

Note: BAFTA 'Best Comedy' Award, March 1989

CAST

Del Trotter . . . . .David Jason
Rodney Trotter . . . . .Nicholas Lyndhurst
Uncle Albert . . . . .Buster Merryfield
Boycie . . . . .John Challis
Mike .Kenneth MacDonald
Trigger . . . . .Roger Lloyd Pack
Marlene . . . . .Sue Holderness
Raquel . . . . .Tessa Peake-Jones
Micky Pearce . . . . .Patrick Murray
Jevon .Steven Woodcock
Chris .Tony Marshall
Nerys .Andrée Bernard
Technomatch agent . . . . .Christopher Stanton
Sonia .Jean Warren
Charles . . . . .Nicholas Courtney
Policeman . . . . .Paul Beringer
Policewoman . . . . .Maggie Norris
Sid . . . . .Roy Heather
Naval officer . . . . .Martin Cochrane
Mrs Sansom . . . . .Jean Challis (Voice only)
Walk-ons: . . . . .Carl Harris, Danny Glass, Dave Owen, Nicky Ezer, Sean Harris, Pete Chesterfield, Nick Hardy, Bert Crome, Venetia Day, Bertie Green, Della McCrae and Evrol Puckerin.

PRODUCTION TEAM

Written by John Sullivan

Title music arranged and conducted by Ronnie Hazlehurst composed and sung by John Sullivan

Stunt Arranger . . . . .Colin Skeaping
Stunt Performers . . . . .Graeme Crowther, Nick Gillard, Paul Heasman, Alan Stuart, Tip Tipping, Chris Webb, Tina Maskell
Make-up Designer: . . . . .Jean Steward
Costume Designer: . . . . .Richard Winter
Properties Buyer: . . . . .Malcolm Rougvie
Visual Effects: . . . . .Graham Brown
Film Cameraman: . . . . .Alec Curtis
Film Sound: . . . . .Michael Spencer
Film Editor: . . . . .John Jarvis
Gaffer: . . . . .Peter Robinson
Camera Supervisor: . . . . .Ken Major
Studio Lighting Director: . . . . . .Don Babbage
Studio Sound: . . . . .Keith Mayes
Technical Coordinator: . . . . . . .Reg Poulter
Videotape Editor: . . . . .Chris Wadsworth
Production Assistant: . . . . .Amita Lochab
Assistant Floor Managers: . . . . .Kerry Waddell and Paul Dale
Vision Mixer: . . . . .Hilary Briegel
Production Managers: . . . . .Adrian Pegg and Gill Anderson
Designer: . . . . .Graham Lough
Directed by Tony Dow
Produced by Gareth Gwenlan

Albert's birthday is approaching so Del hires out The Nag's Head for a few drinks and a bite to eat. When Trigger arrives he stuns everyone with his bright blue suit, bunch of flowers and news that he's got a date, thanks to a new dating agency that's just opened in the High Street. Del decides to investigate further.

He visits the agency and is matched with Raquel Turner, an actress who's looking for a partner. While Del wines and dines her in style at the Hilton, his younger brother is hoping to improve his luck on the female front by adopting the James Dean look. Things are looking up when he meets Nerys, the barmaid at The Nag's Head. But a run-in with a group of punks does little for creating the right ambience. While Rodney's date is a complete failure, Del and Raquel hit it off and so begin a lasting relationship, that is until he discovers – much to his embarrassment – that she works as a strippergram two nights a week. But true love shines through the gloomy moments, even though Del has a spot of bother with the police to sort out first.

Dave

Rodney claims that Dave is one of his buddies from evening class. He makes out that he socialises with him, often frequenting various West End clubs. Mentioned in 'Go West Young Man', Dave is not seen in the sitcom.

Davenport, Miranda

Played by Juliet Hammond

An antiques expert who owns a shop in Chelsea, the attractive, well spoken Miranda, who's in her early thirties, examines a cabinet Del advertises in the local rag during 'Yesterday Never Comes'. Whilst he claims it's a Queen Anne model worth £145, Miranda isn't a fool and points out it's a Queen Elizabeth, circa 1957, and is actually made from Fyffes banana boxes.

'Yesterday Never Comes'

But Miranda – who Grandad has classed as a 'posh tart' – is a guileful lady, and when she spots a valuable painting hanging on the Trotters' wall in the flat, she warms to Del, offering him a partnership in restoring and selling furniture. Before long, Del is wining and dining the lady, whose sole objective in the brief liaison is to get her hands on the painting. In the end, although she achieves her aim, and sells the painting for over seventeen grand at auction, the last laugh is with Del, who tells her that his Gran pinched it from an art dealer.

David

In 'The Miracle of Peckham', David is a cameraman who's asked to film the so-called tears of the Virgin Mary. Although he's classed as a non-speaking character, it does seem as if he's heard replying in the affirmative when his colleague – a reporter – asks if he's got the shots he wants.

Davidson, Roger

Role: Mr Dow
Appeared in 'A Royal Flush'
Born in Sheffield in 1948, Roger worked in advertising before training at the Rose Bruford College, including two years towards a BA in English and Drama in conjunction with the University of Kent.

Roger, who no longer works in the theatre, made his professional acting debut in 1972 at Bristol's Old Vic, before embarking on an extensive journey in repertory theatre, working with all the major regional companies, including Bristol, Birmingham, Edinburgh, Leeds, Farnham and Salisbury. His first small-screen appearance, meanwhile, was in 1975, playing Celia Johnson's grandson in *The Nicest Man in the World*. Since then he's worked frequently in the medium, with credits such as Willy Carson in *The Sea*, Lamb in *The Hothouse*, *Secret Army*, *Paradise Postponed* and *The Bill*. On the big screen he's appeared in the Bond movie, *For Your Eyes Only*, and *The Secret Life of Ian Fleming*. As well as acting, Roger is a member of the Casting Directors' Guild.

Davies, Richard Rhys

Dubbing editor on two episodes: 'Miami Twice' (Parts 1 & 2)
Richard, who was born in the Welsh town of Tenby, graduated from film school in London in 1987. He's always worked as a freelance sound and picture editor, although a lot of his work has been for the BBC, beginning with a spell in BBC Education. Another John Sullivan project he worked on was *Roger, Roger*.

Davis, Ben

Role: Jason
Appeared in S4, episode 1

Davis

In 'To Hull and Back', Davis is the policeman assigned the job of covering Luton Airport with his colleague Skinner during the diamond smuggling scheme. Although we hear about him, he's not seen in the sitcom.

Dawn

Played by Sheree Murphy
In 'Heroes and Villains', Dawn works with a group of muggers as a decoy; while she distracts the victim, the boys grab the valuables.

Debby

Played by Oona Kirsch
Aged 18, the attractive Debby – whom Rodney has been dating – works at the local newsagents and is seen behind the counter in 'Happy Returns'. It turns out she's the daughter of June, who Del dated for a year back in the 1960s; when the two meet up again, Del begins wondering if Debby is his daugh-

MEMORIES OF ONLY FOOLS

★ ★ ★ ★ ★ ★

'Working on *Only Fools and Horses* was not only a fantastic experience but also very educational, and I feel I learnt more about my job from this series than any other. In fact, I turned down the chance to be a production manager of a show because I wanted to work on *Only Fools*, even though that meant remaining as an assistant floor manager for longer; it's just that I thought it was going to be one of the best things I would ever work on, and I was right. I also have John Sullivan and Susie Belbin to thank for giving me my big break into directing because they gave me the opportunity to direct the second series of *Sitting Pretty* in 1993.

'As far as *Only Fools* is concerned, I have vivid memories of "The Jolly Boys' Outing", especially the scenes where the coach blows up. Although it looks as if the vehicle, which was already on its last legs, is blown into a thousand pieces, it wasn't, because we had to make sure we could remove it from the site afterwards. We'd secured the use of a special site [a car park] in Margate, which the fire brigade and police were happy with, and that's where we created the explosion.

'We only had one chance to do it, or so we thought. We were using two cameras for this sequence, but after completing the scene, tension ran high when the Director of Photography appeared from behind the main camera looking very concerned, saying that something technical might have gone wrong with one of the cameras. We were shooting on film and didn't have the luxury of playing back the rushes to check everything was okay, a facility which is more or less taken for granted these days. So poor Chris Lawson, from visual effects, who was looking very sweaty and smoky, said: "Having said you only had one chance for this scene, give me 20 minutes and I'll try and reassemble the coach so that we can have another go." I'm not sure if there was actually a problem with the cameras, but Chris managed to put the bits back together again and we eventually completed the scene, However, it was certainly more difficult removing the coach after it had endured two explosions!

'Working on "The Jolly Boys' Outing" was great fun, and we were very lucky with the weather, too. We filmed in May and were blessed with a mini-heatwave. Margate resembled the South of France for the whole time we were there.

'One final memory concerns the time our day off was altered and we had to carry out a recce of Benbom Brothers' Theme Park. We went along to look at all the rides and had to try a few out. The trouble was, some people – believing they were having a day off – had enjoyed a few drinks the previous evening; now they were having to go on all these rides nursing a hangover! It wasn't fun, I can tell you.

'By the time I worked on "Rodney Come Home", Series 7 and "Miami Twice", I'd been promoted to production manager. In my new position I found myself dealing with the bigger picture, whereas the assistant floor manager was all about working closely with the artists. Now, I was responsible for the safety of the entire crew.

'I also became more involved in finding locations, unless, of course, a locations manager was specifically recruited to the production. I always found that part of the job very enjoyable. One of the reasons the production moved a lot of its location shooting to Bristol was because it had become too well known in the capital; people would toot their horns as they went by and shout things like, "You plonker!", during the takes, which became frustrating. In Bristol, meanwhile, we managed to replicate London but had much more control and freedom.

'In London, moving and parking essential film vehicles can be problematic, obviously parking spaces and meters are like gold dust, so I was surprised when in Bristol the police drove me around and I simply told them the parking meters I would need and they suspended them for me; of course, things might have changed by now but back then Bristol was a location manager's heaven. When it came to getting permission to film at various places, whether it was Bristol or London, we always received a positive response from people. When I went around London trying to secure locations for "He Ain't Heavy, He's My Uncle", I only had a day and half to sort them out. Normally it would take you weeks to organise, but everywhere I went, people said: "*Fools and Horses*? Oh yes, no problem, you can film." You don't get that very often. Everyone was more than happy to help.

'My worst memory of filming in Bristol was when two huge Cherrypickers, extending platforms needed to hold large lamps to light an exterior night shoot outside of Rodney and Cassandra's flat, arrived early during the 5.30pm rush hour. I had nowhere to park them as I had obtained permission to use a car park which was still full of office workers' cars! We had just acquired "mobile phones" the size and weight of car batteries so I made a lot of calls that day.

'Another episode I remember filming is "Three Men, a Woman and a Baby", partly because I visited the hospital in Hillingdon on Boxing Day to see how many babies had been born! The expert, who was our contact point, was called Nurse Nightingale. The hospital staff were really helpful, and they shut down a labour ward so that we could make full use of it.

'We used a baby which had just been born at the hospital – I think it was about two or three days old. The birth scene was hilarious, and Tessa, who didn't have a child herself at that point, had obviously done her research because she got it absolutely right.

'Being involved in *Only Fools and Horses* was like belonging to one big family. We all grew up on it, and people accepted that next time you came back to it, you might have been promoted and were always willing to help.'
ANGELA DE CHASTELAI SMITH

ter, only to learn – much to his consternation – that her father was Albie Littlewood, Del's best friend.

De Chastelai Smith, Angela

Assistant floor manager on one episode: 'The Jolly Boys' Outing'. Production/Location manager on nine episodes: 'Rodney Come Home'; S7 and 'Miami Twice' (Parts 1 & 2)

Angie, who was born in Bristol in 1958, studied Drama at Birmingham University and worked in the theatre before joining the BBC costume department as a holiday relief in 1983. In the early stages of her career she worked on shows such as *Jasper Carrott Live, Playschool, Bob's Full House, The Mary Whitehouse Experience* and *One Foot in the Algarve.*

After 18 years in the profession, she's now a director and recent assignments include directing *EastEnders, The High Life, Grange Hill, Alistair McGowan's Christmas Show* and the second series of *Sitting Pretty.*

De Gaye, Phoebe

Costume designer on six episodes: S1

Pheobe, who was born in the London district of Finchley, studied theatre design at the Wimbledon School of Art. She worked in the theatre world for a time before joining the BBC as a costume assistant in the late 1970s. Her first series as a designer was *Only Fools and Horses,* and she went on to design the costumes for many other productions before leaving the Beeb in 1986 when her daughter was born.

She's been working freelance ever since and recently spent almost a year designing the costumes for the revival of *The Forsyte Saga.* Other productions she's designed for include *Lorna Doone, The Sculptress* and films like *Carry On Columbus* and *Tom and Viv.*

Deirdre

In the mid 1960s Deirdre and Albie Littlewood made up a foursome with Del and June. It transpires that Albie was seeing June behind Del's back, although Del can't grumble because he was returning the compliment and dating Deirdre – who's never seen in the sitcom – on the quiet.

Del

(See 'Trotter, Derek')

Delaney's Club

Mentioned in the scene from the Royal Variety Performance, Delaney's Club is where the Trotters are intending to deliver 12 boxes of whisky. The trouble is they get lost and turn up at the Drury Lane Theatre, making their entrance right in the middle of the performance. Delaney's Club, which used to be a strip joint, is managed by Chunky Lewis, who isn't seen during the short scene.

Dentist, The

Played by Andrew Charleson

In 'Fatal Extraction', the dentist (Mr Ellis) treats a reluctant Del who's suffering from bad toothache.

Denzil

Played by Paul Barber

West Indian-born Denzil – who has five brothers – first appears in 'Who's a Pretty Boy?', at which point he's living in a block of flats with his wife, Corinne. He moved to London with his parents when he was 13, finishing his education at the Martin Luther King Comprehensive in 1962.

'**W**e were up in Hull filming "To Hull and Back" when I learnt Denzil was going to become a regular character. Back at the hotel, one evening, John Sullivan and Ray Butt called me over from the bar; I was just getting a drink when they asked: "How do you feel about Denzil? Do you like the character?" I told them he was great and that it was fun playing him. They said they'd like to include him in more episodes, which was fine with me: from then on I found myself appearing more and more. In fact, it feels as if I've been in every episode, but of course I haven't. I particularly like it when Del takes Denzil for a ride, and that he's always the last one to know what's going on, which is true to character because I'm like that!

'It was lovely working with Corinne, who was Denzil's wife. She was played by the late Eva Mottley, and I'm sorry I only appeared with her the once; she would have gone on to do a lot more had it not been for her tragic death, which was a deep shock. The way she called Denzil's name was great because she used one of those voices which everybody feared; so my way of avoiding Del Boy whenever I saw him was to say: "God, Corinne will kill me if she knows I've been talking to you."

'"To Hull and Back" conjures up a lot of memories, such as driving the articulated lorry. I only drove it over the bridge, which was enough! The actual truck driver was crouched down on the passenger's side, and while we crossed the bridge he'd be saying, "Double-declutch, double-declutch", because it was a 15-geared vehicle, if I remember right. I drove it in third gear, which is like driving an Aston Martin in first gear along the motorway; it was really funny because the driver was shouting, "Go on, put it up another gear," and I'd reply, "Where, where?" The thing was I hadn't had any lessons. When we came to film the scene, Ray Butt asked whether I could drive it, and even though I said no, he told me to get in and do it.

'I also remember the location shooting for "As One Door Closes", especially the butterfly scene where I slap Del's hands, squashing the rare butterfly in the process. We filmed at Ravenscourt Park and were supposed to do a shot of me walking through the park with my ghetto blaster over my shoulder before slapping Del's hands. We rehearsed it and everything went well. Just as we were about to film, the rain began falling, so we took refuge in the pub at the bottom of the park.

'We were all sitting around the tables when Ray turned to me and said: "Don't worry, Paul, as soon as the rain finishes we'll get your shot done." I don't know what made me say it, but I replied: "It would look good on skates." It seemed to me that the scene would be funnier if after Del's hands are slapped, he turns around to see me halfway down the road, not just two feet away because I'm walking. Ray just gave me this look, and as filming was suspended for the day because it had started snowing, he said: "That's it then. I want you to go to the props department, get a pair of roller skates."

'As it turned out, we weren't able to complete the scene for about two weeks because of the weather, so I had to learn to roller skate in the snow. But I did, and everything worked out well; in fact, Ray Butt was so pleased he told me I could keep the skates because it was such a good idea.'

PAUL BARBER

When we first meet Denzil he's planning to decorate his living room, but when Del hears that he's going to hire Brendan O'Shaughnessy for the job he puts him off the Irishman with a pack of lies, thereby securing the job for himself. He's next seen in 'As One Door Closes', speaking to Del in the market *en route* to the Job Centre, and becomes embroiled, once again, in Del's plans.

One of Denzil's biggest flaws is his gullibility, particularly where Del Boy is concerned, and when we see him in 'To Hull and Back', he's just patched up his differences with Corinne and has promised to stop seeing Del, stop getting inebriated, stop gambling, and secure a steady job. But he lacks the inner strength to meet his spouse's demands and by the time he's seen talking in The Nag's Head during 'Fatal Extraction', he's been separated from Corinne for seven years.

An affable, kind-hearted guy, Denzil is one of life's plodders, someone who struggles to get ahead. By Series 6 his luck is low again: he's set up his own haulage business, Transworld Express, but with only a transit, opportunities are limited.

Derbyshire, Clive

Film sound recordist on six episodes: S3, episodes 1–4, 6 & 7
Born in London in 1945, Clive worked for six years in telephone maintenance, initially for the Post Office before moving on to London Transport. He applied to the BBC for the post of trainee assistant film recordist in 1968 and upon being offered the job, worked on shows such as *The Wednesday Play*, the second series of *Monty Python* and *Not Only – But Also…*. He also worked with Ray Butt on *Seconds Out* and spent seven months on *The Singing Detective*.

Clive left the BBC in 1994 and now works freelance. Recent jobs have included various commercials, the comedy drama series, *Chillers*, *Lucky Jim*, *Hot Money* and *Bad Girls*.

Desert Inn

In 'Stage Fright', Eric, the manager of The Starlight Rooms, claims that Raquel has just finished a sell-out season on the same bill as Barry Manilow at the world-famous Desert Inn, in Las Vegas.

Desmond Tutu House

This tower block on the Nyeyre Estate is mentioned by Del in 'Little Problems'. When he's trying to install the video recorder that Rodney believes is wired for the Continent, not the UK market, Del explains that he got an electrical whiz-kid who lives in Desmond Tutu House to fix an adaptor.

Deveney, Pat

Lighting gaffer on four episodes: 'Heroes and Villains', 'Modern Men', 'Time On Our Hands' and 'If They Could See Us Now…!'

'**I**'ll always remember my assistant, who operated the boom, made no secret about wanting to be a recordist; we were filming in a street somewhere in London and he'd been going on, so I said: "OK, you do my job and I'll do yours," so we swapped.

'Ray Butt, the director, joked that with me doing the boom we'd end up with the microphone in the shot! That didn't happen but something equally embarrassing did: whilst filming a tracking shot in the road a wristwatch went off and everything was brought to a halt. Then I realised it was my watch. It was so humiliating, especially right in front of my assistant having swapped jobs.

'Another occasion I particular remember was during a night shoot. We were trying to produce rain in one of the scenes and were using the fire brigade to pump the water. I said to this fireman: "My equipment is only slightly waterproof so please avoid it." But unfortunately the imitation rain soaked the equipment, so I moved over to the light and got a hairdryer to dry it off. Ray Butt ran over and said: "You can't make it work." I told him it was okay, I could dry it out, but he asked me not to because an actor who'd had a death in the family had insisted on coming in, but obviously hadn't got his mind on the job. Ray wanted me to say the equipment didn't work so that we could stop filming.'

CLIVE DERBYSHIRE

'Diamonds are for Heather'

(Christmas Special 1982)

Original transmission: Thursday 30 December 1982, 7.55 pm

Production date: Monday 20 December 1982

Original viewing figures: 9.3 million

Duration: 30 minutes

First repeat: Monday 24 December 1984, 8.25 pm

Subsequent repeats: 20/12/94, 27/10/98, 3/3/00

CAST

Del Trotter . . . . .David Jason
Rodney Trotter . . . . .Nicholas Lyndhurst
Grandad Trotter . . . . .Lennard Pearce
Enrico .John Moreno
Heather . . . . .Rosalind Lloyd
Brian . . . . .Roger Brierley
Waiter (in Indian restaurant) . . .Dev Sagoo
Carol singers . . . . .The Fred Tomlinson Singers
Guitarist in pub . . . . .George Kish
Darren (small boy) . . . . .Daniel Jones
Walk-ons: . . . .(Carol singers) Fred Tomlinson, Fred Lucas, Michael Clarke, Mark Brown, Peter Bamber, Lee Gibson, Bridget Tomlinson, Glenys Groves, Alison McGregor, Jacquie Stillwell. (Barmaid) Julie La Rousse. (People in pub) Chris Breeze, John Holland and 19 extras. (Planetarium commissionaire) George Barnes.(Man's hand in planetarium during scene between Del and Heather) John Holland.

PRODUCTION TEAM

Written by John Sullivan
Title music arranged and conducted by Ronnie Hazlehurst composed and sung by John Sullivan
Audience Warm-up: . . . . .Felix Bowness
Make-up Designer: . . . . .Shaunna Harrison
Costume Designer: . . . . .Anushia Nieradzik
Properties Buyer: . . . . .Peter Sporle
Film Cameraman: . . . . .Alec Curtis
Film Sound: . . . . .Dennis Panchen
Film Editor: . . . . .John Dunstan
Camera Supervisor: . . . . .Ron Peverall
Studio Lighting Director: . . . . . .Don Babbage
Studio Sound: . . . . .Dave Thompson
Technical Coordinator: . . . . . . .Robert Hignett
Videotape Editor: . . . . .Chris Wadsworth
Production Assistant: . . . . .Penny Thompson
Assistant Floor Manager: . . . . .Tony Dow
Graphic Designer: . . . . .Fen Symonds
Vision Mixer: . . . . .Angela Beveridge
Production Manager: . . . . .Sue Bysh
Designer: . . . . .Don Giles
Produced and directed by Ray Butt

Del's love life is on hold again as he sits forlornly at the Spanish night at The Nag's Head, but then he spots Heather and is quick to start chatting her up. When she explains that her friend has failed to turn up, Del plays the gentleman and offers to take her home. Back at her Brixton flat, he discovers she has a young son and that her hubby left her 18 months ago, when he failed to return from a visit to the Job Centre.

Del takes Heather and her little boy, Darren, to

'Diamonds are for Heather'

the zoo, and it seems like he's found true love. The relationship is running along so smoothly that he buys a ring and proposes over a candlelit dinner at an Indian restaurant. But his proposal is rejected: Heather's husband, Vic, who's now living in Southampton and working as a department store's Santa, has written and asked her if she's prepared to give their marriage another try; when Heather passes the ring back, the flame in another of Del's romances is snuffed out.

Dicks, Melanie

Assistant floor manager on one episode: 'A Royal Flush'

Melanie left the BBC in 1992 to become a Features 1st assistant director, and has since worked on a host of films, television programmes and commercials, including *Mike Bassett: England Manager*, *The Commissioner*, *Over Here*, *The English Wife* and *The Snapper*.

Dimond, Andy

Designer on six episodes: S2, episodes 2–7

Born in Kingston-upon-Thames in 1943, Andy attended the Central St Martin's Art College in 1961. Whilst he was studying he gained valuable experience by working at the Margate Stage Company.

On leaving college in 1964, he joined the BBC as an assistant designer, working on programmes such as *It's A Square World*, *Steptoe and Son* and *The Rolf Harris Show*. As a designer, his credits include *Last of the Summer Wine* and *The Two Ronnies*. Andy retired from the BBC in 1994 after 30 years' service.

Dirty Barry

(See 'Barry')

DJ

Played by Mike Read

The DJ introduces 'A Bunch of Wallies', Rodney's old group, on *Top of the Pops*. Their inaugural hit, 'Boys Will Be Boys', has reached number 26 in the charts.

Dockside Café, The

Lil owns the café , which is seen in 'To Hull and Back' when Denzil (who's a long-distance lorry driver) pops in after driving all night.

Dockside Junior School, The

In 'Rodney Come Home' Chris and Mickey Pearce try striking up a conversation with two 'mature' girls in a nightclub. Chris asks one of them if she attended the junior school.

Dockside Secondary Modern

The school is mentioned by Del in 'Modern Men', indicating that it was the place where he finished his education. However, earlier in the series he refers to The Martin Luther King Comprehensive, the name having been changed during Rodney's time at the school.

Doctor, The

Played by Brian Jameson

Based at the local hospital, the doctor examines Uncle Albert in 'Sleeping Dogs Lie', when Del and Rodney suspect he may have eaten some contaminated meat.

Doctor, The

(For the doctor in 'Homesick', see 'Becker, Dr'.)

Doctor, The

Played by James Olver

In 'Modern Men', the doctor takes Mike Fisher through to the treatment room at the local hospital. Mike's burned his head using the hairdryer Del sold him which turned out to be a paint stripper!

Dog owner

Played by Linda Barr

In 'Sleeping Dogs Lie' Del takes a fancy to the dog owner when he sees her walking her dachshund, Sacha, in the park. He starts chatting her up, claiming he knows everything about dogs.

Dominique

(See 'Concierge')

Don

Don's sister, Janice, tells Rodney – who's dating her – about her brother during 'A Slow Bus to Chingford'. Don is a painter for the local council, but doesn't appear in the show.

Dora

(See 'Lane, Dora')

Dosser

Played by Robert Vahey

Asleep, next to Rodney in Sid's Café, the dosser is seen in 'A Royal Flush'. He awakes when Rodney mistakenly takes a sip from his mug of tea. Most television viewings and video releases don't show the tea-sipping.

Double Cream

In 'Stage Fright', Raquel tells Del that she used to be in the duo, Double Cream.

Dow, Mr

Played by Roger Davidson

In 'A Royal Flush', Mr Dow is the snooty manager of the gents' outfitters. The Trotters visit the shop to buy Rodney a suit for his weekend visit to the Duke of Maylebury's country home.

Dow, Tony

Assistant floor manager on 17 episodes: S1, episode 6; S2; S3; 'Diamonds are for Heather' and 'Thicker Than Water'. Production manager on two episodes: 'To Hull and Back' and 'A Royal Flush'. Director on 22 episodes: S6, episodes 1, 3–6; S7; 'Dates'; 'The Jolly Boys' Outing'; 'Rodney Come Home'; 'Miami Twice' (Parts 1 & 2); 'Mother Nature's Son'; 'Fatal Extraction'; 'Heroes and Villains'; 'Modern Men' 'Time On Our Hands' and 'If They Could See Us Now…!'

...orld. 'I did a bit of amateur dramatics at school, then attended art college, but wasn't particularly doing a lot with my life, so just decided to try my luck in the theatre; I applied and was lucky enough to be offered a position.'

Tony began his career as an assistant stage manager, joining Eastbourne's Devonshire Park Theatre in 1966. 'I was a trainee everything, to be honest,' admits Tony. 'I did acting, stage management, sets, lighting – you name it, I did it. I spent six months there and thought: "This is great!"' Wanting to further his knowledge and experience, he attended RADA's course in stage management before heading out into theatreland.

By the time he joined the Beeb he was already an experienced director, albeit in the theatre, which was valuable when transferring mediums. He initiated the change of direction when he realised chances of progression within the theatre were limited. A friend, who worked at the BBC, suggested he tried television. Although he was unsure whether it was for him, he decided to apply. 'I applied to the Drama and Series/Serials areas and was told I could certainly join, but there wouldn't be a position in those divisions for about six months.' In the meantime, light entertainment offered him a job in studio management, which he duly accepted.

'I must admit, I didn't even know what light entertainment meant,' admits Tony, whose extensive list of credits includes directing shows such as *Ain't Misbehavin'*; *Roger*, Roger; *Birds Of A Feather*; *Blind Men* and *The High Life*. 'On my first day I worked on *Blue Peter* and didn't get that right. I remember one day speaking to John Howard Davies and telling him the problem was I knew nothing about cameras – I didn't even have one myself! He replied: "Listen, we've got hundreds of people who know about cameras, but we need people who know about actors." My theatre background meant I'd worked with actors all my working life, and found that part easy. But what I had to learn quickly was how the cameras and the rest of the studio worked.'

After the first week of studio management, Tony was scheduled to join a show entitled *Only Fools and Horses*. 'I'd never heard of it, obviously, and so I went down and trailed Mandie Fletcher, to gain experience.' Little did he know that he would be directing the series in his own right – a job he thoroughly enjoys. 'There's a good amount of trust on the show because we've all worked together for so long. You hear of reputations of actors on other shows, but on *Fools* you don't get anything like that. There's very little aggravation considering how much work we have to do in such a tight timescale.'

Born in Cheshire, Tony – who was educated at boarding school in Caterham, Surrey – has been working freelance since 1988. After working flat-out on *Only Fools* for several months now, he plans to take a little break before moving on to the next project. 'The trouble with doing *Fools* is that people phone up and ask if I'd like to do such and such a project, but I think: "It's not quite as much fun." Though some recent projects I've done, such as the series *Bob Martin* and Lee Evans' *So What Now?* were very enjoyable.'

Down by the Riverside Club, The

Mentioned by Mickey Pearce in 'Yuppy Love', the Club is in Blackheath. Pearce asks Cassandra and Emma – who live in the area – if they've heard of it, only for Cassandra to claim that it's got a terrible reputation and is always full of 'unsavoury characters'.

Our first glimpse of the Club – which is a large, brightly-lit, prefabricated building – is in 'Stage Fright'. Trigger tells everyone at The Nag's Head that his workmate, Tony Angelino, the Singing Dustman, performs there.

Driscoll, Danny

Played by Roy Marsden

One of the Driscoll Brothers, Danny is in his mid-forties and dresses in a three-piece suit and tie, with a gold watch chain hanging across his waistcoat. He is seen in 'Little Problems'.

THINKING UP THE PLACE NAMES

★ ★ ★ ★ ★ ★

'When I used to play football there was a team in one of the lower divisions called The Riverside and I used that when naming **The Down by the Riverside Club**; I don't know why, it just sounded nice. **Nelson Mandela House** came via the fashion which left-wing councils adopted during the late-1970s, early-80s, to change all the street names to African heroes, with the British names becoming taboo. So I thought I'd go for Nelson Mandela, my hero. I was very aware of Mandela's life and thought I'd go for the big cheese. The same happened when it came to naming the **Martin Luther King Comprehensive**. Another school mentioned is the **Dockside Junior School**: the Dockside was the name of the school my dad went to in Bermondsey, so I just used that. **The One Eleven Club** is interesting because it was based on a club in Balham High Road owned by the Richardson brothers. It was number 112 in the road. However, at the time, my wife and I lived at 111 Westmoreland Drive, and thinking one eleven sounded better, I opted for that as the name. **The 121 Club** comes from *Dear John*. I was trying to come up with a trendy name for a club and liked it. Others like **The Monte Carlo Club** and **The Starlight Rooms** are just made up.'

JOHN SULLIVAN

Driscoll, Tony

Played by Christopher Ryan

Classed as a 'pugnacious little sadist', Tony appears in 'Little Problems' and is one of the Driscoll Brothers.

Driscoll Brothers, The

Feared around the streets of Peckham, the Driscoll Brothers (Danny and Tony) are to be avoided at all costs. While trading with Mickey Pearce and Jevon in 'Little Problems', Del gets tangled up with the brothers. When Mike, the landlord of The Nag's Head, asks what they're like, Boycie replies: 'One of them looks like he was evicted from the Planet of the Apes,' while Del adds that the other has one of those faces 'you'd like to slap'.

They had a poor upbringing; their father worked in the stables at a mansion house, earning a pittance. A fire occurred at the house and he was arrested, mainly because he was in possession of jewels from the property. Later, he died in a police cell with a fractured skull. The police claim he tried hanging himself with his braces and smashed his head on the ceiling. The day he died, Tony and Danny vowed they would never be dumped upon, and they would never be poor. The brothers ended up in a young offenders' home, during which time Del looked after their mother with some hookey groceries and other provisions.

Del mentions them in 'Video Nasty' because they're partners in Boycie's first film, *Night Nurse*. And in 'The Frog's Legacy', Del tells Rodney and Albert that he visited the brothers because he's after information concerning Freddy the Frog.

Driscoll, Robin

Role: The Great Ramondo

Appeared in 'The Jolly Boys' Outing'

Robin is a successful writer, performer and co-founder of the Cliffhanger Theatre Company. He co-wrote and appeared in *They Came From Somewhere Else* for Channel 4; *Alas Smith and Jones, Hello Mum, Les and Robert, Sage and Onion* for BBC and both the television series and film of *Mr Bean*.

Other television credits, as an actor, include *Colin's Sandwich, Dear John, Murder Most Horrid, Waiting For God* and *Duck Patrol*.

Drummer

Played by Derek Price

During 'Tea for Three', the drummer helps provide the backing music during the talent night at The Nag's Head.

Drummer

Played by Alf Bigden

The drummer is part of the group entertaining at the Mardi Gras nightclub in Margate during 'The Jolly Boys' Outing'.

Drury, Ken

Role: Midwife

Appeared in S7, episode 6

Upon graduating from the Central School of Speech and Drama, Ken – who was born in 1950 – completed a postgraduate drama course at Manchester. Afterwards, in 1970, he headed north and was first seen in a professional capacity at the Citizen's Theatre, Glasgow, in *Colombe*. Stints with numerous repertory companies followed, such as Leicester, Edinburgh and Bristol, before he made his inaugural television appearance as Sergeant Fowlis in the last series of *Sutherland's Law*, back in 1975. His comprehensive range of small-screen jobs include many favourite roles, such as Louis in *Down Among the Bog Boys*, Cameron Dicks in *Hamish MacBeth*, McNish in Channel 4's production of *Shackleton, Taggart, London's Burning* and *Call Red.*

Ken, whose big-screen credits include *Yanks* and *Four Weddings and a Funeral*, is still busy in all strands of the profession, and has recently played in Shakespeare's *As You Like It* on tour in America.

Dublin Bay Stormers

When members of this resident band at The Shamrock Club in Deptford end up in prison on remand, Del sees a business opportunity and arranges for Rodney's group to sing at the club on St Patrick's Night.

Duggan, Terry

Role: Council cleansing lorry driver

Appeared in S2, episode 2

Terry was born in Shoreditch, London, in 1932 and worked as a printer before attending the Ronnie Curtis Theatre School. In his early days as an actor he appeared mainly on the screen, as well as being involved in stunt work. His debut was in the BBC's 1965 series, *The Illustrated Weekly Hudd.*

Terry has been a busy character actor for some time now, and over the years he's popped up in various episodes of *On the Buses, The Fosters* and *Class Act*, to name just a few. His favourite screen role was playing Bruno Valenta in ATV's 1976 series, *A Place to Hide*. He's also made several excursions into the film world, playing small parts in pictures like *Poor Cow, 2001: A Space Odyssey, The Horror of Frankenstein, Family Life, What's Up Nurse!* and *Murder by Decree.*

MEMORIES OF PLAYING THE MIDWIFE

★ ★ ★ ★ ★ ★

'I was lucky enough to get the part because Ken MacDonald, who played Mike, read the script and noted the character had a Scottish name and required a bald head. He went to Tony Dow, the director, and said: "Look no further than Ken Drury." Tony took Ken at his word, sent me the script and offered me the job. Good old Ken and good old Tony!

'We filmed the birth of Damien between Christmas and New Year at a hospital in Hillingdon. David Jason had just won a Best Comedy Actor Award, so I was a bit nervous, but he put me at ease right away.

'Some unsuspecting mother handed over her new baby and Damien was born. We did have a laugh trying to work out how the wig would come off during the delivery! Fortunately I knew Tessa Peake-Jones, who as Raquel was supposed to be giving birth, because I'd worked with her husband at the National Theatre for a year, so we weren't too embarrassed!'   **KEN DRURY**

Duke

Marlene's Great Dane puppy, Duke, is introduced in 'Sleeping Dogs Lie'.

Duke of Maylebury, The

Played by Jack Hedley

A second cousin to the Queen, the Duke – aka Sir Henry Marsham KBE, MVO, MC, the 14th Duke of Maylebury – lives at the family home, Covington House, in Upper Stanameer, Berkshire. He appears in 'A Royal Flush', when his daughter, Vicky, runs an art stall at the local Peckham market.

Duncan, Sarah

Role: Vicky

Appeared in 'A Royal Flush'

London-born Sarah Duncan trained at The Drama Studio, in the capital, and made her professional debut in *Passion Play* at the Leicester Haymarket and Wyndham's Theatre in the West End. Her first taste of television came just before her appearance as Vicky, when she played Alison Blair in *A Very Peculiar Practice*.

Vicky gave up the theatre in 1987.

Dunstan, John

Film editor on four episodes: 'Diamonds are for Heather', 'A Royal Flush' and 'Miami Twice' (Parts 1 & 2)

After leaving school John, a native of Newcastle upon Tyne, harboured dreams of working in the entertainment world; as the dreams were yet unfocused he decided to train as a solicitor. He qualified in 1966 but was by then confirmed in his original belief that this was not the life for him, and had already made applications to the BBC and Tyne-Tees Television.

He moved to the capital and, concentrating on the film side of the profession, attempted to join the BBC's editing training course only to be told that he lacked professional experience. After writing to a myriad of film companies he was finally given a chance by the Overseas Film and Television Centre in London. During his two-year stay he was occasionally able to assist an editor working on BBC programmes, including *The Frost Report*, *Monty Python's Flying Circus* and *Marty*.

When the 'overseas' side of the work collapsed, John was made redundant but managed to join the BBC in 1969 as a holiday relief assistant film editor. After spending nearly two years working on a current affairs programme, he was, in 1971, appointed to a permanent post and then in '76 promoted to film editor having already begun specialising in comedy.

By the time he left the Beeb in 1995, he'd worked on countless top shows, including *The Dick Emery Show; Porridge; The Two Ronnies; Happy Ever After; The Good Life; Rings on Their Fingers; To the Manor Born; Rosie; Sorry!; Yes, Minister; Bread; One Foot in the Grave; 'Allo 'Allo!* and *Waiting for God*. Since turning freelance, he's continued to work on hit series like *Next of Kin; Roger, Roger* and *Bob Martin*.

Dykes, Alan

Dubbing mixer on one episode: 'A Royal Flush'

London-born Alan Dykes' first job was as a runner at the British Film Institute. He then worked as a projectionist, including two years with the National Film Theatre, before joining the BBC in 1958. His career was interrupted by two years spent completing national service, and by the time he returned to the Beeb he'd developed an interest in sound recording and became a dubbing mixer. After 17 years in the job he left the BBC and worked freelance for four years at Ladbroke Films.

In 1987 he moved to Cornwall and undertook the occasional freelance job, before giving up the profession in 1992.

DVDs

All the DVDs listed are produced by BBC Worldwide

'THE JOLLY BOYS' OUTING'

Catalogue No	BBCDVD1029
Duration	80 mins
Release date	6/11/00
Episode included	1989 Christmas Special

'THE FROG'S LEGACY'

Catalogue No	BBCDVD1041
Duration	59 MINS
Release date	20/11/00
Episode included	1987 Christmas Special

'THE COMPLETE *ONLY FOOLS AND HORSES* – SERIES 1'

Catalogue No	BBCDVD1035
Duration	214 mins
Release date	20/11/00

'THE COMPLETE *ONLY FOOLS AND HORSES* – SERIES 2'

Catalogue No	BBCDVD1045
Duration	231 mins
Release date	2/4/01

'THE COMPLETE *ONLY FOOLS AND HORSES* – SERIES 3'

Catalogue No	BBCDVD1046
Duration	236 mins
Release date	4/6/01

'THE COMPLETE *ONLY FOOLS AND HORSES* – SERIES 4'

Catalogue No	BBCDVD1070
Duration	180 mins
Release date	1/10/01

'TO HULL AND BACK'

Catalogue No	BBCDVD1071
Duration	90 mins
Release date	12/11/01

Earl

Played by Desmond McNamara

A friend of Del, Earl is seen in The Monte Carlo Club during the 1981 Christmas Special, 'Christmas Crackers'. Del gets chatting to Earl, who's the same age, but not as shrewd. He has suffered a rough time of late: not only is his father seriously ill in hospital, after collapsing in The Nag's Head just yards away from where Del and Trigger were enjoying a pint, but his marriage has hit troubled waters, culminating in his wife clearing off to her mother's with the kids. To top it all Earl has just been made redundant.

Easter, Robert J

Business manager (New York) on one episode: 'Miami Twice' (Part 2)

Robert was involved in coordinating arrangements and finance when it came to filming the episode in the States.

Eberle, Scott

Grip on one episode: 'Miami Twice' (Part 2)

America-based Scott Eberle was employed to work on the filming sequences in the States.

Ecstasy

Ecstasy is a supplier of 'adult requisites' – more commonly known as a sex shop. Situated in Walworth Road, it's owned by Dirty Barry. Del, Rodney and Albert visit the establishment in 'Danger UXD' when they're trying desperately to flog 50 inflatable sex dolls, only to discover that the council has revoked Barry's trading licence, forcing the shop's closure.

Eddie

(See 'Chambers, Eddie')

Edwards, David

Played by David Warwick

Referred to as the 'TV presenter' in the scripts, David Edwards presents *London Plus*, a regional news programme. It's on TV when Denzil is waiting for his takeaway at a Chinese restaurant during 'Danger UXD'. Denzil is alarmed to hear Edwards' leading story about 50 highly dangerous inflatable dolls that went missing from a site at Deptford, primarily because he passed them on to Del.

Eels On Wheels

Mentioned in 'The Jolly Boys' Outing', Eels on Wheels is the seafood business that Del established with Jumbo Mills outside The Nag's Head. The business didn't last long, largely due to an unfavourable report from the local health inspector.

Eileen

Eileen's former husband, Roland, attends the funeral of her uncle, Albert Warren, in 'If They Could See Us Now…!' but Eileen herself is not seen.

Ellis, Bryan

Designer on four episodes: S3, episodes 5, 6 & 7; 'Thicker Than Water'

Born in Wallasey, Merseyside, Bryan left school and worked in architectural design before joining the BBC as an assistant designer in 1967. During his national service he worked in a drawing office for the Royal Engineers, helping design, amongst other things, bridges. Upon returning to civvy street he was employed by an architect in Chester for two years, before briefly working in exhibition design prior to joining the Beeb.

Within a couple of years he was promoted to designer and went on to work on shows like *It Ain't Half Hot, Mum; Some Mothers Do 'Ave 'Em; The Dick Emery Show; Dad's Army; The Dave Allen Show* and *Hold the Back Page.*

Bryan took voluntary redundancy from the BBC in 1992 and worked freelance for a while, including projects such as *Absolutely Fabulous* (he'd worked on the first series while still at the Beeb). He's now retired from the business.

Ellis, Caroline

Role: Michelle
Appeared in S1, episode 2

Caroline, who was born in London in 1950, trained at the Aida Foster Theatre School. She made her professional stage debut in a 1962 production of *Puss in Boots*, at the London Palladium. Theatre dominated the early stages of her career: a well as numerous shows in London, she also toured; among her credits are appearances in *Pardon Me, Prime Minister, Peter Pan, Birds of Paradise, Sound of Music* and *Don't Just Lie There, Say Something.* She earned her television break during the mid-1960s in BBC's *Sherlock Holmes*, playing a witness to a murder, and has gone on to appear in productions from *The Many Wives of Patrick* and *The Cut Price Comedy* to *The Unvarnished Truth* and *Freewheelers.* Her favourite role, though, was playing Joy in the American series *The Bugaloos.*

Caroline, who stopped working when she became pregnant with her daughter, Sasha, moved to Spain in 1986.

Ellis, Mickey

Grip on one episode: 'The Jolly Boys' Outing'

Other productions Mickey has worked on include the 1990 movie *Sweet Nothing*, the television mini-series *Sleepers*, in 1991 and *Great Moments in Aviation* for the BBC two years later.

Ellis, Mr

(See 'Dentist, The')

Elly-May

Not seen in the sitcom, Elly-May is mentioned by Del in 'Yuppy Love' – he's not too sure he's got it right but states it was one of those 'long double-barrelled funny names'. An oil baron's daughter from Texas, she met Del when he was a teenager working in the Tower of London doing the Happy Snaps. She asked Del to take a photo of her and a Beefeater, after which they started chatting. Del offered to show her around London and it wasn't long before they fell in love – although he always struggles to remember her name!

Elvis

Rodney's assistant at work in 'The Chance of a Lunchtime', Elvis is not seen, but steps into Rodney's shoes when Alan Parry accepts Rodney's letter of resignation, which he was intending to withdraw before Mr Parry got to see it. The acne-suffering Elvis only left school a year ago and is filling the void until a replacement can be found.

Emma

Played by Francesca Brill

A friend and neighbour of Cassandra, Emma is seen at the disco in 'Yuppy Love'. She's having boyfriend problems with a guy who claimed he had a holiday home near Marbella: it turned out to be a caravan on the Isle of Sheppey. She is mentioned again in 'Rodney Come Home', when Del tells Cassandra that Rodney has taken Tanya to the pictures. Cassandra, who becomes upset, decides to forego her evening class and visit Emma instead because she needs a shoulder to cry on.

English girl

(See 'Wendy')

Englishman

(See 'Ray')

Enrico

Played by John Moreno

A Spanish-singing Cockney, Enrico entertains the clientele during the Spanish night at The Nag's Head. He and his partner make up the flamenco duo, The Magaluf Brothers, and are seen in 'Diamonds are for Heather'.

Enrico

In 'Chain Gang', Boycie and Del are shown to their table in an upmarket Chelsea restaurant by a waiter called Enrico.

Eric

Played by Geoffrey Wilkinson

Eric works as a chauffeur for the Duke of Maylebury and is seen in 'A Royal Flush', collecting Lady Victoria from the Theatre Royal, Drury Lane.

Eric

Played by Trevor Byfield

The pony-tailed manager of The Starlight Rooms is seen in 'Stage Fright'. Eric used to own the business until he sold it to Eugene Macarthy, after a little undue pressure was applied. A tough-looking cockney, Eric is an old friend of Del's and is pleased to meet up with him again, especially as they haven't seen each other for five or six years following a slight misunderstanding which left Eric believing Del had swindled him out of £500. Eric needs Del's help, which shows how desperate he is. He's been let down by a singing duo and asks if Raquel would come out of retirement for one night. When £600 is offered, Del's quick to sign the contract, even though he hasn't even asked his girlfriend.

Eric (the policeman)

Played by Derek Newark

Eric is the policeman who pulls Del, Rodney and Grandad over for doing 60mph in a built-up district during 'The Russians are Coming'. He jokes about whether they've just heard the four-minute warning, unaware that his quip is more apt than he realises. His young co-driver in the police car is Wayne.

Eric is far from scrupulous and instead of booking the Trotters, he informs Del that he's on the look-out for some stolen summer-wear because he's jetting off to Corfu with his wife shortly.

Erotic Estelle

An inflatable doll, Erotic Estelle is one of 50 Del buys from Denzil in 'Danger UXD'.

Escobar, Robert

Role: Francisco
Appeared in 'Miami Twice' (Part 2)

America-based actor Robert Escobar has appeared in various screen productions. On television he's been seen in *Miami Vice, B.L. Stryker, Nostromo* and *Fuego Verde*, while his film career includes appearances in movies such as *Cat Chaser, Folks!, Peace Town* and *The Perez Family.*

Etienne, Treva

Role: Vicar
Appeared in 'Miami Twice' (Parts 1 & 2)

Born in London in 1965, Treva studied electronics at college and did various jobs, including selling ice creams, before becoming an actor. He first worked in children's theatre in 1984, before moving on to appear in various productions in Folkestone, Leicester and Manchester. His first television was as Horace in the ITV series *Prospects*, but his favourite roles have been Mick, in the hit ITV sci-fi series *The Last Train*, and Lloyd in the award-winning BBC2 drama *Holding On.* Other credits include *Casualty, Call Me Mister, The Missing Finger* and *The Lenny Henry Show.*

Treva, who continues to work in theatre and film (including the recent Ridley Scott picture *Black Hawk Down*), also writes, directs and produces. He trained on the BBC TV directors' course.

'Miami Twice'

Eugene

(See 'Macarthy, Eugene')

Evans, Derek

Designer on four episodes: S2, episodes 1, 2, 6 & 7

Born in Ashford, Middlesex, in 1952, Derek left the Twickenham College of Technology with a diploma in exhibition design in 1973. His first job was as a design assistant with a record promotional company, but he left after a year to join the BBC as a holiday relief design assistant. During 21 years with the Beeb, he worked on a multitude of programmes, including *Little and Large*, *Fry and Laurie*, *Ever Decreasing Circles*, *Keeping Up Appearances*, *In the Dark*, *Blue Peter*, *Tomorrow's World*, *Children in Need*, *Grandstand* and *Match of the Day*.

Derek left the BBC in 1996 and worked freelance for a year, but in 1997 decided to change course and attended the Nescott College, Ewell, where he gained the Royal Society of Health Certificate in Pest Control. He's now self-employed and works in landscape gardening, general maintenance and pest control.

Evans, Gail

Production assistant on two episodes: 'Miami Twice' (Parts 1 & 2). Associate producer on one episode: 'If They Could See Us Now…!'

Gail, who was born in Leintwardine in 1962, began her working life in the medical profession. After gaining the Association of Medical Secretaries' Diploma at Bromsgrove's North Worcestershire College, she was employed at Corbett Hospital, Stourbridge, and London's St Mary's Hospital, before opting for a career change and joining the BBC in 1985.

Initially working as a secretary in various capacities, such as for the editor of *That's Life!*, she was soon promoted to production assistant. Some of the programmes she worked on during this time include *Luv*, *The Last Word*, *One Foot in the Grave*, *Sitting Pretty*, *Waiting for God* and *On the Up*. By 1995 she had moved on to become a production manager/associate producer (the role she currently holds), assigned to shows such as *The Last Salute*, *The Brittas Empire*, *A Prince Among Men*, *Next of Kin*, *Chambers* and *The Office*.

Evans, Roy

Role: Harry

Appeared in 'The Jolly Boys' Outing'

Bristolian Roy was born in 1930. After leaving school he worked in the building trade and as a window cleaner before breaking into the entertainment world, initially as a dancer with small acting roles in musicals, beginning with Peter Brook's 1958 production, *Irma la Douce*. His early years were spent in fringe theatre and with Tony Robertson's Prospect Theatre Company, as well as small parts in film and television, with his first role being a bookie in 1965's *Call Me Lucky*.

Other film credits include *The Company of Wolves*, *The Elephant Man*, *Raise the Titanic*, *The Dirty Dozen*, *Jack the Ripper*, *Yellow Beard*, *The Big Sleep* and, more recently, *The Singing Fool* and *The Gathering*.

He seldom works in the theatre these days, but remains busy on television, where his credits range from *Andy Capp*, *Porterhouse Blue*, *Casualty* and *Blackadder* to *Campion*, *Murder Most Horrid*, *Hetty Wainthropp Investigates* and *Bramwell*.

Faber, Duncan

Role: Man in market

Appeared in 'The Frog's Legacy'

Born in London in 1947, Duncan began his working life as a trainee reporter before giving it up to train at the E15 Acting School (1970–73). He made his professional debut the year he graduated as a milkman in an episode of *Dixon of Dock Green*, and then divided his time between the stage and screen. Other screen credits include playing a sailor in *The Naked Civil Servant* (1975); an army sergeant in *The Tomorrow People* (1994); a porter in *Poirot* (1989); a stall holder in *Goodnight Sweetheart* (1993); Ken in *Barbara* (1999); a flower stallholder in *Chucklevision* and a parent in Warner Brothers' film *Harry Potter and the Sorcerer's Stone*, in 2001.

Fan

Tony Angelino's aged fan was scripted for a few words in 'Stage Fright', but the scene was cut from the transmitted version. Eager for the Singing Dustman's autograph, the fan barges past the real Tony Angelino – minus the stage clothes and make-up – in search of the singer.

Fantasy Therapy

In 'If They Could See Us Now…!', Rodney suggests to Cassandra that they try resolving their marital differences with Fantasy Therapy, a treatment introduced by an American and based on 'iconoclastic auto suggestion'. Part of the therapy results in Rodney and Cassandra planning to enjoy a night of passion dressed as a Roman gladiator and policewoman respectively. Then Del turns up!

'Fatal Extraction'

(Christmas Special 1993)

Original transmission: Saturday 25 December 1993, 6.05 pm

Production date: Sunday 28 November 1993

Original viewing figures: 19.6 million

Duration: 85 minutes

First repeat: Tuesday 17 December 1996, 9.30 pm

Subsequent repeats: 15/6/01, 23/6/02

CAST

Del Trotter . . . . .David Jason
Rodney Trotter . . . . .Nicholas Lyndhurst

Uncle Albert	Buster Merryfield
Raquel	Tessa Peake-Jones
Cassandra	Gwyneth Strong
Boycie	John Challis
Trigger	Roger Lloyd Pack
Mike	Kenneth MacDonald
Denzil	Paul Barber
Sid	Roy Heather
Mickey	Patrick Murray
Damien	Jamie Smith
Beverley	Mel Martin
The dentist	Andrew Charleson
Lady on the bus	Kitty Scopes
Arthur	Derek Martin
Mick	Nick Maloney
Vi	Lyn Langridge
Policeman	Linford Brown
Texo	Bryan Brittain
Casino waitress	Lorraine Parsloe
Miguel	Ronald Murray
Walk-ons:	(The Nag's Head bar staff)

Anne-Marie Chevannes and Julie Evans. (Dentist's patient) Eva Coleman-Wood. ('Right Said Fred' girl) Anneli Daniell. (Her boyfriend) Terry Arnold. (Casino staff and punters) Jan Anderson, Amanda Cole, Rob E Ryan and Omar Williams. (Girl in market) Shariena Greaves. (Police/rioters) Stanmore Allen, Carl Pettman, Mike Kent, Adrian Bishop, James Hewson, Gerald Benson, Earl Duforte, Andrew Hallman, J. Galvin, Bill Butcher, Charles Harrison, Mal Tobias, Aaron James, Paul Joy, Mike L'Dell, Bill McCarthy, Toby Merrell, John Curry, Graham Pearce, Glenn Row, Mike Sherwood, Phillip Molyneux, Curtis Rivers, Michael Shute, Sean Saye, Paul Markham, Lionel Phillips, Andy Turvey, Terry Thomas, Alan Sanderson, Mike Praverman, Ernest Ian Smith, Jean Hunt. (Snooty woman in market – scene cut from final version) Cindy Leather.

Extras: (The Nag's Head customers) Tony Amechi, James Appleby, Della Bhujoo, Carrie Brooks, Janette Brown, Malcolm Collop, Malcolm Davey, Angela Delaney, John Delaney, Charlotte Dudley, Irene Frederick, Ricardo Hunt, Akin Jones, Danny Lane, Richard Malado, Eniye Osifo, Nick Parmenter, Matt Pearce, Celia Radband, Victor Richards, Michael Savva, Bejen Ignatius Temba, Mal Tobias, Dave Trevors, Sophie Camara, James Faulkner, Peggy-Ann Fraser, Norma Walker. (Dentist's patients) Graham Ryder, Ted Gold, Penny Graham, Kim Stone, John Emms, Martin Kingston, Barry Lane, L. Gold, Carol Kirkland, Tony Smith, Jeremy Balfour, Renee Smith, Sarah Lincoln, Paul Winteridge, Tricia Stone. (Casino staff and punters) Suzi Amor, Jan Anderson, Alan Barrett, Selwyn Broodie, Gary O'Brien, Kim Buckpitt, Andrew Bullivant, Jacqueline Burrell, Kirsti Ann Calder, Jonathan Cann, Caroline Carro, Mark Cartier, Edward Chester, Amanda Cole, Rebel Dean, Paddy Faulkner, Kathryn Iles, James Harvey, Ron Jacobs, Samuel Jones, Elaine Innocents, Lee Innocents, Kaly Lay, Jackie Leigh, Geoff Lewis, Katherine Loeppky, Suzi Mollett, Nicky Nash, Dave Owen, Chrissie Peart, Simon Peters, Ann Pitt, Gary Rymell, Kevin Bignall, Wendie De Lewis Simeon, June Simmons, Phillip Ticehurst, Maureen Wilmot. (People on bus) Wingrove Broody, M. Waters, Noni Brooke, Kit Hillier, Douglas Johns, Vivien Lesley, Angie Nicholas, Rebecca Sloan, Barrie West. (Sid's Café) Peter Maitland, Harry Perries, Ken Dee, Robert Shield, Ben Armstrong, Mark Dominic, Martin Gilmore, Tommy Martin, Derek Gale, Ken Coombes, Karien Wolf, Steve Ford, Pat Prince, Martin Thomas, Dominic Balasco, Billy Kerr, Delroy Perries, Saka Singh, Lloyd McIntosh, Ossie Brooks, Branwen Iwan, Sonja Sabin, Mary Sansom. (Market) Martino Burgess,

Wynna Evans, Diana Greaves, Debbie Greaves, Patricia Ingram, Marcia Williams, Beth Paramor, Marie Paramor, Leon Miller, Jason Fennell, Roy Ali, Carlo Taylor, Robert Pitman, Richard Morgan, Wayne Hill, Don Leather, Ricky Denfield, Rebecca Roberts, Joanne Miles, Kevin Barber, Amanda Cole, Diana Clay, Corinne Britton, Tricia Stone, David McConnell, Paul Strike, Richard Randall, Ted Shepherd, Matthew Welsh, Vince Clifford. (Rioters) Johnny Shoestring, Wayne McLean, Miles Lavers, James Little, Kurt Glasson, Rodney Hardy Brown, Brian Bowen, Jade Adams, Omar Williams, Guy Calhoun, Kyle Pearce, Lee Gaguano, Kevin Stewart, Vic Baulton, Roger Adamson, Chris Lloyd, Shakeel Hunniford, David Behennah, Marc Valentine, Rubin Richard, Gary Hardy Brown, Timothy Williams, Sylvester Allan, Colin Melbourne, Jonathan Witch, Chuck Mardi, Lyndon Comerosatch, Anthony Edward, Paul Shepherd, Deki Okom, Mano Sol, Ade Glanville, David Chandler, Peter Stephens, Alistair Wood, Vernon Pearce, Simon Campbell, Stuart Budd, Gideon Turner, Mark Sawyers, Eric McCarthy, Jeremy Radall, Miles Chambers.

Child Extras: (Dentist's surgery) Calum Small, Lucy Pelligrini, Kylie Steele, Tia Steele, Richard Cox, Michelle Cox. (On bus) Angie Nicholas and Martin Nicholas.

'Fatal Extraction'

PRODUCTION TEAM

Written by John Sullivan
Title music arranged and conducted by Ronnie Hazlehurst composed and sung by John Sullivan

Additional Music:	Clever Music
Make-up Designer:	Christine Greenwood
Costume Designer:	Robin Stubbs
Properties Buyer:	Graham Bishop
Visual Effects Designer:	Andy Lazell
Casting Adviser:	Judy Loe
Film Cameraman:	John Rhodes
Film Sound:	Michael Spencer
Film Editor:	John Jarvis
Camera Supervisor:	Gerry Tivers
Studio Lighting Director:	Graham Rimmington
Studio Sound:	Laurie Taylor
Resources Coordinator:	Michael Langley-Evans

Videotape Editor:	Chris Wadsworth
Production Assistant:	Tracey Gillham
Location Manager:	Jonathan Paul Llewellyn
Stunt Coordinator:	Andy Bradford
Grip:	James Grimes
Gaffer:	Peter Robinson
Dubbing Mixer:	Michael Narduzzo
Dubbing Editor:	Simon Price
Assistant Floor Managers:	Ali Bryer Carron and Tania Normand
Vision Mixer:	Heather Gilder
Production Manager:	Johanna Kennedy
Production Secretary:	Simon Sharrod
Designer:	Donal Woods
Art Director:	Charmian Adams
Executive Producer:	John Sullivan
Directed by Tony Dow	
Produced by Gareth Gwenlan	

Raquel and Del are experiencing marriage problems: Del never seems to be home anymore and is drinking a lot down The 121 Club, a casino owned by Ronnie Nelson. Raquel is getting worried that Del, the family man, has disappeared forever and he's returned to his old ways. Meanwhile, Cassandra and Rodney are, at long last, more settled in their lives and are even trying for a baby. But it's taking its toll on Rodney, especially when he starts getting calls from Cassandra whilst he's at work, asking him to get home quick because her temperature is right for conceiving!

Worried about his brother's behaviour, Rodney confronts Del, who explains that he's going along to the casino because he's negotiating a deal with the owner, but doesn't want to tell Raquel until it's finalised. The latest in Del's long list of exclusive offers will hopefully be Russian ex-military camcorders, which he later discovers won't exactly fit in your back pocket; to top it all, he also finds out that

'Fatal Extraction'

you need to buy a Russian VCR if you want to view any of the tapes.

Eventually Raquel reaches the end of her tether and leaves Del for the comfort of Rodney and Cassandra's flat. Del is stunned at Raquel's departure but is oblivious to his faults. To prove to himself that he's still got the ability to pull, he asks a dental receptionist, Beverley, out for a date when he reluctantly visits the dentist to have an aching tooth removed. However, before they meet, Del sees the error of his ways and rings Beverley to cancel their appointment.

But it's some time later that Del gives in and contacts Raquel, claiming he's a changed man and that he wants her back. When they agree to resume their relationship, Del celebrates by getting drunk, and then incites a riot on the estate on his return from the pub by singing at the top of his voice, and waking all the neighbours in the process. Always the intrepid businessman, he uses the opportunity to flog his supply of ski visors to both the rioters and the police.

Although Raquel is back in Del's life, all is not well because wherever he goes he spots Beverley and he starts to believe that she's stalking him. She even arrives on his doorstep, saying that she wants to buy Damien's highchair, which was advertised in the local shop. Del really begins to worry when Boycie recognises her from a visit he made some

time back to a psychiatric ward! Unable to stand anymore, Del storms to her place of work and throws accusations all over the place, but she mirrors his actions and claims she'll go to court if he continues to pester her.

Christmas Day finally arrives and just when it seems as if harmony has been restored in the Trotter household, Raquel makes the mistake of letting Rodney try out her present for Del: an answerphone with an unexpected message on it!

Fatty Thumb, The

(See 'Sid's Café')

Fawcett, Beccy

Assistant floor manager on three episodes: 'Heroes and Villains', 'Modern Men' and 'Time On Our Hands'

Felton, Mike

Studio sound supervisor on seven episodes: S1 and 'Christmas Crackers'

Born in the Shropshire town of Newport, Mike joined the BBC in 1962 as a technical operator in radio at Bush House. He transferred to television in 1964 and was promoted to sound supervisor in 1980, since when he's worked on a myriad of shows, including *The Val Doonican Show*, *Wogan* and *Open All Hours*. Mike, who's currently clocked up 39 years' service, still works for the Beeb.

Female passenger

(For 'Female passenger' in 'To Hull and Back', see 'Smuggler')

Female tannoy announcer

Only heard in 'To Hull and Back', she announces the arrival of British Airways flight 417 from Amsterdam.

Ferdinand, Lorence

Role: Mr Hussein
Appeared in 'To Hull and Back'

Lorence, who also appeared in other episodes in non-speaking roles, was born in South Africa. He initially trained as a ballet dancer and worked in that role before opting to travel the world. Settling in the UK, he continued his ballet career and was soon offered work. His credits include an appearance in the big screen version of *Oliver!*

Gradually he started concentrating on acting and stunt work. On the small screen he's appeared in a host of shows, such as *Doctor Who* and *Danger Man*. On the big screen, meanwhile, he worked on many of the Bond movies, including *Dr No*. Lorence has also worked in the theatre.

Ferriday, Chris

Properties buyer on 16 episodes: S1; 'Christmas Crackers', S4 and 'Miami Twice' (Parts 1 & 2)

MEMORIES OF 'MIAMI TWICE'

★ ★ ★ ★ ★ ★

'The remit for a properties buyer is to provide everything that's seen in front of the camera with the exception of costumes, the four walls and ceiling. It could be anything from a light switch to an elephant, the flight deck of a spaceship to the interior of a Georgian drawing room.

'We would take an empty shop and make it into a travel agents one day, repaint it overnight, fill it with props and next morning it could be a private room in a hospital. As a prop buyer, I had two customers: the director, whose requirements were a certain amount of props needed to complete the action – we called these action props. A list was drawn up by the assistant floor manager breaking down the script and identifying what was required. My other customer was the designer, who usually had the bigger list, detailing everything he needed to create the sets. So I would end up with an action list and a dressing list.

'Most of the time I would take the designer with me to the prop houses and between us would select furniture and the dressing items for the sets. Usually the action props are the choice of the prop buyer, although sometimes I'd discuss requirements with the director and, even, the artist.

'When Only Fools started, I couldn't cover the programme because we were short of prop buyers, so I decided to do the job myself. At that time, it was a new, as yet untitled, comedy series; another reason I thought I'd better do it is because in the pipeline were some serious dramas, shows which needed the expertise of more experienced staff. Therefore, I opted for the easier option, which turned out to be Only Fools.

'As we got nearer and nearer to production, I still hadn't got a script so I rang the production office and begged them to let me have a look at one. Because it was still being worked on, they were in short supply, but I borrowed their only copy for a while and sat down to read it. Ideally, I like to see scripts about three weeks before we start filming it because of the time it takes to find items. Usually after completing the location scenes, which can take anything up to three weeks normally, there's a gap, perhaps of a week or two, depending on how tight the scheduling is, before we go into the studio; after that there's usually a weekly turnover as each of the episodes are completed.

'The BBC usually hired in most of their props, which is why a lot of prop companies thrived. Working on Only Fools provided quite a challenge for me, mainly because I was inexperienced as a buyer, but being a contemporary show made life a little easier.

'When it came to obtaining the Reliant van, I turned to a vehicle agent, a company called Action Cars. We didn't want a van which was falling apart, nor did we want one which looked too new. Even the sign-writing had to look right: Del and Rodney wouldn't have done it themselves, they would have got a friend, someone who owed them a favour but was a little drunk, to do it. We didn't want scruffy, nasty, ridiculous sign-writing, we wanted writing which was obviously done by a professional but completed in a bit of a hurry, or while the guy was under the influence of gin.

'Action Cars found the first vehicle we used; I think it was green when they first got it so they sprayed it yellow, had it signed to my spec – the required wording was in the script, of course – and it was delivered on the first morning of location filming. Unfortunately it was looking pristine and freshly sprayed, so I got some sandpaper and an aerosol can and just broke the corners a bit, making it look as if it had been on the streets for a few years.

'The smoke coming from the van was controlled by the visual effects department. They fitted an electric windscreen washer bottle with its motor under the bonnet and filled it with cooking oil. A little tube went back to a tiny inlet valve drilled into the inlet manifold, which David Jason or Nick Lyndhurst would operate whenever they wanted the smoke effect. When we first started, explosive charges were also fitted to the exhaust and control detonated, but it was a long-winded affair and meant taking a visual effects operator with us on location every time we needed to film the van, costing the programme money.

'During the time I worked on the show, Action Cars supplied over three vans because the chassis used to give out and they weren't worth repairing. But they were very reliable and nippy. The BBC rarely bought a vehicle so Action Cars owned the Reliants and I just paid a daily rental whenever we needed it.

'When it came to buying props for the Trotters' flat, we were able to change items from week to week because if Del could sell anything, he would, which meant there was a high turnover of items in the place. That's why we made a point of changing the dining table and chairs from time to time; the only things which remained constant were usually the curtains and a pot which sat on top of the television in which Del kept his cigars. I bought that item from a gift shop in Acton, while the cigarette lighter in the shape of a pistol was bought in a shop in Turnham Green.

'I entered the unknown by working on Only Fools but thoroughly enjoyed it and was more than happy to be allocated Series 4. That's not just because of the success, although everybody likes working on a successful programme, but working with people like David and Nick was great fun. It was a huge happy family and I'm sure my colleagues echo that. **CHRIS FERRIDAY –Properties buyer**

Chris, who was born in London in 1951, always wanted to be a journalist. He joined the BBC in 1970, working in the film department for a few months, but regarded the job as a stop-gap until pursuing the career he really wanted. By the time Chris left the Corporation in 1992, he'd clocked up over 22 years' service.

He moved to a clerical role in the props department in 1975, allocating staff to programmes, before accepting a year's attachment (1977–78) to become a prop buyer. He returned to his allocating role until a dearth of staff saw him switch back to buying, where he remained for the rest of his career, by which time he'd worked on a multitude of productions, including 'Allo 'Allo!, Are You Being Served?, Tenko, Lovejoy, The House of Eliott and Campion.

Chris accepted voluntary redundancy in 1992 and moved to North Devon with his wife, ex-production manager, Clare Graham. He now works for the 'Doctor on Call' service and is deputy station officer with the local coastguard.

Finch, Bobby

Not seen in the sitcom, Bobby Finch is mentioned by Del in 'The Second Time Around'. He married Del's ex-fiancée, Pauline Harris, but later died and is buried in a cemetery in Blackshaw Road. Del is led to believe that his death has become the subject of a police investigation, the results of which establish that he died of food poisoning, all of which is untrue.

First woman

Played by Lyn Langridge
The middle aged woman – who's seen in 'Stage Fright' – rushes after Tony Angelino in The Starlight Rooms, requesting his autograph.

Fisher, Mike

Played by Kenneth MacDonald
Mike – an amiable, easy-going kind of chap – takes over as landlord of The Nag's Head in the episode, 'Who's a Pretty Boy?'. With his friendly face and mild manner, he's quickly accepted by the locals; but his unassuming approach to life is frequently exploited by Del, who can always rely on good old Mike to fork out on whatever useless item he's currently trying to fool the public into buying.

Other than the string of barmaids he employs at the pub, Mike runs the hostelry on his own, having split from his wife some years ago. He was 18 when he met his wife, and sums up his broken marriage by saying 'I had 18 blissfully happy years – then I met her!' Mike had just come home from a three-month stint working as a cocktail waiter on a cruise ship when his wife announced she was two months pregnant. Although we never learn who the father was, it proved to be the final straw as far as Mike was concerned and he packed his bags and left.

Enjoying his bachelor days once again, Mike's smiling face helps create the jovial atmosphere in The Nag's Head, so it's a shock to all the regulars when he's imprisoned for embezzlement. Intent on making a fast buck, he invests his life savings, re-mortgages the pub and puts all the money into the Central American money markets. When the markets crash and Mike loses everything, he's accused by the Fraud Squad of trying to recoup his losses by embezzling money from the brewery. Mike eventually admits to his wrongdoing and is given a custodial sentence, with Sid taking over the helm at The Nag's Head in his absence.

Fleeshman, David

Role: Gas rigger
Appeared in 'To Hull and Back'

David, who's married to *Brookside* actress Sue Jenkins, was born in Glasgow in 1952 but educated in Birmingham. He made his professional debut at Birmingham's repertory theatre in 1973, which launched him into a busy career that has included over 200 stage productions all over the UK, including Malvolio in *Twelfth Night*, Demetrius and Bottom in *A Midsummer Night's Dream* and Rosencrantz in *Rosencrantz and Guildenstern are Dead*.

Equally busy on television, he's played estate agent Peter Haines and Superintendent Jevons in *Coronation Street*, Barry Hill in *Emmerdale Farm*, Derek in *Boys from the Blackstuff*, Frank Taylor in *Truckers*, David Hurst in *Brookside*, Soames in *EastEnders*, Thomas Cromwell in *The Six Wives of Henry VIII* and many more.

Fletcher, Mandie

Assistant floor manager on six episodes: S1. Director on four episodes: S5, episodes 1–4

Mandie was born in Adelaide, South Australia, but came to the UK as a child and was educated in Guildford. Always interested in joining the theatre, she became an assistant stage manager at Exeter's Northcott Theatre upon leaving school, before swapping the stage for television at the age of 24.

At the BBC she was an assistant floor manager for a year, working on shows such as *Butterflies* and *Not the Nine O'Clock News*, before being promoted through the ranks, finally reaching the post of director. *Butterflies*, *Brush Strokes*, *The Fainthearted Feminist* and two series of *Blackadder* are among the shows she's directed.

Mandie left the Beeb in the late 1980s and has worked freelance ever since. For six years she ran her own company producing and directing commercials for companies like Nescafé, Flora and John Smith's Bitter. Nowadays, as well as directing films and commercials she runs an organic farm in Dorset.

Fletcher, Steve

Role: Marcus
Appeared in S2, episode 4

Steve's acting career has seen him appear in a range of television roles, such as a a pageboy in the miniseries *Prince Regent*, a youth in a 1979 episode of *Minder*, Mike Ryan in *Going Out*, Mark in *The Best Years of Our Lives*, Dawes in *Contact*, a punk in a 1985 episode of *Dempsey and Makepeace*, Peter in *Survivors* and Smithy in *Soldier, Soldier*. He's also appeared in a handful of films.

Flower, Gilly

Role: Old lady (No 1)
Appeared in S3, episode 1

London-born Gilly Flower is probably best known for playing the doddery Miss Tibbs in *Fawlty Towers*. She claimed she became an actress accidentally at the age of 12, playing a spirit in a Hampstead Theatre Club's production of *Through the Crack*.

At one point, she gave up the profession and

worked in personnel for six years, but returned to a thespian's life and started clocking up appearances on stage and screen, including episodes of *Steptoe and Son*, *The Fall and Rise of Reginald Perrin*, *Terry and June*, *Juliet Bravo* and 1987's *Hello, Mum*. She retired from the industry in 1991.

Flowers, Alfie

Not seen in the sitcom, Alfie sells some broken lawnmower engines to Del in 'Healthy Competition'. Del later sells the equipment at auction, and the mugs who part with their cash are Rodney and his new business partner, Mickey Pearce.

Foot, Jilli

Role: English girl (Wendy)
Appeared in S2, episode 6

On stage, Jilli has worked around the country in productions such as *Orphea, Leave Him to Heaven, Never Say No, The Mating Game* and *Run For Your Wife*. On television, meanwhile, she appeared regularly on *The Kenny Everett Television Show* and *The Russ Abbot Show*, as well as playing Helga Weir in *The Standard*, Doctor Harper in *Bugs*, Sheila Bennett in *The Jump* and Susan Hall in *Casualty*.

Fortune, Steve

Role: Gary
Appeared in S6, episode 3

Born in 1958, Steve worked as a shoe shop manager and a used-car salesman before deciding to try his luck in the entertainment world. He began his career as a dancer before gradually moving into singing and acting. His first job as a dancer saw him working in cabaret shows in Europe and the Middle East, but his major break came in the West

End show *Underneath the Arches*, understudying the leading role of Chesney Allen, and appearing on several occasions.

He then worked all over the UK in repertory and provincial theatres, mainly in musicals like *Annie, The Music Man* and *Pirates of Penzance*. Steve still works in the theatre. In recent years he's been seen in *Jesus Christ Superstar* at the Lyceum, and *Noises Off* at the Piccadilly Theatre.

MEMORIES OF PLAYING GARY

★ ★ ★ ★ ★ ★

'**A**bout a year before I appeared in *Only Fools and Horses* I was given an audition for a new sitcom called *The River*, which was to star David Essex; I was up to play the part of his best friend. The director was Susie Belbin, one of the BBC's top comedy directors, who'd also directed *Only Fools*.

'The first audition was great, and Susie and I got on very well, but she was concerned that I was a bit young, being only about 28 whereas David was around 40 at the time. However, she called me in again and asked me to read for most of the other episodes of *The River*. At the audition was Tony Dow, who'd worked with Susie as a production manager. Needless to say, the job didn't work out, but about a year later I happened to write a letter to Tony Dow having seen that he was directing *Only Fools and Horses*. He recognised my face and name, and offered me the role of Gary in "Chain Gang". The job involved only two days' filming and a reasonably modest BBC fee – although the repeat fees and video fees have turned it into one of the best paid two days I've ever worked in my life!' **STEVE FORTUNE**

On television, he's been offered a few small parts, beginning with the role of a thug in *Casualty*, Neil in *Crime Ltd*, a biker in *Nelson's Column* and Hancock in *The Jump*.

Foster, Bryony

Set decorator on two episodes: 'Miami Twice' (Parts 1 & 2)

Prior to becoming a set decorator, Bryony was a prop buyer, working on films – such as 1980's *Bad Timing* – and television. Her credits as a set decorator include the 1986 television production *Sword of Gideon*, and the 2000 film *Shanghai Noon*.

Fox, Sandra

Played by Carol Cleveland

The American reporter covers the story of the weeping statue in 'The Miracle of Peckham'.

Fox, Tubby

Not seen in the sitcom, Tubby Fox is mentioned by Albert in 'The Chance of a Lunchtime'. Albert claims that whilst they were docked at Valletta, *en route* to Greece, Fox (the Chief Communications Officer) was charged after the Captain caught him in the radio room with a bottle of gin and a Maltese girl. Court martial proceedings started but were never followed through. Fox remained in the service until he died in Palermo Harbour after dropping a depth charge in nine feet of water.

Francis, Marcus

Role: Charlie
Appeared in S4, episode 4

Marcus started acting early in his life and in 1977 played the lead role in *Graham's Gang*, having previously appeared as Sean Tinnersley in *Going Out*.

Francisco

Played by Robert Escobar

In 'Miami Twice', Francisco is a waiter at a night-club visited by Del and Rodney. Spotting Del's likeness to a top bod in the local Mafia, he refrains from demanding the Trotters leave the members-only club.

Frank

Played by Philip Blaine

Frank is Rodney and Cassandra's neighbour. He's seen in 'Rodney Come Home', appearing at his door to remind Del and Rodney, whose raised voices have woken him up, that it's gone midnight.

Frazer, Mr

Played by James Woolley

Mr Frazer is the barrister representing the Trotters in court during the hearing of Albert's compensation claim in 'Hole in One'.

Fred Tomlinson Singers, The

Role: Carol singers

Appeared in 'Diamonds are for Heather'

Born in Rawtenstall in 1927, Fred Tomlinson was a professional singer who formed his own company, The Fred Tomlinson Singers, supplying singers to stage and TV productions, as well as writing music for other performers to sing.

Fred followed in his brothers' footsteps and became a chorister at Manchester Cathedral just before the war, where he learnt to read music and sing. When war broke out he was evacuated to Thornton, near Blackpool, for a year, before being seconded to King's College, Cambridge, as a chorister for two years.

When the war ended, it took a while before Fred began his singing career, partly because he had to complete his national service in the army, which involved teaching apprentices mathematics and two years in the Far East. Returning to civvy street, he was finally given a break when he joined the famous Mitchell Singers, singing on various radio and television productions.

Eventually Fred decided to branch out on his own, and he arranged, organised and wrote songs for various artists, and was even involved in the famous lumberjack song in *Monty Python*. He also worked on *The Two Ronnies* for many years before retiring from the business at the age of 72.

Freddy the Frog

(See 'Robdal, Freddy')

French girl

(See 'Jackie')

'Friday the 14th'

Original transmission: Thursday 24 November 1983, 8.30 pm

Production date: Sunday 16 October 1983

Original viewing figures: 9.7 million

Duration: 30 minutes

First repeat: Monday 30 July 1984, 8.00 pm

Subsequent repeats: 14/9/91, 26/2/95, 5/6/98, 7/4/00

CAST

Del Trotter	David Jason
Rodney Trotter	Nicholas Lyndhurst
Grandad Trotter	Lennard Pearce
Policeman on moorland road	Ray Mort
Gamekeeper (Tom Witton)	Bill Ward
Robson (Chief of Security) and Madman	Christopher Malcolm
Police sergeant	Michael Stainton
Old rustic yokel	Michael Bilton (edited out before transmission)
Walk-ons:	(Police constables at country police station) James Harvey and David Coles

PRODUCTION TEAM

Written by John Sullivan

Title music arranged and conducted by Ronnie Hazlehurst composed and sung by John Sullivan

Audience Warm-up:	Bobby Bragg
Make-up Designer:	Denise Baron
Costume Designer:	Dinah Collin
Properties Buyer:	Penny Rollinson
Film Cameraman:	Ian Hilton
Film Sound:	Clive Derbyshire
Film Editor:	Mike Jackson
Camera Supervisor:	Ron Peverall
Studio Lighting Director:	Don Babbage
Studio Sound:	Dave Thompson
Technical Coordinator:	Chris Watts
Videotape Editor:	Mike Taylor
Production Assistant:	Penny Thompson
Assistant Floor Manager:	Tony Dow
Graphic Designer:	Mic Rolph
Vision Mixer:	Angela Beveridge
Production Manager:	Andy Smith
Designer:	Antony Thorpe

Produced and directed by Ray Butt

Boycie's lent the Trotters his cottage in Cornwall, which is situated in woodland, not far from one of England's finest salmon rivers. Planning a weekend's fishing, there's more to the trip than simply a touch of relaxation: as usual, there's a financial reason for travelling all the way from Peckham to Tregower, Cornwall. Over dinner at Mario's fish restaurant, the proprietor offers Del and Boycie £10 for every salmon they supply; agreeing to split the money fifty-fifty, Boycie provides the accommodation and Del agrees to catch the fish.

En route to the cottage the Trotters are stopped by police, who are searching for an escapee from the

---

★ ★ ★ CUT SCENE! CUT SCENE! ★ ★ ★

CUT FROM 'FRIDAY THE 14TH'

DAY. A COUNTRY PUB/ VILLAGE GREEN

THIS IS ONE OF THOSE IDYLLIC SCENES STRAIGHT OFF A POSTCARD. OUTSIDE THE OLD PUB WE HAVE A COUPLE OF TABLES AND CHAIRS, THE VAN IS PARKED CLOSE BY. AT ONE OF THE TABLES WE HAVE AN OLD RUSTIC TYPE PUFFING ON A PIPE. AT THE OTHER TABLE SIT DEL AND GRANDAD. DEL IS STILL WEARING HIS CAMEL-HAIR COAT, ETC.

DEL (LIGHTING A CIGAR) This is what it's all about annit, Grandad, eh? This is yer real England!

GRANDAD It's lovely annit? And it's so clean an' all!

DEL And I'll tell you what, shall I? Because the people out here have respect for their environment! (HE THROWS HIS EMPTY CIGAR PACKET AWAY) Men went away in the war and fought and died for this!

GRANDAD I know – I almost did!

DEL You almost died?

GRANDAD No, I almost went away and fought for it!

DEL Oh yeah... I love this life! This is what nature intended. Freshly baked bread, beer from the wood and honest food straight from God's good earth!

RODNEY EXITS FROM PUB CARRYING A TRAY OF DRINKS (PINTS)

ROD (TO DEL) They've never heard of a pina colada and they don't do pizzas!

DEL Don't do pizzas? Stone me – what sort of dead and alive hole is this?

ROD (THINKING THIS MAY OFFEND THE YOKEL) Sshh!...

(TO THE YOKEL) Morning.

YOKEL (STARING OFF INTO DISTANCE) Af'rnoon!

ROD (CHECKS HIS WATCH, TAPS IT) This deep-sea diver's watch still ain't working right!

DEL Leave off, Rodney. (INDICATES YOKEL) He's tryna tell the time by the sun!

ROD But you can tell the time by the sun!

GRANDAD But it's hardly bloody TIM is it!

DEL He's right an all! (TO YOKEL) Lovely weather for a bit of sheep-shearing, eh?

YOKEL Oh arr, fine weather! Soon be turning though!

DEL Will it?

YOKEL You mark my words, sir, before the night is out there'll be a storm the likes of which you've never seen before! There'll be thunder that'll wake the dead from their sleep. Rain and flooding and a wind a'howling so fierce you'd think it came from the mouth of Satan himself!

DEL AND ROD LOOK AT EACH OTHER AND REACT.

GRANDAD Still, it'll be good for the flowers, won't it?

DEL GIVES HIM A DAMNING LOOK.

ROD How do you country people know these things? Is it because the cows are all laying down, or can you tell by the clouds?

YOKEL (TURNS TO FACE RODNEY, WE SEE HE HAS AN EARPIECE WHICH IS CONNECTED TO A RADIO) No, I just heard the forecast on Radio 4!

ROD REACTS.

DEL Come on, drink up!

'The Frog's Legacy'

local institute for the criminally insane. It's ten years to the day since he committed his abhorrent crime, and he's at large once more. While Rodney and Grandad think they should turn around and head home, Del's common sense is blurred by the thought of all those tenners he'd like to get his hands on.

Their first night in the cottage is eventful, with Rodney claiming he heard someone in the bushes upon their arrival, and a face staring through the window – concerns that are mocked by his brother, until there's a knock on the door. The visitor of the night claims to be chief of security at the nearby institute, but turns out to be none other than the mad axe murderer himself.

'Frog's Legacy, The'

(Christmas Special 1987)

Original transmission: Friday 25 December 1987, 6.25 pm

Production date: Wednesday 9 December 1987

Original viewing figures: 14.5 million

Duration: 60 minutes

First repeat: Tuesday 28 June 1988, 9.30 pm

Subsequent repeats: 9/12/90, 10/3/02

CAST

Del Trotter	David Jason
Rodney Trotter	Nicholas Lyndhurst
Uncle Albert	Buster Merryfield
Boycie	John Challis
Trigger	Roger Lloyd Pack
Mr Jahan	Adam Hussein
Vicar	Angus Mackay
Auntie Renee	Joan Sims
Mike	Kenneth MacDonald
Marlene	Sue Holderness
Andy	Mark Colleano
Lisa	Gerry Cowper
Man in market	Duncan Faber
Woman in market	Angela Moran
Walk-ons:	(Pub customers) Denise Dubarry,

Faylin Minell, Tony Amechi, Veronique Chomilo-Edwards, Ulrick Brown, George Canning, Michelle Grand, Gail Abbott, Jazzi Northover, Lawrence Williamson, Peggy Bourne, Blanche Coleman, Ian Bodenham, Alan James, Lee Ryan, Willy Bowman, Jack Crosbie, Albert Welch, John R. Darling, Robin Easther, Charu Bala Chokshi, Ranjot Nakara. (Wedding guests) Yvonne Collier, Trudy Miller, John Alder, Kevin Deakin, Johnny Golde, Mike Charles, Derek Raymond, Andy White, Ned Potts, Arthur Hore, Eddie Tomasso, Steve Palmer, Aubrey Lewin, Jonathan Grey, Vince Rayner, Pearl Hawkes, Beryl Nesbitt, Carol Houghton, Daphne Self, Jean Tomasso, Jane Syder, Valerie Gale, Sue Vasey, Amanda Rickett and Susan Lynch. (Mourners) Norman Fisher, Paul Delaney, Kristina Helga, Kelly Condell, Gwennie Lee and Cyril Crook. (Market crowd) John Gordon-Ash, Teresa Ash, Tom Beresford, Rex Lear, Jean Lear, Lucinda Bathe, Stephanie Miller, Merlin Miller, Wendy Shepherd, Andrew Fox, Sharon Carol, Howard Swinson, Joyce Swinson, Joanna Craven, Marjorie Butters, Terry Treloar, Patricia Marshall, Sue Franklin, Johnny Burslem, Roy Bradley, Patsy Urqhurt, Beverley Smith, Adrian Hutson, Colin Goldring, Tony Dennes, John D. Vincent, Yvonne Marsh, Alison Warden, Diana Rayner and Suzanne Rayner. (Driver of the hearse) Saul Hunnaball.

PRODUCTION TEAM

Written by John Sullivan

Title music arranged and conducted by Ronnie Hazlehurst composed and sung by John Sullivan

Audience Warm-up:	Bobby Bragg
Make-up Designer:	Ann Ailes-Stevenson
Costume Designer:	Robin Stubbs
	and Linda Haysman
Properties Buyer:	Hilary Nash
Film Cameraman:	Rex Maidment
Film Sound:	Michael Spencer
Film Editor:	John Jarvis
Camera Supervisor:	Ken Major
Studio Lighting Director:	Don Babbage
Studio Sound:	Dave Thompson
Technical Coordinator:	Reg Poulter
Videotape Editor:	Ed Wooden
Production Assistant:	Jan Willson
Assistant Floor Manager:	Sue Bishop
Graphic Designer:	Andrew Smee
Vision Mixer:	Heather Gilder
Production Managers:	Sue Longstaff
	and Lesley Bywater
Production Secretary:	Linda O'Connell
Designer:	Paul Trerise
Produced and directed by Ray Butt	

Things aren't going too well for the Trotters with Del's RAJAH computers causing nothing but complaints. Rodney tries out his new job as chief mourner for a local funeral directors, while Albert steps in to help Del by play-acting a miracle cure for the market crowds in an attempt to help sell the latest in body massagers – but his hammy performance is far from convincing.

Their fortunes, however, could be on the way up when they attend the wedding of Trigger's niece, Lisa, and bump into an old friend: Trigger's Aunt Renee, who tells Del the story of Freddy the Frog. Freddy was a bank robber and close friend of the Trotters' mother, and it seems he died leaving everything to her, including the missing gold bullion from his biggest job. Del goes on a crusade to find the gold and make himself a millionaire, while Rodney tries working out the connection between his mother, Freddy and a son who, by now, would be in his mid-twenties!

The crew get ready for another shoot during 'The Frog's Legacy'.

A local hearse was hired for the funeral scenes in 'The Frogs' Legacy'.

MEMORIES OF 'THE FROG'S LEGACY'

★ ★ ★ ★ ★ ★

'I remember with some disbelief an assistant buyer knocking on my door and showing interest in my pale blue, black top, Ford Cortina Mark II, with the registration number TMJ 873R. He said he wanted to take a photo of the car and send it to the BBC, along with a few others, because they were recording an episode of *Only Fools and Horses* ('The Frog's Legacy') in the area and needed some vehicles. If it was selected, he wondered if I would be able to get time off work and drive it to Ipswich in time for filming?

'To cut a long story short, the BBC did use my car and I was offered £200 for its use. I was told where to be on the dates for filming and recall being at a church car park very, very early on the first day of recording. I made contact with a lady from the BBC and she ticked me (well, the car, really!) off her list. For the days I was involved the weather wasn't too kind – a lot of showers – which made for difficult filming, especially when puddles had to be swept away between shots for continuity.

'On the second morning the filming started early but was stopped for rain once again. During that short stoppage the local milkman delivered milk to the doorsteps and somebody had to tap on all the doors to ask the residents to take their milk in because the bottles weren't in the previous shots.

'My Cortina was required for the funeral procession which Rodney led in his big, shiny top hat. The car had to break down in the storyline to embarrass Boycie, who'd sold the vehicle. I thought it was only the car they wanted until the assistant buyer called at my home and rushed my best suit to me as I was required to ride in the chief mourners' funeral car, next to the driver, and there was a chance that I might be caught on camera, hence the suit!

'One thing that sticks in my mind was the excellent food on location. It was a mobile wagon with two young ladies serving up drinks and meals to a very high standard. It was all served up in the car park alongside the church hall, just off Rectory Road.

'My fantasy two days were soon over and at the end of the second day I was thanked and told that I was no longer required. A few weeks later, my family, friends and workmates were eagerly watching the Christmas Special, but there wasn't one glimpse of me and only a few seconds of my car breaking down. But it was well worth it just for knowing I had done my very small bit for *Only Fools and Horses*.'

CHRIS BARKER

'From Prussia with Love'

Original transmission: Sunday 31 August 1986, 8.35 pm

Production date: Sunday 15 June 1986

Original viewing figures: 12.1 million

Duration: 30 minutes

First repeat: Thursday 10 September 1987, 8.30 pm

Subsequent repeats: 25/6/89, 19/12/97, 8/11/00

CAST

Del Trotter	David Jason
Rodney Trotter	Nicholas Lyndhurst
Uncle Albert	Buster Merryfield
Boycie	John Challis
Marlene	Sue Holderness
Mike	Kenneth MacDonald
Anna the German	Erika Hoffman
Maureen	Nula Conwell
Baby	Michael Peters
Walk-ons:	Anthea Ferrell and Felicity Lee

PRODUCTION TEAM

Written by John Sullivan

Title music arranged and conducted by Ronnie Hazlehurst composed and sung by John Sullivan

Audience Warm-up:	Felix Bowness
Make-up Designer:	Elaine Smith
Costume Designer:	Robin Stubbs
Properties Buyer:	Maura Laverty
Film Cameraman:	Chris Seager
Film Sound:	Dave Brabants
Film Editor:	John Jarvis
Camera Supervisor:	Ken Major
Studio Lighting Director:	Henry Barber
Studio Sound:	Anthony Philpot
Technical Coordinator:	Nick Moore
Videotape Editor:	Chris Wadsworth
Production Assistants:	Rowena Painter and Alexandra Todd
Assistant Floor Manager:	Adrian Pegg
Graphic Designer:	Andrew Smee
Vision Mixer:	Heather Gilder
Production Manager:	Sue Longstaff
Designer:	Mark Sevant

Directed by Mandie Fletcher

Produced by Ray Butt

When Rodney arrives home with a homeless 19-year-old student in tow, Del isn't too pleased, especially as Anna – a language student from Germany, who's been thrown out by the family who were employing her as an au-pair - is pregnant. But Del soon has a change of heart when he realises that Anna's impending delivery could provide the perfect opportunity for a little business.

With the German student upset and indicating she wants to put the baby up for adoption when it's born, and Marlene and Boycie desperate for a baby, Del spots the ideal situation for making everyone happy – and earning three grand in the process; but his plan soon backfires.

'From Prussia with Love'

'I remember my father, Richard Funnell, met John Sullivan once and as they talked and reminisced about their childhoods in South London, they remembered orange-flavoured frozen drinks called Jubberlies, with the catchphrase "lovely jubberly". Of course, the saying turned up in *Only Fools and Horses* and I've always wondered if there was any connection.

'Another memory concerning that catchphrase involves a trip I made to Egypt earlier this year. I was visiting the Valley of the Kings when a local man, dressed in traditional costume, asked which country I was from. When I told him England, he gave me the thumbs up and started jumping up and down shouting, "lovely jubbly". It just shows how far the fame of the Trotters has travelled!' **DAWN FUNNELL**

Funnell, Dawn

Role: Helen
Appeared in 'The Jolly Boys' Outing'

Dawn, who was born in the Surrey town of Carshalton in 1966, trained at the Italia Conti Academy of Theatre Arts before making her professional debut as a 'spider person' in a 1980 episode of *The Kenny Everett Video Show*. The early part of her career was spent in children's theatre, although she also appeared in the movie *The Diary of a Serial Killer*, and made the occasional appearance on the small screen. But the lion's share of her time was spent on the stage, with credits ranging from playing Mei Ling in *Demon of Guandong* to Elie in *The Perfect Murder*.

Nowadays, Dawn – who's also completed a course in teacher training – works for a theatre company (Theatre Exchange) in Caterham, Surrey. She's also a part-time drama teacher, where her responsibilites include running a youth theatre in Caterham.

Funny Side of Christmas, The: Christmas Trees

(Christmas Special 1982)
Original transmission: Monday 27 December 1982, 8.05 pm
Original viewing figures: 7.2 million
Duration: 8 minutes
First repeat: Monday 22 August 1983, 6.50 pm

CAST
Del Trotter . . . . .David Jason
Rodney Trotter . . . . .Nicholas Lyndhurst
Grandad Trotter . . . . .Lennard Pearce
Vicar . . . . .John Pennington
Sid . . . . .Roy Heather
Walk-ons: . . . .(Shoppers in market) Chris Breeze, Doris Littlewood, Joan Beveridge, Peter Finn, Jerry Judge and Ann Priestley.

Del's not having much luck trying to flog telescopic Christmas trees, even though he's only charging six quid, inclusive of lights, bangles, beads and baubles. As he says, they're going down 'about as well as Union Jacks in Buenos Aires'. The trouble is, he has 149 to get rid off.

It's been a hard day's trading, so the Trotter boys and Grandad pop down for a quick cuppa to Sid's burger van, which is parked near a church. It's then that Del has a brainwave, and without explaining his ulterior motive, tells his brother the sad tale of how a shortage of money has meant the market traders are unable to donate a Christmas tree to the local church, something they've been doing for years. When he adds that it's the orphans he feels sorry for, especially as they won't be able to hold their annual open-air carol service, Rodney's almost reaching for his hankie.

Leaving his brother to mull the matter over, Del gives Grandad a lift home, leaving Rodney in charge of the trees. Wanting to bring cheer to the little orphans' lives, Rodney gives one of the trees to the Vicar, only to discover that Del's tale of woe is a pack a lies, and a crafty marketing scheme so that he can claim the trees are recommended by the Church of England.

Futafax Machines

Boasting the slogan, 'Futafax. The fax machine of tomorrow – today', these machines cause Del nothing but headaches. He ends up with lots of rejected stock in 'The Class of '62', but Mike – down at The Nag's Head – is fool enough to buy one.

Gamekeeper

(See 'Witton, Tom')

Gandhi Avenue

Mentioned by Del in 'Fatal Extraction', Gandhi Avenue is where a Mr Owens used to have his dental surgery. Discussing the dentist reveals just how many years have passed since Del last visited a dentist because Owens died in 1977, the night of the Queen's Silver Jubilee.

Garcia, Jane

Production assistant on one episode: 'Christmas Crackers'

Gardener, Caroline

Production assistant on four episodes: 'Heroes and Villains', 'Modern Men', 'Time On Our Hands' and 'If They Could See Us Now…!'
Note: Caroline has appeared twice in the series: she was seen on a poster at the beginning of 'Heroes and Villains' and with Jonathan Ross in 'If They Could See Us Now…!'

Garfield, Kelly

Role: Wayne (the policeman)
Appeared in S1, episode 6

Gary

Played by Steve Fortune
Son of Arnie, Gary is seen in 'Chain Gang'. Together with his brother, Steven, they don ambulance men's suits and are part of the con trick involving the gold chains.

Gary

Played by Scott Marshall
In 'Heroes and Villains', Gary is one of the muggers

who attempts to steal the handbags from Councillor Murray and the old lady in the market.

Gas rigger
Played by David Fleeshman

En route to the Dutch coastline in 'To Hull and Back', Del – who's on board the Inge with Rodney and Uncle Albert – dumbfounds a gas rigger by asking the directions to Holland.

Gatland, Steve

Film sound recordist on two episodes: 'Miami Twice' (Parts 1 & 2)

Other shows Steve, who's a freelance sound recordist, has worked on include the 1983 sitcom *No Place Like Home*, the drama *The Rainbow* and television documentaries such as *Inside Story, The Shop* and *Hyperland*.

Geary, Joan

Role: Dora
Appeared in S7, episode 5

The late Joan Geary appeared on stage and screen. Other television appearances included playing Mrs Templeton in 1993's *If You See God, Tell Him* and on the big screen, as a waitresss in 1961's, *The Kitchen*; Mrs Hawkes Fenhoulet in *Up Jumped a Swagman*, four years later; a landlady in 1969's *The Betrayal* and an appearance in 1980's *Moon Over the Alley*.

George

Not seen in the sitcom, George is mentioned by Rodney in 'Go West Young Man'. He's supposed to be one of Rodney's chums from his evening class, who often goes out with him to various West End clubs, but it's debatable whether George actually exists.

George
(See 'Trotter, George')

Gernon, Christine

Production assistant on two episodes: S7, episodes 5 & 6

Born in Warrington in 1963, Christine lived in France before joining BBC Radio as a clerk. She became a production assistant for radio before transferring to work as a production secretary on television, with one of her first jobs being the opening series of *One Foot in the Grave*.

Now a director, recent work assignments have been *Fun at the Funeral Parlour* and *Absolutely Fabulous*.

Gerrard, Mr
Played by Andrew Tourell

Mr Gerrard represents the brewery which owns The Nag's Head during Albert's compensation claim in 'Hole in One'. Whilst in the courtroom, Mr Gerrard examines Albert's naval record and learns that he spent the lion's share of the war stationed in a storage depot on the Isle of Wight.

Gerry the gerbil

The black gerbil escapes from its cage and climbs all over Rodney, who's asleep in the Reliant van during 'Fatal Extraction'. Believing it's a rat, Rodney runs into the dentist's surgery, where Del is receiving treatment, only to discover that the animal is a Christmas present for Damien.

Gibb, Barry

Role: Himself
Appeared in 'Miami Twice' (Part 2)

Barry Gibb, one of the Bee Gees, appeared briefly in 'Miami Twice'; whilst he's outside in his riverside garden, a boat full of eagle-eyed tourists, including Del and Rodney, sails by.

Born on the Isle of Man in 1946, he was the second of five children, some of whom teamed up with Barry to form the internationally acclaimed pop group, The Bee Gees, whose worldwide success includes composing ten UK number ones, and in 1978 penning four consecutive chart-toppers in the States.

Gibson, Lee

Role: Singer
Appeared in 'The Jolly Boys' Outing'

Born in Watford, Lee originally trained as a dancer before turning her attention to singing. Her early work saw her peforming with the Black and White Minstrels and as leading lady at London's Talk of the Town, where she was spotted by Laurie Monk, producer of the BBC's Jazz Club, and offered her first broadcast. During this period, Lee was also studying part-time at university for a philosophy degree.

Since then she's recorded hundreds of times for the Beeb, including recent live transmissions of *Big Band Special* with the BBC Big Band from Leeds, and with the BBC Concert Orchestra on the weekly live broadcast, *Friday Night Is Music Night*, for Radio 2.

Her film and television credits include: *Victor Victoria, Privates on Parade, The Great Muppet Movie, The Two Ronnies, Yentl, The Morecambe and Wise Show, The Benny Hill Show* and seven Royal Variety Shows.

Lee is an internationally acclaimed jazz singer and has performed around the world.

Gilbey, Lennox
Played by Vas Blackwood

Seen in 'The Longest Night', Lennox greets everyone at the Top-Buy supermarket with a smile, even though he's an habitual shoplifter, and has just been released from prison. He claims he's nicknamed 'The Shadow' by police because he's 'fast and fleeting', although it's just another lie. Hiding behind the confident exterior, he's just a callow, confused lad, who's easily led off the straight and narrow.

Lennox lives a life on the dole, not having worked for six years – he was even turned down for a job at Top-Buy. When we meet Gilbey, his latest escapade is to try and rob his local branch of the supermarket. Brandishing a gun, he's holed up in the shop manager's office with the manager, the

'The Longest Night'

head of security and the unfortunate Trotters. It turns out that he remembers Del from his days as a door-to-door shoe salesman, and he eventually explains to him that the idea of raiding the supermarket was the brainchild of Mr Peterson, the shop manager, and Tom Clarke, Top-Buy's Head of Security.

Gilbey, Roseanna

In 'The Longest Night', Lennox, convinces Del that he knew his mum, Roseanna, a West Indian lady who lived in Cutler Road. She suffers from bad feet nowadays and is a deeply religious woman. She is not seen in the sitcom.

Gilder, Heather

Vision mixer on 22 episodes: S4, episodes 1–6; S5; S6, episodes 1, 3 & 4; 'The Frog's Legacy'; 'Miami Twice' (Parts 1 & 2); 'Mother Nature's Son'; 'Fatal Extraction'; 'Heroes and Villains' and 'Time On Our Hands'

Heather, who was one of the BBC's most respected and talented vision mixers, was born in Bournemouth. After finishing school she completed a one-year secretarial course before joining the BBC as a secretary in 1964. Three years later she was working as a production assistant in children's television, but eventually trained to become a vision mixer, a job she did for nearly 30 years.

Although she worked on the whole spectrum of shows during her career, she spent much of her time in light entertainment, from *The Morecambe and Wise Show* and *The Young Ones* to *Top of the Pops* and *Three Of A Kind*.

Heather remained working until 18 months before her death of cancer in 1999.

Giles
Played by Stephen Riddle

Seen in 'A Royal Flush', Giles – who has a flat in Chelsea – is a guest at the Duke of Maylebury's weekend shoot. We see him at the dinner table when he starts chatting to Rodney, but the only thing they have in common is that they both support Chelsea.

Giles, Don

Designer on one episode: 'Diamonds are for Heather'

London-born Don Giles studied graphics at art school in Hornsey. He spent six months working in advertising before realising it wasn't the right career for him. After helping friends design window displays for the London department store Simpson's, he joined the architects department at the London County Council. Before joining the BBC as a design assistant in 1966, he worked as a designer for a wine merchant.

By the 1970s, Don had been promoted to designer and began working on shows such as *Softly, Softly*, *The Onedin Line*, *Miss Marple* and *My Cousin Rachel*, filmed in Italy. He left the Beeb in 1992 and has been working freelance ever since, one of his recent assignments being *Midsomer Murders*.

Gillard, Nick

Stunt artist on one episode: 'Dates'

At the age of 12, Nick ran away from military school and joined a circus. By the time he left that world behind at 18, he was travelling the world with the famous Moscow State Circus.

Upon joining the British stunt register in the late 1970s, work soon came his way. During his career he's been employed on films – including *Superman* and *Indiana Jones* productions – and television, from *The Sweeney* and *The Professionals* to *Casualty* and *The Bill*. In *Only Fools*, Nick drove the American car which chased Rodney and Nerys through the streets and over the humpbacked bridge in 'Dates'.

Nowadays Nick is a second unit director and stunt coordinator, with recent credits covering the recent *Star Wars* movie and *Sleepy Hollow*.

Gillham, Tracey

Production assistant on three episodes: 'Miami Twice' (Parts 1 & 2) and 'Fatal Extraction'. Casting adviser on 'If They Could See Us Now…!'

Since becoming a casting adviser, Tracey has been involved in various television series, including *A Prince Among Men*, *Get Well Soon*, *Spark*, *Dad*, *The Last Salute*, *Jonathan Creek* and *Rhona*.

Gillian

Not seen in the sitcom, Gillian is mentioned by Grandad during 'Strained Relations'. He tells Del and Rodney that he went to comfort Patsy's girl, Gillian, when her husband began working nights; six months later, she set fire to the house, for which she received three months' medical supervision.

Gilpin, Francesca

Assistant floor manager on one episode: 'A Royal Flush'

Among the many shows Francesca worked on is the 1991 comedy series *Bottom*, on which she was a production manager. She now directs, particularly operas.

Ginger Ted

While he's supposed to be decorating Denzil and Corinne's living room, Dell decides to phone Ginger at his Vancouver home. The character is never seen in the sitcom.

Gino

Rico, the son of Vinny Occhetti, talks to Gino on the phone whilst dining at a nightclub in 'Miami Twice'. He then talks to him again later, asking him to bring some clothes along to Del and Rodney's room. It's unclear what position he holds within the Occhetti household and he is never seen.

Girl (1st)

(For the '1st Girl' who appeared in 'Christmas Crackers', see 'Anita').

Girl

Seen briefly at the hotel bar in 'The Unlucky Winner is…', the girl talks to Del before he returns to Cassandra.

Girl

Seen in the wine bar in 'Yuppy Love', the girl is one of the yuppies who frequent the bar. Del tries showing Trigger how to chat up the girls – he believes it's all about technique: your conversation and manner has to ooze money! But Del fails the test.

Girl

Played by Judith Conyers

When Trigger tries chatting this girl up at The Nag's Head in 'To Hull and Back', she tells him, in no uncertain terms, where to go!

Girl in disco

Played by Tracy Clarke

Seen in 'Yuppy Love', the girl is at the disco with her friend. She speaks briefly to Jevon, a chum of Mickey Pearce and Rodney.

Girlfriends

Until Raquel and Cassandra walked into their lives, the Trotter boys were unlucky in love. While Del got through girlfriends like there was no tomorrow, with the occasional serious romance thrown in, Rodney's history in love is littered with a string of one-night stands and dismal failures.

Glass, Chris

Camera supervisor on two episodes: S3, episodes 1 & 4

Glenister, Robert

Role: Myles

Appeared in 'Mother Nature's Son'

Robert's career has involved working in all areas of the profession. His film credits include *Quadrophenia*, *Secret Rapture*, *The Visitors* and *All Forgotten*, while his stage work has seen him appearing as Caliban in *The Tempest* and Vincentio in *Measure for Measure*, both for the Royal Shakespeare Company, as well as many other productions.

On television he's played, among others,

Marion

Met her at the Catford dog track. Yeah, she was a nice girl, but it ended in another wasted ring.

Deirdre

I'll never forgive Albie Littlewood for pulling my bird, June, behind my back. Then again, if he were alive today, he probably wouldn't forgive me for doing the same with his girl, Deirdre. So fair's fair, I suppose.

Elly-May

Elly-May? I think that was her name – it was certainly double-barrelled, anyhow. I was a teenager working as a photographer in the Tower of London when we first met; I took a picture of her with a Beefeater and it wasn't long before we fell in love. It was all short-lived, though. She wasn't short of a few quid because her father was a Texas oil-baron.

Miranda Davenport

This posh tart ran an antiques shop and tried taking me for a ride with a painting; I ask you, do I look like a mug? Still, I had the last laugh and enjoyed telling her she'd just auctioned a stolen picture!

Miranda

Petula

Don't remember much about her, except that we met at a car-boot sale.

Marlene

Have to keep this one hush-hush because Boycie hasn't an inkling about me dating his bird. She might have been around a bit, but she's a good all-rounder, a real sporting girl, if you know what I mean! Got a nice heart and dagger tattoo on her thigh. She dumped me after a month, just when I'd saved up enough dosh to take her off to sunnier climes for a break. I tried talking to her about it but she kept hiding on the roof of the bookies!

Marlene

Janine

I've nothing but bad memories of this red-head, so won't waste any energy recording intimate details here.

Veronique

She worked in Woolies, there's not much else worthy of recording.

Beverley

One to forget! I didn't really date her, thank god. I was on the rebound after Raquel had walked out on me, and was smitten by her smile. All right, I asked her out, but cancelled soon after, so I didn't have anything to feel guilty about when me and Raquel got back together. The stupid cow kept following me, it was a bit of a nightmare in the end!

Trudy

A bit rough, even if I do say it myself. She was also a bit of a boozer. Probably the biggest mistake of my life, as far as the bird front is concerned. I can't believe that we were engaged back in the 1970s – that was until Rodney's pet vole took a liking to her wig!

Pauline Harris

Now she was the true love of my life, or so I thought at the time. If it hadn't been for that geezer with the sportier Vespa, we'd be married now. Mind you, it might have been a blessing in disguise because the two blokes she did end up marrying are both dead! I couldn't believe it when I saw her not so long ago, the first time in 12 years. She was just as gorgeous. I nearly made a fool of myself again, but luckily brought the relationship to an end once and for all.

Pauline

Heather

Met her at a Spanish night in The Nag's Head. A great girl; had a nice kid, too. Could have had a ready-made family there, until her dipstick of a hubby came back on the scene. I'll never know why she agreed to give their relationship another try. Still, at least the engagement ring was on a week's approval!

Rodney's Little Black Book of Romance

Marguerite
Grandad always called her the 'skinny bird'. Everybody thought I was in love with her but it was only an infatuation; still I was able to get a discount on any dry cleaning, being that she worked in the local shop.

Sandra
For once I should have listened to Del. I might like females in uniform, but I should have drawn the line at getting involved with a real-life policewoman! Del did his nut when he found out, and it didn't help matters when she spotted all the stock in the flat was hookie and gave me an ultimatum: get rid of everything or face a visit from the CID.

Shanghai Lil
An old flame from art college days in Basingstoke. Brings back lots of memories whenever I think of her, although most of them are bad, like the time I was expelled from the college when the governors caught us both smoking pot, leaving me with an 18-month suspended sentence. Last time I heard anything about her, she was being deported back to Hong Kong.

Big Brenda
I could kill Del sometimes, and this was one of those occasions. He had the gall to set up a blind date with this monster, who was none other than the Southern Area Shot-put Champion. I'll get him back one day.

Imogen
She was okay but got a bit serious and started talking about engagement. Mind you, she couldn't have been that serious because I caught her with another man. At least it let me off the hook.

Irene Mackay
Another relationship my good old brother put an end to. I wish he'd keep his nose out of my affairs some times. All right, she was a bit older than me, but she was gorgeous, especially when she wore that tight skirt! In hindsight, there might have been some sense in Del's actions, especially when you consider her hubby had served a prison sentence for attempted murder.

Nervous Nerys
Barmaid at The Nag's Head. Attractive but a nervous wreck – well she was by the time we'd finished our date. But that wasn't my fault, you can blame the punks who decided their daily dose of entertainment would be chasing us in their American car; I wouldn't have minded, but I was only driving the Reliant! Obviously this was a very brief relationship.

Linda
Didn't see her after her parents nearly caught us at it. It was a close call. I don't think they'd have suspected anything if I hadn't have put my trousers on back to front in all the panic when they arrived home early.

Debby
Spotted her behind the counter at the local newsagents. She was 18 and very attractive, but Del put paid to this relationship by warning me that Debby could be my niece! I wish he'd get his facts right before he starts shouting his mouth off.

Vicky
I could have been onto a winner here. She was an artist, drove a blue Mercedes and her father was none other than the Duke of Maylebury. I sometimes wonder what would have become of us if it hadn't been for bloody Del again, messing everything up. I think nobility would have suited me.

Helen
Tall, slender, a real beauty. Del, who must be as blind as a bat, had a different opinion, claiming she's known as Helen of Croydon, the face that launched a thousand dredgers. He even classed her as an 'old dog' and a bit 'scraggy' – bloody cheek.

Debby

Bernice
Had to put a stop to this relationship; she was getting a bit too serious. I'm a man of the world, I can't be tied down at my age.

Tanya
Asking her to go to the cinema just because I was having a few problems with Cassandra was a mistake, which is why I cancelled the date. She didn't have much of a personality anyway. Tanya worked as a receptionist at the Peckham Exhaust Centre.

Yvonne

Del was right when he classed her as 'all body and no brains', so why did he have to bribe her into accompanying me to the do at The Nag's Head? Not only did she enjoy the old tipple a bit too much, she embarrassed me rotten in front of my mates by stripping. And all this because I needed to find someone who'd accompany me to the do in order to win a bet, which wasn't worth it in the end.

Yvonne

Janice

I thought Janice and I had a lot in common, considering we were both interested in art. She used to go around braless, which cheered me up. The trouble is Del had a bout of straying eyes.

Monica

She never did take kindly to the policewoman's uniform I bought her. But if it hadn't have been for Mickey Pearce's interference, she might have warmed to the idea. Another one of my girlfriends Del would insist on insulting, referring to her as a 'little tart with fat thighs'. Why I ever listened to Pearce, and agreed on a trial separation, I'll never know, but now realise that he wanted her for himself.

Zoe

After my brief fling with the rather mature Irene Mackay, Zoe seemed very youthful, at just 18. I met her at a roller-disco and she had a great figure.

Inspector Beavers in *Juliet Bravo*, Mr Richards in *Boon*, Detective Sergeant Terrence Reid in *A Touch of Frost*, John Field in *Midsomer Murders* and Chris in *Prime Suspect*.

Glen McDonald Whisky

Produced in Malaysia, the blended scotch whisky is supposed to be 12 years old. The Trotters are meant to deliver 12 boxes to Chunky Lewis, the manager of Delaney's Club, but get lost and turn up at the Drury Lane Theatre instead. The whisky is seen during the Royal Variety Performance scene.

'Go West Young Man'

Original transmission: Tuesday 15 September 1981, 8.30 pm

Production date: Sunday 14 June 1981

Original viewing figures: 6.1 million

Duration: 30 minutes

First repeat: Friday 14 September 1990, 7.35 pm

Subsequent repeats: 3/4/97, 30/4/99

CAST

Del Trotter . . . . .David Jason
Rodney Trotter . . . . .Nicholas Lyndhurst
Grandad Trotter . . . . .Lennard Pearce
Boycie . . . . .John Challis
Aussie Man . . . . .Nick Stringer
Waiter . . . . .Barry Wilmore
Nicky . . . . .JoAnne Good
Michelle . . . . .Caroline Ellis
Walk-ons: . . . . (Male transvestites) Steve Fideli and Frank Cullen. (People in nightclub and disco) Geoffrey Whitestone, Keith Adam and eight extras.

PRODUCTION TEAM

Written by John Sullivan

Title music arranged and conducted by Ronnie Hazlehurst composed and sung by John Sullivan

Audience Warm-up: . . . . .Felix Bowness
Make-up Designer: . . . . .Pauline Cox
Costume Designer: . . . . .Phoebe De Gaye
Properties Buyer: . . . . .Chris Ferriday
Film Cameraman: . . . . .Bill Matthews
Film Sound: . . . . .Dennis Panchen
Film Editor: . . . . .John Jarvis
Camera Supervisor: . . . . .Ron Peverall
Studio Lighting Director: . . . . .Don Babbage
Studio Sound: . . . . .Mike Felton
Technical Coordinator: . . . . . .Robert Hignett
Videotape Editor: . . . . .Chris Wadsworth
Production Assistant: . . . . .Penny Thompson
Assistant Floor Manager: . . . .Mandie Fletcher
Graphic Designer: . . . . .Peter Clayton
Vision Mixer: . . . . .Hilary West
Production Manager: . . . . .Janet Bone
Designer: . . . . .Tony Snoaden
Directed by Martin Shardlow
Produced by Ray Butt

While Rodney is depressed again, this time because of his trial separation from girlfriend Monica, Del's on the lookout, as always, for business opportuni-

ties and turns his attention to the second-hand car market.

While visiting Boycie's garage, Del and Rodney examine an old, rusty Mark II Cortina convertible that's been used as part-exchange for a Vanden Plas. Boycie's asking fifty quid, but Del manages to knock him down to 25 by offering to garage his E-type Jag for a week. The car is a birthday present for Boycie's 'bit on the side'.

After doctoring the milometer, they slap a £199 price tag on their first venture into the second-hand car market, and soon an Australian appears on the scene and shows an interest. Del's unconventional sales patter does the trick and the car is sold.

That evening, Rodney plans to paint the town red, but with no one to join him, he persuades Del to come along. Believing their arrival in a three-wheeled Reliant would do little for their image, Del suggests taking Boycie's E-type for a spin, instead.

The night is far from swinging at the nightclub, and to make matters worse, Del finds himself chatting up a couple of transvestites. But before the evening is out the boys strike lucky and end up arranging a date with Nicky and Michelle, who share a pad in Chelsea. After one of the girls jots down their phone number on Del's cigar pack, it's au revoir until the following Friday. But the brothers' luck runs out on their way home when Rodney accidentally slings the cigar pack – together with the phone number – out of the car window. To top it all, when Del realises what Rodney has done and brakes suddenly so he can run back and retrieve the box, a car smashes into the back of the E-type. And it's none other than the brakeless Cortina convertible.

Goddard, Daphne

Role: Lady at dinner

Appeared in 'A Royal Flush'

Daphne's television credits include playing Violet in *Lost Empires*, a Lady Mayoress in *London's Burning*, a committee lady in *Prime Suspect III*, Miss Barrington in Catherine Cookson's *The Girl*, an irate passenger in *Oh, Doctor Beeching!*, a frail OAP in *This Could Be the Last Time* and Miss Laybourne in *Midsomer Murders*.

Daphne's busy career has also seen her work extensively in the theatre and make the occasional film appearance.

Golden Dragon, The

In 'Time On Our Hands', Del suggests to Rodney and Albert – who have all been visiting the flat in Nelson Mandela House, reminiscing about the old days before becoming millionaires – that they leave their flash cars behind and go for a meal at The Golden Dragon.

Golden Lotus, The

A Chinese takeaway seen in 'The Yellow Peril'. The Golden Lotus is owned by Mr Chin. Del volunteers Rodney to paint the restaurant's kitchen for £150 when the owner is expecting a visit from the health inspector. What Chin doesn't realise is that the anonymous caller tipping him off about the visit was Del, anxious to rid himself of some dodgy paint he bought from Trigger, which turns out to be luminous.

In a later episode ('The Frog's Legacy'), we hear that the restaurant – which is sited near the station – has gone out of business and Del's going along to where the restaurant equipment is being auctioned to see if he can pick up any bargains.

Goldring, Peter

Camera supervisor on two episodes: 'Miami Twice' (Parts 1 & 2)

As a camera supervisor, Peter worked on a range of shows, especially in light entertainment, such as *Terry and June* (1979), *Tanya* (1987), *Keeping Up Appearances* (1990), *As Time Goes By* (1992), *Chalk* (1997) and *Bloomin' Marvellous* (1997).

Gold Rush

The television game show featured in 'If They Could See Us Now…!' and was presented by Jonathan Ross. Del appeared on the show as a contestant hoping to ease some of his financial worries by winning the monetary jackpot. While Raquel and Damien were in the studio audience, Rodney and Cassandra were glued to the box at home, which was just as well because Del nominated Rodney as the person he wanted to phone for his 'SOS Call' when he became stuck on the fifty grand question.

Gomez, Raphael

Role: Pauly in 'Miami Twice' (Part 2)

As well as acting, Raphael is also a stuntman, whose work in this field includes the 1986 movie *Band of*

à la Del

★ ★ ★ ★ ★ ★

'Buenos Aires'

('A Slow Bus to Chingford')

the Hand, and *Innerspace,* a year later. As an actor, he's played a pickpocket in 1990's *Miami Blues,* a NATO officer in *Blue Sky* and Bobby in the TV series *Chains of Gold.*

Good, JoAnne

Role: Nicky

Appeared in S1, episode 2

JoAnne was a dancer before turning her attention to acting. She trained at the Rose Bruford Stage School and made her professional debut in *Gigi* at the Connaught Theatre, Worthing, during the 1970s.

Her first job in television was as a secretary in the BBC series *Potter,* but her favourite role was playing the female mechanic, Carol Sands, in *Crossroads* for four years. Other television roles include several characters in *Casualty,* Rose in *Forgotten,* a TV reporter in *Silent Witness,* Nurse Watts in *The Detectives,* Mrs Copper in *Shine on Harvey Moon,* and Vi in *Last of the Summer Wine.*

In the theatre, she's played Rita in *Educating Rita,*

Josie in *Steaming,* and numerous other characters in the West End, national tours, and the Far East.

Nowadays, as well as her acting, JoAnne presents her own show for BBC South.

Goodwin, Courtney

Focus puller on two episodes: 'Miami Twice' (Parts 1 & 2)

Courtney was part of the American crew assembled to film the episodes in the States.

Goorney, Howard

Role: Knock Knock

Appeared in S7, episode 5

Born in 1921, Howard was a founder member, with Joan Littlewood, of the Theatre Workshop, where he made his professional acting debut in *The Flying Doctor* in 1945.

His extensive acting career has covered all areas of the business. On stage, he's worked throughout the British Isles, including a lengthy period at the National Theatre. His film work, meanwhile, includes *Fiddler on the Roof, Circus of Blood, Where's Jack?* and *The Fool.* On the small screen he's appeared in productions such as *Bramwell, 2 Point 4 Children, All Creatures Great and Small, Under the Sun* and *Nelson.*

Gordon

During 'Three Men, a Woman and a Baby', Del tries selling the bald-headed Gordon one of the rejected wigs he's found himself lumbered with.

Graham, Clare

Assistant floor manager on one episode: 'Christmas Crackers'

Clare – who's married to ex-properties buyer, Chris Ferriday – grew up in Birmingham. Upon leaving school she studied English and Drama at Manchester University before launching a career in stage management. For three years she worked in theatres up and down the country, including Manchester, Chester and Leicester, and then toured as a stage manager, which involved a spell in Barnstaple, North Devon.

In 1980 she was successful in securing a job as assistant stage manager at the Beeb; early shows she worked on include *Kelly Monteith, Hi-De-Hi!, Tenko, The House of Eliott* and *Campion.* During 1982 she transferred to the drama department as a production manager, where she stayed until leaving the Corporation ten years later.

Clare moved to North Devon shortly afterwards, where she ran a bakery for a while. Nowadays she concentrates on raising her family, as well as serving in the local coastguard team with husband, Chris.

Grandad

(See 'Trotter, Grandad')

Grayson, Mr

Played by Peter Rutherford

Seen in 'Chain Gang', Mr Grayson – who's in his mid-fifties – enters The One Eleven Club with a young woman. He's a shady so-called businessman who applies for voluntary liquidation whenever trouble looms.

Great Ramondo, The

Played by Robin Driscoll

The entertainer is seen performing at the Mardi Gras club in Margate during 'The Jolly Boys' Outing'. He's assisted by Raquel, which surprises Del when he pops into the club during his trip to the seaside. As a result of this chance encounter, Del and Raquel rekindle their relationship.

The Great Ramondo was appearing at a holiday camp in Devon when his assistant walked out on him. Raquel's agent put her in touch and she was taken on as a replacement. They secured a three-month contract at the Margate club but Raquel isn't

'The Jolly Boys' Outing'

keen on Ramondo, who's got a filthy temper. When Del later argues with the magician back at Raquel's rented flat, we learn that the entertainer is gay.

Green, Garard

Role: Auctioneer
Appeared in S3, episode 4
A veteran film actor, Garard was frequently seen on the big screen during the 1950s and '60s in pictures such as *Profile*, *Count to Twelve*, *High Terrace*, *The Steel Bayonet*, *Morning Call* and *Emergency*. As well as working on radio, stage and television, he's also a seasoned audio book narrator.

Green, Ron

Camera supervisor on one episode: S6, episode 1
Other programmes Ron has worked on include *The Kenny Everett Television Show* in 1981; *Blackadder II* and *Season's Greetings* in 1986; and *The Importance of Being Earnest*, three years later.

Greenway, Iain

Graphic designer on one episode: S6, episode 4
For the last five years, Iain has been based in New York, where he works for Click 3x as Creative Director. The winner of more than two dozen Broadcast Designer Association awards, he specialises in design, branding and special effects for TV and advertising, with recent projects including producing new identities for BBC America and Bravo.

Born in the Midlands town of Allestree in 1956, he completed a four-year graphic design course and joined the BBC's design department in 1980. During the 16 years he worked for the Beeb, he was assigned to programmes like *Casualty*, *The Lenny Henry Show*, *Tomorrow's World*, *Wogan* and *Crimewatch*.

Greenwood, Christine

Make-up designer on 11 episodes: S7, 'Rodney Come Home', 'Miami Twice' (Parts 1 & 2), 'Mother Nature's Son' and 'Fatal Extraction'
When London-born Christine Greenwood realised that she was too young to apply to the BBC for a job she trained in hairdressing and beauty therapy.

When old enough, she re-applied and her 23-year career in the industry began.

Early productions she worked on include the period drama *Prince Regent* and *Top of the Pops*. Since leaving the BBC in the early 1990s to become a freelance make-up and hair designer, she's worked on many feature films, such as 1997's *Elizabeth*, where she was personal make-up artist and hairdresser to Cate Blanchett, as well as continuing her involvement with television. Recent work on the small screen includes Granada's *Lenny Blue*.

Other productions she's worked on during her freelance career include *Band of Brothers*, *Gormenghast*, for which she won a BAFTA craft award for make-up and hair design, *The George Best Story*, *Shakespeare in Love*, *The Borrowers* and *Bramwell*.

Grimes, James

Grip on one episode: 'Fatal Extraction'
Other shows James has worked on as a grip include *Keeping Up Appearances* and *Oranges Are Not the Only Fruit*.

Groovy Gang, The

The Groovy Gang is seen in 'The Unlucky Winner is…'. Much to his consternation, Rodney becomes a lifelong member for winning the under-15 painting competition organised by the cereal company Mega Flakes. As well as becoming members, the winners win a Mallorcan holiday, on which Rodney pretends to be an over-grown teenager!

Guitarist in pub

Played by George Kish
In 'Diamonds are for Heather', the guitarist helps entertain the punters during the Spanish night.

Gulf War Special

A special sketch was recorded exclusively for the troops during the Gulf War crisis. Penned by John Sullivan, and produced by Gareth Gwenlan, the cast consisted of David Jason, Nicholas Lyndhurst and Buster Merryfield.

The storyline of the short scene centres around the Trotters' attempts to record a message for the troops, while wives and family members of the soldiers stand around watching the proceedings, such as Del trying to explain why he thinks it would be a worthwhile idea shipping over their decrepit Reliant van, remarking on its impressive speed and versatility. The sketch closes on a serious note, with Del Boy telling the soldiers how proud everyone back home is, and wishing them the best of luck.

A copy of the sketch is kept at the War Museum in London and has never been released commercially.

Gunn, Keith

Studio sound supervisor on one episode: S3, episode 2
Keith, who was born in London, joined the BBC straight from school in 1963 as a camera/sound operator. Early shows he worked on include *Z Cars* and *Doctor Finlay's Casebook*. He transferred to outside broadcasts for a time, before returning to the studio in 1973 as sound supervisor. Although he worked on a whole range of programmes, he tended to concentrate on light entertainment, including a year on *Top of the Pops*, *Sykes*, *The Old Grey Whistle Test* and *The Val Doonican Show*.

Keith left the BBC in 1967 and works on freelance projects occasionally, as well as enjoying his semi-retirement.

Gwenlan, Gareth

Producer on 23 episodes: S6; S7; 'Dates'; 'The Jolly Boys' Outing'; 'Rodney Come Home'; 'Miami Twice' (Parts 1 & 2); 'Mother Nature's Son'; 'Fatal Extraction'; 'Heroes and Villains'; 'Modern Men'; 'Time On Our Hands'; 'If They Could See Us Now…!'
Note: Gareth also made an appearance in the sitcom, as a policeman on horseback during the riots in 'Fatal Extraction'
Gareth Gwenlan always wanted to work in the entertainment world, but his parents harboured dreams of seeing him pursue a medical career. Gareth had other ideas, however, and, as soon as he was eligible, he completed his national service instead. 'I did it to escape becoming a doctor,' he admits.

Before returning to civvy street he was offered a place at drama school, but when the news wasn't well received by his parents, he opted for an English degree, which included an element of drama. 'I was only doing it to please my parents. I didn't necessarily want to be an actor but I wanted to be something in the theatre. We're talking about a period in the late 1950s when there wasn't a huge amount of television around, so the theatre seemed to be the place to work.'

As soon as Gareth had satisfied his parents by completing the degree, he used the drama experience he'd gained to secure a job as an actor at a theatre in York. Over the ensuing years spent at reps in cities such as Derby and Manchester he made it known that he wanted to direct. He took his first steps towards becoming a director when Ian Wilson, a theatre director, was looking for an

assistant. Gareth was offered the post, and within a week stepped into the breach to direct his first production. 'Ian was suddenly taken ill,' he says. 'In a sense, it was one of those lucky breaks, and as I didn't screw it up I was given the chance to direct the next two or three shows.'

Upon Wilson's return to the helm, Gareth was appointed the theatre's associate producer/director, a job he did until the venue was closed down for a few months, at which point he headed for pastures new. 'I saw a job in *The Stage* for something called an assistant floor manager. It was a short-term contract for three months at the BBC. I was interviewed for it in London where it was pointed out that I was over-qualified for the job because I was already a director.' Gareth was keen to take the assistant floor manager's job, however, because, firstly, it was a route in to a new medium and, secondly, it paid £4 a week more than what he was earning back in the theatre at Derby.

However, there was a shock in store for Gareth when the first director he was allocated to work for turned out to be someone he'd trained two years previously in the theatre. 'I remember he turned to me and said: "I can't believe you're an assistant floor manager, you know more about directing than I do." And, believe it or not, I was made the 1st assistant director on my first week! What was an extra £4 a week suddenly became an extra £14 and after that I never returned to the theatre.'

Gareth's career took off when he swapped roles with fellow director Ken Riddington, and moved into the comedy department. His first project was *Wodehouse Playhouse*, starring John Alderton and Pauline Collins. 'John and I had been mates since our days in theatre at York, so it was great working with him again. But my big break was working on *The Fall and Rise of Reginald Perrin*, starting in 1976, which was followed by *Butterflies* and *To the Manor Born.*'

By 1983, Gareth was the incumbent Head of Comedy at the Beeb, a job he held until 1990, when he left to work freelance. Since leaving the staff of the BBC, he's worked on many top shows, *Only Fools* and *Waiting for God* to name but two. 'Even though I worked freelance, I always made sure I was available to do *Only Fools,*' Gareth points out.

Reflecting on over a decade working freelance, Gareth is entirely happy with his lot. 'In 1990 when I decided to return to being a working producer/director, I was determined not to do any more babysitting of junior producers and directors; neither did I want to be in a situation of having to do a series simply because I needed to pay the mortgage. So I decided to go freelance and enjoy the freedom of deciding what I want and don't want to do.'

In April 2002, Gareth began a new contract working as comedy adviser for BBC Wales. 'I've got a house in Herefordshire, which is only about 40 miles away from where I'll be working, so it couldn't be better.'

Gwynne-Davies, Ifor

Role: Carter
Appeared in 'A Royal Flush'

Hammond, Juliet

Role: Miranda Davenport
Appeared in S3, episode 4

Juliet, who was born in London in 1953, has appeared on television in a host of roles, including Natalie Chantrens in the 1977 series *Secret Army*, Pella in *Blake's 7*, Emilie in 1982's *Baal*, Irene Kohl in *Blood Money* and Miss Hawk in *Dark Towers.*

Hancock, Lucy

Role: Stewardess
Appeared in S7, episode 1

Lucy's television credits include playing a stage manager in 1985's *Star Quality*, Rosie in *Cover Her Face*, a mini-series the same year and Maria in BBC's 1987 production *Cariani and the Courtesans*. Her film work includes the 1989 picture, *Soursweet.*

Handsome Sansom

Mentioned by Del in 'A Royal Flush', the horse is owned by the Duke of Maylebury, and it's hoped he'll be fit for the Derby.

'Happy Returns'

Original transmission: Thursday 21 February 1985, 8.00 pm

Production date: 20 January 1985

Original viewing figures: 15.2 million

Duration: 30 minutes

First repeat: Saturday 16 November 1985, 8.25 pm

Subsequent repeats: 29/3/86, 19/10/91, 2/4/95, 28/11/97, 4/8/00

Note: BAFTA 'Best Comedy' award, 1986

CAST

Del Trotter	David Jason
Rodney Trotter	Nicholas Lyndhurst
June	Diane Langton
Trigger	Roger Lloyd Pack
Mickey Pearce	Patrick Murray
Debby	Oona Kirsch
Maureen	Nula Conwell
Old lady in newsagents	Lala Lloyd
Jason	Ben Davis
Extras	(Child) Nicholas Grant

PRODUCTION TEAM

Written by John Sullivan

Title music arranged and conducted by Ronnie Hazlehurst composed and sung by John Sullivan

Audience Warm-up:	Felix Bowness
Make-up Designer:	Linda McInnes
Costume Designer:	Richard Winter
Properties Buyer:	Chris Ferriday
Film Cameraman:	Chris Seager
Film Sound:	Dennis Panchen
Film Editor:	John Jarvis
Camera Supervisor:	Ken Major
Studio Lighting Director:	Peter Smee
Studio Sound:	Dave Thompson
Technical Coordinator:	Tony Mutimer
Videotape Editor:	Chris Wadsworth
Production Assistants:	Caroline Andrews and Lesley Bywater
Assistant Floor Manager:	Gavin Clarke
Vision Mixer:	Heather Gilder
Production Manager:	Andy Smith
Designer:	Eric Walmsley

Directed by Susan Belbin

Produced by Ray Butt

When Del stops Jason, a young boy, running into the road, he strikes up a friendship with the lad which eventually leads him to an old flame. Jason's mother, June (whose husband is serving time for stealing) and Del used to date in 1964, and they resume their friendship, while Rodney befriends Debby, who turns out to be June's daughter.

Realising that Debby will soon be celebrating her 19th birthday, Del starts believing that she was conceived whilst he courted her mother, and with his brain working overtime, thinks he must be the father, putting paid to poor old Rodney's relationship.

When he finally broaches the subject with June, he's shocked to find the father is in fact Albie Littlewood, his supposed friend, who died when his bike fell on a live railway line. For years Del had felt partly responsible for Albie's death because he was on his way over to the Trotters' house when the fatal accident occurred – or so he had thought.

Harding, Nick

Art director on three episodes: 'Heroes and Villains', 'Modern Men' and 'Time On Our Hands'

Born in Leicester, Nick studied drama at London University and embarked on an acting career before changing direction. He joined the BBC's visual effects department in 1987, but after eight months transferred to Scenic Design. Employed on a rolling contract, he remained with the Beeb until 1996, when his department closed down and he turned freelance. Recent projects he's worked on include two series of the children's series *The Worst Witch*, the soap *Night and Day*, and *A is for Acid* for Yorkshire TV.

Harrington, Jean

Role: Woman in club
Appeared in 'Rodney Come Home'

'I helped Donal Woods, who was production designer on the three episodes. When it came to dressing the sets, I remember watching some old tapes of the previous series to find out what colours we had to paint the wall and the rest of it. We had a problem with the wallpaper, finding some of the bamboo-style paper, which was meant to be old fashioned when it was first used, so you can understand why we had difficulties. But we eventually found a few rolls. A lot of the props were still with the prop houses, so Graham Bishop, the prop buyer, sorted all that out.

'There were certain items on the set which were quite memorable, so it was important to track them down, whereas the rest of the furniture viewers don't really remember from one series to the next. Also people change their furniture. It was being a detective, really, piecing everything together.

'When we filmed in Bristol, especially for "Heroes and Villains" during the chase scene, there were a lot of estate agents' boards around, so we ended up taking them down whilst we filmed. Part of my job was to look out for things like that, because the director might suddenly decide to film a close-up of Del turning around, and you never know what is going to be in the background. You have to be on the ball all the time, and when we're pretending the setting is Peckham, we don't want Bristol phone numbers appearing on screen.

'I remember recording what we thought was going to be the final episode, "Time On Our Hands", in the studio. It was a sad occasion. We emptied the flat and had to keep it a secret as far as the audience were concerned, so we dropped a black cloth over the set while we emptied it. The scene where the Trotters return to the empty flat is very moving.

'There was a big debate at the time as to whether we should remove the carpet or not, but we decided to keep it there because the flooring underneath wasn't very nice, and that horrible swirly red carpet – which was supplied by a carpet stall in Shepherd's Bush market – is so much a character of the room.' **NICK HARDING**

Among Jean Harrington's other screen credits are appearances as Martina in 1973's movie, *Secrets of a Door-to-Door Salesman,* and Mary Adams in *Deadly Females* three years later. Her television roles include playing a hostess in an episode of the 1978 sitcom *Rings on Their Fingers* and Connie in a couple of episodes of *All Creatures Great and Small.*

Harris, Faith

Production assistant on one episode: S6, episode 1

Harris, Monkey

Monkey doesn't appear, but is mentioned by Del throughout the sitcom. A regular business associate of Trotter senior's, the first reference to his name is in 'The Long Legs of the Law' when we hear about Harris having gone into partnership with Tommy Razzle, erecting false ceilings. On return from fixing a ceiling in a dental clinic in Saudi Arabia, Harris was out on a pub crawl when Del and Rodney bumped into him. A row quickly ensued between Razzle and Harris and all hell was let loose, with tables and chairs flying everywhere. We can only surmise that the Razzle–Harris partnership was short-lived.

Harris lives in a bungalow, not the sort of accommodation one would expect of such a wheeler-dealer, and seems to have a finger in every pie. Making a fast buck is all that matters to Harris, even if the business opportunity isn't entirely kosher, like the time he had Trigger steal some yellow luminous paint from a storage shed at Clapham Junction. This unlikely partnership is ancient history by the time Detective Inspector Slater asks Trigger about Harris in The Nag's Head during 'May the Force be with You'.

Harris – who attended the same school as Del, Denzil, Slater, Boycie and Trigger, and played left back for the school football team – may have formed an enduring business relationship with Del, but that doesn't prevent Del Boy using Harris as an example while trying to flog one of his dodgy wigs to a chap called Gordon. He ridicules the three-quid hair transplant Harris has invested in, claiming it's not a pretty sight.

The character is also mentioned in 'No Greater Love…', 'The Yellow Peril', 'The Class of '62', 'Three Men, a Woman and a Baby', 'Video Nasty', 'The Unlucky Winner is…', 'Modern Men' and 'If They Could See Us Now…!', when Del's keen on sorting out a deal for electronic organisers.

Harris, Pauline

Played by Jill Baker

Del's ex-fiancée turns up in 'The Second Time Around'. In her early thirties, the smartly dressed, blonde-haired Pauline – whose mother was a bus conductress – was the great love of Del's life, and he still has a very soft spot in his heart for her. When he gets chatting to her in The Nag's Head, we learn that they haven't seen each other for 12 years. She married a chap called Bobby Finch, but when he died she headed for San Francisco and became an air hostess. Whilst based in the States, she wedded an American called Baker, who's also deceased. It seems Pauline has had her fair share of heartache, perhaps her comeuppance after breaking Del's heart when, during their Mod days, she ditched him for a bloke with a faster Vespa!

Del and Pauline's whirlwind romance saw them engaged within a week, then split up after a month. This time around, it only takes an evening and Pauline and Del are engaged. She moves into the flat, much to the dismay of the disapproving Rodney and Grandad, and does little for her relationship with them by refusing to cook for them, and confiscating Grandad's teeth to stop him overeating during the day.

Del soon realises too much water has flowed under the bridge for their relationship to be rekindled, but is also frightened off by the suggestion that Bobby Finch's death is being investigated by the police. Pauline's eagerness for Del to take out life insurance also worries him, so he writes a frank letter, giving her five days to clear out of the flat.

Harrison, Gail

Role: Joanne

Appeared in 'The Jolly Boys' Outing'

Gail – who's, perhaps, best known for her role as Isobel Hardacre in three series of *Brass* – played Marion Wilkes in *Emmerdale Farm* for three years (1972–75). Her busy screen career also includes roles such as Hilary Thorpe in the mini-series *The Nine Tailors*, Gaye in *A Roof Over My Head*, Rhonda in *Comeback*, the mother in *Summer in London* and an appearance in Perry and Croft's sitcom *Hi-De-Hi!*

Harrison, Mike

Camera supervisor on one episode: S1, episode 6

Harrison, Shaunna

Make-up designer on eight episodes: S2 and 'Diamonds are for Heather'

London-born Shaunna Harrison was educated at a French school in the capital. She joined the BBC in the 1970s, initially working as a secretary in

the contracts department. When she reached her 21st birthday, she applied to join the internal make-up school and was accepted for a two-year apprenticeship.

Upon successfully completing her apprenticeship she was appointed an assistant make-up designer and gained vital experience working on a range of shows, including dramas like *The Onedin Line* and *How Green Was My Valley?*

Only Fools was one of the first jobs Shaunna undertook as a fully-fledged make-up designer, and although she tended to concentrate on dramas, she went on to work on many other comedies, such as *Butterflies*, and several series with Dave Allen.

Shaunna – who won a BAFTA and RTS (Royal Television Society) award for her work on the TV film *Tumbledown* – left in 1990 when she became pregnant with her second child. Nowadays she splits her time between working freelance (one of her most recent credits was BBC's *The Lost World*) and teaching at the London College of Fashion and Greasepaint School of Stage, Film and Television.

Harry

Played by Robert Vahey

Harry is a furniture restorer employed by Miranda Davenport in her Chelsea antique shop. He's seen in 'Yesterday Never Comes', opening the door of the shop when Del comes calling for Miranda. When Del enquires why the shop isn't open, he is told the place is being fumigated because it's full of woodworm, probably brought into the shop via the wooden cabinet Miranda bought from Del.

Harry

Played by Roy Evans

Old Harry gets drunk *en route* to Margate during 'The Jolly Boys' Outing'; the trouble is he's the coachdriver so Denzil has to take his place behind the wheel.

Harry (the foreman)

Played by Rex Robinson

Harry is the yard foreman at the auction room. He laughs at Rodney and Mickey Pearce for being stupid enough to buy Lot 37, which consists of nothing but broken lawnmower engines.

Harvey, Max

Role: Mr Peterson

Appeared in S5, episode 3

Born in 1942, Max trained at the Webber Douglas Drama School, before making his debut in rep at Leicester during 1970. He moved on to tours, summer seasons and spells in reps at Farnham and Salisbury.

His first taste of television came in the late seventies, playing a visitor in the BBC series *1990*. Other credits include three episodes as Walter Barker in *Strathblair*, a Spanish torturer in *Blackadder II*, Harry in *The Upper Hand*, *Angels*, *Doctor Who*, *The Mistress*, and *Last of the Summer Wine*.

Max has appeared in a few films, such as *84 Charing Cross Road*, playing the Wing Commander, but his various theatre stints have seen him act in *Pack of Lies, A Passionate Woman, Milk and Honey* and *I Have Been Here Before*.

Harvey's

Alan Parry talks about this mail order company during 'The Chance of a Lunchtime'. When Parry's company wins the contract to print all their junk mail, catalogues and office stationery, it means expansion.

Hawley, Dave

Telecine operator on two episodes: 'Miami Twice' (Parts 1 & 2)

Born in Rochester, Kent, Dave joined the BBC straight from school in 1971. He was employed as a technical assistant (a trainee engineer) working on film and video transmissions. In 1976 he was promoted to full engineer status, then six years later became a senior telecine operator, specialising primarily in dramas and documentaries, such as *Pride and Prejudice* and *Horizon*. For a time in the early 1990s, he worked closely with Granada Television, completing drama transfers for the station. Now working as a colourist, Dave has clocked up 30 years' service with the Beeb.

Haysman, Linda

Costume designer on one episode: 'The Frog's Legacy'

Linda, who was born in London, decided she wanted to work for the BBC when she was a teenager. After studying theatre design at the Central School of Art and Design, she left in 1980 and worked in fringe theatre for a short time before achieving her goal by joining the Beeb as a temporary costume assistant in 1981.

By the mid-1980s she'd been promoted to designer and worked on *Grange Hill* for a year, followed shortly after by 'The Frog's Legacy'. Linda, who's been working freelance since 1995, has worked on a host of shows, from comedy to period drama. Credits include *Noel's House Party, May to December, EastEnders, Hero to Zero, Out of the Blue, Prisoners in Time* and the children's BBC series *The Story of Tracy Beaker*, which aired in early 2002.

Hazlehurst, Ronnie

Arranged and conducted the title music

Ronnie is a self-taught musician whose initial instrument was the trumpet. After performing at church halls, Palais and Mecca ballrooms around his native Manchester, he played 'the road' and eventually set up home in London during the late 1950s, playing trumpet for a living, augmented by arrangements here and there.

His activities as a 'ghost' for many well known writers at the time helped him to build a strong enough reputation to be contracted by BBC radio as a composer/arranger, and over the next two years he operated as musical director on many of the BBC's most successful TV and radio programmes.

More than 130 themes for TV programmes are credited to Ronnie, who has frequently performed before royalty and has often conducted the Royal Variety Performance. He has officiated as the host MD for the Eurovision Song Contest several times and has worked around Europe as a musical director on behalf of the BBC. He has vast experience in all areas of popular music and has worked in such diverse fields as plays, documentaries, sitcoms, religious programmes, films, jazz, concerts, live shows and albums of all kinds.

Today, Ronnie lives in the Channel Islands, and continues to write extensively.

'He Ain't Heavy, He's My Uncle'

Original transmission: Sunday 27 January 1991, 7.15 pm

Production dates: 9 and 10 January 1991

Original viewing figures: 17.2 million

Duration: 50 minutes

First repeat: Wednesday 15 April 1992, 8.00 pm

Subsequent repeats: 25/3/94, 22/8/97, 18/5/01

CAST

Del Trotter	David Jason
Rodney Trotter	Nicholas Lyndhurst
Uncle Albert	Buster Merryfield
Raquel	Tessa Peake-Jones
Boycie	John Challis
Trigger	Roger Lloyd Pack
Marlene	Sue Holderness
Mike	Kenneth MacDonald
Dora	Joan Geary
Knock Knock	Howard Goorney
Mechanic	Herb Johnson
Ollie	Tony London

Walk-ons: Lee Farraday, Manda Maylin, Edi Britten, Philip French, Karrie Lambert, Graham Garrett, Barry Dougherty, Mark Flitton, Andy Goff, Dillon O'Mahony, Kay Lyell, Tom Little, Willy Bowman, Lola Morice, James Ash, Helen Jane Ridgeway, Dave Kurley, Tavernier, Robert Sim and Austin Brooks.

PRODUCTION TEAM

Written by John Sullivan

Title music arranged and conducted by Ronnie Hazlehurst composed and sung by John Sullivan

Make-up Designer:	Christine Greenwood
Costume Designer:	Robin Stubbs
Properties Buyer:	Malcolm Rougvie
Casting Adviser:	Judy Loe
Film Cameraman:	Alec Curtis
Film Sound:	Michael Spencer
Film Editor:	John Jarvis
Dubbing Mixer:	Michael Narduzzo
Camera Supervisor:	Ken Major
Studio Lighting Director:	Ron Bristow
Studio Sound:	Alan Machin
Resource Coordinator:	Peter Manuel
Videotape Editor:	Chris Wadsworth
Production Assistants:	Chris Gernon and Amanda Church
Assistant Floor Manager:	Debbie Crofts
Graphic Designer:	Andrew Smee
Vision Mixer:	Sue Collins

Production Manager: . . . . .Angela de Chastelai Smith
Production Secretary: . . . . . . .Katie Tyrrell
Designer: . . . . .Richard McManan-Smith
Directed by Tony Dow
Produced by Gareth Gwenlan

Raquel has reached the seventh month of her pregnancy, while Albert has joined the Over-Sixties' Club on the estate and has his sights set on Dora Lane. Life is going well for everyone, except Rodney, who's jobless and still separated from his wife. For Del, life's looking rosy too: he'll soon be a father, business is booming, he's arranging to buy his flat off the council and become a two-vehicle man when he buys a Ford Capri Ghia – even if its new home should be the nearest scrap yard, which is where it was heading until Boycie saw an opportunity to shift it on to Del.

Rodney is at such a low ebb that he pleads with Del to re-employ him; with no money coming in he's had to take out an overdraft at the bank to maintain his share of the mortgage. Initially Del isn't keen but eventually takes pity on his brother and asks him to get his car-cleaning gear because the new vehicle needs a polish. Dirtying his hands isn't what Rodney was expecting, especially as Del had agreed to his suggestion of being employed as TITCO's new Director of Commercial Development.

Later, after playing dominoes at The Nag's Head, Albert is mugged on his way home. Bruised and suffering from shock, he's so shaken up that he's scared to leave the flat. When Del and Rodney attempt to help their uncle out by playing tough, their plan backfires and he leaves during the night. They scour London and eventually find him and are able to persuade him to return home, but it's not long before Knock Knock comes calling and the real story behind Albert's black eye is heard.

'Healthy Competition'

Original transmission: Thursday 17 November 1983, 8.30 pm

Production date: Sunday 9 October 1983

Original viewing figures: 9.7 million

Duration: 30 minutes

First repeat: Monday 23 July 1984, 8.00 pm

Subsequent repeats: 7/9/91, 19/2/95, 3/11/97, 11/3/00

CAST

Del Trotter . . . . .David Jason
Rodney Trotter . . . . .Nicholas Lyndhurst
Grandad Trotter . . . . .Lennard Pearce
Auctioneer . . . . .Glynn Sweet
Mickey Pearce . . . . .Patrick Murray
Harry (the foreman) . . . . .Rex Robinson
Waiter (Indian restaurant) . . . . .Dev Sagoo
Young Towser . . . . .Mike Carnell

Walk-ons: . . . .(Policeman) Trevor Steedman. (People outside and inside department store) Alan Riches, Angela Delaney, Jay McGrath, Roy Seeley, Heather Downham and 19 extras. (People in Indian restaurant) six extras. (People in pub) John Holland and seven extras. (Barmaid) Julie La Rousse.

PRODUCTION TEAM
Written by John Sullivan
Title music arranged and conducted by Ronnie Hazlehurst composed and sung by John Sullivan
Audience Warm-up: . . . . .Bobby Bragg
Make-up Designer: . . . . .Denise Baron
Costume Designer: . . . . .Dinah Collin
Properties Buyer: . . . . .Penny Rollinson
Film Cameraman: . . . . .Ian Hilton
Film Sound: . . . . .Clive Derbyshire
Film Editor: . . . . .Mike Jackson
Camera Supervisor: . . . . .Ron Peverall
Studio Lighting Director: . . . . . .Don Babbage
Studio Sound: . . . . .Keith Gunn
Technical Coordinator: . . . . . . .Chris Watts
Videotape Editor: . . . . .Chris Wadsworth
Production Assistant: . . . . .Penny Thompson
Assistant Floor Manager: . . . . .Tony Dow
Graphic Designer: . . . . .Mic Rolph
Vision Mixer: . . . . .Angela Beveridge
Production Manager: . . . . .Andy Smith
Designer: . . . . .Antony Thorpe
Produced and directed by Ray Butt

Rodney's got a lot on his mind, which explains why Del nearly gets collared by a policeman for selling items illegally, when Rodders was supposed to be official look-out. He's been taking stock of his life: he's 24, has two GCEs, 13 years of schooling and three terms at an adult education centre behind him and all he's achieved is to become Del's look-out. The time has come to break free of his brother: Rodney announces he's going into partnership with Mickey Pearce. Del accepts the decision reluctantly, but warns his brother that severing all ties with TITCO means he pays his own way in every sense, even when it comes to drinking at The Nag's Head.

The following day, rivalry surfaces when Rodney and Mickey visit an auction that is also attended by Del. When Del advises his brother against bidding for Lot 37, Rodney becomes suspicious; believing Del obviously wants the items himself, he charges full-steam ahead and ends up wasting money on a pile of old broken lawnmower engines, which happen to have been sold on by Del in the first place.

Rodney's partnership is soon struggling, and when Mickey Pearce runs off to Benidorm with all their cash he's left with nothing in life but a load of old scrap, so turns to Del for help.

Heather

Played by Rosalind Lloyd
Heather is first seen sitting at the bar in The Nag's Head. Along with Del, she applauds Enrico, the so-called Spanish singer, when he finishes singing 'Old Shep' during 'Diamonds are for Heather'. After a

girlfriend fails to turn up, she decides to head back to her dingy little flat in Brixton, but not before Del steps in, gets chatting and offers to take her home.

Heather has a three-and-a-half-year-old son, Darren, and is separated from her husband, Vic, who walked out on her 18 months ago. Del quickly falls in love and it's not long before he's wining and dining her at a local restaurant, and offering her an engagement ring, which he's acquired on a week's approval. But she breaks his heart – until the next female comes along – by announcing that she's heard from Vic, who's working as Father Christmas in a Southampton department store, and has agreed to give their marriage another try.

Heather, Roy

Role: Sid
Appeared in 12 episodes: S2, episode 1, 'Christmas Trees', 'To Hull and Back'; 'A Royal Flush'; 'Dates'; 'The Jolly Boys' Outing'; 'Miami Twice' (Parts 1 & 2); 'Fatal Extraction'; 'Heroes and Villains'; 'Modern Men' and 'If They Could See Us Now…!'
Indelibly etched on Roy Heather's mind is the way director Ray Butt introduced him to the character of Sid. 'He said he was a scruffy bugger who ran the local greasy café, then added: "I think you will be just right!"'

Ray fancied using an older actor whose face wasn't instantly recognised by viewers and told Roy

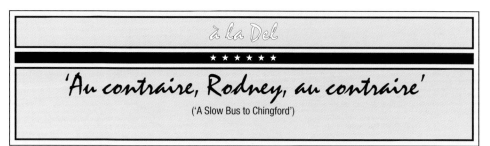

à la Del

★ ★ ★ ★ ★ ★

'Au contraire, Rodney, au contraire'

('A Slow Bus to Chingford')

that he'd be in touch. Roy didn't expect to hear anything further, so was surprised to receive a phone call the following week inviting him for an audition. The reading in front of Ray, John Sullivan, David Jason and Nicholas Lyndhurst was a success and he was offered the part. Always believing it would be a one-off role, he could never have imagined his character would become one of the regulars. 'It was great appearing in the show and I'm proud to be associated with it.'

One of Sid's foibles is his incessant smoking. He's rarely seen without a cigarette hanging precariously from his lips, which isn't ideal for a man who's been trying to quit smoking for years. 'Whenever a new show is commissioned, my wife says: "Oh my god, it's starting again, you'll never be able to give up the cigarettes."' But Roy finds solace in the fact that he's reduced the amount he smokes each day. 'I suppose I could play the part without actually smoking the cigarettes, but people expect the smoke to rise and the ash to go over the bread and butter, the same as they expect hairs to be found in the porridge – they expect that of Sid!'

Playing Sid, the slovenly café owner and temporary landlord, brought much-deserved attention and success for Roy, who'd turned to acting late in his working life, having worked as a warehouse manager in the cosmetics industry for 14 years beforehand. Ever since he was a boy, Roy had a passion for acting but pressure from his father prevented him pursuing an acting career earlier. Roy's father was an engineer who worked for ICI and was vehemently against his son trying his luck as an actor. 'I came from a rather Victorian type of family and he was dead against it,' explains Roy. 'He always believed that all actors were queer and all actresses loose!

'I think my initial desire to act came from the golden days of radio. When I was a kid I listened avidly to all the shows and thought it was something I'd enjoy. I had always been keen and did a lot of acting at school; it's just that it took me a long time to actually achieve my goal by making it my profession.'

Born in the Buckinghamshire town of Stoke Poges in 1935, Roy worked for an asbestos firm for a couple of years after leaving school and before completing national service with the Royal Air Force. Always an active participant in amateur dramatics, he had further opportunities to perform in the RAF. Once demobbed in 1957, he was determined not to return to his previous post and

accepted several dead-end jobs jobs until something better came along. 'I even worked as a Betterware salesman for a while, going from door to door; it was a tough job.'

All the time, Roy maintained his involvement in amateur acting, and it was a performance in the late 1970s that led to him taking the plunge and trying his luck as a professional. He was appearing in a play directed by a professional director who asked Roy if he'd ever considered entering the profession full time. Although the thought had been at the forefront of his mind, giving up a secure job wasn't a decision to be taken lightly. A week later, though, the decision was made for him when Roy was made redundant.

Within days the theatre director came calling and offered him his first professional job. With nothing to lose, Roy accepted the invitation and appeared in a 1978 production of *Rattle of a Simple Man* at Sheringham, Norfolk. 'Initially I'd asked for 48 hours to think about it, but he replied: "You've got ten minutes. I'll be waiting in the pub across the road." I sat there mulling things

MEMORIES OF PLAYING SID

★ ★ ★ ★ ★ ★

'I remember the day Windsor Davies introduced me to director Ray Butt in the BBC bar; he told me about this programme he was directing called *Only Fools and Horses*. My first thought was: "What a strange title for a sitcom!"

'But I love playing Sid, and fans of the sitcom must like him, too, because I get loads of letters from people. They tell me how much they love the character and always say things like, "I know he's disgusting but…". Whenever I go along to the conventions held by the Appreciation Society, people always want photographs of me lighting a cigarette.

'Over the years, I feel I've helped turn the character into the messy bugger he is today. In fact, it was me who evolved the idea of him having a four-day growth on his face. He's the sort of chap who gets up so early in the morning he doesn't feel he has time to shave; so this really down-at-heel character emerged.

'When I consider the sort of characters I've played elsewhere during my career, they couldn't be any further away from Sid. I remember filming "To Hull and Back" in 1985. One incident in particular sticks in my mind: I had a very early call, so after make-up and wardrobe I wandered down to watch the lads dressing the set – an empty ex-dress shop was being used as my café. There I stood, about 5.30am, with the obligatory four-day growth on my chin, hair in its usual shaggy unkempt style and wearing a gravy-stained apron. Suddenly, out of the corner of my eye, I saw two guys who could only be described as "gentlemen of the road", taking up station on a railway sleeper hidden in the grass behind me. After surreptitious glances at me, and a lot of furtive whispering between them, one of them staggered towards me waving an amply filled bottle, slurring: "Here, mate! Have a swig of this, you look like you need it!" In my very best RSC voice, I replied: "Well I never! That really is terribly sweet of you, but I think it's just a teensy bit early just at the moment. Thank you all the same." He gave me the biggest, old-fashioned look imaginable and retired in total confusion to join his mate!

'I love how the character is regarded as something of a regular nowadays. And, of course, he's now running The Nag's Head in Mike's absence. Shortly after poor old Ken died, John Sullivan rang me. Some other members of the cast had said they felt the best thing was to stick Sid in the pub; they must have been reading John's mind because that's what he wanted to do. He asked what I thought and obviously I was more than happy. There had always been this unwritten agreement between Mike and Sid that should anything arise, Sid would run the pub.

'I don't know if we'll ever see the café again; I've got a feeling that Health and Safety officials will close the place down, but only John Sullivan knows the answer to that one. Of course, they never kept the café as one of the stock sets anyway, so every time you see it it appears slightly different. If you're one of these anoraks who looks out for those sort of things you'll notice it couldn't possibly be the same building. And whenever we were on location, all sorts of places were used from an old dress shop and disused factory to real-life truckers' cafés.

'I love the character and am happy to join up with the cast and be part of such a wonderful programme. When it comes to an end, or if it comes to an end, Sid will always be with me. I remember once we'd worked late in the studio, and rather than trudge all the way home, Paul Barber very kindly offered to put me up at his place. In the morning he took me down to his local greasy spoon and introduced me to an original Sid: he was a hell of a nice man. He put this huge breakfast down on the table in front of me and said: "Now you can see what a real breakfast looks like." It was wonderful. As well as trying to give up smoking, I was also attempting to cut down on my cholesterol, so I was forbidden fried food most of the time. I'd been very good but on a morning like that, I couldn't resist having this massive fry-up.

'Meeting up with all my old friends for "If They Could See Us Now…!" was fantastic. When we got down to Weston-super-Mare for some of the location shooting, nearly all of us were staying at the same hotel, so we sat down and had dinner together. And earlier when we had the read-through, everybody was there, except Paul Barber, who was working. It was great seeing all the old faces again, and we spent some time rushing around being very luvvy with each other!

'The content of the storyline didn't surprise me at all. Knowing in my mind the way John Sullivan writes, I knew he'd come up with some magic core of a story. He's just amazing. I went to an awards ceremony once with John Challis and Ken MacDonald. On that particular occasion we had to accept an award for John Sullivan. I remember they passed the mike around and asked whether there was anything we had to say. I just said: "I know it's an overworked word, particularly in television, but John Sullivan is a genius." It got a great round of applause and I knew everyone else agreed; he's the best there is, there's no doubt about that.'

ROY HEATHER

---

over, but really there wasn't anything to think about: I didn't have a job, it was something I'd always wanted to do, and at 44 I knew if I didn't give it a go, I never would, so I accepted his offer. I haven't regretted the decision once.'

Roy's debut as a professional actor was a success, local newspapers the following morning carried nothing but glowing reviews of his performance. 'The director came up to me and threw a paper on the table, saying: "There you go; look at these reviews and you'll understand why I wanted you to play the part." All the reports were about me and they were absolutely wonderful.'

After a spell in rep at Sheringham, Roy joined Newpalm, a production company set up by ex-actor John Newman and his wife, Daphne Palmer, at Chelmsford. From there he did a summer season at Shanklin, on the Isle of Wight, where he became friends with Windsor Davies, who helped him move into television. 'I remember him telling me that I should do some television, so he took me to the BBC Club, where I met Ray Butt. It all helped, especially as I'd only done one thing on television before that.'

His debut in 'Fatty Patty', a 1980 instalment from BBC's *Scene* series, was the springboard to many other small-screen appearances. He played Simpson in the 1985 mini-series *Return to Treasure Island*, Lowe in *Edge of Darkness*, a workman in *Colin's Sandwich*, a transport superintendent in *Poirot*, an old man in *Bottom*, a taxi driver in *As Time Goes By*, a caretaker in *Frank Stubbs Promotes* and the Biscuit Man in *The Legacy of Reginald Perrin*. He's recently been recording another series as the Old Geezer in Sky One's comedy series *Time Gentlemen Please*.

Roy's worked in all mediums but finds it difficult choosing a favourite. 'When I'm doing lots of tele I always want to do more theatre, but when I'm on stage I feel the opposite. Obviously working in the theatre isn't as well paid as television, unless you get involved with one or two big companies, such as the Royal Exchange in Manchester. But you can't beat doing something like *Only Fools*; it's not just work, it's like a family, we all get on so well. A friend of mine, when interviewed once, said: "I look forward to every morning because I wake up and tell myself I'm an actor." That just about sums me up as well!'

Heavy, The

Played by Roy Questel

The non-speaking 'heavy' provides the muscle whenever Mr Ram requires it. The casually dressed Indian is first seen sitting in a car outside the town hall in 'Cash and Curry'. A second dan in karate, he's called into action when Ram confronts Vimmal Malik, but to Rodney's disbelief, Del puts the heavy out of action with an incisive whack in the groin.

Hedley, Jack

Role: Henry

Appeared in 'A Royal Flush'

Veteran film and television actor Jack Hedley was born in London in 1930. His small-screen work has kept him busy over the years, with appearances in shows like *Gideon's Way*, *The Saint*, *Journey to the Unknown*, *UFO* and *Special Branch* in the 1960s to *Colditz*, *Remington Steele* and, more recently, *Dalziel and Pascoe* and *San Paolo*.

On the film front, he's been seen in a number of pictures, including *Room at the Top; Make Mine Mink; The Very Edge; The Longest Day; Goodbye, Mr Chips* and *For Your Eyes Only.*

Helen

Not seen in the sitcom, Helen met Rodney at The Nag's Head disco during 'The Miracle of Peckham'. Older than Rodney, she's tall and slender. Rodney thinks she looks like Linda Evans from *Dynasty*, while Del sees her in a different light: he regards her as an 'old dog', a bit 'scraggy' and about six foot six. He also says she's known as Helen of Croydon, the face that launched a thousand dredgers.

Helen

Played by Dawn Funnell

Seen in 'The Jolly Boys' Outing', Helen works for Mrs Baker in her Margate guest house, the Sunny Sea. The dark-haired waitress is serving dinner when we see her.

Helga

Not seen in the sitcom, Helga's the Swedish girl Mickey Pearce meets in Benidorm when he runs off with Rodney's money, claiming he'll be sorting out some business contracts with Spanish clients for their broken lawnmower engines.

Helga

A faded photo is all Uncle Albert has of Helga, the one girl he truly loved. We never see her, but hear about her in 'Watching the Girls Go By'. It was 1946 and Albert's ship had sailed into Hamburg to pick up prisoners; she was working in a bar near the docks. Helga had lost the little finger on her right hand when her home was bombed – an attack which wiped out her entire family. Albert fell in love with her instantly, and asked her to marry him but she refused, which was just as well since he was still married to Ada at the time.

Hendrix

Chief Inspector Slater refers to Hendrix in 'To Hull and Back', whilst talking to Del. He was the leader of a diamond smuggling outfit, but Slater was forced to let him go due to insufficient evidence, a fact which still irks him.

Henry

Played by Jack Hedley

(For 'Henry' in 'A Royal Flush', see 'Duke of Maylebury, The')

Henry

Played by Gordon Warnecke

In 'The Sky's the Limit', Henry, the concierge at the Gatwick hotel looks after Rodney's needs. A suite has been hired for Rodney and Cassandra to sort out their marital problems, but plans for putting his marriage back on track in style are scuppered when the Malaga flight – on which Cass is returning – is rerouted to Manchester.

Herford, Robin

Role: Man at opera
Appeared in 'A Royal Flush'

Born in Windsor in 1946, Robin – who's also a director – trained at the Bristol Old Vic Theatre School before making his professional debut in 1972 at Bath's Theatre Royal in *Narrow Road to the Deep North.*

After working all around the country in various repertory theatres, including Derby, Nottingham, Harrogate, Manchester, Scarborough and London, he stepped into the genre of television in 1985, playing Ivan Braithwaite, Pandora's father in *The Secret Diary of Adrian Mole*. He was later seen in *The Growing Pains of Adrian Mole.*

Much of Robin's career has been involved with Alan Ayckbourn (he's appeared in more original productions of Ayckbourn's plays than any other actor), and the Stephen Joseph Theatre in Scarborough. He joined the company in 1976 as an actor, was appointed associate director in 1979 and, then, artistic director between 1986 and 1988. More recently, he's directed *The Women in Black* tour of the UK, Japan and America.

Herman, Leslie Eve

Assistant costume designer on two episodes: 'Miami Twice' (Parts 1 & 2)

American costume designer Leslie Eve Herman has built up an extensive list of credits in film and television in the States. In 1980 she worked as production assistant on *Running Scared*, while as a wardrobe supervisor she's clocked up a host of movies, including *Cat Chaser, A Show of Force, Primal Rage, Two Much, First-Time Felon, Thick as Thieves, Play It to the Bone, Gun Shy* and *Joy Ride.*

Her television work covers productions such as *King of Texas* and *Moon Over Miami.*

'Heroes and Villains'

(First part of 1996 Christmas Trilogy)

Original transmission: Wednesday 25 December 1996, 9.00 pm

Original viewing figures: 21.3 million

Duration: 60 minutes

First repeat: Friday 2 January 1998, 7.55 pm

Subsequent repeats: 17/9/99, 22/6/01, 16/2/02

CAST

Del Trotter	David Jason
Rodney Trotter	Nicholas Lyndhurst
Uncle Albert	Buster Merryfield
Raquel	Tessa Peake-Jones
Cassandra	Gwyneth Strong
Boycie	John Challis
Trigger	Roger Lloyd Pack
Mike	Kenneth MacDonald
Marlene	Sue Holderness
Denzil	Paul Barber
Sid	Roy Heather
Councillor Murray	Angela Bruce
Old Damien	Douglas Hodge
Damien	Jamie Smith
Kenny	Steve Weston
Gary	Scott Marshall
Scott	Dan Clark
Kevin	Fuman Dar
Dawn	Sheree Murphy
Old Lady	Bay White
Mayor	Robin Meredith
Photographer	Richard Hicks

Tom (Commissionaire) . . . . .Ted Shepherd
(The scene involving the five actors below was edited out before final transmission)
Market lads . . . . .Lee Barritt and Leonard Kirby
Policeman . . . . .Ray Macallan
Walk-ons: . . . .(Mugging sequence) Debbie Bowman and Abigail

Walk-ons: . . . .(Futuristic sequence) Daniel Thompson, Helen Judson, Vida Garman, Ellie Reece Knight, Richard Grant, Paul Capelli, John Berry, Sharon Douglas, Fred Whitham, Jean Whitham, Kee Yee Lam, Steve Babb, Kask Kumar, Cherron Johnson, Tym Arah. (Sid's Café) Crystal, Adrian Coke, Colin Johnson, James Crooks, Melvyn Campbell, Jane Stevens, Jane Terry, Don Board, Jamie Greaves, James Anderson, Tony Baylis, Kit Edwards, Andrew Bell, Lee Benson, Tom Walker, Tony Birch and Jorge Borrios Silva. (Wake) Maureen Brown, Vivien Lesley, Christopher Smith, Don Leather, Danny Georgeovich, Jean Hall, Eric Hartley, Pauline Millman, Brian Bowen, Lindsay Elliott, Lorraine O'Leary, Nicole Dominic, Liz Young, Terry Arnold, Julie Bateman, Hermine Lewis, Gareth Evans, Steve Maro, Margaret Edwards, Paul Farish, Chris Abbott, Philip Ticehurst, Pete Rayland, Clive Greenaway, Kate Kempton, John Clay, Robbie Payne, Cindy Leather and Fay Williams. (Market) Gavin Wilson, Cherrie Chantell, Maxine Atkins, Marina Johnson, Coral Chapman, Vincent Bell, Bobby Daniel, John Emms, Clare Francis, Johnson Yakoob, Lloyd James Mason, Tracey Ann Ward, Jill Alexanda, Daphne Neville, Kate Kempton, Michael Bell, Paul Anderson, Peter Yakoob, Margaret Davies, Gwyn Blackbird, Anna Farthing, Baby Mabel Moll, Lureen Campbell, Molly Keel, Nathan Lewis, Saeed Esmaeli, Carl Thomas, Paul Howard, Mike Eastman, Christine Murphy, David Dean, Andrew Jones, Angeliki Yannaghas, Badria Timmi, Max Speed, Rosita Mee, Mark Breckon, Chris Palmer and Anne Beardsley. (Chase sequence) Adrian Bennett, Mohinder Ayers, Adrian Bennett, Sandra Forbes, Angela Forbes, Darius Walker, Ian Sutherland, Basil Anderson, Eric McCarthy, Harriett Stagg-Graham, Justine Garner, Bartholomew Lawless, Jonathan Burrows, Colin Whitear, Monica Ramone, Suzie Amor, Debra Mundy, Terry Courtney, Marc Griffiths, Justin Wong and Lucea Eldmiere. (The Nag's Head) James Delaney, Bert Crome, Norman Feakins, Romona Joseph, Lewis Saint Juste, Pat Goode, Lorna Sinclair, Pat Shepherd, Ivan Hunte and George Bailey. (Town hall) Pogus Caesar, Barbara Allen, Rebecca Sloan, Alison Jameson, Tommy Banner, Malcolm Holmes, Peter Lawrence, Nigel Keen, Gerry George, Denise Danielle, Bahar Mohammed, Akbar Bibi, John Brinson, Diana Clay, Roger Bill, Mo Bill, Pat Wayne, Martin Thomas, Monica Thomas, Derek Brunstone, Terry Henry, Lloyd McIntosh and Ted Shepherd.

PRODUCTION TEAM
Written by John Sullivan
Title music arranged and conducted by Ronnie Hazlehurst composed and sung by John Sullivan
Music: . . . . .Graham Jarvis
Make-up Designer: . . . . .Deanne Turner
Costume Designer: . . . . .Robin Stubbs
Properties Buyer: . . . . .Graham Bishop
Art Director: . . . . .Nick Harding
Visual Effects Designer: . . . . . .Andy Lazell
Video Effects: . . . . .Ian Simpson
Casting Adviser: . . . . .Judy Loe
Programme Finance Assistant: .Alison Passey
Fim Sound: . . . . .Roger Long
Film Editor: . . . . .John Jarvis

Camera Supervisor: . . . . .Peter Woodley
Studio Lighting Director: . . . . .Graham Rimmington
Studio Sound: . . . . .Keith Gunn
Studio Resource Manager: . . .Richard Morgan
Videotape Editor: . . . . .Chris Wadsworth
Production Assistant: . . . . .Caroline Gardener
Assistant Floor Manager: . . . .Beccy Fawcett
Floor Manager: . . . . .Vivien Ackland-Snow
Vision Mixer: . . . . .Heather Gilder
Stunt Coordinator: . . . . .Nick Powell
Grips: . . . . .Iain Johnstone
Gaffer: . . . . .Pat Deveney
1st Assistant Director: . . . . . . .David Reid
2nd Assistant Director: . . . . . . .Dominic Bowles
3rd Assistant Director: . . . . . . .Anna Brabbins
Location Managers: . . . . .Lisa McArthur
and Steve Abrahams
Dubbing Editor: . . . . .Paul Bingley
Production Secretary: . . . . .Katie Wilkinson
Production Designer: . . . . .Donal Woods
Photography: . . . . .John Rhodes
Associate Producer: . . . . .Sue Longstaff
Executive Producer: . . . . .John Sullivan
Directed by Tony Dow
Produced by Gareth Gwenlan

Del's depressed: not only has he found himself lumbered with 150 Latvian radio alarm clocks that have a mind of their own, and 200 aerodynamic cycling helmets that are nothing more than horse-riding crash helmets painted red, but he has just had his home improvement grant rejected by the council.

Rodney, on the other hand, is just bushed; he and Cassandra are still going all out for a baby and the punishing 'schedule' issued by the hospital is getting too much for him because he can't stand the pace! With Cassandra getting very broody, Rodney tries placating her by buying her a rabbit called Roger, giving her something to care for until the real thing comes along.

Trigger is probably the happiest of The Nag's Head crowd, because he's just been awarded a medal by the council for services to the public; he's also saved his employer's money by retaining the same broom for 20 years, but what they haven't realised is that it's had 17 new heads and 14 replacement handles in that period.

It's Rodney's birthday and just when he starts thinking no one has remembered, Del – being as generous as ever – has got him a nine-carat gold identity bracelet, disguised as a 24-carat version,

'Heroes and Villains'

with the name 'Rooney' emblazoned on it. Cassandra's parents, meanwhile, have invited her and Rodney to their villa as a birthday treat; so desperate is he to take a break from their 'schedule', he uses the pressures of work as an excuse and ships Cassandra off on her own. This also means that the Trotter boys have a rare weekend together.

Taking the opportunity to have a boys' night out at a fancy dress party organised by a local publican, Del and Rodney don their Batman and Robin outfits and head across town. But *en route* the van packs up, leaving them no alternative but to sprint the rest of the way in their costumes.

Meanwhile, Councillor Murray – who had turned down Del's home improvement grant – leaves work and is set upon by a gang of youths who try to snatch her bag, just as Del and Rodney arrive on the scene. Spotting the caped crusaders running towards them, the muggers take fright and disappear into the darkness, leaving the gobsmacked Murray to thank her masked rescuers.

The Trotters finally make it to the party and are greeted by a sniggering Boycie, dressed in a black suit and tie. Unbeknown to Del and Rodney, the host has just died and a wake is being held instead.

Back at the market the following day, the muggers turn up again, this time picking on a frail old lady and running off with her handbag. Rodney sets off in pursuit, with Del not far behind lugging his suitcase full of goods. When he's cornered with one of the muggers, Rodney chickens out, leaving his big brother to flattens the youth with the help of his trusty old suitcase.

Del's awarded a bravery medal and sees his home improvement grant reconsidered in the light of his heroics. To make the Trotters' day, Cassandra and Rodney have some good news: they will soon be hearing the patter of tiny feet.

Herrington Road

In 'Homesick' Dr Becker suggests the Trotters move to one of the new three-bedroom council bungalows in Herrington Road. In the doctor's opinion, not having to clamber up 12 flights of stairs will work wonders for Grandad's health – even if the old man was only feigning illness in the first place. The road is also mentioned by Del in 'Dates', when Raquel rents a flat at number 18.

Hicks, Richard

Role: Photographer
Appeared in 'Heroes and Villains'
Richard's list of credits includes appearances in *Bean: The Movie*, *Waking the Dead*, *Feast of July* and *Revolution*.

Higgins, Iggy

Not seen in the sitcom, Iggy is mentioned by Del in 'A Royal Flush'. The local villain loans Del a rifle for him to take along to the Duke of Maylebury's shoot.

Highcliffe Hotel

Cassandra stays at this hotel on Guernsey whilst

★ ★ ★ **CUT SCENE!   CUT SCENE!** ★ ★ ★

CUT FROM 'HEROES AND VILLAINS'

John Sullivan says: 'This was part of my original notes for the 1996 Christmas episode, which eventually became "Heroes and Villains". I began to develop the theme but it became too drawn out, so I dropped the hidden treasure idea but kept the Batman and Robin image. The missing treasure idea eventually became the Harrison watch, which made Del and Rodney millionaires.'

DEL AND ROD HAVE BEEN INVITED TO A FANCY-DRESS PARTY AT THE HOUSE OF HARRY MALCOLM, AN 80-YEAR-OLD MAN WHO WAS THE LANDLORD OF THE 'CROWN AND ANCHOR' PUB FOR YEARS. DEL AND ROD ARE NOT TO KNOW, BUT HARRY HAS BEEN TAKEN SERIOUSLY ILL (ON HIS LAST KNOCKINGS) AND THE FANCY-DRESS PARTY HAS BEEN CANCELLED. THE 'PARTY' IS NOW MORE LIKE A WAKE – ALL OF HARRY'S RELATIVES ARE THERE DRESSED IN BLACK OR SOMBRE ATTIRE. THE TROTTERS ARRIVE DRESSED AS BATMAN AND ROBIN.

HARRY'S LIVING ROOM. NIGHT

THE FAMILY AND FRIENDS ARE ALL SEATED ROUND CONSOLING EACH OTHER WHEN THE BELL RINGS.

HARRY'S HALL. NIGHT
BOYCIE OPENS DOOR TO DEL AND ROD (BATMAN AND ROBIN).
DEL All right, Boycie? Sorry we're a bit late.
DEL AND RODNEY ENTER HALLWAY.
DEL What you come as, an undertaker?
ROD Not very original, is it?
DEL Ready?
DEL AND RODNEY EXIT. BOYCIE SMILES TO HIMSELF.

HARRYS LIVING ROOM. NIGHT
BATMAN AND ROBIN BURST INTO THE ROOM.
DEL AND ROD (SINGING THEME SONG) Da da da da da da da da – da da da da da da da – Batman! Da da da…
DEL BECOMING AWARE THAT ALL IS NOT WELL, STOPS SINGING. RODNEY CONTINUES FOR A COUPLE OF BARS.
ROD Da da da da da – Bat (ALSO REALISING THAT ALL IS NOT WELL) …man.
HARRY'S SON TELLS DEL THAT HARRY HAS REQUESTED TO SEE HIM THE MOMENT HE ARRIVES.

HARRY'S BEDROOM. NIGHT
HARRY IS ASLEEP IN BED. HE WAKES WITH ALARM TO

FIND BATMAN AND ROBIN PEERING DOWN ON HIM. HE NOW EXPLAINS WHY HE WANTED TO TALK TO DEL AND GOES ON TO TELL AN INCREDIBLE TALE.
HARRY My great-grandfather went looking for work in America. He lived in Boston, I think. This was in 1861. You remember what happened in 1861?
ROD No.
DEL He can't remember what happened in 1961!
ROD But then again I've got medical reasons, ain't I? I weren't bloody born!
HARRY The American Civil War started in 1861.
DEL See, the American Civil War started in 1861!
ROD I know that, don't I! I studied history at school.
DEL Yeah, a lot of good you were as well! I remember that time you thought Merlin the magician was Houdini's Dad.
ROD That's what you told me!
HARRY Boys, boys! Will you please stop arguing so I can die.
DEL Sorry, Harry. Have some respect, Rodney!
HARRY Grandad couldn't find any work so he joined the Union army. He fought against the Confederates. He fought right through the war; he was actually there at the very end. You know Abe Lincoln?
DEL Did he have a fruit and veg stall at the end of the market?
ROD No! Abraham Lincoln! You've heard of his Gettysburg address.
DEL I never knew the bloke, Rodney, so how do I know where he lived?
ROD Dear God!
HARRY It's not important, Del. The important thing is that during the battle of Bull Run he accidentally discovered something. He came across a burnt out wagon and on the back of this wagon was a metal chest. So he opened it.
DEL What was in it?
HARRY A fortune, Del! A bloody fortune! More wealth than he'd ever seen or was ever likely to see.
ROD What's he do? Did he hand it in to the authorities?
HARRY AND DEL START LAUGHING.
HARRY That's why I wanted Rodney here, Del, so I could die with a smile on me face. No, Rodney, he didn't hand it in to authorities. He wasn't that sort of bloke. He pugged it away in a secret place. A month or so later he met an old mate who was returning home to England, He gave him the chest to fetch home for him. So eventually it arrived back at the family house. Well, they didn't know what was in it, and it was locked anyway, so they shoved it up in the loft to await Grandad's return. Well, he never did return. He died over there, the very last skirmish of the war.
ROD What, he was shot?

HARRY No, apparently he lit the fuse on a field gun and nothing happened. So he looked down the barrel to see if it was loaded… and it was! Well, everyone forgot about that old metal chest, it just lay in the attic for the next eighty-odd years – until my Mum and Dad died in a 1943 bombing raid. Me and my brother Stan were left the old house and we found the chest, forced it open. Blimey, Del Boy, we couldn't believe our eyes. Never seen anything like it in our lives. We were rich, stinking, bloody rich!

DEL Lovely jubbly!

HARRY But we were worried.

DEL Why?

HARRY Well, one, was it legal? And two, how could we protect it? They were dodgy times, Del. People were dropping bombs on us. So Stan, being the elder brother, went off and buried it – said we'd dig it up when the war was over. Stan then went off and promptly got killed in Tripoli.

ROD And you didn't know where it was buried?

HARRY Didn't have a clue, Rodney. Until about a month ago. My nephew, Stan's boy, found a couple of letters addressed to me in Stan's old army rucksack. In one of 'em was a map of where he'd buried the chest. Well, it don't mean a lot to me, Del, in my condition. So I'd like you to have it.

DEL Oh cheers, Harry.

HARRY It's in my bedside drawer.

ROD But why you giving it to Del?

DEL Harry can do what he wants with his own map, Rodney!

ROD But I mean, you've got your own sons and daughters out there.

HARRY Rodney. I see them once a year if I'm lucky. They've never done anything for me.

DEL That's right, ungrateful gits!

ROD Well, they're all here now, ain't they?

HARRY They've just come to see what I'm leaving 'em. I feel like I'm at London Zoo, in the bleed'n vultures' cage! Del boy did something for me years ago. I promised I'd pay you back, didn't I, Del?

DEL (STUDYING THE MAP) Yes, you did, Harry.

HARRY And I've kept me promise. Hide it, Del; don't let that lot see it.

DEL Righto, Harry, whatever you say.

ROD Del, that legally belongs to Harry's children.

DEL No it doesn't! This belonged to his Grandad.

ROD Yeah and he nicked it!

DEL It was the American Civil War, Rodders; I shouldn't think they're still looking for it!

ROD Legally it should be passed down through the family!

DEL No! Harry's simply paying back a favour for what I did for him years ago!

ROD And what did you do for him?

DEL Well, I…! What did I do for you, Harry? Harry!

WE SEE THAT HARRY HAS PASSED AWAY WITH A SMILE ON HIS FACE. DEL AND ROD LOOK UP AT EACH OTHER.

HARRY'S LIVING ROOM. NIGHT

DEL AND ROD ENTER AND JOIN ALL OF HARRY'S RELATIVES WHO ARE WAITING EAGERLY/ HUNGRILY FOR NEWS.

DEL He's gone.

DAUGHTER Oh no! (SHE RUSHES INTO BEDROOM FOLLOWED BY FOUR OR FIVE OTHERS. THEY ALMOST FIGHT EACH OTHER TO BE FIRST OUT OF THE ROOM.)

SON Did he say anything, Del?

DEL No!

SON What, nothing?

DEL No. Not a thing, did he, Rodney?

ROD … No.

SON Well, you were in there a long time! What were you doing?

DEL Waiting for him to say something.

DEL AND ROD NOW EMBARK ON A CRUSADE TO RETRIEVE THE METAL CHEST. THEY FINALLY FIND IT AND DISCOVER IT IS PACKED FULL OF AMERICAN DOLLARS – CONFEDERATE DOLLARS – AND, THEREFORE, WORTHLESS. DEL THEN REMEMBERS WHAT HE DID FOR HARRY. YEARS AGO, WHEN DEL WAS ONLY 16, HE SOLD HARRY SOMETHING COUNTERFEIT AND HARRY HAD SWORN THAT IF IT TOOK HIM TILL HIS DYING DAY, HE WOULD GET REVENGE.

****

John Sullivan says: 'The Whole of Del's opening spiel and the sales pitch to the four lads was cut from "Heroes and Villains".'

THE MARKET. DAY

A WEEK LATER. DEL HAS THE SUITCASE OPEN ON THE GROUND. WE SEE IT IS FULL OF THE RED RIDING HELMETS AND THE BASEBALL CAPS. ROD IS CLOSE BY, LEANING AGAINST THE FRAME OF ONE OF THE STALLS AND READING THE *PECKHAM ECHO*. THE HEADLINE READS: 'COUNCILLOR MURRAY BREATHALYSED AFTER MUGGING CLAIM' SUB HEADLINE READS: "'BATMAN AND ROBIN SAVED ME' CLAIMS TOWN HALL CHIEF'.

DEL IS ALREADY BORED WITH THE REJECTION OF HIS WARES AND IT TELLS IN HIS VOICE.

DEL (FED UP) Aerodynamic cycling helmets. (TAPS ONE FOR US TO HEAR A METALLIC SOUND) as worn by Chris Boardman – and his cousin, Stan. Baseball caps. Straight from L.A, as worn by MC Hammer. Buy the kid a baseball cap for Christmas. Unisex baseball caps, designed especially for your sons or daughters – or your Rottweiler or your goldfish. Baseball caps. (TO ROD) I can't see us doing a lot of business today. Let's sling it all in the van and go home.

AS DELS TURNS BACK TO SUITCASE ETC, WE SEE FOUR LADS (ABOUT 16–17 YEARS OF AGE) ARE STUDYING THE BASEBALL CAPS. THE FOUR LADS ALL WEAR BACK-TO-FRONT BASEBALL CAPS.

DEL D'you wanna buy one?

1ST LAD We've already got baseball caps.

DEL Not like these you ain't. These are a brand new design straight from Los Angeles.

2ND LAD (STUDIES INSIDE OF A CAP) It says here 'Made in Taiwan'.

DEL Yes, made in Taiwan but designed in America. The Bloods and the Cripps are wearing these, they're all the go over there.

1ST LAD Yeah? What's so special about 'em? They don't look any different.

DEL Haute couture is obviouly not your strong point, is it? I'll show you.

HE DIRECTS 1ST LAD TO A SMALL MIRROR WHICH IS HANGING ON END OF STALL. DEL REMOVES LADS BACK-TO-FRONT BASEBALL CAP AND PLACES THE NEW ONE ON HIS HEAD – BUT HE PLACES IT WITH THE PEAK AT THE FRONT.

DEL See, with these ones the peak is at the front!

1ST LAD STUDIES HIMSELF IN THE MIRROR.

1ST LAD Oh yeah, good ain't they?

DEL For two pounds fifty you'll all be instant trend-setters.

1ST LAD Righto, I'll take it.

OTHER LADS Me too.

DEL STARTS TAKING MONEY. WE SEE AN ELDERLY LADY STANDING CLOSE TO A STALL AND PUTTING HER PURSE BACK INTO HER BAG. WE ALSO SEE THE THREE MEN AND GIRL MUGGING TEAM ARE CLOSE BY AND EYEING HER. DAWN MOVES IN AND ASKS THE OLD LADY THE TIME. THE BOYS MOVE IN CLOSER.

ROD Del! Have a look.

DEL What's up?

WE NOW SEE SCOTT AND KEVIN CROWD THE OLD LADY, GARY (THE LEADER) GRABS THE OLD LADY'S HANDBAG AND PULLS IT FROM HER. IN THE STRUGGLE THE OLD LADY FALLS TO THE GROUND.

attending a banking conference. It's not seen, but is mentioned by Del in 'Chain Gang'.

Hignett, Robert

Technical coordinator on ten episodes: S1; S2, episodes 5 & 7; 'Christmas Crackers' and 'Diamonds are for Heather'

Hill, Daniel

Role: Stephen
Appeared in 'The Jolly Boys' Outing'

David – who was born in Bristol – worked in a solicitor's office before training at the city's Old Vic Theatre School. He made his professional debut in *Royal Hunt of the Sun* before working around the country in theatre.

His first taste of television was playing Ivor in BBC's 1975 comedy *Forget-Me-Not Lane*, but his favourite roles, as well as Stephen, are Harvey in *Waiting for God* and Raymond in *No Place Like Home*. Recent television work includes appearing as Jeff Latham in *Hope and Glory* and in *Uprising* for NBC.

Hill, Mike

Engineering manager on one episode: 'A Royal Flush'

Hills, Beverley

Role: Sister
Appeared in 'Modern Men'

Liverpudlian Beverley Hills – whose father was the Nigerian featherweight champion in 1952 – moved, in her teens, to Birmingham, where she joined the city's youth theatre. This led to a spell working in the costume department of the Birmingham Rep.

After several seasons as wardrobe mistress with the RSC, Beverley headed south to London and became a professional actress and jazz singer. Her debut arrived in 1983, playing Maria in *Carmen*, followed by a spell in fringe theatre. She made her first excursion into the world of television with an appearance in BBC's *South of the Border*.

Her varied career has ranged from designing costumes in Italy for an opera company to co-writing a West End musical. Her acting credits include *The Liver Birds*, *The Accused*, *Real Women* and two years on *Brookside*. She's currently very busy presenting the children's show *Storytime* and appearing in *Byker Grove*. She has just completed her first novel and is soon to shoot and star in her first short film, *Whatever's Going On at Number 19?*

Hills, Peter

Camera supervisor on one episode: 'Christmas Crackers'

Hilton, Ian

Film cameraman on six episodes: S3, episodes 1–4, 6 & 7

History of the sitcom

By the time the Trotters arrived in town in their clapped out Reliant, John Sullivan was well aware of the capricious nature of sitcom writing. The joys of achieving success with his first serious offering, *Citizen Smith*, had been muted by the disappointment of seeing his second sitcom, *Over the Moon*, about the manager of Britain's worst football team, cancelled. But he hoped to get back on track with his next idea.

Jimmy Gilbert, who'd been instrumental in helping launch John Sullivan's career by commissioning *Citizen Smith*, had been promoted to Head of Entertainment by the time *Only Fools* – which was originally titled *Readies* – came along. John Sullivan had already discussed the premise for the show with Gilbert, whilst he had been Head of Comedy, but it was a year or so later before the idea was raised again. When John Howard Davies sat down with Gilbert to discuss the idea, the potential was noted immediately. However, Gilbert wasn't particularly happy with the title, which by now had been altered to *Only Fools and Horses* (it had previously been used for an episode of *Citizen Smith*). 'It wasn't the greatest title in the world,' admits Jimmy. 'I'd heard of a similar phrase, "Only birds and idiots fly" from my days in the RAF, but just didn't feel it was ideal for a television programme.' But, just like Howard Davies, he knew the proposal had potential.

'It was an intriguing idea at the time,' says John Howard Davies. 'A story about a London family who wouldn't sponge off the State, wouldn't use the National Health if they could help it and certainly wouldn't use any of the facilities available to them, offered a lot of opportunites for comedy. But on the other hand they wouldn't actually contribute anything in the way of tax: they would be self-sufficient in many ways.'

Jimmy Gilbert was determined to keep Sullivan writing for the Beeb and wasn't going to let his feelings concerning the show's name get in the way, but it was something he wanted to address in due course. 'John was obviously a major new writer and I wanted to keep him employed with the BBC. And, to be honest, the show would have been a success whatever it was called.'

Even when the series was commissioned, concerns regarding the title rumbled on. Gareth Gwenlan, who later produced the series, remembers talking to John Sullivan and Ray Butt, the original producer/director, about the matter. 'When I asked them how it was going, John seemed a little depressed. He knew he'd come up with the right title but had been asked to think of alternatives. So I offered him a bit of advice. He had a meeting with Jimmy Gilbert and John Howard Davies that afternoon, so I told him to say he wanted to use it and they would need to think of something else if they didn't like it. Later on, John returned to my office delighted because the strategy had worked.'

'Actually, I thought *Readies* would have made a good title,' says John Sullivan. 'People like Del never dealt in cheques or credit cards; everything had to be ready cash, so the title seemed appropriate. I'd also considered calling it *Big Brother*, which eventually became the title for the first episode.'

The uncertainty towards the title even made John Sullivan begin questioning the wisdom of his choice. 'Someone ran a straw poll at the BBC Club asking people "What is *Only Fools and Horses*?" The top two answers were: "It's a Shakespearean quote" and "Isn't it Lester Piggott's autobiography?" It kind of backed up the concerns, I suppose, but then someone argued, "But did you know what *Steptoe and Son* was until the series actually started?" Someone else, meanwhile, pointed out that even though it was an unusual title, it was long and would catch the eye, resulting in instant interest, which is half the battle. Once you've got people engaged, hopefully they'll follow up their interest and watch the show.'

The origins of the title phrase are unclear. 'Ronnie Hazlehurst told me it was a northern saying, but then I found out from a newspaper that it was a vaudeville phrase; whether it drifted across the Atlantic and then came back I don't know, but it's something that's been around for ages, and a phrase that my father used to use,' says John.

Looking back, John Sullivan wonders whether Jimmy had taken pity on him when he was commissioned to write a series. 'At that point I didn't have any work because *Citizen Smith* had finished and *Over the Moon* had been scrapped, so I've always wondered whether Jimmy, knowing I had a couple of kids and being aware of the work situation, had given the go-ahead out of kindness.'

But Jimmy is quick to point out that this wasn't the case. 'Pity wouldn't have come in to it; I simply liked the idea behind the show and felt it deserved a chance.'

Eventually the show got underway. Coming up with a surname for the main characters was less tortuous that finding the right title. 'I'd worked with a guy called Trotter, while Del was one of those names I loved. Derek was boring, so I thought I'd alter it to Del, like Del Shannon, just to give it a buzz. As far as Boy is concerned, it was a working-class phrase; a kid who was a bit of a lad was given the name; I thought it would be amusing that he's now in his late 30s, early 40s and he can't rid himself of the name.'

Ray Butt, who had directed *Citizen Smith,* was given the job of producing and directing the first series. In many respects he was the ideal choice to head the team. 'He knew the vernacular for a start,' explains John Howard Davies. 'He was also a very canny man and knew instinctively what would and wouldn't work – he was a very good producer.'

John Sullivan was pleased to be working with Ray once again. 'Ray was from the East End of London and his family had run a market stall, where he'd worked before joining the RAF. I was from the south of London and we both knew the market scene very well. We'd had many conversations about the way of life, and I remember telling him that my favourite character was the fly-pitcher, the guy who'd turn up with a suitcase and a trestle table, and always had a young look-out. It was the way he tried selling his goods that interested me – he was a real entertainer. Then every time a policeman or the market inspector appeared he was off.'

Ray Butt remembers the conversations. 'On one occasion, just after *Over the Moon* had been turned down, I was sat with John in one of my local pubs in Hammersmith. It was a time when all the newspaper headlines were about the black economy, the money the taxman never got hold of. We started talking about this, and that's when John told me about his ideas, which became the genesis of *Only Fools and Horses*.'

John fashioned an idea about a man and his cousin, later altered to be a brother, who sold dodgy items from a suitcase. The age-gap between the central characters was a reflection of the difference between John and his sister. 'I think it was a result of the war: the men went off and so they never had their kids within two or three years of each other, which seems to be the norm now.'

The initial script was written and posted to Ray Butt, who fell about laughing as soon as he began to read it. 'It was an excellent read, so funny,' recalls Ray with fervour. 'The hardest job with a sitcom is writing that first script because in half an hour you have to tell a story which is not only funny, but strong enough to establish all the characters. John achieved that with "Big Brother".'

Ray was pleased to be teaming up with John Sullivan again. 'We became great mates over the years,' he says, 'I even used to babysit for him when his kids were young.' He admired John's writing skills enormously. 'There were three laughs on every page, and you don't see many scripts like that. My only criticism, and he would laugh at this, is that they were always so bloody long! Sometimes for a 30-minute show he'd write an hour's worth. I had to cut reams from his scripts, all brilliant material; mind you, we'd put it in a drawer and try to come back to it later.'

The only other grumble Ray had is that occasionally the scripts would arrive late. 'I remember once I'd gone away filming an episode of *Just Good Friends,* another of John's projects. I'd taken the unit down to Southend-on-Sea without a script. All I did for the first couple of days, because I knew what the script was about even though it wasn't finished, was to shoot some background shots. Then John came on the phone and dictated some scenes to my assistant.'

When Gareth Gwenlan became Head of Comedy he was able to sanction extended episodes lasting 50 minutes, which is something Ray had tried to achieve during his time on the show. 'My controller thought that extending the shows would dilute the comedy, so I told him:

"You ought to see the stuff I'm throwing away."' The annals of television history are littered with sitcoms that failed dismally when extended in duration, often for the big screen. Ray acknowledges that a lot of sitcom writers aren't up to the task, but always felt John Sullivan didn't fall into that category. 'I did three 90-minute Christmas Specials and they all worked, and when Gareth finally managed to get 50 minutes, the show continued to flourish.'

When it came to thinking up episode ideas, John looked around him. One of the prerequisites for any scriptwriter is to have a discerning eye – always to be on the look-out for potential storylines from everyday situations. 'Ideas come from everywhere: something that someone says, a small article you read in the newspaper, anything. It's very rare that I can remember exactly where an idea originated, but occasionally an episode can start from simply a gag or a funny line. You write it down, then record which character said it, then come up with another character's response and the script starts to build. Invariably I find that I record a little incident or passage of dialogue and that's what inspires the story, although more often than not the original piece of dialogue is discarded.'

When it came to planning his work schedule for *Only Fools*, John usually banked on the half-hour scripts taking approximately two weeks to write, even though there were always exceptions: while some took as long as three or four weeks, "The Long Legs of the Law" was completed within six days. 'I used to write all the scripts in longhand,' says John, who'd also pace up and down talking to himself, trying to formulate the dialogue in his mind before committing to paper. Even when he's out shopping his mind is still working. 'My wife often has to nudge me,' he admits, with a smile spreading across his face. 'We might be in Marks and Spencer and my lips are going; I'm not concentrating on the frozen peas or whatever, my mind is somewhere else.'

The advent of the word processor was welcomed in John's office. 'I don't know how I managed before; to rely on a typewriter to produce a script, then to find yourself having to do a rewrite sounds like torture. Life is certainly much easier now.'

Crucial to the success of any television programme is the casting; Ray Butt knew he already had top-notch scripts, so it was imperative that he recruited a cast worthy of such quality. 'John Howard Davies already had Nick Lyndhurst in mind for playing Rodney, so that

one didn't take any thinking about.' Ray knew Nick from *Butterflies* and felt he was right for the part, while John Sullivan had seen him playing Fletcher's teenage son in *Going Straight* and agreed with the decision.

Casting Del proved more difficult. 'Our first choice was Enn Reitel, but when I spoke to his agent I discovered that he was busy filming *Misfits* for Yorkshire Television,' recalls Ray. 'Then John Howard Davies suggested I saw Jim Broadbent in a play at the Hampstead Theatre, London. I did and was very impressed, but when I met up with him afterwards and offered him the role, he turned it down because the play was transferring to the West End. He said he loved the script I'd shown him but didn't think he could give enough concentration and energy to both things at the same time.'

John Sullivan, though, didn't think casting a tallish actor in the part of Del, considering Nicholas Lyndhurst's height, would work. 'It was completely against what I wanted,'says John. 'In my view, they had to be different. If you had a big, tall Del Boy treating a slightly smaller Rodney the way Del treated his younger brother, people would regard him as a bully. I felt you had to have Del smaller than his brother to get away from the bullying aspect.'

While he remained without anyone for the role of Del, Ray Butt turned his attentions towards finding someone to play Grandad. 'Ideally, I was looking for an actor like Wilfrid Brambell, although he wouldn't have been right because he was too well known as Steptoe. Then an agent called Carole James, who's a dear friend, phoned about another client. I told her my predicament and asked if she had anyone suitable. She didn't, but said she knew an actor who'd be just right

for the part. She gave me Lennard Pearce's agent's number, and from there I met Lennard. As soon as he came for an audition both John Sullivan and I knew he was ideal.

'He was a very soft-spoken man. He'd been unwell for some time and was on the verge of packing up the profession; he said to me many times afterwards that he couldn't believe his luck: *Only Fools* had given him the best pension he could ever have expected. He was a lovey person, great fun on the set.'

John Sullivan was equally impressed with Lennard's performance in the audition. 'I loved his voice. We'd seen quite a few people and I can remember nudging Ray's knees to let him know I felt we'd got the right man. He was brilliant.'

With two of the main characters cast, Ray turned his attention back to the role of Del Boy, which was still vacant. Whilst sitting at home watching a repeat of *Open All Hours,* suddenly he saw his Del Trotter. 'It had to be David Jason. Granville was doing a virtuoso performance in the stockroom – it was a great moment. I'd worked on the series as a production assistant so knew David; I felt that in real life he was very similar to Del Boy because he likes to wear gold jewellery. The joke in the studio when we were filming *Only Fools* was that he'd take the real gold off and lock it in his dresser, because it was bloody expensive, and then put on all this cheap rubbish. Anyway, my mind was made up. So I rang John Sullivan but I don't think he was too keen on the idea.'

John wants to point out that any rumours that have sprung up over the years about him not wanting David Jason for the part are unfounded. 'I didn't know David Jason, so I couldn't want or not want him. At the time Ray suggested David I'd only seen him as Peter Barnes, a loser in *A Sharp Intake of Breath*. I didn't know if he could play the sort of style I had in mind for Del, so simply asked some questions. Ray knew David well and was convinced he could play the character well so we invited him in. As soon as I met him I could appreciate why Ray had been so enthusiastic about him.'

But Ray's boss, John Howard Davies, then Head of Comedy, didn't think Jason was such a good idea. 'I was pretty anti it because the two main parts were being played by people who didn't look anything like brothers. Also, David was in *Open All Hours* at the time and I didn't know how Roy Clarke and Ronnie Barker would react if we took one of their pivotal stars to do another series. So I checked with them and fortunately they were both very amenable.'

Ray was relieved he'd received the go-ahead to invite David in to discuss the role. 'I didn't think the concerns about not looking like brothers was anything to worry about because families are different. David wasn't asked in to audition because I had no doubts about his talent, but because there was a triangle of characters: Del, Rodney and Grandad, I wanted to see how he,

Nick and Lennard would gel. I did the same when Lennard died and we brought Buster in. If you have three central characters in a show and one doesn't work, you have problems. Fortunately the chemistry was there almost immediately.'

Integral to the show's success has been the excellent rapport between the sitcom's two leading actors: David Jason and Nicholas Lyndhurst, topped with a superb gallery of supporting players.

John Sullivan was responsible for casting John Challis, whom he'd worked with on *Citizen Smith.* Ray agreed he'd make an ideal Boycie. 'Roger Lloyd Pack was a lucky find,' admits Ray, who'd worked with his father, Charles Lloyd Pack. 'Trigger was described as looking like a horse in the script, so when I happened to see Roger in the play *Moving* (I'd gone along to watch Billy Murray to see if he'd be suitable for Del) appearing on stage with a black Mohican haircut above his long face, he looked just right for the part of Trigger! So I met with him, we had a chat, and he accepted the part.'

Of the other actors brought into the fold as the series progressed, Ray enthuses about their importance to the series. 'People like Sue Holderness and Paul Barber were excellent. I don't know how I came to recruit Paul, but I was bloody glad he came along because he was wonderful to work with – he's such a smashing bloke. When you direct and are working hard, you don't want hassle and with people like Paul around you knew you'd never get any.'

John Sullivan, meanwhile, can remember creating the easy-going character of Denzil. 'I wanted Del to have a black friend from school and Paul Barber joining the cast gave the show another dimension. Denzil had come down from Liverpool and felt, in order to survive, he had to fall in line. He was an incredibly gullible character and Del took him under his wing when he first arrived; now Del can twist him round his little finger.'

Denzil's wife, Corinne, was seen in just one episode before the untimely death of Eva Mottley, who played the character. Had she lived, there's no doubt Corinne would have become a semi-regular, as John explains. 'I loved the idea that Del was frightened of her; whenever she got angry he jumped. Although Eva died not long after appearing in the show, we continued mentioning the character occasionally but made out that she'd separated from Denzil.'

With the first series approved, work began on the location filming. But within a few days the project was hit with producer/director, Ray Butt, being rushed to hospital. He says: 'We'd just finished a night shoot for "Cash and Curry" and when I got home I climbed into bed and had a couple of hours sleep. When I woke up and got out of bed I heard a slight click, no more than that, but I was in terrible pain: a disc has slipped and touched the sciatic nerve. I lived alone in

those day so when I fell to the floor I lay there for about half an hour. Not having a phone by my bed, I had to get into the front room, where I pulled the phone down and rang my production manager, Janet Bone. She got hold of the BBC's doctor, and came around with him to my flat. By then the pain had eased a little and I was able to throw the keys over the balcony so they could let themselves in. Within a short time I was at Charing Cross Hospital, where I spent three weeks in traction.' Two other colleagues: Gareth Gwenlan and Martin Shardlow stepped into the breach until Ray was able to return.

The first series kicked off with 'Big Brother', which was transmitted on 8 September 1981. As well as the main trio, the only other character present who would become one of the regulars was Trigger, played superbly by Roger Lloyd Pack. The roadsweeper underwent subtle changes as the series progressed. 'I started trying to emphasise that he wasn't the sharpest knife around,' explains John.

Once outside filming had been completed and the team moved into the studio, the schedule was hectic, as Ray Butt explains. 'I liked doing the recordings on a Sunday because you tended to get better audiences, perhaps because it was the weekend. In the days I was working on it, you hired an actor for seven days, but they had to have one day off. So I'd begin the read-through on the Tuesday morning and we'd spend the rest of the day blocking, which is when you work out the mechanics, such as where people stand or say particular lines.

'The next day (Wednesday) the actors would come in and hopefully know at least half of their lines, and by Thursday they should know their lines and not need the scripts. At this point, with all the mechanics over, I can really start work, fine tuning the directing bit of it – for example, telling an actor this would be funnier than that, and trying things out. Friday would be the technical run; after the actors have had a quick run through, the technicians – such as the lighting man, senior cameraman and the sound man – would come in and we would work through the plan.

'I'd call the actors in on Saturday morning (if you gave them the day off they would forget their lines), we'd go through it twice, then we'd go round to the pub and have a drink. Then on Sunday we were back in the studio for the recording. While the cast had Monday off, I'd pop into the editing suite to start work on what we'd shot the night before. So for me it was a seven-day cycle.'

In terms of audience figures, the first series didn't set the world alight. On average, each of the six episodes in the initial season attracted just under eight million viewers. 'It bombed out,' admits John Howard Davies, 'but then very few series work from day one. I can only think of two outstanding examples: *Porridge* and *Fawlty Towers.* The BBC had courage in those days to give programmes time to develop.' He isn't surprised the sitcom has been widely acclaimed. 'If you give talent room to germinate, grow and be developed properly, it will go on for a considerable amount of time.'

And that certainly applies to *Only Fools*, which has recently celebrated its 21st birthday. Obviously there are a lot of components that come together to make a programme a success, but, perhaps, the two fundamental aspects are the quality of scripts and calibre of cast. Ray Butt knows he was lucky to have a starting line-up of Jason, Lyndhurst and Pearce. 'John wrote the characters, but on paper they're only two dimensional. You then have to put the personality into them, and that's where casting comes in – getting the right actor to interpret what John has created, and it turned out the combination we got was just right.'

John Sullivan agrees with Ray, before pointing out that he wrote the first six episodes without knowing who was going to play the parts. 'David and Nick brought certain qualities to their characters: David gave Del tremendous energy and was very animated, while Nick took the other approach by hardly moving at all. Eventually their own personalities start coming through and you begin taking that into consideration when you're writing scripts. You've got your basic character established, then the actors add more layers and dimensions.'

There were times when David Jason helped John's confidence as a writer. 'He kept pushing me,' recalls John. 'He'd say things like: "Don't ever be frightened to write anything, just go for it." I remember telling him once that I'd like to write more about emotions and have some pathos in the scripts, which I'd tried out before but found I'd scared actors off because they wanted to play everything with a smile. But David kept saying: "Push the barriers and go as far as you want." That was a tremendous help to know that I didn't have to feel embarrassed about it; I could write something and know full well that the actor was behind it one hundred per cent.

'That's why I started developing the characters because no one was frightened of serious moments, and doing so then gave them greater depth,' explains John. 'If David hadn't said anything to me I would never have explored delicate areas in the characters' makeup. The audience realised Del was an emotional man at heart, which enabled me to cover real-life issues such as grief.'

For a while, John Sullivan doubted the sitcom's long-term future. 'I didn't think the BBC were particularly fond of it, which meant I never thought beyond the series I was working on; in fact, I felt it would be axed at the end of the first season.' So he was surprised to be invited along to John Howard Davies' office and after a brief discussion be offered the chance to write a second series.

The average viewing figures during the second series was just under nine million – again largely insignificant. John Sullivan believes that the lack of publicity was largely to blame. 'No one from the publicity department came to see us; I started thinking that someone didn't want the show to continue so they decided to suffocate the baby at birth.'

Whilst the second season went out with a bang in terms of content, with the Trotters causing irreparable damage to a priceless chandelier, there was a period of silence before John was asked to write any more adventures with the Trotters. 'My agent told me to look around for something else. My wife and I had two kids by then, so we decided to take a caravan holiday in Hastings. I was really down in the dumps.'

During the time the Sullivans were away, two repeats were shown, which ignited the interest in *Only Fools* almost immediately. 'Both episodes went high in the ratings list, so God bless whoever decided to schedule them. From that moment, the show's popularity increased.'

Ray Butt always had faith in the sitcom, even if it took several series to attract a sizeable following. 'It wasn't a blockbuster at the beginning by any means, but the episodes were good and its success was building as it went along,' says Ray, who loved working on the show. 'I just used

to say "Do it, boys", it was the easiest job in the world. I've always said I was so lucky being paid good money to go out to work and laugh. It was an easy job thanks to the quality of the scripts and the calibre of the actors.'

'To Hull and Back' was one of Ray's favourite episodes. 'I remember being ferried out to the Inge (the boat we used for filming) in the pilot boat, by which time David, Nick and Buster were already aboard. As we approached, David and Nick were waiting with straight faces, shouting: "Ray, we've got terrible problems." I asked what was the matter, and they replied: "It's Buster, he's in the back being seasick; he just can't take it, it's terrible." I thought to myself, "Shit! What am I going to do now? We're filming a 90-minute episode and one of my principles can't cope." So I climbed aboard and rushed down to the cabin, opened the door and saw him there feeling rotten.

'I kept asking, "Buster, Buster, are you all right?" He was doing his best to be in pain but then couldn't hold it anymore; I started to realise what was going on, so I poked him and he

laughed out loud. I shouted, "You bastard!" All three of them had wound me up rotten for about ten minutes.'

Ray was surprised to hear about the return of the Trotters when it was announced back in 2001. 'I thought that towards the end of the last run in 1996 it was getting tired and it was time to finish, which is why I thought John had made them millionaires because there's no way back after that. It's interesting to note that when they smuggled the diamonds in "To Hull and Back", the original ending of the script saw them become millionaires. However, I said to John: "If you do that, where do we go from there? Once they've got money we've lost the plot." John agreed and changed the ending, and we saw the Trotters throw the money off the balcony.'

By the time Series 4 was commissioned an average of 10.4 million viewers were watching the adventures of the Trotters; audiences were increasing, but just when things were looking rosy, tragedy struck: Lennard Pearce suffered a heart attack and was rushed into hospital. John Sullivan was the first to hear the bad news. 'I received a phone call from his landlady, so I then had to contact everyone else.'

By the following Sunday, Lennard was dead. Carole James called Ray Butt to inform him of the shocking news. 'The last time I'd seen him

à la Del

★ ★ ★ ★ ★ ★

'Oh bain marie, bain marie'

('Christmas Crackers')

was on a Sunday morning; we'd just finished filming outside the magistrates court in Kingston for "Hole in One". After checking the schedules I realised that Lennard wasn't needed for filming until the following Sunday, so he had a week off. As he was walking away, I shouted: "Here we are, paying you all this bloody money and you aren't going to work for a week!" He turned around and smiled and I told him to look after himself. That was the last time I ever saw him.

'Everyone was distraught; there were lots of tears. We were meant to be doing some filming outside a newsagent's, but I told Susie Belbin, who was directing the series, and the rest of the unit, that I was going to stand everyone down; we were fast approaching Christmas and obviously we had some major problems to overcome – not least John having to rewrite the episodes.'

Ray altered the filming schedule which meant the team would reconvene on 2 January 1985. Creating some breathing space was essential, especially as so many important decisions would have to be made. The following day Ray returned to Television Centre and met with, among others, John Sullivan and Gareth Gwenlan, who'd just taken over as Head of Comedy.

'The options were to push the series back, to cancel it or to recast for Grandad and continue with the scripts I'd already written,' explains John. Realistically, everyone knew recasting wasn't an option. 'We were all too close, too much of a family simply to change the actor.'

'No, it wouldn't have worked,' admits Gareth Gwenlan. The death of Lennard Pearce left an unbridgeable chasm, so the idea of replacing the actor was never a valid option. 'Then John had a thought. He'd looked back at some of the earlier scripts and noticed there was a reference to Grandad's brother, Albert, who was a sailor, so John suggested bringing him into the story, initially attending Grandad's funeral. Everyone liked the idea.'

Writing the funeral scenes in 'Strained Relations' were some of the hardest John Sullivan ever had to complete. 'I knew I had to cover the funeral but I didn't want to start the series off that way: a brand new series and we walk straight into a graveyard. I couldn't do that. So I decided to write an episode where Grandad is supposed to be in hospital; once I've done that I'll go into the funeral with the second script, at which point I'd introduce Uncle Albert.'

Working under tremendous time pressures and under difficult emotional circumstances, John Sullivan's skill as a scriptwriter came to the fore and he produced the moving episode 'Strained Relations'. The rich dialogue focused on how the Trotter brothers handled the loss of their grandfather, but John was also looking for the right moment to inject a little humour. 'I was trying so hard to get that gag; I just had to burst the bubble quickly as far as all the grieving was concerned – I didn't want simply to fade out at the end of the funeral scene without a moment of humour. Then I suddenly thought about using his old hat, and it worked so well. I knew that the audience would be desperate to laugh after a scene like that, so whatever I did I'd probably take the audience along with me. Thankfully it worked.'

After that point, many of the lines allocated to Grandad could simply be reassigned to Uncle Albert. 'I had to change them to compensate for the new character, which resulted in me writing two completely new episodes, but many of the lines could just be altered slightly.' It was a very difficult time for John, who had to write the scripts quickly, whilst still mourning the death of a close friend. 'It was horrible. I felt like a traitor in many ways, but as people kept reminding me, Lennard would have wanted the show to go on.'

Finding an actor to play Uncle Albert began in earnest just after Christmas. Ray Butt returned to his office after spending the festive period quietly in Suffolk to find a pile of letters; all from actors putting themselves forward for

the role. 'I was still very upset, so couldn't face them to start with,' admits Ray. 'But I realised it had to be done some time so I began working my way through the pile.' Then one letter in particular caught his eye. 'As I opened the envelope there was a big photo of an actor called Buster Merryfield – I'd never heard of him. He had this big white beard and looked good. I think John had come up to the office as well, so I showed him the photo. We both liked the look of Buster, he certainly reminded us of an old sailor.'

Ray picked up the phone and called Buster's home. 'Buster picked up the phone and I told him I'd like to meet up. He was appearing in panto at Windsor, so I asked him to come in and see us the following morning. Buster agreed, so I arranged for David Jason and Nick Lyndhurst to be there. I was up against it and needed to find someone for the role as quickly as possible; I'd been after a couple of other people but there was no established actor who wanted to take the part on. Buster read and then went off to appear in a matinée performance of the panto, while we all sat around and chewed the matter over for some time. Finally, we decided to go for it, and Buster was offered the job.'

All concerned were happy with how Buster settled in to the team. 'David and Nick were very generous towards him and helped a lot. Had

they not been, it would never have worked. I was glad we had got Buster, because although he wasn't the greatest actor around, he was a fresh face and the public didn't know him,' says Ray. 'I remember when John came up with the idea of this old sea dog, with his cap and duffle coat, I thought the character could smoke a pipe. But Buster had never touched tobacco in his life, so wasn't keen. I suggested he put an empty pipe between his teeth, which he did for a while but then quickly dropped it.'

Gareth Gwenlan was also happy with how events had turned out. 'The public grew to love him. Obviously he hadn't had 40 years professional acting experience because he'd been a banker, but he'd been in amateur dramatics and was quite good. You have to remember that he was in his mid-sixties and just occasionally he'd be a touch unreliable, like he'd forget the odd line, but even professional actors can be like that; and at the end of the day when it was all mixed together, he looked good and everyone seemed to like him.'

When the fifth series finished with the trans-

mission of 'Who Wants to be a Millionaire' in October 1986, over 18 million people had tuned in to watch Del Boy seriously consider moving to Australia to work for his old chum Jumbo Mills. By the time the sixth season had begun in 1989, two major changes had taken place: Ray Butt had left the BBC and moved on to become Head of Comedy at Central Television, and the episodes were extended to 50 minutes.

Looking back over his years on the series, Ray Butt remembers enjoying it immensely. 'There were so many great episodes; as well as "To Hull and Back" I particularly liked "Diamonds are for Heather", perhaps because I'm a bit of a romantic. For straight comedy, the chandelier scene in "A Touch of Glass" has to be the best visual gag ever. The audience reaction was always very good, but when we showed them that particular sequence, it gave me a major problem because everyone laughed for so long that you couldn't hear another word in the rest of the scene. So when it came to the editing stage, I had to strip off the soundtrack, relay the dialogue and condense the laugh, which no comedy director wants to do – you usually want to lengthen it. But I had no choice because otherwise you wouldn't have heard anything else.'

The team of Gareth Gwenlan producing and Tony Dow – who'd previously worked as an

à la Del

★ ★ ★ ★ ★ ★

'Répondez s'il vous plaît, ain't it?'

('The Long Legs of the Law')

assistant floor manager and production manager on the series – as director was installed for the 1988 Christmas Special, 'Dates'. Gareth was still Head of Comedy at the time. 'There was no one on my staff that was free and suitable when it came to making more episodes of *Only Fools*. Although Tony was a novice as far as directing for television was concerned, he was experienced in theatre work and had the makings of a television director. I couldn't take the show on myself, so we decided to give Tony a chance, while I would babysit him – not that he needed much of that,' says Gareth.

'When Ray left there was a queue around the block to do *Only Fools,* but I know David Jason and John Sullivan were keen, especially considering the episodes were going to be 50 minutes, to get a fresh approach on the show,' explains Tony Dow. 'I think they were keen for me to take over the directing, which, I believe, caused major consternation around the department. But Gareth knew that if I directed it, he could produce it. At that stage, I hadn't done a huge amount of directing: a little bit of *Alas Smith and Jones,* but that was about it. As we had a few months before *Only Fools* started, I was sent off and had a blitz of directing studios, which I had little experience of. I did stuff like *Blankety Blank* and *Top of the Pops*, and then completed the Drama Directors' Course, which was fantastic. It was a major break for me, and I'm sure I put a few people's noses out of joint.'

Gareth Gwenlan realised the enormity of the task he was taking on. 'It was a big job in the sense that it was a very popular programme, but it hadn't yet achieved the cult status it has now – it was just about to take off. It was a big responsibility and that doubled because we went to 50 minutes, which, coincidentally, was the point at which it took off in a big way and became the BBC's most popular programme in terms of audience viewing; you suddenly realised you were responsible for running this, so you had to get it right. But I always had the security of knowing that John Sullivan, to my knowledge, has never written a bad script. Some are wonderful and others are just very good, but he's never delivered one that didn't come up to standard. If you have a reliable scriptwriter, you know that most of your worries are over.'

'He's such a great writer,' adds Tony, who asked John Sullivan to be his best man at his wedding. 'We've moved on together, really. When we did the first series of 50-minuters, there was obviously an opportunity to make the characters slightly more rounded, and add a little drama here and there, which I feel always works well. I'll always remember sitting in the gallery whilst we were recording the final scenes of Rodney's reception in "Little Problems". John was getting nervous because it was all going terribly quiet down on the floor – no one was laughing. I said: "Don't worry, John. No one's laughing because everyone is crying." And it was then that we all realised that you could make a show like *Only Fools* with drama in it as well as the comedy.

Just under 14 million people watched the sixth series kick off with 'Yuppy Love', the first of the 50-minute episodes. The move to a longer duration gave John Sullivan more room to breathe when it came to developing story-lines and meant less material had to be cut from his scripts, but originally he had only appealed for 35-minute episodes. 'I'm terrible because I can't help but overwrite, which meant we spent half the rehearsal time cutting chunks out, getting it down to the bare bones. Finally, David Jason and I went to Gareth and said: "We're not going to do any more after this series unless we get 35 minutes." We thought that the extra five minutes would mean we could keep some of the good material in. Gareth then suggested making it 50 minutes, which would mean we could try selling the programme abroad as an hour-show, taking into consideration the commercial breaks.'

Gareth agrees it was a good idea to move to longer episodes. 'There are episodes in those first few series in which, if you listen carefully, you can sense that something has been cut out which had moved the plot on. But of course when John was given a 50-minute slot, the scripts came in at about 75 minutes!' says Gareth, with a smile. 'That was okay, though, because it's much easier cutting minutes out of a longer script. But as a result of having more screen time, the programmes took on a different status.'

But as John points out, what they didn't allow for was extended rehearsals. 'For that first series of extended episodes we crammed each one into five days. The way David and Nick worked was incredible. Nowadays we've got a ten-day turn-around, but luckily it worked. We were recording on a Sunday as last week's episode was being transmitted. We were attracting some great reviews, which kept the adrenalin going, because otherwise I don't know how the actors would have got through it because it was such hard work.

'But John is brilliant to work with because I know him well. We've had our rows, of course we have, but they're good rows and are soon over!' smiles Tony. 'They're all over different opinions on how scenes should work, or whatever, like the scene where Batman and Robin come out of the mist in "Heroes and Villains". John couldn't understand why we needed all the mist. I told him it was because it would look great. I know John and Gareth weren't too sure but when they saw it, together with the music, they thought it was fantastic.

'John always likes to see things instantaneously, even when he comes on location, where the pace is very slow, but he likes to see it all happen. I keep him away from edits and dubs until we've got a picture and sound, otherwise he hates it.'

Such is the effort John Sullivan puts into his work, he's often working on scripts until the last moment. But this is something Tony Dow takes in his stride. 'But his scripts are always in much better shape than most people's. That's the way he works and you accept that. In the early days you wouldn't hear from him for some time, then he'd call you and be deeply depressed about something in the script. So you'd tell him you were coming down, jump in the car and head to his house. Then when you read the script, it might only take one little amendment to solve the problem. Three days later the script would appear. Working on his own means he hasn't got anyone to feed off, which is what you need sometimes.'

As an experienced director and producer, Gareth had worked with hundreds of actors over the years, including Nicholas Lyndhurst on *Butterflies*, but he'd never worked with David Jason until *Only Fools*. 'They were both growing at different speeds as actors,' he observed. 'David was a more experienced actor when we started, so he was a lot more accomplished and already a

leading comedy actor. Nick, meanwhile, had always had a good instinct as an actor, and although he definitely played second fiddle, he did over the years get better and better. Now, the scenes that they play together really are master-class performances. All young actors should be told to watch them at work – they're just wonderful together.'

Gareth is equally complimentary about the supporting actors. 'They're all very good in their own way. Roger Lloyd Pack is a good actor but he never has to work hard for a laugh; Trigger comes in, says one word, and everyone falls about. I am not diminishing Roger because he's a very good actor, but the part of Trigger, which he's added to enormously over the years, is a gem.

'Boycie is a wonderful character, the sort of person everyone recognises, and John Challis plays him well. And Marlene is played beautifully by Sue Holderness, but they all contribute in their own way – they're all part of the gang.'

When he takes a few moments out of his busy schedule to consider the characters he's created, John Sullivan must be extremely proud. 'They've all worked out so well,' he says. 'When you see Boycie for the first time he's quite different to how he is now; he's based on those car dealers who always had these rather flash women who've gone past their sell-by date. But because they've got money they feel superior, even though they're exactly the same as everyone else, except, maybe, they've got a better house. I could never get my head around that: feeling superior to another human being because you've got a bit more money. I find that absolutely appalling, but a lot of them are like that.

'Having and retaining the three central characters has always been crucial, just as it was important to have a range of ages: the old man who'd seen it all, Del who's at the age where he's still young enough to be ambitious but old enough to know the tricks of the trade, and the younger Rodney, who's still incredibly naïve. Uncle Albert kept that trio going, but once he was gone it was important that we looked for someone else for the new episodes, and that's where Damien comes in.'

In the latter years of *Only Fools and Horses*, we saw a move towards the Trotters boys finally settling down. Both had a string of failed romances to their name, and in Del's case he had enjoyed playing the field. But now they were reaching the time in their lives when they realised there was more to life than seeing how many girls they could chat up at the local nightspot.

Del was the first to find true love, even though he didn't realise at first. 'We began thinking that maybe Del was getting a bit too old for hanging around discos, and I didn't want him to become a dirty old man, so in "Dates" I arranged for him to meet Raquel,' says John Sullivan.

Gareth Gwenlan fully supported John's decision to move the characters on. 'He had this idea

of someone – who turned out to be Raquel – meeting Del and the relationship becoming serious. He didn't want them to get married because he felt that didn't suit Del's image, but he wanted to show that they were growing up and getting older.'

'As well as having steady relationships, I started thinking about having young Trotters running around,' says John. We knew we weren't going to go on forever, so we could start doing things, such as producing a child, even if we never saw him again. We could afford to be a bit daring.'

Del's new girlfriend struck a chord with viewers, particularly women. 'I remember visiting my local baker's a few days after Christmas and the lady who ran it thanked me for introducing such a good female character. I also received a lot of complimentary letters about Raquel, so I started thinking that she was just what we were looking for. She was the right age, the right look – everything was perfect about her.'

At first, John had only intended to use Raquel in 'Dates', but she made such an impact with the public he decided to bring her back in the following year's Christmas Special, 'The Jolly Boys' Outing', where Del spots her assisting the Great Ramondo. 'I then decided to make her a permanent part of the crowd,' says John Sullivan. I suppose it was brave to suddenly bring women into the show in such a strong way but, to be honest, we never really worried about it.'

When it came to casting for the part of Raquel, several actresses were seen, but eventually it was whittled down to just two: Pippa Guard, who went on to play Reen in Sullivan's *Roger, Roger* and Tessa Peake-Jones. Three of us

voted; I won't say who voted for whom, but it went 2–1 to Tessa. Afterwards I was determined to work with Pippa, she's a good actress and would have been great in the part, but Tessa is lovely, and has made a brilliant Raquel.'

At the start of Series 6, Rodney meets his wife-to-be, Cassandra. Rather than opt for a working-class partner for Rodney, John decided that the character would possess more potential if she came from a middle-class background. The part was offered to Gwyneth Strong, but one of the other actresses who attended the auditons was Liz Hurley, as Tony Dow recalls. 'It was quite extraordinary because she looked even more amazing than she does now, but I just couldn't believe that she could be Rodney's girlfriend; it seemed too much for this plonker [Rodney] to be dating this stunningly beautiful woman. That's not to say Gwyneth isn't attractive, but I

went for her because I felt she had a very photogenic face and would be a good member of the company. And it must have been a difficult job for her because she had to become a regular member of the company very fast, but she settled in well. But Liz was divine, very charming, and when I told her my reasons for not offering her the job, she replied: "Really? I don't understand why."'

It wasn't long before Rodney and Cassandra were married, but just like many couples in real-life, they have suffered many ups and downs. 'Rodney is one of those guys who wants to be such a modern-thinking man that he brings problems on himself,' explains John Sullivan. 'I just thought it would be fun, and realistic, to have them face some problems.

'Of course, there's always the unavoidable fact that Cassandra's parents are wealthy, and then Rodney ends up working for her dad. There's a resentment which always causes problems. Then, Cassandra being more ambitious than he is – being a very modern woman – drives him up the wall. But I'm pleased to say that they get over their problems before the forthcoming episodes are over.'

In 1996, it looked as if the sitcom was being brought to an end with the Christmas Trilogy. Each instalment was watched by over 20 million people, with the final episode, 'Time On Our Hands', pulling in a record-breaking 24.3 million. There is no doubting that the series went out with an almighty bang, with plaudits from viewers and critics alike. The scripts were immaculate and showed, once again, the range of John Sullivan's talents. The second instalment in this festive feast, 'Modern Men', revealed his ability to mix pathos and humour within the same scenes. One of the themes explored in this script was miscarriage, as Rodney and Cassandra's dreams of parenthood are shattered when she suffers a miscarriage and is rushed to hospital. As the brothers prepare to enter Cassandra's room, Del plays big brother and tells Rodney to be strong for the sake of his wife, only to burst into uncontrollable sobs himself, with tears squirting everywhere in a very humourous scene; but the entire miscarriage storyline is sublimely acted out and spotlights the agonies involved in the immediate aftermath by both partners, especially the father. 'I knew someone it had happened to, and he said: "No one gives a second thought to the father." Although, quite rightly, much of the sympathy is directed towards the mother, the father often cries alone,' states John Sullivan..

HMS Lock

In 'He Ain't Heavy, He's My Uncle', a photo of *HMS Lock* sinking is found in Uncle Albert's treasure chest. It went down on 27 June 1943. The chest also contains telegrams from the Admiralty to his wife Ada, stating that Albert was lost at sea, presumed drowned.

HMS Peerless

From one of Uncle Albert's tall stories comes the tale of his time serving on *HMS Peerless* in the South China Sea, and the time he was nearly court-martialled.

HMS Spinx

In 'Time On Our Hands', Albert claims he served on *HMS Spinx*, which was under the command of Captain Kenworthy, in the Adriatic.

Hobbs, Peter

Film sound recordist on one episode: S6, episode 3

Hodge, Douglas

Role: Old Damien

Appeared in 'Heroes and Villains'

Born in Plymouth in 1960, Douglas trained at RADA and made his professional acting debut in a 1981 production of *Macbeth*, with Ken MacDonald. Television work soon came his way, in the shape of Raskolnikov for Channel 4's *Crime and Punishment*, Declan McConnachie in the series *Capital City*, James in *True Love*, Tertius Lydgate in the 1994 mini-series *Middlemarch*, Steve Blake in 1997's *The Uninvited* and, the following year, Jack Blakeney in *The Scold's Bridle*.

Douglas, who's also made several films, remains busy on stage and screen, with recent work assignments including *Redcap* and *The Way We Live Now*.

Hodges, Joan

Role: Marion

Appeared in 'If They Could See Us Now…!'

Joan has appeared in a host of television shows, including playing Sheila in *London's Burning*; Marilyn in *Roger, Roger*; Gwyn in *In Deep*; Irene Hagger in *Hot Money* and Barbara in *The Bill*. Her stage work, meanwhile, includes her role as Joyce in *Top Girls*.

Hodges, Peter

Dubbing mixer on two episodes: 'Miami Twice' (Parts 1 & 2)

Hoffman, Erika

Role: Anna

Appeared in S5, episode 1

For four years, Erika played Lesley Bainbridge in *Brush Strokes*, while other television roles include Suzie Anderson in *Tales of the Unexpected*, Faith in *Minder*, Sandra in *No Place Like Home*, a nurse in *Fairly Secret Army*, April in *Home to Roost* and Princess in *The Final Cut*.

Holderness, Sue

Role: Marlene

Appeared in 18 episodes: S4, episode 5; S5, episodes 1 & 5; S6, episodes 5 & 6; S7, episodes 1, 2 & 5 and 'The Frog's Legacy'; 'Dates'; 'The Jolly Boys' Outing'; 'Miami Twice' (Parts 1 & 2); 'Mother Nature's Son'; 'Heroes and Villains'; 'Modern Men', 'Time On Our Hands' and 'If They Could See Us Now…!'

Sue Holderness believes the character of Marlene, the wanton wife of Boycie, was only introduced to the scripts because of a storyline involving a dog. When she joined the cast of *Only Fools and Horses* for the fourth series' episode 'Sleeping Dogs Lie', it was just for one day's filming. 'John Sullivan had the idea of Del and Rodney looking after the Boyce's dog, Duke, whilst they went away on holiday. Up to that point, I'm told it was John's intention not to show Marlene because everybody's idea of her would be better in their imagination.'

Sue was spotted by producer Ray Butt and director Susie Belbin in the sketch show *End of Part One*, and was invited along to play Marlene. 'The offer arrived out of the blue, which was lovely, and I didn't even have to audition,' says Sue, who was consulted when it came to establishing the character's image. 'It was great fun to help create the look, with the high heels, short and very tight skirt, the loud fur coat and masses of make-up and hair.'

Such was the success Sue made of her initial appearance as Mrs Boyce that John Sullivan wrote the character into several episodes over the next three series, as well as the majority of the Christmas Specials, establishing her as one of the regulars at The Nag's Head. 'It was very exciting to know that John had liked the scene and the idea of Marlene, and quite quickly I was allowed to come back and be part of the team.'

Until the arrival of Tyler, one of the running gags through the series concerned the Boyces' infertility problems, which is also the subject of much of Sue's fan mail. 'People still write to me and ask about Tyler, because they were as excited as I was when Marlene was allowed to have a baby. But, of course, the mystery goes on as to whose baby it is. It was a glorious scene when the baby was in the pram and Marlene said, "Wave goodbye to your daddy" and everybody in the bar waved back.'

Unlike her screen character, Sue Holderness didn't harbour an uncontrollable desire to start a family and concentrated on her career until finally, at the age of 36, she felt the time was right for children in her life. 'I was a very dedicated career-woman, but having children definitely alters your life. Everything gets turned upside down and your priorities change totally. I discovered that motherhood is great, and now I couldn't be happier with my lot,' enthuses Sue.

In another John Sullivan series, *Dear John*, Sue played the irascible wife of Ken, work colleague of the star, John, who was played by Ralph Bates. Fourteen episodes were transmitted between February 1986 and December 1987. 'She was foul and always grumpy, but that was probably because she was tired from looking after all those kids. I was sorry I wasn't in more episodes, but what was comforting was knowing John Sullivan had written the part and wanted me to play it. Actors are so pathetically insecure that it's a real confidence boost when someone asks you to play a part, and thrilling when the scripts are brilliant, which John Sullivan's always are.'

Born in London in 1949, Sue always knew she was going to work in showbusiness. 'As a little girl I loved singing and dancing, but quickly realised that

Sue Holderness as a medium in *The New Avengers*

life as a chorus girl was not terrific. I had a few horsey years when I was sure I would become a show-jumper. Then, when I was 16 I started thinking that I'd probably like to be an actress, but wasn't certain.' To find out if acting was right for their daughter, Sue's parents allowed her to attend drama school with the proviso that if it didn't work out, she'd continue her education at university and pursue an alternative career. But within a week of joining drama school, Sue knew it was where she wanted to be.

After graduating from the Central School of Speech and Drama in 1970, she was engaged immediately to play a fairy in *A Midsummer Night's Dream* at Manchester, followed quickly by an appearance in Jack Good's *Catch My Soul* (a rock musical based on *Othello*) as Desdemona. 'There was a whole cast of rock musicians and it was the most extraordinary experience of my life. It was thrilling. I went from being a fairy, a very tiny part, to a leading lady in a rock musical – it was very exciting.'

Sue Holderness with Peter Tilbury in *It Takes a Worried Man*

Sue wasted no time and was soon offered her first taste of television in 1971, playing Gordon Jackson's secretary in Jimmy Perry's sitcom *Lollipop Loves Mr Mole*. Opportunites to work on children's programmes, which she regards as 'a jolly good way to learn', then came her way, with a long-running series, *Tightrope*, as a posh Girl Guide, and *Fly Into Danger*, where she had to undertake lessons flying a small aircraft. 'It was a good way to learn about filming, cameras and studio work. I also enjoyed the role and got a lot of playground credibility through that series.'

Among her favourite small-screen jobs was the role of Marianne in Yorkshire TV's spy series *The Sandbaggers*. Written by Ian MacKintosh and produced by Michael Ferguson, it was a show Sue had watched from its inception in 1978. 'I loved it so was delighted when the opportunity to be a regular character in it came about. But my other favourite job was *It Takes A Worried Man*, a sitcom written by a friend of mine, Peter Tilbury.' As Liz, Sue appeared in the second and third series, playing Philip Roath's girlfriend. 'I was playing Cleopatra IV in a controversial series for BBC called *The Cleopatras* when I was called out of rehearsals to take a call from Thames Television offering me the part of Liz. I didn't have to audition and knew that as soon as I finished *The Cleopatras* I was going straight into a series working with a dear friend of mine on scripts that were wonderfully funny.'

As well as television, Sue continues to work in the theatre and in 2001 appeared in Neil Simon's *The Female Odd Couple*, playing a corpulent policewoman. 'I had my hair cropped and was very butch, with a whole, huge body built around me. In rehearsals the director kept looking at me and didn't think I was big enough. I couldn't do much about it because I was already eating like a horse so a lot of extra padding was needed.'

Since her children, Freddie, 14, and Harriet, 16, have become boarders at school, Sue has more time to concentrate on theatre projects. But, without doubt, she's never happier than when she's playing Marlene, and regards 'From Prussia with Love' as her favourite episode. 'The idea of Del flogging them a baby, who turns out to be black, was a glorious episode to do; it was very truthful: unlike myself, Marlene was the sort of woman who from the age of 14 longed for a baby. There are women like that, whose whole *raison d'être* is to reproduce and when she found she couldn't, it was a big sadness for her. So the possibility of suddenly having a baby in her life mattered more to her than anything. It was a very satisfying part to play because you knew you had these hysterically funny lines, but were playing the truth of a woman for whom this mattered deeply.

'It was one of those nights when the audience's reaction was marvellous. The laughter at John Challis' speech when he tells Marlene that he might be able to con people into buying his cars, and that she had conceived and given birth in seven days flat, but couldn't convince them that his grandad was Louis Armstrong completely brought the

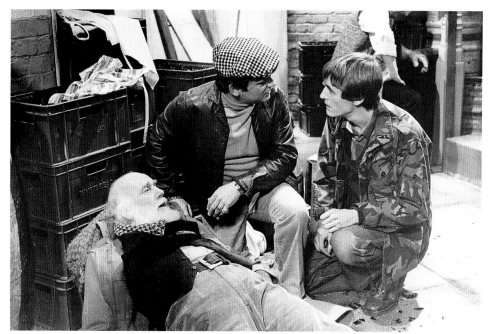
'Hole in One'

house down. Then I had the short but touching scene with Del where I had to turn my back on the baby and leave, so you had the amazing feeling of hearing the audience laugh their socks off, followed by the snuffles and handkerchiefs coming out as I left the room. And that's what the show is all about: it makes people laugh and genuinely makes them cry – it's fabulous.'

'Hole in One'

Original transmission: Thursday 7 March 1985, 8.00 pm

Production date: 12 February 1985

Original viewing figures: 13.4 million

Duration: 30 minutes

First repeat: Saturday 30 November 1985, 8.10 pm

Subsequent repeats: 2/11/91, 16/4/95, 27/3/98, 17/8/00

CAST

Del Trotter	David Jason
Rodney Trotter	Nicholas Lyndhurst
Uncle Albert	Buster Merryfield
Solly Attwell	Colin Jeavons
Mike	Kenneth MacDonald
Judge	Dennis Ramsden
Mr Gerrard	Andrew Tourell
Mr Frazer	James Woolley
Maureen	Nula Conwell
Cockney man	Michael Roberts
Clerk	Les Rawlings
Walk-ons:	(Draymen) Alan Talbot and Tim Milson. (Courtroom stenographer) Jean Channon. (Usher) Cy Town.

PRODUCTION TEAM

Written by John Sullivan

Title music arranged and conducted by Ronnie Hazlehurst composed and sung by John Sullivan

Audience Warm-up:	Felix Bowness
Make-up Designer:	Linda McInnes
Costume Designer:	Richard Winter
Properties Buyer:	Chris Ferriday
Film Cameraman:	Chris Seager
Film Sound:	Dennis Panchen
Film Editor:	John Jarvis
Camera Supervisor:	Ken Major
Studio Lighting Director:	Don Babbage
Studio Sound:	Dave Thompson
Technical Coordinator:	Tony Mutimer
Videotape Editor:	Chris Booth
Production Assistants:	Caroline Andrews and Lesley Bywater
Assistant Floor Manager:	Gavin Clarke
Vision Mixer:	Heather Gilder
Production Manager:	Andy Smith
Designer:	Eric Walmsley

Directed by Susan Belbin

Produced by Ray Butt

You could cut the tension in the Trotters' household with a knife: Del is annoyed with his younger brother for forking out five hundred quid on suntan lotion just when it seems like the Ice Age is returning. To make matters worse, Rodney's squandered the last of Trotters' Independant Trading Company's funds.

Business is dire: the only sale they've made recently is an electric deep-fat fryer to Mike, the landlord at The Nag's Head. Rodney blames their run of bad luck on Albert, claiming his arrival has been coupled with a noticeable down-turn in their fortunes. To top it all, Del thinks they'll now have to cancel the headstone for Grandad's grave due to lack of funds.

A visit to The Nag's Head brings no solace, especially when it's quickly evident that the deep-fat fryer is on the blink, causing Mike a headache. And with Rodney and Del at each other's throats, Uncle Albert is left to mediate, claiming something will crop up to turn their fortunes around, before leaving the Trotter boys to drown their sorrows with alcohol.

But when Albert falls through the open cellar door and remarks that he should sue the brewery for negligence, Del, never one to let an opportunity go by, quickly picks up on Albert's deliberate attempt to make the cash flow in again. What he didn't bargain for is that when the compensation claim reaches court, it's established that Albert had sought to bring 15 previous lawsuits for falling down holes. But Del and Rodney's anger is short-lived when they learn that Albert's attempt at being a stuntman was to help repay them for the kindness they've shown him and to pay for Grandad's headstone.

'Homesick'

Original transmission: Thursday 10 November 1983, 8.30 pm

Production date: Sunday 2 October 1983

Original viewing figures: 9.4 million

Duration: 30 minutes

First repeat: Monday 16 July 1984, 8.00 pm

Subsequent repeats: 31/8/91, 10/2/95, 2/10/98, 4/3/00

CAST

Del Trotter . . . . .David Jason
Rodney Trotter . . . . .Nicholas Lyndhurst
Uncle Albert . . . . .Buster Merryfield
Baz . . . . .Ron Pember
Trigger . . . . .Roger Lloyd Pack
Old lady (No 1) . . . . .Gilly Flower
Old lady (No 2) . . . . .Renee Roberts
Doctor . . . . .John Bryans
Miss Mackenzie . . . . .Sandra Payne
Small boy . . . . .Miles Rinaldi
Walk-ons: . . . .(People in market) Ali Baba, Derek Chabrol, Meg Lindsey, Doreen Taylor, Yvette Rey, Judy Collins and 19 extras.

PRODUCTION TEAM

Written by John Sullivan
Title music arranged and conducted by Ronnie Hazlehurst composed and sung by John Sullivan
Audience Warm-up: . . . . .Felix Bowness
Make-up Designer: . . . . .Denise Baron
Costume Designer: . . . . .Dinah Collin
Properties Buyer: . . . . .Penny Rollinson
Film Cameraman: . . . . .Ian Hilton
Film Sound: . . . . .Clive Derbyshire
Film Editor: . . . . .Mike Jackson
Camera Supervisor: . . . . .Chris Glass
Studio Lighting Director: . . . . .Don Babbage
Studio Sound: . . . . .Malcolm Johnson
Technical Coordinator: . . . . . .Chris Watts
Videotape Editor: . . . . .Mike Taylor

Production Assistant: . . . . .Penny Thompson
Assistant Floor Manager: . . . . .Tony Dow
Graphic Designer: . . . . .Mic Rolph
Vision Mixer: . . . . .Angela Beveridge
Production Manager: . . . . .Andy Smith
Designer: . . . . .Antony Thorpe
Produced and directed by Ray Butt

A strange turn of events finds Rodney elected as Chairman of the Tenants' Committee, a position of responsibility he soon uses to his family's advantage when it appears Grandad's days of living in the tower block and having to climb 12 flights of stairs are numbered. When Grandad's legs give way and he collapses in the lounge, Del tries persuading an initially reluctant Rodney to call Miss Mackenzie, who's responsible for housing and welfare at the local council, to get them moved to one of the new three-bedroom bungalows the council has built in Herrington Road.

Finally, Rodney succumbs to Del's pressure and Miss Mackenzie is only too pleased to help. But when it's discovered that it's all a devious plan, and Grandad is caught partaking in a celebratory dance with Del, Miss Mackenzie promises to put a halt to their move and her friendship with Rodney, who agrees to resign as Chairman of the Tenants' Committee forthwith.

Hookie Street

The etymology of the phrase 'Hookie Street' is uncertain, but the word 'hook' appears to date back to the 19th century and originate from the American language, being used to describe a thief.

'Hookie Street'

The title of the song, sung by John Sullivan, which accompanies the closing credits at the end of each episode.

MOTHER AND SON IN 'HOMESICK'

★ ★ ★ ★ ★ ★

In 'Homesick', a little boy runs past Del's market stall and pinches one of his oranges. The 11 year old was Miles Rinaldi, who undertook photographic work and small acting jobs during his school holidays. Accompanying him at the day's filming was his mother, Judy Collins, who trained at the Royal Ballet School but gave up her career as a dancer and singer to raise a family. Nowadays, she's a background artist and worked as such on the same episode.

When a child was required in the show, a representative from the *Only Fools* production team asked Judy's agent, who suggested Miles. 'Not that long ago you had to be an Equity member to do background work – it was a very closed shop. It's not like that anymore, but in those days it was mostly old dancers, musicians and people like that who were seen floating around in the background.'

Although not expected to learn lines, there are certain requirements expected of background artists, as Judy explains. 'You have to merge into the background as far as your style of clothes and the colours you choose; you don't want to be outstanding in any way, you need to be ordinary. You would never wear reds or anything bright like that, but would opt for dull or pale insignificant colours.'

'On period productions you're fitted for costumes, but in something like *Only Fools and Horses* you're just told to bring along a change of clothes. The artist is expected to know what is required of them.'

Judy enjoyed her short time on the sitcom. 'There weren't too many background artists involved in the scene, so it was nice from that point of view. But we were merely passers-by. I went on to work on several other episodes of the show which was great because it was a very successful show, even back then.' **JUDY COLLINS**

'Hookie Street'

The quarterly newsletter produced by The Only Fools and Horses Appreciation Society, which was founded in 1994 by Perry Aghajanoff, who's now the Society's president.

Horseferry Road Magistrates' Court

In 'The Long Legs of the Law', Del tells Grandad about the punch-up they witnessed between Monkey Harris and Tommy Razzle and how Rodney tried chatting up the arresting officer, a young policewoman. He points out that the only date Rodney was likely to get with her was one at Horseferry Road Magistrates' Court.

Hoskins, Terry (police constable)

Played by Christopher Mitchell

Hoskins is a local policeman who stands guard at the interrogation conducted by Slater during 'May the Force be with You'. Hoskins – who dislikes the Detective Inspector just as much as Del – seems a nice enough chap, and is known by Del, who sold his mother a gas fire recently. He's seen again in 'To Hull and Back', with Slater at the market; he's now employed as the Chief Inspector's driver.

'May the Force be with You'

Hotel Las Palmas

The Trotters stay at this Benidorm hotel in 'It Never Rains…'.

Howard, Sam

Role: Steven
Appeared in S6, episode 3
Other appearances Sam has made include playing

Mr Harvey in 1989's *Press Gang* and Edward in the film *Madame Sousatzka*.

Huddleston's Auction Rooms

In 'Yesterday Never Comes', Del pops over to these Chelsea-based auction rooms to find Miranda Davenport splashing out £3,800 for one of the lots.

Hughes, Alan

Costume designer on one episode: 'Christmas Crackers'

Hulse, Alan

Role: Bridge attendant
Appeared in 'To Hull and Back'

Humphreys, Dean

Dubbing mixer on one episode: 'To Hull and Back'
Since being assigned to *Only Fools*, Dean has worked extensively in the film industry on pictures such as *Cry Freedom*, *Queen of Hearts*, *Frantic*, *Shadowlands* and *The Next Best Thing*. His television work has included *Wagner* (1983), *Kidnapped* (1995) and *Victoria and Albert*.

Hussein, Adam

Role: Mr Jahan
Appeared in 'The Frog's Legacy'
Among Adam's other screen appearances are roles in *The Professionals*, *Dempsey and Makepeace* and *The Doomsday Gun*, while his films include *Navy Seals* and *Ishtar*.

Hussein, Mr

Played by Lorence Ferdinand
Mr Hussein, who's Abdul's cousin, is a diamond merchant based in Amsterdam. He's seen in 'To Hull and Back' and is involved in Abdul, Boycie and Mr Van Kleefe's diamond smuggling racket.

Hyde, Glenn

Dubbing editor on two episodes: 'Miami Twice' (Parts 1 & 2)

'If They Could See Us Now…!'

(For details of this episode, refer to 'The Return of the Trotters' chapter.)

Imogen

Played by Bridget Sutcliffe
Rodney tells Del about Imogen in The Nag's Head during 'To Hull and Back'. He's been dating her, but feels she's getting too serious – she's even talking about engagement. He's wondering whether he should finish the relationship, but whilst he's chewing over the matter, he suddenly sees her in the arms of another man.

Indian restaurant manager, The

Played by Babar Bhatti
The manager breaks the sad news that Mr Ram – who hoodwinked Del into believing he owned the Indian restaurant, and seventeen others – is a fraud.

Indian waiter

Seen briefly in 'Chain Gang', the waiter works in the restaurant where the conman Arnie finally gets his comeuppance.

Inframax Deep Penetration Massager

Del puts all his efforts into selling the massage lamps at the market in the 'The Frog's Legacy'.

Inga

Played by Brigid Erin Bates
Seen in 'The Jolly Boys' Outing', the bad-mannered Inga – who works in the Villa Bella, the worst guest house in Margate – is helping to serve dinner when she's ordered by the owner, Mrs Creswell, to show the Trotters to their room.

Inge

Seen in 'To Hull and Back', the Inge is the boat Del hires for his diamond smuggling jaunt across the North Sea to Holland. The boat is valued at £10,000, but its condition leaves a lot to be desired.

The former fishing boat is now for sale at a boat yard in Mistley, Essex. Its owner, David Foster, would be interested in offers in the region of £500.

The vessel has attracted plenty of interest – even from abroad – ever since it appeared in *Only Fools and Horses*, but as yet hasn't been sold.

After the Beeb finished with the boat it was bought by a local businessman and docked in Gashouse Creech, Harwich, alongside the old rail link between Harwich and Zeebrugge. Colin Crawford, at Sea Containers, asked David to tow it away because it had eventually sunk.

Interviewer

(See 'Cox, Sandra')

'It Never Rains…'

Original transmission: Thursday 25 November 1982, 8.30 pm

Production date: Sunday 27 June 1982

Original viewing figures: 9.5 million

Duration: 30 minutes

First repeat: Tuesday 9 August 1983, 8.30 pm

Subsequent repeats: 30/11/90, 3/2/95, 1/7/97, 18/2/00

CAST

Del Trotter . . . . .David Jason
Rodney Trotter . . . . .Nicholas Lyndhurst
Grandad Trotter . . . . .Lennard Pearce
Alex, the travel agent . . . . . . .Jim McManus
French girl . . . . .Anne Bruzac
English girl . . . . .Jilli Foot
Englishman . . . . .Michael Attwell
Spanish guard . . . . .Anthony Jackson
Barmaid . . . . .Julie La Rousse
Walk-ons: . . . . (People in pub) John Holland and seven extras. (Women in street, although edited out before transmission) Jeanette Lampshire and Barbara Hampshire. (People on Spanish holiday) Judy Cowne, Annette Paris, Graham Cole, Martin Grant, Tom Gandl, Phil Marvin, Tony Snell, Brian Godfrey, Steve Christy, Leon Ross, Adrian Fenwick, Maria Eldridge, Wendy Holker and 25 extras.

PRODUCTION TEAM

Written by John Sullivan
Title music arranged and conducted by Ronnie Hazlehurst composed and sung by John Sullivan
Make-up Designer: . . . . .Shaunna Harrison
Costume Designer: . . . . .Anushia Nieradzik
Properties Buyer: . . . . .Roger Williams
Film Cameraman: . . . . .John Walker
Film Sound: . . . . .Dennis Panchen
Film Editor: . . . . .Mike Jackson
Camera Supervisor: . . . . .Ron Peverall
Studio Lighting Director: . . . . .Henry Barber
Studio Sound: . . . . .Dave Thompson
Technical Coordinator: . . . . . .Derek Martin
Videotape Editor: . . . . .Mike Taylor
Production Assistant: . . . . .Penny Thompson
Assistant Floor Manager: . . . . . Tony Dow

Graphic Designers: . . . . .Peter Clayton and Fen Symonds
Stills photographer: . . . . .John Jefford
Rostrum Cameraman: . . . . .Ivor Richardson
Vision Mixer: . . . . .Angela Beveridge
Production Managers: . . . . . . .Janet Bone and Sue Bysh
Designers: . . . . .Derek Evans and Andy Dimond
Produced by Ray Butt

It's been raining for days and the Trotters are down-beat because it's stopped them working. In The Nag's Head the atmosphere is even more doom-laden because Alex, a local travel agent, is finding business slow with loads of holidays unsold. Del tells him it's all about marketing and persuades Alex to give an 80 per cent discount on a holiday anywhere in the world for the next customer in his shop. Del's got an ulterior motive, though: he fancies a break himself.

'It Never Rains…'

'It Never Rains…'

While Rodney tries earning some much-needed holiday cash by selling sun hats in the pouring rain, Del grabs the cheap holiday, but his destination, Benidorm, does little to excite Rodney.

The holiday doesn't extend to Grandad, but when they realise it would break his heart to be left behind, they arrange for an extra seat on the plane, even if it will cramp their style, which it certainly does when they bring two girls back to their apartment only to have them take fright and scarper when they see Grandad's teeth in a glass. But more trouble erupts when Grandad is arrested and spends hours in a police cell. Just when he thinks his past is catching up on him, he's released after discovering that all he was arrested for was a minor traffic violation.

'It's Only Rock and Roll'

Original transmission: Thursday 14 March 1985, 8.00 pm

Production date: Sunday 27 January 1985

Original viewing figures: 13.6 million

Duration: 30 minutes

First repeat: Saturday 9 November 1991, 5.45 pm

Subsequent repeats: 30/4/95, 13/3/98
(Insert of group singing 'Boys Will Be Boys' recorded in *Top of the Pops'* studio on Wednesday 9 January 1985)

CAST

Del Trotter . . . . .David Jason
Rodney Trotter . . . . .Nicholas Lyndhurst
Uncle Albert . . . . .Buster Merryfield
Policeman . . . . .Geoffrey Leesley
Mental Mickey . . . . .Daniel Peacock
Charlie . . . . .Marcus Francis
Stew .David Thewlis
DJ . . . . .Mike Read
Voice-overs: . . . . .Jean Challis, Bob Sinfield and Kenneth MacDonald

PRODUCTION TEAM

Written by John Sullivan
Title music arranged and conducted by Ronnie Hazlehurst composed and sung by John Sullivan
The song, 'Boys Will Be Boys', composed by John Sullivan and arranged by Steve Jeffries.
Make-up Designer: . . . . .Linda McInnes
Costume Designer: . . . . .Richard Winter
Properties Buyer: . . . . .Chris Ferriday
Film Cameraman: . . . . .Chris Seager
Film Sound: . . . . .Dennis Panchen
Film Editor: . . . . .John Jarvis
Camera Supervisor: . . . . .Ken Major
Studio Lighting Director: . . . . .Peter Smee
Studio Sound: . . . . .Dave Thompson
Technical Coordinator: . . . . . .Tony Mutimer
Videotape Editor: . . . . .Chris Booth
Production Assistants: . . . . . . .Caroline Andrews
                        and Lesley Bywater
Assistant Floor Manager: . . . .Gavin Clarke
Vision Mixer: . . . . .Heather Gilder
Production Manager: . . . . .Andy Smith
Designer: . . . . .Eric Walmsley
Directed by Susan Belbin
Produced by Ray Butt

Rodney is off to rehearse with his band of no-hopers and has to make do with a set of packing cases for drums. When Del hears The Shamrock Club has lost their resident band, he concocts a plan: he calls Liam, the club's owner, and tells him that for 300 sovereigns he can supply the perfect band for the forthcoming St Patrick's night. He soon installs himself as the band's manager by promising new equipment and plenty of gigs, even if he shudders at the sound of the din coming from their rehearsal room.

The gig at The Shamrock Club is a disaster and when a fight ensues the band scarper; next morning, Rodney finds all the equipment has been stolen from the garage. He calls the police, only to discover that Del had the equipment on a sale-or-return basis, and fearing the worst for the band's prospects, he returned the gear.

Rodney's aspirations to be a rock'n'roller are quashed, but he can't believe his eyes when he switches on *Top of the Pops* and sees his old group singing their hit record.

Jackie

Played by Anne Bruzac
Jackie, whom Del mistakes for a French girl, is seen in 'It Never Rains…'. He tries chatting her up at the pool-side bar, but is snubbed when she walks off and joins Ray, an arrogant Englishman who's sunning himself.

Jackson, Anthony

Role: Spanish guard
Appeared in S2, episode 6
Anthony, who was born in Birmingham in 1946, trained at the Rose Bruford College and made his professional debut in a 1962 production of *The Glad and Sorry Season* in the West End. His early years were spent largely on stage and radio, working at The Mermaid Theatre and with the BBC's Radio Drama Company (1965–68).

After making his television debut in 1967, he has gone on to appear in various programmes, including *Bognor, Beyond Belief, Rentaghost, Citizen Smith, EastEnders, Boon, Lovejoy, The Governor* and, his favourite role, Trevor, in *Bless This House*. More recent television credits include *Casualty* and *Doctors*, while on the stage he's been seen in *The Faith Healer*.

Jackson, David

Role: Brendan O'Shaughnessy
Appeared in S3, episode 7
It was during the 1960s that David started making his name on television with appearances in *Redcap, The Avengers, Z Cars, Counterstrike* and *The Liver Birds*. In the 1970s he moved on to *The Sweeney, Space: 1999, Sky, Minder* and *Blake's 7*. The 1980s were equally busy, with roles ranging from Basil in *Lovejoy* to Colonel Lawson in *Edge of Darkness*.

David has also appeared on the big screen in productions including *The Big Sleep, Killer's Moon* and *Breakout*.

Jackson, Laura

Role: Marsha
Appeared in S6, episode 1
Born in London in 1960, Laura graduated from London's Central School of Speech and Drama and spent the early part of her career in the theatre

and making commercials. She made her first appearance in a television programme playing Dawn, a Yellowcoat in *Hi-De-Hi!*, in 1984. She continued dividing her time between the stage and screen, playing small parts in shows like *The Legacy of Reginald Perrin, Nelson's Column* and *Roger, Roger*.

Jackson, Mike

Film editor on 12 episodes: S2, episodes 1, 2, 4–7; S3, episodes 1–4, 6 & 7

Jahan, Mr

Played by Adam Hussein
Mr Jahan – who runs an undertaking business in Peckham – arrives at The Nag's Head in 'The Frog's Legacy', furious with Del because the computer he purchased from him still doesn't work. What Mr Jahan doesn't realise is that the Office of Fair Trading classified the computers as useless. He gives Del one more week to rectify the problem before he returns the machine.

James

(See 'Turner, James')

James, Linda

Role: Neighbour (voice only)
Appeared in 'Rodney Come Home'
On the proviso that she qualified as a teacher, Linda was allowed by her parents to enrol on a drama course at The Royal Academy of Music. Three years later, she graduated as a speech and drama teacher.

She worked in rep before making her television debut in 1969's comedy *The Gnomes of Dulwich*, written by Jimmy Perry. The series about garden gnomes meant her appearance as one of the humans was restricted to shots of her feet. Other television credits include *Keeping Up Appearances, Waiting for God, Dad's Army, Don't Wait Up, Last of the Summer Wine, Some Mothers Do 'Ave 'Em, The Liver Birds* and *The Dick Emery Show*.

In a career spanning 15 years, she was seen mainly in comedy parts. Nowadays Linda – who's married to actor Michael Knowles – is a dialect coach for film and television, and teaches at two drama schools.

Jameson, Brian

Role: Doctor
Appeared in S4, episode 5
Brian has worked on stage and screen, appearing as Brian Epstein in the 1979 film *Birth of the Beatles*, on television in *Terry and June* and as Ronald in *Minder*.

Jamille, Mr

Mr Jamille is Rodney's tutor in computer science, which he's studying at evening class. He's not seen, but is mentioned in 'Little Problems', when Rodney, despondent at failing his exam again, tries to shield his embarrassment by claiming Mr Jamille hasn't marked all the papers yet. When Del returns home with the diploma under his arm, Rodney is overjoyed; what he doesn't realise is that it cost Del £150 before Mr Jamille would issue it!

Janice

Played by Gaynor Ward

Another of Rodney's girlfriends, the braless Janice – who has a brother called Don and a pet corgi called Nero – is seen in the flat during 'A Slow Bus to Chingford'. We get to know little about the brunette's background, other than that she's supposed to be keen on art.

Janine

We never see Janine, but she is mentioned in 'Fatal Extraction' when Del is sat in Sid's Café with Rodney, Trigger and Denzil, desperately trying to remember the name of an ex-girlfriend. Trigger suggests the red-haired Janine, but it seems that Del hasn't got fond memories of her – if his reaction is anything to go by.

Jarvis, Graham

Music on four episodes: 'Heroes and Villains', 'Modern Men', 'Time On Our Hands' and 'If They Could See Us Now…!'

Graham was the musical director and composer on the 1996 Christmas Trilogy. He also played the guitars, while Mark Cumberland and Andy Gibson played trumpet and flugel horn, Philip Hoskins was on drums and Duncan Lamont on alto sax and flute.

Jarvis, John

Film editor on 35 episodes: S1; S4, episodes 1–5 & 7; S5, episodes 1–4; S6, episodes 1 & 3; S7, episodes 1–3, 5 & 6; 'To Hull and Back'; 'The Frog's Legacy'; 'Dates'; 'The Jolly Boys' Outing'; 'Rodney Come Home'; 'Miami Twice' (Parts 1 & 2); 'Mother Nature's Son'; 'Fatal Extraction'; 'Heroes and Villains'; 'Modern Men' and 'Time On Our Hands'

John, who was born in Borehamwood, followed in his father's footsteps when he joined the film industry at the age of 15. Working as a messenger boy for ABPC, based at Elstree, he remained in the job for a year before moving on to Humphrey's Film Laboratories.

After completing national service with the army, he joined Esso's film unit in 1953 as an assistant editor on the company's petroleum documentaries. After 12 years he'd gained experience as a fully fledged editor, so when the unit closed down and he was made redundant, John bought the equipment and established his own company in 1963. Initially most of his work came from Esso, where he continued editing the company's documentaries, but eventually work from the BBC came his way, beginning with *Top of the Pops*, and commercials.

By the time he retired in 1999, John – who now lives in Spain – had 17 cutting rooms, and had edited film sequences for many of the Beeb's top shows, including *Harry Worth; Morecambe and Wise; Open All Hours; The Goodies; Just Good Friends; As Times Goes By; Dear John; Roger, Roger* and *Over Here*.

Jason

Played by Ben Davis

Nine-year-old Jason is seen in 'Happy Returns'. He's just about to run into the road outside Zimbabwe House, when Del grabs him. When he explains he was running because his mum was going to 'kill him', Del gives the little boy – and his brother – 50p to buy an ice cream. He then learns that his mum threatened him because he'd let down the tyres on Del's van. Del takes quite a shine to Jason and when he later sees him sitting on the roadside, claiming he's running away, he discovers his mum is none other than an old flame: June.

Jason

We never see Jason, who works in a unisex hairdresser's in the High Street. While Del is in hospital during 'Sickness and Wealth', he mentions Jason as he cut his hair recently. Desperate to find a reason why he's ended up in hospital, Del wonders if he caught something from the hairdresser, and even suggests AIDS.

Jason, David

Role: Derek Trotter and Vinny Occhetti
Appeared in all episodes as Del and in 'Miami Twice' as Occhetti

Regarded as one of the country's finest actors, particularly in the field of comedy, David Jason's glittering career has included such classic parts as the aged delivery boy Granville in four series of Roy Clarke's *Open All Hours*, Pop Larkin in three series of *The Darling Buds of May* and Detective Inspector Jack Frost in *A Touch of Frost*, while no one can ever forget his portrayal of 63-year-old Blanco in *Porridge*. However, bringing to life Peckham's cheery wheeler-dealer is regarded by many as his best performance to date.

Reflecting on the success of the character in 1985, David told the *Radio Times* that Del was the sort of guy you could meet anywhere. 'The thing about him is that although he's not honest, he's moral. He thinks small, but he's happy-go-lucky – the eternal optimist – and that's why people love him.'

Born in London in 1940, the son of a fish porter at Billingsgate Fish Market, David gained his first taste of acting as a 14 year old in a school play. When he left school the following year, though, he followed his parents' advice and took a trade. He was originally a garage mechanic, but after a year switched professions and began training as an electrician; his evenings, meanwhile, were occupied performing in local amateur productions.

Fellow actor Rex Robinson, who played two separate characters in *Only Fools*, lived just around the corner from David during his amateur-acting days; for a short time they ran a business venture together, carrying out general house maintenance. Even in these early days, Rex could spot David's talents a mile off. 'I used to do the painting while David and his mate did the electrics; it was like listening to *The Goon Show* because a stream of comedy kept coming from him; he was very inventive and could improvise so well, especially with funny voices. I should think that anyone who heard us working must have wondered what was happening – we were more like the Crazy Gang!'

Rex remembers seeing David in an early semi-professional production and knew instantly that he had the potential to go far in the profession. 'His performance was excellent.' Reflecting on the success David has enjoyed, Rex isn't surprised in the slightest. 'He's got an enormous amount of natural talent, and I knew he'd got that all-important spark to succeed.'

David secured his first professional job thanks to his brother Arthur, in 1965. When Arthur was offered a part in *Z Cars*, he had to drop out of a forthcoming production of *South Sea Bubble*, a Noël Coward play at Bromley Rep. He recommended his younger brother to the director, who watched David in an amateur production, was

---

MEMORIES OF ONLY FOOLS

★ ★ ★ ★ ★ ★

'**My** job was to put all the location filming together. The film and soundtrack would arrive at my studio and it would be my responsibility to edit both. Once I was happy with the material, I'd sit down with the director and we'd run through it and make any final amendments; it's never correct first time, it's more an assembly of the best shots. When the director takes it away with him, we have the picture and the dialogue, but by the time it's taken through the dubbing theatre we would have seven or eight different sound tracks, covering all the other sound effects, such as cars and hooters. These would all be obtained from the library and added. The filming sequences are finally shown in the studio on the night of the recording to get the laughter track, and then they're slotted in to the overall episode.

'I thoroughly enjoyed working on *Only Fools*, and it's probably the funniest show I ever worked on, although I also have very fond memories of *Just Good Friends*. I remember when we were working out in Florida on *Miami Twice*, I received the rushes of the filming sequence where the crocodile is behind Del and Rodney. After I looked at them I told Tony Dow and Gareth Gwenlan that they didn't work because the crocodile started walking away and didn't look particularly menacing. As you can imagine, they weren't too pleased at having to go back and set up the scene again with the crocodile!' **JOHN JARVIS – Film editor**

David Jason (back row, second from left) as Dithers in *His Lordship Entertains*

suitably impressed and offered him the job, which was to mark the beginning of an award-winning career spanning nearly four decades.

Other stage work followed, together with spells of unemployment, before he returned to Bromley Rep and a year-long contract which offered him the chance to cut his teeth on a host of character parts and humorous roles.

David made his television debut in 1967's children's comedy *Do Not Adjust Your Set*, alongside Michael Palin, Eric Idle and Terry Jones, after being spotted by television producer Humphrey Barclay in a Bournemouth play with Dick Emery. Humphrey once explained: 'I'd seen a picture of him and his face had an air of innocent comedy about it. Then I saw him on stage and he was four times as amusing. Here was a performer who knew a thousand ways to make you laugh. What I didn't know then was that he could make you sigh and grieve, too.'

After the success of *Do Not Adjust Your Set*, David went on to combine stage and television work for years, with appearances in *Crossroads*, *Doctor at Large*, *Doctor at Sea*, *Lucky Fella*, *The Top Secret Life of Edgar Briggs*, *A Sharp Intake of Breath*, *Porterhouse Blue*, *A Bit of a Do* and *Hark at Barker*, with Ronnie Barker, with whom he'd work so successfully years later.

Hark at Barker spawned a sequel, *His Lordship Entertains*, in 1972. Jason played Dithers again in the seven-part series produced and directed by Harold Snoad, who has fond memories of working with Jason on the programme. 'The series was written by Ronnie Barker, under the pseudonym Jonathan Cobbald. It was all about Lord Rustless (played by Ronnie) deciding to open his home as

a hotel,' explains Harold. 'It was a great success and we were going to do some more, but *Fawlty Towers* arrived and rather took over the comedy hotel world. Anyway, David Jason played Dithers, a gardener-cum-odd-job man who now also had to assume the role of hall porter. David was brilliant in the part – especially as the character was supposed to be almost three times his own age! It was a very happy show and David was much liked by everyone – myself, the rest of the cast and the crew.'

Harold called upon David's talents again for an episode of *The Dick Emery Show*, which contained a 25-minute story centred round a prisoner-of-war camp. 'David played a prisoner who was part of a plot to break out of the camp. We saw him attend a meeting of the escape committee dressed up as a dog (full body costume, head, etc.) and learnt that the plan was that the following morning he would be hiding round the corner of a hut in the compound, and when a fellow prisoner saw the main gates open to let in a German lorry, he would throw a stick out of the open gate and David, as a dog, would dash off after it past the guards. Having got out, he would then contact various people in order to further other escape plans.

'The comedy came from the fact that having watched the dog dash out after the stick, the prisoner who'd thrown it was horrified to see that playing the role of the dog had obviously got under his fellow prisoner's skin because the dog (David) picked the stick up in his mouth, returned back through the camp gates and dashed up to the other prisoner wagging his tail before dropping the stick and waiting for it to be thrown again! It was a very funny sequence.

'At the end of *The Dick Emery Show* I had an out-takes' section which I called *The Comedy of Errors*. This show included two featuring David – one of which occurred when we were filming the aforementioned escape committee meeting. As David came in to the room dressed as the dog, the door closed behind him and pulled his tail off! David burst into hysterical laughter as did Dick and everyone else. Again, it was lovely having David on board and I think he enjoyed himself.'

But it's for the success he's made of playing Del Boy, the finagling market trader, that many people will always remember him. In 1982, he told the *Radio Times*, 'What draws me to Del is that he's a character who's rooted in reality.' A year later, David said: 'Del is a very rich character, one of the most interesting I've played. The writer has developed the character. He's three-dimensional, which is unusual for situation comedy where they normally go for jokes all the time. He shows emotion and all the sides of human endeavour. He's interesting.' David added: 'His character is outrageous but you can't help liking him. He's a little man trying to succeed against all the odds.' These sentiments are echoed by millions of fans around the British Isles who have taken Del Boy to their hearts.

Jayston, Michael

Role: James
Appeared in 'Time On Our Hands'

Michael, who was born in Nottingham in 1935, trained at the Guildhall School of Music and Drama before building a successful career on stage and screen. His television credits include *The Power Game*; *Jane Eyre*; *Quiller*; *Doctor Who*; *Tinker, Tailor, Soldier, Spy*; *A Bit of a Do*; *Casualty*; Ernest Bristow in *The Darling Buds of May*; Bob Willis in *Outside Edge*; *Heartburn Hotel*, *The Bill* and *Holby City*. He's also been seen in several films, such as *Cromwell*, *The Homecoming* and *Follow Me*.

Jean (Cousin)

Played by Maureen Sweeney

Married to Cousin Stan, the snooty Jean is seen at Grandad's funeral in 'Strained Relations'. Far from showing consideration and understanding on such a grief-stricken day, she shows her displeasure at being 'south of the river' and can't wait to get home.

Jeavons, Colin

Role: Solly Attwell
Appeared in S4, episode 3

Colin, who was born in Newport in 1929, trained at the Old Vic Theatre School. Although he's popped up in a handful of films, such as *Absolute Beginners*, *Secret Friends* and *The French Lieutenant's Woman*, he's been busiest on television. His credits in this medium include *Bleak House*, *The Baron*, *Doomwatch*, *Billy Liar*, *Fairly Secret Army*, *The Return of Sherlock Holmes*, *Bergerac*, *Home to Roost*, *Lovejoy* and *The House of Eliott*.

Jeffery, Alan

Technical coordinator on one episode: S2, episode 3

Jefford, John

Stills photographer on two episodes: S1, episode 3 and S2, episode 6

John, who also took the photos for the original title sequence, trained at the Ealing Art School for three years before working in advertising. After seven years he left and joined the BBC as a graphics photographer, a job he kept for 27 years before being made redundant in 1993. He's now enjoying his retirement.

Jeffries, Steve

Steve arranged the song 'Boys Will Be Boys' which is sung by 'A Bunch of Wallies' during 'It's Only Rock and Roll'. The song was written by John Sullivan.

Jelly Kelly

Not seen in the sitcom, Jelly Kelly is mentioned by Uncle Albert in 'The Frog's Legacy'. He was an explosives expert who teamed up with Freddy the Frog and broke into a post office in Plumstead. Unfortunately the robbery went badly wrong and he didn't survive.

Jervis, Dave

Video effects on one episode: S7, episode 1

Dave joined the BBC in 1969 and initially trained as a studio cameraman, working on programmes such as *Doctor Who*, *Dixon of Dock Green* and *Z Cars*. He started getting involved in digital effects during 1971 and has been working in the area ever since, covering a wide spectrum of shows, from dramas and light entertainment to music and arts shows. He continues to work at the Corporation.

Jesse Jackson Memorial Hall

Del books a room at this hall for Raquel and Tony Angelino to rehearse in during 'Stage Fright'.

Jevon

Played by Steven Woodcock

A friend of Mickey Pearce and Rodney, Jevon is seen at the disco in 'Yuppy Love'. He claims he was placed on Earth to bring pleasure and excitement into the lives of attractive young women. He doesn't live up to his proclamation, however, receiving two rejections on the trot upon inviting two girls – including Cassandra – to dance. By the end of the evening he's in luck and smooching along to the last dance.

Also seen in The Nag's Head in 'Sickness and Wealth' and 'Little Problems', Jevon goes into partnership with Mickey Pearce, trading in anything. His name is uttered once more in 'He Ain't Heavy, He's My Uncle' when Rodney tells Del he's going round to Jevon's place.

Jim

Not seen in the sitcom, Jim is mentioned by Rodney in 'Go West Young Man'. He's supposed to be one of Rodney's friends from evening class, whom he meets up with in the West End on nights out.

Joanne

Played by Gail Harrison

Yuppy Joanne is seen in 'The Jolly Boys' Outing'. She's married to Stephen and accompanies him to Rodney and Cassandra's first wedding anniversary bash.

Jobling, Ray

Production operatives' supervisor on two episodes: 'Miami Twice' (Parts 1 & 2)

Johnson, Herb

Role: Mechanic
Appeared in S7, episode 5

Johnson, Malcolm

Studio sound supervisor on one episode: S3, episode 1

London-born Malcolm Johnson worked as a lab assistant in a research laboratory for two years before spotting an advert in the *Radio Times* for engineers at the BBC. His successful application saw him take up the post of technical operator at Bush House on the World Service in 1960.

He transferred to television three years later and worked in technical operations, helping to run the studio crews, before becoming a sound supervisor in the late 1970s. Shows he worked on include the first three years of *Multicoloured Swap Shop* and the beginning of Breakfast TV.

By the time Malcolm retired from the Corporation in 1997, he'd built up 35 years' service and been promoted to Head of Sound for the station's outside broadcasts. Since leaving the Beeb, he has remained busy, working as a consultant for a European microphone company for three years.

Although he's now semi-retired, he's spent much of the last two years running the secretariat for the Institute of Broadcast Sound.

Johnstone, Iain

Grip on three episodes: 'Heroes and Villains', 'Modern Men' and 'Time On Our Hands'

Johnstone, Mike

Responsible for sound on the location video in 'Diamonds are for Heather'

'Jolly Boys' Outing, The'

(Christmas Special 1989)

Original transmission: Monday 25 December 1989, 4.05 pm

Production Date: Friday 2 June – Sunday 4 June 1989

Original viewing figures: 20.1 million

Duration: 85 minutes

First repeat: Sunday 8 July 1990, 4.50 pm

Subsequent repeats: 21/6/00, 22/5/02

CAST

Del Trotter	David Jason
Rodney Trotter	Nicholas Lyndhurst
Uncle Albert	Buster Merryfield
Cassandra	Gwyneth Strong
Boycie	John Challis
Mike	Kenneth MacDonald
Trigger	Roger Lloyd Pack
Denzil	Paul Barber
Marlene	Sue Holderness
Raquel	Tessa Peake-Jones
Mickey	Patrick Murray
Jevon	Steven Woodcock
Sid	Roy Heather
Alan	Denis Lill
Pamela	Wanda Ventham
Stephen	Daniel Hill
Joanne	Gail Harrison
Trainee	Jake Wood
Harry	Roy Evans
Mrs Baker	Katharine Page

'The Jolly Boys' Outing'

Helen	Dawn Funnell
Mrs Creswell	Rosalind Knight
Inga	Brigid Erin Bates
Ramondo	Robin Driscoll
Policeman	Del Baker
Singer	Lee Gibson
Drummer	Alf Bigden
Bass player	Dave Richmond
Organist	Ronnie Price
Eddie	Steve Alder
Tyler Boyce	Danny Billard

Walk-ons: . . . . .Kim Robinson, John Baker, Gregory Ball, Jason Beasley, Bert Crome, Bertie Green, David Hampson, Lloyd Harvey, Teddy Massiah, Nick Sandquest, Jack Street, Mike Vinden, Paul Vaughan-Teague, Tracy Spencer, Norman Warren, Mark Brett, Jim Delaney, Pat Shepherd, Sean McCrory, Natalie Bradley, Lisa Clifton, Felicity Lee, Gloria McGuire, Riccardo Mulhall, Robert Appleby, Ron Barney, Harry Bottom, Darrell Brook, Russell Brook, Peter Gates Fleming, Eric Kent, Michael Leader, Michael Mello, Oscar Peck, Paul Sadler, Philip Sadler, Joe Wells, Stephen Fitzalan, Rachel Chaney, Ray Chaney, Flanagan, Basil Marty, Lee Richards, Avril Dean, Gary Dean, Michael Hicks, Bob Terson, Roger Weightman.

The scene involving the following two actors was edited out before final transmission

Arthur	Michael Bilton
Betty	Fanny Carby

PRODUCTION TEAM

Written by John Sullivan

Title music arranged and conducted by Ronnie Hazlehurst composed and sung by John Sullivan

Closing titles written and sung by Chas and Dave.

Make-up Designer:	Dorka Nieradzik
Costume Designer:	Colin Lavers
Properties Buyer:	Leigh Craig
Stunt Arranger:	Colin Skeaping
Visual Effects:	Chris Lawson
Film Cameramen:	Alec Curtis and Adrian Smith
Film Sound:	John Parry
Gaffers:	Ted Turpin, Peter Robinson and Ted Bird
Grips:	Micky Ellis
Film Editor:	John Jarvis
Camera Supervisor:	Ken Major
Studio Lighting Director:	Don Babbage
Studio Sound:	Keith Mayes
Technical Coordinator:	Paul Thackray
Videotape Editor:	Chris Wadsworth
Production Assistant:	Amita Lochab
Assistant Floor Managers:	Angela de Chastelai Smith and Henry Tomlinson
Vision Mixer:	Sue Collins
Production Manager:	Adrian Pegg
Location Manager:	Duncan Cooper
Designer:	John Anderson

Directed by Tony Dow

Produced by Gareth Gwenlan

It's Rodney and Cassandra's first wedding anniversary and they've organised a dinner party, with Cassandra's 'yuppie' boss and his wife on the guest list in an attempt to assist her promotion.

'The Jolly Boys' Outing'

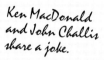

Ken MacDonald
and John Challis
share a joke.

Nicholas Lyndhurst soaks up
the sun during a filming break.

Everyone had a smashing time filming by the sea in sunny Margate.

Unfortunately, Del and Albert are also invited and it isn't long before they're putting their foot in it.

To make matters worse, the annual boys' outing – which Del has arranged – is discussed, and Rodney's desire to participate in the event is frowned upon by Cassandra. But he stands firm for tradition and books his place on the coach. The trip to Margate runs smoothly at first, but the inevitable disaster isn't far away because the coach driver gets drunk *en route*, Rodney gets arrested for kicking a ball at a policeman and the coach blows up when the radio, supplied by Trotters Independent Traders, catches fire. With no alternative transport to hand, the revellers find themselves scouring the seaside town's guest houses for an unexpected night's stay.

All is not doom and gloom, though, because Del spots his long-lost love, Raquel, who's working as a magician's assistant in the Mardi Gras nightclub. Del's love life may be rekindling, but Rodney's fades fast when he arrives home the following day to find Cassandra entertaining her boss; jumping to all the wrong conclusions, he throws a punch at Stephen, whose motives for being at the flat are, in fact, legitimate.

★ ★ ★ CUT SCENE! CUT SCENE! ★ ★ ★

CUT FROM "THE 'JOLLY BOYS' OUTING"

THE TROTTERS FOLLOW INGA UPSTAIRS. MRS CRESWELL FOLLOWS THEM. DEL LOOKS INTO THE SEMPRINI ROOM AT A SAD-FACED COUPLE (ARTHUR AND BETTY).

DEL Are you guests or has she hired you to cheer the place up?

ARTHUR No, we're guests.

BETTY Guests, aye.

DEL This place is no Club Med, is it?

ARTHUR It's really 'orrible here. The food's awful.

BETTY Awful food.

ARTHUR And not much of it, either.

BETTY No. She only allows you one jacket potato a day.

DEL Well, you never know, she might give you an extra lump of custard with yer afters.

ARTHUR Well, she hasn't previous years.

BETTY No.

ARTHUR Aye.

DEL Well, stay lucky

DEL ASCENDS THE STAIRS.

Jones, Daniel

Role: Darren (small boy)

Appeared in 'Diamonds are for Heather'

It would appear that Daniel never pursued acting as a career.

Jones, John Pierce

Role: Biffo

Appeared in S5, episode 2

Born in Anglesea in 1946, John trained at the University College of North Wales. Originally he wanted to pursue a career in teaching, but during his last year the artistic director of the Welsh Theatre Company saw him in a play and offered him the chance to join the company as a trainee. He took up the post in 1972.

He made his debut in a tour with other trainee students, and soon after appeared in a television sitcom, *Doctor*, for HTV. Later on, he worked for the channel's children's department for six years, presenting *Lots of Fun*, a puppet series.

His favourite television role was a long-running series in Wales, *Come on, Midfield*, a sitcom about a local football team, with John playing the lead. He appeared as the manager for eight years.

Other jobs in the medium include *Blackadder II*, *Drover's Gold*, *Sixteen Ounces* and *The Secret Life of Michael Fry*.

Jones, Michael G

Role: Pub customer (Paddy)

Appeared in S2, episode 3

Michael's recent work has been on the stage, working with the Royal Shakespeare Company in productions such as *Julius Caesar* and *Desire Under the Elms*, as well as the New Shakespeare Company and, among other venues, the Chichester Festival Theatre. On the small screen, meanwhile, he played Big Jake in the children's programme *Chucklevision*.

Joyce (the barmaid)

Played by Peta Bernard

A barmaid at The Nag's Head, Joyce serves Del and Rodney in the opening episode, 'Big Brother', and is seen again in 'The Second Time Around'. Clad in a leopard-skin blouse, and wearing earrings the size of footballs, her tarty appearance is commented on by Del, who has a soft spot for her, even though he classes her as an 'old dog'. He adds that he likes old dogs because you know where you stand with them, 'they never ask if you still respect 'em in the morning, and they'll always lend you a nicker for petrol!'

Juan

Actor not named on the cast list

Del calls the barman Juan, although it's uncertain if that is his real name, and asks for a pina colada with ice and Alka Seltzer. He's seen in 'The Unlucky Winner is…', working at the hotel in Mallorca, the place where Rodney, Del and Cassandra stay after Rodders wins a competition organised by Mega Flakes cereal company.

Judge

Played by Dennis Ramsden

The judge presides over Uncle Albert's compensation claim in court during 'Hole in One'.

Jules

Played by Paul Opacic

The 25-year-old gay set designer is working on the production of *As You Like It*, when Raquel auditions for a part. He appears in a café during 'The Chance of a Lunchtime', wearing leather trousers and jacket.

Julie (the barmaid)

Played by Julie La Rousse

A red-headed barmaid at The Nag's Head, Julie is first spotted in 'A Losing Streak', serving Del, Rodney, Boycie and Trigger when they're discussing gambling. She's later seen in 'No Greater Love…', 'It Never Rains…', 'Diamonds are for Heather' and 'Healthy Competition'.

Jumbo Mills

(See 'Mills, Jumbo')

June

(See 'Snell, June')

Justin

Played by Kim Wall

Justin represents the Trotters at the bankruptcy court in 'If They Could See Us Now…!'.

Kahjoo, Chua

Role: Tony (Chinese takeaway owner)
Appeared in S5, episode 5
Chua's list of credits include playing Choy in a 1980's episode of *The Professionals*, two roles in *Doctor Who* (a party guest and a stuntman) and Wong's aide in the 1983 film *High Road to China*.

Kandy Dolls

In 'It's Only Rock and Roll', Del is trying to sell the 'Kandy Doll – Your Talking Friend'. Made in Taiwan, the dolls talks, but sounds like Bugs Bunny!

Karen (the barmaid)

Played by Michèle Winstanley
The straight-faced Karen is seen pulling pints behind the bar at The Nag's Head in 'May the Force be with You' and 'Wanted'. The only time we hear her is when she tells Del – who's chatting to Boycie and Trigger – that there's a phone call for him. She's seen again in 'Who's a Pretty Boy?', when she complains to Del that the coat he sold to her dad has a big hump in the back. She even accepts Del's ridiculous excuse that it's because the coat is genuine camel-hair.

Katis, Diana

Role: Dale
Appeared in S6, episode 1
The early part of Diana's career was spent with the Youth Action Theatre, a company run by young actors between the ages of 16 and 25. She appeared in a host of plays with the company, such as *A Midsummer Night's Dream* and *Measure for Measure*, in which she played Mariana. On screen, she's played Anne in the 1982 film *Privileged*, and a bicycle rider in *Film (A Screenplay by Samuel Beckett)* in 1979.

Kawahara, Takashi

Role: Chinese takeaway owner
Appeared in S6, episode 2
Takashi has made occasional television appearances in the UK, most notably playing Shinya in the BBC drama *Tenko*. Other credits include *Bon Voyage*, *A Very Peculiar Practice* and *Virtual Murder*. His film work has seen him appear in *Eat the Peach*, *Road to Ruin* and *Massacres*, amongst others.

Kellgren, Lusha

Role: Trudy
Appeared in S6, episode 4
Born in London in 1972, Lusha trained at the Anna Scher Stage School before making her debut as an extra in the film *1984*. She broke into television playing Ethel, an orphan, in *The British Rebellion*, but gave up the profession to qualify as a nurse.

Kemp, Mike

Role: Stan (Cousin)
Appeared in S4, episode 2
Mike's television credits include playing a policeman in *The Professionals*, a fisherman in *Bergerac*, a publican in *Lovejoy*, Clayton in the 1982 miniseries *The Hound of the Baskervilles* and a mayor in the 2000 production of *Don Quixote*.

Kennedy, Johanna

Production manager on one episode: 'Fatal Extraction'
Johanna, who's married to director Richard Valentine, was born in Chichester. After leaving school she trained in business studies, but she always retained an interest in the theatre and went on to be stage manager at the Tower Theatre, Islington, a well respected amateur theatre.

She joined the BBC's personnel department in 1982 before moving in to the production side of the Corporation, initially as a floor assistant. By the time she left the Beeb in 1997 to raise a family she was a production manager and had worked on shows such as *Last of the Summer Wine*, *The Fast Show*, *Honey for Tea*, *Blackadder Goes Forth* and the *Paul Daniels' Magic Show*.

Johanna is now back working occasionally as a freelance floor assistant.

Kennedy, Ricky

Role: Tommy
Appeared in S4, episode 6
Ricky's other television appearances include playing Santa Claus in the 1974 production *Don't Open 'Til Christmas*.

Kenny

(See 'Malcolm, Kenny')

Kenworthy, Captain

Not seen in the sitcom, Captain Kenworthy was in charge of the corvette that Uncle Albert served on in the Pacific during the Second World War.

Kenworthy wore a wig, although you could only tell when the seas were rough and it slid to one side. The wig actually saved Albert's life, although its owner didn't fair so well. When a Japanese kamikaze pilot crashed his plane into the vessel, the crew abandoned ship and managed to make their way to a remote island; the islanders caught sight of Kenworthy's wig and thought it had magical powers. Wanting to get their hands on their remarkable find, they shot the captain but in the ensuing excitement lost interest in the other sailors, who escaped unharmed.

Kenworthy is mentioned again by Albert in

'Time On Our Hands'; this time he delves further into his naval past to the time they served together on the frigate HMS *Spinx*, in the Adriatic. Albert tells Del how his old captain used to allay his crew's worries about U-boats and sharks by creating a 'counter-worry', such as the time he warned there was a cholera epidemic aboard – not the most effective way to handle the sailors' concerns.

Note: The character was named after showbiz journalist Christopher Kenworthy, a friend of John Sullivan's, who was the first person to write about *Only Fools*.

Kevin

Not seen in the sitcom, Kevin is mentioned by Uncle Albert in 'Strained Relations'. He tells Del and Rodney that he lived with Kevin and his wife, Audrey, for a year, until one day they sent him down to Sainsbury's and emigrated whilst he was away.

Kevin

Played by Fuman Dar
In 'Heroes and Villains', Kevin is one of the muggers who attempts to steal the handbags from Councillor Murray and the old lady in the market.

Khalil, Ahmed

Role: Vimmal
Appeared in S1, episode 3
Ahmed, who's now living in India, has appeared in various television programmes: he played a businessman in *EastEnders*, a shopkeeper in *The Bill*, a chemist in *Heartstones*, Mr Patel in *Casualty*, an Arab sheikh in *Civvies*, an Embassy attaché in *Home James*, an Arab ambassador in *The Piglet Files*, Sheikh El Hamid in *Mind Your Language*, Khan in *Gangsters* and Mr Singh in *The Secret Diary of Adrian Mole Aged 13¾*.

His film appearances have seen him play a horse owner in 1997's *Shooting Fish* and Otter Pilot in *Son of the Pink Panther*.

Kidd, Barbara

Costume designer on one episode: 'To Hull and Back'
Barbara joined the BBC at the age of 20 and worked as a costume assistant for just a year before being promoted to costume designer. Over the years she worked for the Beeb she covered numerous shows, but particular favourites include *Doctor Who* and *Blake's 7*. She left the BBC in 1985 and continues to work freelance.

Kings' Avenue

This peaceful, suburban road is seen in 'Yuppy Love' when Del and Rodney stop to take a look at the plush properties. Del regards the road as the 'crème de la menthe' of the community, symbolising everything about the life he craves: a sumptuous house and huge disposable income. The only residents we get to know are the Boyce family, who live at number 17, while next door resides a high-ranking police officer, not the ideal neighbour for Boycie.

Kirsch, Oona

Role: Debby
Appeared in S4, episode 1

Oona's other television work includes playing Sandy Copeland in *The Professionals*, Margaret in *The Bill*, Claire in *Bergerac*, Anne in *Covington Cross*, Heidi in the first series of *Auf Wiedersehen, Pet*, Maureen in *Forever Young*, Julia in *East of Ipswich* and WDC Tilly Spink in *The Paradise Club*.

Her film appearances range from Maggie in *Sacred Hearts* to Valerie Caldwell in *A Certain Justice* for Anglia Television, while on stage her credits include playing Lydia in *Pride and Prejudice* and Denise Tricointe in *Court in the Act*.

Kish, George

Role: Guitarist in pub
Appeared in 'Diamonds are for Heather'

Kljuco, Cynthia

Designer on three episodes: S1, episodes 2 & 5 and 'Christmas Crackers'

Cynthia, who was born in Bloxwich, West Midlands, trained at the Birmingham College of Art. Upon seeing an advert for designers at the BBC, she applied and was offered a design assistant's role in 1964. Although she covered a wide spectrum of programmes, she preferred working on dramas, and among her credits are shows like *Dr Finlay's Casebook*, *The Brothers*, *Z Cars*, *Poldark*, *Dixon of Dock Green* and *The Songwriters*.

Cynthia left the Beeb in the early 1980s, and although she worked freelance at Anglia TV for a while, she took a break from the industry whilst she raised her family. Nowadays, she lives in France, overlooking the Pyrenees.

Knight, Rosalind

Role: Mrs Creswell
Appeared in 'The Jolly Boys' Outing'

Born in London in 1935, Rosalind studied at London's Old Vic Theatre School. She made her acting debut at Coventry, in a Midland Theatre Company's production of *Hobson's Choice*, playing Ada Figgins, before moving on to other rep compa-

nies, such as Ipswich, West of England Theatre Company (based in Exmouth), Amersham and Hornchurch.

Rosalind's television debut was in a 1955 production of *Nicholas Nickleby* and her favourite roles include Great Aunt Effie in 1997's series *Berkeley Square*, and Beryl Merit in BBC's *Gimme, Gimme, Gimme*.

She's appeared in several films, among them *Carry On Nurse*, as Nurse Nightingale; *Carry On Teacher*, as Felicity Wheeler; *Blue Murder at St Trinian's*, as Annabel and *Tom Jones*, as Mrs Fitzpatrick.

Rosalind still works in all strands of the profession with recent appearances including *Jack and the Beanstalk* for the Henson Organisation.

Knock Knock

Played by Howard Goorney

Seen in 'He Ain't Heavy, He's My Uncle', Knock Knock – who acquired his nickname because dominoes is not his forte – is an old school friend of Uncle Albert's. He's a regular attendee at the Over-Sixties' Club and down at The Nag's Head.

Kouchalakos, Tom

Role: Salvatore
Appeared in 'Miami Twice' (Part 2)

Tom, who was born in Miami in 1961, graduated from the University of Miami in 1983 and soon began working in the industry. On American television he's been seen in *Miami Vice*, *B.L. Stryker*, *Superboy*, *The Cape*, *First-Time Felon*, *Red Wind* and the mini-series *From the Earth to the Moon*. His film work includes appearances in *Let It Ride*, *Cocoon: The Return* and *Trading Hearts*.

Kristos

Not seen in the sitcom, Kristos is on the phone to Del during 'From Prussia with Love'. Del tries to convince him to buy a cordless phone, even if it is faulty.

Kylie

(See 'Lane, Kylie')

'La Dolce Vita'

The name of the Italian men's shirts – which are actually made in Malaya – that Del hopes to sell to Monkey Harris in 'The Unlucky Winner is…'.

Lady at dinner

Played by Daphne Goddard

Sat next to Del at dinner in 'A Royal Flush' is a plummy-voiced woman who's shocked when he tells her that Rodney and Lady Victoria are soon to be engaged.

Lady on the bus

Played by Kitty Scopes

In 'Fatal Extraction', the old lady is sat next to Rodney on the doubledecker when Mickey Pearce arrives and comments on how tired Rodney is looking. When the old lady agrees, Rodney gets annoyed.

Lamb, Constance

Role: Sister Shelley
Appeared in S7, episode 6

On television, Constance has appeared in various roles, including Polly (a councillor) in *Edge of Darkness*, Mrs Ackerman in *Woof!*, W P Sergeant in *An Actor's Life for Me*, Hanna in *A Shadow of an Angel*. More recently she's devoted her time to working on the stage in productions such as *Celebs*, as Julia, *The Case of the Crushed Petunias* (Dorothy), *10,000 Broken Mirrors* (Diana) and *Romeo and Juliet* (Lady Montague).

Lambeth, Mayor of

The Mayor is not seen in the sitcom, but in 'From Prussia with Love' we learn that Boycie's prison sentence when he was younger was in part due to his attempt to bribe the Mayor.

Lane, Bronco

Played by Ron Aldridge

Bronco – a painter and decorator who lives with his partner, Sandra, their daughter, Kylie, – is seen in 'The Sky's the Limit'. He's just finished a £400 job for Boycie who refuses to cough up the cash because he's made such a mess. At one point, life looked rosy for Bronco, when he bought a flat in Lordship Lane: eventually, though, he was

---

MEMORIES OF PLAYING MRS CRESWELL

★ ★ ★ ★ ★ ★

'One thing I remember about filming "The Jolly Boys' Outing" was the time we were working very late at night in a decrepit, condemned, deserted house in Ramsgate. I was playing a landlady and a scene required me to open the door of this ghastly boarding house and say: "Yes?". When I did it, there was nothing but silence and then David Jason and Nicholas Lyndhurst burst into spontaneous hysterical laughter; exactly the same thing happened on the second take, which was, of course, very gratifying, but it meant that neither of these takes could be used, and I never managed to achieve the same spookiness and energy again in that particular scene.' **ROSALIND KNIGHT**

evicted by the building society and now lives at the Hotel Schubert, a bed and breakfast establishment near Gatwick. His luck is still on a downward spiral because rent arrears have meant he can't even wash his overalls as the landlord has cut off the electric.

Bronco, who's Boycie's brother-in-law, put a lot of effort in to establishing his business, but luck isn't a commodity he's ever been blessed with: a roof he retiled collapsed and a flat he recently rewired caught fire. But despite all the setbacks he feels he's worked hard since being released from Wandsworth Prison, where he served time for speeding down Streatham High Road in a stolen JCB. A psychiatrist examined him after the incident and diagnosed paranoia.

Considering Bronco is Marlene's brother, Boycie's aggressive attitude towards the painter and decorator does little to strengthen their ties of kinship.

Lane, Dora

Played by Joan Geary

Dora is the 68-year-old woman Albert takes a fancy to in 'He Ain't Heavy, He's My Uncle'. He meets Dora – who's Marlene's mother – at the Over-Sixties' Club on the estate; the queen of the blue rinses, she's always immaculately attired.

Lane, Kylie

Sandra and Bronco's daughter is not seen in the sitcom, but is mentioned in 'The Sky's the Limit'. All we learn about her is that she broke her arm climbing out of a chair to look at a plane.

Lane, Sandra

We never see Sandra, but she lives with Bronco, a painter and decorator, and is mentioned in 'The Sky's the Limit'; life isn't easy for them and their little daughter, Kylie. Evicted from their flat in Lordship Lane, they're struggling to maintain the payments at the bed and breakfast hotel they're staying in.

Langley-Evans, Michael

Resources coordinator on two episodes: 'Mother Nature's Son' and 'Fatal Extraction'

Michael's experience of working on the studio floor ranges from productions like Sir Michael Tippet's opera, *New Year*, and *The Paul Daniels Magic Show* to Alan Bennett's *Talking Heads* series and an independent production of the Royal Ballet's *Three Sisters* and *Winter Dreams*. Other credits include *The Generation Game, Just Good Friends, Dear John, Absolutely Fabulous, Wogan, Top of the Pops, Bread, The Sky at Night* and *I, Claudius*. Michael now works freelance.

Langridge, Lyn

Roles: First woman and Vi

Appeared as First woman in S7, episode 3 and as Vi in 'Fatal Extraction'

Lyn's other television work includes playing a nurse in *Juliet Bravo*, a Spanish teacher in *This Is David Harper*, a cashier in *If You See God, Tell Him*, Marion in *Ballroom* and Mrs Howells in the 1983 series *The Citadel*.

Langton, Diane

Role: June

Appeared in S4, episode 1 and 'A Royal Flush'

Diane trained at the Corona Academy and started her professional career as a dancer. Nowadays she's regularly seen on television, most notably, perhaps, as Ruby Rowan, Nick's mother in *Heartbeat*. However, she's also appeared in shows such as *The Rag Trade, The Bill, Joking Apart, How To Be A Little Sod, EastEnders, Chicago* and *Holby City*.

Her stage credits include playing Miss Lucy and Pearl Lamonte in *Sweet Bird of Youth* and *Johnny On A Spot* respectively, at the Royal National Theatre; Vi in *Steaming* and Viv Nicholson in *Spend, Spend, Spend* at the Piccadilly Theatre.

She's also appeared in a handful of films, such as *Don't Just Lie There, Say Something; Percy's Progress; Eskimo Nell; Confessions of a Pop Performer; Trial By Combat* and *Carry On England*.

La Rousse, Julie

Role: Julie (the barmaid)

Appeared in S2, episodes 3, 4 & 6; 'Diamonds are for Heather'; S3, episode 2

Julie's other credits include appearing as an extra in an episode of *Dr Who*.

Lassie

In 'Thicker Than Water' Rodney describes Del's latest girlfriend as Lassie. He jokes that when she went to Tenerife it took two weeks to get her out of quarantine. We never see her or hear anything more about her.

Lavers, Colin

Costume designer on one episode: 'The Jolly Boys' Outing'

Colin began his career at L & H Nathan, the theatrical costumiers, working with designers in theatre, film and television. When Joan Ellacott designed *The Forsyte Saga*, Colin organised the fitting and making of all the men's costumes, an 18-month assignment.

He joined the BBC in 1972 as an assistant cos-

MEMORIES OF 'THE JOLLY BOYS' OUTING

★ ★ ★ ★ ★ ★

'This Christmas Special was filmed on location in and around Margate earlier in the year than the story was set, which meant it was sometimes colder and certainly windier and wetter than we all would have liked.

'Most of the story takes place on one day; the filming, however, took about three weeks. This gives an immediate problem to the costume department. Filming is expensive, but even more expensive if everyone is ready on location but the leading man's suit is being dried off with a hair dryer because of a sudden rain storm.

'Most of the actors had scenes on the coach or on a particular location but didn't work every day. They came down to location and returned home during the filming. David and Nicholas were with us every day and in virtually every scene. Both of their suits were duplicated and an allowance made for fitting thermal underwear

underneath for the night filming. I also bought duplicate shoes as filming days are long and uncomfortable enough without having to put up with damp shoes. Some other pieces of costume were duplicated, but one was unique and by good fortune it never got caught in the rain. The unique suit is, of course, Trigger's – man-made fibre at its worst and a shade of blue that hurts your eyes if you look at it for too long.

'The design element on an established show like *Fools and Horses* is to continue the look of the characters so the fans won't notice any change in their wardrobe. One outfit I did design for the episode was Raquel's. I had it made in a somewhat old-fashioned, variety-theatre style rather than a modern, lycra fabric, which was the latest style. I thought this would help with the impression given in the script that she wasn't appearing in a first-class act.' **COLIN LAVERS**

tume designer and worked on a range of programmes. Promoted to costume designer five years later, Peter – who designed Peter Davison's costume as *Doctor Who* – continued to be assigned a variety of productions, some of which were filmed abroad.

Laverty, Maura

Properties buyer on six episodes: S5

Maura worked for the BBC until 1997. When the Corporation's design department closed down, she became a freelance prop buyer. Among the productions she's worked on are *A Perfect Spy*, *Not A Penny More*, *The Men's Room*, *Between the Lines* and *Henry IV*, whilst employed by the Beeb, and *Close Relations*, *Forgotten*, *People Like Us* and *Time Gentleman Please* on a freelance basis.

Lawson, Christopher

Visual effects designer on two episodes: S7, episode 1 and 'The Jolly Boys' Outing'

Chris was born in Thailand and moved to England at the age of five. He left school and studied business and accountancy at night school with the intention of pursuing a career in that field. Two years later, he realised it wasn't for him and changed direction, joining the BBC instead. Initially he worked as a storeman before transferring to the visual effects department in 1973. Early shows he worked on as an assistant include *Dr Who*, *The Goodies* and *The Survivors*.

Chris left the BBC in 1999 to work freelance and recent projects include *Jonathan Creek*, *Midsomer Murders* and *One Foot in the Grave*.

Lazell, Andy

Visual effects designer on two episodes: 'Fatal Extraction' and 'Heroes and Villains'

Andy, who was born in London in 1950, joined the BBC in 1968 as a technical assistant in television news, based at Alexandra Palace. His early years were spent largely working as a vision mixer on live broadcasts, before moving on to shows like *The Goodies*, *Dr Who*, *Blake's 7* and *'Allo 'Allo!*

He joined the visual effects department in 1974. Now a visual effects supervisor, recent jobs have seen him working as set and staging designer on *The World's Strongest Man* and *Britain's Strongest Man* competitions.

Leake, Annie

Role: Ruby

Appeared in 'To Hull and Back'

Annie was particularly busy during the 1970s and was seen playing Lil in 1973's *Love Thy Neighbour*, Wully Harris in *Beryl's Lot* and a tweedy lady in *Man About the House*. In 1985, she was cast as Mrs Pickles in the series *The Bright Side*.

Leesley, Geoffrey

Role: Policeman

Appeared in S4, episode 4

Geoffrey, who was born in Manchester in 1949, graduated from RADA in 1972 and went on to establish a healthy list of credits, especially on tele-

vision, where his roles include Dr Warren in *Target*, Mr Roper in *All Creatures Great and Small*, a taxi driver in *As Time Goes By*, Gilbert Prestcote in *Cadfael*, Frank Beckshaw in *Heartbeat*, Crosby in *Peak Practice*, Geoff Travis in *Albion Market*, Mr Pinky in *Cows* and plenty of policeman: Detective Sergeant Dickerson in *This Is David Harper*, D C Wilson in *Bergerac* (1981–87) and First Constable in *Black Carrion*.

He's also played paramedic Keith Cotterill in *Casualty* for three years and John Harrison in *Brookside* for a year.

Lennox

(See 'Gilbey, Lennox')

Leroy

Played by David Rhule

A West Indian guy who drags Del into an alley during 'No Greater Love…', Leroy is a friend of Tommy Mackay. He lends him a helping hand whenever some muscle is required, although it's doubtful whether Mackay, who's served time for various crimes involving violence, really needs it.

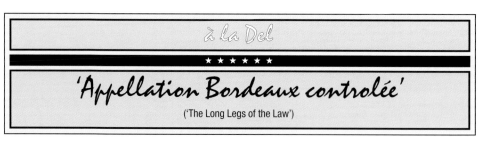

à la Del

★ ★ ★ ★ ★ ★

'Appellation Bordeaux controlée'

('The Long Legs of the Law')

Leroy

Del speaks to Leroy on the phone in 'The Sky's the Limit'. We find out little about him except that he's unhappy with a mobile phone he bought from TITCO, so Rodney suggests he gives Del a call.

Leverick, Peter

Camera supervisor on one episode: S1, episode 5

Peter was born in Woking, Surrey, in 1943 and worked in electronics before joining the BBC in 1963. He's now a director of photography, and has worked freelance since leaving the Beeb in 1992 .

Lewis, Chunky

Not seen in the sitcom, Chunky is mentioned by the Trotters in the scene from the Royal Variety Performance. He is the manager of Delaney's Club.

Lewisham Grove

During 'Fatal Extraction', Del is sat in Sid's Café with Rodney, Trigger and Denzil, trying to recall the name of an ex-girlfriend who had a tattoo of a heart pierced by a dagger on her thigh; her dad was a tattooist and she worked in a betting shop in Lewisham Grove.

Liam

Owner and manager of The Shamrock Club in Deptford, Liam is never seen in 'It's Only Rock

and Roll', but he's scripted as trying to sort out a fight at his club, although his voice is inaudible in the TV recording. Del also speaks to him on the phone, earlier in the episode. Liam has been let down by a band called The Dublin Bay Stormers, and is desperately searching for an alternative act for St Patrick's night. Del recommends Rodney's band.

Liddement, Robert

Role: Damien

Appeared in 'Mother Nature's Son'

Light of Nepal Restaurant, The

Mentioned by Del in 'The Frog's Legacy', the restaurant is sited in Wilmot Road.

Lijertwood, Lucita

Role: Mrs Murphy

Appeared in S3, episode 4

The late Lucita Lijertwood, who was born in Trinidad in 1921, appeared in films and on television. On the small screen she played Alice in an episode of *The Fosters* back in 1976, while she was

Jo Jo in the 1977 series *The Rag Trade*. Her movie roles included playing a wailing lady in *Leo the Last*, Bopsie in *Pressure*, a smash and grab lady in *Pink Floyd: The Wall* and Delgado's Mum in *Water*.

Lil

A non-speaking member of the Over-Sixties' Club, Lil is seen at The Nag's Head in 'He Ain't Heavy, He's My Uncle'. Mike, the barman, refers to her as 'old Lil with the 'airy wart' when he asks Del which of the old ladies Albert has his eyes on.

Lil

Played by Rachel Bell

Seen in 'To Hull and Back', Lil owns the Dockside Café. She serves Denzil when he pulls up in his lorry, but when she notices he's tired, she tries giving him some advice about working too hard.

Lill, Denis

Role: Alan Parry

Appeared in S6, episode 6; S7, episodes 1 & 2; 'The Jolly Boys' Outing'; 'Rodney Come Home'; 'Miami Twice' (Parts 1 & 2) and 'Mother Nature's Son'

Born in Hamilton, New Zealand, in 1942, Denis worked as an airframe mechanic in the Royal New Zealand Air Force for seven years, during which time he became involved in amateur dramatics. After leaving the forces, he decided to pursue an acting career, making his professional debut in his homeland with a national tour in 1967.

The same year he moved to England and continued acting, concentrating on the theatre, with a tour of northwest England, and spells at Leicester and Canterbury.

He made his break into TV during 1970 as Captain Alfred Slingsby in the BBC series *The Regiment*. He's been seen playing numerous characters on the box ever since, his favourite jobs being Bertie in *Lillie*, Charles Vaughan in *Survivors*, Major Benjy in *Mapp and Lucia* and Dennis in *Outside Edge*.

Denis has also appeared in a few films, such as *The Eagle has Landed*, *Batman* and *Evita*. More recently, he's spent a lot of time working in the theatre, with assignments including tours and West End productions of *An Inspector Calls*, *Kafka's Dick* and *When We Were Married*.

Limpy Lionel

During 'A Royal Flush', Rodney wants tickets to take Vicky to see *Carmen* at the opera. Del tells him he'll get them from the ticket tout Limpy.

Linda

Not seen in the programme, Linda's another of Rodney's girlfriends, and is mentioned in 'Ashes to Ashes'. Rodney's tired and blames it on lack of sleep because he's worried, but it turns out he was at Linda's house the previous evening when her parents returned home earlier than expected, almost catching Rodney and Linda in the act! They nearly managed to sort themselves out, but Linda's father did notice that Rodney's trousers were on back to front.

Linda

Trigger talks about Linda in 'The Sky's the Limit', but she is never seen in the show. They worked at the same council depot and struck up a relationship, but split two years ago. In Trigger's eyes, Linda was a real highflier: she held a management position and was the person he saw whenever he wanted a new broom. She suggested spending a weekend together at a little hotel near Henley-on-Thames, but the rendezvous must have been a disaster because afterwards she never wanted to see Trigger again.

Trigger was enamoured of Linda despite her funny eye, which meant that when she glanced in his direction he didn't know if she was looking directly at him or seeing if a bus was coming.

Lisa

Played by Gerry Cowper

Seen in 'Tea for Three', Lisa is Trigger's niece. She lives in the country, a few miles from Winchester, but decides to spend a few days with her uncle. She's now 25 and no longer the scruffy little girl Del and Rodney remember. The Trotters know the family well, especially as Del once dated her mother – Reen.

Lisa's seen again in 'The Frog's Legacy' at her

'Little Problems'

wedding in Hampshire. The ceremony was planned for the previous year when she thought she was pregnant, but when she discovered it was a false alarm, she put the wedding off for a while.

Little girl

(See 'Trudy')

'Little Problems'

Original transmission: Sunday 12 February 1989, 7.15 pm

Production dates: Saturday 4 and Sunday 5 February 1989

Original viewing figures: 18.9 million

Duration: 50 minutes

First repeat: Friday 13 October 1989, 7.30 pm

Subsequent repeats: 26/2/92, 11/2/94, 4/9/96, 14/6/98, 18/8/99, 9/3/01

CAST

Del Trotter	David Jason
Rodney Trotter	Nicholas Lyndhurst
Uncle Albert	Buster Merryfield
Cassandra	Gwyneth Strong
Boycie	John Challis
Trigger	Roger Lloyd Pack
Mike	Kenneth MacDonald
Denzil	Paul Barber
Marlene	Sue Holderness
Mickey	Patrick Murray
Jevon	Steven Woodcock
Danny Driscoll	Roy Marsden
Tony Driscoll	Christopher Ryan
Alan Parry	Denis Lill
Pamela Parry	Wanda Ventham
Comedian	Jeff Stevenson
Registrar	Derek Benfield
Walk-ons:	Bertie Green, Jack Street,

Maggie Mitchell, Roger Weightman, Richard Francis, James Delaney, Ella Cerri and Della McCrae.

PRODUCTION TEAM

Written by John Sullivan

Title music arranged and conducted by Ronnie Hazlehurst composed and sung by John Sullivan

Make-up Designer:	Jean Steward
Costume Designer:	Richard Winter
Properties Buyer:	Malcolm Rougvie
Visual Effects:	Graham Brown
Camera Supervisor:	Ken Major
Studio Lighting Director:	Don Babbage
Studio Sound:	Alan Machin
Technical Coordinator:	Reg Poulter
Videotape Editor:	Chris Wadsworth
Production Assistant:	Amita Lochab
Assistant Floor Managers:	Kerry Waddell and Sue Bishop
Vision Mixer:	Bill Morton
Production Manager:	Adrian Pegg
Designer:	Graham Lough

Directed by Tony Dow

Produced by Gareth Gwenlan

Despite having just announced his engagement, Rodney is down in the mouth. He thinks he's failed his Diploma in Computer Science again, which could impact on a job he's been offered by Cassandra's father, who's expanding his company's computer department. Rodney was banking on the job because he's found a flat, requiring a £6000 deposit. Two thirds of the sum will come from Cassandra's parents and her own bank account, while it's down to Rodney to stump up the rest.

Del comes to the rescue as the bringer of good news: Mr Jamille has given him Rodney's diploma and asked him to apologise for being late in marking the test paper; furthermore, Del is prepared to call in all his debts so he can give Rodney the two grand needed for the flat. Later, when Rodney has gone to the cinema with Cassandra, Albert – knowing what Del is like – asks how much he paid Mr

Jamille for the diploma. One hundred and fifty pounds is the reply!

Del runs into trouble calling in his debts, and is told by Mickey Pearce and Jevon (who are both sporting broken limbs) that the infamous Driscoll Brothers believe he's trying to con them on a business deal. When the Brothers catch up with Del, they demand two grand, but a little good fortune buys him more time, enabling him to fool Boycie into coughing up for some dodgy video recorders he'd supplied.

But not everything goes to plan and it's a battered and bruised Del who plays Best Man at Rodney's registry office wedding, before sharing a tear-jerking few moments with his younger brother as he prepares to leave for his honeymoon in Rimini.

Littlewood, Albie

Not seen in the sitcom, Albie used to be Del's best friend when they were youngsters. In 'Happy Returns', Del discovers that later in life, when he was dating a girl called June, Albie had a fling with her, and that Debby – who works at the local newsagent's – was the result of the liaison.

Littlewood died in 1965, after his bike fell onto a live rail whilst he took a shortcut across a railway line. Del had always thought that his friend was on his way to see him, but it turns out he was *en route* to June's.

Llewellyn, Jonathan Paul

Location manager on one episode: 'Fatal Extraction'

Born in Haverfordwest in 1959, Jonathan had a brief stint in advertising before graduating from the University of Exeter and joining the BBC in 1982. His early years in the Corporation were spent working on shows like *EastEnders, Casualty, Carrott Confidential, The Kenny Everett Television Show, Keeping Up Appearances, Troublemakers, Grange Hill, Waiting for God, Honey for Tea, One Foot in the Grave* and *Absolutely Fabulous.*

After 18 years in the industry, Jonathan is now a producer for BBC's comedy department, producing the last series of *One Foot in the Grave* in 2000, which won a BAFTA nomination, and the fourth series of *Absolutely Fabulous* in 2001.

Lloyd, Lala

Role: Old lady in newsagents and Old lady

Appeared as Old lady in newsagents in S4, episode 1 and as Old lady in S4, episode 2

Among Lala's many television credits are roles as Mrs Hollins in *Upstairs, Downstairs;* Miss Daniels in *Shoestring;* Nanny Melville in *Nanny;* Mrs Ford in the 1972 mini-series *Emma* and an old woman in *Calling the Shots.* However, her screen work dates back to the late 1940s when she made an uncredited appearance in the 1948 film *London Belongs to Me.* Other movie roles include Amelia Adams in *Fiend Without a Face* (1958) and a nurse in *Secret Places* (1984).

Lloyd, Rosalind

Role: Heather

Appeared in 'Diamonds are for Heather'

Rosalind's other television appearances include playing Queen Xanxia in an episode of *Doctor Who* back in 1963, Sally Campion in a 1984 episode of *Bergerac,* Fenella in *Minder* in the same year, as well as films such as *The Wild Geese, Horror Planet* and *Who Dares Wins.*

Lloyd-Jones, Bernard

Designer on one episode: 'To Hull and Back'

Born in the Welsh town of Rhyl in 1942, Bernard worked in architecture before joining the television industry in 1964. Early programmes he worked on at the BBC include *Morecambe and Wise, Dr Who, Hi-De-Hi!, Are You Being Served?, The Two Ronnies, When the Boat Comes In* and *Dear John.*

After 36 years in the business, Bernard is now a production designer for television and film, after leaving the BBC to work freelance in 1992. Recent work includes *As Time Goes By, Bloomin' Marvellous, So Haunt Me* and *EastEnders.*

Lloyd Pack, Roger

Role: Trigger

Appeared in 37 episodes: S1, episodes 1 & 4; S2, episodes 2, 3 & 5; S3, episodes 1, 5 & 6; S4, episodes 1, 2 & 6; S5, episodes 4 & 5; S6, episodes 1, 2, 3, 5 & 6; S7, episodes 1–6 and 'To Hull and Back'; 'A Royal Flush'; 'The Frog's Legacy'; 'Dates'; 'The Jolly Boys' Outing'; 'Miami Twice' (Parts 1 & 2); 'Mother Nature's Son'; 'Fatal Extraction'; 'Heroes and Villains'; 'Modern Men'; 'Time On Our Hands' and 'If They Could See Us Now…!'

Being accepted by the Royal Academy of Dramatic Art is a dream come true for most aspiring thespians, but for Roger Lloyd Pack, who decided to follow his father, Charles, into the acting profes-

sion instead of attending university, it was a mixed blessing. 'It was a difficult period for me; acting is a lot to do with learning about yourself and there was much I didn't know,' admits Roger. 'I was a very awkward teenager, not very coordinated, so my time at RADA was a mixture of fun and anxiety.'

Despite such apprehension, Roger didn't let his feelings deflect from his sole ambition: to graduate

as a professional actor. 'I never questioned my decision to act; even in the darkest days I clung on to my belief that this was the job for me.'

As a boy, Roger – who was born in London in 1944 – showed aspirations for his future career by organising regular puppet shows for family and friends. 'I don't know when I made the decision to go into the profession, but I was always acting at home and at school.' When he attended Bedales, a private school in Hampshire, to study for his A-levels, his interest deepened. 'It was then that I realised I enjoyed acting enough to try and make a career out of it.'

After graduating in 1965, Roger spent several years in rep, a real learning curve. 'I learnt how to play a range of different characters at places like Northampton, Coventry and Leatherhead, then I joined the Royal Shakespeare Company and received a great deal of verse training, which has held me in good stead ever since.'

By now, Roger had a clear vision of where his future lay. At this early point in his career, being an actor was all about treading the boards in theatres up and down the country. Such was his belief and determination to follow his chosen path, he even turned down his first television offer. 'I had a rather puritan attitude towards my work and set ideas about what I was going to do – and that was rep. When I was offered an episode of *Dixon of Dock Green* and I turned it down, my agent was very put out, but I was determined to work in the theatre, which always seemed the orthodox thing to do.'

During a busy career, Roger has worked in all mediums, but is undecided on his favourite. 'I just say it's the one I'm doing at the time, although if I'm pressed it's probably between theatre and film. Television is my bread and butter so I love it for that, but it doesn't have the excitement and intensity of filming or provide the opportunities to study a script in depth like the theatre. However, I enjoy meeting the technical demands of television.'

Although he prefers stage and film work to television, the power of the medium has inevitably resulted in Roger being recognised largely for his small-screen creations. He's uncertain in which programme he made his debut, but believes it could have been an episode of *Dixon of Dock Green,* even though he'd turned down an earlier part. 'I played a lot of villains in those days, not much comedy,' says Roger, who's made up for it since. In *2 Point 4 Children* he played Jake Klinger, he was Owen Nesbitt in *The Vicar of Dibley* and, of course, Trigger in *Only Fools,* a job which came about by chance.

Ray Butt, the original director of the sitcom, was in the audience one night to watch a performance of *Moving,* a play in which Roger was appearing in the West End. Ray was actually there to watch another actor – Billy Murray – who he was considering for the part of Del prior to David Jason's appointment. But it wasn't long before Roger's performance caught the director's attention. 'He offered me the part of Trigger the following day, which was a lucky break.' The rest is history.

On the drama front, Roger has appeared in a myriad of television programmes, including *Kavanagh QC, Survivors, Inspector Morse, Oliver Twist, Heartbeat, The Chief, The Bill* and *Tom Jones.* But when it comes to selecting favourite jobs, it's his work on *The Naked Civil Servant*; the Pinter play *One for the Road, Longtitude* and *The Gravy Train* which spring to mind. Meanwhile, on stage, appearing in *The Caretaker* and *The Speakers* are just two highlights from an extensive career.

Today, Roger enjoys dividing his time between stage and screen. 'I never like to leave the theatre for too long because you can loose your nerve; so much of acting is confidence and performing on stage regularly helps in this respect. I've done a lot of theatre recently and would now like to do a bit more television, but we'll have to wait and see.'

Roger agrees that nothing is likely to eclipse the role of Trigger. 'Whatever else I do, he's what I'll be remembered for; he's become a myth in his own right. I've been lucky and such an opportunity is unlikely to happen again, so in that respect it has to be the highlight of my career.'

Lochab, Amita

Production assistant on eight episodes: S6, episodes 1, 3–6; 'Dates'; 'The Jolly Boys' Outing' and 'Mother Nature's Son'

Amita – who was born in New Delhi – entered the television industry in 1977. Shows she was involved in during the early part of her career included *Hypnosis, Bleak House* and *Three Up, Two Down,* but she regards *Only Fools, Alas Smith and Jones* and *Blackadder* as favourite programmes to have worked on.

She left the Beeb in 1997 and now works for the independent production company Initial. Recent assignments include filming in Kavos for *Bar Wars* and *Ed Stone is Dead.*

Locarno

In a conversation between Grandad and Del during 'Thicker Than Water', we learn that Del and Rodney's mother had met a musician at the Locarno just before Rodney was born, fuelling speculation over the true identity of his father.

Locations

As with most situation comedies, locations played their part in the overall success of the show, freeing it from the claustrophobic feel sometimes associated with studio-based programmes. Obviously the decision to incorporate outside filming into a programme brings its own challenges: not only does it swallow up a large chunk of the budget, but there are the difficulties of finding the right locations. And even then, once all the necessary agreements have been reached with the authorities, proprietors and members of the public who own the chosen location, there are the inevitable logistics behind actually shooting the scenes to overcome.

Production manager Janet Bone was responsible for finding locations for the first two series: 'As a production manager on the programme I'm sure it was an advantage having been born and bred in London, as there were to be few exotic locations: Docklands, back alleys, etc. seemed to be destined for me!

'During my career, one of the funniest locations I had to find was the wall of a London prison, on which "Wolfie" Smith was to spray "Freedom for Tooting". I spent a whole Saturday afternoon driving from prison to prison taking polaroids of their walls. I got some very funny looks.

'Fortunately, I have a good memory for places so it was not too difficult to know the right areas in which to search for locations for *Only Fools and Horses.* When I received the scripts from John Sullivan I'd make a list of all the locations required.

Sometimes it would simply be a request for a location because he was still completing the script. What followed was a fairly gruelling four weeks or so of searching and organising the shoots.

'Permissions have to be obtained and contracts drawn up for virtually every location; even street filming, in the quietest road, has to have permission from the local council and, of course, be sanctioned by the police. If you had the good fortune to find a location in an out-of-town area (such as Dorset for "A Touch of Glass" and "It Never Rains…") we would try to kill as many location birds with one stone as it saves time travelling; it's also amazing how a few strategically placed props can create the right impression.

'The first tower block I looked at for the Trotters' home was in Brentford, Middlesex. However, when Ray Butt and I finally took the lift to the roof, the view to the south was straight across the Thames and Kew Gardens – quite beautiful but definitely not Peckham. The view to the north was ideal, so we moved a couple of miles north-east to Acton and settled the Trotters' home there. I think we only filmed from the roof of the block once and that was for the nuclear fallout shelter in "The Russians are Coming", the remainder of the home-based filming in Acton being safely grounded.

'The reason we did not film in Peckham was because BBC Television is based in West London and the amount of time and money spent travelling across London every day would have been prohibitive.

'The two most memorable locations, though, had to be the house used for the famous chandelier-dropping scene in "A Touch of Glass" and, for me especially, the siting of the boys' mother's grave in "The Yellow Peril". The two got inextricably mixed in one week.

'My colleague Sue Bysh had found the location for the stately home (a difficult task) in Dorset – a boarding school which was willing to have us. This was without doubt one of the most nail-biting film sequences to shoot. We had, of course, a beautiful, highly valuable and highly insured crystal chandelier, as well as a brilliant facsimile. It was a wonderful prop made of cheap, old glass pudding bowls, tubes of aluminium and bits of old glass, which, from a distance, looked just like the real thing. Tension was very high that afternoon. Both chandeliers were in place. We had at least four cameras in strategic positions, so it was covered from all angles, and, of course, Del and Rodney were on top of their ladders. The atmosphere was electric as, obviously, we could only do it once. Ray Butt called "Standby", then "Turn Over" and, finally, "Action". The bolt was knocked out of the prop chandelier in the floorboards above and it fell. It was perfect. The deathly hush that had fallen over us all seemed to continue until Ray said, "Cut", then the broad smiles broke out and chatter began. It was actually an emotional moment.

I also had another little problem on my mind: for some time I had been looking for a graveyard or cemetery that was surrounded by railings and not

122

Getting ready to film another scene in and around the streets of London

brick walls. The catholic cemetery at Kensal Green, where we'd shot "Mum's" grave previously, was not suitable, so on the way to and from work I looked at most of the graveyards in West London. None of the local authorities was willing to let us film in their cemeteries at night. It was becoming quite a problem. So the day after dropping the chandelier I headed back to London, leaving the unit to complete the Dorset shoot, to take a look at local parks, which do have railings and where we wouldn't be intruding on the neighbourhood's sensitivities. So Walpole Park, Ealing, was chosen because it had large black wrought iron gates and a broad path beyond, on which we could set up Mum's gravestone. With some earth over the path, a few other stones sat around and some clever lighting, the scene worked a treat, especially when the stone was covered in Del Boy's luminous paint.

'Over the years I've come across some awful scripts but John Sullivan's were just a joy to work with. He's an excellent writer and a wonderful perceiver of people; he must sit quietly, watch and take it all in because his characters are so good.'

Listed below are a selection of the locations used during the series.

'BIG BROTHER'
- The block of flats featured in the opening credits of the series, as well as early exterior shots involving Nelson Mandela House, were in North Acton, just off Bollo Bridge Road.
- The market scenes, meanwhile, were shot at Chapel Market, Islington.
- The first exterior shots of The Nag's Head were, in fact, a pub (The Alma) in Chapel Market, close to the Angel tube station.

'CASH AND CURRY'
- The venue for the Peckham and Camberwell Chamber of Trade's dinner/dance was a community centre in Cuckoo Hill, Hanwell.

'A SLOW BUS TO CHINGFORD'
- The bus depot used in the episode and referred to as the Tyler Street Bus and Coach Depot was actually the Grey-Green Coach Station, 55 Stamford Hill, London.

'THE RUSSIANS ARE COMING'
- The roof-top scene, where the Trotters are hiding away in their nuclear fall-out shelter, was filmed on the top of the North Acton flats acting as Nelson Mandela House for the early part of the sitcom.

'ASHES TO ASHES'
- The Peckham Bowling Club was, in reality, a bowling green in Hanwell, while the River Thames was used for the scene where Rodney and Del row out to try and drop the ashes into the water.

'NO GREATER LOVE…'
- The alleyway where Del is assaulted by Tommy Mackay was in Bedford Road, West Ealing.

'THE YELLOW PERIL'
- The cemetery scene, where Del paints his mother's tombstone with luminous paint, was recorded in Walpole Park, at the back of Ealing Film Studios.
- The Golden Lotus chinese restaurant, which also suffered at the hands of the Trotters and their glowing paint, was actually a café in Hanwell, London.

'IT NEVER RAINS…'
- The Trotters' Spanish hotel is the Knoll House Hotel, Studland Bay, near Swanage, Dorset.

'A TOUCH OF GLASS'
- Ridgemere Hall, home of Lord and Lady Ridgemere, was an old school, Clayesmore School, in Iwerne Minster, near Blandford Forum.

- The building used at the beginning of the episode where the Trotters attend a sale is the village hall at Sutton Waldron.

'HOMESICK'
- The hall where the Tenants' Committee meet to discuss their business is St Nicholas' Church Hall, Chiswick. It was also used by the team for rehearsals.

'FRIDAY THE 14TH'
- The location scenes when the Trotters are staying at Boycie's cottage were filmed in and around Iwerne Minster.
- The police station seen in the episode was actually residential housing in The Chalks, Iwerne Minster.

'STRAINED RELATIONS'
- Grandad's funeral took place at a cemetery just off Field Road, Hammersmith, London.

'HOLE IN ONE'
- The scene where Uncle Albert falls through the hole into the pub cellar was filmed outside a pub in Kensal Road, London W10.
- The magistrate's court in Kingston was also seen in the episode, when the Trotters attend court to try and win compensation.

'SLEEPING DOGS LIE'
- The scene in the front garden of Boycie's house was filmed in Harrow-on-the-Hill.

'AS ONE DOOR CLOSES'
- The park where the Trotters catch the rare butterfly is Ravenscourt Park, London.

'TO HULL AND BACK'
- Hull railway station was used for the scene where Albert is met off the train.
- Other locations chosen in the area include an alleyway between the station and town – for the scene where the Trotters argue about clothes – the Humber Bridge and St Andrew's Dock.
- Sammy's Point, near Hull, was used for the scene in which Denzil looks out to sea and spots Del on the Inge.
- A nearby branch of Barclays Bank was used to represent Amro Bank.
- Some of the sets, including The Nag's Head and the Trotters' flat, were constructed inside the former Armstrong's factory, which is now derelict.

'THE MIRACLE OF PECKHAM'
- Two churches were used to represent the church where the statue of the Virgin Mary and her baby supposedly sheds tears. One of these was St Alphedge, King James Street, Southwark – which has since been demolished.

'A ROYAL FLUSH'
- Much of the location work was completed in and around Salisbury, including the scene in the gentlemen's outfitters where the Trotters look for

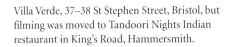

the correct garb for Rodney's weekend with his rich girlfriend.

- The Duke of Maylebury's country estate is actually Clarendon Park, Wiltshire.

'THE FROG'S LEGACY'

- Many of the outdoor locations were in and around Ipswich, including Seymour Road, which was used for the market scenes. Rectory Road was used for the cortège.
- St Mary's Church, to the south of Helmingham Hall, was seen at the end of the episode, while the Hall was used for the interior shots of Trigger's niece's wedding reception.

'DATES'

- Del meets Raquel for the first time at Waterloo Station. However, he first hears about her via a

Helmingham Hall was the venue for the wedding in 'The Frog's Legacy'.

dating agency. The scene which shows the Trotter van parked outside the agency was filmed at Kelter Recruitment, 46 Old Market Street, Bristol. The property is now empty.

- Rodney, meanwhile, dates Nervous Nerys, but finds himself being chased by a group of yobs driving an American car. The scene where the van jumps over a hump in the road whilst being chased was intended to be recorded at Fishpool Hill, Brentry, Bristol, but was finally recorded at Talbot Road, Isleworth.
- The Italian restaurant where Trigger meets his date was Pasta Park, Gloucester Road, Bishopston, Bristol.
- Outdoor scenes involving the police taking Del away from The Nag's Head after he's attempted to rip off a policewoman's blouse were filmed at The Waggon and Horses, 83 Stapleton Road, Easton, Bristol. It's also the setting for Del and Raquel's argument in the car park.
- When Del is led into the police station after being arrested, he's actually walking into Winchmore Hill Police Station, Green Lanes, London.

- The London Hilton was used for scenes where Del enjoys a meal with Raquel.

'YUPPY LOVE'

- The scene at the disco where Rodney dances with Cassandra was filmed at The Parkside Club, Bath Road, Bristol.
- A building occupied by Acer, Freeman and Fox at 48 Queen Charlotte Street, Bristol, was used to represent the education centre where Rodney first meets Cassandra whilst attending evening classes.
- The scenes where Del shows Rodney the opulent houses in Kings' Avenue, and where Cassandra later drops Rodney off in the pouring rain, were filmed in Broad Walk, Winchmore Hill, London.
- A set was used for the hilarious scene where Del falls through the gap in the bar, but the outside scenes of the pub were filmed at The Granary, Bristol.

'DANGER UXD'

- The scene where Rodney, whilst dining with Cassandra, hears that the sex dolls are faulty was filmed at the Conservatory Bar, Parkside Hotel, Bath Road, Bristol.
- The scene where the Trotters take the sex dolls out to the van was recorded outside the block of flats used to represent Nelson Mandela House, on the Duckmore Road Estate, Duckmore Road, Ashton, Bristol.
- Dirty Barry's sex shop was set in Hanover Street, at the side of the Bristol Hippodrome.
- The scene where the Reliant explodes was filmed at a British Gas site at Canon's Marsh, Bristol.

'CHAIN GANG'

- The Parkside Club, Bath Road, Bristol was again used to represent The One Eleven Club.
- The restaurant where Arnie suffers his first fake heart attack was originally intended to be the

Villa Verde, 37–38 St Stephen Street, Bristol, but filming was moved to Tandoori Nights Indian restaurant in King's Road, Hammersmith.

'THE JOLLY BOYS' OUTING'

- Scenes at the Mardi Gras nightclub were recorded at The Top Hat Club, Northfield Avenue.
- Margate Station was used for the station scene and Benbom Brothers' Theme Park in the town was also seen.
- The pub (The Halfway House) where the boys enjoy a pint was The Roman Galley, Thanet Way, Chislet, near Herne Bay, Kent.
- The scene where the coach explodes was filmed at Bungalow Car Park, Palm Bay, Margate. At that moment, Rodney is using the phone in a call box to contact Cassandra. Her scenes were recorded at the Marina Resort Hotel, Harbour Parade, Ramsgate.
- The market scenes were shot at Dumpton Greyhound Stadium, Hereson Road, Ramsgate, which has since been demolished and replaced by a housing estate.
- Mrs Creswell's guest house, the Villa Bella, and Mrs Baker's Sunny Sea guest house, were filmed at Dalby Square, Margate.
- Rodney's flat in the episode was at Rebecca Court, Lower Northdown Avenue, Margate.

'RODNEY COME HOME'

- The nightclub scenes were shot at The Parkside Club, Bath Road, Bristol.
- Scenes at Alan Parry's printing company were filmed at Gemini Graphics and Print, York Street, Bristol.
- The shopping centre where Del tries to sell his dolls was the Broadwalk Shopping Centre, Knowle, Bristol.

'THE CHANCE OF A LUNCHTIME'

- The scene where Rodney helps the inebriated Trudy from The Nag's Head into the taxi was recorded outside The White Horse, a pub in Chesil Street, Bedminster. The pub had been used for The Nag's Head in an earlier episode.
- The restaurant seen when Raquel meets the theatre producer was Henry Africa's Hothouse, Whiteladies Road, Bristol.
- The floating restaurant where Rodney dines with Cassandra is Shoots, Bristol.

'STAGE FRIGHT'

- The scenes where Tony Angelino sang at the Down by the Riverside Club were actually filmed at the Courage Social Club in Willway Road, Bedminster, Bristol, now called The Fiddlers.
- The nightclub where Tony and Raquel sing was the Locarno in Bristol. The club no longer exists.

'HE AIN'T HEAVY, HE'S MY UNCLE'

- The scenes where Del and Rodney hunt for Uncle Albert were shot around London, including

Tower Bridge, *HMS Belfast*, Portobello Green, Acklam Road East, Malton Road and Portobello Road Market.

'MIAMI TWICE'
- Most of the location work was shot in Miami, but two different churches were used at the beginning of the programme for Damien Trotter's christening. The interior scenes took place at St John's Church in Ladbroke Grove and the exterior shots at St John's Church, Kentish Town.

'MOTHER NATURE'S SON'
- The Grand Hotel, Brighton, and the esplanade were used, while The White Admiral at Lower Bevendean, took on a different guise, becoming The Nag's Head.
- An allotment in Natal Road, Lower Bevendean, meanwhile, was used as Grandad's forgotten patch of land where the great discovery takes place.
- Swain's Farm Shop, Henfield, was also used in the episode as Myles' organic shop, Nature's Way.

'FATAL EXTRACTION'
- The block of flats used as Nelson Mandela House where the riots take place is in Duckmore Road, Ashton, Bristol.
- When Rodney and Del walk to the dentist's surgery they actually cross Brunswick Square in Bristol.
- The market scenes were filmed in the car park at Bristol City's football ground, Ashton Gate.
- The hospital scenes, where Del talks to the dental receptionist, were completed in a hospital near Bristol.
- The casino frequented by Del was actually The Old Granary, Welsh Back, Bristol.

'HEROES AND VILLAINS'
- When the Trotters break down in their Reliant whilst dressed as Batman and Robin, they're at the Broadmead Shopping Centre in the heart of Bristol.
- The scene where Councillor Murray leaves work was filmed at the Bristol Coroner's Office, Backfields, Upper York Street, Bristol. The car park used by Ms Murray was sited just across the road from the coroner's office and is owned by a meat company.
- After coming to the councillor's aid, the caped crusaders race off down York Street, towards Brunswick Square in Bristol.
- The scene where Rodney is chasing the muggers from the market was filmed in and around Park Avenue, Bedminster, Bristol, while the market itself was actually Borough Market, Lambeth.
- The Peckham Post Office was actually a post office in St John's Lane, Bedminster, Bristol, while the fruit stall where all the produce gets knocked over in the chase was the Banana Boat, Totterdown, Bristol.

'MODERN MEN'
- The scene where Del and Rodney are standing outside Nelson Mandela House and Dr Singh turns up was recorded at Duckmore Road, Bristol.
- The hospital scenes, where Cassandra is recovering after suffering a miscarriage, were recorded at Ham Green Hospital, near Bristol.

'TIME ON OUR HANDS'
- The famous garage scene where Raquel's father discovers the old discarded watch was recorded at the block of flats in Duckmore Road, Bristol. The council-owned garage is used by Terry Dite.
- After picking up their fortune from the auction house, the Trotter brothers head for the car showrooms and purchase a Rolls Royce from Boycie's company. The setting for this scene was Miles' Motor Company in Marsh Road, Ashton.
- The large property Del buys after becoming a millionaire was situated in High Weald, West Sussex.

'IF THEY COULD SEE US NOW...!'
- The Hotel De Paris, Golden Square, Place du Casino, Monte Carlo, was used for the French hotel scenes.
- For Justin's office and the court house corridor, the Old Council Chamber at North Somerset Council's Town Hall, Oxford Street, Weston-super-Mare was used.
- The two houses used for the funeral scenes were situated in Woodland Road, Weston-super-Mare.
- The bistro used by Rodney and Cassandra when they discuss experimenting with a new sex therapy to help solve their marital problems was the Dragon's Kiss restaurant, Regent Street, Weston-super-Mare.
- Whitemead House, Duckmoor Road, Ashton, Bristol was again used to represent Nelson Mandela House.
- When Del and Rodney are in a taxi being taken to see Justin, they're driving around the Shaftesbury Avenue area of London.
- The *Goldrush* scenes were filmed at Pinewood Film Studios.

NELSON MANDELA HOUSE IN BRISTOL
'I suppose you could have described our three blocks of flats in Bristol as something of a backwater as far as council high-rise dwellings were concerned. Nearly all of us being classified as "elderly" residents, the only children we ever heard were usually passing along the adjacent main road on their way to and from the local school. Even with the local football ground right next door, other than on seasonal Tuesdays and Saturdays, the only noise pollution we generally experienced was from the traffic using our main road as a "rat run" preferred option to the A38 Winterstoke Road.

'So when we learnt that the BBC wanted to film an episode of the immensely popular *Only Fools and Horses* programme right inside and outside our flats we wondered what we could *possibly* be letting ourselves in for, when, following the production team's consultation with both the Council and our own local Residents' Association, we decided to say "yes".

'After all, nothing very exciting ever happened in our neck of the woods. And most of us enjoyed watching *Only Fools and Horses* on the telly anyway. That was how it all started, and very shortly what appeared to be an unusually large amount of vehicles, technical equipment and people descended upon us. Since we didn't have any genuine graffiti on our outside walls (or on our inside ones hopefully) some temporary graffiti substitution was imported. In the interests of realism the names of our flats were changed (again temporarily) to Nelson Mandela, Desmond Tutu and Robert Mugabe Houses.

'There were occasions when we even had "derelict cars" abandoned on our site, thankfully a situation we have been spared in our normal everyday life. As I was in those days still a working person, I unfortunately saw very little of the daytime filming activity that was to be enjoyed by our residents, from either their windows' high-rise vantage point, or at ground level beyond the filming area.

'During the protracted day and evening shooting sessions we all realised how many times a scene had to be "shot" before it became a "take". It was only then that we could begin to appreciate the considerable amount of time some actors had to wait around doing nothing in between takes. Some of the perceived showbiz "glamour" dissipated at that point, especially when it was raining, as it was when Del Boy was featured singing over and over again, the rather plaintive song "One voice, Singing in the darkness", as he staggered somewhat the worse for a drink or two, back to his flat. Sometimes it was cold and frosty and the

Two residents of the flats that were used to represent Nelson Mandela House.

actor's breath could be clearly seen condensing in the air. No, it was probably not all fun being a television star!

'In my opinion one of the most humorous sequences filmed was when the two inflatable dolls suddenly became inflated and quite unexpectedly popped up first of all from behind the sofa, and later on in the rear window of the Reliant three-wheeler as it drove away.

'Probably the most graphic episode of the Christmas Specials included the scene when "the riot" was filmed in the centre of our three blocks.

'More recently we found an establishment in a side street called "Trotters' Bar", the interior of which was decorated with numerous pictures of the stars and also had a yellow Y-registered Reliant three-wheeler parked in the road (in much better nick than Del Boy's) with "Trotters' Independent Trading, Paris, Peckham and Puerto Pollensa", painted on the side. Those Trotters seem to get everywhere.

'We really enjoyed having David Jason, Nicholas Lyndhurst, Buster Merryfield and all of the other stars, as well as the BBC production crew, among us on the occasions when they selected our blocks of flats as the location for filming such a popular series. We even enjoyed the temporary disruption to our normal routine, like having to keep silent when the cameras were rolling and staying behind certain barriers to keep out of camera range. Sometimes being unable to enter or leave the flats by our usual doorway was not a problem, and the increase in bustling activity did not bother many of us either. Absolutely no one objected to putting up their Christmas decorations a little earlier than intended, at the request of the BBC.

This scene was shot repeatedly over several hours, and the realism was such that personally it made the hairs stand up on the back of my neck.

'For some time, along with my wife and my sister, I watched from our seventh floor balcony and the effects were startling. The noisy crowd scenes with the rioters shouting and banging ashbin lids, the mounted policemen lashing out with their batons, the horses in the thick of it, and then the arrival overhead of the *real* police helicopter with its searchlight shining on the frightening mêlée below from just above roof-top level, along with the artificial smoke and fires from burning cars appeared to be as near to an actual riot as was possible to simulate, and *much* too realistic for my comfort. And then, the multi-tone horn on that eye-catching pale green Capri Ghia sounded, a mounted policeman shouted: "Hold it, hold it, hold it, it's Del Boy." The noise suddenly ceased, and the crowd parted to let Del and Raquel drive up to the door of the flats. Surely a classic situation comedy.

'A number of residents permitted their flats to be used by various members of the cast for specific parts of the story line. A great favourite was Uncle Albert, the late Buster Merryfield, a lovely man.

'There was even one of our neighbours who allowed the press to take pictures of the filming from the window of the flat, a fact that was not appreciated too much by the production team, and which resulted in a well aimed spotlight being directed towards the window in question. This had the immediate effect of somewhat detracting from the quality of the pictures, and most certainly a source of great discouragement to the camera operator.

'The episode when Del and Rodney purchased their green Capri Ghia "company car" was the first occasion on which my council garage was used as a location. In the Christmas Special "Time On Our Hands", my garage was again called into service to

provide the setting for the discovery of the extremely rare Harrison pocket watch, which enabled the two brothers to finally achieve Del Boy's oft-stated dream of becoming a millionaire.

'I cleared the garage of all our accumulated bits and pieces including the family car, and this was replaced by an even larger and more varied assortment of BBC props to create the setting for Del, Rodney and Raquel's father to discover the now famous watch. And how unusual it was to have a Rolls Royce *and* a Jaguar car parked near our flats!

'Some years afterwards, while on holiday in Majorca, we noticed many of the bars and restaurants in the resort where we were staying, were showing videos of *Only Fools and Horses*. It was more than a little strange to walk into a place and see people watching a piece of film actually showing the place we lived in, and knew so well.

'David Jason was an extremely nice person to have around. He took the opportunity to talk to many of the residents when conditions permitted, and often posed for photographs with them. He came across more like the "ordinary genuine person" he generally portrays on the television screen, than the successful big star he obviously is. And that famous laugh of his could frequently be heard above the other sounds of filming preparation. Nicholas Lyndhurst was just a little quieter, less outgoing and was not so often seen when not rehearsing or off camera. Buster Merryfield was very popular with some of the more elderly lady residents, who would rather have liked to adopt him!

'*Only Fools and Horses* would be welcome to call back anytime.'

TERRY DITE – Resident

Loe, Judy

Casting adviser on 13 episodes: S7, 'Miami Twice' (Parts 1 & 2), 'Mother Nature's Son', 'Fatal Extraction', 'Heroes and Villains', 'Modern Men' and 'Time On Our Hands'

Judy joined the BBC in 1951 as a trainee secretary working in the overseas department. She transferred to the drama script department as a junior secretary, and after gaining experience in other sections, moved into light entertainment before the decade was out. She became a production secretary and worked for Dennis Main Wilson and then Sydney Lotterby, an association which lasted for over 30 years, by which time she had worked on many successful shows, such as *Butterflies*, *Porridge* and *Last of the Summer Wine*.

Always keen on casting, she moved into this field during the mid-1980s and helped cast shows, including John Sullivan's *Over Here*, until she retired from the Beeb in 1998.

Lombardi, Louis

Played by Anthony Morton

The Italian owns a pet shop and is seen in 'Who's a Pretty Boy?'. When the Trotters decorate Denzil and Corinne's sitting room and kill their canary in the process, by allowing the bird to breathe in paint fumes, Grandad is sent down to Lombardi's shop to buy a replacement.

London, Tony

Role: Ollie

Appeared in S7, episode 5

Tony, who was born in London in 1961, started his working life as a carpenter, but upon deciding he wanted to try his luck as an actor, enrolled at The Anna Scher Theatre School. He made his acting debut in a 1977 production of *The Destructors*, since when he's worked mainly in films and television. His small-screen credits include playing a youth in the 1978 mini-series *Pennies from Heaven*, a drunken youth in *Minder*, Lewis in *The Bill* and Levey in *Dempsey and Makepeace*. On the big screen, meanwhile, he's played Adam in *The Class of Miss MacMichael*, Woods in *Scum*, Jimmy in *That Summer*, a young porter in *The Elephant Man*, a cockney soldier in *Secret Places* and Leon in *24 Hours in London*.

'Long Legs of the Law, The'

Original transmission: Thursday 21 October 1982, 8.30 pm

Production date: Sunday 23 May 1982

Original viewing figures: 7.7 million

Duration: 30 minutes

First repeat: Tuesday 26 July 1983, 8.30 pm

Subsequent repeats: 19/10/90, 13/1/95, 3/6/97, 18/9/98, 14/1/00

CAST

Del Trotter	David Jason
Rodney Trotter	Nicholas Lyndhurst
Grandad Trotter	Lennard Pearce
Sid	Roy Heather
Sandra	Kate Saunders
Walk-ons:	(People in café) six extras

à la Del

★ ★ ★ ★ ★ ★

'You've no… "tres bien ensemble", as the French say'

('The Yellow Peril')

PRODUCTION TEAM

Written by John Sullivan

Title music arranged and conducted by Ronnie Hazlehurst composed and sung by John Sullivan

Make-up Designer:	Shaunna Harrison
Costume Designer:	Anushia Nieradzik
Properties Buyer:	Roger Williams
Film Cameraman:	John Walker
Film Sound:	Dennis Panchen
Film Editor:	Mike Jackson
Camera Supervisor:	Ron Peverall
Studio Lighting Director:	Henry Barber
Studio Sound:	Dave Thompson
Technical Coordinator:	Derek Martin
Videotape Editor:	Chris Wadsworth
Production Assistant:	Penny Thompson
Assistant Floor Manager:	Tony Dow
Graphic Designers:	Peter Clayton and Fen Symonds
Vision Mixer:	Bill Morton
Production Managers:	Janet Bone and Sue Bysh
Designer:	Derek Evans
Produced by Ray Butt	

Del and Grandad can't believe their ears when they hear that Rodney is dating a policewoman called Sandra. With Grandad concerned about what the neighbours will think, and Del more worried about his business coming under the scrutiny of the Old Bill, Rodney's news is far from welcome. As Del admits to Grandad, 'One wrong word from that plonker Rodney and I could end up doing five years!'

Del's blood pressure rises even more when Rodney brings Sandra back for a nightcap after the pictures. Then when he learns that Rodders has given his girlfriend one of his red-hot watches, he nearly does his nut and deliberately pours gin all over her to enable him to reclaim the watch and state he'll get her a replacement.

The tense evening draws to a close and Rodney escorts Sandra home, but he's in for a shock when she tells him she recognised many of the items in the flat from Scotland Yard photos and *Police Five*, and gives him 24 hours to clear the flat of stolen goods before she informs CID.

Long, Roger

Film sound recordist on three episodes: 'Heroes and Villains', 'Modern Men' and 'Time On Our Hands'

Roger, who was born in Cheltenhan in 1946, started his BBC career on the World Service, before becoming an assistant film recordist when BBC2 expanded its coverage. His early work was on pro-grammes such as *Z Cars*, *Monty Python*, *Dad's Army* and *Play for Today*.

Roger transferred to BBC Bristol in 1974, where he worked for nearly 20 years, before leaving to become a freelance sound recordist. In this capacity his first assignment was *Only Fools and Horses*, but he's since worked on numerous shows, including documentaries and history programmes, like *Battlefields* for BBC2.

'Longest Night, The'

Original transmission: Sunday 14 September 1986, 8.35 pm

Production date: Sunday 8 June 1986

Original viewing figures: 16.7 million

Duration: 30 minutes

First repeat: Thursday 24 September 1987, 8.30 pm

Subsequent repeats: 9/7/89, 1/9/97, 8/12/98, 22/11/00

CAST

Del Trotter	David Jason
Rodney Trotter	Nicholas Lyndhurst
Uncle Albert	Buster Merryfield
Tom Clarke (Security officer)	John Bardon
Mr Peterson (Store manager)	Max Harvey
Lennox Gilbey	Vas Blackwood
Woman in kiosk	Jeanne Mockford
Checkout girl	Catherine Clarke
Walk-ons:	Gaynor Seago, Kelly Hurst, Brian West, James Muir, Walter Turner, Mark Brett, Mark Howard, Mike Vinden, Ray Lavender, Wyn McLeod, Olwyn Atkinson, Margaret Braden, Renee Barr, Rachel Chaney, Pamela Dale, Nancy Adams, Belinda Lee, Nicola Bacon, Gilly Foss, Pauline Lewis-John, Venicia Day, Nicky Hooper, Pearl Gilham, Jean Channon, Barbara Hampshire and Felicity Lee.

PRODUCTION TEAM

Written by John Sullivan

Title music arranged and conducted by Ronnie Hazlehurst composed and sung by John Sullivan

Audience Warm-up:	Felix Bowness
Make-up Designer:	Elaine Smith
Costume Designer:	Robin Stubbs
Properties Buyer:	Maura Laverty
Film Cameraman:	Chris Seager
Film Sound:	Dave Brabants
Film Editor:	John Jarvis
Camera Supervisor:	Ken Major
Studio Lighting Director:	Henry Barber
Studio Sound:	Anthony Philpot
Technical Coordinator:	Nick Moore
Videotape Editor:	Chris Wadsworth

'The Longest Night'

Production Assistants: . . . . .Rowena Painter
                                  and Alexandra Todd
Assistant Floor Manager: . . . . .Adrian Pegg
Graphic Designer: . . . . .Andrew Smee
Vision Mixer: . . . . .Heather Gilder
Production Manager: . . . . .Sue Longstaff
Designer: . . . . .Mark Sevant
Directed by Mandie Fletcher
Produced by Ray Butt

The Trotters are accused of shoplifting when they complete their weekly shopping at the local Top-Buy supermarket. With no receipt to hand, they have nothing to support their protestations. They're soon joined in the manager's office by Lennox Gilbey, a 20-year-old habitual shoplifter, who takes everyone by surprise by pulling a gun. It transpires that Del knows the gunman and his mother, and tries persuading him to throw in the towel. But it turns out that Lennox's attempt to raid the supermarket safe was the idea of the Head of Security, Tom Clarke, and manager, Mr Peterson – they even supplied the toy gun.

When the scheme falls apart, Del agrees not to spill the beans to the police about Clarke and Peterson's involvment so long as Lennox – who has never had a proper job – is given the role of Head of Security once the current incumbent, Tom Clarke, retires. He also demands to be classed as the retailer's millionth customer, thereby winning a grand in the process.

Longstaff, Sue

Production manager on 11 episodes: S5; 'To Hull and Back'; 'The Frog's Legacy'; 'Miami Twice' (Parts 1 & 2) and 'Mother Nature's Son'. Associate producer on three episodes: 'Heroes and Villains'; 'Modern Men' and 'Time On Our Hands'
Sue, who's a Liverpudlian, was born in 1958. She

started her career at the BBC as a secretary, a position she held for six months, before moving on to become a floor assistant. Early programmes she worked on include *Top of the Pops*, *Blake's 7* and *Seconds Out*, where she first worked with Ray Butt.

Now a production manager, Sue has particularly enjoyed working on *Three Of A Kind*, the last series of *Noel's House Party* and *Only Fools and Horses*, while recent assignments have included *The Weakest Link*, *2 Point 4 Children* and Lee Evans' *So What Now?*

Lordship Lane

Mentioned by Del in 'The Sky is the Limit', Lordship Lane is where Bronco, a painter and decorator, bought a flat before being evicted by the building society.

Lorraine, Marie

Role: Woman in crowd
Appeared in S6, episode 3
Actress/singer Marie Lorraine, who was born in Barking in 1932, has spent most of her career in the theatre. Her first West End musical was *The Sound of Music* at the Palace Theatre in 1961, and her last West End performance was at the Adelphi Theatre in *Me and My Girl*, which closed in 1993. Since then she has completed a few tours and filmed several commercials, including one for Pimms.

Now, Marie considers herself retired from the theatre; her long career began when she trained at the Max Rivers Stage School and the Guildford School of Music, but she originally worked as a shorthand typist.

She made her professional acting debut in variety in 1953, before moving into the theatre and roles such as Olga in a national tour of *The Merry Widow* in 1957. Other stage credits include *Seven Brides for Seven Brothers*, *The Ivor Novello Story* and *Kismet*, while her few television appearances include *Dear John* and *Touch of Spice*. Marie has also spent many years as an entertainer on major cruise liners.

'Losing Streak, A'

Original transmission: Thursday 4 November 1982, 8.30 pm
Production date: Sunday 30 May 1982
Original viewing figures: 7.5 million
Duration: 30 minutes
First repeat: Tuesday 19 July 1983, 8.30 pm
Subsequent repeats: 2/11/90, 10/5/96, 17/6/97, 28/1/00

CAST

Del Trotter . . . . .David Jason
Rodney Trotter . . . . .Nicholas Lyndhurst
Grandad Trotter . . . . .Lennard Pearce
Trigger . . . . .Roger Lloyd Pack
Boycie . . . . .John Challis
Pub customer (Paddy) . . . . . . .Michael G. Jones
Julie (Barmaid) . . . . .Julie La Rousse
Walk-ons: . . . .(People in pub) Sonia Benjamin
                                  and Brian Braithwaite

PRODUCTION TEAM

Written by John Sullivan
Title music arranged and conducted by Ronnie Hazlehurst composed and sung by John Sullivan
Audience Warm-up: . . . . .Felix Bowness
Make-up Designer: . . . . .Shaunna Harrison
Costume Designer: . . . . .Anushia Nieradzik
Properties Buyer: . . . . .Roger Williams
Camera Supervisor: . . . . .Ron Peverall
Studio Lighting Director: . . . . .Henry Barber
Studio Sound: . . . . .Dave Thompson
Technical Coordinator: . . . . . .Alan Jeffery

'A Losing Streak'

Videotape Editor: . . . . .Mike Taylor
Production Assistant: . . . . .Penny Thompson
Assistant Floor Manager: . . . . .Tony Dow
Graphic Designers: . . . . .Peter Clayton and Fen Symonds
Vision Mixer: . . . . .Shirley Coward
Production Managers: . . . . .Janet Bone and Sue Bysh
Designer: . . . . .Andy Dimond
Produced by Ray Butt

Del has turned to gambling and is losing money like there's no tomorrow. He's £150 out of pocket from the previous night's poker session and is still planning to host the next session at his flat. His luck seems to be going from bad to worse, seemingly losing everything to Boycie, including all his money, Grandad's cash, his van, jewellery and even the odd few pennies collected from the return of some empties from a long-forgotten party. But Boycie's run of good fortune is soon to change as he finally gets his comeuppance for cheating his way through the poker games.

Lough, Graham

Designer on six episodes: S6, episodes 1, 3–6 and 'Dates'
London-born Graham Lough joined the BBC upon leaving Cambridge University with a degree in architecture. His first position, back in 1974, was design assistant, and he worked on shows including *Poldark, Dr Who, Secret Army* and *The Des O'Connor Show.*

After being made redundant from the Beeb in 1974, he moved to Bristol and joined the John Lewis Partnership, the retail department store, where he works as a visual merchandise manager.

Louis

(See 'Lombardi, Louis')

Lunt, Patrick

Role: TV announcer
Appeared in 'Rodney Come Home'

Patrick has been a broadcaster, narrator and voiceover artist for over 25 years, and his voice has been heard on a myriad of programme trails on the BBC and various awards ceremonies. He's worked on Radio 2 for over two decades as a programme presenter, newsreader and continuity announcer, and has been employed by BFBS Radio since the 1970s.

Lurch

Played by Dave Corey
Lurch, who's seen in 'Miami Twice', is one of Vinny Occhetti's henchmen.

Lusty Linda

A doll seen in 'Danger UXD', Lusty Linda is one of 50 Del bought from Denzil, without realising that they were the inflatable kind!

Lyndhurst, Nicholas

Role: Rodney Trotter
Appeared in all episodes
Playing Rodney Trotter has been a happy experi-

'As One Door Closes'

ence for Nicholas Lyndhurst, who was first choice for the role. As he explained to the *Radio Times* during an interview in 1983, he finds Sullivan's lines so funny that sometimes he can't look at the other actors when he is speaking. 'I will always look somewhere else. If we catch each other's eyes, we laugh.'

The character's deadpan grin and dry sense of humour have been adeptly exploited by Nicholas, who's been acting since boyhood. Born in 1961 at Emsworth, West Sussex, he trained at London's Corona Drama Academy from the age of ten. He stayed eight years, paying his fees from money earned making commercials.

His first television work was for BBC Schools productions, and was followed by more expansive roles: in the period drama *Anne of Avonlea*, a leading role in the BBC's 1974 six-part adaptation of *Heidi* and, aged 14, the lead in *The Prince and the Pauper*. Directing *Heidi* was June Wyndham Davies: 'I remember Nick, then 12, coming to play Peter in the series. Even then he was as tall as a beanpole, growing taller every day. Everybody loved him. He was extremely professional, knew his lines and managed to keep some very chirpy goats in order. At the end of the shoot party, he had hit 13, and I remember him dancing with the make-up ladies, who adored him.'

When he was 17 he landed the role of Raymond, Fletcher's gormless son in *Going Straight*, the sequel to Dick Clement and Ian La Frenais' earlier success, *Porridge*, but his big break came in the shape of Adam Parkinson in Carla Lane's highly

rated sitcom *Butterflies*, the same year. Four series were made and by the time the closing episode was transmitted, five years later, Nicholas' was a familiar face to television viewers across the nation.

John B Hobbs, whose extensive list of credits as a producer and director include such series as *Terry and June; Three Up, Two Down; Brush Strokes; Bread* and *Laura and Disorder* with Wendy Craig, was production manager on the first series and directed the final season of *Butterflies*. He holds fond memories of working with Lyndhurst on the sitcom. 'He's a very dedicated actor and easy to work with. It was early in his career and he was very enthusiastic and a good team player, getting on with everyone on the set. I remember that as soon as Gareth and I met Nicholas during the casting process we were enthusiastic about him. He has a nice dry sense of humour, and the young teenagers liked him; I remember he had quite a large following, and always had large mail bags.'

Other small-screen appearances include *The Two of Us, Spearhead, A Mother Like Him, Gulliver's Travels, To Serve Them All My Days, The Piglet Files* and playing Gary Sparrow in *Goodnight Sweetheart*, but for millions of fans around the world, nothing will ever top his portrayal of Rodney Trotter, a role that Nicholas enjoys playing. In 1983 he told the *Radio Times* that 'this is the only programme I'm in that I like to watch… I don't like watching myself, but the lines are marvellous.' And on his screen character, he said: 'Rod is a bit of a plonker. He's a nice chap with a conscience who is trying to do right. He knows that Del is doing wrong, but he's usually talked or bribed into joining him. It's the big brother syndrome. But he means well. I love it.'

Lynn, Ann
Role: Audrey
Appeared in 'Time On Our Hands'

Ann, who was born in London in 1939, has built up an extensive list of credits, particularly in film and television. On the small screen her roles include Ann Beaumont in *Gideon's Way*, Ivy Williams in *Redcap*, Marie Spring in *The Saint*, Inga Kalmutt in *The Champions*, Frau Muller in *Special Branch*, Rose in *Minder*, Claire Williams in *The Others* and Rita Pinner in John Sullivan's *Just Good Friends*.

Her film work includes *Piccadilly Third Stop* (1960), *Strip Tease Murder* (1961), *A Woman's Privilege* (1962), *Doctor in Distress* (1963), *The Uncle* (1965), *Baby Love* (1968) and *Screamtime* (1983).

Mac
Played by Willis Knickerbocker

Mac is seen in the second instalment of 'Miami Twice'. He owns the car rental firm, through which the travel agent who organises the Trotters' trip to Miami books a car.

Macarthy, Eugene
Played by Roger Blake

Seen in 'Stage Fright', Eugene is a local villain and unpopular around the vicinity. The expressionless criminal is 45 and, when we meet him, has owned The Starlight Rooms for three months, after forcing Eric – who's now the manager – to sell him the property.

Macarthy, Lil
Actor not named on the cast list

Lil, who's 82, is Eugene's mother and is seen in 'Stage Fright'. It's the old girl's birthday and she's celebrating it at The Starlight Rooms, which is owned by her son, Eugene. Fortunately for Del, who's arranged the night's cabaret, Mrs Macarthy loves the act.

MacDonald, Kenneth
Role: Mike Fisher
Appeared in 30 episodes: S3, episode 7; S4, episodes 2, 3 & 6; S5, episodes 1, 4, 5 & 6; S6, episodes 2–6; S7, episodes 1–6, 'To Hull and Back'; 'The Frog's Legacy'; 'Dates'; 'The Jolly Boys' Outing'; 'Miami Twice' (Parts 1 & 2); 'Mother Nature's Son'; 'Fatal Extraction'; 'Heroes and Villains'; 'Modern Men' and 'Time On Our Hands'

Seeing the postman squeeze the latest *Only Fools and Horses'* script through the letterbox was always a welcome sight for Kenneth MacDonald, as his widow, Sheila, recalls. 'Actors are notorious for never reading their scripts properly; when they arrive, they'll thumb through and look for their bit. But as soon as one of John Sullivan's scripts arrived, Ken read every page; he absolutely loved them and would sit on his own just laughing. He loved the whole concept of the programme because John, being such a clever writer, made it an all-round story – almost like a novelette.'

When a new batch of scripts arrived, Ken was more interested in finding out how the whole story panned out, than what contribution he'd be making; it was this unselfishness that helped to create the loyalty and felicity which surrounded the production. Ken created a well-loved character whose naïvety saw him constantly succumb to Del's sales patter: time and time again he'd end up dishing out a wad of notes in exchange for some utterly useless item.

When Sullivan decided it was time The Nag's Head needed a landlord, Ken was delighted to be offered the part, even though he assumed it was a one-off job. 'He was first seen in "Who's a Pretty Boy?", right at the end of the third season, and as no one knew whether there was going to be another series, Ken automatically thought it was a one-episode role,' explains Sheila.

Although he was seen in numerous other television roles – including several series of *It Ain't Half Hot, Mum,* playing Gunner Clark – Sheila regards Mike Fisher as her late husband's favourite small-screen character. 'He did lots of things and found many very rewarding but when it came to *Only Fools and Horses,* he always enjoyed going to work.'

The sheer magnitude of the success enjoyed by *Only Fools and Horses* surprised everyone, not least Ken. He once said: 'I get a tremendous response from fans of the show. They're always coming up to me or shouting across the street, things like: "Clean your pipes out, Mike" or "How's Del Boy?". That familiarity is nice because you know the nation loves the show so much.'

Although he was inundated with fan mail, he always tried to reply personally. 'He made the effort,' says Sheila. 'He was always charming and had time for people because he felt the public made his career; it amazed me how patient he was sometimes: he wouldn't go out of his way to look for the attention and, at times, it could be intrusive, especially if you're out with your family, but he would always be gracious and have time for fans.'

Ken held fond memories for all the episodes he appeared in, especially the Christmas Trilogy in 1996. 'Doing the last episodes was very sad because you just couldn't believe it would ever come to an end. By the finish, everyone was in tears.'

Born in Manchester in 1950, Ken completed his A-levels but instead of considering university or drama school he took a series of small jobs, including working at a Kellogg's Cornflakes factory, a building site and a department store, all to try and help his mother, Emily. His father, Bill MacDonald, a Scottish heavyweight wrestling champion, had died when Ken and his older sister, Jeanette, were still teenagers, so he was keen to stay in Manchester and do what he could.

His long-held ambition, however, was to become an actor and after a while he decided it was time to try his luck, so with the blessing of his mother, he headed south and joined the National Youth Theatre. 'His mother knew he wanted to act and she'd been wonderful. Although her husband had died when Ken was 13, she'd managed to keep him at boarding school until he'd completed his A-levels.'

After a spell with the National Youth Theatre,

Ken's first job was with Theatre and Education; together with a group of fellow performers, he'd tour the country in a little van performing at schools. This earnt him his Equity card at which point he moved into repertory theatre, gaining valuable stage experience at places such as Leatherhead, in the early 1970s.

Television roles soon followed, including small parts in *Z Cars; Softly, Softly; Coronation Street; Upstairs, Downstairs; Last of the Summer Wine; Dad's Army; The Famous Five* and *Oh No – It's Selwyn Froggitt.* Later television appearances included playing Cyril, an informant, in ITV's police drama *Touching Evil,* and appearances in *The Thin Blue Line, Crocodile Shoes, Moll Flanders, Heartbeat, Heartburn Hotel, David Copperfield, The Mrs Bradley's Mysteries, The Sins, Peak Practice, Merseybeat* and 23 episodes of *Brookside.* The last time he worked for television was for an episode of ITV's police comedy drama *The Last Detective,* playing a hotel doorman.

But it was *It Ain't Half Hot, Mum* that gave Ken his big break in the medium. 'He was very lucky to play a character like Gunner Clark at quite a young age; he certainly hadn't done a lot of rep work before he was offered the part, so it was a great opportunity for him.'

A week after parading with the rest of the theatrical troupe for the last time in Jimmy Perry and David Croft's sitcom, he was pulling pints behind the bar at The Nag's Head. 'It was a very busy period in his career,' says Sheila, who first met Ken whilst working as a costume assistant at a theatre in Crewe. 'It was 1976 and I was still a student, but I was gaining experience as a wardrobe assistant at the rep. Ken was working there and my first impressions were of a mature, confident working actor. He was 26 when we first met, I was only 20, and before long we went out on our first date. I

then returned to college in Liverpool, Ken went back to London but we kept in touch.'

Although the lion's share of Ken's career was spent in television, he did enjoy returning to the stage and went on to appear in some major productions, such as *My Night With Reg* at The Royal Court in 1994, before transferring to the West End's Criterion Theatre. Other stage credits include *Say Goodnight to Grandma* at the Belgrave Theatre, Coventry; a tour of *The Day War Broke Out* and *It Ain't Half Hot, Mum; Macbeth* and various productions for the National Theatre: *Animal Farm; Guys and Dolls; The Way of the World; Cleo; Camping* and *Emmannuelle and Dick.* He also made a handful of film appearances, like *The Class of Miss McMichael, A Hitch in Time, Breaking Glass, Cor Blimey!* and *Dream.*

Tragically, in 2001, Ken died of a heart attack at the age of 50 whilst holidaying in Hawaii with his wife, Sheila, their son, William, and daughter, Charlotte. The success of *Only Fools and Horses* and other shows he worked on, however, means Ken's face is regularly popping up on the screen. Fortunately the MacDonald family are still able to take pleasure in the enjoyment he brought to millions of viewers.

When the Trotters returned to Nelson Mandela House in 'If They Could See Us Now…!' on Chrismas Day 2001, fans quickly learnt that Mike Fisher hadn't been killed off; instead, his fate was an open prison for trying to recoup money he'd lost on the Central American money markets by embezzling money from his brewery. When John Sullivan called Sheila to discuss his plans for the jovial landlord, she was delighted. 'It would have been so final just to say he'd been in a car crash or something. To have seen him die in the show as well as in real life would almost have been like two deaths.' Sheila also feels the storyline makes sense.

'Like most of the characters, Mike was *just* on the right side of the law, but possibly wouldn't have been totally honest about everything. In one episode he was involved in a decorating scam with Del, where they fleeced an Irish decorator. It wasn't totally dishonest, but it was slightly underhand. So fiddling the books is the sort of crime I could see Mike committing, so it's a clever way to deal with a difficult situation.'

Machin, Alan

Studio sound supervisor on 12 episodes: S6, episodes 1, 3–6; S7 and 'Mother Nature's Son'

Bradford-born Alan Machin left school after completing his A-levels and joined the BBC in 1963, working at London's Television Centre. Upon completing his probationary period as a trainee technical operator, he moved into the sound department, initially as a floor operator. He was promoted to sound supervisor in 1973, whilst still only 25. Most of his career has been spent working on classic comedy shows like *The Liver Birds; Whatever Happened To The Likely Lads?; It Ain't Half Hot, Mum; 'Allo 'Allo!; Dad's Army; Bread* and *Yes, Minister*.

In the 1990s, Alan got more involved in drama, but has recently been working on shows such as *They Think It's All Over, Crimewatch, Watchdog, Blue Peter* and *Chambers*. Alan still works for the BBC.

Mackay, Angus

Role: Vicar
Appeared in 'The Frog's Legacy'

Angus is a busy character actor whose many screen appearances include playing Professor Lewin in *Doomwatch*, Alec Prosser in *The Sweeney*, Dr Winner in *The Gentle Touch*, Jeffries in *Dempsey and Makepeace*, an art teacher in *One Foot in the Grave* and a doctor in *If You See God, Tell Him*.

On the big screen he's been seen in several films, including *Percy, Quest for Love, Percy's Progress, Clockwise* and *King Ralph*.

Mackay, Irene

Played by Gaye Brown

Forty-year-old Irene – whose husband has been serving time in Parkhurst for GBH, attempted murder and wounding with intent – is seen in 'No Greater Love…'. When we first see her she's been living in the area a month, after moving from East London. She's taken over a flat from Mrs Singh, which surprises Rodney when he calls at the flat intending to try and flog cheap clothes to the previous incumbent. When Irene – who has a 16-year-old son, Marcus – learns that Rodney's samples include lingerie, she invites him in, so beginning a brief romance. Impressed by the tight skirt, Rodney falls for Irene in a big way, so when he later discovers that Del has put an end to the relationship, he's fuming. Del tries telling Rodney it's for his own good because her husband has just been released from prison, which could mean trouble for him if he finds out about the relationship.

Mackay, Marcus

Played by Steve Fletcher

Irene and Tommy Mackay's 16-year-old son Marcus, is a punk who's first seen in The Nag's Head during 'No Greater Love…'.

Mackay, Tommy

Played by David Daker

Husband of Irene who isn't the sort of guy to mess around with. He's served time at Parkhurst Prison for GBH, attempted murder and wounding with intent, and is released during the episode 'No Greater Love…'. Aware that a guy called Rodney Trotter has been playing around with his wife whilst he's been inside, Mackay is on the war-path, but a case of mistaken identity results in Del being assaulted instead.

Mackenzie, Margaret

Played by Sandra Payne

In charge of housing and welfare at the local town hall, Margaret is smartly dressed, attractive, in her thirties and seen in 'Homesick'. When she left school she had ambitions of becoming a choreographer, studying at Knightsbridge's London School of Dance for two years, but ended up working for the council. Rodney – who got to know Margaret through his role as Chairman of the Tenants' Committee – and Del are both smitten with her, especially when she supports their request for one of the new council bungalows in Herrington Road in the interests of Grandad's health. She soon changes her mind, however, and breaks off her friendship with Rodney, upon discovering there's nothing wrong with Grandad and that their transfer request is a hoax.

Madman

(See 'Robson, Chief')

Magaluf Brothers, The

Seen and heard in The Nag's Head during 'Diamonds are for Heather', the flamenco duo entertain the pub's clientele during the Spanish night. Enrico – although he's really a Cockney in disguise – makes up one half of the duo.

Maidment, Rex

Film cameraman on one episode: 'The Frog's Legacy'

Although he was born in Basingstoke, Rex grew up in Bournemouth and worked as a stills photographer in the commercial and industrial fields for six years, before moving to Jersey and working as a camera assistant for a while. In 1969 he joined the BBC as a camera assistant, based in Belfast, and was promoted to film cameraman five years later.

He moved to work at Ealing in 1981 and remained with the Beeb until 1994, when he left to work freelance. Among his credits whilst employed by the BBC are *Enchanted April, The Grass Arena* and *A Dark Adapted Eye*, and *The Hanging Gale, Rebecca, Kavanagh QC, Cider With Rosie* and *Murder Most Horrid* as a freelancer.

Major, Ken

Camera supervisor on 27 episodes: S4, episodes 1–5 & 7; S5; S6, episodes 2–6; S7; 'Dates'; 'The Frog's Legacy'; 'The Jolly Boys' Outing' and 'Rodney Come Home'

Malcolm, Christopher

Role: Madman/Chief of Security
Appeared in S3, episode 3

For many people, busy screen actor Christopher Malcolm is best known for playing Justin in several episodes of *Absolutely Fabulous*, but he's also been seen in *Whoops Apocalypse, The Comic Strip Presents, A Midsummer Night's Dream, Beau Geste, The Moneymen, War and Remembrance* and *Over Here*.

His film appearances include *Welcome to the Club, Diamonds on Wheels, The Spiral Staircase, Force 10 from Navarone, Ragtime, Superman III, Highlander* and *Eat the Rich*.

Malcolm, Harry

Harry, the 80-year-old publican at The Crown and Anchor, is mentioned by Mike Fisher in The Nag's Head during 'Heroes and Villains', but is never seen. Each year the local publicans organise a fancy dress party and in 1996 it's Harry's turn. But his untimely death means the celebration is cancelled and a wake is organised instead; unfortunately Rodney and Del don't hear about his demise and feel like real 'plonkers' when they turn up dressed as Batman and Robin.

Note: John Sullivan wrote a scene showing Harry on his death bed in 'Heroes and Villains', telling Del and Rodney about some hidden treasure buried by his late brother, Stan. A metal chest packed with American dollars, which had supposedly been found by Harry's great-grandfather during the American Civil War, found its way back to England and had been secretly hidden by Stan. Harry later found a map showing where it was buried and he wants Del to have it. However, the Trotters are on a wild goose chase. When Del was only 16, he sold a counterfeit item to Harry, who swore that he would get revenge. Content in the knowledge that he has done this, Harry duly dies with a smile on his face. (See the 'Cut Scene' after the episode review.)

Malcolm, Kenny

Played by Steve Weston

Kenny is the son of Harry Malcolm, the landlord of The Crown and Anchor, and is seen in 'Heroes and Villains'. Harry was supposed to be hosting the annual fancy dress party, but his sudden death forces the re-organisation of the party, as a wake.

Male customs worker

Played by Jon Rust

In 'To Hull and Back', the customs worker runs to assist a female passenger who's just arrived on an Amsterdam flight. Little does he know that her suitcase opening, depositing its contents all over the floor, is a deliberate act to deflect the official's attention from her partner, who walks through customs unchallenged.

Malibu Reef

Del drinks a Malibu Reef cocktail at The Nag's Head in 'Little Problems'.

Malik, Vimmal

Played by Malik Armhed Khalil

Del meets up with Vimmal at the Peckham and Camberwell Chamber of Trade Dinner/Dance in 'Cash and Curry'. New to the area and apparently affluent, Vimmal is on the look-out for business opportunities, and Del tries exploiting the situation for the benefit of Trotters' Independent Trading Company. It transpires that Malik's business affairs have nose-dived recently, and he's far from prospering. When he's stopped by Mr Ram outside the town hall, whilst in the company of Del and Rodney, it's evident his life isn't as smooth as he leads people to believe.

The Maliks and Rams are families who've been in dispute ever since the British Empire dominated India, with the Maliks accused of stealing land from the Rams, selling it, then establishing a successful business from the proceeds. The only item remaining of Mr Ram's family's heritage is a porcelain statuette, which he's desperate to reclaim. It later turns out that Malik is in partnership with Ram, touring the country looking for unsuspecting mugs like Del, who's out of pocket by two grand by the end of the episode.

Maloney, Nick

Role: Mick

Appeared in 'Fatal Extraction'

Nick was born in Liverpool in 1953 and trained for three years at London's Drama Centre. He made his acting debut in 1976, performing in *Juno and the Paycock* at Stoke's Victoria Theatre. Repertory work followed up and down the country, at places such as Chester, Stoke, Lancaster and Manchester.

His first excursion into the world of television came with an appearance as a rent collector in the series *Boys from the Blackstuff*. Other small-screen work includes playing Rev Worthington in four series of *Out of Tune*, Piggy Pearson in *Outside Edge*, PC Symons in *Coronation Street*, Laverick in *One Foot in the Grave*, a police sergeant in *The Upper Hand* and, amongst others, appearances in *Dangerfield*, *The Detectives*, *The Brothers MacGregor*, *C.A.T.S. Eyes* and *Terry and June*.

Although Nick rarely works on the stage these days, he's clocked up a number of appearances over the years, including spells in *The Norman Conquests*, *Seasons*, *Having A Ball* and *Drink the Mercury*.

Man at opera

Played by Robin Herford

Seen in 'A Royal Flush', the annoyed gentleman is disturbed, like the rest of the audience, by Del's constant chatter at the Theatre Royal, Drury Lane.

Man in church

Played by James Richardson

After waiting for days for the statue of the Virgin Mary to shed a few tears in 'The Miracle of Peckham', the supposed miracle finally happens and the man in the church – who's a reporter – calls David, his cameraman, to capture the momentous occasion on film.

Man in crowd

Played by Doug Rowe

When Del tries selling electronic trimming combs at the market in 'As One Door Closes', the man listens to his banter before asking if the combs are sharp. To demonstrate, Del tests it out on Rodney's hair.

Man in hospital

Played by Phil Cornwell

The drunken yob mouths off about the service he's getting, and the state of the health service, in 'Modern Men'. He complains just once too often so Del, who's upset because Cassandra has just lost her baby, flattens him with a solitary punch.

Man in market

Played by Paul McDowell

Seen in 'A Royal Flush', the man irritates Del by challenging the validity of his sales pitch for some Malaysian-made cutlery sets.

Man in market

Played by Duncan Faber

When Del's demonstrating his deep penetration massager in 'The Frog's Legacy', the man suggests he tries it out on Uncle Albert, who happens to walk by with a bad stoop, at the opportune moment.

à la Del

★ ★ ★ ★ ★ ★

'The "crème de la menthe" of the painting and decorating world'

('The Yellow Peril')

Man in pub

Played by Ian Barritt

In 'Chance of a Lunchtime', the man asks Mike, the landlord at The Nag's Head, to order a taxi for Trudy, the inebriated blonde, whose raucous laughter echoes around the pub.

Man on rig

(See 'Gas rigger')

Manager

The manager appeared in the script for 'The Class of '62' but the scene was cut before transmission. He's organising the auditions at a nightclub, which Raquel attends. Sadly, when the owner of the club realises she's pregnant, he turns her down.

Manuel, Peter

Technical coordinator on nine episodes: S7; 'Rodney Come Home' and 'Miami Twice' (Parts 1 & 2)

One of the shows Peter has worked on recently at the BBC is *EastEnders*.

Marcus

(see 'Mackay, Marcus')

Mardi Gras, The

Eddie Chambers' club in Margate is first discussed in the gents' toilet during 'The Jolly Boys' Outing'. There are cheap tickets available, so the boys on the annual trip decide to see what the club is like; for Del it's lucky he made the effort to go along because the night's entertainers are the Great Ramondo and his new assistant, Raquel, Del's former girlfriend.

Marguerite

A girlfriend of Rodney's who works in the local dry cleaners, Marguerite is not seen in the show, but is referred to as a 'skinny bird' by Grandad in 'No Greater Love…'. Rodney claims he was never in love with her, it was just an infatuation.

Marilyn

Not seen in the show, Trigger's cousin, Marilyn, is mentioned during 'Wanted'. In The Nag's Head, Del, Trigger and Boycie chat, and one of the subjects of conversation is Rodney's unfortunate experience with Blossom: the woman was plastered and started screaming for help when Rodney tried preventing her from falling over. Trigger goes on to explain that the woman also accused Marilyn of touching her. His cousin (who spent some time at Greenham Common) is a tomboy who wore a crew cut, braces and smoked a pipe when he last saw her.

Mario

Played by Frank Coda

Seen in 'Chain Gang', Mario is the head waiter of an upmarket restaurant in Chelsea, where Arnie is supposedly meeting Mr Stavros in connection with the sale of gold chains. Even though the restaurant is busy, he manages to find a table for Del and Boycie – although Del slipping him a few quid obviously helped.

Mario

Mario owns a fish restaurant and is mentioned in 'Friday the 14th' when Del explains that he met

Boycie at the restaurant and was offered the second-hand car salesman's weekend cottage in Cornwall for a break. But the offer wasn't out of generosity, it was all to do with business: as the cottage is sited near one of the finest salmon fishing streams in England, Mario agrees to pay Del and Boycie (who'll split the cash fifty-fifty) £10 for every salmon they can supply. Mario is not seen in the sitcom.

Marion

When Del's trying to remember the name of one of his old girlfriends while sat in Sid's Café during 'Fatal Extraction', Rodney suggests Marion. Del met Marion, whom we never see, at the Catford dog track, and must have liked her, because he bought her a ring.

Marion

Played by Joan Hodges
Marion, who appears in 'If They Could See Us Now…!', used to do a bit of cleaning for Albert at his seaside home. She's seen at the house the Trotters visit before attending the funeral. The trouble is, the Trotters arrive at the wrong house and the Albert in question is Albert Warren, not Uncle Albert.

Mario's restaurant

Owned by Mario, this fish restaurant is mentioned in 'Friday the 14th'.

Marlene

(See 'Boyce, Marlene')

Marley Road

In 'Yuppy Love' Del tells Rodney about the time he was a kid with two paper rounds and had to deliver a copy of *Spick and Span* to a weirdo in this road.

Marr & Son Ltd, J

The crews' entrance to this company is seen in 'To Hull and Back'.

Marriner, Keith

Dubbing mixer on two episodes: 'Miami Twice' (Parts 1 & 2)
Born in Perivale, Greater London, Keith started as an engineer in BBC Radio in 1977, moving to the Corporation's film department at Ealing as an assistant dubbing mixer three years later. He began on current affairs programmes, such as *Panorama*, but worked on a range of shows during his career with the Beeb, which ended in 1995. He now works freelance and runs two companies: Martyr Sounds, a post-production company in London, and his own sound editing firm.

Marsden, Roy

Role: Danny Driscoll
Appeared in S6, episode 6
Roy, who was born in London in 1941, has had a busy career on stage and screen. His television appearances include playing Blick in *Frank Stubbs*

Promotes, George Osborne in the mini-series *Vanity Fair*, Neil Burnside in *The Sandbaggers*, Jack Ruskin in *Airline* and Chief Supt Adam Dalgleish in several productions, including *Death of an Expert Witness*.

Among the films he's appeared in are *Tomorrow*, *The Squeeze* and *Dangerous Lady*.

Marsha

Played by Laura Jackson
In 'Yuppy Love', the attractive Marsha and her pal, Dale, pull up at a wine bar in a Porsche. Wearing the latest fashion gear, they enter the bar and are standing at the counter when Del – who spotted them entering – makes his move. Unaware that the girls are taking the mickey out of him, he tries chatting them up but fails dismally.

Marshall, Tony

Role: Chris
Appeared in 'Dates', 'Rodney Come Home' and 'Mother Nature's Son'
Although he was born in Birmingham, Tony grew up in Oldham and attended the Oldham Theatre Workshop. He'd already appeared in four episodes of *Coronation Street*, playing Len Fairclough's assistant, when he moved to London and enrolled at the Drama Centre.

Five years of children's theatre around London was followed by more television work, including three years as Diesel in *All Quiet on the Preston Front*, and appearances in *The Paradise Club*, *Bostock's Cup*, *The Flint Street Nativity*, *Second Thoughts*, *Nelson's Column* and *Casualty*. He's recently spent over two years co-presenting two children's programmes, *Numbers Plus* and *Think About Science*.

In addition to television, Tony's also a regular in fringe theatre.

Marshall, Scott

Role: Gary
Appeared in 'Heroes and Villains'
Scott, who was born in London in 1977, started acting at 13. He trained at the Sylvia Young Theatre School and whilst establishing his acting career

worked in various other jobs, such as assisting in a clothes shop in London's Oxford Street and painting and decorating on building sites.

His professional acting debut was playing a rebellious schoolboy in *EastEnders*, but he's since gone on to appear in a string of shows, including several appearances with Harry Enfield, *Crimewatch*, *The Bill* and *The Thin Blue Line*. He's also appeared in a few films, such as *Bar Room*.

Marsham-Hales, Lady Victoria

(See 'Vicky')

Martin, Derek

Technical coordinator on four episodes: S2, episodes 1, 2, 4 & 6

Martin, Derek

Role: Arthur
Appeared in 'Fatal Extraction'
Born in London, Derek worked in several other jobs before turning to acting. He made his professional debut in a 1962 episode of *Z Cars*, playing a drinker in a pub. His career has been dominated by television and film work, and he's never worked in the theatre.

On the big screen, his roles have included Harry in *Piggy Bank*, Big Jake in *The Gift* and Uncle Benny in *The Cutter*. On television, meanwhile, his credits include *Shoestring; Terry and June; It Ain't Half Hot, Mum; Potter; Upstairs, Downstairs; The Professionals;* lead roles in *King and Castle; The Chinese Detective; Law and Order;* playing Gary Marshall in *The Governor* and Charlie Slater in *EastEnders*.

Martin Luther King Comprehensive, The

This nondescript Peckham school where Del, Trigger, Denzil, Roy Slater and Boycie finished their education, only has one moment of fame in the series. This occurs in 'The Class of '62' when Del worries about whether their old headmaster, Benson, organised the school reunion, especially when it appears that no one is going to turn up.

MEMORIES OF PLAYING GARY

★ ★ ★ ★ ★ ★

'When I auditioned for the part of Gary, I was already in contention for the lead in a sitcom. Believing I would be offered the lead role, I was a little downhearted because I really wanted *Only Fools* as it was both my wife's and my favourite programme of all time. By the time I got home I had received a call from my agent offering me the part of Gary – I was ecstatic.

'When it came to the scenes running through the streets, being chased by Rodney, it was painful for me because I'd broken my toe two days earlier playing football. I had to have therapy on my toe the night before at the hotel.

'One of the funniest memories relates to filming the chase scene. Nick Lyndhurst was belting along behind me in front of lots of the general public when he suddenly slipped over; everyone just fell about laughing. Thankfully, the Beeb's *Auntie's Bloomers* hasn't got hold of it – yet!'

SCOTT MARSHALL

Denzil, however, says it's impossible because the doctor stated Benson should never be allowed back into society after having been convicted of an undisclosed crime.

In 'Modern Men', however, Del refers to the Dockside Secondary Modern as being his final school, so we can only surmise that the establishment changed names.

Martin, Mel

Role: Beverley

Appeared in 'Fatal Extraction'

Mel's busy career has included a long list of television credits. She's been seen in *Hazell*, *Bergerac*, *Minder*, *Inspector Morse*, *Poirot*, *Lovejoy*, *Boon*, *The Big One*, *Darling Buds of May*, *A Touch of Frost*, *Cadfael*, *Heartbeat*, *Silent Witness*, *Cold Feet* (playing Heather Childs), *Poldark* and *The Pallisers*.

Her film credits include *Quincy's Quest*, *Business as Usual* and *Tom's Midnight Garden*.

Maskell, Tina

Stunt artist on one episode: 'Dates'

London-born Tina Maskell – who doubled for Rodney's date, Nervous Nerys, during the car chase in 'Dates' – was a nursery nurse for ten years before swapping jobs and working in children's theatre.

Screen work soon followed, beginning with the movie *Greystoke*, in which she played an ape. Eventually she began receiving offers on television for progammes such as *Coronation Street*, *EastEnders*, *Mr Bean*, *'Allo 'Allo!*, *One Foot in the Grave*, *Peak Practice*, *London's Burning* and *Wycliffe*; she's also regularly employed as a double.

As well as continuing to work as a stunt artist, Tina has branched out into coordinating stunts and has just finished working on the film *Crush*, which was released in 2002.

Matthews, Bill

Film cameraman on six episodes: S1

The late Bill Matthews worked on a host of shows during his career with the BBC, including *The Liver Birds* back in the 1960s.

Matthews, Seymour

Role: Auctioneer

Appeared in 'Time On Our Hands'

Seymour, who was born in Brighton, trained at East 15 Acting School. Upon graduating he joined the Royal Shakespeare Company and spent the next two and half years in the theatre, his preferred medium. The last 13 years have been dominated by his stage work at the National Theatre where he's appeared in 14 productions, most recently *The Cherry Orchard*.

In 2001 he was cast in his first major feature film, playing a doctor in *Secret Passage*, set in 16th century Venice, which entailed three months filming on location. On the small screen, his credits include playing Alan Hunt in *Softly, Softly*; Chief Inspector Henderson in *Sorry!*; Ronnie in *Bergerac*;

Derek Wallace in *Boon*; Trotter in the 1987 mini-series *Vanity Fair*; DCI Morris in *The Jump* and, in 2000, a role in *Dinner of Herbs*.

Maureen

Played by Nula Conwell

Maureen – who Del classes as a 'saucy little cow' – is a barmaid at The Nag's Head, and is first seen in 'Happy Returns', when she serves Del, who's entertaining an old girlfriend, June. She's also seen in four other episodes.

'May the Force be with You'

Original transmission: Thursday 8 December 1983, 8.30 pm

Production date: Sunday 13 November 1983

Original viewing figures: 10.7 million

Duration: 30 minutes

First repeat: Monday 13 August 1984, 8.00 pm

Subsequent repeats: 28/9/91, 12/3/95, 11/9/98, 28/4/00

CAST

Del Trotter . . . . .David Jason
Rodney Trotter . . . . .Nicholas Lyndhurst
Grandad Trotter . . . . .Lennard Pearce
Trigger . . . . .Roger Lloyd Pack
Detective Inspector Roy Slater .Jim Broadbent
Boycie . . . . .John Challis
PC Hoskins . . . . .Christopher Mitchell
Karen (the barmaid) . . . . .Michèle Winstanley
Walk-ons: . . . .(Customers in pub) Ray Sumby
and seven extras. (Policeman in police station and customer in pub) Terry Bradford

PRODUCTION TEAM

Written by John Sullivan
Title music arranged and conducted by Ronnie Hazlehurst composed and sung by John Sullivan
Audience Warm-up: . . . . .Felix Bowness
Make-up Designer: . . . . .Denise Baron
Costume Designer: . . . . .Dinah Collin
Properties Buyer: . . . . .Penny Rollinson
Camera Supervisor: . . . . .Ron Peverall
Studio Lighting Director: . . . . .Don Babbage
Studio Sound: . . . . .Dave Thompson
Technical Coordinator: . . . . . .Terry Brett
Videotape Editor: . . . . .Chris Booth
Production Assistant: . . . . .Penny Thompson
Assistant Floor Manager: . . . .Tony Dow
Graphic Designer: . . . . .Mic Rolph
Vision Mixer: . . . . .Angela Beveridge
Production Manager: . . . . .Andy Smith
Designer: . . . . .Bryan Ellis
Produced and directed by Ray Butt

The unpopular Detective Inspector Slater is back on Del's patch, where he used to walk the streets as a bobby. This time he's on the hunt for a stolen microwave and is already keeping a close eye on his chief suspect: Del Boy, whom he's known since they went to school together.

When Slater gets chatting with Rodney – who doesn't know he's a copper – in The Nag's Head and says he hasn't seen Del for years, Rodney

invites him round to the flat and is shocked when Del nearly suffers a seizure. Discovering he's let a policeman through the door, Rodney tries making amends, but it's too late, especially as the stolen microwave is in full view on the sideboard.

The Trotters are arrested and interrogated; when Slater discovers Rodney has a criminal record he corners Del by threatening to implicate Rodney in a fictitious crime of possessing drugs. Del seems to have little alternative but to become a police informer and tells Slater who supplied the stolen goods, but not before receiving an immunity from prosecution for his family.

Mayes, Keith

Studio sound supervisor on two episodes: 'Dates' and 'The Jolly Boys' Outing'

Born in Welwyn Garden City, Keith began studying electronics but left before completing the course. In 1977 he joined the BBC as a trainee sound assistant and gained vital experience working on shows such as *Doctor Who* and *Grange Hill*.

During a 13-year career with the Beeb he worked on a host of programmes, including *Top of the Pops*, *Hi-De-Hi!*, *To the Manor Born* and *Blackadder*. He left to work freelance in 1990, by which time he'd reached the position of senior sound supervisor. In a freelance capacity he's been involved in *Drop the Dead Donkey*, *Red Dwarf* and a myriad of music shows, including the MTV Music Awards.

Mayor

Played by Robin Meredith

In 'Heroes and Villains', the Mayor presents Del with his medal for bravery after he apprehended a mugger.

McArthur, Lisa

Location manager on three episodes: 'Heroes and Villains', 'Modern Men' and 'Time On Our Hands'

McBride, Hazel

Role: Snobby girl

Appeared in S6, episode 1

Born in Enfield in 1949, Hazel gained a teaching qualification before deciding her future lay in acting. She made her professional debut in children's theatre during 1971, before moving into rep.

Her first stint in television was a 1974 episode of *Within These Walls*, but her favourite part was playing Madeleine in the series *Secret Army*. Other small-screen roles include Blink in *Good Behaviour*, Claire in *Hart to Hart*, DI Latham in *The Locksmith*, Elspeth Hayes in two episodes of *Family Affairs* and, more recently, Mrs Green in *Hollyoaks*.

Hazel's theatre credits include *The Mousetrap*, a tour of Sweden in *Who Killed Santa Claus?*, *An Inspector Calls* and *Little Women*.

McCullum, Mr

Played by Ken Drury

Seen in 'Three Men, a Woman and a Baby', Mr McCullum is the male midwife who's in charge at the delivery of Del and Raquel's baby. When he first arrives on the scene at the hospital, Del finds it hard to believe that the midwife could be a man, so asks if he's a pervert or something, wanting to be around at the birth.

McDowell, Paul

Role: Man in market
Appeared in 'A Royal Flush'

Paul, who was born in London, left school and trained to be a painter at Chelsea Art College. During his student days, he formed a band, The Temperance Seven, and went on to enjoy success with six hit singles, including 'You're Driving Me Crazy', which went to number one in 1961. When Paul tired of the band, he left and worked at The Establishment, a satirical club in London, as a writer/actor, which introduced him to the world of acting.

Upon leaving the club, he worked in the United States for five years with an improvisational group, The Second City, before returning to England and writing for *The Frost Report*. His first small-screen appearance as an actor was in the second series of *The World of Beachcomber*, with Spike Milligan. On the box, he's worked predominantly in comedy, including many series with Dave Allen, *The Good Life*, *Porridge*, *The Two Ronnies* and four series of LWT's sitcom *The Two of Us*, playing Nicholas Lyndhurst's father, Colin Phillips. He was frequently cast as policemen.

He's also appeared in several films, including the role of a Scottish laird in *The 39 Steps*, with Robert Powell, and a postman in 1980's *Rough Cut*.

Nowadays, Paul spends most of his time writing or teaching T'ai Chi around the world; he's also had a novel published and hopes it will shortly be adapted for the screen.

McGough, Philip

Role: Arnie
Appeared in S6, episode 3

Philip's career has involved working in all mediums. On the stage he's worked at many of the top theatres, including the National in productions like *The Pied Piper* and *Black Snow*, while his film credits include *Number 27*, *Les Misérables*, *Don't Go Breaking My Heart*, *Us Begins With You* and *Killing Joe*, which was nominated for an Oscar.

On the small screen he's played a range of characters, from Charlie Dawson in *Brookside*, Edwin Woodall in *The Monocled Mutineer*, Brian Pearce in *Inspector Morse* and Hibbert in *The Magician* to Marcus in *Wilderness*, Peter Mansell in *The Bench*, Plato in *Gulliver's Travels* and three years as Dr Malcolm Nicholson in *Bad Girls*.

McGuire, Mickey

(See 'Mental Mickey')

McInnes, Linda

Make-up designer on seven episodes: S4

Born in London, Linda worked as a science technician for five years before enrolling at the London School of Fashion. After graduating she joined the BBC in the mid-1970s, beginning a 15-year career with the Corporation. She accepted redundancy in 1992, by which time she'd worked on numerous shows, such as *Just Good Friends*, *The Onedin Line*, *Play for Today* and *The Kenny Everett Television Show*.

Since raising a family she's worked on a freelance basis, concentrating mainly on commercials.

McKern, Roger

Role: Owner of club
Appeared in S7, episode 4

Although Roger was cast in the episode, the scene was cut before transmission.

McManan-Smith, Richard

Designer on nine episodes: S7, 'Rodney Come Home' and 'Miami Twice' (Parts 1 & 2)

Other shows Richard has worked on include *Doctor Who* and the *Multicoloured Swap Shop*.

McManus, Jim

Role: Alex (the travel agent)
Appeared in S2, episode 6

In recent years, Jim's career has been dominated by work in the theatre, including playing Tony Hancock on tour in *Hancock's Last Half Hour* and a tour with his own one-man show, *Jim McManus as Charles Dickens*.

On television he's played Ronnie Lee Davis in *Casualty*, Sergeant Brown in *Underworld*, Brian Merry in *Goodnight Sweetheart* and Doctor Don't in *Don't Try This At Home*, while more recently he appeared in the feature film *The Lawless Heart*, playing a chef.

McManus, Patrick

Role: Damien Trotter
Appeared in S7, episode 6

Patrick's brief appearance as Baby Damien didn't, as far as my research can establish, lead to any further television work, which isn't surprising considering he was only days old.

McNamara, Desmond

Role: Earl
Appeared in 'Christmas Crackers'

Desmond, born in 1938, managed a printing company before trying his luck in the acting profession. He studied at RADA and made his professional debut in the late Leslie Sand's play *Investigation*, in 1968.

The next two-and-a-half years of his career were spent at the Birmingham rep, during which time he had his first job in television, playing a writer in a 1969 episode of *Nearest and Dearest*. His favourite roles in the medium are Cousin Tel in *Hazell* and Lem in *Roll Over Beethoven*.

Desmond is still working in all strands of the business. His two latest films were *Shakespeare in Love* and *Lucky Break*, while on television he's recently been seen in *The Bill*, *Casualty* and *The Last Detective*.

Meadows, Dr

Played by Ewan Stewart

In 'Sickness and Wealth', Albert advises Del, who's suffering stomach pains, to see the Scottish doctor. When he eventually attends the surgery, he finds out that Meadows left general practice two years ago and is now working at the local hospital. His replacement is Dr Shaheed. Down at the hospital, Robbie Meadows – who's in his late thirties and a reformed gambler who used to frequent The One Eleven Club – finally examines Del and confirms he's got irritable bowel syndrome.

Mechanic

Played by Herb Johnson

Seen in 'He Ain't Heavy, He's My Uncle', the mechanic works for Boycie at Boyce Auto Sales and Car Accessories. He enters the sales office and asks his boss if he wants an old banger taken to the scrap yard. But there is a change of plan when Boycie thinks he can palm the old wreck off on Del, who's looking for a run-around for Raquel.

Mental Mickey

Played by Daniel Peacock

The lead singer in Rodney's rock group, Mickey once bit a piece off a bloke's ear and has served time in Broadmoor. This wild and dangerous character, whose full name is Mickey McGuire, is seen in 'It's Only Rock and Roll'.

Merchandise

Any books, videos, DVDs and audio cassettes that have been released commercially are listed under those headings

Over the years, plenty of merchandise has been produced by both the BBC and the Only Fools and Horses Appreciation Society.

The Society's extensive range of products have included posters, phone covers, car accessories, badges, key rings, lighters, bookmarks and mouse mats. For full details of the items available, contact the Appreciation Society (see 'Only Fools and Horses Appreciation Society, The').

For full details of official BBC merchandise, contact the Beeb direct.

Meredith, Robin

Role: Mayor
Appeared in 'Heroes and Villains'

Born in Chalfont St Peter in 1943, Robin trained at Italia Conti before making his professional stage debut in a 1963 production at Butlin's holiday camp in Pwllheli, North Wales. The next two years were spent in the theatre before he made his first small-screen appearance as a furniture repairer in *The Mask of Jonus*. His favourite roles include the barber in *Merchant of Venice*, with Lord Olivier, and Mr Evans in *Golden Hill*.

Robin – who's also been seen in a handful of films, such as *Little Dorrit* and *The Fool* – is now artistic director of New Directions Theatre Company, a script production facility founded in 1994. He also continues to act.

Merryfield, Buster

Role: Uncle Albert

Appeared in 37 episodes: S4, episodes 2–7; S5; S6; S7; 'To Hull and Back'; 'A Royal Flush'; 'The Frog's Legacy'; 'Dates'; 'The Jolly Boys' Outing'; 'Rodney Come Home'; 'Miami Twice' (Parts 1 & 2); 'Mother Nature's Son'; 'Fatal Extraction'; 'Heroes and Villains'; 'Modern Men'; 'Time On Our Hands' and the Comic Relief Special

Even for an actor whose entire professional life had been spent treading the boards, taking on the role of Uncle Albert, the senior citizen in the Trotter household whose interminable reminiscences of life in the navy are met with drawn-out yawns, would have been a daunting task. So one could have excused Buster Merryfield, who had only turned to professional acting upon retiring from his career as a bank manager, if he'd suffered a severe bout of nerves before joining the production for the first time at the funeral of his screen brother in 'Strained Relations'. But Buster's matter-of-fact approach to work placed him in good stead for the task ahead.

In 1985 he told the *Radio Times*, 'Uncle Albert is in no way a replacement for Grandad. He is irreplaceable and this is why an entirely new character has been written into the series.' Inevitably fans mourned the loss of the acerbic Grandad Trotter, and some would unfairly make comparisons between him with the truculent old sea dog brought to life so adroitly by Buster.

Sandy Ross-Brown, Buster's long-standing friend and manager, started representing him shortly after he'd been offered the part, and explains how she approached the job. 'He was terribly respectful of what Lennard Pearce had brought to the show and wasn't even going to try and compete in the same vein. I don't think Buster took very long to settle in to the role. Within a short space of time he'd come to grips with the character, and the way he felt John Sullivan wanted him to be played.'

Playing Uncle Albert in his sixties was the highlight of Buster's professional acting career and led to a myriad of requests to help with charity work, offers to perform in pantomimes and the occasional television role. But Buster had reached the time in his life where he valued more than ever the days spent with his wife, Iris, daughter, Karen, son-in-law, Rodney, and grandchildren, Stuart and Jonathan, and though he was always keen to work hard, he didn't want to contemplate spending long periods away from his Dorset home. Helping and advising throughout, Sandy – like all good agents – helped to coordinate his acting career. 'Left to his own devices he would have spent every day doing as much work as he could, so we had to be selective. Sometimes I'd have to say to him: "Look, this is ridiculous, you've got to pace yourself." There were times when I'd have to literally tell him (because he was a strong character) that he wasn't going to do anything for a couple of days because he needed to take a rest.'

The relationship Sandy enjoyed with Buster was unlike any other she'd had with her clients. 'He was

Buster Merryfield with his close friend and manager, Sandy Ross-Brown

my idea of a grandfather,' she says with a warm smile. 'We got to know each other very well and he became a close friend of the family. One of the things I loved enormously about him was that he appreciated every day of his life, and always wanted to make the most of it. His zest for each day was a tonic and an inspiration to me and all that knew him.'

And Buster certainly did make the most of his life. Born Harry Merryfield (the nickname 'Buster' was coined when he weighed in at over nine pounds at birth) in Battersea in 1920, he was educated locally. During his schooldays he developed an interest in boxing, which later saw him become a Southern Command champion in 1945.

Other than during the Second World War, when he served in the Royal Artillery, Buster worked for the Westminster Bank, but as Sandy Ross-Brown points out, his banking career – which saw him rise to managing his own branch at Thames Ditton – wasn't his first love. 'It simply paid the bills and was by far a more secure profession,' she explains. Buster had always been an enthusiastic amateur actor, an interest he developed further in the army when he accepted the role of entertainments officer. But with a wife and young daughter to support, acting could only remain a deep-rooted passion which he would satisfy by regular jaunts in various amateur productions, including the time he formed his own theatrical company, The Characters.

In the late 1970s, however, when he opted for early retirement from the bank at the age of 57, he found himself with the time and energy to pursue his ambition to act professionally. His first job was on stage at Worthing, and he frequently returned to tread the boards, especially during the pantomime season. He also started to receive offers for commercials and the occasional spot on television. As well as playing Albert in *Only Fools*, he was seen as Uncle Jim in the BBC series *Hannah*, the Bishop in *Strangers and Brothers*, Professor Challis in *The Citadel*, Sir Miles Honeyman in Anglia's *Shroud for a Nightingale* and Sir Joshua Stakes in *Lovesong*.

But not even in his wildest dreams could Buster

have envisaged becoming a national figure in his sixties. He once commented, 'The most pleasurable thing is that I can walk down any street and people smile at me and say: "There's Uncle Albert." That's magic.'

As Sandy points out, however, such stardom never went to his head. 'Yes, he thoroughly enjoyed the recognition but was never conceited about it all – he just loved the attention, and more importantly how, being well known, there were innumerable ways in which he could contribute to others.'

Buster's death in 1999, shortly after being treated for a brain tumour, shocked not just his family and close friends, but his adoring public, too. Sandy misses him terribly. 'I was very fortunate to have looked after him. He was very gentle and incredibly kind. In all the time I knew him he never had a bad word to say about anyone. His legacy to me and many others is that there is only one performance on the stage of life, as he always said, "This is not a rehearsal: I commend you to live it to the full." Throughout his career his wife, Iris, gave him unfailing support and he always said she was the wise head that kept his feet firmly on the ground.'

Metro Café, The

Emblazoned across the window of Sid's Café in 'Dates', the café trades under this name.

Mexican barman

Not seen in the sitcom, the barman is mentioned in 'Yesterday Never Comes'. He lives in the flat above the Trotters and gives Del a recipe for a drink called a tequila sunset.

'Miami Twice'

Part 1: 'The American Dream'

(Christmas Special 1991)

Original transmission: Tuesday 24 December 1991, 7.30 pm

Production dates: 14 and 15 December 1991

Original viewing figures: 17.7 million

Duration: 50 minutes

First repeat: Wednesday 29 April 1992, 8.00 pm

Subsequent repeats: 15/4/94, 29/12/98, 26/5/01, 19/7/02

CAST

Del Trotter	David Jason
Rodney Trotter	Nicholas Lyndhurst
Uncle Albert	Buster Merryfield
Raquel	Tessa Peake-Jones
Cassandra	Gwyneth Strong
Alan	Denis Lill
Pam	Wanda Ventham
Mickey	Patrick Murray
Vicar	Treva Etienne
Trigger	Roger Lloyd Pack
Boycie	John Challis
Marlene	Sue Holderness
Mike	Kenneth MacDonald
Denzil	Paul Barber
Sid	Roy Heather
Baby Tyler	Danny Rix
Baby Damien	Grant Stevens

Richard Branson . . . . .Himself

Walk-ons: . . . .(Barmaid) Sandra Tavernier. (People in pub) Lewis St Juste, Piers Gielgud, Alexander Fodor, Simi Russ, Gladness Nkosi, Vicki Collins, Lesley Guinn, Peggy Ann Fraser, Alexander De Quince, Joy Roston, Steve Little, Kim Dare, Zoe Walsham, Pat Worth, Beef Constantine, Mike Brown, Paul Joy, Jack Burns, Krissie Ducann, Natalie Tomlinson, Tina Olaloko, Tom Little, Inga Daly and Ricky Gallahad. (People in café) Luke Jinadu, Beef Constantine, Mike Brown, Paul Joy, Jack Burns, Baz Billington and Krissie Ducann. (Bag lady in café) Mimi Gale. (Flight passengers) Mike Wade, Colin Thomas, Alison McGuire, Chris Abbott, Pat Varley, Pat Le Clerc, Shirley English, Melita Clarke, Andrew Tyler, Lauren Dean and Danny Lade.

'Miami Twice'

Part 2: 'Oh to be in England'

(Christmas Special 1991)

Original transmission: Wednesday 25 December 1991, 3.10 pm

Production dates: 14 and 15 December 1991

Original viewing figures: 14.9 million

Duration: 95 minutes

First repeat: Saturday 9 May 1992, 6.25 pm

Subsequent repeats: 16/4/94, 30/12/98, 2/6/01

CAST

Del Trotter . . . . .David Jason
Rodney Trotter . . . . .Nicholas Lyndhurst
Uncle Albert . . . . .Buster Merryfield
Raquel . . . . .Tessa Peake-Jones
Cassandra . . . . .Gwyneth Strong
Boycie . . . . .John Challis
Marlene . . . . .Sue Holderness
Trigger . . . . .Roger Lloyd Pack
Mike .Kenneth MacDonald
Alan . . . . .Denis Lill
Mickey Pearce . . . . .Patrick Murray
Denzil . . . . .Paul Barber
Sid . . . . .Roy Heather
Baby Damien . . . . .Grant Stevens
Vicar .Treva Etienne
Barry Gibb . . . . .Himself
Francisco . . . . .Robert Escobar
Carlotti . . . . .Roger Pretto
Pauly .Raphael Gomez
Lurch .Dave Corey
Tony .Jay Amor
Mac .Willis Knickerbocker
Rico .Antoni Corone
Salvatore . . . . .Tom G. Kouchalakos
Also:
Alberto Vasquez . . . . .Mario Ernesto Sanchez
Jorge Herrera . . . . .Alfredo Alvarez Calderon
First police officer . . . . .John Archie Peak
Second police officer . . . . .Rob Stuart Fuller
Lady driver . . . . .Dee Dee Deering
First diner . . . . .Jeff Gillen
Second diner . . . . .Janice Tesh
News reporter . . . . .Renee Sweeney
Everglades ranger . . . . .D. L. Blakely
News cameraman and
sports voice-over . . . . .Damian Chuck
Tyler (child in USA) . . . . .Joshua Rosen

Cab driver . . . . .Jackie Davis
Others: . . . .(Driver and pilot) Billie J Mitchell. (Boat skipper and police voice on radio) Eric Loren. (Woman on plane and Tyler's voice) Sharon Mayer.
Walk-ons: . . . .(Builders at church) Mike Brown and Paul Joy. (Romanian lorry driver) Basil Patton. (Customers at The Nag's Head) Ricky Gallahad, John Clay, Natalie Tomlins, Alex Fodor, Inga Daly, Tom Little, Trevor P Wayland, Krissie Duncann, Garry Heath, William Kwatia, Danny Lane, Sandra Tavernier, Gladness Nkosi, Piers Gielgood, Nicole Jackson and Shirley Patterson. (Plane passengers) Godwin Ohajah, Kenneth Coombs, Susan Scott, Kristina Overton, Alison McGuire, Phillip Howells, Carole Careford, Albin Pahernik, Juliette St David, Greg Pichery, Selwyn Pitcher, Eric Edwards, V Obaseki, Spencer David, Lorence Ferdinand, Joe Wells, Colin Bourner, Nick Scott, Chris Underhill, Tony Starr, Julian Hudson, Taryn Dielle, Judy Duggan, Imran Shafi, David Larkin, Sue Paule, Nina Diamond, Vivienne Jay, Pearl Hawkes, Mavis Wright, Ziggy Williams, Jack Burns, Pat Varley, Colin Thomas, Pat Le Clerc, Shirley English, Melita Clarke, Trisha Clarke, Andrew Tyler, Lauren Dean, Scott Smith, Tina Olakoko, Norman Cleary, Chris Abbott, Jonathan Cann, Gary Dean, Rachel Llewelyn, Maureen Waters, Jean Frances and Thien Tran. (Hotel receptionist) Tasha Bertram. (Hotel Guests) David Edgell, Kit Hillier, Richard Westcott, Bobby Daniels, Harjit Singh, Cliff Obaseki, Kim Jackson, Noel Butler, Cynthia Powell and Rosemary Banks. (Virgin Atlantic stewardesses used in vision) Jackie Mundell, Britt Strong and Rebecca Woods. (USA stunt drivers) Ken Collins, Brady Michaels and Joe Hess.

PRODUCTION TEAM (for both instalments)

Written by John Sullivan
Title music arranged and conducted by Ronnie Hazlehurst composed and sung by John Sullivan
Audience Warm-up: . . . . .Jeff Stevenson
Graphic Designer: . . . . .Andy Carroll
Casting Adviser: . . . . .Judy Loe
Casting Director: . . . . .Dee Miller, CSA
Set Decorator: . . . . .Bryony Foster
Properties Buyer: . . . . .Chris Ferriday
Properties Master: . . . . .Charles Guanci, Jr
Production Operatives'
Supervisor: . . . . .Ray Jobling
2nd Assistant Director: . . . . . .Udanne Uditis
1st Assistant Director: . . . . . . .Ken Bruns
Location Manager: . . . . .Gail Bruns
Grip: .Scott Eberle
Lighting Gaffer: . . . . .Colonel Dave Harris
Focus Puller: . . . . .Courtney Goodwin
Business Manager (New York): .Robert J Easter
Production Secretary: . . . . .Katie Tyrrell
Assistant Floor Managers: . . . .Debbie Crofts
and Charles Whaley
Telecine Operator: . . . . .Dave Hawley
Lighting Director: . . . . .Ron Bristow
Studio Sound: . . . . .Tony Revell
Resources Coordinator: . . . . . .Peter Manuel
Camera Supervisor: . . . . .Peter Goldring
Vision Mixer: . . . . .Heather Gilder
Videotape Editor: . . . . .Chris Wadsworth
Dubbing Editors: . . . . .Kevin Ahern, Glenn Hyde
and Richard Rhys Davies
Dubbing Mixers: . . . . .Peter Hodges, Keith Marriner
and Lee Taylor
Make-up Designer: . . . . .Christine Greenwood

Assitant Costume Designer: . . .Leslie Eve Herman
Costume Designer: . . . . .Robin Stubbs
Production Assistants: . . . . .Gail Evans and Tracey Gillham
Music Producer: . . . . .Jez Coed
Music by . . . . .The Gutter Brothers
Sound Recordist: . . . . .Michael Spencer
Production Managers: . . . . .Angela de Chastelai Smith
and Sue Longstaff
Assistant Film Editor: . . . . .Simon Price
Film Editors: . . . . .John Jarvis and John Dunstan
Photography: . . . . .John Rhodes
Film Sound: . . . . .John Parry and Steve Gatland
Film Camera: . . . . .John Walker BSC and Alec Curtis
Designer: . . . . .Richard McManan-Smith
Executive Producer: . . . . .John Sullivan
Directed by Tony Dow and Gareth Gwenlan
Produced by Gareth Gwenlan

It's Damien Trotter's christening, but business doesn't even stop on this special occasion as Del puts together a deal with the vicar to distribute pre-blessed wine – imported from Romania – to churches around the country.

Rodney's life is still up in the air and, on the advice of a Relate councillor, he's living with Del and Raquel during the week, then returning to his wife at weekends in the hope that gently easing himself back into her life will help patch up their marital differences.

As usual, Del can't help interfering in Rodney's life and when he sees a 'two for one' holiday to Miami for £250, he suggests Rodney whisks Cassandra off on a long overdue break. But he has an ulterior motive for showing such unusual signs of thoughtfulness: he already knows Cassandra won't be able to make it due to a banking conference, leaving the door open for him to accompany his brother across the Atlantic. His devious plan works.

Out in Miami, all is going well for the Trotter boys until a Mafia family spot a striking resemblance between Del and their father, who's awaiting trial for numerous heinous crimes. This sets a cunning scheme in motion to swap their father with Del and then arrange for his murder, resulting in the subsequent abandonment of Vincenzo Occhetti's trial. Del, however, seems to have a guardian angel watching over him on the trip because all the attempts on his life fail.

Meanwhile, back at The Nag's Head everyone is oblivious to their plight and therefore shocked when they hear a TV news report about America's most notorious gangster and find it's none other than Del's mug which appears on the box.

After days of believing they're just being shown good old-fashioned American hospitality, Rodney and Del eventually get wise to the plot and desperately try to escape the clutches of the gang. They make it to the Everglades National Park only to be confronted by an angry looking alligator. But help is soon at hand in the shape of Boycie, Marlene and Baby Tyler, who are on the second leg of their American holiday.

Relieved to be back home, the Trotters unlock the door to their flat to find it packed to the rafters with crates of rejected Romanian plonk. Del's plan to sell the drink to the Church has turned sour because white wine is unsuitable for Holy Communion!

Michaels, Christina
Roles: Programme seller and Woman at window
Appeared as Programme seller in 'A Royal Flush' and as Woman at window in 'Ashes to Ashes'
Born in Hertfordshire in 1936, Christina was a clerical worker before turning to acting in the early 1960s, making her debut as a background artiste in *The Benny Hill Show*. Most of her early work concentrated on television, and one of her favourite roles was playing a barmaid in the first series of *The Likely Lads*. Other small-screen appearances include *Just Good Friends*, one of her last appearances in that medium.

Michelle
Played by Caroline Ellis
Seen in 'Go West Young Man', Michelle is one of the two girls Del and Rodney chat up in a nightclub. She shares a flat in Chelsea with her friend Nicky, and plans to meet up with the boys the following Friday. Even though they supply their phone number, it's the last we see of them because Rodney loses the number, which was written on Del's cigar box, when he throws the box out of the car window by mistake.

Michelle
Played by Paula-Ann Bland
Seen in 'Rodney Come Home', Michelle – who prefers filing her nails to secretarial duties – is Rodney's secretary when he works for Alan Parry. She's new to the company and won't survive long if she doesn't alter her attitude.

Mick
Played by Nick Maloney
Mick lives in the same tower block as the Trotters and is awoken by a drunken Del when he returns home at 2.30am during 'Fatal Extraction'.

Mickey
(See 'Pearce, Mickey')

Midwife
(See 'McCullum, Mr')

Miguel
Played by Ronald Murray
In 'Fatal Extraction', Miguel is the non-speaking barman at The 121 Club.

Mike
Not seen in the sitcom, Mike is mentioned by Rodney in 'Go West Young Man'. He's supposed to be one of Rodney's friends at evening class, whom he often socialises with in the West End.

Mike (The landlord)
(See 'Fisher, Mike')

Miles, Mrs
Played by Kate Williams
Mrs Miles works as a cook at the Duke of Maylebury's country home in Berkshire. She's seen in 'A Royal Flush' when she cooks a meal for Uncle Albert.

Miller, Dee
Casting director on two episodes: 'Miami Twice' (Parts 1 & 2) Other productions Dee has helped cast include *The Heavenly Kid*, *The New Kids*, *Whoops Apocalypse*, *Rumpole's Return*, *Spring Break*, *Police Academy 5* and *Wrestling Ernest Hemingway*.

Mills, Jumbo
Played by Nick Stringer
First seen at The Nag's Head in 'Who Wants to be a Millionaire', Jumbo is one of the 'old gang' and used to be Del's partner before emigrating to Australia in 1967. Now a successful businessman, he knows a good investment when he sees one, but his Achilles' heel is his lack of ability in the PR field: he annoys everyone in sight. His rather flash personality and appearance see him dripping in gold jewellery, wearing garish clothes and having one of the loudest mouths around.

Jumbo has returned to his birthplace to buy some cars from Boycie, but as well as moving into the auto trade, he's also a major shareholder in an office-cleaning company and owns a chain of fast-food restaurants. He's become a success and has rewarded himself with an apartment overlooking Sydney Harbour. Mills wants Del to come into partnership with him again, fronting his business in Australia, importing prestige European cars. This once-in-a-lifetime offer is very appealing to Del but he eventually declines his friend's proposal when Rodney – who was going to tag along with him – is refused a permit due to his criminal record.

Del talks about Jumbo again in 'The Jolly Boys' Outing', when he tells Rodney about the time they set up a seafood stall outside The Nag's Head. They called their business Eels on Wheels and had big plans, but never made much money, partly due to a scathing report they received from the health inspector.

'Miracle of Peckham, The'
Original transmission: Sunday 7 September 1986, 8.35 pm
Original viewing figures: 14.2 million
Duration: 30 minutes
First repeat: Thursday 17th September 1987, 8.30 pm
Subsequent repeats: 2/7/89, 6/3/98, 15/11/00

CAST
Del Trotter . . . . .David Jason
Rodney Trotter . . . . .Nicholas Lyndhurst
Uncle Albert . . . . .Buster Merryfield
Father O'Keith . . . . .P G Stephens
Biffo .John Pierce Jones
Australian reporter . . . . .Peter Wickham
American reporter . . . . .Carol Cleveland
Man in the church . . . . .James Richardson

PRODUCTION TEAM
Written by John Sullivan
Title music arranged and conducted by Ronnie Hazlehurst composed and sung by John Sullivan
Make-up Designer: . . . . .Elaine Smith
Costume Designer: . . . . .Robin Stubbs
Properties Buyer: . . . . .Maura Laverty
Film Cameraman: . . . . .Chris Seager
Film Sound: . . . . .Dave Brabants
Film Editor: . . . . .John Jarvis
Camera Supervisor: . . . . .Ken Major
Studio Lighting Director: . . . . .Henry Barber
Studio Sound: . . . . .Anthony Philpot
Technical Coordinator: . . . . . . .Nick Moore
Videotape Editor: . . . . .Graham Taylor
Production Assistants: . . . . . . .Rowena Painter
                                        and Alexandra Todd
Assistant Floor Manager: . . . . .Adrian Pegg
Graphic Designer: . . . . .Andrew Smee
Vision Mixer: . . . . .Heather Gilder
Production Manager: . . . . .Sue Longstaff
Designer: . . . . .Mark Sevant
Directed by Mandie Fletcher
Produced by Ray Butt

Del makes a rare visit to the confession box and discovers St Mary's, the local hospice, is becoming dilapidated, and unless a further £185,000 can be raised, the place will close. As a result, all the sick and old people who rely on the services offered by the hospice will be left to fend for

'The Miracle of Peckham'

PRODUCTION TEAM

Written by John Sullivan
Title music arranged and conducted by Ronnie Hazlehurst
composed and sung by John Sullivan
Music: .Graham Jarvis
Audience Warm-up: . . . . .Bobby Bragg
Make-up Designer: . . . . .Deanne Turner
Costume Designer: . . . . .Robin Stubbs
Properties Buyer: . . . . .Graham Bishop
Art Director: . . . . .Nick Harding
Casting Adviser: . . . . .Judy Loe
Programme Finance Assistant . .Alison Passey
Film Sound: . . . . .Roger Long
Film Editor: . . . . .John Jarvis
Camera Supervisor: . . . . .Peter Woodley
Lighting Director: . . . . .Graham Rimmington
Studio Sound: . . . . .Keith Gunn
Studio Resource Manager: . . .Richard Morgan
Grips: . . . . .Iain Johnstone
Gaffer: . . . . .Pat Deveney
1st Assistant Director: . . . . . . .David Reid
2nd Assistant Director: . . . . . .Dominic Bowles
3rd Assistant Director: . . . . . . .Anna Brabbins
Dubbing Editor: . . . . .Paul Bingley
Photography: . . . . .John Rhodes
Location Managers: . . . . .Lisa McArthur and
Steve Abrahams
Videotape Editor: . . . . .Chris Wadsworth
Stunt Coordinator: . . . . .Nick Powell
Production Assistant: . . . . .Caroline Gardener
Assistant Floor Manager: . . . .Beccy Fawcett
Floor Manager: . . . . .Vivien Ackland-Snow
Vision Mixer: . . . . .Hilary Briegel
Production Manager: . . . . .Andy Smith
Production Secretary: . . . . . . .Katie Wilkinson
Production Designer: . . . . .Donal Woods
Associate Producer: . . . . .Sue Longstaff
Executive Producer: . . . . .John Sullivan
Produced by Gareth Gwenlan
Directed by Tony Dow

MEMORIES OF 'THE MIRACLE OF PECKHAM'

★ ★ ★ ★ ★

'I had a fantastic time working on this episode. We used two churches in the end, one in Blackfriars, the other near the Blackwall Tunnel, where we actually built a false roof, enabling us to look up through the belfry to reveal that the lead had been nicked.

'During filming we found out that one of the churches wasn't deconsecrated. It had needed bringing back to life a little, so we had hired in the confessional, cleaned the church up and redressed it. Then, at the last minute, the director had felt it looked *too* clean so we had had to dirty it down a little. After the filming had been completed we suddenly received a letter from someone high up in the Church complaining about how disrespectful we'd been to a functioning church. In the end, I had to find some good French polishers to visit the church and bring it back to its original state. But I have fond memories of this episode because I feel we were able to create the atmosphere of a softly lit church.'   **MARK SEVANT – Designer**

themselves. As the staff at the hospice nursed Del's mother and grandad, he takes the matter seriously.

Later, when it's rumoured that the church's statue of the Virgin Mary and Child is weeping, Del suggests that this fantastic opportunity should be exploited to help raise the money needed to save the hospice.

It's not long before the national press and television are poised, waiting for the tears to fall, and Del is lapping up all the attention. But then the true source of the tears comes to light.

Mitchell, Christopher

Role: PC Hoskins
Appeared in S3 episode 5 and 'To Hull and Back'

The late Christopher Mitchell, who was born in 1947, is probably best remembered for his time playing Gunner Parkin in Perry and Croft's sitcom *It Ain't Half Hot, Mum*. However, other television work included playing Simms in an episode of *The Professionals*, while his film credits contain such productions as *Here We Go Round the Mulberry Bush, A Promise of Bed, The Sex Thief* and *What's Up Superdoc?*, in which he played Dr Todd.

Mockford, Jeanne

Role: Woman in kiosk
Appeared in S5, episode 3

London-born Jeanne worked in a bank for 18 months before joining RADA. Her first job was in a tour of *St Joan*, followed by stints at various reps, including Manchester, Liverpool, Oldham and Bath.

She made her TV debut in the 1950s before appearances in numerous shows such as *Up Pompeii!, Dixon of Dock Green, Angels, The Liver Birds, Hi-De-Hi!, Dear John* and *Last of the Summer Wine*. Nowadays she mostly works in the theatre, her preferred medium.

'Modern Men'

(Second part of the 1996 Christmas Trilogy)

Original transmission: Friday 27 December 1996, 8.00 pm
Original viewing figures: 21.3 million
Duration: 60 minutes
First repeat: Friday 16 January 1998, 8.00 pm
Subsequent repeats: 24/9/99, 29/6/01, 19/2/02

CAST

Del . . . . .David Jason
Rodney . . . . .Nicholas Lyndhurst
Uncle Albert . . . . .Buster Merryfield
Raquel . . . . .Tessa Peake-Jones
Cassandra . . . . .Gwyneth Strong
Trigger . . . . .Roger Lloyd Pack
Mike .Kenneth MacDonald
Boycie . . . . .John Challis
Marlene . . . . .Sue Holderness
Denzil . . . . .Paul Barber
Sid . . . . .Roy Heather
Dr Singh . . . . .Bhasker Patel
Damien . . . . .Jamie Smith
Mickey Pearce . . . . .Patrick Murray
Man in hospital . . . . .Phil Cornwell
Stunt double for
Man in hospital . . . . .Ray Nicholas
Sister . . . . .Beverley Hills
Doctor . . . . .James Olver
Nurse . . . . .Corinne Britton
Receptionist . . . . .Lorraine Ashley
Walk-ons: . . . .(The Nag's Head) Rachel Adamson, Gail Abbott, Carol Desmond, Maggie Mitchell, David Bradley, Ray Brook, Harry Holland, Bill Farrow, Adam Russ, Lee Bevan, Matthew Barney, Teddy Massiah, Pat Shepherd, Lorna Sinclair, Lewis St. Juste, Patricia Goode, Ramona Joseph, Beverley Jennings, Katy Jarratt, Jack Street, Yvonne Stroud. (Sid's Café) Jorge Borrios Silva, Adrian Coke, Colin Johnson, James Crooks, Melvyn Campbell, Jane Stevens, Don Board, Jamie Greaves, James Anderson, Tony Baylis, Kit Edwards, Andrew Bell, Lee Benson, Tom Walker, Winnie Crooks, Cosmo Crooks and Lloyd McIntosh. (Hospital) Prince Green, Sharon Dean, Peter Yakoob, Johnson Yakoob, Miriam Humphries, Hector Eugene, Eric McCarthy, Wayne McLean, Binda Singh, Roselle Gowan, Claire Rhodes, Nichola Beer, Michael Booth, Dainton Bowner, Stephen Hirst, Nick Tregoning, Eric Bottomley, Jaskarn Sanhera, Marie Paramour, Susan Bentley, Kay Zimmerman, Ian Adamson, Gary O'Brien, Bobby Civil, Sarah O'Keefe, Norman Blezard, Simon Lewis, Joy Johnson, Norma Blezard, Margo Lawrence Greene, Rose Croom Johnson, Ian Sorley, Derek Parkes,

Del's flavour of the week is a book called 'Modern Men', which tells him all he needs to know about being positive and decisive, and wooing women – not that he feels he requires any advice in this area. Though if the way he tries flattering Raquel when she dresses up to celebrate the news of Rodney and Cassandra's baby is anything to go by, he needs as much guidance as possible!

Now that the baby is on the way, Rodney wants more responsibility; he's also concerned that since reading his book, Del is making too many rash decisions. Feeling his future lies elsewhere, Rodney

'Modern Men'

applies for another job, unaware that Del has placed the advert in an attempt to find some help for Rodney, who he realises will need time off shortly to be beside his wife.

Del's rash decisions aren't only confined to business: he now thinks it's his duty as a man to have a vasectomy; he's stuck on the idea until he experiences a nightmare about Dr Singh, who's been chasing him around Peckham concerning some dodgy paint, being the surgeon to perform the operation. And with the size of the injection almost bringing tears to his eyes, Del decides that perhaps he's being just a little too hasty.

Before the day is out, Del has to provide a shoulder for his brother to cry on, when Rodney receives a call from the local hospital informing him that Cassandra has been rushed in suffering a miscarriage. His dreams of fatherhood are shattered; stunned and upset he heads for the hospital, together with Del. Unsure what he can say to his devastated wife, Rodney turns to Del, who advises him to show a stiff upper lip and give Cassandra all the support she deserves. Being strong for Cassandra is difficult for Rodney, though, especially when Del ends up blubbering all over the place.

Monica

An unseen girlfriend of Rodney's, Monica is mentioned in 'Go West Young Man' and is described as a 'little tart with fat thighs' by Del. Rodney has only known her two weeks when the relationship hits troubled waters, partly because Rodney's fetish for women in uniform sees him splashing out on a policewoman's uniform for her. Foolishly taking Mickey Pearce's advice, Rodney and Monica agree on a two-week trial separation – within days she's dancing the night away at The Nag's Head disco with none other than Peckham's agony uncle, Mr Pearce.

Monique

Del's ex-girlfriend Monique is mentioned by Rodney in 'Dates'. When Del is angry upon seeing his new love, Raquel, turn up at The Nag's Head as a stripagram, Rodney tries calming him down by referring to Monique, reminding him that she went around wearing next to nothing, too. But Del points out that she was a lifeguard.

Monk

We never see Monk, but Del speaks to him on the phone and persuades him to take his Kandy Dolls during 'It's Only Rock and Roll'.

Mont Chernobyl Champagne

From the vineyards of the Ukraine, the champagne is bought by Del to celebrate Cassandra's pregnancy in 'Modern Men'. Sadly, she loses the baby.

Monte Carlo Club, The

A rough nightclub in New Cross, The Monte Carlo Club is described as all 'tinsel and tat, the kind of place that looks good with the lights out'. Bored stiff with Christmas, Rodney suggests to Del that they drive over there for the evening in 'Christmas Crackers'. Initially, Del is against the idea, but when Grandad decides to head over to the local community centre, he takes Rodney up on his offer.

Moore, Nick

Technical coordinator on six episodes: S5

★ ★ ★ CUT SCENE! CUT SCENE! ★ ★ ★

CUT FROM 'MODERN MEN'

AFTER CASSANDRA LOSES THE BABY.

ALB I know how they're feeling.

DEL I don't think you do, Unc.

ALB I do, Del. Years ago the same thing happened to me. So I know how young Rodney and Cassandra are feeling.

DEL Is that when you were married to Aunt Ada?

ALB Yeah.

DEL I'm sorry, Albert. I didn't know. I'm really sorry.

ALB Long time ago, son.

DEL You never said anything about it.

ALB Oh, you know me, Del, I don't like talking about the past.

DEL Is that what broke you and Ada up?

ALB No, son. But it would have if she'd found out about it!

DEL What, it weren't Aunt Ada?

ALB No, it was some woman I met in Honolulu. Long time ago, boy, and ain't worth talking about.

Moran, Angela

Role: Woman in market (Gwen)

Appeared in 'The Frog's Legacy'

After graduating from the Guildhall School of Music and Drama, Angela – who was born in Warwickshire in 1943 – began her career as an opera singer, before making her debut as an actress in 1979's *A Little Night Music*.

She had worked in various repertory theatres, including Birmingham and Chester, when her first TV role (Mrs Fiorelli in *The Fear*) came along. Other appearances on the small screen include Liz in *No Place Like Home*, Rose Lincoln in *The Practice*, several characters in *The Bill* and her favourite, Maria in *Forever Green*.

On the stage, her numerous appearances have seen her play Violet in *Steaming*, Sheila in *Relatively Speaking*, Sybil Berling in *An Inspector Calls*, Miss Bourne in *The Ghost Train* and Maggie in *Inner City Jam* amongst others.

Moreno, John

Role: Enrico

Appeared in 'Diamonds are for Heather'

John was born in 1939, and trained at the Strasbourg in France. He took part in amateur dra-matics from the age of 12, then spent his early career in repertory companies, including Margate, Plymouth, Newcastle and Sunderland. In 1963, he appeared at the Mermaid Theatre in *Eastward Ho*.

John had appeared in two films before any tele-vision work came his way. He's since worked on a range of programmes, such as *The Troubleshooters, Out of the Blue, Darling Buds of May, Northern Lights, The Saint, Squadron* and *The Sweeney*. His favourite role was a leading part in the series *Kessler*, for the BBC.

His work on the big screen includes *Chimes at Midnight* with Orson Wells, and the James Bond movie, *For Your Eyes Only*.

Nowadays, John – who's an Equity registered fight director – teaches stage fighting in drama schools across Europe, as well as stage fighting for the theatre in Madrid and Vienna.

Morgan, Richard

Studio resource manager on three episodes: 'Heroes and Villains', 'Modern Men' and 'Time On Our Hands'

Morris, Dave

Properties buyer on one episode: 'To Hull and Back'

Dave, who was born in London, worked at Pearl Insurance for a year before securing a job as a clerk with the BBC. He returned to the post after com-pleting national service, thus beginning a 37-year career with the Beeb.

He moved to the props department in 1956 and over the years worked on numerous shows, including *When the Boat Comes In, The Singing Detective, Love in a Cold Climate* and *Wives and Daughters*. He's been freelancing since being made redundant and one of his recent work projects was *The Lonely Years*, an independent production for the BBC.

Morris, Lennie

Not seen in the sitcom, Lennie Morris is father to the child whose Christening Del attends during 'Diamonds are for Heather'. The occasion makes Del realise how much he misses not having a family of his own.

Mort, Ray

Role: Policeman

Appeared in S3, episode 3

Ray, who died in 1994, was a regular face on televi-sion. Among his credits are appearances as Bernard Driscoll in *The Sweeney*, a fisherman in *The Good*

Life, Mr Wiggins in *All Creatures Great and Small*, George in *Duty Free*, Campie in *Lovejoy*, Gerry Thompson in *Sounding Brass* and Raggles in the 1987 mini-series *Vanity Fair*.

Morton, Anthony

Role: Louis Lombardi (the pet shop owner)
Appeared in S3, episode 7

Morton, Bill

Vision mixer on six episodes: S2, episodes 1, 2 & 4; S6, episodes 5 & 6; 'A Royal Flush'

Born in Reading, Bill grew up in Edinburgh, where he became interested in amateur theatre. After national service he worked for a printing firm in the city, but quit his job to join a touring theatre revue company, the Fol-de-Rols, as assistant stage manager. It was there he met his future wife Julie, who was a dancer with the show.

In 1964 they married and Bill had become resident Stage Director at the Alexandra Theatre in Birmingham, also playing minor roles in rep and pantomime.

In 1966 he and Julie moved to London where Bill joined BBC Television as an assistant floor manager and after two years transferred to vision mixing. During his years with the BBC he was the vision mixer on many classic programmes, such as *Monty Python's Flying Circus*, *The Good Life*, *Fawlty Towers* and of course *Only Fools and Horses*. By the time he left the BBC in 1989 he'd also had his first taste of directing, including *Bob's Full House* and *Noel Edmonds' Christmas Show*.

As a freelance director he's worked for the last ten years with Bruce Forsyth on *The Generation Game*, *Play Your Cards Right* and *The Price is Right*. Other directing credits include *Rolf's Amazing World of Animals*, *Denis Norden's Laughter Files* and *The BAFTA Awards*.

'Mother Nature's Son'

(Christmas Special 1992)

Original transmission: Friday 25 December 1992, 6.55 pm

Production date: Sunday 20 December 1992

Original viewing figures: 20.1 million

Duration: 65 minutes

First repeat: Saturday 9 January 1999, 9.00 pm

Subsequent repeat: 8/6/01

CAST

Del Trotter	David Jason
Rodney Trotter	Nicholas Lyndhurst
Uncle Albert	Buster Merryfield
Raquel	Tessa Peake-Jones
Cassandra	Gwyneth Strong
Denzil	Paul Barber
Boycie	John Challis
Myles	Robert Glenister
Marlene	Sue Holderness
Mike	Kenneth MacDonald
Trigger	Roger Lloyd Pack
Damien	Robert Liddement
Alan Parry	Denis Lill
Chris	Tony Marhsall
Mickey Pearce	Patrick Murray
Pamela Parry	Wanda Ventham
Newscaster	Richard Whitmore (voice only)

PRODUCTION TEAM

Written by John Sullivan	
Title music arranged and conducted by Ronnie Hazlehurst composed and sung by John Sullivan	
Additional Music:	Clever Music
Audience Warm-up:	Denny Hodge
Make-up Designer:	Christine Greenwood
Costume Designer:	Robin Stubbs
Properties Buyer:	Malcolm Rougvie
Casting Adviser:	Judy Loe
Film Cameraman:	John Rhodes
Film Sound:	Michael Spencer
Film Editor:	John Jarvis
Dubbing Mixer:	Aad Wirtz
Dubbing Editor:	Graham Bevan
Camera Supervisor:	Gerry Tivers
Studio Lighting Director:	Don Babbage
Studio Sound:	Alan Machin
Resources Coordinator:	Michael Langley-Evans
Videotape Editor:	Chris Wadsworth
Production Assistant:	Amita Lochab

THE ROLE OF VISION MIXER

★ ★ ★ ★ ★ ★

'In simple terms, a vision mixer's job is to switch the pictures on a television screen from one source to another, in accordance with the programme director's intention. This bald description belies the complexity of a job that is part technical and part artistic. Nowadays, with the technical advances in electronics, many programmes that were previously made in studios, particularly dramas, are now shot on location with single cameras, but a vision mixer works with a multi-camera studio or outside broadcast.

'In the Control Room, or Gallery, the vision mixer operates a control panel (also called a vision mixer) of buttons, faders, switches and electronic effects, in order to switch or dissolve between any number of incoming sources to produce a single output on your television screen at home. The control room has a bank of television monitors showing all the vision sources available to the production. These picture sources can range from just two cameras, as on the *EastEnders* lot, to 42 cameras on a major outside broadcast, plus many other incoming pictures, such as film and pre-recorded tape inserts, other outside broadcasts, graphics, still captions, computer animations and so on. So a vision mixer must have eyes everywhere, as all these sources must be previewed to make sure they are ready, before they are cut up "on air".

'On unscripted programmes, the vision mixer will work either to verbal instructions from the director, or have freedom to cut the pictures within a framework of shots planned by the director as the action proceeds. On scripted programmes, the director will have prepared a camera script, with his preferred shots marked against the dialogue. With these programmes, the performers and technical crews will have the opportunity of a short period of rehearsal together, before committing the show to tape. This is particularly important with situation comedy, such as *Only Fools and Horses*, which uses five or six cameras in the studio, as the cameramen and vision mixer must get on the same wavelength as the director and the actors, so that the technical coverage compliments the performance.

'The one thing that sets light entertainment shows apart from other forms of television output is the presence of an audience in the studio. This is an important aspect of television comedy, as the actors need the laughs and reaction of a live audience to enhance their performance. With a show like *Only Fools and Horses* you can predict to a certain extent, from the script, how and where an audience will react, but until the performance takes place, you cannot be entirely sure. It's always said that the secret of good comedy is timing, and the timing that has been rehearsed may not entirely work on the night. Comedy actors will subtly change their performance and timing to suit the reaction they are getting from the audience, and the vision mixer must be aware of this and change his cutting points accordingly. We are talking of fractions of a second here, because in any one second of time there are 25 places to make a cut. It's possible to kill a joke stone dead by cutting in the wrong place, so this puts the vision mixer in the unique position of being the bridge between the skill of the performer and their television audience.

'The cast of *Only Fools and Horses*, led by David Jason and Nicholas Lyndhurst, are a hugely talented team and for them, and the technical crew, every performance is a first night, because, unlike a stage performance, they have only one opportunity to get it right. Certainly, with today's sophisticated editing techniques, retakes can be done and repairs made, but the first time an audience sees a performance is when they laugh best. Once they have seen the joke, they will never react so well a second time and the spontaneity can be lost. A film or videotape editor has the opportunity to rehearse his cuts and adjust them as many times as he wishes, before making the final decision, but the vision mixer in a situation comedy does not have that facility and must make his or her decisions instantly as the performance proceeds.

'The important thing about the job is to ensure the smooth continuity of the visual narrative and the secret of the success of their work is that it's never noticed.'

BILL MORTON – Vision mixer

Assistant Floor Manager: . . . . .Jenny Penrose
Location Manager: . . . . .Susannah Bartlett
Vision Mixer: . . . . .Heather Gilder
Production Manager: . . . . .Sue Longstaff
Designer: . . . . .Donal Woods
Executive Producer: . . . . .John Sullivan
Directed by Tony Dow
Produced by Gareth Gwenlan

It's a year after the Trotters' brush with the Miami Mafia, Cassandra has finally got her promotion, Raquel has got post-natal depression and Del and Rodney are stressed out at having no money.

Del seems to have lost his motivation for business and when Rodney confronts him to find out why, it seems a long-forgotten application to buy his council flat in Nelson Mandela House has finally been approved, leaving Del with a mortgage to pay which is double the rent: he needs to find a quick route to some dosh. To make matters worse, he's receives a summons to clear out his late Grandad's allotment, which has become a health hazard. Reluctantly, Del accepts his duties and sets about clearing up the mess. He unearths some hazardous-looking drums of yellow liquid which,with the help of Trigger and Denzil, are disposed of during the night.

Meanwhile, Rodney tells Del about one of his old friends who's made millions opening a chain of organic food shops, and a trip to one of the shops sparks off an idea in Del's devious mind. Noticing the exorbitant prices of the spring water, Del manages to convince Myles, who's vice-president of SWANS (Spa Water and Natural Spring Committee) that he's discovered a natural spring on his allotment, and with his newly acquired certificate of purity in his pocket, he starts marketing Peckham Spring Water.

Such is the demand for the spring water that there is soon a mini-industry taking shape inside the Trotters' abode; little do people know that Del's major discovery is none other than tap water, which explains why the water board believe there is a major pipe leak because so much water is being drawn off in the area.

At last the Trotters have some spare cash in their pockets, and Raquel, being in the money, is soon being invited along to Marlene's coffee mornings. Cassandra suggests a weekend away with Rodney to unwind, but Del jumps on the bandwagon and is quick to invite himself and Raquel on the trip to Brighton; he even books connecting rooms. Both couples are set for a romantic night in when news breaks that there has been a major contamination of water back home because drums, looking suspiciously like those that Del disposed of, are pulled from the local reservoir.

Mottley, Eva

Role: Corinne
Appeared in S3, episode 7

Eva, who was born in Barbados, became a familiar face on television playing Bella O'Reilly in the hit ITV drama *Widows*, by which time she'd already

appeared in several shows, including *Bergerac*. The same year as appearing in *Widows*, she was seen in the movie *Scrubbers*, playing Pam.

Eva would, undoubtedly, have made further appearances as Denzil's wife but for her tragic death after a drugs overdose in Miami in 1985.

Mountbatten House

Rodney mentions Mountbatten House in 'Yuppy Love' when he reminds Del of the time he sent his younger brother there to sell DIY gas conversion kits. North Sea Oil had been introduced to the area, but the property was all electric.

Murphy, Mrs

Played by Lucita Lijertwood

Mrs Murphy, who lives in the same block of flats as the Trotters, is first mentioned in 'Healthy Competition', when Del tells Grandad he's finally managed to sell some technicolour woollen tea cosies. With Mrs Murphy's help, all the holes were stitched up and he managed to sell them to the West Indian lads down at the youth centre.

Her first appearance is in 'Yesterday Never Comes', when we see her coming out of a lift. Albert mentions her again in 'Fatal Extraction', because she told him the police had gone to get their horses to help control the riot which had started outside Nelson Mandela House, thanks to Del.

Murphy, Sheree

Role: Dawn
Appeared in 'Heroes and Villains'

Sheree, who was born in London in 1975, trained at the Sylvia Young Theatre School. She made her stage debut at the age of 11 in a musical, *The Rink*, at London's Cambridge Theatre, while her first screen role was Florrie, a nanny in BBC's costume drama *Berkeley Square*. At present, Sheree is a regular in *Emmerdale*, playing Trisha Fisher.

Murray, Patrick

Role: Mickey Pearce

Appeared in 18 episodes: S3, episodes 2 & 6; S4, episodes 1 & 6; S5, episode 5; S6, episode 1, 5 & 6; 'Dates'; 'The Jolly Boys' Outing'; 'Rodney Come Home'; 'Miami Twice' (Parts 1 & 2); 'Mother Nature's Son'; 'Fatal Extraction'; 'Modern Men'; 'Time On Our Hands' and 'If They Could See Us Now…!'

Born in Greenwich, London, in 1956, Patrick's appearance in a Pizza Hut advert caught the eye of John Sullivan, who invited him to audition for the part of Mickey Pearce, who was finally brought to life on screen after being mentioned in the scripts on many previous occasions.

Patrick took his first steps towards an acting career when, at the age of 15, he noticed a theatrical agency advertising in a daily paper. Within a week of registering with the agency, he was appearing in a play, marking the beginning of a busy work period.

As well as playing Mickey Pearce, other television credits include Johnny in *New Scotland Yard*, Blackie in *Keep It In the Family* and appearances in shows like *The Bill*, *The Upper Hand* and *Hale and Pace*. He's also been seen in a few films, such as *The Class of Miss MacMichael*, *Breaking Glass*, *The Curse of the Pink Panther* and a leading role in *Scum*.

Murray, Ronald

Role: Miguel
Appeared in 'Fatal Extraction'

Mustapha

Del mentions Mustapha during 'Three Men, a Woman and a Baby', but he is never seen. He works in the Bangladeshi butcher's shop and has a nephew who works for a top West End wigmaker. Del buys a box of seconds from the company, with the intention of selling them to all the 'old tarts' down The Nag's Head.

Mutimer, Tony

Technical coordinator on seven episodes: S4

Born in London in 1948, Tony joined the BBC in 1967, working as an engineer before joining the operational department as a technical coordinator. Shows he has worked on include *Grandstand*, *Sportsnight*, *EastEnders*, *A Very Peculiar Practice*, *Blue Peter*, *The Late Show*, *Call My Bluff*, *Wogan*, *Jim'll Fix It* and *That's Life*.

After 29 years with the Beeb, Tony left in 1997, and is now retired, although he occasionally carries out freelance work.

Myles

Played by Robert Glenister

During 'Mother Nature's Son', Del is depressed with his lot, so Rodney tells him how Myles – a dynamic, bright, go-ahead individual he met whilst attending evening classes a couple of years back – found a gap in the market. Keen on growing his own vegetables and very health conscious, he developed an idea for a centre where you could buy natural fertilizer and health foods. In two-and-a-half years he's become a millionaire who owns four centres, with another opening shortly in Maidenhead.

His company is called Nature's Way and Rodney ends up buying a few items there, which is when we first see the flat-capped Myles, who's also vice-president of SWANS (the Spa Water and Natural Spring Committee). When Del pretends to have discovered a natural spring in Peckham, Myles is so excited he gives a certificate of purity to Del, unaware that the water supply is coming straight from the tap!

Nag's Head, The

First seen in the opening episode, 'Big Brother', the pub is the Trotters' local hostelry. We don't discover who runs the pub until the third series, when we have the first sighting of Mike Fisher, the new incumbent landlord.

Built on the site of a public grave which contains victims of The Great Plague, the pub is the social hub of the district. With something for everyone, from Friday night's disco to special theme nights, it's the meeting place for the Trotters and their fellow market traders, as well as Boycie, Marlene, Trigger et al.

For the Trotters, it seems a day doesn't go by without them popping down The Nag's Head; although much of their private lives revolve around the pub, it's also the place where Del seals many of his business deals.

When Mike gets tangled up in embezzlement and is given a custodial sentence, the pub is handed over to Sid to take temporary charge in the landlord's absence.

Narduzzo, Michael

Dubbing mixer on six episodes: S7, episodes 1–3, 5 & 6 and 'Rodney Come Home'

Michael was born in Harpenden and worked in a music shop for a year before joining Cresswell Film Unit in Hemel Hempstead, which specialised in films for the oil industry. By 1976 he'd moved on to Universal Sound, a dubbing studio, where he gained his first experience as a dubbing mixer on documentaries and comedies, including the episodes of *Only Fools*.

Inside The Nag's Head

Nowadays he owns his own company, 5XP, and works freelance. Since September 2001 he's been working on the BBC's *Holby City*, based at Elstree Studios.

Nash, Hilary

Properties buyer on one episode: 'The Frog's Legacy'

Naval officer

Played by Martin Cochrane

In 'Dates', the naval officer gatecrashes Uncle Albert's birthday shindig at The Nag's Head. He arrives on the scene and pretends to arrest Albert for dereliction of duty in 1941, before introducing the stripagram, who's none other than Raquel.

Neighbour

Played by Linda James

In 'Rodney Come Home', the neighbour's voice is heard whilst Rodney and Del are talking outside the entrance to Rodney and Cassandra's block of flats. She reminds them that people are trying to sleep.

Nelson, Conrad

Role: Mike Wallace

Appeared in 'If They Could See Us Now…!'

Most of Conrad's recent work has been in the theatre, with roles including Benedick in *Much Ado About Nothing*, Edgar in *King Lear*, Mark in *A Passionate Woman*, Tom in *Mad And Her Dad* and Oedipus in *Omma* at the Young Vic Theatre. However, in 1999 he was seen in *Casualty*, playing Tony Williams, and in *The Bill*, as Greg Stanley.

Nelson Mandela House

The Trotters live on the 12th floor of the 26-floor flats in Peckham. Immediately above them is a Mexican barman, while in the flat below lives Mrs Obooko. The tower block is one of many on the Peckham estate.

Nelson, Ronnie

We never see Ronnie in the series, although he is mentioned several times. In 'Danger UXD', Del tells Rodney that Ronnie's gone up in the world. He once owned Ron's Cash and Carry but is now managing director of Advanced Electronics Research and Development Centre. In Del's opinion – for what it's worth – all the big business opportunities occur at the Research and Development Centre. He subsequently conducts some business with Nelson, buying 50 video recorders at £50 a time.

We hear of him again in 'Fatal Extraction': by now he owns The 121 Club, a casino Del frequents whilst trying to conduct his business: he's trying to put together a deal for 650 Russian army camcorders through one of the proprietor's other businesses, Nelson's TV and Video Company.

By 'Heroes and Villains', Del is considering whether to continue trading with Ronnie because the answerphone he supplied is playing up which meant Raquel's parents were unable to leave a message.

Nero

During 'A Slow Bus to Chingford', Del tries making out that Janice's corgi, Nero, is an ex-police dog. He wants Rodney to drive a tourist bus around London's ethnic sites during the day, even though he's already working as a night watchman at the local bus and coach garage. To help his younger brother get some much-needed shut-eye at the garage, thereby enabling him to drive the bus during the day, Del suggests employing Janice's corgi as a guard dog. Far from being a snarling, brute of an animal, Nero keeps Rodney up all night wanting to go 'walkies'.

Nerys

(See 'Sansom, Nerys')

Newark, Derek

Role: Eric (the policeman)

Appeared in S1, episode 6

Derek, who was born in Great Yarmouth in 1933, entered the industry late after having already enjoyed a varied career. He spent three years in the merchant navy before joining the army. After serving with the Coldstream Guards he spent time in Singapore during the Malayan emergency and ran a radio show there playing country and western records, giving him his first taste of the entertainment world. On his return to England he knew where his future lay and joined RADA.

As soon as he graduated he worked in rep for many years before television and film work came his way. Early credits included *Z Cars*, *Out of this World*, playing a mess sergeant in *Redcap*, a reporter in *Front Page Story*, *The Baron*, *Man in a Suitcase*, *The Avengers*, *The Saint*, *Callan*, *The Champions*, *Rising Damp*, *Department S*, *Jason King*, *Budgie*, *Doctor Who* and *Coronation Street*. He also appeared in several films, including *The Hill* and *Where Eagles Dare*.

He continued working in the theatre and the high point in his career came in the early 1980s when he was invited to join the National Theatre. He remained with the theatre for over a decade.

Derek died of a heart attack in 1998.

Newsreader

Played by Richard Whitmore

Former newscaster Richard Whitmore reads the news during 'The Sky's the Limit', informing viewers that a radar transmitter dish has been stolen from the end of Gatwick's primary runway.

Bronco supplied the dish to Del, who's horrified to hear the news.

He's later heard reading the news again in 'Mother Nature's Son', while the Trotters, Raquel and Cassandra spend a weekend in a top Brighton hotel. The news report tells of drums of chemicals found dumped in the local reservoir back home, the same drums as those recently removed from Del's allotment.

Nicky

Played by JoAnne Good

Nicky is one of the two girls Rodney and Del chat up in a West End disco during 'Go West Young Man'. It turns out they share a pad in Chelsea, and when they agree to meet up the following Friday, they write their phone number on Del's cigar box – only for Rodney to toss it out of the car window on the way home.

Nieradzik, Anushia

Costume designer on eight episodes: S2 and 'Diamonds are for Heather'

Anushia, who was born in Poland, came to England in the 1960s and went to boarding school, followed by art college, where she won an Art Council Award, enabling her to spend a year at the Young Vic.

Initially, she worked freelance on productions including *Ballroom of Romance*, then joined the BBC in the early 1980s. Anushia, who also paints and has her own studio in Hackney, remained with the Corporation for about ten years, before returning to freelance designing. Productions she's worked on over the years include *Middlemarch*, *Madame Bovary*, *Ghosts*, the feature film *Circle of Friends* and, more recently, *Lucky Jim* for ITV.

Nieradzik, Dorka

Make-up designer on one episode: 'The Jolly Boys' Outing'

Dorka is an experienced make-up, hair and visual effects designer who's worked extensively in films, television and the visual arts, including photographic shoots and commercials.

Trained at the BBC, she moved quickly through the ranks to become a make-up and hair designer, working on numerous productions, such as *Cold Comfort Farm*, *Circle of Friends* and *Karaoke*. She has received several BAFTA and Royal Television Society Awards. In 2000 she was presented with the BAFTA Special Award for outstanding creative contribution to film and television.

Now working freelance, assignments have taken

à la Del

★ ★ ★ ★ ★ ★

'Jeux sans frontières'

('The Yellow Peril')

her all over the world. Countries she's worked in include Brazil, Chile, France and Austria.

Night Nurse

This cheap home movie is made by Mickey Pearce in 'Video Nasty'. Its leading, and only, star is the punkette Amanda, whose nurse's attire and stockings and suspenders make it clear just what type of film Pearce is shooting.

Nine Elms, The

A hostelry mentioned by Del at Ridgemere Hall during the episode 'A Touch of Glass', The Nine Elms is frequented by many of the market boys.

'No Greater Love…'

Original transmission: Thursday 11 November 1982, 8.30 pm

Production date: Sunday 13 June 1982

Original viewing figures: 8.6 million

Duration: 30 minutes

First repeat: Tuesday 5 July 1983, 8.30 pm

Subsequent repeats: 9/11/90, 20/1/95, 24/6/97, 4/2/00

CAST

Del Trotter . . . . .David Jason
Rodney Trotter . . . . .Nicholas Lyndhurst
Grandad Trotter . . . . .Lennard Pearce
Irene Mackay . . . . .Gaye Brown
Julie (the barmaid) . . . . .Julie La Rousse
Marcus Mackay . . . . .Steve Fletcher
Ahmed . . . . .Raj Patel
Leroy . . . . .David Rhule
Tommy Mackay . . . . .David Daker
Zoe .Lisa Price
Walk-ons: . . . .(Police constable) Derek Chafer.
(People in pub) David Jessiman, Elaine Ford, Liz D'Esterre, Brian Braithwaite and nine extras.

PRODUCTION TEAM

Written by John Sullivan
Title music arranged and conducted by Ronnie Hazlehurst composed and sung by John Sullivan
Audience Warm-up: . . . . .Felix Bowness
Make-up Designer: . . . . .Shaunna Harrison
Costume Designer: . . . . .Anushia Nieradzik
Properties Buyer: . . . . .Roger Williams
Film Cameraman: . . . . .John Walker
Film Sound: . . . . .Dennis Panchen and Nigel Woodford
Film Editor: . . . . .Mike Jackson
Camera Supervisor: . . . . .Ron Peverall
Studio Lighting Director: . . . . .Henry Barber
Studio Sound: . . . . .Dave Thompson
Technical Coordinator: . . . . . .Derek Martin
Videotape Editor: . . . . .Mike Taylor
Production Assistant: . . . . .Penny Thompson

Assistant Floor Manager: . . . . .Tony Dow
Graphic Designers: . . . . .Peter Clayton and Fen Symonds
Vision Mixer: . . . . .Bill Morton
Production Managers: . . . . . . .Janet Bone and Sue Bysh
Designer: . . . . .Andy Dimond
Produced by Ray Butt

Rodney's in love again. This time he's fallen head over heels for an older woman: the 40-year-old Irene Mackay, whose hubby is serving time at Parkhurst. When she dumps him, he's heartbroken, although Del thinks it's for the best, seeing as her husband has just been released. When Rodney discovers that Del has been interfering in his love life again, he's livid. Worried about his little brother's well-being, bearing in mind Tommy Mackay's release, Del persuades Irene to ditch Rodney.

But a case of mistaken identity finds Del taken for Rodney when Tommy Mackay – aware the young Trotter has been entertaining his wife – arrives back on the streets. A violent altercation leaves him battle-scarred, but alive to find his fight has been in vain: Rodney has found a new love in his life.

Nomad cordless telephones

In 'From Prussia with Love', Del's latest sales drive sees him trying to flog boxes of damaged Nomad cordless telephones.

Norland, The

Mentioned in 'To Hull and Back', *The Norland* is the cross-channel ferry that travels between Hull and Zeebrugge.

Normand, Tania

Assistant floor manager on one episode: 'Fatal Extraction'

Norris, Lennie

In 'Time On Our Hands', the Trotters return to the flat in Nelson Mandela House just one final time. Whilst they're there, the phone rings: it's Lennie Norris, who hasn't heard that they've moved out; he's trying to flog 250 electronic carpet steamers and will let the Trotters have them for £25 each, even though they normally retail for £115. Del reluctantly informs him that TITCO has ceased trading.

Norris, Maggie

Role: Policewoman
Appeared in 'Dates'

After being born in Birmingham, Maggie's family headed for Nairobi, where her father worked as a missionary. They stayed two years before returning to the UK in 1961.

Upon leaving school, Maggie knew she wanted to become an actress and gained a degree in drama and dance. Her first job was a six-month assignment as an actress/musician for an acting company touring old-age pensioners' homes. Television work came early in her career, beginning with a small part as Jane, a secretary, in *Jury*, followed by *Brookside*, playing a tarty DJ. Other television credits include *Bergerac*, *All Creatures Great and Small*, *Coronation Street*, *Where the Heart Is*, *Peak Practice* and *Casualty*, playing Madam Rosa, her favourite role.

As well as an extensive list of theatre appearances, Maggie writes, directs and has started producing, and is currently developing a feature film. Among her writing credits are musicals such as *Ferry Cross the Mersey*, *Hot Stuff* and *Rock Hard*, while she's directed plays like *Dust*, *Josephine* and *The Assignment*.

Nurse

Played by Ann Bryson
The nurse works at the local hospital and is seen in 'Sickness and Wealth', enquiring into why Del hasn't eaten his dinner.

Nurse

Played by Corinne Britton
In 'Modern Men', the nurse appears in Del's vasectomy nightmare.

MEMORIES OF PLAYING THE POLICEWOMAN

★ ★ ★ ★ ★ ★

'At the time I appeared in *Only Fools and Horses* my dad was a Methodist minister and he had a little church in Brightlingsea, a fishing village near Colchester. We were all big fans of the programme and Dad was so proud I was in it that he told his congregation, so everyone decided to watch my appearance.

'After the programme had been aired, I had a phone call from my dad and he was flabbergasted that I hadn't said that I was in my underwear. If I'd told him he wouldn't haven't mentioned it to the congregation. No one worried about it but I think my dad felt a bit vulnerable having his daughter on prime time television on Christmas Day in her flimsies!'
MAGGIE NORRIS

Obooko, Mrs

Although she never makes an appearance in the sitcom, Mrs Obooko, who lives in the flat below the Trotters, is mentioned in 'The Russians are Coming'. After collecting boxes of lead from the site of an old derelict building, Del is worried that if they store too many of the boxes in their flat the floor might give way and they might find themselves crashing through the ceiling.

We hear of her again when Del refers to her as 'the old girl downstairs', during 'Christmas Crackers'; Del asks Grandad if he has binned the giblets from the turkey because he had promised them to Mrs Obooko for her cat.

Occhetti, Vinny

Played by David Jason

In 'Miami Twice', the cantankerous Vinny Occhetti – whose nickname is The Chain – is a senior figure in the local Mafia, striking widespread fear wherever he goes. He's been released on bail pending a trial for numerous heinous crimes.

O'Connell, Linda

Production secretary on one episode: 'The Frog's Legacy'

O Fura-Vidas

The success of *Only Fools and Horses* is worldwide; its popularity in Portugal has seen it spawn a Portuguese adaptation, titled *O Fura-Vidas*. The sitcom was set in Sapadores, an old region of Lisbon, with Quim Fintas (played by Miguel Guilherme) and Joca (Ivo Canelas) replacing Del and Rodney respectively.

Other cast members included Canto e Castro as Grandad, Fernando Ferrao as Pirilampo (Trigger), Orlando Costa as Vilela (Boycie), Maria Joao Abreu as Graciete (Marlene), Carlos Magassela as Wilson (Denzil), Dinarte Branco as Valentim (Mickey Pearce) and Americo Silva as Cabral (Mike). New artists who joined the cast for the second series included Joao Lagarto as Helder (Alan), Luisa Cruz as Mimi (Pam), Joana Seixas as Patricia (based on Cassandra) and Ana Bustorff as Isabela (Raquel).

The show, which was adapted by Antonio Pinho and Leonor Tenreito, was directed by Jorge Queiroga for SP Filmes.

O'Keith, Father

Played by P G Stephens

The Catholic priest runs the confessionals when Del visits the church during 'The Miracle of Peckham'. He suffers from persistent corns and claims they're the bane of his life. It's from Father O'Keith that Del hears the sad news concerning the fate of St Mary's, the local hospice.

Old Damien

Played by Douglas Hodge

In the opening scenes of 'Heroes and Villains', Rodney has a nightmare in which Old Damien is ruling the Trotter empire with a rod of iron – and in a white suit, too!

Old lady

Played by Lala Lloyd

Attending Grandad's funeral in 'Strained Relations', the old lady comments to Del that she loves a good funeral. Del advises her to hang around, as there's a couple more scheduled.

Old lady in newsagents

Played by Lala Lloyd

Del gets chatting to the old lady in a newsagents during 'Happy Returns'. She asks how Grandad is getting on in hospital.

Old lady (No. 1)

Played by Gilly Flower

In 'Homesick', the old lady buys three oranges for 25p from Del at the market.

Old lady (No. 2)

Played by Renee Roberts

The old woman is seen in 'Homesick' and enquires whether Del has any pineapples for sale; after informing her he hasn't, he tries selling her oranges, claiming they have a similar taste!

Old lady

Played by Bay White

In 'Heroes and Villains', the old lady is mugged in the market by the same gang who attempted to steal Councillor Murray's handbag.

'Old Shep'

Heard twice in 'Diamonds are for Heather', the song is one of Del's favourites, especially when he's feeling melancholic. In the episode it's sung by The Magaluf Brothers during the Spanish night at The Nag's Head, and later by the carol singers.

The music and lyrics of this old-time classic were written by Foley and Westpar. Various artists have recorded the song, including Elvis Presley and Clinton Ford, who saw his version reach 27 in the British charts back in October 1959.

The inspiration behind the song was a border collie. In 1936, a shepherd was hospitalised in Montana, USA. His faithful working dog kept a vigil outside the hospital, but his master died. The dog would have accompanied the shepherd's body back East for burial, but was prevented from boarding the train. It's believed that the dog met each passenger train arriving at the station for the next five and a half years in the hope that his master would appear. When Shep died in 1942, he'd become so famous that national newspapers carried his obituary.

Oliver, Mike

Role: Otto
Appeared in S6, episode 3

Ollie

Played by Tony London

Seen in 'He Ain't Heavy, He's My Uncle', Ollie – whose nickname is Oily Ollie – is leader of the biker's gang who are swilling pints and making a lot of noise at The Nag's Head. Among the other visitors at the pub that evening are the Trotters, Boycie, Trigger, Marlene, Raquel and a group of skinheads. Del, who knows Ollie, calls him over to the bar and asks if he knows anything about the group of skinheads who've started frequenting the pub.

Olver, James

Role: Doctor
Appeared in 'Modern Men'

James was born in Maidstone, Kent, in 1971, and made his acting debut in a 1992 production of *The King and I* at the Aberystwyth Arts Centre. His first TV role was in the 1995 police drama *Back Up*. James now works for a financial services company.

One Eleven Club, The

A licensed gambling club seen in 'Chain Gang', The One Eleven Club concentrates on card games and one-armed bandits. The décor is all chandeliers, crystal-effect table lamps and Georgian chairs, while the clientele consists of people like Del Boy and Trigger.

121 Club, The

The casino, which is owned by Ronnie Nelson, is seen in 'Fatal Extraction'. Del frequents the establishment a little too often for Raquel's liking, especially as he usually fritters away all the housekeeping.

Only Fools and Horses Appreciation Society, The

Founded in 1994 by Perry Aghajanoff, who's the Society's president, the Only Fools and Horses Appreciation Society has over 6000 members at present. However, the seeds for an association to celebrate John Sullivan's classic sitcom were sown some years previous, courtesy of Paul and Clifford Galley who laid the foundations for what has metamorphosed into today's Society.

An informative quarterly magazine – *Hookie Street* – is produced by the team, which at the time of writing this entry consisted of Perry Aghajanoff (President), Keith Bishop (Joint Vice-President and Web Page), Peter Burton (Joint Vice-President and Features Editor), Wendy Burton (Video Librarian), Jackie Rayner (Merchandise) and Melanie Ritson (Proof Reader).

At present, the Society's annual subscription is £7, and all enquiries should be sent to PO Box 92, Romford, Essex RM6 5DN. Remember to enclose a SAE if you require a reply to your correspondence. You can also make contact via the website www.onlyfools.net

Only Fools and Horses Museum

The Only Fools and Horses Appreciation Society have opened their own museum dedicated to the sitcom. Launched in early 2002, it was originally intended to be based in Essex, but society member John Mansfield struck upon the idea of creating a mobile museum by housing it inside an old double-decker.

After scouring the 'For Sale' columns in the local press and specialist magazines in search of a replica of the vehicle used by the Trotters in 'A Slow Bus to Chingford', they struck gold when they purchased a 1967 PD2 from a company in Wales; the only significant difference between this bus and that seen in the 1981 episode was that it has a roof, a prerequisite considering the bus would be touring the country carrying valuable items of memorabilia.

Travelling under the banner, 'Trotters' Ethnic Tours', the bus has already been sprayed in the famous Trotter yellow and has the familiar sign-writing emblazoned across the length of the vehicle. As the Society's president, Perry Aghajanoff, wrote in the editorial of the Winter 2002 edition of *Hookie Street* (the Society's fanzine), 'The upper deck will contain a hospitality lounge for the actors and sleeping quarters for the staff. Downstairs is where it will get very exciting.' He adds: 'The back of the bus will be a recreation of the Trotter flat.'

PERRY AGHAJANOFF is founder and president of the Only Fools and Horses Appreciation Society, which boasts over 6000 members worldwide, from Fiji to Finland, Alaska to Australia, Jamaica to Jersey and Belgium to Botswana. Here he answers some questions about his love for the series.

How long have you been a fan of the sitcom?
Since day one – although it was probably around the mid-1990s that you could say I became hooked and started watching at least an episode a day. I've seen them all so many times now that I'm word perfect.

What caught your interest?
The superb quality of the writing and the way plots interweave. Something mentioned in one episode would become relevant a year later. I also loved the scenes in the flat which remind me very much of Morecambe and Wise.

How did you set up the Society?
I was unemployed at the time, had a computer and always fancied desktop publishing. It was around the time football fanzines first hit the scene and I wondered if I could do one on *Fools*; the answer was yes, and to my amazement people loved it and wanted more – we're now up to a full-colour publication with lots of contributions from cast members and production. At first, I found filling the publication a daunting thought but now it virtually writes itself. If there isn't any news on the *Fools* front we make our own with reports of conventions, meetings, interviews, etc.

Do you have a lot of personal memorabilia?
Yes, a whole host of stuff collected over the years, including a Reliant Regal used by the BBC, Del's bar and numerous original items of clothing worn by members of the cast, such as Del Boy, Rodney, Uncle Albert, Trigger, Mike, Denzil, Boycie, Mickey Pearce, Marlene and Sid. I've also got hundreds of signed photos of everyone who's ever appeared in the show, as well as signed scripts. Then there are various *Peckham Echos*, Trigger's broom and dolphin from Margate, blueprints of set designs and about fifty various props used over the years. We plan to display most of this in the mobile museum during 2002.

Perry Aghajanoff (right) on the set of the Trotters' flat

What's your most treasured item?
A photo of me in the Trotter Flat, with Keith Bishop and Peter Burton to my left (see above).

Do you get a lot of support from the actors involved in the sitcom?
Yes, an enormous amount. Ken MacDonald was a staunch supporter over the years. So far we have received help, support and encouragement from all the cast, production team and the writer.

What's your favourite episode?
'The Class of '62'. Slater was such a fantastic character; I loved the way John Sullivan wrote him as being Raquel's husband – typical Sullivan. Top quality writing.

Least favourite?
'A Royal Flush' which desperately needed a studio audience; having said that, if it had an audience it would probably be one of my favourites. The scene in the theatre and the shotgun section are pure class.

How many hours of your day are spent involved in running the society?
Twenty-four hours, seven days a week – it's constant. The phone rings all day long and sometimes I receive around one hundred letters a day! You can't switch off.

I understand you have your own yellow Reliant Regal van?
I have 15!

If you could have one wish, what would it be?
That dream came true when I was booked as an extra in the recent episodes.

The BBC and all the production staff of *Only Fools*, both past and present, have been very helpful on this; be prepared to see some fantastic items.'

Costumes, memorabilia, autographs and items from the Society's archives will adorn the walls. 'We'll be playing videos and have *Only Fools* fruit machines installed, too. Oh yes, it's going to be pukka and, best of all, it's going to be free.' The museum will also have its own website (www.trottersethnictours.com).

Opacic, Paul

Role: Jules
Appeared in S7, episode 2

Born in Halifax in 1966, Paul worked as a bar manager before enrolling at the Drama Centre, London. He made his professional debut at Plymouth's Theatre Royal in 1990, playing Angelo in the English Shakespeare Company's production of *Comedy of Errors*. He spent a long period with the Company, working all over the UK, as well as in Moscow, Kiev and Jerusalem.

His appearance as Jules in *Only Fools and Horses* marked his arrival in television and he's since gone on to appear in numerous shows, including his favourite roles as Steve Marchant in *Emmerdale* and Dr Mark Kershaw in *Peak Practice*. Other credits include playing Mark Waddle in *Bad Girls*, Graham Rysinski in *Heartbeat*, Rick in *Doctors* and a hairdresser in *Birds of a Feather*.

Paul continues to work in the theatre and in 2000 won the Manchester Evening News Theatre Award for 'Best Actor' for his appearance in *The Mysterious Mr Love* at the Oldham Coliseum.

Organist

Played by Ronnie Price

The organist, who's seen in 'The Jolly Boys' Outing', is part of the group entertaining at the Mardi Gras club in Margate.

Orlando

Seen in 'Watching the Girls Go By', Orlando is the barman at the nightclub where Yvonne chats up Rodney as part of Del's bet.

O'Shaughnessy, Brendan

Played by David Jackson

The tough-looking painter and decorator, who's in his thirties, Brendan is seen at The Nag's Head in 'Who's a Pretty Boy?'. He drives an old transit and is responsible for supplying Del with battleship grey paint instead of apple white! Not the brightest of guys, O'Shaughnessy was heading back to Dublin until he won the contract for painting The Nag's Head.

His departure must have been delayed, however, because he's mentioned again in 'As One Door Closes'. O'Shaughnessy has just won a contract to fit out and decorate a new housing estate at Nunhead, and Del intends selling his louvre doors to him – but with little luck.

Otto

Played by Mike Oliver

A doorman at The One Eleven Club, Otto – a burly thug-like character – is seen in 'Chain Gang'.

Owens, Mr

Mentioned in 'Fatal Extraction', Mr Owens was Del's last dentist. His surgery was in Gandhi Avenue, but he's been dead since the night of the Queen's Silver Jubilee in 1977, which reveals just how much time has elapsed since Del last had a check-up.

Owner

Played by Roger McKern

The owner of the nameless nightclub in 'The Class of '62' rejects Raquel as soon as she turns sideways during her audition and he notices that she's several months pregnant.

Paddy

Played by Michael G Jones

An Irish labourer who pops into The Nag's Head for a drink in 'A Losing Streak', Paddy is the subject of a bet between the luckless Del Boy and Boycie. Del claims that he'll order a pint from the bar, while Boycie opts for a short, and comes out the winner.

Paddy the Greek

Not seen in the sitcom, Paddy is a local wheeler-dealer who's first mentioned by Rodney during a conversation with Del at a nightclub in 'Go West Young Man'. Rodney, who likes women in uniform, bought Monica, his ex-girlfriend, a blue serge suit from Paddy for her birthday. It was just one step in Rodney's master plan to get Monica to dress up as a policewoman. The plan failed miserably.

Del mentions him again in 'The Miracle of Peckham' during his confessionals to Father O'Keith. Del bought some lead off him only to find out it was from the church roof. And in 'Watching the Girls Go By', Rodney informs Del that he bought his white jacket, black shirt and white tie, the outfit he hopes (laughingly) will win him a girlfriend, from Paddy. But what he doesn't realise is that Del sold the outfit to Paddy in the first place.

Del is still trading with Paddy in 'Heroes and Villains', having bought some nine-carat gold bracelets from him; one is given to Rodney for his birthday, although he tries convincing his brother it's 24-carat.

Page, Katharine

Role: Mrs Baker
Appeared in 'The Jolly Boys' Outing'

Glaswegian Katharine Page was born in 1908. She worked in teaching before turning to acting; after graduating from the Guildhall School of Music and Drama, she worked in a myriad of reps around the country, beginning at Bexhill-on-Sea.

Her television debut came in 1936, playing the title role in *Marigold*, and it's this medium that she concentrates on today, with recent credits including Agatha in *Couplings*, an old lady in *Dinnerladies*, Hannah Brown in *Cider With Rosie* and Nora Oakes in *Peak Practice*.

MEMORIES OF PLAYING JULES

★ ★ ★ ★ ★

'As you know, Jules was a camp set designer, so excessive blonde highlights, make-up and leather pants were deemed necessary. However, after we'd finished filming in Bristol, I didn't take my make-up off properly, and travelled all the way back to – and across – London with tousled blonde hair, smudged eyeliner and a tight white t-shirt, to be met by my girlfriend with the immortal words: "You look like a f****** rent boy!".

'After the episode was shown, I was walking down the street the following day, when this builder shouted: "Oi! Weren't you in *Only Fools and Horses* last night?" Feeling pretty chuffed, I replied: "Yeah, I was actually." The builder smiled, saying: "Yeah, I thought it was you." He then paused, before shouting: "Poof!"'

PAUL OPACIC

Painter, Rowena

Production assistant on six episodes: S5

Born in Bulawayo, Zimbabwe, in 1951, Rowena worked in animation and advertising before joining the BBC as a secretary in 1978. Her aim was to become a production assistant and after she achieved her goal worked on shows including *Last of the Summer Wine*, *Omnibus* and various sports programmes. She left the Beeb in 1986 and worked freelance for a time, but has now changed career and is employed by Social Services in Devon.

Palmer, Toni

Role: Blossom

Appeared in S3, episode 6

Toni, who was born in 1932, originally trained as a dancer and made her professional debut, aged 12, in a 1944 panto in Torquay. Other early shows she appeared in as a dancer include *Guys and Dolls*, *Kiss Me Kate* and *Can Can*.

Toni is still working on television and was recently seen on the children's programme *Harry and the Wrinklies* for Scottish TV. To date, she has played Dot in two series.

Other small-screen credits include Doreen in series one and two of *Real Women*, Mrs Trapp in *The Cuckoo Sister*, *The Rag Trade*, *Randall and Hopkirk (Deceased)*, *Goodnight Sweetheart*, *Paul Merton's Hancock Show* and *Bergerac*.

Her film work covers such productions as *The French Lieutenant's Woman*, *Ellis Island* and *The Young Americans*.

Pamela

(See 'Parry, Pamela')

Panchen, Dennis

Film sound recordist on 19 episodes: S1, episodes 1–5; S2, episodes 1, 2, 4–7; S4, episodes 1–5 & 7; 'Diamonds are for Heather' and 'To Hull and Back'

The late Dennis Panchen worked on countless shows during his career with the BBC, including many sitcoms, such as *Terry and June* and *Only Fools and Horses*.

Parker, PC

Played by Jeff Stevenson

Hoskins speaks to PC Parker in 'To Hull and Back', asking him to get a car and meet him around the front of the police station; together with Chief Inspector Slater, they're heading off to follow up reports of three men breaking into the back of a lorry, unaware it's Del, Boycie and Abdul. He's seen later in the episode when Chief Inspector Slater arrives at The Nag's Head to meet Del, Boycie et al.

Parry, Alan

Played by Denis Lill

The first reference to Mr Parry – who owns a villa in Spain – is during 'Chain Gang', when Cassandra (his daughter) tells Del about him at The One Eleven Club. His first appearance is when he enters The Nag's Head to see Del in 'Little Problems'. He's in his forties and has an expensive

Denis Lill as Alan Parry

taste in clothes. Despite his success – he has his own printing company and employs Rodney for a time – he's retained his Cockney accent and enjoys returning to his roots, having been brought up on a council estate in the area. His big weakness, however, is alcohol.

Parry, Cassandra

(See 'Trotter, Cassandra (née Parry)')

Parry, John

Film sound recordist on three episodes: 'The Jolly Boys' Outing' and 'Miami Twice' (Parts 1 & 2). Worked on many other episodes as assistant sound recordist

John was born in Rochford, Essex, and worked in ballistics photography before spotting an advert for job vacancies at the Beeb. He joined in 1977 and worked on shows such as *Nationwide*, *The Duchess of Duke Street*, *Blue Peter*, *One Foot in the Grave*, *Waiting for God*, *The Singing Detective*, *Absolutely Fabulous*, *French and Saunders*, *Hi-De-Hi!* and *'Allo 'Allo!*.

After 19 years' service with the Beeb, John left in 1996 and now works as a producer/director in film and television, and has gone on to win four Royal Television Society Awards.

Parry, Pamela

Played by Wanda Ventham

Cassandra's mother is seen in 'Little Problems' at the registry office. She's smartly dressed and in her early forties.

Parsloe, Lorraine

Role: Casino waitress

Appeared in 'Fatal Extraction'

Lorraine, who was born in Gloucester in 1962, graduated from Bulmershe College, Reading, with a BA (Hons) in Film and Drama. She made her professional debut in the Pandemonium Theatre Company's production of *The Silver Chair* before gaining valuable experience on small-scale national tours of productions such as *Gaslight*, and in a self-devised children's show, *Rainy Daze*, at local venues.

Her first appearance on television was playing a car accident victim in a 1989 episode of *Casualty*, but her favourite role was Cowpat the Peasant in *Maid Marian and Her Merry Men* for the BBC in 1990. Most recent work assignments include providing voices for the BBC's cartoon *Prince of Atlantis*, and the French animated movie *Children of the Rain*.

Since September 2001 Lorraine been a full-time mother to her son, John.

Partridge, Elsie

Played by Constance Chapman

Mentioned by Rodney in 'The Unlucky Winner is…', Elsie goes out with Albert; he met the elderly widow with 11 children, at bingo. She's seen for the first time in 'Sickness and Wealth', where we learn

---

MEMORIES OF 'TO HULL AND BACK'

★ ★ ★ ★ ★ ★

'I remember setting off on the Inge one morning and the weather was atrocious. There was a great deal of conjecture as to whether we should be eating a hearty breakfast or none at all, so there was great indecision at the caterer's, but those of us who opted for something to eat finished our breakfast and then set forth on the trawler. The boat wallowed an awful lot, and as it was supposed to be carrying just three people, it meant in many of the shots everyone had to hide except for the shooting crew. As the assistant recordist I was standing on the prow of the boat, literally, and it was bobbing up and down.

'As we were shooting one of the scenes, the dresser suddenly shot out of one of the lockers where he'd been hiding – the diesel fumes had gotten to him – and hit the side of the boat and started throwing up. As the waves were coming over, of course, his vomit was coming back as fast as it was going over the side. The waves also took his wig off, which proceeded to wash around the deck, together with the vomit and the sea water, with three or four people trying to stamp on it! It was very funny.

'At times it was difficult to film, and I remember the make-up girl having trouble trying to keep the actors' colour constant.'
JOHN PARRY

that Albert's lady friend is a spiritualist. In the early 1960s she held regular meetings in a hall above John Colliers, in Peckham. So popular were the meetings that people travelled miles to attend, paying thousands to use her powers of communication; Elsie donated the money to Battersea Dogs' Home.

Elsie isn't seen again but she's mentioned in 'Little Problems' when Uncle Albert tells Del on the phone that he's at the woman's house. He later heads off to live with her at the seaside until his death in 2001, by which time Elsie has been residing in a rest home for six months, probably as a direct result of having the old seafarer under her feet for too long!

Passey, Alison

Programme finance assistant on three episodes: 'Heroes and Villains', 'Modern Men' and 'Time On Our Hands'

Alison, who was born in Peterborough, decided against a career in the WAAF and became an office junior in a solicitor's office upon leaving school. At 19, she enrolled on a secretarial course in Huntingdon, and when she attended a lecture given by a BBC representative, she realised her future lay in the television industry.

Within two weeks of leaving college in 1986 she was an employee of the Beeb, working in the personnel department. After 18 months she had completed a drama producer's secretarial course and was working with George Gallaccio on shows such as *Bergerac* and *Miss Marple*.

After several administrative positions, Alison became a finance assistant in the entertainment department, a job she held for eight years, before being promoted to production manager within the music and entertainment departments in 2000. Programmes she's worked on in this capacity include *The League of Gentleman* and *The Fast Show*.

Pat

We never get to see Pat, who's celebrating St Patrick's night at the Shamrock Club during 'It's Only Rock and Roll'. A voice-over is used for the character, but is almost inaudible in the actual TV recording.

Pat

Wife of Arnie, Pat's not seen in the series, but her husband mentions her in 'Chain Gang' whilst talking to Del.

Patel, Bhasker

Role: Dr Singh
Appeared in 'Modern Men'

Born in the Ugandan capital, Kampala, in 1956, Bhasker began training at Studio '68 of Theatre Arts, in Kensington, London, in 1979. However, he started getting work whilst still a student, including the 1981 play *The Garland*, for the *Play for Today* series, which earnt him his Equity card. After completing his first year at drama school, he left to pursue his career, beginning in children's theatre, then progressing to radio and television dramas.

His extensive list of credits covers all areas of the profession. On the radio he's worked on a myriad of productions, including *The Bandit Queen*, *Night Runner of Bengal* and *The Jury*, while on stage he's been seen in, among other shows, *A Map of the World*, *Comedy of Errors* and *Macbeth*. On the big screen, his movie work includes Rashid in *Mad Dogs*, a house boy in *Octopussy* and Nitai in *Flight*, while his television appearances range from Rahim Shah in *Crown Court*, Aziz Hussein in *Boon* and a karate freak in *The Lenny Henry Show* to Karim in *Between the Lines*, Nawaz Hamoud in *Brookside* and Mr Kumar in *Wavelength*.

Patel, Mrs

In 'Fatal Extraction', Beverley – the dental receptionist – tells the dentist, Mr Ellis, that Mrs Patel, who's one of his patients, has cancelled her four o'clock appointment. She's never seen in the sitcom.

Patel, Raj

Role: Ahmed
Appeared in S2, episode 4

Raj's other credits include playing Sanjay in 'Who's Taking You Home Tonight?', a 1995 episode of *Goodnight Sweetheart*, a doctor in *Framed* and appearances in the films *The Butterfly Effect* and *The Accountant*.

à la Del

★ ★ ★ ★ ★ ★

'Oh mon dieu, mon dieu'

('A Touch of Glass')

Patel's Multimart

When he's fed up with poor service at Top-Buy supermarket, Del declares in 'The Longest Night' that the Trotters will frequent Patel's shop in future; although it's more expensive, you do receive service with a smile. The establishment is mentioned again by Del in 'The Unlucky Winner is…'.

Patsy

Not seen in the sitcom, Patsy is mentioned by Uncle Albert during 'Strained Relations'. He tells Del and Rodney the story of how he tried comforting Patsy's daughter, Gillian, while her husband worked nights. However, he obviously didn't help much because within six months she'd torched the house.

Patterson

Played by Arnold Peters

Patterson works for the Duke of Maylebury in 'A Royal Flush' and is asked to arrange for an extra place at the dinner table when Del arrives on the scene uninvited.

Pauline

(see 'Harris, Pauline')

Pauly

Played by Raphael Gomez

Pauly is one of the gangsters on Vinny Occhetti's payroll, and is seen in 'Miami Twice'.

Payne, Sandra

Role: Miss Mackenzie
Appeared in S3, episode 1

Cambridge-born Sandra Payne spent a few months at the Italia Conti Stage School before accepting her first professional job in panto at Weymouth during the Christmas of 1960. Rep work followed, beginning at Cromer, where her stage manager was Gareth Gwenlan. He's since employed her several times. She also worked at Northampton and Croydon rep before TV started to dominate her career.

Sandra, whose mother was an actress and father a solicitor, made her TV debut in a 1963 episode of *Compact*. Her other TV credits include *The Troubleshooters*, *Riviera Police*, Pam in the pilot of *Roger, Roger*, Marion in five series of *Waiting for God*, Christine Harris in two series of BBC's *Triangle*, *The Professionals*, Belinda Leydon in *Never the Twain*, Mrs Micawber in *David Copperfield*, Caroline Ackland in the TV film of *Jack the Ripper*

with Michael Caine and four years as Janet Langley in BBC's early soap *The Newcomers*.

In the mid-1970s she lived in New York, before returning to England and resuming her career, which in recent years has included a lot of Shakespeare.

Peabody Buildings

As mentioned in 'It Never Rains…', Grandad's family used to live at Peabody Buildings, Peckham Rye, in austere conditions: no money, no food, no future. Fed up with life, Grandad ran off to join the Foreign Legion with a friend, Nobby Clarke.

Peach daiquiri

Del orders a peach daiquiri at The Nag's Head in 'The Sky's the Limit'.

Peacock, Daniel

Role: Mental Mickey
Appeared in S4, episode 4

Born in 1958, Daniel spent a year at the Central School of Speech and Drama before he was asked to leave. But the incident never held him back and by his early twenties, he'd already made his television debut as Baines, an office boy, in a BBC drama, *Plain Murder*. Around the same period he was given his first film role, playing a mod in *Quadrophenia*. Other films he's appeared in include *Party, Party*; *Ghandi* and *Jewel on the Nile*.

For a short time, he worked at the Royal Court Theatre, appearing in two plays, including *Sugar and Spice*, but his career gradually moved towards television, his preferred medium.

Daniel, who has written since the age of 15, has been making his living from writing since he was 27. At the age of 35, he began to direct his own plays.

Peake-Jones, Tessa

Role: Raquel Turner/Slater/Trotter
Appeared in 17 episodes: S7; 'Dates'; 'The Jolly Boys' Outing'; 'Rodney Come Home'; 'Miami Twice' (Parts 1 & 2); 'Mother Nature's Son'; 'Fatal Extraction'; 'Heroes and Villains'; 'Modern Men'; 'Time On Our Hands' and 'If They Could See Us Now…!'

Tessa will never forget the day the birth scenes were filmed in 'Three Men, a Woman and a Baby', one of her favourite episodes. Arriving at the hospital one morning after enjoying a huge breakfast, a midwife asked if it would help if she watched a video of a real birth. 'I didn't have a child of my own back then, so had no idea of what went on. I told her it might help, but I think she was only expecting, perhaps, Tony Dow – the director – and myself to watch it, but David, Nick and Buster tagged along as well.'

With their fry-ups hardly settled in their stomachs, they sat down and waited for the video to begin. 'It was very graphic, of course, with loads of blood and gunge,' recalls Tessa. 'At first, we were horrified and concerned about all the pain the woman was enduring, but gradually our thoughts turned towards things like, "I wish I hadn't had that egg!" By the end we were all feeling green and it put us off our lunch.'

Raquel was first seen in the 1988 Christmas Special, 'Dates'. A woman with a flagging acting career, she resorts to appearances as a stripagram to help pay the bills. One scene saw Raquel performing her act dressed as a policewoman, but Tessa was more nervous about singing in tune than removing her uniform. 'I was terrified because I'm all right holding a song, but can occasionally go a bit flat. I remember thinking: "My god, it will be embarrassing if I don't sing well, especially with all my friends watching!"'

Although she loved bringing Raquel to life, Tessa didn't see any future for the character beyond the one episode. 'She was introduced to give Del Boy a little romance, but I don't think John Sullivan had any intention of making her a regular character. I auditioned with some other actresses and was lucky enough to get the part, but I only ever saw it as a one-off appearance.'

Regardless of whether the character had a future in the sitcom, Tessa was impressed with the part.

'She was fantastic and we had a ball filming it. When the episode was transmitted, and there was a favourable reaction from everyone, I think John Sullivan started thinking about whether it was time to let Del Boy have somebody a little more permanent in his life.'

Raquel returned the following Christmas, appearing as a magician's assistant in 'The Jolly Boys' Outing', and remained with the show thereafter. A popular addition to the regular cast, the strength of the character and the adroitness with which Tessa played her, added an extra dimension to life around Nelson Mandela House.

Being watched by millions of viewers each week had a marked affect on Tessa's life. 'When I first joined the cast, people said I wouldn't be able to use the Tube anymore; I wondered what they were going on about, and continue to use the trains to this day, partly because I'm determined not to let the success make a difference to my life. But I had never been in a show with so many viewers before and wasn't prepared for the impact it had. However, it's all part of the job and you quickly get used to the attention.'

Fortunately, fans of the show are respectful of Tessa's privacy, especially if she's out with her partner, actor Douglas Hodge, and their ten-year-old daughter, Mollie. 'People might make a little comment but tend not to come over, so that hasn't been a problem. Anyway, Mollie takes it all in her stride because she's used to us being on television.'

Tessa's ambitions veered towards acting when she realised she wouldn't make it as a dancer, her original aim in life. 'It was pointed out to me that I wasn't the right shape: I didn't have brilliant legs

and wasn't terribly thin; also ballet wasn't my greatest strength, which was vital if you wanted to take up dance professionally; I preferred jazz and tap.' The dancing school she attended had recently opened a drama section, and when Tessa met up with the teacher, who introduced her to Shakespeare and poetry, she knew where her future lay.

Ironically, before attending the Central School of Speech and Drama, Tessa, who was born in Hammermith, London, in 1957, earned her Equity card as a dancer by appearing in pantomime at Redditch and completing a summer season at Bristol, in between earning a few pounds temping in offices.

She has nothing but fond memories of her days at the Central School. 'It was so fantastic to be with a group of people who all felt as passionate about acting as you. It felt like a luxury, really, to be given a grant for three years to go and do something I loved doing every day.'

After graduating in 1978, Tessa landed herself a ten-month job on television, appearing in *Telford's Change*, a ten-part drama series for BBC2, starring Peter Barkworth and Hannah Gordon. 'Barry Davis, the director, was looking for someone to play a tiny part in the series and, fortunately, he happened to see me playing a lead role in my final year at drama school. He offered me the part, and although there wasn't much to do, I learnt so much by just watching all the guest actors coming in each week.'

The late director, Barry Davis, played a huge part in shaping Tessa's career, as she explains. 'I don't think I would have got the part in *Only Fools* if it hadn't been for Barry because he cast me in another one of his shows, *What the Butler Saw*, which Tony Dow happened to see. Then he cast me in the lead role for another series, *The Bell*, which opened up lots more opportunities.'

After a string of television roles, Tessa knew it was time she started gaining experience on the stage. 'I started finding that whenever I went along for jobs in the theatre, people would recognise all the television work I'd done, but comment on the lack of stage work. So I wrote a long letter to Alan Ayckbourn, because I loved his plays, asking if he'd audition me.' Tessa proved that persistence is the name of the game in the acting world. 'I wrote so many times to Alan that he now calls me a pen pal because I wouldn't stop writing until he saw me!' Tessa spent a year with Ayckbourn's company in Scarborough.

Her career has encompassed stage and screen. In the theatre, she regards her time playing Ophelia in the RSC's tour of *Hamlet* and Belinda in Ayckbourn's play *Season's Greetings,* among her favourites. Although she hasn't worked on stage for a while, she's always keeping her eyes open for the right opportunity to come along. 'I don't think I would want to tour at the moment, but I always read the plays that come my way so something might take my fancy.'

On the small screen, her roles include Mary Bennett in *Pride and Prejudice*, a reporter in *Bergerac*, Julia in *The Two Gentlemen of Verona*, DCI Munson in *The Bill*, Anita in *Quatermaine's Terms* and Nancy Holmes in *When We Are Married*. She's also played Maria in *Up the Garden Path*, Sally Rokeby in *So Haunt Me*, Mrs Hunter in *The Demon Headmaster*, Sarah Lawton in *Midsomer Murders*, Maggie Latham in *Holby City* and Hilda Summerlee in *The Lost World*.

When it comes to selecting a favourite medium, Tessa is undecided. 'I love them all, especially theatre, although I haven't done it for three or four years because of family commitments. There is nothing like the feel of all those people sitting there and watching your every move. But at the same time, I think television can be wonderful; I'm happy doing anything, I just like acting.'

Tessa admits, though, that she would like to be offered more drama roles, after enjoying her time playing Sandra Lyle in 1999's *Summer in the Suburbs*, and Molly in the black comedy *Births, Marriages and Deaths*, the same year. 'I'd also like to do some films; I never seem to go up for them, but would love to do a "proper" movie.'

Reflecting on the success of *Only Fools and Horses*, Tessa is quick to point out that playing such a prominent character in the long-running sitcom hasn't held back her career in any way. 'Getting that much exposure can only help, really,' she says. 'In this business, out of sight is also out of mind. Very often, brilliant actors go off and spend five years or so with the Royal Shakespeare Company, probably working harder than they ever did on television, and are forgotten by directors and casting advisers, purely because they're not seen on the box. So I think that every time your face appears on the screen can only help.'

Pearce, Lennard

Role: Grandad Trotter
Appeared in 23 episodes: S1, episodes 1, 2, 4–6; S2; S3; 'Christmas Crackers'; 'Diamonds are for Heather'; 'Thicker Than Water' and 'Christmas Trees'

From the moment Lennard Pearce walked through the audition room door, John Sullivan warmed to him. 'When we were casting for Grandad, a lot of men were seen, but when it came to Lennard's turn, the first thing I took to was his voice. He had a lovely voice, reminiscent of everyone's grandad from where I grew up. He was also great at adopting a gravelly South London accent, which was ideal for the show.'

John knew immediately he was the one for the part. 'He just looked right; in fact, he actually came in looking a bit scruffy, which was clever: he hadn't shaved and was already beginning to develop the character. In my original notes, I'd described an "unshaven man who doesn't care too much because he's seen it all before". Lennard had taken that on board.' As Lennard left the room, John turned to director Ray Butt and voiced his approval.

Through working together, Lennard and John became good friends. 'He was like one of the family, a smashing man whom we all liked. He used to send my kids presents and they started thinking they had not just two grandfathers but three!' John remembers attending a parents' evening to talk to his son's teacher. 'After telling us how our son was getting on, she said he was always talking about his *three* grandfathers.' I told her that as well as Grandad John (my father) and Grandad Charlie (my wife's father), he always regarded Grandad Trotter as a grandfather.'

After years spent treading the boards at various theatres up and down the country, Lennard finally received the big break which had eluded him for so long when he was offered the part of Grandad. He became famous in the last years of his life, yet despite having spent most of his career as a jobbing actor, he didn't let subsequent stardom affect him, as John Sullivan points out. 'He was proud that he was suddenly being recognised. He said to me once: "I've been in the business since I was 15 and the other week was the first time I was recognised in a supermarket; people came over and made a fuss of me." It was such a tragedy that within a few years he was dead.'

His most notable legacy in terms of his acting career will always be the gloriously acerbic Grandad, a character he helped to shape. As soon as John Sullivan saw him step into the character's shoes for the first time, he started writing towards the qualities that Pearce possessed. It was Lennard who introduced the idea of wearing the pyjama jacket under his jumper, as well as donning the trilby, which was originally borrowed from his old friend Fred

---

MEMORIES OF PLAYING RAQUEL

★ ★ ★ ★ ★ ★

'Raquel is an excellent character. Although her life with Del is pretty much conventional in terms of child rearing and cooking the meals, they're equal in terms of personality, which interests me. They're both tough when they want to be, and she isn't afraid to tell him where to go, which is great because it gives Del Boy something to play off.

'When I first appeared on the show I was very nervous. Up until that point, I wasn't very familiar with the programme because I'd been doing lots of theatre, so tended not to be around much in the evenings. Therefore, I didn't have any pre-conceptions about what I was going into. There are always nerves with any part because you really want to do it well, but I was even more nervous than usual because I loved the character and the script so much, I was desperate to do my best. Any new job is like starting at a new school, with lots of people you've never met before; but I needn't have worried because I felt at home almost immediately.

'I can't think of a single part I haven't enjoyed playing, but I'm particularly fond of Raquel, partly because of her, and John Sullivan's writing, but also because of the teamwork involved in the show. That makes such a difference because it colours the way you feel about your work. The scripts are wonderful, though. John can have you laughing hysterically one moment, but can then turn your emotions like a coin, so that you suddenly think: "I shouldn't be laughing at this." He's very clever in that way.

'It was so lovely getting back together for the recent episodes. It's the sort of team where you can have a five-year gap, but it only feels like yesterday when you meet up again. There's a sort of shorthand amongst the cast, enabling you to pick up from where you left off, regardless of how long it's been. The sad difference, of course, is that we don't have Buster or Ken, and that's very noticeable. There is no question, it doesn't feel the same because they're not around, but having said that, life goes on and they would have both wanted the show to continue.'

TESSA PEAKE-JONES

Lennard Pearce (left) with his friend Fred Mossman, who owned Grandad's trilby

with The Court Players in productions such as *The Return of Peggy Atherton* (as Challis) and *Sauce for the Goose* (as Alf Crane), while in the early sixties he understudied Doolittle in the original production of *My Fair Lady* and went on to play the part on more than 150 occasions: he also played Colonel Pickering during the run.

In 1965 he joined the National Theatre and appeared in a string of plays, such as *Much Ado About Nothing*, *The Royal Hunt of the Sun*, *Rosencrantz and Guildenstern are Dead* and *Tartuffe* as well as playing an orderly in Chekhov's *Three Sisters* and a courtier in *As You Like It*.

Other stage roles included Tribunes in *Titus Adronicus* at the Aldwych Theatre; Major Blake in *Tonight at 8.30* at the Bristol Old Vic; Cinna (the poet) in *Julius Caesar,* Euphronius in *Antony and Cleopatra*, the fourth senator in *Coriolanus* and a merchant in *Comedy of Errors,* all with the Royal Shakespeare Company; Peter Grimstone, a financial journalist, in *Ring of Jackals* at the Theatre Royal, Brighton, and Detective Superintendent Baxter in 1965's *Busy Body,* a play which also had a certain David Jason amongst the cast. Ten years later, he was Owl in *Winne the Pooh* at London's Phoenix Theatre, while in 1977 he was cast as Harper and Mr Witherspoon in *Arsenic and Old Lace,* a revival of the comedy thriller at the capital's Westminster Theatre.

Mossman, who ran a bookshop in London's St Martin's Lane.

Wanting to be around the hub of theatre land, where he was likely to meet fellow thespians and producers, Lennard occasionally helped in the West End bookshop. 'I needed some assistance in the shop, and because he wanted to be around the area, he offered to help,' explains Fred, who got to know Lennard soon after the war. 'We became great friends. He was a lovely person and nothing like the character he played. Unlike Grandad, he had a Noël Coward-style voice.'

Until the part in *Only Fools* came along, Lennard earned his living playing predominantly small parts. Fred states that Lennard realised his heavy smoking didn't help his chances of attracting more substantial roles. 'He knew he smoked too much and that his voice wasn't very strong; he became despondent about it for a while. Then he got the part of Grandad, but took it all in his stride. He was very happy to get the job, was earning money and working steadily at long last.'

Appearing on television in what was to become a highly successful series had its financial rewards, which meant that for the first time in his acting career he was able to take life a little easier. As he admitted to the *Radio Times* in an interview, this couldn't have come at a more apposite moment in his life. Whilst rehearsing at the Bristol Old Vic, he'd become seriously ill and

was nearly forced to quit the profession. He said: 'I lost my balance and kept falling asleep when I shouldn't. It was hypertension. I was a workaholic, never took a holiday and never relaxed; it was 18 months before I could work again and I nearly gave it up. Then *Only Fools and Horses* came along and gave me a new lease of life.'

Lennard – who was born in London in 1915 – enjoyed his time playing Grandad and admired the writing talents of Sullivan. In an interview prior to the screening of the third season, he remarked: 'The first two series were so beautifully thought out that I was a bit dubious about doing a third. I wondered how the writer could keep it up. But the standards are the same.'

During the war, Lennard served with the army: as well as spending time as a member of SEAC (South East Asia Command), he was an active member of the entertainment unit, BESA (Bengal Entertainment Services Association), with whom he acted and produced several productions. Upon returning to civvy street it wasn't long before he was back applying the greasepaint and making a living as a jobbing actor, primarily on the stage. In 1947 he was working at the Shakespeare Memorial Theatre at Stratford, during which time he played Lord Fitzwater in *Richard II*, Salanio in *The Merchant of Venice* and Helicanus in *Pericles*, as well as minor roles in *Dr Faustus*, *The Tempest*, *Twelfth Night*, *Measure for Measure* and *Romeo and Juliet*.

During the 1950s his credits included a spell

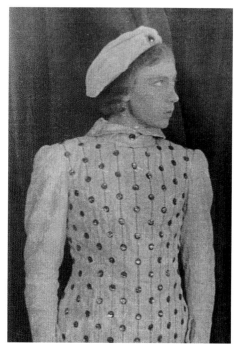

A young Lennard Pearce

During the early 1970s, one of the theatres at which Lennard worked was the Thorndike in the Surrey town of Leatherhead. The pianist and musical director at the time was Peter Durrent, who became great friends with the actor. 'It was 1971 when I first met him, while he was playing the Wicked Wizard in pantomime. He was very amusing and had a marvellous sense of humour,' recalls Peter. 'We used to meet up in London for a drink and a snack, most weeks. Two friends of his, Flo and Freddie Jones, had a florist shop in St Martin's Lane, which they turned into a snack bar and named The Lunch Box. Many a jacket potato was eaten there by Lennard and I.'

Peter remained friends with Lennard until he died, and remembers the day he started being recognised in the street for playing Grandad.

'One day I was waiting with him for a bus that took him back to Holloway, where he lived in Caedmon Road. Several rather boisterous ladies stepped off the bus; one of them looked at Lennard and said: "'Ere, I know you, don't I?"

'Lennard just smiled and said: "Maybe, eh?"

'The lady replied: "Yes, you're Grandad, aren't you?" He laughed. I think he felt pleased to be recognised, although he was very modest. It seemed to be so ironic that he became a TV star

so late in life. Sadly, it was to be the last thing he ever did, as an actor.'

Although playing Grandad was the pinnacle of Lennard's career, it wasn't the only time he worked in the medium, He was seen playing Clerk of the Court in an episode of *Bless Me, Father*; and supporting roles in shows like *Cathy Come Home, Take Three Girls, Dr Finlay's Casebook, Coronation Street, Minder* and the P. D. James' thriller *A Shroud for a Nightingale*.

A bachelor all his life, Lennard died in December 1984, just as filming on the fourth series had begun. An actor who had yearned for the success that was achieved in the final years of his life, he had enjoyed such a brief taste of fame. At the time of Lennard's death, Gareth Gwenlan, then Head of Comedy at the BBC, stated: 'Lennard was a wonderful actor who made a great contribution to the series.'

His friend, Peter Durrent, was also shocked by the news of his death. 'Shortly after he went into hospital after suffering the heart attack I visited him; he was sitting up in bed, looking very healthy. He said: "Peter, I don't know why I'm in here, I feel so well." On calling in again, a few days later, I found him in a confused state, with an oxygen mask on. He was saying: "I must learn this script." I had to leave him, and the last thing he said to me, was "be good".

'His funeral was a fairly sombre occasion. David Jason and Nicholas Lyndhurst attended, and I was there with my dear friend Hetty Ward, for whom Lennard had acted as best man at her wedding in India.'

John Sullivan's poignant comments to a reporter for *The Sun* expressed how deeply Lennard Pearce was missed. He said: 'Writing a script without him is like trying to put my coat on with only one arm. It just doesn't work anymore. After Christmas we will have to get together and decide what to do about it.'

What John did about it was to create Uncle Albert and the rest is history, but there is no doubting the magnitude of the loss suffered with the death of Lennard Pearce.

MY MEMORIES OF LENNARD PEARCE

★ ★ ★ ★ ★ ★

'I first met Lennard in the Everyman Theatre, Cheltenham, at a readthrough of a play entitled *The Farmer's Wife*. This was my first ever professional play and I was absolutely terrified. A readthrough is, as any actor will tell you, a nerve-wracking ordeal, but for me whose only other experience on stage was as a ballet dancer in the Royal Ballet Company, it was especially so.

'I had received no formal acting training and had no idea how to use my voice on stage, and I felt incredibly vulnerable and lonely. On that first day it was Lennard who immediately came to my aid. He took me under his wing, introduced me to everyone and made me feel one of the company. I honestly believe that it was through Lennard and his support that I survived that first job.

'During rehearsals, seeing my obvious lack of experience, he used to give me help with my performance, as well as breathing and voice lessons. He also – when, during the run, I came down with a terrible cold and had to face a matinée – introduced me to the joys of the actor's remedial tipple, port and brandy. I don't know if it cured me but I certainly flew through the show and even today if I get struck down I'll pour myself a port and brandy, but usually *after* the show these days!

'Lennard was a very accomplished actor, with fantastic timing, a real "stage presence" and a unique voice. He could, in the best rep tradition, play anything: Shakespeare, farce, musicals. Whilst at Cheltenham I acted with him in *The Farmer's Wife* (a comedy), *The Boyfriend* (a musical), and a good old traditional repertory pantomime – he was brilliant and totally different in all of them.

'He was a natural company person, an unobtrusive leader whom everyone respected and listened to and a joyous companion, full of fun and wonderful stories but without an ounce of malice. I never heard him criticise or be spiteful about anyone – he was a gentleman. I always think of Lennard wearing "soft" clothes: suede shoes, corduroy jacket and an old brown felt hat – he never seemed to dress up even when we used to go to the theatre, which we did quite often back in London after Cheltenham. He was always just himself, Lennard, and I loved him for that.

'Just when he thought that his career was over, along came *Fools and Horses* and made him happier than he had ever imagined he could be. Suddenly,

Jan Francis

instead of being the lonely, hard up, ex-actor he had dreaded, he was busy in a successful show that he loved, being recognised and appreciated wherever he went. He told me it was the best present he could have received and he couldn't think what he'd done to deserve it.

'When I got married and had my first baby, Lennard used to come and visit for tea. Never lunch or dinner, he liked the convenience of tea time "not too early and not too late". We lived quite a way from each other and he always came in a taxi, a treat he felt he could afford as he was now doing *Fools* and for the first time in his life didn't have to watch the pennies so carefully. When he died, Jo, my daughter aged about two, asked: "Did he go to heaven in a taxi?" as she'd never seen him travel any other way. He adored children and they adored him – he was a happy, interested person and kids sensed this and responded to him. Jo couldn't say Lennard when she knew him and called him Lemmon, which is how we still refer to him today.

'I feel privileged to have met and worked with Lennard and even more to have become his friend. He was one of those special people who touch your life and even though they have gone, never leave it. Whenever I think of him or talk about him, I feel calm and happy and I smile.'   **JAN FRANCIS**

Pearce, Mickey

Played by Patrick Murray

A so-called friend of Rodney's, Mickey – who dresses like a Mod – is an untrustworthy, obnoxious individual, who reveals his true colours by advising Rodney to have a two-week trial separation from a girl called Monica, only to end up spending an evening with her himself at The Nag's Head disco. Although we don't see Mickey until the third series, we learn that he's lived with a woman and, therefore, feels qualified to offer his services as an agony uncle.

Rodney, however, always forgives Mickey and by 'Christmas Crackers' they're back on speaking terms and Rodney has borrowed a book from Pearce, entitled 'Body Language: The Lost Art'.

Their capricious friendship has strengthened by 'Healthy Competition' when Mickey and Rodney set

Mickey Pearce with Del

up in partnership together. Their inexperience finds them coming unstuck at their first auction, however, where they end up owning a pile of old, rusting lawnmower engines. Although he's supposed to be financial director in the company, Mickey is financially inept and when the business begins to struggle, instead of standing firm alongside Rodney, he sneaks off to Benidorm with all the money, leaving Rodney no option but to abandon the partnership.

Mickey is soon back in the UK, however, because Grandad mentions his name in 'Yesterday Never Comes', and he's seen at The Nag's Head with Rodney in 'Wanted', trying to summon the courage to chat up a couple of girls.

Mickey's personality is tarnished by a malevolent streak, which surfaces from time to time, like the occasion he ridicules Rodney, teasing him about never having a girlfriend.

Rarely seen without his trademark pork-pie hat, he's also an incessant liar, especially concerning his supposed conquests with the opposite sex. His friends, like Rodney and Jevon, are fed up with his lying, so much so that at the disco in 'Yuppy Love', Rodney reminds him that the last time he dated a girl he took her to a Bay City Rollers' concert.

Mickey – who lives on the Nyerere Estate, Peckham and is a member of the Down by the Riverside Club – flits between jobs as if there was no tomorrow. As well as going into partnership with Jevon, he also worked for a time at the World of Leather, before getting the sack (and deciding to become a vegetarian). Other jobs on his never-ending

CV include working for Boycie, delivering and collecting videos, working Saturday mornings on the photo desk in Boots, and selling double glazing.

Peckham

A former village in Surrey, Peckham is now a district in the London borough of Southwark. The borough's population in 1999 stood at 237,300.

Although it's uncertain what the name Peckham actually means, experts believe it originated from two Old English names, 'peac', meaning hill, and 'ham' meaning 'village', resulting in, perhaps, 'village by a hill'.

Peckham was mentioned in the Domesday Book and was once separated from the City of London by fields, orchards and farms, but the migration of people towards the city in search of work, marked the demise of such open spaces. Nowadays, most of the houses and flats are owned by Southwark Council, but during the last century, the lion's share of housing was run by private landlords.

Peckham and Camberwell Chamber of Trade Dinner/Dance

Del dons a flashy evening suit and attends the event in 'Cash and Curry' in an attempt to strike up a

WHY PECKHAM?

Just why did John Sullivan pick Peckham as the place where the Trotters would live? 'When I was a teenager, it was the toughest area I knew. It was a place you avoided, if you could.'

business relationship with Vimmal Malik, an Indian businessman whom Del thinks is loaded. The dinner/dance is held at the local town hall and Malik, who's new to town, attends.

Peckham Bowling Club

We see the Club in 'Ashes to Ashes'. Trigger's late grandfather, Arthur, was a lifelong member of the bowling club and the Trotters, in Trigger's absence, decide to scatter his ashes in the middle of the green. But when the plan fails, they concoct another doomed scheme: to bury him in St Catherine's Dock.

Peckham Car Rentals

Mentioned in 'He Ain't Heavy, He's My Uncle', the car rental company owns the Ford Capri that Del buys for Raquel.

Peckham Courier Service

(See 'Transworld Express')

Peckham Echo

The Trotters' local paper, mentioned in 'The Miracle of Peckham' when Del suggests that Rodney calls the paper telling them that the statue

is weeping. Raquel is seen reading it in 'He Ain't Heavy, He's My Uncle'.

Peckham Exhaust Centre

Mentioned by Del in 'Rodney Come Home', this is where Rodney takes the van for a replacement exhaust. Whilst there, Rodney – who at that point is experiencing marital difficulties – asks Tanya, the new receptionist, out on a date. We never see the girl in the episode, but Del is desperate to stop his brother dating her, although he needn't have worried, because Rodney eventually comes to his senses and cancels the rendezvous.

Peckham General Hospital

Whilst the Trotters were millionaires, they spent some of their money on a new ward for the local hospital. Officially christened the Trotter Ward, it is mentioned in 'If They Could See Us Now…!'.

Peckham Pouncer

Del makes up this nickname for Rodney during 'Wanted'. An unstable woman has accused Rodney of touching her up and Del is trying to frighten him about the incident.

Peckham Spring Water

In 'Mother Nature's Son', Del fools Myles, who's the vice-president of SWANS (the Spa Water and Natural Spring Committee) into issuing a certificate of purity so that he can market Peckham Spring Water. The bottled water takes off and a major supermarket chain trials it, even though the true source of Peckham Spring, which sells for 45p, is the tap in Del's kitchen!

Pegg, Adrian

Assistant floor manager on six episodes: S5. Production manager on 14 episodes: S6, episodes 1, 3–6; S7; 'Dates', 'The Jolly Boys' Outing' and 'Rodney Come Home'

Born in Bishops Stortford, Hertfordshire, in 1958, Adrian studied theatre stage management for two years at the Central School of Speech and Drama. His first job upon graduating was assistant stage manager with The Royal Ballet in Covent Garden, before experiencing repertory theatre and the West End.

After two years of working in reps all around the country – including Coventry, Derby and Manchester – Adrian felt he needed to change course and joined the BBC in 1983. He progressed quickly to become an assistant floor manager and production manager. From 1990, he worked freelance on shows including the comedy drama *Love Hurts*, and the first two series of *Gladiators*, before returning to the Beeb in 1995.

Programmes he worked on during the early days of his BBC career include *Just Good Friends*, *Dear John*, *Blue Peter*, *On the Up* and *Lame Ducks*.

Having worked in television for 14 years, Adrian is now the editorial director of the BBC's commercial website, www.beeb.com, and for the last five years has created websites based around BBC programme bands, including comedy.

'Having the opportunity to work on a John Sullivan show was a unique experience, and it's a time I remember fondly. Just waiting for the scripts to arrive in the production office was like the anticipation a child feels waiting for Christmas to come. You knew that the postman (or the fax machine) would bring something that would be a joy to read and that once again it would be a pleasure to be part of the team who would make it come alive. I clearly recall the laughter echoing around our BBC production office as each of us relished the words that had just arrived.

'John Sullivan is truly brilliant at planting an idea in the minds of the audience very early on in the story, but not revealing the true significance of that idea until very much later on. In "The Miracle of Peckham", for example, the idea is planted right at the beginning that Del has lead to

sell, but it isn't until the end of the show that you connect that piece of information with the crying Madonna and the church's leaky roof!

'For my part, having the script in my hands meant that I could start breaking it down to work out what exactly we would need for each scene. Would it be filmed on location or recorded in the studio? What locations would we need? Was there anything in the script that would require special permission from the police or local authorities? How about special effects – such as rain for the scene where Cassandra gives Rodney a lift "home" to Kings' Avenue? Or stunts, like when the Trotters' van leaps over a hump-backed bridge like General Lee in *Dukes of Hazzard*, or Del hang-gliding, or blowing up a coach in a car park!

'I look back on my time working on *Only Fools* with enormous pleasure. I helped make several series and Christmas Specials, initially as assistant floor manager, when one of my biggest tasks was to make sure the right actors were at the right place at the right time with all the

props they needed. Later, I became production manager on the series, taking on responsibility for the budget, the locations, the schedule and the safety of the unit on location and in the studio. Somehow it doesn't seem right that we could have so much fun at the same time as working, but we always did, and I can't think of a single member of the team who wouldn't have given their right arm to work with David and Nick.

'If there is one show in particular that stands out for me it is "The Jolly Boys' Outing", made for Christmas Day in 1989. I recently found some of the photographs I took of Margate and Ramsgate when Duncan Cooper (another production manager) and I first went to look for locations there. The weather was truly appalling: gale-force winds and lashing rain that pretty much obscured everything we photographed. Still, we did eventually find the film locations we needed in Margate, with the exception of the club where Del, Rodney and the others discover Raquel and The Great Ramondo performing (which was in Ealing) and soon enough we were on our way to start filming.

'We needed two identical coaches for the show. One had to be safe and roadworthy – we were to spend many uncomfortable hours crushed inside filming the scenes travelling down to Margate, and the scene outside the pub where Rodney gets arrested. The other coach was handed over to the visual effects team to be rigged up to explode on cue. We shot the explosion using three cameras to capture several alternative angles at the same time; cutting quickly between these shots is a trick to make the explosion look much bigger than it actually was, when we exploded the coach the visual effects team had to put it back together again and clean it up! Fortunately we didn't need to call on the fire brigade, who were standing by just in case.

'Once, stuck in Margate on a day off, we decided to go fishing for the day. Tony Dow, Duncan Cooper, David, Nick and I hired a boat and set off. It was a nice day out for everyone, but as you can see from the pictures, Nick had the best day of all. David, I'm afraid, didn't!'

ADRIAN PEGG – Production manager

Pember, Ron

Role: Baz

Appeared in S3, episode 1

Born in London in 1934, Ron began acting at school before going on to perform Shakespeare in Durham pubs. He worked extensively in rep before moving into television and films in 1960, often playing villainous roles.

Ron's career has included a host of television appearances in shows including *The Avengers*, *Dear John*, *Black Beauty*, *Crown Court*, *The Two Ronnies*, *The Fall and Rise of Reginald Perrin*, *The Secret Army* and *The Chief*. He's also appeared in a few films, such as *Young Winston*. Ron retired from the business after suffering a stroke in 1992.

Pennington, John

Role: Vicar

Appeared in 'Christmas Trees' and S4, episode 2

Born in Nottingham in 1939, John taught mathematics for seven years before quitting the teaching profession and joining the Rose Bruford College.

He spent several years in repertory theatre, making his debut at the Bristol Old Vic in 1970. A few years later, he moved into the medium of television and was seen in two episodes of *Colditz*.

John – who's also appeared in a handful of films, including *Juggernaut*, as a passenger, and *A Nightingale Sang in Berkeley Square*, as a detective – has a healthy list of credits to his name. On the stage he appeared in a recent Agatha Christie season at the Palace Theatre, Westcliff, while other television roles include Mr Dean in *Peak Practice*, Geoff Mullins in *Casualty*, a detective in *Keeping Up Appearances*, an estate agent in *Lovejoy*, as well as four episodes of *Yes, Minister*.

Penrose, Jenny

Assistant floor manager on one episode: 'Mother Nature's Son'

Born in Newcastle upon Tyne in 1964, Jenny trained as a dancer until a hip problem forced a career change. She took a job working behind the scenes in the theatre, but after writing a letter to the head of drama at the BBC asking for career advice, she was offered a job as a runner in the department.

She was successful in gaining a floor assistant's position in 1988 and worked on various shows, such as *One Foot in the Grave* and *Last of the Summer Wine*. After 14 years in the television industry, Jenny is a production manager, and amongst the various shows she's been assigned to is *Fun at the Funeral Parlour*, a sitcom for BBC Choice. Her favourite jobs to date are *Last of the Summer Wine*, *Only Fools and Horses* and *Ain't Misbehaving*.

Perkins, Mr

Played by Michael Fenton Stevens

Alan is the representative from Mega Flakes who travels to Mallorca with the winners of the art competition during 'The Unlucky Winner is…'. Whilst the rest of the party is made up of parents and children, the Trotter party consists of Del (acting as Rodney's father), Cassandra (as his common-law stepmother) and Rodney, who's supposed to be 14 years old after winning the Under 15's category.

Perllman, Dawn

Role: Amanda

Appeared in S5, episode 5

Born in London, Dawn left school at 15 and took up acting immediately, beginning with *TV Club*, a BBC schools programme. Other TV credits include *Are You Being Served?*; *The Sweeney*; *Slinger's Day*; *Home, James!*; *General Hospital*; *Dempsey and Makepeace*; *Shine On Harvey Moon* and *The Gentle Touch*. She has also worked in the theatre. Nowadays Dawn – who has recently been seen in *The Bill* – does a lot of corporate work.

Peters, Arnold

Role: Patterson

Appeared in 'A Royal Flush'

Arnold – who's the voice behind Jack Woolley in the long-running radio series *The Archers* – was born in London in 1925. He joined a dance band as a schoolboy until being called up to the RAF during the Second World War. Returning to civvy street, he became a professional actor and entertainer, with his first job being on radio's *Children's Hour*, in a programme called *Hastings of Bengal*.

Offers of work were plentiful and he joined the BBC Drama Repertory Company in Birmingham. As well as radio and theatre work, Arnold is also a busy screen actor. His television appearances include: *Citizen Smith*; *Dad's Army*; *Please, Sir!*; *The Siege of Golden Hill*; *Shoulder to Shoulder*; *United!*; *The Tomorrow People* and, in 1998, the BBC series *Prince Among Men*.

Arnold has had a long-standing interest in English folk music and plays in a folk dance band.

Peters, Michael

Role: Baby

Appeared in S5, episode 1

Peterson, Mr

Played by Max Harvey

D. A. Peterson manages the Trotters' local branch of Top-Buy supermarkets and is seen in 'The Longest Night'. He's kept firmly under the thumb of his domineering wife, Valerie, whom we never see.

It transpires that Peterson dreamed up the idea of robbing the safe in the supermarket, with the dim-witted Lennox Gilbey being an easy target when it came to finding someone to execute the plan. He admits to Del that he did it for the money, mainly because his wife has extravagant tastes (solarium, swimming pool), which have led to huge debts.

Peterson, Valerie

Not seen in the sitcom, Valerie's husband, Tom, has a conversation with her on the phone during 'The Longest Night'. It seems Valerie wears the trousers in the Peterson household and spends her husband's money as if there was no tomorrow.

Petula

In 'The Unlucky Winner is…', we learn from Rodney that Del is out on a date with Petula, whom he met at a car boot sale. She is never seen in the series.

Peverall, Ron

Camera supervisor on 18 episodes: S1, episodes 1–4; S2; S3, episodes 2, 3, 5–7; 'Diamonds are for Heather' and 'Thicker Than Water'

Among the many shows Ron has worked on is *Blackadder*.

Philpot, Anthony

Studio sound supervisor on five episodes: S5, episodes 1, 2, 3, 5 & 6

Born in Penzance, Tony wanted to follow a musical career but failed his music A-level. His father suggested he found out what the BBC had to offer and in 1965 he was offered a position as technical operator.

After spending some time at the Corporation's engineering college at Evesham, he returned to London, elected to concentrate on television sound and joined a studio crew, working on shows including *Top of the Pops*, *Blue Peter*, *The Forsyte Saga* and *Doctor Who*. In 1973 he was promoted to studio sound supervisor and added shows like *The Old Grey Whistle Test*, *Play School*, *Open All Hours* and *Nationwide* to his ever-increasing list of credits.

He took redundancy in 1997 and has been working freelance ever since. Recently he's worked for S4C and plenty of music shows; he's also recorded the incidental music for *Last of the Summer Wine* for many years.

Photographer

Played by Richard Hicks

When Del is awarded a medal in recognition of his bravery in apprehending a mugger during 'Heroes and Villains', the photographer is at the awards' ceremony to take Del's picture for the local rag.

Pianist

Played by Fred Tomlinson

In 'Tea for Three', the pianist is seen at The Nag's Head playing the piano during the talent night.

Pilblad, John

Camera supervisor on one episode: 'A Royal Flush'

Playthings

In 'Danger UXD' Denzil collects 50 dolls from Playthings. thinking that it is a toy shop. He is surprised, therefore, to find they are inflatable sex dolls.

Policeman

Played by Paul Beringer

In 'Dates', the policeman is involved in a car accident caused by Rodney, who's driving his Reliant like a maniac in order to escape the punks. What upsets the policeman more than anything else is that he only took delivery of the panda car the previous day.

Policeman

Played by Andy Readman

The policeman is seen patrolling the market in 'A Royal Flush'. When Del spots him, he makes a quick exit.

Policeman

Played by Geoffrey Leesley

The policeman pops round to the Trotters' lock-up when Rodney reports the theft of his band's instruments in 'It's Only Rock and Roll'. But when Del

climb on to the coach for Margate after stopping off at a pub for a quick pint. When Rodney, who's playing with a ball, accidentally hits the policeman in the head, he is arrested.

Police sergeant

Played by Michael Stainton

The sergeant, who's based at a rural station in Cornwall, appears in 'Friday the 14th'. He's on duty when Rodney and Grandad believe they've captured the madman, who's tied up, gagged and in

'It's Only Rock and Roll'

admits the equipment was returned to the retailer, the policeman is annoyed with Rodney for wasting police time.

Policeman

Played by Linford Brown

In 'Fatal Extraction', the policeman tries his utmost to stop the rioters but is fighting a losing battle.

Policeman

Played by Ray Mort

The policeman stops the Trotters *en route* to Boycie's weekend cottage in Cornwall during 'Friday the 14th'. He checks they haven't given a man a lift in the area because a patient has escaped from the local institute for the criminally insane; ten years ago that very night he murdered a party of weekend fishermen.

Policeman

Played by Del Baker

In 'The Jolly Boys' Outing', the policeman walks over to Del and the boys, who are just about to

the back of their van. He breaks the news that their prisoner is not the escapee from the local institute for the criminally insane, but Tom Witton, the gamekeeper.

Policewoman

Played by Maggie Norris

Seen in 'Dates', the policewoman – together with her male colleague – is involved in a shunt when Rodney, who's driving like a mad man, races by in his three-wheeler while being pursued by a bunch of punks. She later appears at The Nag's Head, and confronts Del as the owner of the Reliant. Unfortunately, Del believes the policewoman is a stripagram and tries helping her undress, only to find himself in handcuffs and being carted off to the police station for molesting a police officer.

Pope, Philip

Role: Tony Angelino
Appeared in S7, episode 3

Born in 1956, Philip was first seen on stage professionally in *Oedipus* at the Edinburgh Festival and

the Oxford Revue. He spent a great deal of his career touring with a revue show *Radio Active* in regional theatres and Australia, with Angus Deayton, Geoffrey Perkins and Michael Fenton-Stevens among the cast.

He first experienced television in *Not The Nine O'Clock News* in 1981, and went on to appear in many roles, his favourites being a referee in *11 Men Against 11*, a fading rock star in *Shelley* and, of course, Tony Angelino.

Recent work includes several roles in Radio 4's *Old Harry's Game* and *Revolting People*; Philip also writes music for television, film and radio.

Poulter, Reg

Technical coordinator on seven episodes: S6, episodes 1, 3–6; 'Dates' and 'The Frog's Legacy'

Reg – who was born in Kingston, Surrey – worked for the Post Office in Birmingham before moving down to London and joining the BBC in 1951. He worked as a technical assistant on a host of programmes, and was promoted to technical coordinator in 1982. Reg retired from the Beeb in 1989.

Powell, Nick

Stunt coordinator on two episodes: 'Heroes and Villains' and 'Modern Men'

Born in Dudley, Nick left school and began training as an engineer, but after two years realised it wasn't the job for him and left college in Sheffield – even though he'd already been offered a place at the city's university – and joined a London drama school.

After graduating from the East 15 Drama School he took a postgraduate course at the Drama Centre, finishing in 1984. Two years working as an actor followed, including spells at Edinburgh and other reps, before qualifying as a stunt artist. Initially he combined the two jobs until stunt work gradually began to dominate. Upon completing six years as a stunt perfomer he began to concentrate on coordinating, which he continues to do today.

As a stunt coordinator he's worked on shows such as *Gladiator* (organising all the fight sequences); *Braveheart; The Mummy; Micawber*, with David Jason, *EastEnders* and *A Touch of Frost*. To date, Nick has coordinated over 150 television shows and more than 30 feature films.

Powick, Teresa

Production assistant on four episodes: S7, episodes 1–3 and 'Rodney Come Home'

Pretto, Roger

Role: Carlotti
Appeared in 'Miami Twice' (Parts 1 & 2)

American-based Roger Pretto's television credits include *Miami Vice, Superboy, B.L. Stryker* and *Law and Order*, while his film appearances have seen him play a commando lieutenant in *Running Scared*, a senator in *A Show of Force*, Lieutenant Morgan in *American Rickshaw* and a racquetball colleague in *Cape Fear*.

Price, Derek

Role: Drummer
Appeared in S5, episode 4

Price, Lisa

Role: Zoe
Appeared in S2, episode 4

Price, Ronnie

Role: Organist
Appeared in 'The Jolly Boys' Outing'

Ronnie, who was born in Manchester in 1923, was 25 before he became a professional musician. His first job as a session musician came along in 1953, by which time he'd already worked with local bands. He'd also been a member of the Teddy Foster Band for two years and worked with the Tito Burns Sextet, a jazz outfit. With the band he toured around the world, before joining the resident band at the American Services' Club in London's Regent Park.

Whilst working with Sidney Lipton at Grosvenor House, he reached an important juncture in his career when Peter Knight, who arranged for Lipton, offered Price his first studio recording session. As a session musician he went on to work with top stars like Sammy Davis Jnr, Burt Bacharach, Henry Mancini, John Barry, Petula Clark, Shirley Bassey and Bing Crosby. He also studied at the Harrow School of Music in order to learn more about classical music and arranging.

Ronnie, who worked extensively in television, died in 1997.

Price, Simon

Dubbing editor on one episode: 'Fatal Extraction'.
Assistant film editor on two episodes: 'Miami Twice'
(Parts 1 & 2)

Simon, who was born in a British military hospital in Germany, intended to train as a lawyer but soon realised that he wanted to pursue a career in films. He began his working life with an independent production company, Wheeler's, in 1984, working as a runner and, finally, assistant film editor on the *Holiday* show for BBC.

He diversified and became an assistant director on various commercials and the movie *Empire of the Sun*, before returning to film editing with John Jarvis Associates, based in London. During the eight years he spent with the company, his credits include *Ripping Yarns, As Time Goes By, Brush Strokes, Last of the Summer Wine* and *Ain't Misbehavin'*.

Simon now works as a freelance sound editor in film and television.

Pritchard, John

Film sound recordist on two episodes: S1, episodes 5 & 6

Producer

Played by Richard Braine

The producer is in control of the television programme *Goldrush*, when Del becomes a participant during 'If They Could See Us Now…!'.

MEMORIES OF 'MIAMI TWICE'

★ ★ ★ ★ ★ ★

'Knowing that we'd have a threshold of only three weeks between shooting and transmitting on this episode, the schedules were going to be very tight. Combined with the fact that it would be expensive getting the "rushes" back from America, the BBC realised it was going to be cheaper to have the editor and myself actually on the ground over there.

'It was an enjoyable time in America, although we worked hard, of course, throughout the two months we were there. John Jarvis, the editor, and I would get up about six in the morning, go for a quick swim, and get into work about seven to review the rushes. By the time we finished, which was usually about six or seven in the evening, Tony Dow and John Sullivan, and occasionally the actors, would come up and review the filming from the previous day; by this time, of course, we'd have everything cut in so that they could see exactly where they were going and judge what was working and what wasn't.

'We were very well treated over there. The editing crew worked at a place called Continental Film Labs, a very good film laboratory. They set us up and gave us a room and treated us well: in fact, they were so in awe of the BBC that they gave us priority over the other companies, who had to wait in the queue whilst we sorted out our rushes first.

'I remember Tony Dow wanted a kind of montage sequence at the beginning of the episode, showing how good Miami looked, with the beaches and pretty girls. The days they went out to shoot those scenes the sun wasn't shining, so they ended short of girl shots. One of the lab guys suggested using some of his 35mm film which he kept in his garage, so two of the shots in the montage were actually shots of his girlfriend and members of the American crew.

'It was a great experience working on *Only Fools*. I particularly admired the writing talent of John Sullivan. At recording time, John Jarvis and I would be invited up to the gallery to make sure the filming was running right, and because we'd be doing the film inserts on the series. Apart from ourselves, Tony Dow, and the other people involved in the mechanics of the programme, the only other person there was John Sullivan, sitting in a booth on his own, just smoking. This was the comic genius that we all revered, but no one could have been more nervous, waiting for that laugh to happen and dying if it didn't – it was agony to watch him, really.

'John Sullivan is a wonderful man, definitely one of *the* writing talents. To be clever enough to create phrases that have become colloquial language is a great epitaph to him. It just leaves you with a huge smile on your face when you're walking around and hear people using his phrases in everyday conversation.

'It was also great working with Tony Dow, who's incredibly hard-working. I remember a late-night working session at John Jarvis' cutting room. We were working on a Christmas episode, and were running out of time. The room we were using was small and rather confined; we were stepping over each other to get to the various pieces of equipment, and Tony was keen to complete more and more scenes, but all the time it was getting later and the coffee was running out! Suddenly there was a crash and a yell from round the corner. John and I looked at each other and then noticed Tony had disappeared. He'd fallen into one of the trim bins (which is shaped like a laundry basket and holds the film) on top of all the film, cut his ear open on the way down, leaving blood all over the film, which we had to clean off. He'd split his ear open but his attitude was just to apply a plaster and carry on. He'd fallen head first into the bin, and being quite a big man, it took quite a while to get him out!'

SIMON PRICE

Production Team

(Only the individuals whose names appear in the closing credits are listed below.)

PRODUCERS

Ray Butt (S1–S5; 'Diamonds are for Heather'; 'Thicker Than Water'; 'To Hull and Back'; 'A Royal Flush'; 'The Frog's Legacy'); **Bernard Thompson** ('Christmas Crackers'); **Gareth Gwenlan** (S6–S7; 'Dates'; 'The Jolly Boys' Outing'; 'Rodney Come Home'; 'Miami Twice' (Parts 1 & 2); 'Mother Nature's Son'; 'Fatal Extraction'; 'Heroes and Villains'; 'Modern Men'; 'Time On Our Hands'; 'If They Could See Us Now…!')

EXECUTIVE PRODUCERS

John Sullivan ('Mother Nature's Son'; 'Fatal Extraction'; 'Heroes and Villains'; 'Modern Men'; 'Time On Our Hands'; 'If They Could See Us Now…!')

ASSOCIATE PRODUCERS

Sue Longstaff ('Heroes and Villains'; 'Modern Men'; 'Time On Our Hands'); **Gail Evans** ('If They Could See Us Now…!')

DIRECTORS

Martin Shardlow (S1; 'Christmas Crackers'); **Ray Butt** (S3; S5, episodes 5 & 6; 'Diamonds are for Heather'; 'Thicker Than Water'; 'To Hull and Back'; 'A Royal Flush'; 'The Frog's Legacy'); **Susan Belbin** (S4); **Mandie Fletcher** (S5, episodes 1–4) **Tony Dow** (S6, episodes 1, 3–6; S7; 'Dates'; 'The Jolly Boys' Outing'; 'Rodney Come Home'; 'Miami Twice' (Parts 1 & 2); 'Mother Nature's Son'; 'Fatal Extraction'; 'Heroes and Villains'; 'Modern Men'; 'Time On Our Hands'; 'If They Could See Us Now…!')

DESIGNERS

Tony Snoaden (S1, episodes 1, 2, 4, 5 & 6); **Cynthia Kljuco** (S1, episodes 3 & 5; 'Christmas Crackers'); **Derek Evans** (S2, episodes 1, 2, 6 & 7); **Andy Dimond** (S2, episodes 2–7); **Don Giles** ('Diamonds are for Heather'); **Anthony Thorp** (S3, episodes 1–4); **Eric Walmsley** (S4); **Bryan Ellis** (S3, episodes 5–7; 'Thicker Than Water'); **Bernard Lloyd-Jones** ('To Hull and Back'); **Mark Sevant** (S5; 'A Royal Flush'); **Graham Lough** (S6, episodes 1, 3–6; 'Dates'); **Donal Woods** ('Mother Nature's Son'; 'Fatal Extraction'; 'Heroes and Villains'; 'Modern Men'; 'Time On Our Hands'); **Richard McManan-Smith** (S7; 'Rodney Come Home'; 'Miami Twice' (Parts 1 & 2)); **Paul Trerise** ('The Frog's Legacy'); **John Anderson** ('The Jolly Boys' Outing'); **David Hitchcock** ('If They Could See Us Now…!')

PRODUCTION MANAGERS

Janet Bone (S1; S2); **Jo Austin** ('Christmas Crackers'); **Sue Bysh** (S2; 'Diamonds are for Heather'); **Andy Smith** (S3; S4; 'Thicker Than Water'; 'Modern Men'); **Tony Dow** ('To Hull and Back'; 'A Royal Flush'); **Sue Longstaff** (S5; 'To Hull and Back'; 'The Frog's Legacy'; 'Miami Twice' (Parts 1 & 2); 'Mother Nature's Son'); **Olivia Bazalgette** ('A Royal Flush'); **Adrian Pegg** (S6, episodes 1, 3–6; S7; 'Dates'; 'The Jolly Boys' Outing'; 'Rodney Come Home'); **Lesley Bywater** ('The Frog's Legacy'); **Gill Anderson** (S6, episodes 1 & 3; 'Dates');

Johanna Kennedy ('Fatal Extraction'); **Angela de Chastelai Smith** (S7; 'Rodney Come Home'; 'Miami Twice' (Parts 1 & 2)); **Simon Spencer** (S7, episode 6)

UNIT MANAGER

Caroline McCarthy ('If They Could See Us Now…!')

ASSISTANT PRODUCTION MANAGER

Jo Alloway ('If They Could See Us Now…!')

VISION MIXERS

Hilary West (S1; 'Christmas Crackers'); **Bill Morton** (S2, episodes 1, 2 & 4; S6, episodes 5 & 6; 'A Royal Flush'); **Shirley Coward** (S2, episode 3; S4, episode 7); **Angela Beveridge** (S2, episodes 5, 6 & 7; S3; 'Diamonds are for Heather'; 'Thicker Than Water'); **Heather Gilder** (S4, episodes 1–6; S5; S6, episodes 1, 3 & 4; 'The Frog's Legacy'; 'Miami Twice' (Parts 1 & 2); 'Mother Nature's Son'; 'Fatal Extraction'; 'Heroes and Villains'; 'Time On Our Hands'); **Sue Collins** (S7; 'The Jolly Boys' Outing'; 'Rodney Come Home'); **Hilary Briegel** ('Dates'; 'Modern Men'); **John Barclay** ('If They Could See Us Now…!')

GRAPHIC DESIGNERS

Peter Clayton (S1; S2; S6, episode 3; 'Christmas Crackers'); **Fen Symonds** (S2; 'Diamonds are for Heather'); **Mic Rolph** (S3; 'Thicker Than Water'); **Andrew Smee** (S5; S7; 'To Hull and Back'; 'A Royal Flush'; 'The Frog's Legacy'); **Iain Greenway** (S6, episode 4); **Andy Carroll** ('Miami Twice' (Parts 1 & 2))

PROPERTIES BUYERS

Chris Ferriday (S1; S4; 'Christmas Crackers'; 'Miami Twice' (Parts 1 & 2)); **Roger Williams** (S2; 'A Royal Flush'); **Peter Sporle** ('Diamonds are for Heather'); **Penny Rollinson** (S3; 'Thicker Than Water'); **Dave Morris** ('To Hull and Back'); **Maura Laverty** (S5); **Hilary Nash** ('The Frog's Legacy'); **Malcolm Rougvie** (S6, episodes 1, 3–6; S7; 'Dates'; 'Rodney Come Home'; 'Mother Nature's Son'); **Leigh Craig** ('The Jolly Boys' Outing'); **Graham Bishop** ('Fatal Extraction'; 'Heroes and Villains'; 'Modern Men'; 'Time On Our Hands'); **Marvin George** ('If They Could See Us Now…!')

COSTUME DESIGNERS

Phoebe De Gaye (S1); **Alan Hughes** ('Christmas Crackers'); **Anushia Nieradzik** (S2; 'Diamonds are for Heather'); **Richard Winter** (S4; S6, episodes 1, 3–6; 'Dates'); **Dinah Collin** (S3; 'Thicker Than Water'); **Barbara Kidd** ('To Hull and Back'); **Robin Stubbs** (S5; S7; 'A Royal Flush'; 'The Frog's Legacy'; 'Rodney Come Home'; 'Miami Twice' (Parts 1 & 2); 'Mother Nature's Son'; 'Fatal Extraction'; 'Heroes and Villains'; 'Modern Men'; 'Time On Our Hands'); **Linda Haysman** ('The Frog's Legacy'); **Colin Lavers** ('The Jolly Boys' Outing'); **Jack Levy** and **Pam Maddox** ('If They Could See Us Now…!')

ASSISTANT COSTUME DESIGNER

Leslie Eve Herman ('Miami Twice' (Parts 1 & 2))

MAKE-UP DESIGNERS

Pauline Cox (S1); **Jean Speak** ('Christmas Crackers'); **Shaunna Harrison** (S2; 'Diamonds are for Heather');

Denise Baron (S3; 'Thicker Than Water'); **Linda McInnes** (S4); **Vivien Riley** ('To Hull and Back'); **Elaine Smith** (S5; 'A Royal Flush'); **Ann Ailes-Stevenson** ('The Frog's Legacy'); **Jean Steward** (S6, episodes 1, 3, 5 & 6; 'Dates'); **Sylvia Thornton** (S6, episodes 3 & 4); **Dorka Nieradzik** ('The Jolly Boys' Outing'); **Christine Greenwood** (S7; 'Rodney Come Home'; 'Miami Twice' (Parts 1 & 2); 'Mother Nature's Son'; 'Fatal Extraction'); **Deanne Turner** ('Heroes and Villains'; 'Modern Men'; 'Time On Our Hands'; 'If They Could See Us Now…!'); **Lori Misselbrook** ('If They Could See Us Now…!')

STILLS PHOTOGRAPHER

John Jefford (S1, episode 3; S2, episode 6)

LOCATION VIDEO FOR S4, EPISODE 7 AND 'DIAMONDS ARE FOR HEATHER'

Len Stephens (lighting); **Mike Johnstone** (sound); **Mike Winser** (cameraman); **George Wagland** (vision supervisor)

ASSISTANT FLOOR MANAGERS

Mandie Fletcher (S1); **Tony Dow** (S1, episode 6; S2; S3; 'Diamonds are for Heather'; 'Thicker Than Water'); **Clare Graham** ('Christmas Crackers'); **Gavin Clarke** (S4; 'To Hull and Back'); **Adrian Pegg** (S5); **Francesca Gilpin** ('A Royal Flush'); **Melanie Dicks** ('A Royal Flush'); **Paul Dale** ('Dates'); **Kerry Waddell** (S6, episodes 1, 3–6; 'Dates'); **Gary Sparks** (S6, episode 4); **Sue Bishop** (S6, episode 5 & 6; 'The Frog's Legacy'); **Henry Tomlinson** ('The Jolly Boys' Outing'); **Angela de Chastelai Smith** ('The Jolly Boys' Outing'); **Debbie Crofts** (S7; 'Rodney Come Home'; 'Miami Twice' (Parts 1 & 2)); **Miles Cherry** (S7, episodes 1–3; 'Rodney Come Home'); **Charles Whaley** ('Miami Twice' (Parts 1 & 2)); **Jenny Penrose** ('Mother Nature's Son'); **Ali Bryer Carron** ('Fatal Extraction'); **Tania Normand** ('Fatal Extraction'); **Beccy Fawcett** ('Heroes and Villains'; 'Modern Men'; 'Time On Our Hands')

FLOOR MANAGER

Vivien Ackland-Snow ('Heroes and Villains'; 'Modern Men'; 'Time On Our Hands'; 'If They Could See Us Now…!')

PRODUCTION ASSISTANTS

Penny Thompson (S1; S2; S3; 'Diamonds are for Heather'; 'Thicker Than Water'); **Jane Garcia** ('Christmas Crackers'); **Caroline Andrews** (S4, episodes 1–5 & 7); **Lesley Bywater** (S4; 'To Hull and Back'; 'A Royal Flush'); **Rowena Painter** (S5); **Alexandra Todd** (S5); **Caroline Gardener** ('Heroes and Villains', 'Modern Men'; 'Time On Our Hands'; 'If They Could See Us Now…!'); **Jane Willson** ('The Frog's Legacy'); **Amita Lochab** (S6, episodes 1, 3–6; 'Dates'; 'The Jolly Boys' Outing'; 'Mother Nature's Son'); **Gail Evans** ('Miami Twice' (Parts 1 & 2)); **Tracey Gillham** ('Miami Twice' (Parts 1 & 2); 'Fatal Extraction'); **Faith Harris** (S6, episode 1); **Teresa Powick** (S7, episodes 1–3; 'Rodney Come Home'); **Chris Gernon** (S7, episodes 5 & 6); **Amanda Church** (S7, episodes 5 & 6)

PRODUCTION COORDINATOR

Claudia Cuffy ('If They Could See Us Now…!')

VIDEOTAPE EDITORS
Mike Taylor (S1, episodes 1 & 5; S2, episodes 3, 4 & 6; S3, episodes 1, 3 & 7); Chris Wadsworth (S1, episodes 2, 3, 4 & 6; S2, episodes 1, 2, 5 & 7; S3, episodes 2, 4 & 6; S4, episodes 1, 2, 5 & 7; S5, episodes 1, 3, 4 & 5; S6, episodes 1, 3–6; S7; 'Thicker Than Water'; 'Dates'; 'The Jolly Boys' Outing'; 'Rodney Come Home'; 'Miami Twice' (Parts 1 & 2); 'Mother Nature's Son'; 'Fatal Extraction'; 'Heroes and Villains'; 'Modern Men'; 'Time On Our Hands'; 'If They Could See Us Now…!'); Graham Sisson ('Christmas Crackers'); Chris Booth (S3, episode 5; S4, episodes 3, 4 & 6); Graham Taylor (S5, episodes 2 & 6); Ed Wooden ('A Royal Flush'; 'The Frog's Legacy')

TECHNICAL COORDINATORS
(later retitled resources coordinators)
Robert Hignett (S1; S2, episodes 5 & 7; 'Christmas Crackers'; 'Diamonds are for Heather'); Derek Martin (S2, episodes 1, 2, 4 & 6); Alan Jeffery (S2, episode 3); Chris Watts (S3, episodes 1–4 & 7); Terry Brett (S3, episode 5); Bob Warman (S3, episode 6);

à la Del

★ ★ ★ ★ ★ ★

'Oh toujours la politesse, toujours'

('A Touch of Glass')

Tony Mutimer (S4); Peter Valentine ('Thicker Than Water'); Nick Moore (S5); Reg Poulter (S6, episodes 1, 3–6; 'Dates" 'The Frog's Legacy'); Paul Thackray ('The Jolly Boys' Outing'); Peter Manuel (S7; 'Rodney Come Home'; 'Miami Twice' (Parts 1 & 2)); Michael Langley-Evans ('Mother Nature's Son'; 'Fatal Extraction')

STUDIO RESOURCE MANAGERS
Richard Morgan ('Heroes and Villains'; 'Modern Men'; 'Time On Our Hands'); Kim Jowitt ('If They Could See Us Now…!')

STUDIO SOUND SUPERVISORS
Mike Felton (S1; 'Christmas Crackers'); Dave Thompson (S2; S3, episodes 2–7; S4; S5, episode 4; 'Diamonds are for Heather'; 'Thicker Than Water'); Malcolm Johnson (S3, episode 1); Keith Gunn (S3, episode 2); Anthony Philpot (S5, episodes 1, 2, 3, 5 & 6); Brian Robinson ('A Royal Flush') Alan Machin (S6, episodes 1, 3–6; S7; 'Mother Nature's Son'); Graham Wilkinson ('Rodney Come Home'); Keith Mayes ('Dates'; 'The Jolly Boys' Outing'); Tony Revell ('Miami Twice' (Parts 1 & 2)); Laurie Taylor ('Fatal Extraction'; 'If They Could See Us Now…!'); Nick Roast ('If They Could See Us Now…!')

LIGHTING DIRECTORS
Don Babbage (S1; S3; S4, episodes 3, 5–7; S6, episodes 1, 3–6; S7; episodes 1–4; 'Christmas Crackers'; 'Diamonds are for Heather'; 'Thicker Than Water'; 'The Frog's

Legacy'; 'Dates'; 'The Jolly Boys' Outing'; 'Rodney Come Home'; 'Mother Nature's Son'); Henry Barber (S2; S5); Peter Smee (S4, episodes 1, 2 & 4); Ron Bristow (S7, episodes 5 & 6; 'Miami Twice' (Parts 1 & 2)); Graham Rimmington ('Fatal Extraction'; 'Heroes and Villains'; 'Modern Men'; 'Time On Our Hands'); Mark Kempton ('If They Could See Us Now…!')

CAMERA SUPERVISORS
Ron Peverall (S1, episodes 1–4; S2; S3, episodes 2, 3, 5–7; 'Diamonds are for Heather'; 'Thicker Than Water'); Peter Leverick (S1, episode 5); Mike Harrison (S1, episode 6); Peter Hills ('Christmas Crackers'); Chris Glass (S3, episodes 1 & 4); Ken Major (S4, episodes 1–5 & 7; S5; S6, episodes 2–6; S7; 'Dates'; 'The Frog's Legacy'; 'The Jolly Boys' Outing'; 'Rodney Come Home'); Ron Green (S6, episode 1); John Pilblad ('A Royal Flush'); Peter Goldring ('Miami Twice' (Parts 1 & 2)); Gerry Tivers ('Mother Nature's Son'; 'Fatal Extraction'); Peter Woodley ('Heroes and Villains'; 'Modern Men'; 'Time On Our Hands'; 'If They Could See Us Now…!')

FILM EDITORS
John Jarvis (S1; S4, episodes 1–5 & 7; S5, episodes 1–4; S6, episodes 1 & 3; S7, episodes 1–3, 5 & 6; 'To Hull and Back'; 'The Frog's Legacy'; 'Dates'; 'The Jolly Boys' Outing'; 'Rodney Come Home'; 'Miami Twice' (Parts 1 & 2); 'Mother Nature's Son'; 'Fatal Extraction'; 'Heroes and Villains'; 'Modern Men'; 'Time On Our Hands'); Mike Jackson (S2, episodes 1, 2, 4–7; S3, episodes 1–4, 6 & 7); John Dunstan ('Diamonds are for Heather'; 'A Royal Flush'; 'Miami Twice' (Parts 1 & 2)); Jacqui Bass (S7, episode 6); John Wilkinson ('A Royal Flush')

ASSISTANT FILM EDITOR
Simon Price ('Miami Twice' (Parts 1 & 2))

FILM SOUND RECORDISTS
Dennis Panchen (S1, episodes 1–5; S2, episodes 1, 2, 4–7; S4, episodes 1–5 & 7; 'Diamonds are for Heather'; 'To Hull and Back'); Ron Brown (S1, episode 3); John Pritchard (S1, episodes 5 & 6); Nigel Woodford (S2, episodes 2, 4, 5 & 7); Clive Derbyshire (S3, episodes 1–4, 6 & 7); Dave Brabants (S5, episodes 1–4); Michael Spencer (S6, episodes 1–3; S7, episodes 1–3, 5 & 6; 'A Royal Flush'; 'The Frog's Legacy'; 'Dates'; 'Rodney Come Home'; 'Miami Twice' (Parts 1 & 2); 'Mother Nature's Son'; 'Fatal Extraction'; Peter Hobbs (S6, episode 3); John Parry ('The Jolly Boys' Outing'; 'Miami Twice' (Parts 1 & 2)); Steve Gatland ('Miami Twice' (Parts 1 & 2)); Roger Long ('Heroes and Villains'; 'Modern Men'; 'Time On Our Hands'); Reg Mills ('If They Could See Us Now…!')

FILM CAMERAMEN
Bill Matthews (S1); John Walker (S2, episodes 1, 2, 4–7; 'Miami Twice' (Parts 1 & 2)); Alec Curtis ('Diamonds are for Heather'; 'Dates'; 'The Jolly Boys' Outing'; 'Rodney Come Home'; S6, episodes 1–3; S7, episodes 1–3, 5 & 6; 'Miami Twice' (Parts 1 & 2)); Ian Hilton (S3, episodes 1–4, 6 & 7); Chris Seager (S4, episodes 1–5 & 7; S5, episodes 1–4; 'To Hull and Back'; 'Time On Our Hands'); John Rhodes ('Miami Twice' (Parts 1 & 2); 'Mother Nature's Son'; 'Fatal Extraction'; 'Heroes and Villains'; 'Modern Men'; 'Time On Our Hands'); Keith Burton ('A Royal Flush'); Rex Maidment ('The Frog's Legacy'); Adrian Smith ('The Jolly Boys' Outing'); Alan Stevens (S6, episode 3)

DIRECTOR OF PHOTOGRAPHY
John Rhodes ('If They Could See Us Now…!')

CAMERA OPERATOR
John Hembrough ('If They Could See Us Now…!')

ROSTRUM CAMERAMAN
Ivor Richardson (S2, episode 6)

BOOM OPERATOR (only credited on one episode)
John Lewis ('If They Could See Us Now…!')

LIGHTING GAFFERS (FILM)
Joe Ryan ('To Hull and Back'); Peter Robinson ('A Royal Flush'; 'Dates'; 'The Jolly Boys' Outing'; 'Rodney Come Home'; 'Fatal Extraction'); Ted Turpin ('The Jolly Boys' Outing'); Ted Bird ('The Jolly Boys' Outing'); Colonel Dave Harris ('Miami Twice' (Parts 1 & 2)); Pat Deveney ('Heroes and Villains'; 'Modern Men'; 'Time On Our Hands'; 'If They Could See Us Now…!')

VISUAL EFFECTS DESIGNERS
Graham Brown (S6, episode 6; 'Dates'); Christopher Lawson (S7, episode 1; 'The Jolly Boys' Outing'); Andy Lazell ('Fatal Extraction'; 'Heroes and Villains')

ENGINEERING MANAGER
Mike Hill ('A Royal Flush')

VIDEO EFFECTS
Dave Jervis (S7, episode 1); Ian Simpson ('Heroes and Villains'; 'Time On Our Hands')

LOCATION MANAGERS
Gail Bruns ('Miami Twice' (Parts 1 & 2)); Duncan Cooper ('The Jolly Boys' Outing'); Susannah Bartlett ('Mother Nature's Son'); Jonathan Paul Llewellyn ('Fatal Extraction'); Lisa McArthur ('Heroes and Villains'; 'Modern Men'; 'Time On Our Hands'); Steve Abrahams ('Heroes and Villains'; 'Modern Men'; 'Time On Our Hands'); Peter Chadwick ('If They Could See Us Now…!')

PRODUCTION SECRETARIES
Linda O'Connell ('The Frog's Legacy'); Amanda Church (S7, episodes 1–4; 'Rodney Come Home'); Katie Tyrrell (S7, episodes 5 & 6; 'Miami Twice' (Parts 1 & 2)); Simon Sharrod ('Fatal Extraction'); Katie Wilkinson ('Heroes and Villains'; 'Modern Men'; 'Time On Our Hands')

CASTING ADVISER

Judy Loe (S7; 'Miami Twice' (Parts 1 & 2); 'Mother Nature's Son'; 'Fatal Extraction'; 'Heroes and Villains'; 'Modern Men'; 'Time On Our Hands'); Tracey Gillham ('If They Could See Us Now…!')

CASTING DIRECTOR

Dee Miller, CSA ('Miami Twice' (Parts 1 & 2))

MUSICAL DIRECTOR

Kennedy Aitchison (S7, episode 3)

MUSIC PRODUCER

Jez Coed ('Miami Twice' (Parts 1 & 2))

MUSIC

Graham Jarvis ('Heroes and Villains'; 'Modern Men'; 'Time On Our Hands'; 'If They Could See Us Now…!')

GRIPS

Mickey Ellis ('The Jolly Boys' Outing'); Scott Eberle ('Miami Twice' (Parts 1 & 2)); James Grimes ('Fatal Extraction'); Iain Johnstone ('Heroes and Villains'; 'Modern Men'; 'Time On Our Hands'); Dave Holliday ('If They Could See Us Now…!')

SET DECORATOR

Bryony Foster ('Miami Twice' (Parts 1 & 2))

PRODUCTION OPERATIVES SUPERVISOR

Ray Jobling ('Miami Twice' (Parts 1 & 2))

3RD ASSISTANT DIRECTORS

Anna Brabbins ('Heroes and Villains'; 'Modern Men'; 'Time On Our Hands'); Scott Bunce ('If They Could See Us Now…!')

2ND ASSISTANT DIRECTORS

Udanne Uditis ('Miami Twice' (Parts 1 & 2)); Dominic Bowles ('Heroes and Villains'; 'Modern Men'; 'Time On Our Hands'); Anna Brabbins ('If They Could See Us Now…!')

1ST ASSISTANT DIRECTORS

Ken Bruns ('Miami Twice' (Parts 1 & 2)); David Reid ('Heroes and Villains'; 'Modern Men'; 'Time On Our Hands'); Marcus Catlin ('If They Could See Us Now…!')

FOCUS PULLER

Courtney Goodwin ('Miami Twice' (Parts 1 & 2))

BUSINESS MANAGER (New York)

Robert J Easter ('Miami Twice' (Parts 1 & 2))

TELECINE OPERATOR

Dave Hawley ('Miami Twice' (Parts 1 & 2))

DUBBING EDITORS

Kevin Ahern ('Miami Twice' (Parts 1 & 2)); Glenn Hyde ('Miami Twice' (Parts 1 & 2)); Richard Rhys Davies ('Miami Twice' (Parts 1 & 2)); Graham Bevan ('Mother Nature's Son'); Simon Price ('Fatal Extraction'); Paul Bingley ('Heroes and Villains'; 'Modern Men'; 'Time On Our Hands')

DUBBING MIXERS

Dean Humphreys ('To Hull and Back'); Alan Dykes ('A Royal Flush'); Michael Narduzzo ('S7, episodes 1–3, 5 & 6; 'Rodney Come Home'); Peter Hodges ('Miami Twice' (Parts 1 & 2)); Keith Marriner ('Miami Twice' (Parts 1 & 2)); Lee Taylor ('Miami Twice' (Parts 1 & 2)); Aad Wirtz ('Mother Nature's Son')

STUNT COORDINATORS

Andy Bradford ('Fatal Extraction'); Nick Powell ('Heroes and Villains'; 'Modern Men'); Colin Skeaping ('Dates'; 'The Jolly Boys' Outing')

ART DIRECTORS

Charmian Adams ('Fatal Extraction'); Nick Harding ('Heroes and Villains'; 'Modern Men'; 'Time On Our Hands'); Les McCallum ('If They Could See Us Now…!')

PROGRAMME FFNANCE ASSISTANTS

Alison Passey ('Heroes and Villains'; 'Modern Men'; 'Time On Our Hands'); Honor Newton ('If They Could See Us Now…!')

RESEARCHERS

Mona Adams ('Time On Our Hands') Christopher Kenworthy ('If They Could See Us Now…!')

FRENCH FIXER

Dominique Combe ('If They Could See Us Now…!')

Programme seller

Played by Christina Michaels

When Rodney takes Lady Victoria to see *Carmen* at the opera, he buys two programmes from the seller, not realising they cost £4 each.

Props

(For Del's various cocktails, see 'Cocktails')

Over the years, numerous props have been required for the series. McCallum Jones, a Twickenham-based company which specialises in producing graphic props for the film and television industry, was often called upon to provide a host of items. Faye McCallum, a partner and designer in the company, explains her company's involvement.

Faye McCallum with various props made by her company

An example of McCallum Jones' handiwork

'We first started working on the programme in 1992, supplying items for the Christmas Special "Mother Nature's Son". We were asked to design box graphics for all the dodgy gear, including an alarm clock box, which had to be very old fashioned in appearance, from Latvia, "Free Nelson Mandela" t-shirts, betamax video boxes and many other items for around the flat.

'Peckham Spring Water labels and boxes were the main items we were asked to concentrate on. We initially had a meeting in the Grand Hotel, Brighton, where we looked at a range of spring waters available in the supermarket, and decided on a suitable bottle shape to work on. I remember driving back from Brighton with a car-load of assorted bottles, one of every water available on the market at the time. We don't really get involved with the actual filming or with the crew; in general, production designers and buyers approach us with their graphic requirements list and we take it from there.

'I remember a surprise delivery turning up one day on the largest heavy goods vehicle you can imagine. The driver wanted to despatch thousands of bottles on pallets to our small graphic design studio, in readiness to apply the Peckham Spring Water labels that we were printing. The driver stepped out of his cabin and calmly asked me to send round our forklift truck. Not the sort of machinery graphic designers keep handy out back! So I had to send him away to Television Centre where the chance of unloading these bottles was a little more likely.

'Over the last ten years we have worked on all the episodes, including the Christmas Trilogy in 1996. We were responsible for designing the TITCO logo and applying it to many graphics, such as the aeroplane photo-edit of Trotter Air, which was a super-plane we'd created for the billboards, together with a Meatfingers brand and a range of condoms called Trotterex. Of course, we've been very busy recently supplying more items for the latest episodes, including more 'dodgy' items like KozyGlo fire graphics and *Peckham Echo* newspapers.'

Pub customer

(See 'Paddy')

Pussycat Willum

In the episode 'Healthy Competition' this cat spits at Del as he runs down the alley, trying desperately to escape from a chasing policeman.

Questel, Roy

Role: The heavy
Appeared in S1, episode 3

à la Del

★ ★ ★ ★ ★ ★

'A la mode, a la mode'

('A Touch of Glass')

Rachmann

In 'The Sky's the Limit', Del likens Bronco's landlord to the notorious sixties landlord Rachmann.

Rajah Computers

Del is selling these Mauritius-made computers in 'From Prussia with Love', but they can't be shifting quickly because he's still got 25 left when we see him trying to flog them to Mike Fisher, down at The Nag's Head, later on in 'The Frog's Legacy'. Normally retailing at £399, Del's letting them go for £150, with a free joystick thrown in.

Having only sold five machines in over a year, Rodney admits that their sales campaign took a tragic blow when the Office of Fair Trading announced to the press that the computers don't work.

Ram, Mr

Played by Renu Setna

A small, smartly dressed Indian, Mr Ram is first spotted by Rodney, sitting in a car in the town hall car park during 'Cash and Curry'. Together with his accompanying heavy, Mr Ram confronts Vimmal Malik, who's spent the evening discussing business opportunities with Del. Before the evening is out, Del ends up eating at an Indian restaurant with Mr Ram and the heavy. It transpires that he owns 18 restaurants and plenty of land, and proceeds to tell Del about his long-running dispute with the Malik family, a feud that dates back to the days of the old British Empire. Ram claims Malik's family stole their land, sold it and formed a business empire from the proceeds. He's appeared on the scene to reclaim the sole remaining item of his birthright: a porcelain statuette of the Hindu god of wealth, Kuvera. Although it's only valuable in religious and sentimental terms, he's so desperate to acquire the statuette that he'll pay £4000 to get it back.

It all turns out to be a con, though, as Del finds out to his cost. Ram was in partnership with Vimmal all the time and diddles Del out of a fortune.

Ram Jam Club

Del refers to the club in 'The Longest Night'. The Ram Jam was a famous West Indian club in the sixties and seventies.

Ramondo
(See 'Great Ramondo, The')

Ramsden, Dennis
Role: Judge
Appeared in S4, episode 3
Born in Leeds in 1918, Dennis was intending to follow his father's footsteps into the world of journalism but his plans were scuppered when war broke out and he spent six years in the RAF, where he experienced his first taste of acting. After demob, Dennis joined a friend who was running the Dundee rep for two years.

His busy career has included spells in theatre, film and television, where he made his debut in children's shows; he was regularly spotted on *Crackerjack* in Eamonn Andrews' era.

Other small-screen credits include *Robin's Nest, George and Mildred, The Fall and Rise of Reginald Perrin, To the Manor Born, The Fosters, Terry and June* and *As Time Goes By*. Recently he's been concentrating on theatrical directing.

Ranji
Seen but not heard in the sitcom, Ranji is an Indian who Del speaks to briefly at The Nag's Head in 'Who's a Pretty Boy?'. As Del crosses to the bar, he tells Ranji that he saw his wife the other day and noticed she had a bad spot on her forehead, before telling Karen, the barmaid, that Ranji's a 'nice bloke' because he took him and Rodney to an Asian song contest in Southall recently.

Raquel
(See 'Turner, Raquel')

Rawlings, Les
Role: Clerk
Appeared in S4, episode 3
The late Les Rawlings' career saw him appear in many programmes, including a long-running part in *The Black and White Minstrel Show*.

Razzle, Tommy
Not seen in the sitcom, Tommy is mentioned in 'The Long Legs of the Law'. Del tells Grandad about him, after seeing him in a pub during a night out. Razzle used to live in Cathles House and worked on the Underground when the Trotters knew him. Nowadays, he's in partnership with Monkey Harris installing false ceilings, and has just returned from an assignment in Saudi Arabia, fitting a ceiling in a dental clinic.

Ray
Played by Michael Attwell
An arrogant Englishman who's seen in 'It Never Rains…', Ray is holidaying in Benidorm at the same time as the Trotters. He's also staying at the same hotel, and when it transpires he's with the girl Del has been chasing, Del deflates his blow-up poolside chair with a quick stab of his cigar.

Read, Mike
Role: DJ
Appeared in S4, episode 4
A household name for many years, top DJ Mike Read has won ten National Broadcaster of the Year awards during his radio career, which now involves presenting the breakfast show on Jazz FM. On television, he's fronted shows such as *Saturday Superstore, Pop Quiz, Top of the Pops* and *Pop Quest*.

Mike's career has also extended beyond his radio work, and to date he's written the music and lyrics for six stage musicals, had songs recorded by many top artists and has penned several books.

Readman, Andy
Role: Policeman
Appeared in 'A Royal Flush'
Born in Chippenham in 1955, Andy worked as a waiter in Stratford before accepting a place at the Rose Bruford Drama School in Kent; he left the course early when offered 44 weeks' work – earning him full Equity status in the process – with Second City Theatre in Birmingham. It was here that he made his first stage appearance in *Vandals*. After a spell at the Bubble Theatre, London, he worked in reps around the country for five years.

A decade after waitering in Stratford, Andrew returned as a professional actor, working with the likes of Kenneth Branagh. Over a year later, he started focusing on the small screen, with his first appearance being in Yorkshire TV's 1982 drama *Airline*. Favourite screen work since includes an appearance in *Cracker*; playing Superintendent Brian Lee in six episodes of *Burnside*; Dr Halliday in *Heartbeat*; Martin Hutton in *Where the Heart Is*; Tim King in *Hillsborough* and seven episodes as Detective Constable Cannon in *Coronation Street*.

Andrew still works in the theatre and, in 2001, went on an eight-state theatre tour of America playing Leontes in *The Winter's Tale*.

'Sleeping Dogs Lie'

Receptionist
Played by Debbi Blythe
The attractive blonde receptionist works at the veterinary practice that Del and Rodney take Duke, the Great Dane, to in 'Sleeping Dogs Lie'.

Receptionist
Played by Lorraine Ashley
The receptionist – who works at the local hospital – is seen in 'Modern Men' and has the unenviable task of dealing with a loud-mouthed lout – although Del finally gives her a helping hand!

MEMORIES OF PLAYING THE POLICEMAN
★ ★ ★ ★ ★ ★

'This was my eighth television appearance and one of the most widely seen and lucrative. At the time of the engagement I was working at the Young Vic and appearing in Shakespeare's *Julius Caesar*. I was told that a car would pick me up at curtain down on a Saturday night and take me to a hotel ready to film the following day. The next day dawned and the weather was so bad that the BBC rescheduled the filming for the following weekend. I went back to the Young Vic for another week and then we went through the same routine. Again the weather was bad and we were forced to abandon. On the third weekend we finally got the scene.

'This, of course, meant that my contract had to be issued three times and, consequently, I received three times the original fee with the resultant knock-on effects in terms of future royalties. All in all, I did very well for such a minor appearance and that was to say nothing of the enjoyment we all had whilst filming.

'Both David and Nick were very easy to work with. I'd worked with Nick on *The Two of Us* prior to this and, consequently, was invited to relax with them in their caravan whilst on set. The whole experience crystallised something within me. Previously I had been determined to become a Shakespearean leading actor and had already spent time with the RSC. I'd observed that I got a lot more satisfaction as a performer playing to small groups in a studio environment and got less and less from playing the main house. What with my passion for film and work at the old "Other Place" in Statford, I'd realised that intimacy and subtlety were my new interests.

'Once I got on set I realised that I was at home and became determined to find more work on film. I changed my agent and my focus. I was already a bit fed up that audiences at Stratford were paying a fortune, were limited and often tourists who were sometimes sharing two seats between ten, coming and going in relays just to say that they'd "been". Straight to pseud's corner then when it dawned on me that the new popular theatre medium sat in the corner of people's living rooms.' **ANDREW READMAN**

Redford, Ian

Role: Adrian
Appeared in S7, episode 2

Ian, who was born in Carshalton in 1951, trained at the Bristol Old Vic Theatre School and secured his first professional job as an acting ASM (assistant stage manager) at the Liverpool Playhouse for two seasons in 1972.

Much of his early work was on the stage but his television break was playing Nick in Granada's *A Raging Calm*. He's since appeared numerous times on the small screen, including playing Tom in *Robin of Sherwood*, Mr Legge in *Grange Hill*, Harry Wreitz in *Van der Valk*, Terry Upton in *The Bill*, Aiden McCloy in *Spender*, Joe Canty in *The Prince and the Pauper*, Mick Davies, a soldier, in *Bergerac*, Larry Coiter in *The House of Eliott*, Jarvis in *Bread or Blood* and Jimmy Plinth in *September Song*. On the big screen, meanwhile, he's worked on films such as *Three Men and A Little Lady* and *Remains of the Day*.

On stage, he's appeared in classics to comedies. Among his theatre credits are roles such as Hotspur in *Henry V*, Nikolai in *The Mother*, Nick in *Some Explicit Polaroid* and, more recently, assignments at The National Theatre and the Soho Theatre, London.

Reg

(See 'Trotter, Reg')

Reid, David

1st assistant director on three episodes: 'Heroes and Villains', 'Modern Men' and 'Time On Our Hands'

London-born David Reid was 17 when he first worked for the BBC in its finance department, before leaving to study music and drama. A succession of jobs followed after which he found himself temping back at the Beeb on *That's Life*, which led to a spell working for the drama department as a runner.

He quickly progressed through the ranks and was a 1st assistant director when he left the Corporation in 1995 to work freelance. Gradually he found himself concentrating more and more on the film world and is now Head of Production at Ska Films, working on films such as *Lock, Stock and Two Smoking Barrels*, *Snatch* and *Mean Machine*.

Renee, Aunt

Played by Joan Sims

First mentioned by Trigger in 'Chain Gang', Aunt Renee pawned a necklace to help raise the cash Trigg needed to join the consortium investing in the gold chains that Arnie is selling. She also makes an appearance in 'The Frog's Legacy' at her niece Lisa's wedding.

Since 1965, she's lived in Hampshire, after moving there because she couldn't endure another day on the Peckham estate. Renee Turpin was one of Joan Trotter's best friends, so she's well liked by the Trotter boys, especially Del, who's rumoured to

have had a brief affair with the woman. However, the manner in which they talk to each other at the wedding reception makes one wonder if they were simply good friends, not lovers.

Registrar

Played by Derek Benfield

Seen in 'Little Problems', the registry office official conducts proceedings at Rodney and Cassandra's wedding.

Repeats

Of the regular repeats, excluding sketches recorded for special broadcasts (e.g. Comic Relief or 'Christmas Trees' for 'The Funny Side of Christmas'), the least repeated episode is 'Christmas Crackers' which has been repeated only once since its original transmission in 1981. Meanwhile, at the time of writing, four episodes have been repeated on seven occasions, sharing top spot for the most repeated episodes: 'Yuppy Love', 'Chain Gang', 'Sickness and Wealth' and 'Little Problems'.

REPEATS	EPISODE
1	'Christmas Crackers', 'The Funny Side of Christmas: Christmas Trees'
2	'A Royal Flush', 'The Jolly Boys' Outing', 'Mother Nature's Son', 'Fatal Extraction'
3	'Go West Young Man', 'Cash and Curry', The Second Time Around', 'A Slow Bus to Chingford',' The Russians are Coming', 'It's Only Rock and Roll', 'To Hull and Back', 'Who Wants to be a Millionaire', 'The Frog's Legacy'
4	'Diamonds are for Heather', 'Yesterday Never Comes', 'Thicker Than Water', 'From Prussia with Love', 'The Miracle of Peckham', 'Tea for Three', 'Video Nasty', 'Dates', 'Rodney Come Home', 'The Sky's the Limit', 'The Chance of a Lunchtime', 'He Ain't Heavy, He's My Uncle', 'Miami Twice – Part 1: The American Dream', 'Miami Twice – Part 2: Oh to be in England', 'Heroes and Villains', 'Modern Men', 'Time On Our Hands'
5	'Big Brother', 'Ashes to Ashes', 'A Losing Streak', 'No Greater Love…', 'The Yellow Peril', 'It Never Rains…', 'Homesick', 'Healthy Competition', 'Friday the 14th', 'May the Force be with You', 'Wanted', 'Who's a Pretty Boy?', 'Strained Relations', 'Hole in One', 'Sleeping Dogs Lie', 'Watching the Girls Go By', 'The Longest Night', 'Danger UXD', 'The Unlucky Winner is…', 'Stage Fright', 'The Class of '62'
6	'The Long Legs of the Law', 'A Touch of Glass', 'Happy Returns', 'As One Door Closes', 'Three Men, a Woman and a Baby'
7	'Yuppy Love', 'Chain Gang', 'Sickness and Wealth', 'Little Problems'

Revell, Tony

Studio sound supervisor on two episodes: 'Miami Twice' (Parts 1 & 2)

Tony, who was born in London, joined the BBC as a sound trainee straight from school in 1974. Early

shows he worked on include *The Dick Emery Show* and *Monty Python*, and he worked as grams operator on the first series of *Only Fools*. He was promoted to sound supervisor in 1992 and now works in light entertainment; recent events he's covered include Children in Need and Comic Relief.

Reynolds, Victor

Role: Bill (Captain of the bowling club)
Appeared in 'Ashes to Ashes'

Rhodes, John

Film cameraman on seven episodes: 'Miami Twice' (Parts 1 & 2), 'Mother Nature's Son', 'Fatal Extraction', 'Heroes and Villains', 'Modern Men' and 'Time On Our Hands'. Director of photography on one episode: 'If They Could See Us Now…!'

Born in Jamaica in 1953, John began his career in 1973, working for Town and Country Productions, a small documentary film company in Chelsea, combining his duties as assistant film cameraman with helping repair films in the company's film library.

He joined the BBC in 1978 and has worked on a host of programmes from *Nationwide* and *Blue Peter* to *Play for Today* and *Play of the Month*. He's also covered many current affairs, documentaries and dramas, with recent projects including *Rockface*. He left the BBC to work freelance in 1993.

Rhule, David

Role: Leroy
Appeared in S2, episode 4

Among David's other screen appearanes are roles in *The Young Ones*, *Cribb* and the 1988 film *Empire State*.

Richards, Danny

Not seen in the sitcom, Danny is mentioned by Rodney during 'It's Only Rock and Roll'. His eldest sister, Viv, signed some cricket bats that the Trotters tried selling, claiming they were signed by the legendary cricketer Viv Richards.

Richards, Viv

Oldest sister of Danny, she's mentioned in 'It's Only Rock and Roll'. She signed some cricket bats so the Trotters could claim they were signed by Viv Richards – though not *the* Viv Richards.

Richardson, Ivor

Rostrum cameraman on one episode: S2, episode 6

Richardson, James

Role: Man in church
Appeared in S5, episode 2

Born in the Hampshire town of Gosport in 1951, James moved between jobs before deciding his future lay in the acting profession. He worked as a bank clerk in the 1960s, and was a sewing machine salesman before managing one of the company's shops.

He trained at the Guildhall School of Music and Drama, and made his professional debut in a 1978 production of *Merchant of Venice*. A year later he was first seen on television as Geoff in *Shelley*. Offers of work increased whilst he continued working on the stage, particularly in regional theatre. Recent work assignments include playing Dr Bradley in Sky Television's *Dream Team*.

Richmond, Dave

Role: Bass player

Appeared in 'The Jolly Boys' Outing'

Born in the West Sussex town of Shoreham by Sea in 1938, Dave joined a business studies course at Torquay's South Devon Technical College upon leaving school. But deciding his future didn't involve the business world, he joined the RAF when his mother heard a radio announcement that the Air Force were looking for men to train as musicians. Between 1955 and 1960, he studied the clarinet and double bass, before leaving the Forces and pursuing a musical career on civvy street, beginning with a world cruise as a member of a liner's resident band.

In 1963 he became a founder member of the rhythm and blues group the Mann-Hugg Blues Brothers, which later became Manfred Mann. After the hit record, '5–4–3–2–1', Dave left to pursue a session career, recording for records, films, TV and radio. Among the dozens of artists he's recorded with are Elton John, Dusty Springfield, Cilla Black, Tom Jones, Cliff Richard, Val Doonican and Lulu, while the various television shows he's worked on include *The Two Ronnies*, *The Cliff Richard Show*, *The Rolf Harris Show*, *Blue Peter*, *Are You Being Served?* and *Last of the Summer Wine*, where he plays fretless bass guitar on the incidental music.

Nowadays he's playing with the new Bert Kaempfert Orchestra.

Rico

Played by Antoni Corone

Rico, who's seen in 'Miami Twice', is the son of Vinny Occhetti.

Riddle, Stephen

Role: Giles

Appeared in 'A Royal Flush'

Ridgemere Hall

Home of Lord and Lady Ridgemere, the 17th-century mansion is seen in 'A Touch of Glass'. Its original structure dates back to 1642 and impresses the Trotters whose brief brush with historical buildings sees them being hired to clean the priceless chandeliers, with the inevitable disaster just around the corner.

Ridgemere, Lady

Played by Elizabeth Benson

Lady Ridgemere's car breaks down in a country lane during 'A Touch of Glass', just as Del, Rodney and Grandad pass by in their van after attending an auction. Seeing the lady needs a helping hand, they end up towing her car back to Ridgemere Hall, before outstaying their welcome.

Ridgemere, Lord

Played by Geoffrey Toone

Seen in 'A Touch of Glass', Lord Ridgemere owns Ridgemere Hall, a 17th-century mansion situated in acres of ground. He takes an instant dislike to Del Boy when he arrives on the scene after towing Lady Ridgemere's car back to the Hall. His Lordship is frugal when it comes to monetary affairs, and after being given an extortionate estimate for cleaning valuable crystal chandeliers, he hires the Trotters to do the job, unaware of their inexperience in the field – a decision he lives to regret.

Riley, Vivien

Make-up designer on one episode: 'To Hull and Back'

Vivien has worked as make-up designer on many television programmes and films, including *Relatively Speaking*, *Uncle Vanya*, *The House of Eliott*, *Dad*, *Nice Town*, *Over Here*, *Madame Bovary* and *Pas de Trois*.

Rimmington, Graham

Lighting director on four episodes: 'Fatal Extraction', 'Heroes and Villains', 'Modern Men' and 'Time On Our Hands'

Graham, who was born in Derby, joined the BBC straight from school in 1964, initially as a technical operator, before joining the lighting team in the mid-1960s. His early credits include working on shows such as *The Billy Cotton Band Show*, *Z Cars* and with singers like Cilla Black, Cliff Richard and Olivia Newton John.

Graham, who spent most of his career in light entertainment, was promoted to lighting director in 1985. His first job in this capacity was *EastEnders*, followed by a string of others, from *French and Saunders* to *As Time Goes By*.

In 1999, Graham resigned from the Beeb after 35 years' service, and has worked freelance ever since, including the third series of *Coupling*, *Absolutely Fabulous*, *Time Gentlemen Please* and the latest series of *As Time Goes By*.

Rinaldi, Miles

Role: Small boy

Appeared in S3, episode 1

As a boy, London-born Miles Rinaldi did photographic and acting jobs during the school holidays. His mother, Judy Collins, a former dancer and singer who's also a background artist, was employed in the same episode of *Only Fools*, and when a child was required as well, her agent suggested Miles.

Aged 11 at the time of the recording, Miles went on to complete a music degree at Leicester University, and later studied for a second degree, in psychology. Since 1996 he has been working for the NHS in mental health.

River policeman

Played by John D. Collins

The policeman is patrolling St Catherine's Dock on the River Thames when Rodney and Del row out in 'Ashes to Ashes'. Hoping to deposit Trigger's grand-father's ashes over the side of the boat, they're prevented from doing so by the river police, who escort the Trotters back to shore.

Rix, Danny

Role: Baby Tyler

Appeared in 'Miami Twice' (Part 1)

Danny, who was born in Lewisham, was four when he appeared in 'Miami Twice'. His grandfather owned a butcher's shop backing on to a drama school in Catford, London, and when the woman who owned the school spotted Danny, she told his mother that the BBC were looking for a child to play the part of Tyler in the Christmas Special.

Danny went along to several other auditions after playing Tyler, but he was unsuccessful and didn't remain in the highly competitive world of child acting. He now has ambitions of joining the army.

MEMORIES OF PLAYING TYLER

★ ★ ★ ★ ★ ★

Danny, who was four when he played Tyler, remembers little about his time playing the Boyce's son, but does remember being taken along to location shooting in a rather 'posh car'. His mother, meanwhile, recalls the simple tricks used by members of the production team to ensure the shooting went to plan. 'There wasn't much acting involved, it was just standing still with Maltesers in his hand! He held a Malteser in each hand and was told to keep still and not let the sweets melt, which helped him to concentrate.'

'The cast were really nice, especially Sue Holderness who really took Danny under her wing.'

DANNY RIX

Robdal, Freddy

Not seen in the series, Freddy, who's nicknamed Freddy the Frog because he used to be a frogman, is mentioned during 'The Frog's Legacy'. Trigger's Aunt Renee talks about him to Del at her daughter's wedding and it turns out that Del's mother met the petty criminal in 1959.

Freddy originated from Rotherhithe and, with his love for French wine and paintings, was regarded as a 'gentleman thief' by Renee. He owned a holiday chalet in Hampshire and it's reputed that when the police broke into it, expensive paintings adorned the walls.

In August 1963, Freddy became a little more ambitious and with his gang broke into the vaults of a London bank; they slipped away with over a quarter of a million pounds worth of gold bullion. While the rest of the gang were caught, Freddy escaped the clutches of the law. However, he was later killed in a freak accident whilst robbing a post office in Plumstead, and his will revealed that he'd left all his belongings to Joan Trotter.

Roberts, Michael

Role: Cockney man
Appeared in S4, episode 3
Michael's credits include playing a boy in the 1968 film *Finders Keepers, Lovers Weepers!*, but his recent work has been primarily on the stage, where he's been seen in *In Praise of Love, A Funny Thing Happened on the Way to the Forum, A Saint She Ain't, Talking Turkeys* and *Angels in America*.

Roberts, Renee

Role: Old lady (No 2)
Appeared in S3, episode 1
During her career, the late Renee Roberts appeared on stage and screen, but she'll probably be best remembered for playing the eccentric Miss Gatsby in *Fawlty Towers*.

Robinson, Brian

Studio sound supervisor on one episode: 'A Royal Flush'
Brian, who was born in Isleworth in 1944, joined the BBC straight from college. For three years he worked on overseas' broadcasts at Bush House before transferring to television and becoming a sound assistant in 1966.

During his time at the BBC, Brian worked on a host of programmes, from the Queen's speeches and Wimbledon to FA Cup finals and cricket matches. Although he's now retired from the Beeb (he left in 1997), Brian still works freelance as a senior sound supervisor and his recent assignments have included *Casualty* and horse racing.

Robinson, Peter

Lighting gaffer on five episodes: 'A Royal Flush', 'Dates', 'The Jolly Boys' Outing', 'Rodney Come Home' and 'Fatal Extraction'
Peter, who's now a freelance lighting gaffer, was born in London. He completed an electrician's apprenticeship before joining Rainbow Lighting, which took him into the film industry for six years.

His career with the BBC's film unit began in 1977 and continued for 22 years, before he was made redundant in 2000. Programmes he's worked on include all the series of *Jonathan Creek*.

Robinson, Rex

Roles: Harry (the foreman) and Vicar
Appeared as Harry in S3, episode 2 and as the Vicar in S5, episode 5
Born in Derby in 1926, Rex trained at the Old Vic School and made his professional debut at the venue in a 1951 production of *Othello*. His early years were dominated by the theatre, including three seasons at Stratford and spells at numerous theatres up and down the country, such as Glasgow, York and Chichester.

Rex – who worked with David Jason when he was still an amateur actor – made his television debut playing a scientist in *Doctor Who*, and has since been seen in various shows, including *Terry and June; Upstairs, Downstairs; The Professionals; Sink or Swim; Yes, Minister* and his favourite role, playing the chief engineer in *Warship*.

Rex retired from the profession after becoming visually impaired. He moved to Spain in 1988, but returned to England in 1999, when his second eye became damaged.

Robson, Chief

Played by Christopher Malcolm
(Also referred to as 'Madman' and 'Chief of Security')
In 'Friday the 14th', the real-life Chief Robson, who's in charge of the institute for the criminally insane, is not seen, and we later find out that he's at the hospital: the escapee knocked him on the head and stole his uniform and identity papers. Masquerading as the Chief, the madman, who was tagged the Axe Murderer after killing a group of weekend fishermen in the area ten years previously, arrives at Boycie's weekend cottage, which is occupied by the Trotters.

Amid all the confusion, Del ends up being alone with the madman, while Rodney and Grandad transport poor old Tom Witton, the local game-keeper, who they think is the escaped patient, to the police station. In the final few moments of the episode, the madman gives an insight, perhaps, of why he turned to crime, explaining that his father forced him to win at everything. He adds: 'But people challenge winners. You become vulnerable, you feel open to attack.'

Although we don't see his recapture, Del escapes the clutches of the madman, but not before betting a tenner a frame that he'll beat him at snooker.

Rodney

(See 'Trotter, Rodney')

'Rodney Come Home'

(Christmas Special 1990)
Original transmission: Tuesday 25 December 1990, 5.10 pm
Production date: Friday 9 November – Sunday 11 November 1990
Original viewing figures: 18 million
Duration: 75 minutes
First repeat: Sunday 8 December 1991, 8.05 pm
Subsequent repeats: 5/3/92, 9/9/00, 23/3/01

CAST

Del Trotter	David Jason
Rodney Trotter	Nicholas Lyndhurst
Uncle Albert	Buster Merryfield
Cassandra	Gwyneth Strong
Raquel	Tessa Peake-Jones
Mickey	Patrick Murray
Alan	Denis Lill
Michelle	Paula-Ann Bland
Frank	Philip Blaine
Chris	Tony Marshall
Woman in club	Jean Harrington
Neighbour	Linda James
TV announcer	Patrick Lunt

Walk-ons: (Barman in disco) Ross Thomas. (Second woman in disco) Jenny Fleming. (Yuppies) Mark Collingwood and Linda Slade. (Shoppers) Diana Dean, Mary Fieldhouse, Anne Schofield, Val Caren, Morag Deyes, Cindy Leather, Sonja Sabin, Jill Dicken, Carol Gentle, Gaye Hopkins, Johnny Walker, Eddie Roberts, Pete Rayland, Michele Brittan-Jones, Rex Forster, Al Fresco, Paul Strike, John Magee, Richard Morgan, Peter Steadman. (Mr Coleman) Llewellyn Williams. (People in disco) Christine Murphy, Clade Edwards, James Anderson, Kit Benjamin, James Caddell, Phillip Racz, Ian Adamson, Martin Samuels, Leon Brazil, Brandon Brazil, Simon Alford, Christopher Cadden, Marcus T Elliott, Ian Tapper, Chris Manvers, Fez Harrison, Sebastion Thomson, Martin J Wills O Toole, Titus Cadden, Layla, Ruth McClaughry, Giancarla, Theresa Robart, Emma Collier, Mary Stanton Gleaves, Laney Ashton, Norma Sharpe, Mark Richards, Rich Pickens, Binda Singh, Will Brown, Rakie Ayola, Paul Anderson, Isaac Maynard, Lindi Oliver, Debbie Sutton, Annabel Thornly, Delia Jones, Victoria Lindley, Caroline Burnett, Michelle Oakey, Carla Mann, Jo Carthey, Sara Roche, Pebs Jones, Caroline Lyndsay, Lizeena Rees, Amanda Clifford, Chelsey Walker and Diane Collier. (Print Workers) Mike Eastman, Paul D'Monaco, Paul Rutter, Ali Williams and Robert Booker. (Passerby) Robin Ardra, Rex Holdworth and Valerie Wayne.

PRODUCTION TEAM

Written by John Sullivan
Title music arranged and conducted by Ronnie Hazlehurst composed and sung by John Sullivan

Closing Music:	Joan Armatrading
Audience Warm-up:	Bobby Bragg and Jeff Stevenson
Make-up Designer:	Christine Greenwood
Costume Designer:	Robin Stubbs
Properties Buyer:	Malcolm Rougvie
Film Cameraman:	Alec Curtis
Film Sound:	Michael Spencer
Film Editor:	John Jarvis
Dubbing Mixer:	Michael Narduzzo
Camera Supervisor:	Ken Major
Studio Lighting Director:	Don Babbage
Studio Sound:	Graham Wilkinson
Resources Coordinator:	Peter Manuel
Videotape Editor:	Chris Wadsworth
Production Assistant:	Teresa Powick
Assistant Floor Managers:	Debbie Crofts and Miles Cherry
Vision Mixer:	Sue Collins
Production Managers:	Adrian Pegg and Angela de Chastelai Smith
Production Secretary:	Amanda Church
Designer:	Richard McManan-Smith
Gaffer:	Peter Robinson

Directed by Tony Dow
Produced by Gareth Gwenlan

Since Rodney landed a job with Cassandra's father, Albert has become Del's right-hand man, acting as lookout while Del tries selling a case full of baby dolls, manufactured in Britain but curiously having Korean voices!

You would think that Rodney had it all nowadays: a good job and a great wife, but things aren't going too well at home. Cassandra's career seems to take priority, and he's rather miffed as to why all

'Rodney Come Home'

she wants to do is attend work-related functions. To make matter worse, tea isn't on the table when he gets home from work in the evenings.

Del's life, on the other hand, is looking up: Raquel's back in town after a theatre tour of the east coast of America, and she's agreed to live with him. Wanting the same happiness for his brother, and worried about losing the perk of getting cheap printing from Alan Parry's printing company if Rodney gets the sack, Del decides to play matchmaker. But by the time he's finished interfering, all he succeeds in doing is making Rodney homeless for the third time in 18 months.

Roedean School

The Brighton-based boarding and day school for girls aged between 11 and 18 is mentioned by Del in 'The Russians are Coming'. While the Trotters test out their nuclear fall-out shelter on top of their tower block, they fantasize about surviving a nuclear war with a bunch of schoolgirls.

Roger the Rabbit

Seen in 'Heroes and Villains', Cassandra's white rabbit is christened Roger. It's a present from Rodney to give her something to care for whilst they struggle to start a family. What happens to it after Cassandra and Rodney finally announce in the episode that they'll soon be hearing the patter of tiny feet around their flat, is uncertain.

Roland

Played by Colum Convey

Roland was married to Albert Warren's niece, Eileen, and is seen with the funeral party in 'If They Could See Us Now…!' when the Trotters turn up at the wrong house. He winds Del up by joking about the deceased, although we later discover they're talking about entirely different Alberts!

Rollinson, Penny

Properties buyer on eight episodes: S3 and 'Thicker Than Water'

Born in Leigh-on-Sea, Penny earned a degree in psychology, but having always had an interest in costume design, she began working in the theatre from the age of 21, designing costumes. After taking a friend's advice she completed a course in Theatre Design and Wardrobe at Wimbledon School of Art, before joining the BBC's costume department in 1980.

Believing that her academic degree would restrict her chances of progression within the department, she transferred to become a prop buyer in 1983. By the time she'd left the Beeb in 1990, she had worked on numerous shows, including *Blackadder* and *Just Good Friends*. After ten years of working as a freelance prop buyer, Penny has given up the business and concentrates on buying and selling properties.

Rolph, Mic

Graphic designer on eight episodes: S3 and 'Thicker Than Water'

Mic studied graphic design at Canterbury College before joining the BBC in 1966. After seven years he turned freelance, and remained in the television industry until 1989, working mainly in light entertainment and on science shows.

Nowadays Mic – together with his partner, who's a science professor – publishes science books for children. They have over 18 titles to their names, many of which have been published around the world.

Ron's Cash & Carry

Del and Rodney talk about the old firm in 'Danger UXD'. The owner, Ronnie Nelson, is now Managing Director of the Advanced Electronics Research and Development Centre.

'Rose, Auntie'

Played by Beryl Cooke

Del and Rodney's Auntie Rose lived in Clacton and in 'The Second Time Around'. Rodney and Grandad go to her address after having enough of sharing the flat with Pauline Harris. It's not long before Del's had enough of his intended, too, and joins them at the cottage. The trouble is, 'Auntie Rose' has trouble remembering who her visitors are, which isn't surprising as the real Auntie Rose moved on ages ago!

'The Second Time Around'

Rosen, Joshua

Role: Tyler Boyce

Appeared in 'Miami Twice' (US scenes)

Rougvie, Malcolm

Properties buyer on 14 episodes: S6, episodes 1, 3, 4, 5 & 6; S7; 'Dates'; 'Rodney Come Home' and 'Mother Nature's Son'

Malcolm, who was born in London, served seven years in the army after leaving school. Upon returning to civvy street in 1971, he spent five weeks working as a security guard before joining the BBC as a props buyer. Early work assignments included *Dad's Army*, *The Onedin Line*, *Duchess of Duke Street* and *Steptoe*.

He remained with the Beeb until 1991, when he left to work freelance. Recent work has included *The Bill* and 15 months on Channel 5's *A Mind to Kill*, filmed in Cardiff.

Rowe, Doug

Role: Man in crowd

Appeared in S4, episode 7

'Royal Flush, A'

(Christmas Special 1986)

Original transmission: Thursday 25 December 1986, 7.05 pm

Original viewing figures: 18.8 million

Duration: 75 minutes

First repeat: Sunday 6 December 1987, 7.45 pm

Subsequent repeat: 31/8/92

CAST

Del Trotter	David Jason
Rodney Trotter	Nicholas Lyndhurst
Uncle Albert	Buster Merryfield
Man in Market	Paul McDowell
Vicky	Sarah Duncan
Trigger	Roger Lloyd Pack
Policeman	Andy Readman
Sid	Roy Heather
Dosser	Robert Vahey
Eric	Geoffrey Wilkinson
Ticket collector	Alan Cody
Programme seller	Christina Michaels
June	Diane Langton
Man at opera	Robin Herford
Lady at opera	Richenda Carey
St John's Ambulance man	Gordon Salkilld
Mr Dow	Roger Davidson
Henry	Jack Hedley
Charles	Peter Tuddenham
Patterson	Arnold Peters
Carter	Ifor Gwynne-Davies
Mrs Miles	Kate Williams
Lady at dinner	Daphne Goddard
Giles	Stephen Riddle
Others:	Fred Tomlinson whistled for David Jason over the opera scene

Walk-ons: (At the shoot) Derek Fincham, James Harvey, Ian Elliott, Howard Major, Tony Birch, Dave Venture, Ray Bennett, Phil Maggs, Pat Fincham, Mavis Linter, Shirley Morgan, Julian Hudson, Vaughan Collins. (The maids) Chrissie Conway, Marianne Bergin and Sue Bartlett. (The loader) Robert Crake. (The café scene) Bill Brown. Peter James, Chris Smith and Graham Pritchard were paid but their contribution was cut from the programme. (The market) Hazel Marks, Iris Jerry, Mary Germany, Sandra Oakley, Sally Burnett, David M. Young and Michael Rose. (Policewoman) Sandra Lane. (The kitchen scene – the maids) Chrissie Conway and Sue Bartlett. (The dining room scene and hall) Pat Fincham, Sandra Kneller, Irene Campbell, Denise Marland, Ruth Stewart, Mavis Linter, Sally Kneller, Ian Elliot, Tony Birch, James Harvey. Marianne Bergin and Chrissie Conway as the maids, and in the hall, Linnzie Drew as the 'lungs'. (The opera bar scene) Anthony Child as the barman and Susie Mollett as the barmaid. Colin Burns, Patrick Travis, Betty Francis, June Simmonds and Cindy Dukes. (Exterior/interior of foyer at opera) Liz Adams, Juliette James, Tessa Landers, Iris Everson, Jilly Nicholson, Janet King, Tina Simmonds, Tiffany Suchard, Belinda Lee, Sheila Power, Laurie Good, Robert Pearson, Don Paul, John Baker, Colin Thomas, Tom Gandle, Ian Sheridan, Alan Crisp, Ray Sumby, Peter Whitaker and James Clements. (Drivers) Tim Parry and Tony Snell. (Approximately 300 supporting artists were used in the episode.)

PRODUCTION TEAM

Written by John Sullivan

Extract from Carmen by Kent Opera

Title music arranged and conducted by Ronnie Hazlehurst composed and sung by John Sullivan

Make-up Designer:	Elaine Smith
Costume Designer:	Robin Stubbs
Properties Buyer:	Roger Williams
Engineering Manager:	Mike Hill
Sound Supervisor:	Brian Robinson
Lighting Gaffer:	Peter Robinson
Film Cameraman:	Keith Burton
Film Sound:	Michael Spencer
Film Editors:	John Dunstan and John Wilkinson
Dubbing Mixer:	Alan Dykes
Camera Supervisor:	John Pilblad
Videotape Editor:	Ed Wooden
Production Assistant:	Lesley Bywater
Assistant Floor Managers:	Francesca Gilpin and Melanie Dicks
Graphic Designer:	Andrew Smee
Vision Mixer:	Bill Morton
Production Manager:	Tony Dow and Olivia Bazalgette
Designer:	Mark Sevant

Produced and directed by Ray Butt

When Rodney chats to Vicky, an artist, at the local market, little does he know that his friendship will see him fraternising with Royalty at the Duke of Maylebury's country home.

Vicky is the Duke's daughter and she's impressed when Rodney gets his hands on the much sought-after opera tickets to see a production of *Carmen* at London's Theatre Royal. She's less impressed when Del turns up with the busty June, his peroxide blonde girlfriend, and spends the entire evening munching crisps, sucking ice cream and chatting.

When Rodney is invited along to a weekend shoot at the Duke's country home in the Berkshire countryside, he doesn't expect his brother to gate-crash the event. Just as Rodney is looking forward to developing his friendship with the well heeled Vicky, Del drinks too much vino and embarrasses him beyond belief, ruining any hopes he had of continuing a relationship with his little rich girl.

Royal Variety Performance, The

During the 1986 Royal Variety Performance the Trotters (Del, Rodney and Uncle Albert) appeared on stage. The storyline saw them them arriving in a

---

MEMORIES OF ONLY FOOLS

★ ★ ★ ★ ★ ★

'One of my jobs was to find a green Capri. John Sullivan had written it into the scripts, and the designer added all the bits like pink fluorescent windscreen wipers, the pink floppy aerial and the tiger skin interior. The car was originally a bronze colour so we had it painted green by TeleFilm Cars in Burnley, who were cheaper, even when you added the expense of bringing the vehicle down to London.

'When I started on the series, the main Trotters' van was housed in the Cars for Stars Museum in Keswick, so I went up and took a few photos for reference purposes. I bought another three-wheeler – which was dark red – for about a hundred quid from Harlow, arranged for Bob Randall at TeleFilm Cars to spray it yellow, got him to MOT and service it, then I added the same number plate as the one in the museum for purposes of continuity.

'For another episode, "Danger UXD", I had to get a lot of sex dolls, which I bought from a sex shop in Soho. I just walked in and asked this girl, who was full of interest and enthusiasm, reading her magazine – if she had any blow-up dolls. She showed me where to look and I noticed they had black ones and white ones, but I asked if she had any Chinese ones as well! Then I got one out and started blow-ing it up. She said: "You can't do that in here!" But I wanted to make sure it wasn't too horrific, which it wasn't, so I bought five of each, as well as a lot of other stuff to stock out Dirty Barry's sex shop – I spent over a grand in there. Of course, I never told her all the equipment was for an episode of *Only Fools and Horses*.

'I always used to be around for the recordings, partly to make sure all the items in the sets were stored away safely. Some of the items, whilst extremely cheap and not particularly good quality, were irreplaceable. We often kept several copies of the same item: for example, we had three examples of the dog on the TV, in which Del kept his cigars. Although it only cost about £3, it was fragile and very prominent so you couldn't afford not to have it for an episode.'

MALCOLM ROUGVIE – Properties buyer

London street to deliver 12 boxes of whisky to Chunky Lewis, the manager of Delaney's Club. When they dump the boxes of alcohol on the stage, they don't realise they've gatecrashed the Royal Variety Performance and have to do a bit of grovelling as they retrace their steps back to the van.

Ruby

(See 'Slater, Ruby')

à la Del

★ ★ ★ ★ ★ ★

'Ordre du jour!'

('A Touch of Glass')

Russell, Elliott

Role: Baby Tyler
Appeared in S7, episodes 1 & 2

'Russians are Coming, The'

Original transmission: Tuesday 13 October 1981, 8.30 pm
Production date: Saturday 11 July 1981
Original viewing figures: 8.8 million
Duration: 30 minutes
First repeat: Friday 12 October 1981, 7.35 pm
Subsequent repeats: 27/5/97, 28/5/99

CAST

Del Trotter . . . . .David Jason
Rodney Trotter . . . . .Nicholas Lyndhurst
Grandad Trotter . . . . .Lennard Pearce
Eric (the policeman) . . . . .Derek Newark
Wayne (the policeman) . . . . . .Kelly Garfield

PRODUCTION TEAM

Written by John Sullivan
Title music arranged and conducted by Ronnie Hazlehurst composed and sung by John Sullivan
Audience Warm-up: . . . . .Felix Bowness
Make-up Designer: . . . . .Pauline Cox
Costume Designer: . . . . .Phoebe De Gaye
Properties Buyer: . . . . .Chris Ferriday
Film Cameraman: . . . . .Bill Matthews
Film Sound: . . . . .John Pritchard
Film Editor: . . . . .John Jarvis
Camera Supervisor: . . . . .Mike Harrison
Studio Lighting Director: . . . . .Don Babbage
Studio Sound: . . . . .Mike Felton
Technical Coordinator: . . . . . .Robert Hignett
Videotape Editor: . . . . .Chris Wadsworth
Production Assistant: . . . . .Penny Thompson
Assistant Floor Managers: . . . .Mandie Fletcher and Tony Dow
Graphic Designer: . . . . .Peter Clayton
Vision Mixer: . . . . .Hilary West
Production Manager: . . . . .Janet Bone
Designer: . . . . .Tony Snoaden
Directed by Martin Shardlow
Produced by Ray Butt

Del gets his hands on a grand's worth of lead from the site of a disused factory which produced prefabricated structures, but when Rodney informs him that it's a do-it-yourself nuclear fall-out shelter, he thinks his little bruv is pulling his leg – until he sees the brochure.

With Rodney's ever-increasing concern regarding the threat of another world war, he asks Del what he'd do if he heard the four-minute warning. Del plays the sceptic and belittles Rodney's comments as sheer fantasy. Nevertheless, the Trotters end up testing out their ability to react in the event of hearing the warning and attempt to reach Grandad's allotment within the allotted time. Although time is tight, Del's confident of achieving their objective, but that's before they're pulled over by the police for speeding.

Rutherford, Peter

Role: Grayson
Appeared in S6, episode 3
The late Peter Rutherford's credits include appearances in *Doctor Who*, *The Professionals*, *Minder*, *Poldark*, *Highlander*, *King and Castle* and *The Hound of the Baskervilles*.

Ryan, Christopher

Role: Tony Driscoll
Appeared in S6, episode 6
Christopher, born in London in 1950, trained at E15 for three years. He graduated in 1971 and secured a place in rep at Glasgow's Citizens' Theatre.

For several years he worked in repertory theatres up and down the country, interspersed by the occasional small part on television, with his first appearance being Bill Badger in a Rupert Bear game during a Christmas edition of *The Generation Game*.

On the small screen, his favourite roles to date are Mike in *The Young Ones*, Hedgehog in *Bottom* and Marshall in *Absolutely Fabulous*. His film credits include *Santa Claus: The Movie* and *Dirty Weekend*.

Christopher is still a regular on screen and stage, and one of his most recent appearances was in the new series of *Absolutely Fabulous*.

Ryan, Joe

Lighting gaffer on one episode: 'To Hull and Back'
Joe was a qualified electrician when he joined the BBC in 1964. After working on light entertainment and dramas for some years he transferred to filming and became a lighting gaffer. He took early retirement in 1994, worked freelance for five years, but is now enjoying his retirement.

Sacha

This dachshund is being walked in the park during 'Sleeping Dogs Lie'. We learn that he has a tendency to chew up the carpet.

Sadler, Dougie

Not seen or heard in the sitcom, Dougie Sadler owns a stationery shop in the High Street. In 'Big Brother', Del thinks he'll be able to sell him some of the dodgy briefcases he's foolish enough to buy from Trigger. During a phone conversation with Sadler, though, Del has to think on his feet when it becomes apparent that the briefcases were stolen from his shop in the first place.

Sagoo, Dev

Role: Waiter (in Indian restaurant)
Appeared in S3, episode 2 and 'Diamonds are for Heather'
Dev, who was born in Uganda, arrived in the UK in 1965. After completing his education he was two years through an apprenticeship to become a pipe-fitter welder when he was given the sack, which was a blessing in disguise because it meant he could pursue his true interest, to work in the world of entertainment.

He trained for two years at the Birmingham Theatre School, graduating in 1973, by which time he'd already played a leading role in a television play, *A Touch of Eastern Promise*. His career quickly progressed and offers of work came from all mediums, including spells with the Royal Shakespeare Company, the National Theatre and a presenting role on *Play School*.

Dev is still acting, but is spending more time directing, having recently completed a short feature, *Close to Home*.

Salkilld, Gordon

Role: St John's Ambulance man
Appeared in 'A Royal Flush'
Born in London in 1927, Gordon had several jobs before becoming an actor. As well as serving in the army, he worked in a factory, and was a salesman, an engineer and a company director. He made his first acting appearance as a pantomime dame in 1973, his television debut two years later in *Dixon of Dock Green*, and worked around the country in theatre in the early stages of his career.

Although he rarely works on the stage these days, he's still busy on the screen, recently appearing in *A Touch of Frost*, while previous credits include *Ever Decreasing Circles*, *Never the Twain*, *Odd Man Out*, *Potter*, *Singles*, *Happy Ever After*, *Rings on Their Fingers*, *Open All Hours*, *Return of the Saint*, *A Very Peculiar Practice*, *Poldark*, *EastEnders* and *Crossroads*.

Salvatore

Played by Tom Kouchalakos

Salvatore is employed as Vinny Occhetti's lawyer and is consulted by the Mafia Chief in 'Miami Twice'.

Sandra

Played by Kate Saunders
Appeared in S2, episode 1

Sandra is Rodney's new girlfriend in 'The Long Legs of the Law'. Having a fetish for women in uniform, especially policewomen, Rodney is chuffed to have pulled a girl who's also a copper. The news causes deep depression in the Trotters' home, with Grandad concerned about what the neighbours will think, and Del more worried about the police getting too close to his dodgy business affairs. His worries are well founded because after Rodney brings Sandra back to the flat for a nightcap, she notices that the place is littered with stolen goods. At the door of her flat, after Rodney has seen her home, she broaches the subject and tells Rodney he has 24 hours to clear the place of the items, before she comes around with the CID.

Sandra

(For 'Sandra', who's mentioned in 'The Sky's the Limit', see 'Lane, Sandra')

Sansom, Mrs

Played by Jean Challis

Mother of barmaid Nerys, Mrs Sansom collars Rodney (although we only hear the voices) outside Sid's Café in 'Dates'. After a high speed chase in the Reliant van, Nerys, who was supposed to be out on a date with Rodney, returned home a bag of nerves, so Mrs Sansom demands to know the reason. We never see her in the sitcom.

Sansom, Nerys

Played by Andrée Bernard

Seen in 'Dates', Nerys is a barmaid at The Nag's Head who's fool enough to agree to a date with Rodney, while he's going through his James Dean stage. As expected (particularly as she's nicknamed Nervous Nerys), she's a little jittery before they start out on their drive, but after being chased through the streets of Peckham by a gang of foulmouthed punks, her nerves have been ripped to shreds.

Saunders, Kate

Role: Sandra
Appeared in S2, episode 1

Born in London in 1960, Kate made her profes-

sional acting debut in 1974, and spent many of her early days in the profession working at the Royal Court Theatre. Her first job on television was playing a student nurse in BBC's *Angels* in 1977, but her favourite role was Sandra in *Only Fools*.

Kate always harboured a dream to write novels and in 1985 gave up the acting profession to pursue her new career. To date, she has written several successful novels, including *The Marrying Game*. She's also a respected journalist, having written for many national papers, including *The Sunday Times*.

Sayeed

Abdul's brother, who now lives in France, is mentioned in the back room of The Nag's Head by Abdul during 'To Hull and Back'. Sayeed – whose wife is expecting their first baby shortly – has conducted business with a man from Amsterdam (Mr Van Cleef) whom Abdul, Boycie and Del are considering doing business with.

Scopes, Kitty

Role: Lady on the bus
Appeared in 'Fatal Extraction'

Kitty, who was born in Exeter in 1918, trained at the Central School of Speech and Drama and also completed a one-year course in singing at the Fay Compton Academy.

She made her professional acting debut at the Old Vic in a 1938 production of *Measure for Measure*, before working with ENSA during the war years. She returned to the stage after the war, but didn't make her small-screen debut until 1969, as a walk-on in *Crossroads*.

Kitty has enjoyed a long and varied career as a character actress, and although she no longer works in the theatre, she oversees an amateur group, and remains busy on screen: as well as commericals, she's recently completed a film, *Derek*, and has been seen in *Crimewatch*. Other small-screen credits include: *Peak Practice*; *Boon*; *Outside Edge*; *Auf Wiedersehen, Pet* and *Big Meg Little Meg* for Granada.

Scott

Played by Dan Clark

In 'Heroes and Villains', Scott is one of the muggers who attempt to steal the handbags from Councillor Murray and the old lady in the market.

Scott, Janice

Played by Jessica Willcocks

Married to Ian, Janice has a three-year-old daughter, Mel, and lives in Newquay. She's a contestant on *Goldrush* in 'If They Could See Us Now…!'.

Seager, Chris

Film cameraman on 12 episodes: S4, episodes 1–5 & 7; S5, episodes 1–4; 'To Hull and Back' and 'Time On Our Hands'

Born in Leicester in 1949, Chris completed a photographic course and a two-year diploma in film and television at the Guildford Art College between 1968 and 1971.

He joined the BBC as a studio camera operator in 1973, and after completing his training worked on shows such as *Top of the Pops*, *The Two Ronnies*,

---

MEMORIES OF ONLY FOOLS

★ ★ ★ ★ ★ ★

'John Walbeoffe, a film operations manager at the BBC, recommended me to Ray Butt, the director. Taking me on board, Ray gave me my first break into the comedy department, which helped me move on to drama productions. I started off working on *Just Good Friends* with Ray, who told me that if he felt I'd done a good job on that, he'd use me on the show's Christmas Special and also *Only Fools and Horses*. He must have found me okay because he used me for the next two years.

'I remember working on the show when Lennard Pearce died. It was a shock to us all and we suspended filming for a couple of weeks. When we returned to the production, John Sullivan had written an episode about his funeral. We were all a bit apprehensive because funerals are a touchy subject to cover in situation comedy. It was a cold, crisp winter's day; grey with an inch or two of snow – a near perfect day for a funeral! The way that Grandad's hat became the focus of the humour was truly wonderful. The filming day which had started very tense ended in laughter; I think we all went to the local pub and had a wake for Lennard.'   **CHRIS SEAGER – Film cameraman**

The Shirley Bassey Show, *The Old Grey Whistle Test*, *Nationwide* and *Grandstand*. In 1978, he joined the BBC film department at Ealing as a film camera assistant, and within three days was filming a *World About Us* documentary in Syria.

He was promoted to film cameraman in 1984 and remained in the position until 1994, when he completed his final assisgnment (shooting John Schlesinger's TV movie *Cold Comfort Farm*) before leaving the BBC to work as a freelance Director of Photography. His first job in this capacity was *Stonewall* in America.

Chris continues to work freelance, shooting commercials, feature films and television drama, with recent credits being BBC1's *The Way We Live Now*, *Lenny Blue* for Granada and the feature film *Ashes and Sand*.

Sean

During 'It's Only Rock and Roll' Sean's name is called by a woman during a brawl in The Shamrock Club. Sean is not seen in the sitcom.

'Second Time Around, The'

Original transmission: Tuesday 29 September 1981, 8.30 pm

Production date: Sunday 28 June 1981

Original viewing figures: 7.8 million

Duration: 30 minutes

First repeat: Friday 28 September 1990, 7.35 pm

Subsequent repeats: 12/5/97, 14/5/99

CAST

Del Trotter . . . . .David Jason
Rodney Trotter . . . . .Nicholas Lyndhurst
Grandad Trotter . . . . .Lennard Pearce
Trigger . . . . .Roger Lloyd Pack
Joyce, the barmaid . . . . .Peta Bernard
Pauline . . . . .Jill Baker
'Auntie Rose' . . . . .Beryl Cooke
Walk-ons: . . . .(Shoppers in market) Debbie
Ann Reed, Lee Montgomery, Margaret Braden, Michaela Welch,
Kathleen Heath, Reg Woods, David Harris. (People in pub) John
Cannon, Alf Mangan, Alan Talbot, Trevor Wedlock, Rory O'Connor,
Roberts Sands, Josephine Hughes, Karen Burch, Sheila West and
six extras.

PRODUCTION TEAM

Written by John Sullivan

Title music arranged and conducted by Ronnie Hazlehurst
composed and sung by John Sullivan

Audience Warm-up: . . . . .Felix Bowness
Make-up Designer: . . . . .Pauline Cox
Costume Designer: . . . . .Phoebe De Gaye
Properties Buyer: . . . . .Chris Ferriday
Film Cameraman: . . . . .Bill Matthews
Film Sound: . . . . .Dennis Panchen
Film Editor: . . . . .John Jarvis
Camera Supervisor: . . . . .Ron Peverall
Studio Lighting Director: . . . . .Don Babbage
Studio Sound: . . . . .Mike Felton
Technical Coordinator: . . . . . .Robert Hignett
Videotape Editor: . . . . .Chris Wadsworth
Production Assistant: . . . . .Penny Thompson

'The Second Time Around'

Assistant Floor Manager: . . . . .Mandie Fletcher
Graphic Designer: . . . . .Peter Clayton
Vision Mixer: . . . . .Hilary West
Production Manager: . . . . .Janet Bone
Designer: . . . . .Tony Snoaden
Directed by Martin Shardlow
Produced by Ray Butt

Taking a break from flogging hankies at the local
street market, Del pops down to The Nag's Head
for a quick drink to be greeted by Trigger's news
that Del's ex-fiancé, Pauline Harris, is back in town.
It's 12 years since they last met, and Del's as keen as
ever to resume a relationship with her, even though
she was responsible for breaking his heart: in their
days as Mods, she walked out on him when she
found a man with a faster scooter. Now, he lets
himself be influenced by his heart rather than his
brain, and within no time they announce their
engagement, much to the disgust of Grandad and
Rodney. But there's worse news to come: he's asked
Pauline to move in with them!

Relations are strained in the Trotters' flat, with
Pauline refusing to cook for Rodney and Grandad,
and hiding the old man's teeth because he eats too
much during the day. But when she starts suggesting Grandad is placed in a home, it's the last straw
for Rodney and Grandad who head off for Auntie
Rose's cottage in Clacton. But when Del hears that
the death of Pauline's last husband, Bobby Finch, is
being investigated – or so he thinks – by the police,
and she's eager for Del to take out life insurance, he
decides he's had enough, too, and heads off to
Clacton as well, but not before leaving Pauline a
note, giving her five days to pack her bags.

My dearest darling Pauline

*The engagement is off, the wedding is off
and, as you can gather from this letter,
I'm off! I'll give you five days to clear out
of the flat, and don't ever come back...
you money-grabbing old murderess.*

*All my love
Del Boy! XXX*

'The Second Time Around'

Setna, Renu

Role: Mr Ram

Appeared in S1, episode 3

On television, Renu has appeared in shows such as *I, Claudius; Open All Hours; Minder; The Return of Sherlock Holmes; Stay Lucky; The Bill; Holby City* and *Ruth Rendall Mysteries: The Lake of Darkness*. His film credits, meanwhile, include playing Mr Raji in 1976's *Shout at the Devil*, a junk shop owner in *Moonlighting* (1982) and Mr Ramdas in the award-winning *Bridget Jones's Diary*.

Sevant, Mark

Designer on seven episodes: S5 and 'A Royal Flush'

Born in Cambridge in 1945, Mark worked as an interior designer for a company he set up with two friends before disbanding the firm in the mid-1970s. He retrained as a jeweller and designed jewellery on commission until joining the BBC in 1979.

As a design assistant he worked on a host of shows, including *Crackerjack, Miss World, The Onedin Line* and *No Country for Old Men*. Subsequently, as a designer, he worked on dramas, comedies, light entertainment and children's programmes.

Mark retired from the BBC in 1995 having been a design manager for some three years. He now pursues his interest in design and jewellery making.

Seventh Heaven Sauna Parlour, The

Del suggests that Rodney mentions this local business in the film he's making for the art class. We hear about the establishment in 'Video Nasty', but it is never seen.

Shaheed, Dr

Played by Josephine Welcome

Dr Shaheed replaced Dr Meadows as the Trotter's GP. She's from New Delhi and took over from

---

MEMORIES OF ONLY FOOLS

★ ★ ★ ★ ★ ★

'I enjoyed working on *Only Fools and Horses*. As soon as I received a script I would make a rough studio plan and identify what sets would be required. Initially you'd see what stock sets could be re-used, even though they might need refurbishing.

'Often the turnaround times were so tight you didn't have a chance to carry out any real research and simply had to whack the sets out as quickly as possible. For example, there wasn't much time to research the supermarkets when it came to "The Longest Night" in 1986, and, in my opinion, I designed the manager's office too big. There just seemed to be too much room and it should have been a little more claustrophobic.

'Another set that ended up being rather more spacious than I'd originally intended was the Chinese takeaway in "Video Nasty". Originally it was going to be a restaurant with a take-away area, so there would be people sat in the foreground; that was altered late in the day which left us with quite a large set.

'Talking about large sets, "The Royal Flush" involved filming at Clarendon Park, near Salisbury. At the time, the main house was empty so we had to dress the entrance hall, the kitchen and, of course, the dining room. The Trotters' flat, meanwhile, was built in a warehouse so that if it was raining and we couldn't shoot one of the market scenes, we could return to the warehouse and film one of the flat scenes. In fact, the weather turned against us quite frequently whilst filming the action in the market and we ended up having to re-set that about five times – it dragged on and on.

'With the weather poor, David Jason suffering from a bad throat and me with flu, I wondered if we would get the episode completed in time for Christmas! In the end it was incredibly tight.

'It really was a super project to work on, though: all the actors were terrific, the locations were well managed and everyone worked well together.'

MARK SEVANT – Designer

Meadows when he left general practice to work at the local hospital. She's seen in 'Sickness and Wealth'.

Shallard, Michael

Role: Adrian

Appeared in S6, episode 2

Born in Yorkshire in 1951, Michael grew up in London and secured a place at RADA, before earning his first wage as an actor with the New Shakespeare Company in 1973.

Other stage roles include Mick in *The Caretaker* at the Royal National Theatre, a sub editor in *Exclusive* at the Strand Theatre, Smith in *The Ghost Train* at the West Yorkshire Playhouse and Paul in *The Liver Birds* at Blackpool's Winter Gardens.

His first role on TV was playing Taffy Morgan in BBC's *By the Sword Divided*, and he's gone on to appear in other shows, such as *Crime Monthly* as a forensic scientist, a reporter for *The Times* in *Yes, Prime Minister* and a postman in *The Bill*.

Shamrock Club, The

This nightclub in Deptford features in 'It's Only Rock and Roll'.

Shane

Not seen in the sitcom, Shane is mentioned by Grandad in 'Christmas Crackers'. He's a son of Terry and Brenda, whose Christmas card is accidentally delivered to the Trotters' flat; the family is unknown to the Trotters.

Shanghai Lil

Not seen in the sitcom, Shanghai Lil is mentioned during a heated argument between the Trotter brothers. Lil is an old girlfriend of Rodney's from his art college days at Basingstoke. In the course of a shouting-match, Del remarks spitefully that Rodney had to drug her before he could have his wicked way. Although there's uncertainty over the sexual side of the relationship, the brief affair led to Rodney's expulsion from a one-year art course when the Board of Governors, whilst carrying out their annual inspection, found him and Lil spaced out in his room after smoking a joint. The brush with drugs also left him with an 18-month suspended sentence.

Shanghai Lil, meanwhile, was deported to Hong Kong after the drugs trial. Upon rowing with Del in

'Sickness and Wealth'

HOW I BECAME INVOLVED WITH ONLY FOOLS

★ ★ ★ ★ ★ ★

Martin Shardlow was called in at the eleventh hour to direct the first series of *Only Fools and Horses*. Ray Butt, who had intended wearing the director's hat, had hurt his back and was unable to undertake the task.

'I was due to do something else – I can't remember what it was now – and had just started setting it up when John Howard Davies called me in to his office one morning. He told me that Ray had hurt his back and asked if I would go out that night and take charge of the shoot. Apparently Gareth Gwenlan had been out the previous night but wasn't able to do a second day. Filming was taking place in a bus garage, a location I hadn't seen, other than in photographs shown to me by Janet Bone, so it was a bit worrying. I was given the scripts for the whole series and I sat in my office, read them, and then tried compiling a shooting script from the few photos I'd seen. In many ways, I felt I went out to do that night's shoot blind.

'But the shoot went well and I stayed around to complete the series; after a bit, Ray was able to turn up for technical runs, and things like that, but on the whole he left it to me. Overall, I enjoyed the experience of working on the show. The only person I didn't know when I started was Lennard, but he was such a brilliant guy that anyone could get on with him. Like all series, the first episode is difficult because you're finding your way, but it seemed

Martin Shardlow (right) discusses the script with the actors

quite successful at the time, and they commissioned a second series, after which it took off.

'We never had to tinker with John's scripts. Sometimes you work on a show and have to do so much to the scripts, you wonder why you haven't got a writer's credit too. But we didn't have to do that with *Only Fools*. The basic storylines were all very solid, and my favourite is "The Russians are Coming".

'That episode was difficult to shoot because we had to film within the shelter. It was such a confined space it was virtually impossible to film without losing some of the claustrophobic feel. This episode proved how strong the writing was: there wasn't a need for lots of visual gags, the dialogue was funny by itself.' **MARTIN SHARDLOW – Director**

'Big Brother', Rodney tells Grandad he's leaving home to seek out his old flame, but he's back after six days, having not made it beyond Stoke Newington.

Shangri La, The

Rodney stays in this doss house in Stoke Newington after storming out of the flat following a row with his older brother during 'Big Brother'. Although he intended backpacking to the Far East to rekindle the relationship with his college-days' sweetheart, Shanghai Lil, this is as far as he gets.

Shardlow, Martin

Director on seven episodes: S1 and 'Christmas Crackers'

Born in the Cheshire town of Whitby, Martin embarked on an 18-month management course in Lewis', a department store in Liverpool, before packing in his job to join the Birmingham School of Speech and Drama. He graduated in 1963, by which time he'd already acted and stage managed at the Birmingham rep. He remained with the company until 1964, when he decided his future lay in stage management.

After a year at Kidderminster rep, he toured the country – including a summer season at Ilfracombe – as production manager for David Kirk Productions performing Agatha Christie plays.

Between 1966 and 1967, he worked with Ray Cooney at the Opera House, Jersey, but when the production company toured South Africa, and crew members weren't required, Martin had to look elsewhere for employment. In 1968 he found work in the form of a three-month contract as a holiday relief assistant floor manager for the BBC. The early productions he worked on included the news from Alexandra Palace and Dora Bryan shows, before spending three years on *Dixon of Dock Green*.

Martin was promoted to production manager in the '70s and began working for the respected director/producer Sydney Lotterby, on shows like *Some Mothers Do 'Ave 'Em* and *Last of the Summer Wine*; it was during an episode of this perennial sitcom that he gained his first taste of directing, when Lotterby gave him the opportunity to direct a few scenes. Martin was later promoted to director and worked on numerous shows, including *Are You Being Served?*

He left the BBC in 1989 and has worked as a freelance director ever since, most recently in a sitcom, *Give My Head Peace*, for BBC Northern Ireland. Martin now lives in Spain.

Sharrod, Simon

Production secretary on one episode: 'Fatal Extraction'

Shaun

Not seen in the sitcom, Shaun is mentioned by Grandad in 'Christmas Crackers'. He's a son of Terry and Brenda, whose Christmas card is acci-

dentally dropped into the Trotters' flat; the family is unknown to the Trotters.

Sheila

Played by Catherine Clarke

Sheila works as a checkout girl at the Top-Buy supermarket that Del and Rodney visit in 'The Longest Night'. Del makes a sarcastic comment about her demeanour when she serves them.

Shepherd, Ted

Role: Tom (the commissionaire)

Appeared in 'Heroes and Villains'

Shirley

Not seen in the sitcom, Shirley is mentioned by Grandad in 'Christmas Crackers'. She's the daughter of Terry and Brenda, whose Christmas card is accidentally dropped into the Trotters' flat; the family are unknown to the Trotters.

'Sickness and Wealth'

Original transmission: Sunday 5 February 1989, 7.15 pm

Production dates: Saturday 28 and Sunday 29 January 1989

Original viewing figures: 18.2 million

Duration: 50 minutes

First repeat: Friday 6 October 1989, 7.30 pm

Subsequent repeats: 19/2/92, 4/2/94, 28/8/96, 4/8/99, 2/3/01

CAST

Del Trotter . . . . .David Jason
Rodney Trotter . . . . .Nicholas Lyndhurst
Uncle Albert . . . . .Buster Merryfield
Cassandra . . . . .Gwyneth Strong
Boycie . . . . .John Challis
Mike . . . . .Kenneth MacDonald
Trigger . . . . .Roger Lloyd Pack
Marlene . . . . .Sue Holderness
Mickey Pearce . . . . .Patrick Murray
Jevon . . . . .Steven Woodcock
Nerys . . . . .Andrée Bernard
Elsie Partridge . . . . .Constance Chapman
Dr Shaheed . . . . .Josephine Welcome
Dr Meadows . . . . .Ewan Stewart
Nurse . . . . .Ann Bryson
Walk-on: . . . . .Leone Amis

PRODUCTION TEAM

Written by John Sullivan

Title music arranged and conducted by Ronnie Hazlehurst
composed and sung by John Sullivan

Make-up Designer: . . . . .Jean Steward
Costume Designer: . . . . .Richard Winter
Properties Buyer: . . . . .Malcolm Rougvie
Camera Supervisor: . . . . .Ken Major
Studio Lighting Director: . . . . . .Don Babbage
Studio Sound: . . . . .Alan Machin
Technical Coordinator: . . . . . . .Reg Poulter
Videotape Editor: . . . . .Chris Wadsworth
Production Assistant: . . . . .Amita Lochab
Assistant Floor Managers: . . . . .Kerry Waddell and Sue Bishop
Vision Mixer: . . . . .Bill Morton

Production Manager: . . . . .Adrian Pegg
Designer: . . . . .Graham Lough
Directed by Tony Dow
Produced by Gareth Gwenlan

Del's suffering stomach pains but blames it on PMA – positive mental attitude. He claims that, just like all the other yuppies, he was psyching himself up for the following day's challenge, and that all the sweating and holding his belly is nothing to worry about.

The truth behind the pains is probably the letter that arrived from the council housing department, threatening eviction unless the three months' overdue rent is paid immediately. Business is far from booming for TITCO. Albert tries comforting Del by assuring him that something will turn up; that something could be Elsie Partridge – Albert's lady friend – a retired spiritualist whose reputation in the field has seen people paying large sums to experience her powers of communication.

Before long, Del has arranged with Mike, the landlord of The Nag's Head, for Elsie Partridge to use a room above the pub for a séance. Concerned about Del's health, Albert asks Elsie to lie, and claim she is receiving messages from Del's late mother (the only person he'd listen to), advising him to visit the doctor. Del's happy to make money from the séances, but believes it's all a load of claptrap, especially as she claims to have been contacted by Boycie's father, telling Boycie to look after his child when it's well known around town that Boycie is infertile. But when Marlene announces that she's expecting, Del has second thoughts and visits the doctor, only to end up in hospital, He's eventually released with Irritable Bowel Syndrome, but another shock is in store for him: Rodney announces he's getting married.

Sid

Played by Roy Heather

Sid – who used to work on the buses – owns the greasy café that Del and Rodney frequent in 'The Long Legs of the Law'. A regular reader of the *Greyhound Express*, his establishment wouldn't win any prizes for 'Most Hygienic Café in Town'. The middle-age proprietor wears a filthy apron, smokes whilst serving behind the counter and rarely bothers to pass the time of day with his customers, who are mostly lorry drivers, building labourers or tramps. While Rodney opts for the 'usual bacteria on toast', Del splashes out on a massive fry-up. As well as the caff, Sid occasionally runs a burger bar at the side of the road.

In 'To Hull and Back' we see Sid serving Chief Inspector Slater when he drags Rodney and Del into the café to present them with a proposition: he wants them to keep their ears to the ground and let him know who's involved in the latest smuggling racket. Sid pops up in several other episodes: the 1982 Christmas Sketch, where he's also operating a burger van, hoping to attract some custom from the local market, 'A Royal Flush', 'Dates', 'The Jolly Boys' Outing', 'Miami Twice', 'Fatal Extraction', 'Heroes and Villains', 'Modern Men' and 'If They Could See Us Now . . .!', by which time he's been

handed the responsibility of running The Nag's Head whilst Mike is doing porridge.

We learn little about Sid's background, other than from 'The Jolly Boys' Outing' when he tells Albert that during the war he was captured on a Greek island and became a prisoner of war.

Sidney

Not seen in the sitcom, Trigger's cousin is mentioned in The Nag's Head during 'Wanted'. Trigger, Del and Boycie are involved in the conversation.

Sid's Café

This local café is seen in several episodes (see 'Sid' entry for further details).

In 'To Hull and Back', it's where Chief Inspector Slater buys a reluctant Del and Rodney a cup of tea. It's affectionately known as The Fatty Thumb by its clientele, and in 'Dates' we see from the window that it's also called the Metro Café. A typical truckers' stop, where the meals swim in grease and the tea cups carry the stains from yesterday's brew, it's certainly not the place to impress a potential client or partner.

Simone

Mentioned by Del in 'Danger UXD', Simone is never seen. She works at the cut-price butcher's, and Del had a date with her until, left with a load of dangerous inflatable dolls on his hands, he had to cancel. What made things more disappointing is that she was going to give him a bag of liver!

Simpson, Ian

Video effects on three episodes: 'Heroes and Villains', 'Modern Men' and 'Time On Our Hands'

Ian, who was born in Bradford, graduated from university with an engineering degree and joined the BBC in 1982 as a trainee broadcast engineer based in Manchester. Two years later he moved to

Television Centre, London, and worked in studio lighting, on shows from *Top of the Pops* and *Play School* to *Crimewatch* and *Live and Kicking*.

Now a digital effects supervisor, he spends a lot of time designing effect shots for drama and documentaries, with a recent project seeing him reconstructing shots of 19th century London for a documentary about the life and times of Charles Dickens.

Sims, Joan

Role: Aunt Renee
Appeared in 'The Frog's Legacy'

Joan Sims was born in 1930 and became a household name, primarily for her roles in the *Carry On* films, but her film, stage and television appearances away from the Peter Rogers' productions revealed her versatility as a comedy actress.

Joan was accepted at RADA on her fourth attempt, but when she graduated in 1950, an early appearance as a nurse in *Doctor in the House* and several other films in that series brought her to the attention of Rogers, who cast her in his second *Carry On* film, *Carry On Nurse*. Joan was to appear in 24 of the films, making her the longest-serving female member of the cast.

Her extensive CV covers television appearances in shows such as *The Goodies, In Loving Memory, Doctor Who, Hetty Wainthropp Investigates, On the Up* and *As Time Goes By,* while other movie roles include Nellie Trotter in *The Iron Maiden,* Harriet in *Twice Round the Daffodils,* Ann Foster in *Watch Your Stern* and Miss Tipdale in *Not Now, Darling.*

Joan died in 2001 after a long illness.

Singer, The

Played by Joan Baxter

In 'Tea for Three', the singer tries her best to entertain during a talent night at The Nag's Head, but her efforts are in vain.

MEMORIES OF ONLY FOOLS

★ ★ ★ ★ ★ ★

'I got my stint on the "original" last three shows by accident. The production team were already talking to Dave Jervis about the effects work required but it became clear that due to prior commitments he wouldn't be available for the location work. I got lucky and landed the job since I was available for the shoot, and so it was logical that I supervise the effects work and do the post-production for the shots, too.

'The two sequences I was particularly involved in were Rodney's dream about the Trotter empire in the future, and the final shot of Del, Rodney and Albert walking off into the sunset.

'The opening to Rodney's dream sequence was a tilt down from a building labelled Trotter Towers to see the future Rodney come into shot and a futuristic helicopter fly overhead. The bottom half of the building is Battersea Power Station with its chimneys removed – well, actually, if you look closely you can still see the back ones! The top

half is a major repaint and distortion of the Shell Tower on the Thames.

The night shoot at Battersea was very cold but quite amazing – the size of that place is awe inspiring. The helicopter was completely computer-generated 3D animation – we even went as far as putting the Reliant van's registration number on the bottom of the helicopter, but you never saw it because of the flight path it took. Sad, really, as it would have been a nice in-joke.

'The sunset sequence was a combination of a night shoot in Bristol (it was very wet, cold and about 12.30am as we did that final shot) and a blue-screen shoot a few weeks later. The inspiration for the final framing came from the designer who had a picture taken from a book that I had also come across called *The Art of Warner Bros. Animation*. There is a great background plate in it used for Bugs Bunny walking off into the sunset. I "borrowed" the look and feel from that.' **IAN SIMPSON – Video effects**

Uncle Albert	Buster Merryfield
Raquel	Tessa Peake-Jones
Alan	Denis Lill
Boycie	John Challis
Mike	Kenneth MacDonald
Trigger	Roger Lloyd Pack
Marlene	Sue Holderness
Bronco	Ron Aldridge
Henry	Gordon Warnecke
Stewardess	Lucy Hancock
Newsreader	Richard Whitmore
Baby Tyler	Elliot Russell

Walk-ons: (Airport passengers) Stephen Chandler, Billy Moore, Bill Spencer, Bertie Green, April Ford, Maggie Mitchell, Vanessa O'Neil, Keli Nolan, Catherine McMahon, Keli Richards, Tina Simmons, Karen England, Madeline Simpson, Penny Lambirth, Stephanie Chambers, Sarah Lloyd, Russell Brook, Darrell Brook, Donnachadh McCarthy, Greg Ball, Paul Barton, Peter Richmond, David J Ross, Basil Marty, Ken Coombs, Peter Roy, Pat Shepherd, Jack Street, Trevor St John Hacker, Ron Barney, Gerry Benson, Tony Carlton, Graham Hunter, Andy Smart, Mark Wardell, Danny Lawrence, Susan Acetson, Jill Bradley, Kristie Walker, Tricia Vincent, Gail Abbott, Jayn May, Serena Destouche, Jean Beswick, Janine Lesley, Felicity Lee and Fiona Lewis. (Pub customers) Pearl Hawkes, Charlie Gray, Billy Hughes, Russell Brook, Darrell Brook, Patrick Ford, Paul Ellison, Justin Cleverley, Bill Spencer, Lewis St Juste, Patrick Shepherd, Jon Baker, Mark Brett, Steve Eke, George Broad, Harry Holland, Lloyd Harvey, Jane Frisby, April Ford, Serena Destouche, Elizabeth Phelan, Tracey O'Connor, Diane Keene, Terry Cavanagh and Hannah Warner.

PRODUCTION TEAM
Written by John Sullivan
Title music arranged and conducted by Ronnie Hazlehurst composed and sung by John Sullivan

Make-up Designer:	Christine Greenwood
Costume Designer:	Robin Stubbs
Properties Buyer:	Malcolm Rougvie
Visual Effects:	Christopher Lawson
Film Cameraman:	Alec Curtis
Film Sound:	Michael Spencer
Film Editor:	John Jarvis
Dubbing Mixer:	Michael Narduzzo
Camera Supervisor:	Ken Major
Studio Lighting Director:	Don Babbage
Studio Sound:	Alan Machin
Resources Coordinator:	Peter Manuel
Video Effects:	Dave Jervis
Videotape Editor:	Chris Wadsworth
Production Assistant:	Teresa Powick
Assistant Floor Managers:	Debbis Crofts and Miles Cherry
Graphic Designer:	Andrew Smee
Vision Mixer:	Sue Collins
Production Managers:	Adrian Pegg and Angela de Chastelai Smith
Production Secretary:	Amanda Church
Designer:	Richard McManan-Smith
Casting Adviser:	Judy Loe
Directed by Tony Dow	
Produced by Gareth Gwenlan	

MEMORIES OF ONLY FOOLS

★ ★ ★ ★ ★

'I had a few things to organise on "The Jolly Boys' Outing", but my main memories involve "Dates" and setting up the chase between the Trotters' three-wheeler and the American car. With all car chases you block the roads off during the particular piece of chase, you position the vehicles in relation to each other and shoot it section by section.

'There wasn't any natural bridge we could find which would give the vehicles enough height, but we used one in Twickenham and, by building a ramp on the other side, both vehicles appeared to become airborne for quite some distance. When the Trotters' van landed, the wheel was pushed up under the bodywork. It was a bit of a suck-it-and-see job because I was uncertain what would happen jumping a three-wheeler as no one had done it before, as far as I knew. We were prepared for the fact that the car would probably collapse. And, of course, the car was unusable after the scene.' **COLIN SKEAPING – Stunt coordinator**

Singer, The

Played by Lee Gibson

Part of the group entertaining at the Mardi Gras club in Margate, the singer is seen during the Christmas Special, 'The Jolly Boys' Outing'.

Singh, Dr

Played by Bhasker Patel

At The Nag's Head in 'Modern Men', Mike tells Del that an irate Dr Singh was in earlier wanting to find him due to a problem over some paint. Del laughs it off but tells Mike to say that he's gone to New Zealand if he enquires again. Dr Singh eventually catches up with Del and explains that he's annoyed about the paint Del supplied for his surgery: it's past its sell-by date and is already peeling off.

Singh, Mrs

Not seen in the sitcom, Mrs Singh returned to Bangladesh without paying the Trotters for a dinner service and two Persian rugs. Her flat is occupied by a new tenant – Irene Mackay – by the time Rodney arrives on the doorstep in 'No Greater Love…'.

Sir Alan

In 'A Royal Flush', Mr Dow, the manager of the upmarket gents' outfitters, is talking to Sir Alan on the phone when the Trotters enter his shop. He has to finish the call quickly but reassures Sir Alan, who is never seen, that his boy will be around to collect his garment that afternoon.

Sisson, Graham

Videotape editor on one episode, 'Christmas Crackers'

Born in Bolton in 1943, Graham trained in electronic engineering at Bolton Technical College before joining the BBC in 1963. He began his career in film recording before moving to video tape some six years later, where he pursued his interest in becoming an editor. Among the shows he worked on are *Blankety Blank*, *The Generation Game* and *Open All Hours*, which he edited.

Graham joined London Weekend Television in the early 1980s and became a prominent member of the editing team, working on most of the Saturday night light entertainment and drama shows, including all the Cilla Black shows.

Graham died in the late 1980s.

Sister

Played by Beverley Hills

When Del and Rodney arrive at the hospital to visit Cassandra in 'Modern Men', the sister ushers them through to her room.

Sister Shelley

Played by Constance Lamb

Seen in 'Three Men, a Woman and a Baby', Sister Shelley assists at the delivery of Del and Raquel's baby boy.

Skeaping, Colin

Stunt arranger on two episodes: 'Dates' and 'The Jolly Boys' Outing'

Colchester-born Colin Skeaping considered a career as a PE teacher but became disillusioned with the prospect and left college before completing his course. He signed up with various stunt agencies and his first job was a Persil commercial, filmed in Hastings. Small television engagements followed, as well as work on films such as *The Charge of the Light Brigade,* before he embarked on a 15-month production of *The Four Musketeers.*

In 1972, when the stunt register was established, work started flooding in and soon Colin was completing over 250 jobs a year. Recent assignments include *Midsomer Murders*, *The Bill* and *Ultimate Force*, a film about the SAS. After 34 years in the business, Colin – who's 57 – now concentrates on coordinating stunt work.

Skinner

The policeman is mentioned by Hoskins in 'To Hull and Back', but is never seen.

'Sky's the Limit, The'

Original transmission: Sunday 30 December 1990, 7.15 pm

Production date: Monday 19 and Tuesday 20 November 1990

Original viewing figures: 15 million

Duration: 50 minutes

First repeat: Wednesday 11 March 1992, 8.00 pm

Subsequent repeats: 18/2/94, 1/8/97, 30/3/01

CAST

Del Trotter	David Jason
Rodney Trotter	Nicholas Lyndhurst

The Trotter flat is crowded, especially as Del's latest girlfriend, Raquel, has moved in, and Rodney's sleeping on the sofa after leaving his wife. While Rodney's contemplating the future in Nelson Mandela House, Cassandra is in sunny Spain with her mother, staying at the family villa.

Rodney's separation has led him to drink and days off work nursing hangovers. Alan Parry – Cassandra's father and Rodney's boss – has become so concerned that he arranges to meet Del at The Nag's Head. Alan admits he always had high hopes for Rodney and Cassandra, and anticipated leaving the business to them when he retires to Spain.

Eager to see Rodney and Cassandra – who have been married for 18 months – reunited, Alan suggests a second honeymoon at a luxury hotel not far from Gatwick Airport, where Cassandra and her mother are due to arrive. Del knows the manager and believes he could fix it all up and Rodney agrees it's a good idea.

Rodney forks out £250 for the night, only to be told at the airport that Cassandra's flight has been re-routed to Manchester, meaning he's splashed out for nothing. But then the real reason for the plane's diversion is established, and Del is right in the thick of it!

Slater, Harry

Husband of Ruby and father to Roy, Harry is mentioned by his wife in 'To Hull and Back' when she's sat next to Albert Trotter, watching an old black and white war movie.

Slater, Rachel

(See 'Turner, Raquel')

Slater, Roy (Detective Inspector)

Played by Jim Broadbent

One of the most unpopular policemen in the area, Roy Slater is known as 'Bulldog' at the Met because he can never let matters drop once he's got his teeth into them. Disliked by colleagues and small-time crooks, he doesn't even endear himself to his own family: he nicked his father for having a defective rear light on his bike! In 'May the Force be with You', he's seen hanging around The Nag's Head, keeping his watchful eye on Rodney and Trigger.

Roy completed his education at the Martin Luther King Comprehensive in Peckham, along with Boycie, Trigger, Denzil and Del, whom he sat next to in class. After leaving school he plumped for a police career, and rose to the rank of Chief Inspector by the time he retired from the force, although it's rumoured that he was forced out due to bad publicity after cajoling a black guy into claiming he was a peeping Tom. When the case reached court it was established that the man was registered blind.

What finally sounded the death-knell of his career was his involvement in the diamond smuggling racket he was supposedly investigating in 'To Hull and Back'. He was handed a five-year custodial sentence, which he served at Parkhurst.

When he's released, after serving just three and a half years, he becomes a born-again Christian and spends time working for an undertaker in Chelmsford. Eager to re-establish friendships with Del, Trigger, Boycie and Denzil, characters who were foes during his police days, he arranges a school reunion in 'The Class of '62'. Del's feelings towards Slater seem to be mellowing until he finds out from Raquel that they were married for four years. The truth behind Slater's sudden departure from his normal repugnant manner is unearthed when it is established that the school reunion was just a façade. Slater – who'd established via the Poll Tax register that Raquel was living with Del – had used the reunion to worm his way into Del's flat and to get Raquel to sign a post-nuptial agreement. But Del has the last laugh and sends him packing.

Slater, Ruby

Played by Annie Leake

Roy Slater's elderly mother is seen in 'To Hull and Back', sitting next to Albert in The Nag's Head, engrossed by an old black and white war film. Her husband, Harry, was put away some years ago; Ruby believes it was when their son, Roy, decided to join the police force that his illness struck.

'Sleeping Dogs Lie'

Original transmission: Thursday 21 March 1985, 8.00 pm

Production team: 17 February 1985

Original viewing figures: 18.7 million

Duration: 30 minutes

First repeat: Saturday 7 December 1985, 8.00 pm

Subsequent repeats: 16/11/91, 26/5/95, 12/12/97, 20/9/00

CAST

Del Trotter	David Jason
Rodney Trotter	Nicholas Lyndhurst
Uncle Albert	Buster Merryfield
Boycie	John Challis
Marlene	Sue Holderness
Dog owner	Linda Barr
Receptionist	Debbi Blythe
Vet	John D Collins
Doctor	Brian Jameson
Walk-on	Patricia Clark

PRODUCTION TEAM

Written by John Sullivan

Title music arranged and conducted by Ronnie Hazlehurst composed and sung by John Sullivan

Audience Warm-up:	Felix Bowness
Make-up Designer:	Linda McInnes
Costume Designer:	Richard Winter
Properties Buyer:	Chris Ferriday
Film Cameraman:	Chris Seager
Film Sound:	Dennis Panchen
Film Editor:	John Jarvis
Camera Supervisor:	Ken Major
Studio Lighting Director:	Don Babbage
Studio Sound:	Dave Thompson
Technical Coordinator:	Tony Mutimer
Videotape Editor:	Chris Wadsworth
Production Assistants:	Caroline Andrews and Lesley Bywater
Assistant Floor Manager:	Gavin Clarke
Vision Mixer:	Heather Gilder
Production Manager:	Andy Smith
Designer:	Eric Walmsley

Directed by Susan Belbin

Produced by Ray Butt

Boycie and Marlene are off on their hols and have persuaded Del to babysit their new puppy, although he didn't need much persuading when £60 a week was mooted. The Trotters soon find that they've taken on more than they can chew, especially when Marlene tells them that her Great Dane needs walking three times a day, a blanket draped over him at bedtime, talking to, a daily vitamin pill and plenty of steak, chicken, veal, etc.

During a walk in the park, Rodney is concerned about the dog's lack of energy and believes he's on his way out, with Del commenting: "Boycie and Marlene ain't even got the top off their suntan oil and we're burying their dog!". There's no option but a visit to the vets, even if it'll cost them a packet. It transpires that pork they reheated for Duke's breakfast might be the cause – as the vet explains, if it wasn't reheated thoroughly it would be the perfect breeding ground for salmonella poi-

'Sleeping Dogs Lie'

soning. But before the meat can be examined, Albert eats the final morsels, so a trip to the hospital is required. But a case of accidental pill-swapping between Albert's sleeping pills and Duke's vitamin tablets explains why Albert's full of zest and Duke is comatose.

'Slow Bus to Chingford, A'

Original transmission: Tuesday 6 October 1981, 8.30 pm

Production date: Sarturday 4 July 1981

Original viewing figures: 7 million

Duration: 30 minutes

First repeat: Friday 5 October 1990, 7.35 pm

Subsequent repeats: 19/5/97, 21/5/99

CAST

Del Trotter . . . . .David Jason
Rodney Trotter . . . . .Nicholas Lyndhurst
Grandad Trotter . . . . .Lennard Pearce
Janice . . . . .Gaynor Ward

PRODUCTION TEAM

Written by John Sullivan

Title music arranged and conducted by Ronnie Hazlehurst composed and sung by John Sullivan

Audience Warm-up: . . . . .Felix Bowness
Make-up Designer: . . . . .Pauline Cox
Costume Designer: . . . . .Phoebe De Gaye
Properties Buyer: . . . . .Chris Ferriday
Film Cameraman: . . . . .Bill Matthews
Film Sound: . . . . .Dennis Panchen
 and John Pritchard
Film Editor: . . . . .John Jarvis
Camera Supervisor: . . . . .Peter Leverick
Studio Lighting Director: . . . . . .Don Babbage
Studio Sound: . . . . .Mike Felton
Technical Coordinator: . . . . . . .Robert Hignett
Videotape Editor: . . . . .Mike Taylor
Production Assistant: . . . . .Penny Thompson
Assistant Floor Manager: . . . . .Mandie Fletcher
Graphic Designer: . . . . .Peter Clayton
Vision Mixer: . . . . .Hilary West
Production Manager: . . . . .Janet Bone
Designers: . . . . .Tony Snoaden
 and Cynthia Kljuco
Directed by Martin Shardlow

Produced by Ray Butt

Del has found a new job for Rodney: he's secured him the position of Trainee NSO with a new security firm. All Del's ideas are formed with number one in mind, and it turns out the new company is Trotter Watch, his new security firm, and the position is Nocturnal Security Officer. The reality finds a unenthusiastic Rodney donning an old traffic warden's uniform and patrolling the bus and coach garage in Tyler Street.

While Rodney is still adjusting to working nights, Del tells him about his next hair-brained scheme: Trotters' Ethnic Tours. He intends running coach trips round the ethnic sites of London, including such unmissable places as Lee Valley Viaduct. Del sees it as a family enterprise with Grandad dishing out advertising leaflets, himself as courier and Rodney as coach driver – even though he's shattered after working all night.

Despite protestations, Rodney is dragged into the world of tourism, but the experience is short-lived because no customers turn up for the launch, which is hardly surprising because Grandad's distribution of promotional leaflets got no further than the dust chute!

Small boy

Played by Miles Rinaldi

The boy runs past Del's market stall and steals one of his oranges in the process. He doesn't speak in the episode.

Smee, Andrew

Graphic designer on 15 episodes: S5, S7, 'To Hull and Back', 'A Royal Flush' and 'The Frog's Legacy'

Born in Colchester in 1949, Andrew worked for Aldridge Associates before setting up The Drawing Room, a design group, with colleagues. When the firm closed he went freelance and began receiving commissions from a friend who worked for the BBC. By 1979, Andrew was on a full-time contract with the Corporation.

Initially he worked mostly on light entertainment programmes, beginning with *Little and Large* and progressing to *The Two Ronnies*, including their short film *By the Sea*. But his favourite assignments include *Absolutely Fabulous*, *French and Saunders* and Comic Relief.

Andrew took voluntary redundancy in 1999 and has since opened a bed and breakfast in Suffolk.

Smee, Peter

Lighting director on three episodes: S4, episodes 1, 2 & 4

During his BBC career in the lighting department, Peter has worked on numerous shows, including *The Liver Birds*, *Porridge*, *Open All Hours*, *No Place Like Home* and *Three Up, Two Down*.

Smith, Adrian

Film cameraman on one episode: 'The Jolly Boys' Outing'

Born in Middlesbrough, Adrian joined the BBC as a trainee assistant cameraman shortly after leaving school in 1974. Shows he has worked on include *The Brothers*, *All Creatures Great and Small*, *Pebble Mill at One*, *Angels* and, his favourites, *Bergerac*, *Horizon* and *Blue Peter*.

After 25 years working in the industry, Adrian left the Corporation in 2000 and is now a house-husband.

Smith, Andy

Production manager on 16 episodes: S3, S4, 'Thicker Than Water' and 'Modern Men'

Smith, Ben

Role: Damien Trotter

Appeared in 'If They Could See Us Now…!'

Ben – who was born in Edgware, London, in 1989 – began acting at the age of five when he joined a local drama group. He's already appeared many times on television, including roles in *Second Sight*, *Holby City* and *Goodnight Mister Tom*. He also imitated Kenny Everett on a Michael Barrymore show, four years ago.

Smith, Elaine

Make-up designer on seven episodes: S5 and 'A Royal Flush'

Born in the Lake District, Elaine studied art for four years in Edinburgh and taught in secondary education before spotting an advert from the BBC's make-up department. She joined the Corporation in 1970, completed her training in the make-up school and spent 26 years in the job, working on a range of shows.

Elaine left the BBC in 1996 and now works freelance, with recent projects including *Respectable Trade*.

Smith, Jamie

Role: Damien Trotter

Appeared in 'Fatal Extraction'; 'Heroes and Villains'; 'Modern Men' and 'Time On Our Hands'

Jamie, who was born in Watford in 1990, moved to the Dorset town of Wimborne at 14 months. After a local photographer told his mother – Charlie Smith, who's a bus driver at Bournemouth Airport – that Jamie's photogenic face would secure him modelling work, Charlie sent pictures of her son off to a London agency. He was soon offered a commercial for Persil washing liquid, followed by another for Japanese Airlines, but his break came when he was offered the part of Damien Trotter, back in 1993, an experience he thoroughly enjoyed.

Jamie is currently at middle school and is interested in sports and technology. Although it's still early days, he's already told his mother that he'd like to pursue a career in television upon leaving school.

Smuggler

Played by Jane Thompson

Having arrived on flight 417 from Amsterdam, the smuggler walks through customs in 'To Hull and

Back'. Her suitcase falls open, depositing its entire contents on the floor as a means of distracting airport officials, thereby allowing her colleague to walk through customs untroubled.

Snell, June

Played by Diane Langton

Appearing in 'Happy Returns', June is an old flame of Del's; they went out together for a year during the 1960s, before breaking up shortly after their friend Albie Littlewood died.

June – who lives in Zimbabwe House – has a teenage daughter, Debby, who works in a local newsagent's. For a while Del wonders if the teenager is his offspring, but he then discovers that June had an affair with Albie Littlewood, who was the father.

June's husband is serving a prison sentence for stealing watches, and is due for release in six months' time. They've been married seven years, but she feels the marriage never really worked and plans to divorce him upon his release.

She's seen again in 'A Royal Flush', accompanying Del to watch a production of *Carmen* at the Theatre Royal, Drury Lane. It's apparent from their relaxed mood when they're together that theirs is a deep-rooted friendship.

Snoaden, Tony

Designer on five episodes: S1, episodes 1, 2, 4, 5 & 6

After serving with the RAF during the Second World War, London-born Tony Snoaden studied art at Camberwell Art School before enrolling on a one-year teaching course at London University. He taught art and crafts for ten years in London schools, then worked with the *Daily Express* and at Olympia exhibitions as a designer before finally joining the BBC in 1965.

During his 21-year career with the Beeb, he worked on a host of programmes, before leaving in 1986 and working freelance, including spells with Channel 4 and ITV's *TV-am*. In 1988 Tony decided to retire from the profession and moved to Plymouth, where he currently resides.

Snobby girl

Played by Hazel McBride

Drinking at a wine bar Del frequents in 'Yuppy Love', the girl's unimpressed when Del, who's trying to show off in front of Trigger, tries chatting her up with money talk.

Solly

(See 'Attwell, Solly')

Sonia

Played by Jean Warren

In the Christmas Special, 'Dates', Sonia is seen hanging around Waterloo Station. When Del is waiting for the arrival of his blind date, Raquel, he wonders for a moment if the tarty Sonia is the woman he's waiting for; it soon becomes obvious that she's a woman of the night and Del gives her the cold shoulder.

DESIGNING THE TROTTERS' HOME

★ ★ ★ ★ ★ ★

Tony Snoaden was the original production designer on *Only Fools and Horses*. He worked on all but one of the episodes in the first series, establishing the look and feel of the sets which would be used throughout the life of the sitcom. Future designers inherited the stock sets created by Tony, and although subtle alterations took place over the years, the style and basic structure of the Trotters' high-rise home, The Nag's Head and other regularly seen sets remained just how Tony had drawn them, back in 1981. Here, he answers some questions about his time working on John Sullivan's sitcom.

How did you get involved with *Only Fools*?
I was just allocated the job. One day the first script arrived on my desk and that was it.

When it came to building the interior of the Trotters' flat, did you carry out any research?
Yes, I went with Ray Butt to a block of flats just over Kew Bridge in London. There were three identical blocks next to each other, all about 20 storeys high, and that was where I was introduced to the programme. Ray told me this was the sort of place he imagined the Trotters living in, so long as we

didn't look back towards Kew, which was a bit upmarket. The caretaker took me up to an empty flat, showed me around, I took some notes and then returned to the office and started work.

How did you transfer your thoughts into sets?
I'd mull everything over for a couple of days; I found I could consider the task more carefully in my spare time rather than in the office. I'd often stroll across to a park or somewhere I could think carefully; slowly I would build up an idea, then put it down into rough form and discuss it with the producer.

What about the view from the Trotters' balcony?
Balconies are very useful to designers for two reasons: you don't have to worry about the groundline (which is always a problem in a studio) and it also gives you a nice recesssion, a sense of perspective, with the items in the room a foreground, then the window, then the balcony, the block of flats behind and finally, maybe, a skyscape.

Was the Trotters' flat a difficult set to build?
No. The main challenge was to get the characterisation as interesting as possible. In the later series I noticed the feel of the room was much more subtle. The Trotters had no 'taste' at all, so the décor I used was very brash (for the wallpaper I

looked through all the cheaper wallpaper books) as well as being untidy, being an all-male environment with unlikely items in unlikely places (motor car wheels in the living space, etc). Once I'd completed full working drawings with all the costs approved, I passed them over to the workshops responsible for building the set.

What about The Nag's Head?
The first market scenes were filmed at Chapel Street Market in Islington. I remember the local lads, who had stalls there, dressed part of the location for me. There's a little pub in the street which had a lovely Victorian frontage, which was used for the first exterior shots of The Nag's Head. I went inside the pub, had a look round, and realised that the layout was almost like a studio set, which meant I could virtually copy the actual layout. I then designed the studio set with rather sombre colours, like a typical Victorian pub!

What other memories of that first series stick in your mind?
The final episode, 'The Russians are Coming'. We had to assemble the fall-out shelter on top of the high-rise flats and because the individual pieces were too big to get up the staircase or in the lift, they had to be winched up the side of the building on ropes – it was a windy day, too!

TONY SNOADEN - Designer

Soweto Road

In 'To Hull and Back', someone calls Chief Inspector Slater to report three men breaking into the back of a lorry parked at a transport café in Soweto Road. The three men are none other than Del, Boycie and Abdul.

Spanish guard

Played by Anthony Jackson

In 'It Never Rains…', the Spanish guard unlocks Grandad's prison cell when Del Boy and Rodney come visiting.

Sparks, Gary

Assistant floor manager on one episode: S6, episode 4

Sparrow, Walter

Role: Barry
Appeared in S6, episode 2

Walter, who was born in London in 1927, was a popular character actor who was rarely out of work. On television he was seen in boundless shows, playing characters like Billy Bones in *The Onedin Line*, Harry Harris in *Rumpole of the Bailey*, a taxi driver in *Shoestring*, Roland Strong in *All Creatures Great and Small*, George in *One Foot in the Grave*, Grandad in *The Famous Five*, a pensioner in *The Thin Blue Line*, William in *Peak Practice* and Harry Barstow in an episode of *Dalziel and Pascoe*.

On the big screen he was seen as a stage manager in *Zeta One*, Ben Weatherstaff in *The Secret Garden*, Fred Paxford in *Shadowlands*, Old Creedle in *The Woodlanders* and Ben Gunn in *Treasure Island*.

Walter died in May 2000.

Speak, Jean

Make-up designer on one episode: 'Christmas Crackers'

Jean, who was born in Lytham St Annes', trained as a beautician before moving to London and joining the BBC's make-up school in 1968. She went on to work for the Corporation for 29 years, before leaving in 1987. Among the shows she worked on are 1982's *Shackleton*, *Fawlty Towers* and *The Two Ronnies*.

She now works freelance, with recent projects including *Lorna Doone* and *Bait* with John Hurt.

Spencer, Michael

Film sound recordist on 16 episodes: S6, episodes 1–3; S7, episodes 1–3, 5 & 6; 'A Royal Flush'; 'The Frog's Legacy'; 'Dates'; 'Rodney Come Home'; 'Miami Twice' (Parts 1 & 2); 'Mother Nature's Son' and 'Fatal Extraction'

Michael, who was born in Bolton in 1945, worked in accountancy and retailing before joining BBC Wales in Cardiff as a freelance sound recordist in August 1968. Learning his craft 'on the job', his early years were spent recording location reports for news and current affairs, magazine and farming programmes.

In 1973 he joined the BBC's film department at Ealing and began working on a whole range of programmes, from *Omnibus*, *Bookmark* and *Arena* to *Hi-De-Hi!*, *Bread* and *First of the Summer Wine*.

Other credits include *Lovejoy*, *The Legacy of Reginald Perrin*, *A Bit of Fry and Laurie*, *Alas Smith and Jones* and two other Sullivan shows, *Over Here* and *Roger, Roger*.

Michael – who's married to actress Laura Jackson, who played Marsha in 'Yuppy Love' – was made redundant from the Beeb in 1995, since when he's been working freelance. One of his most recent assignments has been 13 weeks filming *Wyrdsister College* for Children's ITV.

Spencer, Simon

Production manager on one episode: S7, episode 6

Since working on *Only Fools*, Simon has gone on to direct a Rory Bremner series and write for the long-running children's series *Grange Hill*.

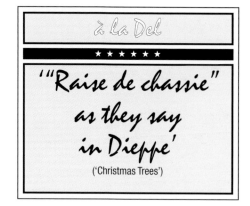

à la Del

★ ★ ★ ★ ★ ★

'"Raise de chassie" as they say in Dieppe'

('Christmas Trees')

Spiros

Del Boy speaks to Spiros on the phone during 'Big Brother'. When Del gets landed with 25 unlockable briefcases, he scours his contact book for any credulous fool who might just be daft enough to fall for a little soft-soaping and a bucketful of lies. But Spiros isn't one of them and wants nothing to do with the cases.

Sporle, Peter

Properties buyer on one episode: 'Diamonds are for Heather'

Born in London, Peter began training as a draughtsman before establishing a career in showbusiness as a singer. He appeared in various productions, sang for an opera company and appeared with the Black and White Minstrels before changing course at the age of 35.

In 1963 he joined the BBC as a holiday relief in the properties department and stayed 23 years. The first production he was allocated was *Cider with Rosie*, before working on a host of light entertainment productions, including Cilla Black shows. He later concentrated on dramas, such as *Pennies from Heaven* and *The Pallisers*. He was working on *EastEnders* when he retired from the Beeb.

St John's Ambulance man

Played by Gordon Salkilld

The aged St John's Ambulance man is seen briefly in 'A Royal Flush', escorting June – who was sick during a performance of *Carmen* – from the Theatre Royal in Drury Lane.

St Juste, Lewis

Role: Black man
Appeared in 'To Hull and Back' and other episodes as a non-speaking character

Lewis, who was born in St Lucia, worked as a BT operator and technician before attending a drama school in London. He made his professional debut in the late 1960s, playing a postman in ITV's *Girls About Town*, but his favourite screen roles have been as a 'Man on the phone' in Channel 4's *Desmond's* and as a dancer in the James Bond movie *Live and Let Die*. Nowadays he continues to work in film (he'll be appearing in the new James Bond movie and the next Harry Potter film) and television as well as photographic work.

St Mary's

Due to lack of funds, the St Mary's hospice is threatened with demolishment in 'The Miracle of Peckham'.

St Nick's

Rodney's group rehearse in this community hall during 'It's Only Rock and Roll'.

St Stephen's Hospital

In 'Chain Gang', Rodney mentions the hospital because it's where he lost sight of the ambulance he was chasing. He was desperately trying to keep up with the vehicle because inside was Arnie, who had feigned a heart attack while trying to stich up Del's consortium.

'Stage Fright'

Original transmission: Sunday 13 January 1991, 7.15 pm
Production dates: Monday 10 December and Tuesday 11 December 1990
Original viewing figures: 16.6 million
Duration: 50 minutes
First repeat: Wednesday 1 April 1992, 8.00 pm
Subsequent repeats: 4/3/94, 29/11/96, 15/8/97, 27/4/01

CAST

Del Trotter	David Jason
Rodney Trotter	Nicholas Lyndhurst
Uncle Albert	Buster Merryfield
Raquel	Tessa Peake-Jones
Boycie	John Challis
Mike	Kenneth MacDonald
Trigger	Roger Lloyd Pack
First woman	Lyn Langridge
Eric	Trevor Byfield
Eugene Macarthy	Roger Blake
Tony Angelino	Philip Pope
Walk-ons:	(In nightclub, Tony's fans)

Maureen Waters, Ina Clare, Valerie Eve, Jo Jolson. (In nightclub, male dancers) Jack Talbot and Anthony Sandford. (In pub) Beverley Jennings, Helena Clayton, Alphia Anthony, Christopher Paul, Patrick Edwards and Pat Shepherd. (Punters in nightclub) Branwen Iwen, Jared Morgan, Pete Blacker, Pete Chesterfield, Jonathan Sheaff, Pete Travers, Laurie Hornsby, Tony Phillips, Hogen Ottery, Marylou Fontaine, Janet Bridgewater, Dinah Glaskin, Cyma Feldwick, Jeanne Mattocks, Christine Russ,

Tina May, Jane Quy, Christine Murphy, Tony Caron, Steve Newton Collier, Stony Garrett, Rob Ryan, Dave Leggett, Pete McStein, Andrew Devoille, Peter Devoille, Ricky Denfiled, Roger Bill, Tim Hooper, Ian Erastmus, Terry Courtney, John Christopher-Wood, Edward J Ludford, Don Leather, Nicole Dominic, Jeanne Hylton, Dave Bilton, Toby Longworth, Lorraine Parsloe, Caron Szulc, Katherine Reeve, Margaret Edwards, Stormy Tempest, Carl Harris, Sheila Mary, Gwen Edmondse, Marian Reed, Maureen Rivers, Samura Khann, Marie Campbell, Bonny Denfield, Sue Simmonds, Jane Bishop, David Lee Jay, Sheila Lorraine, Cherry Gilchrist, Terrie Fearis, Anne Pitt, Gaye Hopkins, Sonja Sabin, Jill Dicken, Barry West, Tony Mann, Waydon Croft, David Dooley, Dave Hopkins, Roland Kitchen, Brian Knight, Chris Rowbury, Jane Lloyd, Suzie Amor, Annie Amesbury, Vivian Lesley, Suzi Mollett, Fay Williams, Amanda Lawes, Judy Leonard, Nicola Maddock, Jackie Kelly, Sharon Broady, Nadger Webb, Clive Durham, Doug Brazier, Bill Zorn, Graham Gadd, Derek Parkes, Martin Dee, Marlene Rabin, Stephanie Debret, Jean Hall, Krissie Ducann, Valerie Wayne, Paula Stringer, Jack Burns, John Clay, Roger Adamson, Vanessa Dodd, Jill Birch, Barbara de Paulis, Irene Reilly, Carol Kirkland and John Yeates. (Diners in nightclub) Tony Baylis, Bob Gibbons, Daisy Bell and Rich Edwards.

PRODUCTION TEAM
Written by John Sullivan
Title music arranged and conducted by Ronnie Hazlehurst
composed and sung by John Sullivan
Musical Director: . . . . .Kennedy Aitchison
Audience warm-up: . . . . .Denny Hodge

Make-up Designer: . . . . .Christine Greenwood
Costume Designer: . . . . .Robin Stubbs
Properties Buyer: . . . . .Malcolm Rougvie
Film Cameraman: . . . . .Alec Curtis
Film Sound: . . . . .Michael Spencer
Film Editor: . . . . .John Jarvis
Camera Supervisor: . . . . .Ken Major
Studio Lighting Director: . . . . . .Don Babbage
Studio Sound: . . . . .Alan Machin
Resources Coordinator: . . . . . .Peter Manuel
Videotape Editor: . . . . .Chris Wadsworth
Production Assistant: . . . . .Teresa Powick
Assistant Floor Managers: . . . . .Debbie Crofts and Miles Cherry
Graphic Designer: . . . . .Andrew Smee
Vision Mixer: . . . . .Sue Collins
Dubbing Mixer: . . . . .Michael Narduzzo
Production Managers: . . . . .Angela de Chastelai Smith
                                                        and Adrian Pegg
Production Secretary: . . . . .Amanda Church
Designer: . . . . .Richard McManan Smith
Casting Adviser: . . . . .Judy Loe
Directed by Tony Dow
Produced by Gareth Gwenlan

Rodney is still unemployed but has brighter news on the accommodation front. With Raquel pregnant, he'll need to find an alternative abode and has just been offered an LDA by the council – which is good news, if only he knew what the acronym stood for! When he discovers it means

'Stage Fright'

'Low Demand Accommodation' he's depressed and turns the offer down.

Del believes his future, meanwhile, is bright – at long last: business is booming, he has new projects in the pipeline and he's building a reputation around town, as confirmed by his old pal, Eric, the manager of The Starlight Rooms.

Eric has been let down by a singing duo who were booked at his club for a birthday party cabaret, and wonders if Raquel would come out of retirement to help? Del declines the request until he hears that £600 is on offer! Raquel is far from struck with the idea, mainly because her previous experiences as an entertainer were a nightmare, particularly the time she appeared at The Talk of the Town, Reading. She forgot her lines and the tune, and when last orders were announced, the audience cheered. When she informs Del that a singing partner would help, he promises to find someone, even though the performance is the following evening.

Del then discovers that The Starlight Rooms are actually owned by a Eugene Macarthy, a local villain best avoided. The cabaret evening is to celebrate his mother's 82nd birthday and she's expecting a terrific show – if not, there will be trouble, which leaves Del shaking in his shoes.

Raquel's singing partner is found in the shape of Tony Angelino, the Singing Dustman, but what Del doesn't realise until it's too late is that he has pronunciation problems. Fearing the worst, Del panics and rushes home, believing that Eugene's mother will hate the act. So it's a relieved man who receives a phone call from Eugene wanting to book Raquel and Tony for a five-week stint at the club because his mother hasn't laughed so much for years.

Stainton, Michael
Role: Police sergeant
Appeared in S3, episode 3
Michael, who was born in Halifax in 1935, spent the early years of his career on stage, appearing with various rep companies and in theatres around the country, but the lion's share of his recent work has been on television. In 1997, he played Edgar Sturgeon in *Dalziel and Pascoe*, while two years earlier he was seen as George in *Prime Suspect*. Other productions include *Dad's Army*, *Jekyll and Hyde*, *Fellow Traveller* and six series of *Metal Mickey*, playing the father. He's played several policemen during his career, including an episode of *Juliet Bravo*, back in 1980.

Stamford Road
The road is mentioned by Trigger in 'Mother Nature's Son' when he advises Del, Rodney and Uncle Albert that there's a 24-hour disposal depot in the road, where they might be able to get rid of the dangerous drums which have been dumped on the allotment that Grandad used to dig. The trouble is, as Trigger later explains, it's not open at night! The drums contain an unknown chemical and later make the national news when they're retrieved from the local reservoir.

Stan (Cousin)

Played by Mike Kemp

Cousin Stan attends Grandad's funeral during 'Strained Relations', representing the north London side of the family. Married to Jean, he owns his own mobile home and works in the insurance business. Uncle Albert lived with them for 18 months before moving in with Del and Rodney.

Stanton, Christopher

Role: Technomatch agent
Appeared in 'Dates'

Christopher trained at Hull University and has appeared in various television shows, including playing Mr Milligan in *The Wild House*, Rev Peters in *Midsomer Murders*, Stuart Black in *The Jump*, James Barker in *EastEnders*, Doctor Ashmore in *Peak Practice* and Mr Stephenson in *The House of Eliott*.

He's also completed extensive improvisional and comedy work, such as writing and performing in *News Revue* at the Canal Café, London, and appearing as Captain Slapstick in *The Slapstick Zone* at the Bloomsbury Theatre.

Star of Bengal

During 'From Prussia with Love', we hear that Rodney took Anna (the German student) to the restaurant before bringing her back to the flat.

Starlight Rooms, The

This dinner and dance club in Peckham is seen in 'Stage Fright'. Eric, the manager, is an old friend of Del's, while it is owned by Eugene MacCarthy, a local villain. The club's promotional slogan is 'Dine and dance to top-class international cabaret'.

Stavros, Maxi

Arnie tells Del and Rodney about Maxi Stavros in 'Chain Gang'. Arnie, who's a retired jewellery trader, obtained 250 18ct gold chains for Maxi, but it isn't surprising that Stavros is a figment of Arnie's imagination, invented as part of the gold chain scam.

Stephen

Played by Daniel Hill

When we see Stephen with his wife, Joanne, at Rodney and Cassandra's first wedding anniversary party talking about economic growth areas in 'The Jolly Boys' Outing', he's assistant head of the overseas' investment bureau, and Cassandra's boss at the bank. Rodney hates the guy and classes him as a 'yuppy' and a 'prat'.

He's mentioned again by Del and Cassandra in 'Three Men, a Woman and a Baby'. Stephen – who Rodney punched on the nose in a moment of madness – started sporting a ponytail; thinking all the young executives are wearing them in the City, Del believes it's a style which attracts 'sophisticated, intelligent young ladies'; Rodney can't see the appeal but borrows one for a meeting with Cassandra.

Stephens, Len

Responsible for lighting on location video in 'Diamonds are for Heather'

Stephens, P G

Role: Father O'Keith
Appeared in S5, episode 2

Born in the west of Ireland in 1923, Stephens worked in the family's hardware business before developing a career in acting. He'd already gained experience of the stage as an amateur actor, but decided he wanted to turn professional and moved to Dublin where he made his debut in 1955, alongside Cyril Cusack; he worked at the Abbey Theatre, Gate Theatre, the Bristol Old Vic and with the Royal Shakespeare Company during the early part of his career. His first taste of television came in 1955 in a production with Margaret Rutherford. He's still busy in the profession, with one of his most recent jobs being in *Uncle Vanya*.

Steven

Played by Sam Howard

Youngest boy of Arnie and Pat, Steven's seen in 'Chain Gang'. Together with his brother, Gary, they don ambulance men's suits and are part of the con trick involving gold chains.

Stevens, Alan

Film cameraman on one episode: S6, episode 3

Born in Wallington, Surrey, Alan left school at 18 and trained at photographic college. He joined the BBC's film department in 1963 as a trainee assistant film cameraman. Two years later, he was an acting cameraman, and by the time he was promoted to become a fully fledged film cameraman in 1974, he'd already won the prestigious News Film Cameraman's Award of the Year in 1968.

Early productions he worked on ranged from *The Onedin Line* to *Panorama*, although most of his time was spent on news and documentaries. In light entertainment he was part of the team for *Monty Python*, *Q3*, *Ripping Yarns*, *Not the Nine O'Clock News* and *Last of the Summer Wine*, which he worked on for 12 years until 1991.

Alan left the BBC in 1992 after more than 30 years' service. He worked freelance for a while but has now retired from the industry.

Stevens, Grant

Role: Baby Damien
Appeared in 'Miami Twice' (Part 1)

Stevens, Michael Fenton

Role: Mr Perkins
Appeared in S6, episode 4

Michael didn't set out to become an actor, and trained as a lawyer. But he fell into revue with friends from university, and after a successful performance at Edinburgh, was offered a radio pilot for Radio 4. So, after qualifying, he dropped law and pursued an acting career.

Comedy revue has featured heavily in his career: he's appeared in eight series for Radio 4 with a company called Radioactive, together with four other actors including Angus Deayton and Geoffrey Perkins. He's also made numerous television appearances, his break arriving with BBC2's *KYTV*. Other parts include Hank in *The Legacy of Reginald Perrin*.

Stevens, Mr

Not seen in the sitcom, Mr Stevens is head of the art group that Rodney attends at evening classes.

Stevenson, Jeff

Roles: PC Parker and Himself
Appeared as PC Parker in 'To Hull and Back' and as Himself in S6, episode 6

Born in London in 1961, Jeffrey trained at the Barbara Speake Stage School as a teenager, making his professional acting debut as a kid on a bike during a Piggy Malone sketch for *The Two Ronnies* in 1974.

Jeffrey, who also appeared as Louis in the *Bugsy Malone* movie, is primarily a comedian who's flirted with the occasional acting part, like his favourite job, hosting a LWT series, *Knees Up*. Other TV appearances include *Barrymore*, *Five's Company*, *Des O'Connor Tonight*, *Talking Telephone Numbers* and *Live From Her Majesty's*

> **MEMORIES OF PLAYING MYSELF**
> ★ ★ ★ ★ ★ ★
> 'I was doing the warm-ups before the studio recordings when John Sullivan asked me to read for a part that he thought I'd be right for; when I was told it was the part of a bad stag comic, I didn't know if it was a wind-up. However, for what was really a small part, it's a job that has got me a lot of work as a stand-up comic. *Only Fools and Horses* is the best comedy show for many years and I'm proud to have played a small part in its success.'   **JEFF STEVENSON**

He's worked in most areas of the business such as theatre, cabaret and corporate functions as an after-dinner entertainer. Over the years, he's toured the UK many times as opening act for Shirley Bassey, Johnny Mathis, The Shadows, Tom Jones and Howard Keel. He's also travelled the world entertaining British Forces in the Falklands, Belize and Germany, and is an experienced warm-up artist.

For many years he was a regular panto player but has since taken a break; his recent work has seen him starting out on the comedy circuit under a new name – Harvey Oliver.

Stew

Played by David Thewlis

Stew plays acoustic guitar in Rodney's group in 'It's Only Rock and Roll'.

Steward, Jean

Make-up designer on five episodes: S6, episodes 1, 3, 5 & 6 and 'Dates'

Born in Fulham, Jean's first job at the BBC was as a foreign news' clerk at Broadcasting House in 1968. She transferred to the make-up department as a stock-keeper before joining the internal make-up school in 1969.

As a make-up designer she worked on shows such as *The Two Ronnies, Porridge, Seven of One* and *One Foot in the Grave*, and by the time she left the Beeb in 1992, she was a design manager.

Jean now works freelance and recent projects include *Jonathan Creek*.

MEMORIES OF ONLY FOOLS

★ ★ ★ ★ ★ ★

'On Boxing Day 1988 I fell down some steps and broke an ankle; I also badly sprained the other one. I was off work for three weeks. On my first day back, I hobbled along to the rehearsal room at Acton, where we were due to have a technical run. I couldn't understand it when I walked into the room and found it empty; I could only assume that it had been cancelled, which was very disappointing because I was so enthusiastic about working on the show. To my utter surprise, everyone soon appeared, but they were all sporting plaster casts on their arms or legs! It was hilarious.' **JEAN STEWARD – Make-up designer**

Stewardess

Played by Lucy Hancock

In 'The Sky's the Limit', the stewardess breaks the news to Rodney that flight 475 from Malaga – on which Cassandra is returning to the UK – has been diverted to Manchester.

Stewart, Ewan

Role: Dr Meadows

Appeared in S6, episode 5

Born in Edinburgh in 1957, Ewan trained at the Central School of Speech and Drama; his first professional job was in a 1977 commercial for matches, before gaining stage experience with the Durham Theatre Company. An early television assignment, meanwhile, came in the shape of a drunk squaddie in a 1978 *Play for Today*, entitled *Soldiers Talking Cleanly*.

Ewan's career has been divided evenly between the stage and screen. In theatre, he worked at the Royal Court in productions like *Sacred Heart* and *Trade and Bluebird*, and at the National in *Racing Demon* and *The Murderer*. Television audiences have seen him in programmes such as *Spender, The Advocate, Biting the Hand, Flight to Berlin, The Professionals* and *Rain on the Roof*.

His film credits include *Titanic, Rob Roy, Paradise Postponed* and *All Quiet on the Western Front*.

'Strained Relations'

Stormers, The

(See 'Dublin Bay Stormers')

'Strained Relations'

Original transmission: Thursday 28 February 1985, 8.00 pm

Production date: 3 February 1985

Original viewing figures: 14.9 million

Duration: 30 minutes

First repeat: Saturday 23 November 1985, 8.35 pm

Subsequent repeats: 26/10/91, 9/4/95, 5/12/97, 11/8/00, 30/6/02

CAST

Del Trotter . . . . .David Jason
Rodney Trotter . . . . .Nicholas Lyndhurst
Uncle Albert . . . . .Buster Merryfield
Trigger . . . . .Roger Lloyd Pack
Boycie . . . . .John Challis
Mike .Kenneth MacDonald
Vicar .John Pennington
Cousin Jean . . . . .Maureen Sweeney
Cousin Stan . . . . .Mike Kemp
Old lady . . . . .Lala Lloyd
Maureen . . . . .Nula Conwell
Walk-ons: . . . .(At funeral) Dennis Jennings, Derek Hunt, Lola Maurice, Linda Anderson, Peter Roy, David Rolfe, Rick Fisher, Esme Dear, George Barnes, Jimmy Muir, David J Ross, Iris Fry, Margaret Adams and Joe Philips.

PRODUCTION TEAM

Written by John Sullivan
Title music arranged and conducted by Ronnie Hazlehurst composed and sung by John Sullivan
Audience Warm-up: . . . . .Felix Bowness
Make-up Designer: . . . . .Linda McInnes
Costume Designer: . . . . .Richard Winter
Properties Buyer: . . . . .Chris Ferriday
Film Cameraman: . . . . .Chris Seager
Film Sound: . . . . .Dennis Panchen
Film Editor: . . . . .John Jarvis
Camera Supervisor: . . . . .Ken Major
Studio Lighting Director: . . . . . .Peter Smee
Studio Sound: . . . . .Dave Thompson
Technical Coordinator: . . . . . . .Tony Mutimer
Videotape Editor: . . . . .Chris Wadsworth
Production Assistants: . . . . .Caroline Andrews and Lesley Bywater
Assistant Floor Manager: . . . . .Gavin Clarke
Vision Mixer: . . . . .Heather Gilder
Production Manager: . . . . .Andy Smith
Designer: . . . . .Eric Walmsley
Directed by Susan Belbin
Produced by Ray Butt

Grandad's death has shocked the Trotter boys and the whole community. At the funeral, the forlorn figures of Del and Rodney stand beside his grave, accompanied by the old boy's family and friends, including cousins Jean and Stan, representing the North London branch of the family, and Uncle Albert, Grandad's brother.

Back at the flat, during the wake, Rodney is deep in mourning, unable to comprehend the laughter he hears from the other mourners congregated in the tiny living room. Uncle Albert tries to comfort Rodney with a myriad of naval yarns.

Later, when it appears all the guests have departed, a hungover Uncle Albert appears from the bathroom. With Stan and Jean (with whom he lived) long gone, there's only one alternative: he'll have to spend the night at the Trotters' place. But the following day, as Del struggles through the London rush-hour to drive him home, they find Stan and Jean

186

'Strained Relations'

have moved their mobile home, probably spotting a chance to rid themselves of Albert.

Del is reluctant to let Albert stay with them at the flat, so tries shipping him off to the local Seamen's Mission, but when he returns clutching his holdall, claiming it's been razed to the ground to make way for luxury flats and a marina, it looks like Del and Rodney have a new lodger.

Stringer, Nick

Role: Aussie man and Jumbo Mills
Appeared as Aussie man in S1, episode 2 and as Jumbo Mills in S5, episode 6

Born in 1948, Nick spent six months as a trainee accountant with Shell Mex and BP, nine months with Lloyds Bank, and twelve as a stage hand at Birmingham's Alexandra and Hippodrome theatres, and Butlins in Finley, before joining the Guildhall School of Music and Drama.

He made his professional debut in two small parts in a 1973 production of *Juno and the Paycock* at Liverpool's Everyman Theatre; his first few years were spent in repertory theatre at Liverpool, Exeter, Manchester, Nottingham and Newcastle, a period which saw him earn his first role on television as a jury foreman in a 1974 episode of *Crown Court*.

He's since appeared a lot on the screen, playing characters such as Max Derwin in *Family Affairs*, Jumpin Jacki in *Coronation Street*, Tommy Kingdom in *Goodnight Sweetheart*, Mr Curtain in *Famous Five*, Bill Turner in *Blind Justice*, Piglet in *Dempsey and Makepeace* and Roger in *The Collectors*.

Nick has also been recruited for several films, such as *Clockwise*, *The Shout* and *Personal Services*.

Strong, Gwyneth

Role: Cassandra Trotter (née Parry)
Appeared in 19 episodes: S6; S7, episodes 2, 5 & 6; 'The Jolly Boys' Outing'; 'Rodney Come Home'; 'Miami Twice' (Parts 1 & 2); 'Mother Nature's Son'; 'Fatal Extraction'; 'Heroes and Villains'; 'Modern Men'; 'Time On Our Hands' and 'If They Could See Us Now…!'

Gwyneth admits that she wasn't prepared for the impact that playing Cassandra would have on her life. The morning after she'd made her debut in the episode 'Yuppy Love', someone shouted to her from across the street. 'I was popping down to buy some milk and within minutes of closing the front door, somebody shouted: "How's Rodney?" People have been shouting "Rodney" and "Cassandra" ever since.'

Although, ideally, Gwyneth would prefer not to be in the spotlight, she appreciates it comes with the job, especially if you're involved in a hit programme. 'I'm very bad at handling it: whereas Tessa Peake-Jones, who's become a good friend of mine, is a much kinder person towards the public, I'm rather grumpy, although I try not to be. In the beginning the attention was a real shock and I wasn't really ready for it, perhaps because it coincided with having children; Oscar, who's now 14, and Lottie, who's 11, have never walked down the street without somebody shouting something at their mother – I would rather they didn't have that. On the other hand, you can't have both: we have a very nice lifestyle and they go to good schools, which all comes from a job like playing Cassandra. So you have to accept it.'

No sooner had Gwyneth decided to return to work after having her first child, than she was offered the part of Rodney's girlfriend. 'When Oscar was six months old I felt ready to return to work, so I tentatively phoned my agent and told her about my decision. Then Cassandra came along, which was fantastic.'

Expecting the role to last no more than a couple of episodes meant Gwyneth readily accepted the job offer. 'All I was told was that she was a girlfriend of Rodney, that's all. I would always have wanted to play the character, but if you're offered a long-running part, it's inevitable that you're going to question whether you want to commit for that long. But I didn't go through that thought process; it was just for a couple of episodes and then it grew from there, which was great.'

Only Fools and Horses was Gwyneth's first taste of situation comedy. 'It's a very technical way of working because you're performing for the audience in the studio and the actual cameras. I get very nervous about it but once I've said my first few lines I love it – it's a real challenge. It's such a thrill when you pull it off and everything comes together. When you've hit the mark and the audience laugh is a wonderful feeling.'

In the early days of playing Cassandra, the help and support of David Jason and Nicholas Lyndhurst were welcomed by Gwyneth. 'Having never worked in a sitcom, they were a great help; you learn by simply watching people, and they were always generous and interested in my thoughts and opinions.'

Although new to that field of television, Gwyneth had been working as an actress from the age of ten. Born in the London suburb of East Ham in 1959, it's hardly surprising she wanted to tread the boards with both her parents working at the BBC. As they were reluctant to send their daughter to drama school, Gwyneth divided her time between working in the theatre and continuing her education in local schools. 'My parents were encouraging, but were careful what work I did because they didn't want a precocious brat for a daughter! They probably thought I'd get tired of acting, to be honest, but of course I didn't.'

Even in those early days, she was being cast in a range of diverse roles. She played Mary Valley in Rank's *Nothing But the Night*, a 1972 horror movie with Gwyneth starring alongside Christopher Lee, Peter Cushing and Diana Dors, while on stage she was appearing in plays at the Royal Court. Meanwhile, on the small screen she was seen in a host of predominantly children's shows, playing Jan in 14 episodes of *The Flockton Flyer* in 1976–77, an adventure series set around a West Country railway line, and Minnie in 1975's *Edward the King*.

Unlike many child actors who struggle to adapt to more adult roles, Gwyneth's seamless transition saw her move effortlessly from one job to the next, covering all mediums. Her extensive list of television credits include playing a jury member in an episode of *Minder*, DS Bailey in *A Touch of Frost*, DI Richards in *An Unsuitable Job for a Woman*, Linda in *Rainy Day Women*, Tina Kitson in *Paradise Postponed*, Linda Thompson in *Nice Town*,

WPC Rachel McMahon in *The Missing Postman*, Hetty in *Lucy Sullivan is Getting Married* and, one of her favourite roles, Janet in *Real Women*.

On the big screen, she's made a handful of film appearances, such as Wanda in *Crimetime*, and *Cry Freedom*. Her long list of stage credits, meanwhile, have seen her play roles like Masha in *The Three Sisters* and Kitty in *Ancient Lights*, at the Hampstead Theatre.

She's worked in every strand of the profession, but doesn't have a preferred medium. 'When my children were first born, I went for about nine years without doing theatre work. Then when I returned to the stage it was so frightening; I'm trying to do a play a year at the moment because it's just the most fantastic way of getting your acting muscles going.'

Although Gwyneth has been acting for over 30 years, she's enjoying her work as much as ever. 'If I hadn't had my children I don't think I would enjoy it quite as much. If acting was my whole life, I wouldn't be so happy; but as a contrast to bringing up two children, it's wonderful.'

As yet, neither of Gwyneth's children have shown signs of following her footsteps into the profession. 'I think I've achieved my goal in putting them off!' she laughs. 'No, they don't show any interest at all. When they see me on television, they take it all very casually; sometimes they hardly even last a whole episode, I'm afraid.'

Stuart, Alan

Stunt artist on one episode: 'Dates'

Alan – who crashed a police car during 'Dates' – began his working life as a professional musician, performing with Tommy Steele and the Steelemen all around the world, and playing the saxophone in jazz bands.

He didn't move into the world of stunts until he was 30, when he doubled for Peter Sellers in *Dr Strangelove*. Alan eventually gave up his career as a professional musician and concentrated on stunt work in film and television. Now a stunt coordinator, recent work projects have included *Casualty*, *Cry*, *Fogle's War* and *The Bill*.

Stubbs, Robin

Costume designer on 22 episodes: S5; S7; 'A Royal Flush'; 'The Frog's Legacy'; 'Rodney Come Home'; 'Miami Twice' (Parts 1 & 2); 'Mother Nature's Son'; 'Fatal Extraction'; 'Heroes and Villains'; 'Modern Men' and 'Time On Our Hands'

Robin worked as a draughtsman before changing direction and joining the BBC. In 1966, whilst helping his wife run the crowd wardrobe for a film titled *Privilege* in Birmingham, the costume designer suggested Robin applied for a job. Within months he had started his television career as a dresser, and by 1974 had climbed the ladder to become a costume designer.

Born in Redditch in 1940, Robin worked on a multitude of shows during his 25 years' service with the Beeb, including *The Two Ronnies*, *Fall of Eagles*, *Doctor Who* and *Blue Peter*, as well as a host of drama films. He left the BBC in 1990 and

---

---

worked freelance for five years, before partnering his wife in Jacqui Stubbs Associates, a garden design company. In 2000 they took a year out and travelled to Australia and New Zealand, where they are now in the process of buying a house.

Stuntman/Double for Del

Played by Ken Barker

The stuntman doubles for Del when he goes hanggliding in 'Tea for Three'.

Sullivan, John

Writer of all episodes and the theme tune. Executive producer on six episodes: 'Mother Nature's Son', 'Fatal Extraction', 'Heroes and Villains', 'Modern Men', 'Time On Our Hands' and 'If They Could See Us Now…!'

John Sullivan admits he spent most of his schooldays living in a secret world. 'I'm one of those people who has a tendency to switch off when something bores me, like a dinner or reception; I close the area down in my mind and drift off into another world, which I did at school, purely because I hated it so much.'

Until the arrival of Jim Trowers – an English teacher who brought the subject alive for the first time in John's entire school life – life was grim. 'In English lessons we'd be handed one of the classics, such as *Pride and Prejudice*, but none of us could get to grips with the text, partly because it was people we didn't understand,' explains John. 'All the kids came from rough areas and now, all of a sudden, we were hearing about middle-class people through a language which was archaic; we had no empathy for the characters and couldn't relate to them. The trouble was, if we didn't understand there was always some kind of punishment, a form of reprisal at the end, so you'd sit there in dread.'

When Trowers walked into John's life, though, the subject took on a different complexion. 'Rather than just forcing us to read the text, Jim acted it out with accents; suddenly stories I'd struggled with until that point became clear and funny.' Trowers also introduced John Sullivan to the world of Charles Dickens, an author who played an important role in his development as a writer. 'Dickens wrote about areas I knew in London; although the writing dated back to the early 19th century, I felt this guy knew where I'd been and I began realising just how special his books were.'

John is keen to point out that he owes so much to his former teacher. 'Jim was an excellent teacher who never resorted to punishments like the cane. Everybody liked him because he made us laugh.' He also showed John the richness of Dickens' work, as well as its comic side. 'All these rather tough kids were suddenly enjoying the lesson.'

John witnessed comedy beyond the classroom, too. He believes he's got his father to thank for his sense of humour. Born in 1946, John grew up in Balham, South London. While his mother, Hilda, occasionally worked as a charlady, his father, also John, was a plumber. 'I was brought up with humour all around me,' says John. 'My mother was a timid woman, perhaps because my dad was such a powerful figure. He was a very funny man and I loved his dry sense of humour; he was always looking at life from a different angle. In fact, most of my family, who originated from Cork, were a laugh, even my aunties, which made for very enjoyable times, especially around Christmas when we all gathered together.'

Coming from a working-class background blinkered his outlook towards a future career. When he left school at 15 he did what was expected of him and looked for an everyday job which would bring in some welcome cash to the Sullivan household. Although he'd enjoyed writing at school, it never entered his mind to pursue it as a potential career. 'I had a cousin who was doing very well as a tailor in Saville Row, so I started attending interviews for a tailor's apprentice, but all the positions were geared more towards selling, which wasn't for me.'

Then his brother-in-law suggested working for the press, so he applied for a job at Reuters in Fleet Street and was successful in securing his first position. After a brief spell working as a messenger he transferred to the company's photographic department, before moving on to an advertising agency – Collett, Dickinson and Pearce – again as a messenger.

By the time John Sullivan seriously began considering writing as a way of earning a living he was employed by Watney's Brewery. 'It was a dull life. I worked in this large hall filled with beer crates moving around on a conveyor belt. A bell would ring, a red button would flash and the belt would start. As a crate came around I would grab it and stack them up. There were long periods when we'd just be sat around and it became boring.' During these periods of boredom, John and his colleague, Paul Saunders, an old school friend, began talking about writing comedy. Reading about the financial success scriptwriter Johnny Speight was enjoying with shows like *Till Death Us Do Part* made them contemplate whether they possessed the necessary skills to follow in his footsteps. 'Paul was a very funny man, a great comedian, and after seeing an article in the paper about how much Speight was earning for every episode he wrote, he said: "We've got a sense of humour and make each other laugh, let's have a go." So I agreed.'

After bouncing a few ideas around, they came up with the premise for a comedy script, so John popped along to a second-hand shop in Tooting and bought a typewriter for £2, 10 shillings. After a couple of months, the crisp, freshly typed script was placed in an envelope and posted to the BBC.

'We waited and waited but nothing happened. Paul was always optimistic and would say things like: "They've got it and it's so good they're just waiting to get in touch."' Eventually the script was returned with a brief note stating they weren't interested. 'Paul lost interest after that,' explains John. 'I suggested doing something else but he didn't want to know.' But John had enjoyed his brief flirtation with the idea of becoming a writer and had acquired the taste for more. 'I loved the process of creating characters, storylines and dialogue, so I decided to continue on my own.'

A change of job came along when John began working with his dad in plumbing, but he's the first to admit it wasn't the right career for him. 'I didn't want to make a living out of plumbing; the fact I flooded so many houses showed I wasn't very good at it – my heart just wasn't in it.' But he was interested in writing. 'In the end, it was the only job I felt I would be able to do, and do well enough to earn a living, so my main hope in life was to sell a

à la Del

★ ★ ★ ★ ★ ★

'Entende, I'm sure'
('Homesick')

'Oh mon dieu, mon dieu'
('Homesick')

script and earn enough money to provide for myself and my future wife and children, whenever they came along.'

But John had a struggle on his hands if he was to make even the first steps towards achieving his goal. An attitude existed amongst many people who felt it wasn't 'the done thing' for a working-class lad to gravitate towards writing as a career; this restricted outlook could easily have shackled his ambitions, yet he remained determined to succeed, spurred on by his role models: Ray Galton, Alan Simpson and Johnny Speight. 'They came from working-class backgrounds and didn't let their success change them, which inspired me even more. I suppose if I'd come from a middle-class school nobody would have batted an eyelid, but growing up where I did you were laughed at by some people; consequently, you don't tell anyone about your dream or what you wanted from life.'

The Beatles played their part in inspiring John, too. 'They were enjoying their first hits and I can remember lying in bed and hearing one of their songs, "From Me to You", playing somewhere down the street. I'd never heard anything like it before, it was such a different sound. I'll always remember thinking: "Aren't the Americans clever." I automatically assumed that any new sound, anything good

originated from the States, so when I found out that they were four working-class boys from a few hundred miles up the road, I was really inspired.'

Working with his father had its advantages: although the money was poor and John realised he could have earned more elsewhere, the nature of the job presented opportunities to write – little windows of time which were filled at the typewriter. 'We'd do two or three jobs and then have the rest of the day off. I'd spend entire afternoons just writing.' Some friends regarded John as 'a bit strange' wanting to dedicate so much of his time to writing. 'My whole life was about writing and football, and while friends were out drinking, I'd be training or out doing cross-country runs; I'd like to have been in the pub with my mates but didn't have the money.' Even his wife, Sharon, didn't take John's goals seriously at first when they began dating. 'I didn't tell her what my ambitions were straight away,' he admits, 'but eventually plucked up the courage. She told me later that she thought: "Oh no, he's a weirdo!" But she still kept on seeing me so couldn't have felt I was that bad.'

John kept churning out different ideas. 'There was one about a family who were living off the state big time, but after about a year or so I realised it would never work because there was no sympathy for them.'

Between 1966 and 1975 John had generated seven different ideas for a comedy series, but all had been rejected by the Beeb, many without a reason, something which frustrated him deeply. 'I couldn't get feedback from anyone; I just wanted somebody to give me some advice, even if it was simply to point out that I was useless. In the end, I spoke to a guy I knew who worked at the BBC and he offered me a job, perhaps as a way of finding out what television was all about. Giving up my job as a plumber to join the BBC changed my life.'

Starting in the props department, John moved on to work as a scene shifter, bringing him closer to the hub of television production. 'Not only could I see how scripts were written but was able to see how it transferred from rehearsal to production; it was so enlightening for me.'

The turning point in his life came whilst he was enjoying a drink at one of the BBC bars. 'Talk about fate, I didn't realise the BBC Club had two bars: one mostly frequented by the jeans-and-boots-type workers, the other where mainly producers, directors and actors visited. One Sunday I was sitting at a table when this man walked through to the bar. A guy said to me: "Do you know who that is? It's Dennis Main Wilson." Up until that point all I knew were the names of people who had the authority to accept and reject scripts, but now I was able to put a face to a name.' John knew this was the opportunity he'd long been waiting for; a moment he couldn't afford to waste. 'I made two attempts to go across and introduce myself, but aborted both of them. When my nerve went on the third attempt I thought it was time to go home.' As he headed for the exit, Main Wilson looked up and their eyes made contact. 'I turned towards him and it must have become quite obvious that I was heading over to speak to him. It was too late to stop now, so I introduced myself and said: "We'll be working together soon." When he asked on what, I replied: "On this thing I'm writing." I wouldn't have been surprised if he'd sacked me, but he didn't, he just laughed and we got on very well.'

Main Wilson had liked John's barefaced cheek. 'I was frightened of him at first,' confesses John, 'because he'd produced so many top shows and had an incredible track record. I've met some producers since then who've said they would have told me where to go, but Dennis was just mad enough to laugh and admire my nerve.'

The veteran producer listened to what John had to say and advised him to gain some vital experience by trying his luck at sketch writing. At this point, John was scene shifting on *Porridge*, so grabbed the opportunity to ask Ronnie Barker for advice. John told him that he had some ideas for sketches, and Ronnie asked him to bring them in. The following week John handed them over to Ronnie Barker, who took them home to read. Come the following Sunday, John Sullivan was offered a contract to write for *The Two Ronnies*. John had finally found his metier and went on to submit sketches for *The Dave Allen Show* (which wre all rejected).

He recalls the first sketch he did for Messrs Corbett and Barker. 'It was the public bar philosophers in a sketch titled, "I'm not God". The characters worked so well they reappeared from time to time. I ended up working on five series. These two old guys used to talk about how they'd change the world if they were God. To be honest, they just rambled on and hadn't got to grips with what was

happening in the world. I based the characters on my father and his friends down the pub having a few drinks and what they'd like to see change.'

By this time, John had already developed the idea for what was to become his first sitcom for television: *Citizen Smith*. Buoyed by the news he'd been offered a contract to write for *The Two Ronnies*, his good fortunes continued when Dennis Main Wilson issued him a contract to write a pilot script. 'It was strange: after ten years of trying I was suddenly offered two contracts within days of each other. I was ecstatic.'

John took annual leave from the Beeb and wrote the pilot script at his wife's parents' home. The genesis of the idea behind *Citizen Smith* came from John's days frequenting a pub in London's King's Road. 'The Nelson Arms was a real old-fashioned London pub. You'd get a lot of actors in there, also a lot of Bob Dylan types. There was one guy – I never knew his name – who could play the guitar to a point, and would always want a drink from

you before going on about the revolution he was going to start as soon as the pub closed. In the next breath he'd say he was cutting his first album the following week. Suddenly he's a successful popstar. I just thought he was an idiot, although he fascinated me. I started wondering where he went after leaving the pub.'

The image of this man had stuck in the back of John Sullivan's mind, and now it was going to influence his future. Sat in front of the typewriter he started bringing the character of Wolfie Smith alive. 'Basically he was a guy who wanted to be a British Che Guevara, hence the beret – and who never bought a drink; he was also planning to be a revolutionary but wouldn't mind being a millionaire as well, if possible,' says John.

John found that because he'd been nuturing the idea for some time, the process of actually writing the pilot script was an easy exercise, although he admits it was too long and contained 'stupid errors'. 'I loved American comedy and watched a lot of the shows, where each scene usually begins with a shot of the front of the house, or whatever, just to set the scene. So I littered my script with every scene starting with a shot of the house or pub. When I was later asked why I did this, I explained because of the American shows. What I didn't realise, though, was this was because of the com-

mercial breaks. So I made amateurish mistakes like that, as well as a script which was far too long, and a final scene which closed on Shirley's parents, not Wolfie, which had to be rewritten.'

However, Main Wilson liked the script, so too did his boss, Jimmy Gilbert, who was then Head of Comedy. 'I remember Dennis telling me he'd met this chap, who was a scene shifter at the BBC, who'd written a script,' explains Jimmy. 'We were flooded with scripts, but Dennis insisted it was worth looking at. Dennis was absolutely brilliant and normally an excellent judge, so I agreed to read it; it didn't take long for me to realise that it was good; you didn't need to touch it, it was extraordinary.'

Such was his confidence in John Sullivan's writing that Jimmy popped upstairs to see the Controller of BBC1 and asked whether he had a free slot in the schedules because here was a script worth piloting straight away. When a space was found, Jimmy commissioned a back-up script, which was delivered within days, and then commissioned a full series. 'Within six weeks of me seeing the pilot, there was a second script complete and a whole series commissioned. In fact, when Alasdair Milne was Director-General and he received criticism about the BBC being under a cloud of bureaucracy, he always quoted the timescales associated with *Citizen Smith*.'

Reflecting on what he liked about the work, Jimmy points to the quality of the writing. 'It was original, and the quality was amazing for a script coming out of that field; John's a very rare writer of comedy: he just has the ability to create characters who are funny and ring true.'

The pilot episode was transmitted on 12 April 1977 under the *Comedy Special* umbrella, the successor to the *Comedy Playhouse* series, which aired pilot scripts in the hope that they'd strike a chord with the public and result in a full series being commissioned. John struck gold with *Citizen Smith* and was asked to write a full series, which was transmitted in November and December 1977.

To give himself the time to think and write, John opted to pack in his scene-shifting job and concentrate on being a full-time writer, but Jimmy Gilbert tried dissuading him. 'Jimmy said: "Don't give up your job; we'll arrange for you to have all the time you need away from your job; that way if it doesn't work out, you'll have a safety net."' John appreciated Jimmy's generosity, but felt it unfair on his colleagues left in the department. 'I wouldn't be doing the work but would be picking my wages up each month. Besides, it didn't fit into the overall plan I'd been dreaming of for the last ten years, where certain events would happen: I'd be discovered, be offered a contract, given a series and then become a success and go to America. That's how I saw it working out. I was very confident and said I'd resign and become a writer, although I was told after they reluctantly accepted my resignation that there would still be something for me if it didn't work out, which was reassuring because at least I'd be able to feed the family!'

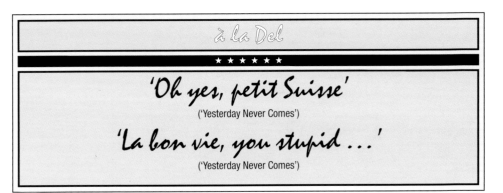

à la Del

★ ★ ★ ★ ★ ★

'Oh yes, petit Suisse'
('Yesterday Never Comes')

'La bon vie, you stupid ...'
('Yesterday Never Comes')

190

John Sullivan never looked back and the adventures of the Tooting Popular Front set him on the road to success. Over three years, 30 episodes were transmitted and although it wasn't a ratings sensation, John was pleased with how *Citizen Smith* had gone. 'I was perfectly happy with it and it became a cult programme, attracting a lot of attention, which meant the BBC wanted me to continue with it. By the time we'd reached the fourth series, though, we were all wanting to move on and getting on each other's nerves, so it seemed the right time to leave it.'

John's fortunes received a temporary setback with his next script, *Over the Moon*, a pilot about the manager of the worst football team in Britain. 'The BBC used to give me this contract whereby I'd finish writing a series and then have to come up with a pilot script for, potentially, my next project. The central character, Ron Wilson, was to be played by Brian Wilde. Ron wasn't a leader of men, suffered with his nerves and had ulcers, but away from football he ran a bed and breakfast with this woman, who'd been on the stage years ago, and had a reputation for having helped the Americans out during the war! But the whole idea of the show was that as soon as they closed the door at home, they became the people they wanted to be: while she considered him to be a strong leader, he thought of her as a true lady; but it was only behind closed doors that they could be who they wanted to be. The rest of the time they were objects of ridicule.'

The pilot script was accepted and John was given a contract to write the second episode. He'd almost completed a third script when Bill Cotton, then Controller of BBC1, came back from America and made the decision to cancel *Over the Moon*. '*Seconds Out*, with Robert Lindsay, was about boxing and it was felt there wasn't room for two sitcoms about sport and, unfortunately, mine was dropped.'

The decision left John Sullivan in a serious predicament: he found himself without any work. By now, he was on contract to the BBC, so he was still picking up a pay cheque despite having nothing to write. In need of inspiration, John thought about all the conversations he'd had with Ray Butt, who'd directed *Citizen Smith*, about life in the London markets – something they had both experienced firsthand. After mulling over these memories in his mind, he began formulating the basic structure of what was to become, arguably, his most successful creation, *Only Fools and Horses*.

Little did John know, when he settled down to pen that first script, that he was beginning a 21-year journey leading to over 60 episodes. But by the end of the 1980s, John would have another three hit shows under his belt: as well as *Only Fools*, he went on to write *Just Good Friends* and *Dear John*.

Between 1983 and '86, 22 episodes of *Just Good Friends* were transmitted. The main characters, Vince Pinner and Penny Warrender, were played by Paul Nicholas and Jan Francis, while Ray Butt was, once again, at the helm for the lion's share of the episodes. The premise of the sitcom was perfectly drawn by John Sullivan: after getting cold feet and

leaving his fiancée, Penny, standing at the altar, Vince heads off for a new life; five years later they meet again and although they intend remaining 'just good friends', they can't shut out their true feelings for one another: the sitcom culminated with the long-term sweethearts tying the knot.

The speed at which the BBC hierarchy accepted the idea for *Just Good Friends* amazed John. 'I've never known anything like it, because it was commissioned in about 35 minutes. John Howard Davies wasn't in his office so I left the new script on his desk and went to Ray Butt's office and chatted about a host of things. Suddenly the phone rang and John said: "I want a series."'

Although John is uncertain exactly how the idea for the series came about, he believes he read an agony letter in one of his wife's magazines. 'With the mists of time, I'm not entirely sure that was how it happened or whether it just made good

TEACHING JOHN SULLIVAN

★ ★ ★ ★ ★ ★

'John Sullivan and I were both "new boys" at Telferscot Secondary School, Balham in 1958. John established himself very early on; within 20 minutes of joining the school, in fact. He stood up for himself in the playground and was involved in a fight, refusing to back down to what he considered to be unfair treatment. This was a trait – one that I admire in people, incidentally – that was to lead him into a number of minor scrapes throughout his school career. To appreciate and admire the distance he has come you have to understand both his environment and the educational machine of that time.

'John lived in Zennor Road, Balham. In the late 1950s that road was almost a no-go area for the local police. The culture could probably be best summed up in the statement: "What use is education? Get yourself down the market and get a proper job!" You can almost hear the echo in "Only fools and horses work"! He was one of the many thousands who had been through the now discredited and unfair 11+ selection process. A secondary school curriculum was often a watered down copy of the grammar school and, as such, bore little or no relation to the lives of the pupils. When I first knew John and his classmates they were being given *Pride and Prejudice* to read on their own. Not only was this

not relevant, but no attempt was made to make it at least an enjoyable experience.

'He and his peers were left to struggle with difficulties such as punctuation and its usage. Despite this, John's interest in English, in particular, and History survived. I recall I was given the task of introducing his class, not the easiest group in the school, to Dickens. The characters that Dickens created, although from a previous century, were relevant to the conditions that this group experienced in their environment. John took to the stories like a duck to water. I can remember his enthusiasm as the stories unfolded, and he was usually the first with his hand up either to answer or to ask a question. His interest in writing continued to grow and when he left Telferscot in June 1963 he was determined against all opposition to become a writer.

'That he has talent is an undisputed fact. That he kept that talent alive against heavy odds to become the successful writer he dreamed of being, is entirely down to his own tenacity and perseverance. He knew he could do it and he was not going to let anyone tell him otherwise. He took a stand just like he did in the first 20 minutes in Telferscot, but the rewards were very different!'

JIM TROWERS – John's former teacher

publicity,' smiles John. 'But back in the days when I grew up people didn't have cars and so you never moved that far. As a result, everyone met their future wives or husbands within a four-mile radius. I know lots of cases of people meeting, parting and then meeting again; it was all very parochial and I thought an interesting idea for a comedy. Leaving someone at the church must be one of the worst things you can do to anyone, and then to try and win them back must be the greatest challenge in the world. Then I thought about this guy, Vince, and whether he could ever get her back.'

By the time Vince and Penny were taking their wedding vows, John Sullivan had another sitcom up and running, *Dear John* starring Ralph Bates. 'As well as the six or seven scripts for the current sitcom I was doing at the time, I had to come up with this extra one as a pilot. It was John Howard Davies' plan because he always wanted me to have a second string. I used to find it a real pain because you'd finish writing a series, you'd have your money, but then there was this other script hanging over you which had to be a brand new idea. But, in a way, it was a godsend because it forced all those little ideas or inklings out of you, which you had to do to get your money. It was good therapy and as much as I hated it, *Just Good Friends* and *Dear John* came through this method.'

The idea behind *Dear John* was based on John's sister's experiences of attending a social gathering for singles and divorced people not too dissimilar to the sessions attended by John, the sitcom's main character. 'She only went once and thought it was awful. Then I started realising that almost all the people I knew were divorced; I hadn't appreciated just how big divorce had become and that helping divorced people was a huge industry.'

A script was delivered but it wasn't developed into a series straight away. 'Suddenly *Only Fools and Horses* and *Just Good Friends* were way up in the ratings and people thought I had the Midas touch! They dragged anything they could of mine off the shelve: they wanted to do *Over the Moon*, this time with Leonard Rossiter, but sadly he died. Anything I'd written became gold dust and *Dear John* was one of the next things brought off the shelf.'

The series ran to 14 episodes, and after it came to an end in 1987, it was sold to NBC in the United States, who made 90 episodes of their own version. This side of the pond, a third series was on the cards until the untimely death of Ralph Bates – who'd became a good friend of John Sullivan's – put paid to the idea.

The 1990s remained equally busy for John: 13 episodes of *Sitting Pretty*, starring Diane Bull as Annabel Briggs, a good-time girl from the swinging sixties who has to confront destitution, were shown between 1992 and 1993, while *Roger, Roger* and *Heartburn Hotel* occupied much of the latter half of the decade.

One author who has always been a key influence in John Sullivan's life from his days as a schoolboy is Charles Dickens. His favourite character from the Dickens' canon was Micawber, the genteel landlord from *David Copperfield*, and during Christmas 2001, John saw a long-term project come to fruition with the showing of his *Micawber*. 'When I was 50, my wife gave me a full set of leather-bound books by Dickens. I've been in the business so long now that when I read books I can't help but thinking about casting the characters. When I started reading *David Copperfield* I immediately thought David Jason would make a brilliant Micawber.'

John started realising there was mileage in the idea of writing a show based on the character so he discussed the possibilities with Jason, who was equally enthused by the idea. Originally intended for the BBC, the project was finally completed for ITV. 'I literally took Micawber and his family out and focused on their lives; originally I planned using some of the others characters, like David Copperfield and Uriah Heep, but David Reynolds, the producer, suggested I forget the other characters else I might have found myself trapped in the world depicted in the book.' The end result was a four-part drama series screened over the festive period, with Jason playing the lead and Annabelle Apsion as his screen wife, Emma Micawber.

A string of success stories has, undoubtedly, lifted John Sullivan into the higher echelons of scriptwriting, and he's regarded as one of the nation's top writers. Success doesn't come easily and John finds his new projects always seem to be compared to the success of the Trotters. 'When I started writing *Roger, Roger* someone in one of the daily papers wrote, "This isn't *Only Fools and Horses*", so I wrote back and said: "No, it's blinking *Roger, Roger* – that's why I called it that."'

Although there are tremendous pressures associated with scriptwriting, it's a process John enjoys. In creating a little world, not only does the writer have to draw the characters who will live out their lives through the scripts, but there are a myriad of shops, cafés, towns and clubs to name as well, a process John Sullivan particularly relishes. 'Coming up with all these new names for shops and such like is exciting.

Reflecting on the success he's achieved to date, though, John's unassuming manner reveals a man who's proud, yet slightly embarrassed about the fuss his creations have brought. Whilst he's able to enjoy all the trappings of a successful life, including properties in Surrey, Sussex and a villa high in the mountains of Majorca, he's never forgotten his roots. 'I'm not the sort of person who gives many interviews or seeks publicity; I like the quiet life. But it's nice to hear people complimenting the shows.'

One of the consequences of achieving success in his field is having to attend functions, including award dinners, something John avoids as much as possible, especially if a speech is involved. 'I hate award dinners. I think it's wonderful that people want to award you with something, but I just like to go up on stage and get off as quickly as possible. But as soon as that pressure is lifted I have a wonderful time and celebrate like hell.

'I remember winning a writer of the year award for *Just Good Friends*. I was told in advance I could prepare a speech, and when the introduction started I stood up and went on to the stage; Ronnie Barker was the host and he told me I wasn't supposed to come up yet because clips were being shown of the show, but no one had told me. I just didn't know what to do, but they showed the clips and then Ronnie, who'd heard something through his earpiece, said: "John, we have to cut the speech." I thought: "Oh, there is a god." It was a wonderful moment.'

John's parents were also proud of what their son achieved, as he recalls. 'When I picked up one of the BAFTA awards – I think it was for *Just Good Friends* – my mum and dad looked after the children for us. When we got home they congratulated me, but later on I asked the kids what nanny and grandad did when I went up on stage to collect the award, and they both replied: "Oh, they cried." That showed just how proud they were.'

Sunglasses Ron

In 'The Miracle of Peckham', Del mentions Ron to Father O'Keith during his confessionals. He's not seen in the episode, but it seems Del bought some lead from him only to find out it's hot property, especially as it came from the church roof. His name crops up again in 'To Hull and Back' on Slater's office whiteboard at the police station, where he's listed the possible suspects involved in the diamond smuggling racket.

Sunny Sea guest house

Owned by Mrs Baker, the Margate guest house is where the Trotters try to stay in 'The Jolly Boys' Outing'. Unfortunately no rooms are available, but the kindly proprietor suggests trying Mrs Creswell at the Villa Bella, across the street.

SWANS

Mentioned in 'Mother Nature's Son', we learn that Myles, who has made a fortune from his Nature's Way chain of stores, is vice-president of the Spa Water and Natural Spring Committee.

Sweeney, Maureen

Role: Cousin Jean
Appeared in S4, episode 2

Maureen's other roles on television have included playing Mrs Medhurst in *The Sweeney*, Gloria in *Dempsey and Makepeace*, Gloria Radford in *She's Out*, a waitress in *Touching Evil* and Eileen in the series *Romany Jones*, while recently she's been seen in *The Law* and *Real Women*. She's also made a handful of film appearances, such as playing Mavis in the 1973 production *Holiday on the Buses* and a sauna receptionist in *The Squeeze*.

Sweet, Glynn

Role: Auctioneer
Appeared in S3, episode 2

Glynn, who was born in Brighton, trained at the Bristol Old Vic School before working in various repertory theatres around the country, beginning with a year and a half at Worthing.

Although primarily a theatre actor, Glynn – who's recently completed a season at The Royal Shakespeare Company – has enjoyed his fair share of television roles, including appearances in *The Bill* and *London's Burning*.

On stage, meanwhile, his favourite roles include Uriah Heep in *David Copperfield* and Sir John Brute in *The Provok'd Wife*. Other productions he's appeared in range from *The Rivals* and *A Doll's House* to *Enemy of the People* and *Peter Pan*.

Sylvester

Denzil and Corinne's canary is seen in 'Who's a Pretty Boy?', but he frustrates his owners when he won't utter a word.

Symonds, Fen

Graphic designer on eight episodes: S2 and 'Diamonds are for Heather'

Fen trained for four years in heraldry and calligraphy at Reigate Art School before joining the BBC's graphic design department in 1974. After three years she left to work freelance, returning to the BBC as Peter Clayton's assistant. In 1986 she gave in her notice and freelanced once again before moving to South Devon. She no longer works in the profession.

Synth player

Seen at The Down by the Riverside Club in 'Stage Fright', the synth player is part of the backing group for Tony Angelino, the Singing Dustman. When Tony finishes his session, the synth player takes to the mike.

Talk of the Town, The

An establishment in Reading, this is where Raquel gave her sole performance as a solo singer: she forgot the words and the tune, and the people cheered when 'last orders' was finally announced.

Tanya

An unseen character in 'Rodney Come Home', Tanya is the new receptionist at the Peckham Exhaust Centre. Whilst experiencing marriage problems, Rodney asks her out to the cinema, even though he admits she hasn't much of a personality. In the end he realises he's making a mistake and cancels the date.

Tarifa

In 'It Never Rains…', Grandad says he was imprisoned just outside Tarifa – a Spanish town – along with Nobby Clarke, back in the 1930s.

Taylor, Graham

Videotape editor on two episodes: S5, episodes 2 & 6

Taylor, Laurie

Studio sound supervisor on two episodes: 'Fatal Extraction' and 'If They Could See Us Now…!'
Born in Wrexham, Laurie joined the BBC straight from school at the age of 18. As a technical operator, based in London, his early work included spells on shows such as *Juke Box Jury*, *Z Cars* and *Dixon of Dock Green*. He was promoted to sound supervisor in 1970 and worked on many of the top programmes of the day, such as *The Generation Game*, *The Good Life* and *The Onedin Line*. Other credits include *Hi-De-Hi!*, *Don't Wait Up*, *Keeping Up Appearances*, *Dinnerladies*, *Never Mind the Buzzcocks*, *Blankety Blank* and *The Clarkson Show*. Laurie still works for the BBC.

Taylor, Lee

Dubbing mixer on two episodes: 'Miami Twice' (Parts 1 & 2)
Lee, who was born in Ilford, left school and worked as a sound engineer for five years with Theatre Projects, touring with rock and jazz bands, such as The Boomtown Rats and E.L.O. He moved on to West End theatre productions, before joining the BBC as an assistant sound recordist in 1980. By the late '80s he'd been promoted to dubbing mixer,

'Tea for Three'

working on a range of shows, including *Lovejoy* and *Between the Lines*.

He left the Beeb in 1994 and works for Interact Sound Limited in London, with recent projects including *Inspector Linley* for the BBC.

Taylor, Mike

Videotape editor on eight episodes: S1, episodes 1 & 5; S2, episodes 3, 4 & 6; S3, episodes 1, 3 & 7
Mike, who still works at the BBC, joined the Corporation in 1974 and worked on numerous programmes before moving on from post-production to another division of the BBC.

Taylor, Roy

Not seen in the sitcom, Roy was a friend of Rodney's when he was little. He's mentioned in 'The Long Legs of the Law' by Grandad, who recalls the story of when Rodney got upset because his friend Roy had a new pair of Jacko roller skates. The following day, Del acquired a pair for Rodney, but forgot to tell him that he'd pinched Roy's pair, resulting in Rodney getting a good hiding from Taylor's older brother.

'Tea for Three'

Original transmission: Sunday 21 September 1986, 8.35 pm

Production date: Sunday 22 June 1986

Original viewing figures: 16.5 million

Duration: 30 minutes

First repeat: Thursday 1 October 1987, 8.30 pm

Subsequent repeats: 1/1/89, 1/12/98, 29/11/00

CAST

Del Trotter . . . . .David Jason
Rodney Trotter . . . . .Nicholas Lyndhurst
Uncle Albert . . . . .Buster Merryfield
Trigger . . . . .Roger Lloyd Pack
Mike . . . . .Kenneth MacDonald
Lisa . . . . .Gerry Cowper
Andy .Mark Colleano
Pianist . . . . .Fred Tomlinson
Singer . . . . .Joan Baxter
Drummer . . . . .Derek Price
Stuntman/Double . . . . .Ken Barker
Walk-ons: . . . . .Mark Burgess, Jonathan Truss, Nicola Miles, Denise Reynolds, Raymond Sargent, Rick Bonner, Denise Dubarry, John Raymond, Rosemary Banks, James Charlton, Larry Bishop, Celia Breckon, Elaina Legrand, Des Williams, Lyndon Lloyd, Patrick Edwards, Raymond Dunstan, Anthea Ferrell, George McCarthy, Charles Gilliard, Robin Easther, David Hoyle, Ricky Kennedy, Felicity Lee, Karen Newsome and Diane Gurney.

PRODUCTION TEAM

Written by John Sullivan
Title music arranged and conducted by Ronnie Hazlehurst composed and sung by John Sullivan
Audience warm-up: . . . . .Felix Bowness
Make-up Designer: . . . . .Elaine Smith
Costume Designer: . . . . .Robin Stubbs
Properties Buyer: . . . . .Maura Laverty
Film Cameraman: . . . . .Chris Seager
Film Sound: . . . . .Dave Brabants
Film Editor: . . . . .John Jarvis
Camera Supervisor: . . . . .Ken Major
Studio Lighting Director: . . . . . .Henry Barber
Studio Sound: . . . . .Dave Thompson
Technical Coordinator: . . . . . . .Nick Moore
Videotape Editor: . . . . .Chris Wadsworth
Production Assistants: . . . . .Rowena Painter and Alexandra Todd
Assistant Floor Manager: . . . . .Adrian Pegg
Graphic Designer: . . . . .Andrew Smee
Vision Mixer: . . . . .Heather Gilder
Production Manager: . . . . .Sue Longstaff
Designer: . . . . .Mark Sevant
Directed by Mandie Fletcher
Produced by Ray Butt

'Tea for Three'

Trigger's 25 year-old niece, Lisa, is staying with him for a few days. She was a scruffy little nipper when Del and Rodney last saw her so their eyes are on stalks when the luscious beauty walks into The Nag's Head. Both brothers fancy their chances and end up inviting her for tea; to ensure he spends the evening with her, Del tries putting his brother out of action by turning up the heat control on his sunbed.

With his face resembling a beetroot, Rodney is desperate for retaliation, so he tells Lisa that Del – who claims he's keen on hang-gliding just to impress her – would like to meet Lisa's hang-gliding friends and, as his 46th birthday is approaching, perhaps even give it a try. Del regrets claiming he was a paratrooper when he spends three hours up in the air before returning to earth with a bang!

Technomatch Agent

Played by Christopher Stanton
The agent runs the new computer dating agency in the High Street. Seen during 'Dates', he interviews Del when he pops in to see who's on offer.

Technomatch Friendship and Matrimonial Agency

In 'Dates', Trigger turns to the agency for female companionship and causes a stir at The Nag's Head when he arrives carrying a bunch of flowers and sporting a bright blue suit, and all because he's got a date.

The company have opened an office in the High Street and for £25 Trigg thought it was worth a try, especially as he decided to falsify a few of his details, like claiming he was a bus inspector.

Desperate for a little romance himself, Del tries his luck at Technomatch and comes up trumps when he's put in touch with Raquel.

Teddy

Played by Johnny Wade
Teddy is drinking at the bar in The Nag's Head in 'To Hull and Back'. Del sells him a new watch.

Teddy

In 'As One Door Closes', Rodney tells Uncle Albert that Del's mate Teddy manages a joinery and can supply louvre doors till the cows come home.

Terry

Not seen in the sitcom, Terry is mentioned by Grandad in 'Christmas Crackers'. He's married to Brenda and has three children: Shirley, Shaun and Shane. Their Christmas card is accidentally dropped into the Trotters' flat.

Texo

Played by Bryan Brittain
Seen in 'Fatal Extraction', Texo is one of the rioters outside Nelson Mandela House who halt their free-for-all to allow Del, Raquel and Damien through. On the way to his garage, Del tells Texo that he now has the Russian VCR to accompany his camcorder, so we can only assume that Texo is a man with limited grey matter, considering he's doing business with the Trotters.

Thackray, Paul

Technical coordinator on one episode: 'The Jolly Boys' Outing'
Upon joining the BBC in 1979, Bradford-born Paul Thackray worked in radio for seven years. Seeking a new challenge, he transferred to television and began working as a technical coordinator. He's worked on a myriad of shows in his time with the Beeb, from *Play School* and *Blue Peter* to *Ever Decreasing Circles* and *Keeping Up Appearances*. More recently, his credits include *They Think It's All Over*, *This Is Your Life* and *The Frank Skinner Show*.

Theme Tune

The original theme tune, which was written and conducted by Ronnie Hazlehurst, was recorded on 6 August 1981 at Lime Grove. The musicians hired to play the music were Alf Bigden on drums; Paul Westwood, bass guitar; Don Hunt, piano; John Dean, percussion; Judd Proctor, guitars, with Eddie Mordue and Rex Morris on saxophone.

After the first series it was decided to change the tune, with John Sullivan writing the new version and Ronnie, once again, arranging and conducting the piece, as he explains. 'John is what you call a whistling composer: he whistled the tune on to tape and I straightened it out, harmonised it and then orchestrated it. John wrote the words and sung it, too.' Ronnie had worked with John before, on the signature tune for *Citizen Smith* and *Dear John*, and felt the *Only Fools*' theme tune successfully captured the mood of the programme.

The revised signature tune was recorded – again at Lime Grove – by a four-piece band on 11 May 1982. This time the musicians were John Horler playing piano; Dave Richmond, bass guitar; Alf Bigden, drums and Judd Proctor on guitars.

> *à la Del*
> ★ ★ ★ ★ ★ ★
> 'It's "oeuf sur le plat" as the French say!'
> ('Thicker Than Water')

'Ronnie did a perfectly decent piece of music but it wasn't the modern rock style I wanted. Everyone was saying it wasn't what they thought it would be like, so as I'd recorded on tape what I wanted it to sound like, I took it along to Ray Butt's office.'

Ray accepts responsibility for the way events had turned out, but points out that it was because he'd spent time in hospital with a slipped disc. 'John hated it, I hated it. It just wasn't right. So when

John brought along his version on tape, I thought it sounded great.'

The theme tune was altered in time for the second series, but hopes of Chas and Dave singing on the theme tune – which John Sullivan had hoped for – were dashed because they were enjoying chart success with their single 'Ain't No Pleasing You', which reached number two in the Top 40. Ray gave John an ultimatum: if he wanted to alter the theme tune, he'd have to sing. 'After many hours of trying to persuade him to do it, he finally agreed to give it a go. We went along to Studio H at Lime Grove. Ronnie Hazlehurst had completed the arrangement, had laid the band's track down before sending them to the bar. Then John and I went into the vocal booth and after quite a few attempts, he did it and it worked out well. Given that the guy is not a singer, I thought it was great. Ideally I would like him to have done

OPENING THEME 'ONLY FOOLS AND HORSES'

Stick a pony in me pocket
I'll fetch the suitcase from the van
Coz if you want the best 'uns
But you don't ask questions
Then, brother, I'm your man

Coz where it all comes from is a mystery
It's like the changing of the seasons
And the tides of the sea

But here's the one what's driving me berserk
Why do only fools and horses work
La la lala – la la la la la (to fade)

CLOSING THEME 'HOOKIE STREET'

We've got some half-price cracked ice
    and miles and miles of carpet tiles,
TVs, deep freeze and David Bowie LPs,
Pool games, gold chains, whatsanames
    and at a push,
Some Trevor Francis tracksuits from a mush in
    Shepherd's Bush

Bush, bush, bush, bush, bush, bush…

No income tax, no VAT,
No money back, no guarantee,
Black or white, rich or broke,
We'll cut prices at a stroke.

God bless Hookie Street,
Viva Hookie Street,
Long live Hookie Street
C'est magnifique, Hookie Street,
Magnifique, Hookie Street,
Hookie Street (to fade)

'Thicker Than Water'

a harmony line, but there was no way he'd do that so we left it like it was.'

It was an experience John Sullivan wouldn't ever want to repeat. 'I hated it. I remember I had about nine pints of lager the night before just to try and calm my nerves, but when I went in to the studio I was stone cold sober – that's what serious nerves do to you, you can't get drunk!' he smiles.

'There's a Rhino Loose in the City!'

Rodney isn't impressed with this, the title that Del gives his idea for a film in 'Video Nasty'. Detecting Rodney's lack of enthusiasm towards his suggestion, Del later adapts it to 'There's a Rhino Loose Somewhere Out in the Sticks Where No Sod Lives', which meets with the same lack of fervour.

Thewlis, David

Role: Stew
Appeared in S4, episode 4
David's other television credits include roles in *The Singing Detective*, *A Bit of a Do*, *Prime Suspect* and *Dandelion Dead*. He's also appeared in several films over the years, such as *Goodbye, Charlie Bright*; *Whatever Happened to Harold Smith?*; *Divorcing Jack*; *Seven Years in Tibet*; *Black Beauty* and *Life Is Sweet*, while on stage he's worked at many of the top theatres, including the National and Royal Court.

'Thicker Than Water'

(Christmas Special 1983)
Original transmission: Sunday 25 December 1983, 9.35 pm
Production date: Sunday 20 November 1983
Original viewing figures: 10.8 million
Duration: 30 minutes
First repeat: Tuesday 1 January 1985, 8.40 pm
Subsequent repeats: 30/12/94, 25/9/98, 19/5/00

CAST
Del Trotter . . . . .David Jason
Rodney Trotter . . . . .Nicholas Lyndhurst
Grandad Trotter . . . . .Lennard Pearce
Reg Trotter . . . . .Peter Woodthorpe
Karen (the barmaid) . . . . .Michèle Winstanley
Extras: . . . .(People in pub) 11 extras

PRODUCTION TEAM
Written by John Sullivan
Title music arranged and conducted by Ronnie Hazlehurst
composed and sung by John Sullivan
Audience Warm-up: . . . . .Felix Bowness
Make-up Designer: . . . . .Denise Baron
Costume Designer: . . . . .Dinah Collin
Properties Buyer: . . . . .Penny Rollinson
Camera Supervisor: . . . . .Ron Peverall
Studio Lighting Director: . . . . .Don Babbage
Studio Sound: . . . . .Dave Thompson
Technical Coordinator: . . . . . .Peter Valentine
Videotape Editor: . . . . .Chris Wadsworth
Production Assistant: . . . . .Penny Thompson
Assistant Floor Manager: . . . . .Tony Dow

Graphic Designer: . . . . .Mic Rolph
Vision Mixer: . . . . .Angela Beveridge
Production Manager: . . . . .Andy Smith
Designer: . . . . .Bryan Ellis
Produced and directed by Ray Butt

The Trotters' home is certainly not the place for festive cheer when Reg Trotter – Del and Rodney's long-lost father – turns up out of the blue. It transpires he's been living in Newcastle for the last year, and after being admitted to the Newcastle Infirmary recently, was diagnosed as suffering from a hereditary blood condition. Needing to inform his sons, he tracks down Del and Rodney to break the news. Fortunately, subsequent medical tests prove negative, so they've nothing to worry about; however, the results also unearth some earth-shattering news for the Trotter brothers: they don't have the same blood types. Through all the confusion it could well be that Rodney and Del have different fathers. Just before Reg and their mother split up they were rowing a lot, leading to their mother's liaisons with other men. When Reg breaks the news that Del is the mystery child, the Trotter family is in turmoil, until a visit to the family doctor, Dr Becker, reveals that life for Del isn't as gloomy as it seemed.

Thomas, William

Role: Barman
Appeared in S6, episode 1
Born in Swansea in 1946, William began studying art before deciding his future lay in the acting profession. He trained at the Guildhall School of Music and Drama, and made his professional debut in a 1971 production, *Geneva*; his first taste of television came a year later playing a spy in a BBC Wales production.

His early days as an actor were largely spent in theatre, including a spell at The Mermaid in London, but during his career he's experienced all mediums: his film work includes playing the lead, Bryn Cartwright, in *Twin Town* and Detective Inspector Jarvis in *Darklands*, while his small-screen appearances extend from Ivor in the series *Fun at the Funeral Parlour* for BBC Choice, and a vicar in *Coronation Street* to Probert in *Magnificent Evans* and a desk sergeant in *EastEnders*.

William remains busy in the profession, especially on television.

Thompson, Bernard

Producer on one episode: 'Christmas Crackers'
Bernard's career in the entertainment world began with acting, and a two-year tour of America and Canada. On his return he began working behind the scenes, initially with Granada Television, and then the BBC as a floor manager. But he's best remembered for his credits as a director, working on shows like *Potter*, *Rosie*, *Whatever Happened to the Likely Lads?* and *Last of the Summer Wine*.

When he left the BBC, he re-joined Granada, directing, amongst others shows, *The Brothers McGregor*. Bernard died in 1998.

Thompson, Dave

Studio sound supervisor on 23 episodes: S2; S3, episodes 2–7; S4; S5, episode 4; 'Diamonds are for Heather' and 'Thicker Than Water'
Ever since he visited the BBC on a school trip, Dave was hooked on the idea of working for the Corporation. He achieved his goal when he started at Bush House, in 1963, as a technical operator.

Born in Nottingham in 1942, Dave worked at Bush House for two years before applying for a transfer into television. He was successful and moved into TV sound, where he began working on shows including *Doctor Who* and the original *Doctor Finlay's Casebook*. Now a senior sound supervisor, with a long list of credits to his name, he classes *Dad's Army*, *Morecambe and Wise* and *The Two Ronnies* among his favourites. Recent work has involved Reeves and Mortimer and *Shooting Stars*.

Thompson, Jane

Role: Smuggler
Appeared in 'To Hull and Back'

Thompson, Penny

Production assistant on 22 episodes: S1, S2, S3, 'Diamonds are for Heather' and 'Thicker Than Water'
Penny completed a secretarial course after her A-levels and joined the BBC in 1954 as a shorthand typist. For three months she was assigned to an engineering department before moving on to Television News, then based at Alexandra Palace, where she stayed for nine years.

Penny's ambition was to work on outside broadcasts and she achieved this when she left News and joined the *Grandstand* production team. Fifteen months later, she moved to light entertainment, where she worked until taking early retirement from the Corporation in 1990. During those years, she worked on a myriad of shows, including *The Basil Brush Show*; *Call My Bluff*; *The Frost Report*; *The Liver Birds*; *'Allo 'Allo!*; *You Rang, M'Lord?* and *Hi-De-Hi!*.

Thornton, Sylvia

Make-up designer on two episodes: S6, episodes 3 & 4
Born in London, Sylvia qualified as a hairdresser and worked in a salon in London's Notting Hill before joining the BBC in the mid-1960s, while in her twenties. After the obligatory three-month training course at the Beeb, she moved into the make-up department and completed a further 21 months on-the-job training. As an assistant make-up artist, she worked on numerous productions, including *Henry VIII*. She was then promoted to make-up artist and worked on many top shows, such as *Bar Mitzvah Boy* in 1976, and *Nancy Astor* six years later, which earnt her a BAFTA. Sylvia was still employed by the BBC when she died of cancer in 1991.

THE ROLE OF PRODUCTION ASSISTANT

★ ★ ★ ★ ★ ★

'The basic production unit consisted of the producer – who sometimes directed the programme as well – the production manager, who sorted out locations, ran the studio floor during rehearsals and recordings and did most of the arranging, including compiling a budget for the programme, the production assistant (a job which was originally titled production secretary) and then the assistant floor manager, who organised – amongst other things – all the props and the marking up during rehearsals, providing an outline of where all the sets would be on the set.

'When as production assistant I went out on locations I'd make notes of all the shots taken, which would be passed on to the film editor; I'd also look out for continuity so that if someone had been in one shot with a suitcase in his right hand he had to have it in the same hand for the next shot. Then, when the programme is over, you have to cost the programme, based on the budget the production manager has put together. Another responsibility of the assistant is to produce a camera script, which records all the camera directions needed. In addition to this, each cameraman – and there were usually five – needed their own set of camera cards which picked out their actual shots, such as a close-up of David Jason. And on the day of recording, you're in the control room timing every shot, and often cueing in the film or video inserts.

'That's the team in the production office, but of course you'd have a designer allocated to the project, who'd be available for consultation at any time, as well as a number of other people. Everyone was professional and made the job of working on the show an enjoyable experience.'

PENNY THOMPSON – Production assistant

Thorp, Anthony

Designer on four episodes: S3, episodes 1–4
One of the many shows the late Anthony Thorp worked on as production designer was *Blackadder*.

'Three Men, a Woman and a Baby'

Original transmission: Sunday 3 February 1991, 7.15 pm
Production dates: 20 and 21 January 1991
Original viewing figures : 18.9 million
Duration: 50 minutes
First repeat: Monday 23 December 1991, 7.10 pm
Subsequent repeats: 22/4/92, 8/4/94, 13/12/96, 7/4/99, 25/5/01

CAST
Del Trotter . . . . .David Jason
Rodney Trotter . . . . .Nicholas Lyndhurst
Uncle Albert . . . . .Buster Merryfield
Raquel . . . . .Tessa Peake-Jones
Cassandra . . . . .Gwyneth Strong

Trigger . . . . .Roger Lloyd Pack
Mike . . . . .Kenneth MacDonald
Midwife . . . . .Ken Drury
Sister Shelley . . . . .Constance Lamb
Baby Damien . . . . .Patrick McManus
Walk-ons: . . . . .Tom Little, Angie Alaimo, Terry
Davy, Lee Richards, Judy Collins, Elaine le Grand, Helena
Clayton, Michelle Grand, Beverley Jennings, Victoria Locke,
Christopher Paul, Bob Heath, Pietro Celoro, Graham Brooks,
Raymond de Haan and Kathleen Heath.

PRODUCTION TEAM
Written by John Sullivan
Title music arranged and conducted by Ronnie Hazlehurst
composed and sung by John Sullivan
Make-up Designer: . . . . .Christine Greenwood
Costume Designer: . . . . .Robin Stubbs
Properties Buyer: . . . . .Malcolm Rougvie
Film Cameraman: . . . . .Alec Curtis
Film Sound: . . . . .Michael Spencer
Film Editors: . . . . .John Jarvis and Jacqui Bass
Dubbing Mixer: . . . . .Michael Narduzzo
Camera Supervisor: . . . . .Ken Major
Studio Lighting Director: . . . . . .Ron Bristow
Studio Sound: . . . . .Alan Machin
Resources Coordinator: . . . . . .Peter Manuel
Videotape Editor: . . . . .Chris Wadsworth
Production Assistants: . . . . .Chris Gernon
                                              and Amanda Church
Assistant Floor Manager: . . . . .Debbie Crofts
Graphic Designer: . . . . .Andrew Smee
Vision Mixer: . . . . .Sue Collins
Production Managers . . . . .Angela de Chastelai-Smith
                                              and Simon Spencer
Production Secretary: . . . . .Katie Tyrrell
Designer: . . . . .Richard McManan-Smith
Casting Adviser: . . . . .Judy Loe
Directed by Tony Dow
Produced by Gareth Gwenlan

Life is still looking bleak for Rodney, especially
after he takes Cassandra to Hampton Court and
she gives him the elbow for good, after accusing
him of never trying to adapt to married life and
lacking ambition. But Rodney cheers up temporarily when he discovers that Del's latest
scheme – trying to flog some wigs he bought on
the cheap – isn't going to be so easy because his
intended customers (a bunch of 'old tarts at The
Nag's Head') won't be happy with men's wigs! Any
hilarity is short-lived when Rodney – who's
turned veggie – gets on his soapbox and preaches
to everyone about the state of the planet: forests
are being suffocated by carbon monoxide, the
polar ice cap is melting, the continental shelves
are shifting, the sea is being poisoned, and he
hasn't had 'a bit' in months!

While Del and Raquel are considering baby
names, Rodney receives a call from Cassandra
asking him to come round and see her. Attempting
to play it cool by telling her he'll pop round sometime doesn't work when he's *en route* within minutes, sporting a stick-on ponytail in the hope that
his new attachment will impress her. He soon dis-

'Three Men, a Woman and a Baby'

'Time On Our Hands'

covers that she feels such items are only fashionable with lame brains. Soon Rodney and Cassandra are embracing; but their night of lust is interrupted by Del's phone call, asking for Rodney's presence at the hospital because Raquel's time is up – their baby is on its way.

Ticket collector

Played by Alan Cody
The ticket collector checks Rodney's opera tickets when he takes Lady Victoria to see *Carmen* in 'A Royal Flush'.

'Time On Our Hands'

(Third part of the 1996 Christmas Trilogy)

Original transmission: Sunday 29 December 1996, 8.00 pm

Original viewing figures: 24.3 million

Duration: 60 minutes

First repeat: Friday 23 January 1998, 8.00 pm

Subsequent repeats: 1/10/99; 6/7/01; 23/2/02

CAST

Del Trotter . . . . .David Jason
Rodney Trotter . . . . .Nicholas Lyndhurst
Uncle Albert . . . . .Buster Merryfield
Raquel . . . . .Tessa Peake-Jones
Cassandra . . . . .Gwyneth Strong
Trigger . . . . .Roger Lloyd Pack
Boycie . . . . .John Challis

Mike . . . . .Kenneth MacDonald
Marlene . . . . .Sue Holderness
Denzil . . . . .Paul Barber
Mickey Pearce . . . . .Patrick Murray
Damien . . . . .Jamie Smith
James . . . . .Michael Jayston
Audrey . . . . .Ann Lynn
Auctioneer . . . . .Seymour Matthews
Tony . . . . .Jotham Annan
Walk-ons: . . . .(Customers in The Nag's Head)
Matthew Barney, Teddy Massaih, Harry Holland, Ron Street, Jack Burns, Jason Swaden, Joe Wells, Jim Groves, Marc Robinson, Jane Lester, James Delaney, Adam Ross, Yvonne Stroud, Bill Farrow, Pat Shepherd, Pat Goode, Lorna Sinclair, Lewis St Juste, Jack Street, Maggie Mitchell, Penny Lambirth, Gail Abbott, Melinda Clancy, Barbara Edwards, Hannah Warner, Jill Goldston, Rosalind Hartley, Astrid Johnson, Tina Simmons, Sally Sinclair. (Outside Sotheby's) Darren Morgan, Jo Jo Lewis, Angel Wilnan, Parnjit Singh, Victor Reynolds, Rosalind Hartley, Hannah Dea Warner, Lloyd Harvey, Keith Swaden, Joanne Shaw. (Inside Sotheby's) Julian Sua, Suresh Maru, Joanne Asker, Jeremy Fowler, Cass Inami, Arnold Zarom, Ryozo Kohira, J L Chong, Kanako Morishita, Nila Myin, Janet Lisa House, Penny Chan, Marianne Hewitt, Peter Law, Michael Sen, Basil Chung, Michelle Charley, Lea Rochelle, Lemoy Agostini, Dulara Kmatun, Ashraf Elabor, Marue Aykan, Nigel Fowler, Martin Harrison, Amanda Foster, Ted Durante, Barry Alan, Mike Mungaruan, Jack Frost, Mair Coleman, David Bulbeck, Hilary Klein, Eric Corlett, Bickers Clark, Barbie Clark, Jane Lester, Ray Severn, Ann Woods, Paul Woods, Hugh Gallagher, Jenny Rose, Ron Harrison, Penny

Lambirth, Clive Norman, Ron Oliver, Jim Groves, Brian Cole, Paul Keys, Jerry Baker, Paul Vincent, Paul Ellison, Christine Vincent, Robert Pearson, Paul Bannon, Maureen Walters, Bobby Bernard, Lester Adams, Ina Clare, Peter Jessup, Molly Seyforth, Rachel Montfort, Michael Montfort, Barbara Edwards, Hilda Durante, Brenda Baker, Frank Johnson, David Ross, Hilary Montfort and Mark Brett. (Boycie's receptionist) Sue Vyse.

PRODUCTION TEAM

Written by John Sullivan
Title music arranged and conducted by Ronnie Hazlehurst composed and sung by John Sullivan
Music: . . . . .Graham Jarvis
Researcher: . . . . .Mona Adams
With thanks to Jonathan Betts and the Greenwich Maritime Museum
Make-up Designer: . . . . .Deanne Turner
Costume Designer: . . . . .Robin Stubbs
Properties Buyer: . . . . .Graham Bishop
Art Director: . . . . .Nick Harding
Video Effects: . . . . .Ian Simpson
Casting Adviser: . . . . .Judy Loe
Programme Finance Assistant: .Alison Passey
Film Cameraman: . . . . .Chris Seager
Film Sound: . . . . .Roger Long
Film Editor: . . . . .John Jarvis
Camera Supervisor: . . . . .Peter Woodley
Studio Lighting Director: . . . . . .Graham Rimmington
Studio Sound: . . . . .Keith Gunn
Studio Resource Manager: . . . .Richard Morgan

'Time On Our Hands'

Grips:	Iain Johnstone
Gaffer:	Pat Deveney
1st Assistant Director:	David Reid
2nd Assistant Director:	Dominic Bowles
3rd Assistant Director:	Anna Brabbins
Location Managers:	Lisa McArthur and Steve Abrahams
Dubbing Editor:	Paul Bingley
Photography:	John Rhodes
Videotape Editor:	Chris Wadsworth
Production Assistant:	Caroline Gardener
Assistant Floor Manager:	Beccy Fawcett
Floor Manager:	Vivien Ackland-Snow
Vision Mixer:	Heather Gilder
Production Secretary:	Katie Wilkinson
Production Designer:	Donal Woods
Associate Producer:	Sue Longstaff
Executive Producer:	John Sullivan

Directed by Tony Dow

Produced by Gareth Gwenlan

Rodney is finding it difficult coming to terms with the loss of his baby, bottling his emotions tightly inside. Del, meanwhile, realising he has to help his brother adapt to the situation, tries to get Rodney to open up about his true feelings, in an attempt to start the long process of healing.

At the same time, Raquel is experiencing emotions of a different kind: panic. Her parents are visiting the flat for dinner: rekindling their relationship with their daughter, and meeting her new man in the process. The atmosphere is tense as Mr and Mrs Turner settle down for dinner around the rather large table Del has borrowed from the town hall. Del does little to impress the Turners, while the evening is marred by Uncle Albert's culinary ineptitude: he mixes up the coffee and the gravy powder, with dire results.

The following day, Raquel's father comes around to collect his car, and finds Del and Rodney sorting through their garage. Being an antiques

John Sullivan says: 'The speeches beneath the dotted lines were never used. I didn't put them in the script, although I had intended to, because we were running long.'

THE LIFT. NELSON MANDELA HOUSE
THE LIFT IS STILL BROKEN AND DEL AND ROD ARE STILL TRAPPED INSIDE. DEL AND RODNEY HAVE BOTH REMOVED THEIR COATS AND UNBUTTONED THEIR SHIRTS. THEY ARE BOTH SWEATING. DEL PACES, HIS CLAUSTROPHOBIA REACHING BREAKING POINT.
DEL They're not here yet, are they?
ROD Give 'em time. Sit down and take it easy.
DEL SITS NEXT TO RODNEY.
ROD Let's play a game.
DEL A game? You got a ball on you then?
ROD No, I mean, some other sort of game. I spy.
DEL I spy!
ROD Yeah. Go'n, you can go first.
DEL All right, dopey! I spy with my little eye something beginning with W.
ROD Er…walls?
DEL Yes! Well, that's the end of that game ainnit!
ROD Well, you choose the game.
DEL How about hide 'n' seek?
DEL NOW STANDS AND PACES AGAIN.
— — — — — — — — — — — — — — — — — — — —
ROD I remember years ago when we all played hide 'n' seek. It was Jubilee Day and I hid in that old chest you'd bought.
DEL Oh yeah. Bloody good hiding place that was, no one thought of looking there.
ROD No. You lot all went down the pub in the end, didn't you? Left me.
DEL We got fed up looking for you.
ROD Four and arf hours I was in that chest.
DEL You took the game too far. I mean, we'd all finished playing.
ROD No sod told me though, did they?
DEL How could we? We couldn't find you!
ROD That chest had a dodgy lock.
DEL How was I supposed to know that? When I bought it I didn't climb inside and lock the bloody thing on meself!
ROD I thought I was gonna suffocate.
DEL Why didn't you knock on the lid or shout?
ROD Cos then you'd have known where I was hiding!

John Sullivan says: 'Boycie's lines outside the car showroom were cut from "Time On Our Hands", while the scene in the Trotters' lounge with Raquel, Cassandra and Albert was cut from the script at any early stage and never recorded.'

CUT FROM 'TIME ON OUR HANDS'

UPMARKET LONDON STREET. SOTHEBY'S. DAY. WE SEE THE THREE-WHEELED VAN PARKED AT A METER. A SIGN IN VAN'S WINDOW READS: 'MIDWIFE ON EMERGENCY CALL'. WE SEE DEL AND ROD APPROACHING. THEY HAVE JUST LEFT THE AUCTION AND ARE IN A STATE OF DEEP SHOCK. THEY CLIMB INTO THE VAN (DEL DRIVING).

THREE-WHEELED VAN. DAY
DEL AND ROD JUST SIT QUIETLY FOR A MOMENT. THEY ARE BOTH VERY CALM – SHOCKED.
DEL So, what was the final outcome?
ROD It was bought by an anonymous bidder. He's giving it to the Maritime Museum at Greenwich. So, at least it stays in the country.
DEL Oh good! I meant, what was the final score? How much exactly did it go for?
ROD (TAKES SOME PAPERWORK FROM POCKET) Six point three million.
DEL CLOSES HIS EYES AS ACID DIGESTION GRABS HIM.
ROD Just over three million pound each.
DEL Well, we've had worse days, ain't we?
ROD Oh yeah… D'you wanna go first or shall I?
DEL How about together?
ROD All right then. One, two, three.
NOW THEY BOTH GO ABSOLUTELY POTTY – SCREAMING, PUNCHING THE AIR, HURLING THEMSELVES ABOUT. WE SEE A PASSER-BY WITNESS THIS LUNACY.
DEL Right, calm down. We better go home and tell the girls, but let's break the news gently, we don't want to spoil a nice day like this by taking one of them to the cardiac-arrest unit.
ROD (VENGEFUL) No, there's somewhere else I wanna go first.
DEL STARTS ENGINE.

BOYCIES'S CAR SHOWROOMS. DAY
THIRTY MINUTES LATER. THE SIGN ABOVE THE SHOWROOM TELLS US THIS IS: 'BOYCE AUTOS – USED CARS OF DISTINCTION'. THE OPEN FRONT AND ENCLOSED SHOWROOMS ARE FILLED WITH MIDDLE RANGE CARS: ASTRAS, MONDEOS, THE OCCASIONAL MERC AND RANGE ROVER, ETC, ALL IN THE TWO- TO FIVE-YEAR-OLD BRACKET. THE CAR OF THE MONTH IS A FINE-LOOKING ROLLS ROYCE. WE SEE BOYCE PLACING A PRICE STAND ON A CAR'S ROOF. HE LOOKS UP TO SEE THE THREE-WHELLED VAN PULLING TO A HALT ON HIS FORECOURT. HE SMILES TO HIMSELF. DEL AND RODNEY APPROACH THE SHOWROOM.
BOYCIE Oh no! Talk about the barbarians at the gates. Do you have to leave that van outside my showrooms? Customers might think I've been reduced to advertising the local cinema – they're showing The Flintstones.
DEL If only you knew, Boycie, if only you knew!
BOYCIE Gimme the keys.

DEL CHUCKS HIM THE VAN KEYS AND MOVES TO THE ROLLS ROYCE. BOYCIE CALLS TO HIS 18-YEAR-OLD CAR CLEANER.
BOYCIE Tony, drive that van around the corner, will you?
TONY You sure? It might get nicked.
BOYCIE Nicked? Who's gonna nick that thing, other than a recently arrived Albanian joy-rider? It certainly ain't gonna be used in a ram-raid is it? (LAUGHS)
WE NOW SEE THE OBJECT OF DEL'S INTEREST. IT IS A THREE-YEAR-OLD ROLLS ROYCE. A SIGN ON IT READS 'CAR OF THE MONTH'. IT IS PRICED AT £80 000. DEL IS NOW SEATED IN THE ROLLS ROYCE.
DEL Beautiful, annit? Luxury and style. Very me, don't you think?
ROD Yeah. Buy it!
DEL Shall I?
ROD You like it, buy it.
DEL (BOTTLE GOES) Na, I'll wait until the cheque's cleared. I've got a horrible feeling this entire deal's gonna go pear-shaped.
RODNEY BUYS THE ROLLS ROYCE FOR DEL.
ROD Little present. Just to say – thanks.
DEL TURNS AND LOOKS AT THE CAR LOVINGLY – EMOTIONALLY, THEN HE HUGS RODNEY TIGHTLY.

INTERIOR. TROTTERS' LOUNGE. DAY
RAQUEL, ALBERT AND CASSANDRA WAIT ANXIOUSLY FOR DEL AND RODNEY'S RETURN.
RAQ (CHECKING HER WATCH) Where the hell are they?
CASS Perhaps they're in discussion with the directors at Sotheby's.
RAQUEL GIVES HER A WITHERING LOOK
CASS No, perhaps not.
RAQ Maybe they're talking with the curator at the museum.
CASS Maybe.
ALB (ON PHONE) Thanks a lot. (REPLACES RECIEIVER) They're not at The Nag's Head.
CASS I guessed Rodney wouldn't be in The Nag's Head, Albert.
RAQ Has he stopped drinking?
CASS No, he's been barred.
WE HEAR THE FRONT DOOR CLOSE AND NOW DEL AND RODNEY ENTER. RAQUEL, CASSANDRA AND ALBERT LOOK AT THEM EXPECTANTLY – IS IT GOOD NEWS OR BAD NEWS? DEL AND RODNEY DON'T WANT TO JUST BLURT OUT THE NEWS AND CAUSE HEART ATTACKS AND SO WE HAVE A KIND OF MEXICAN STAND-OFF.
RAQ Well?
DEL Yeah, fine thanks.
RAQ No! I meant, what happened?
ROD Oh, at the auction?
CASS Yes, at the auction! Did it sell?
ROD Yeah, it sold, didn't it, Del?

DEL Yeah we sold it.
ALB I knew it. Beautiful piece of machinery… How much'd you get?
DEL Guess.
RAQ Oh come on, just tell us!
ROD No, go on, guess.
ALB Five thousand pounds?
DEL No.
RAQUEL AND CASSANDRA'S SPIRITS VISIBLY SAG IN DISAPPOINTMENT.
ALB Six thousand?
DEL Close. Add a nought.
CASS Sixty thousand pounds?
DEL You can tell she works in a bank, can't you?
ROD Hardly any hesitation… No, not sixty thousand. Add another nought.
ALB But that's… What is that, Cassandra?
CASS Six hundred thousand pounds?
DEL No! Will you tell them or shall I?
ROD Erm, you can have the privilege, Derek.
DEL Thank you, Rodney. You two girls hold on to your stays… add one more nought.
RAQUEL, CASSANDRA AND ALBERT EXCHANGE DISBELIEVING GLANCES. CASSANDRA JUST STARES WIDE-EYED AT RODNEY. RODNEY RETURNS A GENTLE NOD, RAQUEL LOOKS AT DEL AND SHAKES HER HEAD. DEL SMILES AND NODS HIS HEAD. DEL HANDS THEM THE SOTHEBY'S PAPERWORK. THEY NOW LOOK UP AT DEL AND RODNEY.
DEL (TO ROD) Call intensive care.
RAQUEL STANDS.
RAQ Six million pounds?
DEL Mmmmh.
PAUSE. RAQUEL NOW BURSTS INTO TEARS, RUSHES TO THE COCKTAIL BAR FOR A TISSUE.
DEL (TO ROD) Told you she'd be happy.
ALBERT AND CASSSANDRA SIT IN STUNNED SILENCE. WE NOW SEE DAMIEN STARING AT RODNEY. RODNEY REACTS. DAMIEN NOW SMILES AT RODNEY. RODNEY'S REACTION IS ONE OF 'DID DAMIEN TURN THIS ROUND FOR US?'
DEL Now we've gotta take things nice and easy – no going mad and splashing it around on anything that grabs our fancies. I know six million sounds a lot but it'll be very easy to blow it on silly luxuries.
RAQ But we can go out in the week and look for a house, can't we?
DEL Of course we can, Darling. Any day except Wednesday, that's when my Rolls Royce is being delivered.

The story behind the watch

Two people who were key in developing the storyline for 'Time On Our Hands', which, at the time, was expected to be the final instalment in the Trotters' colourful televisual life, were historical consultant Mona Adams, who was employed by the BBC, and Jonathan Betts, Curator of Horology at the National Maritime Museum, Greenwich. Between them, they formulated the idea which appealed to John Sullivan and was pursued through the episode's storyline. Here, Mona and Jonathan recall the process they went through to dream up the idea of the Trotters winning the jackpot by discovering the long-lost Harrison timepiece gathering dust inside their garage.

Mona recalls…

'I'd worked with John Sullivan on *Over Here,* a drama series he wrote. I had been the historical consultant on that and John was great to work with. I was holidaying in the South of France when I got a call from the director, Tony Dow, telling me that John wanted to finish *Only Fools* with a good story; he wanted the lads to get rich and was looking for a memorable storyline.

'When I got back to London, I rooted around my various records, looking for something unusual that they might discover. I didn't want anything obvious like a picture or a win on the Pools; it had to be something that would fit into their particular lifestyle of collecting rubbish, but where one of these bits of rubbish could be turned into a sack load of crisp tenners.

'I'd devised a storyline about the discovery of some ivory tusks buried in the mud of a Docklands rubbish tip where the Trotters had scavenging rights. Del and Rodney would find them, take them home and store them away. The tusks, brought from the New World by an early explorer and lost when being unloaded from his ship, were to be carved and painted in a particular way, making them unique and very valuable. I wrote up the storyline for John, but about five days before I was due to deliver my idea, I turned on the *News at Ten* to hear Trevor McDonald saying: "And finally, builders were working in the mud of London today and they discovered some ivory tusks!" I just couldn't believe what I was hearing. I would have to start again from scratch. With so little time left, this had the makings of a nightmare.

'In a panic, I phoned a chum of mine, Jane Bendall, who worked at the Maritime Museum, Greenwich, and told her my sorry tale. Could she help? For a moment or two, there was an ominous silence. Then she said: "Hang on, I've just had an idea." She called back within the hour and suggested I come to the museum to meet Jonathan Betts, the Curator of Horology. They'd just been talking and had come up with a glimmer of a story I might be interested in.

'When I saw Jonathan, he told me about the Harrison timekeepers, but because they were so well known, I feared they wouldn't do. My heart sank. With deadlines getting closer by the moment, despair was setting in. Then Jonathan mentioned – almost as a throwaway – Harrison's

plan to construct another smaller timepiece which he referred to as his 'lesser watch'. The sketches which Jonathan showed me were impressive and convincing but he stressed that there was no evidence it had even been made. Eureka! As there was also no proof that it *hadn't*, I knew this was our story.

'I wrote it up for John Sullivan and he liked it very much. Subsequently, we visited the museum, looked at the Harrisons – and the rest, as they say, is history!'

MONA ADAMS –
Historical consultant

Later, the museum held an exhibition in the Royal Observatory, Greenwich, and borrowed the BBC's mock-up watch. Officials couldn't believe it when the event attracted huge numbers of visitors, with queues around the block. The episode of *Only Fools and Horses* focused people's attention on the Harrisons. The museum had never seen such good numbers for a particular exhibition. That year, Jane Bendall won a prize for initiating the project which attracted the most visitors. She shared her prize (two pairs of designer silk knickers) with Mona.

Now, Jonathan recalls his memories of being asked to help the BBC bring the curtain down on one of the most successful programmes of all time.

Jonathan recalls…

'It was real "cloak and dagger" stuff. In October 1996 I had a call from my colleague Jane Bendall, whose friend, Mona Adams, was on the production team of *Only Fools and Horses,* though I wasn't told which programme until later. Mona wanted to talk to the curators at the National Maritime Museum about ideas for valuable historical objects which were now missing and which might one day be re-discovered.

'We curators had no idea what this was about, and Mona wasn't ready to enlighten us: all she would say was that she was on the production team of a "well known TV situation comedy" and the main character needed to "find" something of immense value which would make his fortune. They had considered his winning the lottery, but this was too obvious, too predictable. Apart from the need for secrecy, one thing was made very clear: whatever the suggestion, it had to be something which was genuinely believed to exist and which really might be found; an imaginary Leonardo painting found in granny's attic would not do. There was a lot of head-scratching among the curators. A number of possibilities immediately suggested themselves but were equally quickly discounted because they were artefacts which had been *stolen*, and we were assured that "the character" had to discover something he could sell legitimately (quite a novelty for him, though I didn't realise it at the time!). Then I remembered the world of horology's great hero John Harrison.

'Those who are familiar with Dava Sobel's best selling book *Longitude*, and the Channel 4 film based on it, will know that Harrison solved that great navigational problem of the 18th century: how to find one's longitude (one's east–west position) at sea, by creating the world's first accurate marine timekeeper. This watch is today known as H4,

and was the fourth in his series of five wonderful prototypes. H1 to H4 are still to be seen on display at the Royal Observatory, part of the National Maritime Museum at Greenwich, and H5, the same size as H4, is on display at the Clockmakers' Company Museum in the Guildhall, London. H4 was built between 1755 and 1759 and won for Harrison the coveted £20,000 prize offered by the British government for a solution to the problem. In fact, H4 was also the world's first truly accurate watch and is considered today to be the most important timekeeper ever constructed. When Harrison told the government's official board (the splendidly titled "Board of Longitude") that he intended to improve on his first three attempts at a marine timekeeper, he said he would: "…make *two* watches, one of such a size as may be worn in the pocket & the other bigger…".

'The "other bigger" was H4, but what was the one that "may be worn in the pocket"? A manuscript drawing, made by Harrison himself at the time to show the mechanism of this smaller watch, still survives in the Clockmakers' Company collection, and in later manuscript writings, Harrison refers several times to this "lesser watch" ("lesser" meant smaller in the 18th century). On one occasion he described something as being "like that in my lesser watch", which certainly suggests that the watch was already made. So where is it now? Nobody knows. There has been no word of it since Harrison's time, but if it were found it would be of immense interest and value, that's for sure.

'Nevertheless, I considered it a bit unlikely as a suggestion for the production team: too unusual and specialist to appeal. So it was quite a surprise when Mona immediately jumped on the idea and wanted to know more. Over the next few weeks the details of the idea were developed and I did a short statement about Harrison and the watches, which would be used in the script writing. Then we had a visit from the props makers who wanted sketches and dimensions of what the watch should look like, along with details of what the correct signature should be on the watch. They were determined to get it all just right. In fact, three watch props were made, the "dirty" watch as found in the garage and chucked into the frying pan by Del Boy; a second watch which would open to reveal the gilt brass mechanism and the "restored" watch, held up by the porter in the saleroom.

'Then came the question of what such a watch would be worth. Of course, as museum curators we are instructed never to discuss the financial value of museum objects and are unqualified anyway to give valuations on other people's objects. So it was a difficult one, but we agreed that if such a watch were to be found, and was sold at auction, it could easily run into millions of pounds. To try and pin me down, the question was asked: "Did I think it was impossible that such a watch could fetch six million pounds?", to which I could only answer: "…not *impossible*, no…" and the price was fixed. As it turned out, we have since seen a number of astonishing record prices made at auction for clocks and watches, the most recent being $10 million for a Swiss watch sold in New York in 1999, so it was certainly not an over estimation. By this time I had been tipped off that Del Boy was the mysterious man in question and that this was to be the final episode of *Only Fools and Horses*. All was now clear!

'All went quiet until the fateful day, 29 December 1996, when the final episode went out. Apparently 24.35 million viewers watched the episode, more than the Queen's speech on Christmas Day and more than the England vs Germany match in Euro '96 that year! Needless to say, I was fascinated to see what the production team would make of the story and was enthralled by the outcome. Not only did the script get it right but it was great fun too, the scene at Sotheby's being a particular favourite among the horological fraternity. The eventual home for the watch was, appropriately enough, the National Maritime Museum at Greenwich. If the watch were ever found we like to think this is exactly where it would go.

'Then there was the aftermath. I had been warned that there might be some press interest, but I wasn't prepared for the storm of enquiries we received. First there was the press itself, keen to know whether this really was an object which could be found (how wise the team were to be firm on that point), though reporters were continually frustrated by my refusal to state for certain what such a watch would be worth, and in some cases putting words in my mouth. There was interest from the radio too, but not exactly at a convenient time: New Year's Day. Like many people, on the morning of 1 January 1997, I was recovering from a very jolly celebration and had only been in bed a couple of hours when the telephone rang. It was Radio 4 wanting me to go for a live interview at Broadcasting House that morning. No chance, but I heard myself agreeing to a telephone interview at the museum, and so it was that I staggered in to work a couple of hours later to answer questions about Harrison and his lesser watch.

'The papers were full of the story of the missing watch. I was "quoted" as saying: "I'd advise people to have a root around for it"! Not quite how I phrased it, I'm fairly certain. Of course, the inevitable result was that the museum received another storm of enquiries, this time from people who believed they had found the watch. In spite of careful descriptions of what the watch would look like (signature of John Harrison, date about 1759, etc) any silver watch bearing a name similar to Harrison, whatever its date, seemed fair game for "discovery". We even received a couple of calls from solicitors, telephoning on behalf of clients, wishing to discuss their good news and negotiate a sale to us. Naturally all calls were taken seriously until we could determine details of the watch in question, but (up to the present) no genuine article has surfaced.

'But the fact remains, the watch could still be out there. So while "a root around" may not reveal the watch in your bedside table, we live in hope that one day the lesser watch may be discovered, for example, among an old watchmakers' possessions or, who knows, even in a lock-up garage in Peckham!'

JONATHAN BETTS –
Curator of Horology, National Maritime Museum, Greenwich

'Time On Our Hands'

dealer, he's always looking for hidden treasures, but can't believe his eyes when he spots an old watch, which the Trotters obtained from a house clearance, 16 years ago.

James Turner thinks they've been sitting on a fortune for all these years because this is the long-lost 18th-century Harrison marine watch, but suggests they get it authenticated. Mr Turner's views are confirmed and the watch is soon auctioned at Sotheby's, making the Trotter boys multi-millionaires when it sells for a staggering £6.2 million.

After a life of scrimping and saving they've finally achieved their ambitions and joined the millionaire club; sumptuous houses and top-of-the-range cars soon follow, but it's not long before Del and Rodney are hankering after the past. In a quiet moment, back at the cold, empty flat in Nelson Mandela House, Del admits to his brother that a life full of riches isn't all it's cracked up to be: he misses the thrill of the chase and needs some excitement again. Just as they head back to their respective homes, Del's new venture comes to him: investing in the futures market. As they walk off into the sunset he explains that next year they could be billionaires!

Tipping, Tip
Stunt artist on one episode: 'Dates'

Tip was born in Beckenham, Kent, in 1958, and became a Royal Marine upon leaving school. When he left the services he worked as a child's entertainer and as a clown in a circus, enabling him to gain his Equity card.

Tip always wanted to become a stuntman: his

à la Del

★ ★ ★ ★ ★ ★

'Ménage à trois!'

('Hole in One')

time in the Marines and then Special Forces (21 SAS) helped him gain the physical experience needed, which he added to once leaving the forces to aid his application to the stunt board.

During his career as a stunt artist he worked on numerous shows, including *Inspector Morse, Drop the Dead Donkey* and *999*. He died of multiple injuries in 1993, at the age of just 34. He was re-enacting a sky diving accident for television, when the stunt went tragically wrong.

TITCO

(See 'Trotters' Independent Trading Company')

Titles

One of the trademarks of *Only Fools and Horses* is the memorable title sequence, which blends graphics with photographic images to form a style apposite for the type of sitcom it accompanies. Peter Clayton was the graphic designer whose expertise was sourced when Ray Butt was tasked with launching the programme. After being given a rough idea of what the programme was about, Peter decided to photograph a number of locations that he thought would represent the kind of world the market-trading wide-boy lived in. 'I ended up photographing markets, a bar, a second-hand car lot, various things like that, and they eventually formed the background for the turning images I developed later,' recounts Peter.

The imaging which saw the actors' names peel back and fly off the screen, almost as if they were being blown by the wind, was another of Peter's ideas. This treatment, as Peter explains, is a metaphor for the vagaries of the Trotters' lifestyle. 'It was all about having money and seeing it slip away; Del made money but lost it just as quick because much of the stuff he bought had something wrong with it, which meant he couldn't flog it, or if he could it was at a reduced price. I think I even considered designing actual five-pound notes with Del's face on it, which would be used instead of the labels.'

One of the challenges facing any new sitcom is establishing the main characters as quickly as possible; once the audience feels familiar with them and their idiosyncrasies, there is a chance the show has a future. Peter was aware of this when he styled the credits. 'We were introducing three main characters to a new sitcom, so we wanted to have them established on the titles.'

Peter prepared a storyboard, which depicted his ideas via drawings, and presented his plans to Ray Butt, who was impressed. 'I then had to sit down and work out logistically how I was going to achieve it! The backgrounds were easy because I just went out with a photographer to various locations, often where they were going to be filming, and took a range of shots. But I then had to think about constructing the actual sequence. We're talking about 1981, way before any computer graphics or fancy technology was available; the budget wasn't enormous, either. So the titles were never actually edited, they were shot by a rostrum

camera, frame by frame. And with 25 frames a second, for titles lasting about 35 seconds, it took some effort.'

Once he knew in his mind how he wanted the titles to work, Peter employed a professional animator, Brian Stephens, to create the actual turning of the labels. 'I designed the front of the labels, which carried, for example, the actors' names, and Brian developed it further by creating the movement. It was then photographed by Doug, a cameraman at Trevor Bond Associates, a company I used for most of my work. The actual job from start to finish took about six weeks.'

At the time, the title sequence Peter developed for *Only Fools* was regarded as a complicated piece of work. 'Today, with computer graphics, it would have been far easier to create. Just a few years after the *Only Fools* titles, it became possible to create a page turn in an edit suite, which would have made my life a lot easier. We were using 35mm film, and it wasn't ideal to start cutting film up because it affects the quality of the final product.'

Over the sitcom's life, the opening title sequence was altered, and most times Peter returned to the show to carry out the work. 'When we did *Christmas Crackers*, the first Christmas show, I remember re-cutting the whole sequence and inserting baubles, cards, wrapping paper, crackers, things like that. And when Lennard Pearce died and Buster Merryfield joined the cast, another alteration was required. This also allowed us to update the pictures of David and Nick. For that, we got David, Buster and Nick into a photographic studio and took pictures of them. Initially, we had got David to wear his camel coat and hold a bundle of notes, which he fluttered through his hand, while Nick's character, who never had any money, looked a bit bewildered and started pulling his empty pockets out. It was all shot on motor-drive, which explains the stop-start style.'

As for the closing credits, a little less ingenuity was called for. 'We eventually changed to a straightforward roller caption. In those days, you used a machine in the studio which rolled the credits from top to bottom, with the camera stuck in front of it filming. Initially I used the notes peeling away for the closing credits, too, but it became too time-consuming, bearing in mind the names of the people recorded in the credits were changing all the time.'

The eagle-eyed viewer may have noticed that subtle changes took place to the closing credits over the years. The flyaway labels were replaced with the more straighforward rolling format for 'The Russians are Coming', with the names of performers and crew superimposed over the final scene. This format was only short-lived, however, and for 'Christmas Crackers' a return to the more familiar style, with the exception that the names were superimposed on to a set of Christmas cards, was seen.

The first permanent change accompanied the transmission of Series 2, with all the lettering in white, set against a black background. It seemed

the dawning of a new series always led to some minor alteration to the style used to bring the episodes to a close, and Series 3 saw the introduction of a few additional symbols and designs; for Series 4, meanwhile, these small designs were dropped in favour of a more sombre style: plain white lettering on a black background.

'What happens with something like the closing credits is that initially the graphic designer sets the style, but then it's a job which is allocated to an assistant to take responsibility for making the week-in, week-out alterations, such as name changes. Slowly, alterations were made to the design,' explains Peter.

Other changes, albeit minor, which occurred over the show's lifetime saw the lettering superimposed on a black and white background for Series 5, only to return to the original black background for the next season. For Series 7, however, the titles were placed instead over a still frame of the final scene.

Tivers, Gerry

Camera supervisor on two episodes: 'Mother Nature's Son' and 'Fatal Extraction'

Gerry, who now works freelance, has supervised a number of television productions including *Victoria Wood's All Day Breakfast* in 1992, *Victoria Wood Live In Your Own Home* in 1994 and *The Corrs: Live at the Royal Albert Hall* in 1998. Among the programmes he worked on as a camera operative are several episodes of *Star Cops* in 1987 and *Later with Jools Holland* in 1992.

'To Hull and Back'

(Christmas Special 1985)

Original transmission: Wednesday 25 December 1985, 7.30 pm

Original viewing figures: 16.9 million

Duration: 90 minutes

First repeat: Thursday 1 January 1987, 8.00 pm

Subsequent repeats: 1/1/93, 12/6/00, 9/6/02

CAST

Del Trotter	David Jason
Rodney Trotter	Nicholas Lyndhurst
Uncle Albert	Buster Merryfield
Smuggler	Jane Thompson
Male customs worker	Jon Rust
Calvin	Dennis Conlon
Imogen	Bridget Sutcliffe
Mike	Kenneth MacDonald
Vicky	Kim Clifford
Teddy	Johnny Wade
Ruby	Annie Leake
Boycie	John Challis
Abdul	Tony Anholt
Trigger	Roger Lloyd Pack
Denzil	Paul Barber
Slater	Jim Broadbent
Hoskins	Christopher Mitchell
Sid	Roy Heather
Mr Biggastaff	Norman Kay

MEMORIES OF 'TO HULL AND BACK'

★ ★ ★ ★ ★ ★

'It was a difficult special from my point of view because all the well established sets, from the pub to the living room in the flat, had to be transported to Hull and built in a warehouse, part of a derelict factory, which became our base and recording studio. Normally, of course, you'd complete your location work and then return to record it in front of a studio audience, but this episode was different because it was recorded entirely on location. Three or four container lorries were hired to transport everything up to Hull – it was quite a task.

'The warehouse was a dreadful place and was adjacent to a soap factory; the smell was awful, it was like rotting flesh, and it permeated the air all the time! Being there a few weeks meant it turned our stomachs. Another problem associated with the warehouse was that when the lorries, carrying all the sets and props, arrived, a roller door on the building was jammed and the lorries couldn't get in, so some work was needed on the doors.

'Some of the locations hadn't been found, so it fell to me and my team to create them, in and around the base area, such as the lorry park, the market caff and the car showrooms, which had been a service bay for the vehicles from the derelict factory. I built this cabin with glass partitioning inside the service bay and that was used as a car showroom. Late on during the filming, I was asked to recreate the fishing boat (it had to be a direct match) in our warehouse – and it had to rock, too! This was the most difficult aspect. Ray said he wanted me to build the whole forecastle of the trawler, and when I asked how long I had, he told me about three or four days! I didn't think we could do it in the time, but when I asked the chippies, they said they could do it. The buyer had to search the docks to find matching pieces of equipment to match the Inge, the boat they filmed on. It was supposed to be night time, so the scene was shot against a black backcloth and, if I remember right, we had people rocking the structure of the boat.

'I also had to build a Dutch diamond merchant's office and happened to find a room, which had a beautiful fireplace in it and some lovely panelling. Then we had to dress the set, but didn't have the time to return to London to pick up items such as foreign telephones and the like, so the buyer asked a Hull lorry driver, who he found in a caff, to bring back a telephone and phone directories from his next trip, which he did.

'The lorry driver also brought us back some pieces of dressing which we used for the bank scenes – set in a bank in the town, I believe.

'The people of Hull were really helpful and when it came to finding things like compasses and other such equipment for the mock boat I had to build, they would always point us in the right direction. The lads on the docks gave me a port and starboard lamp off one of the fishing smacks, which I've kept as a memento.

'On the whole, it was an enjoyable experience, although there was a lot to do. My assistant and I designed a sweatshirt, which we had made whilst in Hull. We had about 30 made, coloured yellow on dark blue. "To Hull and Back" and the Trotters' car were emblazoned across the front and it was a nice memento of our time up there, although sadly I've lost mine.'

BERNARD LLOYD-JONES – Designer

Mrs Biggastaff	Brenda Mortine
Colin	Mark Burdis
PC Parker	Jeff Stevenson
Bridge attendant	Alan Hulse
Lil	Rachel Bell
Boatman	Joe Belcher
Boatman's friend	Johnnie Allen
Gas rigger	David Fleeshman
Van Kleefe	Philip Bond
Mr Hussein	Lorence Ferdinand
Girl	Judith Conyers
Black man	Lewis St Juste
Woman in crowd	Blanche Coleman
Walk-ons:	(People in pub) Rastas: Claud

Bowell, Alex Cruise. (Blonde walking past bar) Julie Evans. (Male smuggler) Fernand Monast. (Smugglers' taxi driver) Ron Barney. (Customs) Johnnie Ellis, Jennifor Stanton and Linda Lee Walsh. (Workmen at Denzil's traffic jam) Jim Molsom and Art Taylor. (Policeman) Pat Gorman. (Van Kleefe's heavies) David J Nichols and Jackson Greene. (The police trap for Slater) Gary Dean and Ray Knight. (Bank tellers and security guards at Van Kleefe's arrest) Mac Ballentine, Patrick Nixon, Paul Goodall, Kinglsey Dean. (Airport announcement voice over) Linda James.

PRODUCTION TEAM
Written by John Sullivan
Title music arranged and conducted by Ronnie Hazlehurst composed and sung by John Sullivan

Make-up Designer:	Vivien Riley
Costume Designer:	Barbara Kidd
Properties Buyer:	Dave Morris
Film Cameraman:	Chris Seager
Sound Recordist:	Dennis Panchen
Film Editor:	John Jarvis
Dubbing Mixer:	Dean Humphreys
Lighting Gaffer:	Joe Ryan
Production Assistant:	Lesley Bywater
Assistant Floor Manager:	Gavin Clark
Graphic Designer:	Andrew Smee
Production Managers:	Tony Dow and Sue Longstaff
Designer:	Bernard Lloyd-Jones

Produced and directed by Ray Butt

When Boycie and Abdul tell Del that they're planning to buy some diamonds from a Mr Van Kleefe in Amsterdam, he can't believe his ears. Although they'll be forking out fifty grand for the stones, they intend making a handsome profit because the current market value is around £150,000. They want Del involved and ask him if he'll act as courier, taking the money across the North Sea and delivering it personally to Van Kleefe, before returning with the stones. Del is quick to turn them down, until he hears there is £15,000 in it for him. He drags Rodney into the job, but when the gang hear Chief Inspector Slater is investigating the drug smuggling and believes Abdul and Boycie are involved, everyone starts worrying. They need a secret hideaway to finalise their plans, so Del suggests somewhere no one would dream of looking: the back of Denzil's lorry.

The meeting draws to an end, but before Del can get out of the lorry, Denzil jumps in the cab and begins his long journey to Hull, with Rodney in hot pursuit in his Reliant Regal. Del's unexpected visit to the North Sea fishing port isn't a total waste of time: he suddenly has an idea to fool Slater, who's so keen to catch the courier he has men patrolling all major airports. Del hires a boat, as well as an experienced sailor, Albert, to steer the boat across the North Sea to Holland. Inevitably, Del and Rodney's troubles may be just around the corner, especially as Abdul and Boycie have supplied counterfeit notes, and they're relying on Albert's non-existent navigational skills. But just when it looks as if they've achieved their goal, Chief Inspector Slater arrives on the scene. But the bane of Del Boy's life is soon to get his comeuppance.

Todd, Alexandra

Production assistant on six episodes: S5

Tom (the commissionaire)

Played by Ted Shepherd
Tom is a grey-haired security officer who works at the council offices in 'Heroes and Villains'. Councillor Murray speaks to him briefly as she leaves the building.

Tom (the security officer)

(See 'Clarke, Tom')

Tomlinson, Fred

Role: Pianist
Appeared in S5, episode 4 and 'Diamonds are for Heather'
(See 'Fred Tomlinson Singers, The')

Tomlinson, Henry

Assistant floor manager on one episode: 'The Jolly Boys' Outing'
Henry, who's the son of the late David Tomlinson, was born in Aylesbury and gained a vast amount of experience in the theatre before turning to television. As an assistant stage manager he toured Australia and Japan with *Starlight Express* and was involved in several Derek Nimmo tours and various productions at the Chichester Theatre.

He moved into television in the mid-1980s and quickly progressed to 1st assistant director, by which time he was working freelance. Nowadays he's producing films and television shows: he's spent three years as associate director on *London's Burning*, produced the movie *Goldfish Bowl*, co-produced *Yellow Bird* and been involved in a host of other pictures, including *A Christmas Carol, Dial 9, In Custody* and *The Final Passage*.

Tommy

Played by Ricky Kennedy
A mate of Del's, Tommy is seen in The Nag's Head during 'Watching the Girls Go By'. Del tells Tommy he's not forgotten about his wife's sandwich-maker and will drop it round the following day.

Tony

Not seen in the sitcom, Tony is mentioned by Rodney in 'Go West Young Man'. Rodney claims he's a friend from evening class, whom he often shares a drink with on his nights out in the West End. Whether he really exists is uncertain.

Tony (the waiter in the Indian restaurant)

Played by Dev Sagoo
Appeared in 'Diamonds are for Heather' and S3, episode 2
The waiter serves Del and Heather at The Star of Bengal when Del proposes, only to find his hopes of married bliss dashed when she turns him down. He's seen again in 'Healthy Competition', and in both episodes Del calls him Tony, so we can only assume that it's his real name.

Tony (Chinese takeaway owner)

Played by Chua Kahjoo
Tony owns the Chinese take-away the Trotters frequent in 'Video Nasty'. Del gets annoyed with him because he's taking forever to cook his order.

Tony

Played by Jay Amor
In 'Miami Twice', Tony is one of Vinny Occhetti's employees.

Tony

Played by Jotham Annan
In 'Time On Our Hands', Tony is employed by Boycie as a car cleaner; when Rodney and Del come visiting to take a look at a Rolls Royce, Boycie – worried that the Trotters parking their Reliant van outside his garage will tarnish his so-called image – asks Tony to drive the van round the corner.

Note: The scene involving Tony was edited out of the final transmitted programme.

Toone, Geoffrey

Role: Lord Ridgemere
Appeared in S2, episode 7
Geoffrey, who was born in Dublin in 1910, has been working on stage and screen since the 1930s, with early film appearances including Bill Brown in *Sword of Honour*, Lieutenant Stocken in *Queer Cargo*, Johnny Carson in *Night Journey* and David in *Poison Pen*. Among the other roles he's played on the big screen are Count Cambia in *The Woman's Angle*, Martin Mallison in *The Man Between*, Sir Edward Ramsay in *The King and I*, Harold Hubbard in *The Entertainer* and Roche in *Blaze of Glory*.

On television, he's been seen in *The Westerner, The Persuaders, All Creatures Great and Small, Jeeves and Wooster, Casualty, The High Life, Anna Karenina, War and Remembrance* and *The Apocalypse Watch*.

Top-Buy supermarkets

The Trotters buy their weekly shopping at this supermarket in 'The Longest Night', and become involved in a plan by the Head of Security and manager of the branch to raid the supermarket safe.

★ ★ ★ ★ ★ ★

'The BBC were most cooperative and took care not to disrupt the everyday life of the school. They arrived, if my memory serves me correctly, about 7am on the morning of filming and finished shortly after lunch.

'The signpost on the opening shot was situated on the Child Okeford–Iwerne Minster Road, and shortly after we have a scene with Lady Ridgemere's broken down vehicle. This was originally intended to be a Rolls Royce but because the towing scene required Del's Reliant Regal to tow the vehicle back to Ridgemere Hall (aka Clayesmore School) and it was found that it

couldn't pull the weight, a Volvo was used as a substitute – and even that was difficult! The Rolls can be seen parked in the background when the Volvo is being untied from Del's car.

'His Lordship calling from an upper window was, in fact, in the staff quarters of the House Mistress of Bower House Flat, which is no longer used for that purpose. Moving to the scene in the lounge (drawing room), the fireplace is the original but the majority of furnishings were supplied by the BBC's props department, although one or two background pieces belonged to the school. His Lordship informs Del that the house was built in 1642, but, in fact, Wolverton Manor (Clayesmore School) was built in the last decade of the 19th century.

'The more general location showing the oak staircase, the library, drawing room, ante-room, together with the stone mosaic floor and the two chandeliers, form the main scene of action. Grandad had to go up the oak staircase to the landing above and remove floorboards to get to the bolts holding the hall lights (not as grand as the chandeliers but equally effective for the school hall), so that they could be removed and replaced by the valuable BBC chandeliers.

'I was fortunate enough to observe the whole scene from when the wrong chandelier was prepared for releasing from the ceiling to the actual dropping of the "valuable" chandelier, which came crashing to the floor with a resounding explosion and breaking of glass. To see this was a most hilarious situation which brought great laughter from those who were lucky enough to watch the scene.'

ASSISTANT BURSAR, Clayesmore School (1974–94)

Getting ready to record 'A Touch of Glass' (above and below)

'Touch of Glass, A'

Original transmission: Thursday 2 December 1982, 8.30 pm

Production date: Sunday 6 June 1982

Original viewing figures: 10.2 million

Duration: 30 minutes

First repeat: Tuesday 16 August 1983, 8.30 pm

Subsequent repeats: 7/12/90, 17/5/96, 8/7/97, 4/9/98, 25/2/00

CAST

Del Trotter . . . . .David Jason
Rodney Trotter . . . . .Nicholas Lyndhurst
Grandad Trotter . . . . .Lennard Pearce
Lady Ridgemere . . . . .Elizabeth Benson
Wallace, the butler . . . . .Donald Bisset
Lord Ridgemere . . . . .Geoffrey Toone
Walk-ons: . . . .(People outside auction hall)
Tony Campbell, Alex Reid, Suzy Lyle and Lee Bennett.

PRODUCTION TEAM

Written by John Sullivan
Title music arranged and conducted by Ronnie Hazlehurst composed and sung by John Sullivan
Audience warm-up: . . . . .Felix Bowness
Make-up Designer: . . . . .Shaunna Harrison
Costume Designer: . . . . .Anushia Nieradzik
Properties Buyer: . . . . .Roger Williams
Film Cameraman: . . . . .John Walker
Film Sound: . . . . .Dennis Panchen
and Nigel Woodford
Film Editor: . . . . .Mike Jackson
Camera Supervisor: . . . . .Ron Peverall
Studio Lighting Director: . . . . . .Henry Barber
Studio Sound: . . . . Dave Thompson
Technical Coordinator: . . . . . . .Robert Hignett
Videotape Editor: . . . . .Chris Wadsworth
Production Assistant: . . . . .Penny Thompson
Assistant Floor Manager: . . . . .Tony Dow
Graphic Designers: . . . . .Peter Clayton and Fen Symonds
Vision Mixer: . . . . .Angela Beveridge
Production Managers: . . . . .Janet Bone and Sue Bysh
Designers: . . . . .Derek Evans and Andy Dimond
Produced by Ray Butt

Driving home from an auction, the Trotters stop to help a fellow motorist, whose car has broken down. The unfortunate woman is none other than Lady Ridgemere, wife of Lord Ridgemere, who owns a local estate. Although she's grateful for their assistance in towing her car back to Ridgemere Hall, they soon outstay their welcome. Whilst at the mansion, Del eavesdrops on a phone conversation his Lordship

★ ★ ★ ★ ★

'**A**fter a month or so of preparation, since deciding the entrance hall was the right place to be, the day had finally arrived for the one-off chandelier drop. My experts had set everything from the real chandelier from Louis Koch, who were entrepreneurs in classic furniture, to the copy made by a company called Trading Post, with its beautiful cut glass fruit salad bowls from Woolies! (I may have had the ideas but then I needed people like Louis Koch and Trading Post to make it happen) Incidentally, in order for Trading Post to be able to copy the chandelier, we had to take the original along to their workshops, and getting it there was a major exercise in itself.

'We only had the one chance to get it right and if it had gone wrong, my head was on the block! My lads did all the decorating of the hall, putting up the screens, paintings and suits of armour, but the actual work involving the chandelier drop was left to Trading Post (whose CV includes blowing up a train on the film *Lawrence of Arabia*).

'Waiting on the ground floor were three cameras, ready to film the moment. I sat myself down on the staircase for a grandstand view, then Ray Butt, the director, called "Action!" and gave the signal for the electrical bolt to fire. We had just a few seconds to the drop and at that moment I turned away. Then I heard the sound of breaking glass followed by 30 seconds of deathly silence. Should I look back? Suddenly people were clapping and mayhem broke out – it had gone to plan.' **ANDY DIMOND – Designer**

'Healthy Competition'

is having with a firm specialising in cleaning chandeliers. He quibbles over the estimate they've given for cleaning the crystal chandeliers at the Hall, believing it to be too expensive. Seizing the opportunity to earn some dosh, Del claims the Trotters are specialists in the field, and agrees to clean the chandeliers in the drawing room for £350, to devastating effect!

Tourell, Andrew

Role: Mr Gerrard
Appeared in S4, episode 3

Born in London in 1946, Andrew worked as a merchant banker before opting for an actor's life and training at the Webber-Douglas drama school.

He made his professional stage debut in a 1967 production of *Jane Eyre* at Palmer's Green, before setting off for various repertory theatres throughout the UK.

His first involvement in television came in the mid-1970s, playing a policeman in *Bouquet of Barbed Wire*. His favourite small-screen roles have been Napley in *It Takes a Worried Man*, Anthony in *No Place Like Home*, Graham in *Just Good Friends*, and five series as Geoffrey in *Waiting for God*.

Andrew's recent work engagements include working in his own children's theatre company.

Townsend, Nipper

Not seen in the sitcom, Nipper is mentioned by Uncle Albert in 'From Prussia with Love'. He was stationed in Malta and had trouble raising a family.

Towser, Young

Played by Mike Carnell

Towser, who's a friend of Del's, is seen in 'Healthy Competition', initially buying something from the auction attended by Del, Rodney and his new business partner, Mickey Pearce. He later pops into The Star of Bengal, an Indian restaurant in which Del is finishing off a meal; Del Boy calls him over and asks a favour: concerned about Rodney's failing partnership with Mickey Pearce, he does his younger brother a favour by giving Towser some money to buy the useless broken lawnmower engines they've lumbered themselves with.

Young Towser is married and has recently been nicked for fly-dumping, so wants to be careful what he gets himself involved in, but when Del suggests he gives the engines back to Alfie Flowers, and there's £20 in it for him, he agrees to help.

The character is mentioned again in 'Stage Fright', when Del tells Rodney (who's just been offered some council accommodation) that if he needs any furniture, Young Towser has some quality three-piece suites.

Trainee

Played by Jake Wood

Seen in 'The Jolly Boys' Outing', Rodney's gormless trainee works for him at Alan Parry's printing business.

Transworld Express

In 'Danger UXD', we learn that Denzil has set up his own haulage company with the motto: 'Any time, any load, anywhere'. He planned to call the business Peckham Courier Service but foolishly listened to Del, who told him 'There is no place in the modern world for small thinkers'.

★ ★ ★ ★ ★

'**I**n November 1984 I was just finishing an enjoyable stint on another John Sullivan/Ray Butt collaboration, *Just Good Friends*, when Ray leaned over and muttered that I might look okay in a wig, a euphemism for playing Prosecuting Counsel in 'Hole in One', an episode in the fourth series. I looked forward with relish to cross-examining Lennard Pearce, an actor I greatly admired. Watching *Only Fools and Horses* over the years, Grandad is the character that interests and amuses me more than any other in the cast.

'Shortly after my conversation with Ray Butt, Lennard Pearce suddenly died, the episode was postponed and re-written a couple of months later involving Uncle Albert. Buster Merryfield was an affable man but it was a difficult and contrived situation for him and the chemistry could never be the same as it was between the original three principals. Ray was later to tell me that within days of Lennard Pearce's death, he received hundreds of applications from actors offering to replace him; he was so upset he hurled the lot across the office.

'As for the episode itself, it was just a few days' work with a friendly cast, a long time ago. But it's been repeated so many times since the original screening that it feels more recent and more substantial. My fee was only moderate but if my other work had attracted similar residual payments on a pro-rata basis, I would now be a rich man.

'During the actual recording I remember David Jason, Nicholas Lyndhurst and Kenneth MacDonald cracking up with laughter and a good time was had by all. Some sitcom actors are uneasy about addressing a studio audience directly, but David Jason was quite the reverse. He was ultra hyped-up and if acting work had ever proved elusive for him he would have been a natural warm-up man. Not very likely! A decade previously an elderly director friend of my wife had told her that he was working with a youngster called David Jason, who should do quite well.

'Since the '80s, of course, Gareth Gwenlan – a man I like and respect – has taken over from Ray Butt as producer, the episodes have stretched to 50 minutes and the regular cast has grown, but in my opinion this is not always for the good. The sharpness of the earlier scripts is often diffused, and the supporting acting ranges from the commendable to the clichéd and to the forced. Kenneth Macdonald belongs firmly to the former category, remaining consistently watchable throughout the entire run, combining both wit and integrity in his performance. This has always satisfied me as he was a pleasure to work with during my short association with the show; so when I heard the news of his early death last year I was particularly sad.' **ANDREW TOURELL**

Trerise, Paul

Designer on 'The Frog's Legacy'

Born in Altrincham in 1944, Paul worked for a shopfitting company in Manchester before joining BBC Manchester in 1965. During the 29 years he was employed by the Beeb, he worked on a range of programmes, from further education series and religious programmes to *Top of the Pops* and sitcoms. Other credits include *Blankety Blank, Bob's Full House, Wogan, Three Of A Kind, Blue Peter, Doctor Who* and a *Bread* Christmas Special. But his first programme as a designer was *Sooty*, followed by the children's programmes *Monster Music Mash* and *Whoosh!*

In 1975 he returned to BBC Manchester and became games designer on *It's A Knockout* and *Jeux Sans Frontières*, before returning to the capital two years later as production designer on *The Generation Game*.

Paul, who retired from the BBC in 1994, has worked in television for over 37 years and is now a freelance production designer. Recent work has seen him help to set up the current Network News.

Trigger

Played by Roger Lloyd Pack

First seen in The Nag's Head during 'Big Brother', Trigger is the local dullard, who got his nickname for looking like a horse. He earns a meagre living as a road sweeper, whose patch includes the streets used by the market traders. He's rewarded for his service to the community when Councillor Murray presents him with a medal, which he proudly displays on his chest.

Trigger, who is in his thirties when we first meet him, isn't the brightest guy around, and has a poor memory, especially when it comes to people's names – particularly Rodney, who he's forever calling Dave. Often seen donning his trademark donkey jacket, he isn't beyond dabbling in petty crime, an unfortunate trait which fades as he reaches middle age. In 'Big Brother' he arrives on the scene and conducts a little business with Del: he has 25 imitation leather briefcases to dump on some unsuspecting mug, which is probably the reason he turned to Del. Trotter Senior ignores his younger brother's protestations and snaps them up for £8 each; to his dismay, he later discovers they're rejects and can't be opened because the paperwork detailing the combination is locked inside; to make matters worse, they were stolen from Dougie Sadler's stationery shop in the High Street, something Del only discovers when he tries flogging them back to him.

Trigger's dealing in stolen goods again in 'The Yellow Peril', this time in the form of yellow paint. It's not until Rodney has used it to paint the kitchen of The Golden Lotus restaurant that they learn it's luminous and was pinched from a storage shed at Clapham Junction.

Trigger – who has a younger sister – endured a turbulent childhood. Because he never knew his father (he once explained that he died a couple of years before Trigger was born), he was brought up

One of Trigger's trademarks was that he would constantly refer to Rodney as Dave. What was the reasoning behind this? 'At first, it was Trigger's way of dismissing Rodney, really,' explains John Sullivan. 'Rodney often thought that he wasn't part of the scene: he felt he was still treated like a child, his opinions didn't matter and no one took him seriously, which was always his grouch. Then I decided to play on Trigger's stupidity and used it again. The audience chuckled, so I decided to make it part of the character's dialogue whenever he met Rodney.'

by his grandparents when his mother died. He has very fond memories of his grandparents, especially his grandfather, who was also a road sweeper and taught Trigger the trade.

He completed his education at the Martin Luther King Comprehensive in 1962, but shortly after found himself serving 18 months in a Young Offenders' Home when Roy Slater, while serving with the police, planted 3000 Green Shield stamps on him.

On the romance front, Trigger – who had a crush on Julie Christie – doesn't enjoy much luck, either. He's a bachelor and the situation is unlikley to change; even his attempts to form a relationship via a dating agency don't last, and the only liaison we ever hear about involves Linda, a lady road sweeper at the council depot. Trigger classed her as a highflyer because you had to consult her when you wanted a new broom. But that relationship broke up several years ago.

For Trigger, the loneliness of life is temporarily relieved by frequenting The Nag's Head, something he's been doing since the age of 16, excepting the period he was barred by Mike, the landlord, for stealing a pork pie. When he walks through the doors he knows he's in the company of friends.

MEMORIES OF PLAYING TRIGGER

★ ★ ★ ★ ★ ★

'When I received my first *Only Fools* script, Trigger was described as someone who looked like a horse. That was all I had to go on when it came to deciding how to play the character; not much, I know, but I knew it was a promising sidestep if I could play someone like that. I also realised from the start that it was clearly a good script. Obviously no one could foresee just how successful the programme would become, but it was certainly a show with plenty of potential.

'In the beginning, Trigger was much more involved in the plot lines, helping push the story along. But over the years the character was honed down to his bare essentials and he became less and less actively involved. Other characters developed around him who were more able to lead the storyline, while Trigger appeared to become something of a peripheral figure, yet retaining the ability to influence events. As people got to know him they realised it was increasingly unlikely that he'd be involved in running a scam. He became more and more detached from reality, which made him even funnier.

'I can't remember when I realised the show was really taking off, but I suppose it was when the episodes increased to 50 minutes. The stories became epics, possessing a degree of grandeur. It showed the strength of the characters because not many half-hour shows can be expanded in that way.

'I receive more fan mail now than ever before. It's astonishing. A new generation of kids are watching the show, which is great. Luckily, I've never received any untoward mail, nothing offensive – usually just endearing tributes. Trigger brings out the best in people. Somebody once said that you can tell what sort of person someone is by the way they respond to Trigger, which is quite an astute thing to say because he's the sort of person who's easy to make a fool of; in a way, he's a blank canvas on which your own personality can be reflected.

'A lot of people recognise me as Trigger, which is something I have to deal with. The mood I'm in at the time will determine whether I go along with it, ignore it or deal with it in some other way. It can be galling to be tied in with just one character, but at the same time it's been my bread and butter for years, which has been wonderful. *Only Fools and Horses* has dominated my career and altered the direction it has taken; who knows what I would have done but for Trigger. However, I'm grateful for how things have turned out.

'Whenever I play the character, I use certain qualities of myself, like what my father used to call dumb insolence. Whenever I got into trouble as a boy I'd adopt a blank expression, something I used for Trigger. From day one I tried making him believable. He says the most ridiculous things, so finding some truth in the character is where I started. I didn't want to play him stupid, that wouldn't be funny; I played him from his point of view, as if he was intelligent.

'It's hard to believe that it's 21 years since the first episode was recorded. When I think back I can still recall the rehearsals down in Chiswick; the actual room is still vivid in my mind. We'd rehearse in the morning and finish at lunchtime; old Lennard Pearce smoking his cigarettes; David Jason full of energy, bouncing around like a rubber ball and Nick quite shy. I also remember the uncertainty of it all: I don't think John Sullivan had finished writing the scripts for the rest of the first series when we recorded number one; I was in the opening instalment but didn't know if I'd be in the next.

'When it comes to special memories from a particular episode, it must be the famous scene where Del falls through the bar. I like to think of it as the scene where "I react to Del falling through the bar", rather than "Del falling through the bar". I'm very proud of the way I hold the scene until he gets back on his feet. The scene wasn't even in the script originally: the episode was short by several minutes at the readthrough, so John Sullivan said he'd write a couple of scenes with Trigger at the bar.

'On the whole, playing Trigger has helped my career. It's meant I've never been forgotten, which is the worst thing that can happen to an actor. There are certain roles that would be hard for me to do now because of the influence of Trigger, such as documentary-style dramas, but I've appeared in many other shows like *Longitude* and *Oliver Twist*, which are completely different, so I've established another persona.' **ROGER LLOYD-PACK**

Trotter Air

In the opening scenes of 'Heroes and Villains', a poster depicts a Trotter Air jumbo jet, with the slogan: 'Trotter Air Gets You There'. It's all part of Rodney's dream.

Trotter, Albert

Played by Buster Merryfield

Grandad's brother, who's in his mid-sixties, is first seen in 'Strained Relations'. Although he didn't talk to his brother for years, just like he didn't talk to his wife, Ada, he feels he should pay his last respects and attends the funeral.

Never one to be lost in a crowd, courtesy of his bushy white beard, Albert – who's fond of a tipple, especially rum – is an old sea-dog, having served in both the Royal and Merchant Navy. However, being a proponent of tall stories, most of his tales – including the one about being torpedoed five times, earning him the nickname Boomerang Trotter because he always came back – have to be taken with a pinch of salt, especially as we find out in 'Hole in One' that he spent most of the war years stationed on the Isle of Wight at a storage depot.

Such is his propensity for spinning a yarn that

no one knows what to believe. Among his many tales is that of the time, in 1941, aged 17, he joined the navy and travelled the South China Sea aboard *HMS Peerless* as part of the Royal Pacific Fleet. His spell on the ship was a disaster because he ended up being considered for court martial after wan-

tonly abandoning his duties, which led to the sinking of *HMS Peerless* and damage to the American aircraft carrier *USS Pittsburg*.

Then there were the claims of helping sink the *Graf Spee* at the Battle of the River Plate, the raid of Telemar, as well as being part of a marine parachute unit, specially formed for missions behind enemy lines. A cunning old geezer, he once executed a plan to earn himself some much-needed cash by swindling a string of public houses into paying out compensation after he'd supposedly fallen down into their cellars and hurt himself in the process. Even the post he held in the navy is questionable: different accounts have him working in a storage depot, involved in laundry matters and as a boiler maintenance man, which is his excuse for not being able to read navigational charts while crossing the North Sea in the Inge.

Born in Tobacco Road, down by the docks in South London, Albert Gladstone Trotter – who is Del's godfather – moved in with the Trotter boys at Nelson Mandela House shortly after Grandad's funeral. He had been residing with Jean and Stan until they moved away and left him homeless.

His father was a deserter from the army, but Albert always showed an affinity with the sea, and his first job upon leaving school at 15 was working on a tramp-steamer.

When the Harrison watch affair left him a millionaire, he didn't hesitate to head for the coast, where he saw out his final years, shacked up with Elsie Partridge.

Trotter, Cassandra (née Parry)

Played by Gwyneth Strong

Cassandra Louise Trotter works for a bank, specialising in overseas investment until she becomes a millionairess when Del and Rodney find a much sought-after watch in their garage. Her father – Alan Parry – has his own printing workshop.

Rodney's wife is first seen in 'Yuppy Love'. She attends an evening class at the Adult Education Centre the same evening as Rodney; they get chatting when a mix-up finds Rodney taking Cassandra's overcoat by mistake. In those days she drove her father's BMW around, and lived in Blackheath.

Later on, she enjoys her first dance with Rodney at a disco and so begins a relationship which, at times, is rocked by some stormy seas. They finally tie the knot in 'Little Problems', but their lives together remain far from settled, and the fragility of their marriage is continuously tested, including a trial separation (when Rodney returns home and Cassandra jets off to the family villa to contemplate her future) and a miscarriage to contend with.

Cassandra begins to realise that life with Rodney will never be a bed of roses, while Rodney holds the firm belief that the root of all their difficulties is Cassandra's drive for a banking career. Always on the look-out for an opportunity to better herself,

MEMORIES OF PLAYING DAMIEN

★ ★ ★ ★ ★ ★

Jamie Smith clocked up four instalments of the sitcom playing Damien, more than anyone else. He was just three and a half when first seen in 'Fatal Extraction', but the opportunity arose by accident, as his mother, Charlie Smith, explains.

'When Jamie was 12 months old he had some photos taken at a local photographers; the man there said he was very photogenic and gave me this number to call, which was a child's modelling agency in London. We decided to give it a try and were invited up for an audition. We were told that Jamie wasn't really what they were looking for, but they decided to take a few photos and keep him on the books.

'He got an advert almost straight away for Persil liquid, but we decided to move on to another agency and got some more work quite quickly, beginning with some stills for Japan Airlines. He was on billboards all over Europe.

'Then the auditions went ahead for Damien and on the second set of auditions, the agency sent Jamie's picture along and he was invited to see the director and that was it. By the time we'd got home we had a message on the answerphone saying he had the job. He's a bright boy for his age and he took things in very easily; he was also very well behaved.

'When it came to recording, Jamie and I would stay with family in Barnet, and the BBC would send a taxi to pick us up. It was a strange experience being with people like David Jason, Nicholas Lyndhurst and Buster Merryfield, who I got on really well with, partly because he lived quite near us.

'Jamie loved the whole experience, although he was very shy at times, especially when it came to filming the scene where he stands at the bottom of Rodney and Cassandra's bed; the scene had to be re-shot several times because Jamie had such a serious face it made Nicholas laugh.

'When the last episode had been recorded, Jamie and I were invited along to a party in London. Of course, no one knew there were going to be further episodes, so it was almost a farewell party before everyone went their separate ways. Jamie got so upset he cried his eyes out, he was beside himself,' explains Charlie. 'Terry Dow came up to me and whispered, "I think you'd better take him home." He was so upset at the thought of not working with them all; sadly, though, we missed the party!

'After playing Damien in *Only Fools and Horses* he never did anything else and concentrated on his school work. He's 11 now and has started asking about going to theatre school, but we can't afford to send him; we might, however, find out if we can get him sponsored so that he can attend drama school.

'But Jamie isn't a natural actor, you can tell by just watching the show. He's a very shy little boy who was the right age, had the right looks and was around at the right time but as far as acting ability is concerned, there's still a long way to go. You cannot take it too seriously at his age, you have to treat it as fun, which is what we did.'

CHARLIE SMITH

her attitude creates, perhaps, pangs of jealousy within her husband.

By the time 'Mother Nature's Son' is screened, Cassandra's been rewarded for her hard graft and is in charge of small business investment at the Peckham branch; although it's not ideal in Cassandra's eyes, it's certainly a step up the bank's protracted promotional ladder.

A strong-minded, assured woman who provides the backbone in her relationship with Rodney, Cassandra is an instantly likeable individual.

Trotter, Damien

Played by Patrick McManus ('Three Men, a Woman and a Baby'); Grant Stevens ('Miami Twice'); Robert Liddement ('Mother Nature's Son'); Jamie Smith ('Fatal Extraction', 'Heroes and Villains', 'Modern Men' and 'Time On Our Hands'); Douglas Hodge (in Rodney's dream as Old Damien in 'Heroes and Villains'); Ben Smith ('If They Could See Us Now…!')

Del and Raquel's baby boy – Damien Derek – is born during the closing scene of 'Three Men, a Woman and a Baby'. When deciding on names for their new arrival, they settle on Sigourney, but are less decisive when it comes to a boy's name: Rodney and Troy are considered before Rodney jokingly floats the idea of Damien, which to his surprise they both like. His christening takes place in 'Miami Twice'.

Jamie Smith as Damien

Trotter, Derek

Played by David Jason

Derek, 'Del Boy' Trotter is the quintessential wide-boy, always on the look-out for any opportunity to earn a quick buck, even if it means helping to fuel the violence during the Brixton riots by selling paving stones to the rioters. Appositely, his business motto is 'Mine is not to reason why, mine is but to sell and buy'.

The gregarious Cockney – who has a penchant for meaningless or inappropriate phrases – is one of life's eternal wheeler-dealers but his garish dress sense and ostentatious behaviour fools no one, except those dim-witted enough to be taken in by his banal sales patter. A supplier of everything under the sun, from telescopic Christmas trees and dodgy computers to Russian camcorders and unlockable briefcases, he's seen regularly at the local market, although he's an unlicensed trader: ever since he had a disagreement with a magistrate, the official has prohibited all the councils from issuing him a licence.

Del is streetwise and resilient, a true survivor, but he's not one of the brightest or luckiest men around: when he read in a Sunday newspaper that diving was hip with the yuppies, he bought a diving-suit, thinking the reporter meant deep-sea diving, not scuba-diving. His lack of substance upstairs wasn't helped by being a habitual truant at school, hence his family's amazement when he returned home one day claiming he had eight O-levels at grade A. All was clear, however, when a letter arrived, explaining that grade 'A' meant absent; whilst everyone else was taking their exams, Del was down the market flogging LPs.

No one could ever describe Del as work shy, and for years he slogged away – even if some of his actions were illegal – to establish the family's import/export business. Such is the volatility of the company's finances, however, that he's often had to resort to pawning all his jewellery. Although he'll forever struggle to get ahead in life, it won't be through lack of trying. Del's father always had confidence in him, believing he would reach the top, although as Grandad pointed out, Del's father's judgement wasn't that impressive: he thought Millwall would win the FA Cup.

Despite Del's hard work, TITCO remains an ineffectual company, heading nowhere fast; and Del seemed destined to eke out a life from the 12th floor of Nelson Mandela House, where he's been living since 1962 – save for a brief period when he lived the life of Riley upon becoming a millionaire. In 'A Touch of Glass', Del reflected on how hard graft had got him nowhere in life, saying: 'We live 'alf a mile up in the sky in this Lego set built by the council, while we run a three-wheel van with a bald tyre.'

For all his wheeling and dealing, and the bravado, Del's easily made a mug of, especially where women are concerned. Unaware of this flaw, he regards himself as a real ladies' man, someone

who sets pulses racing every time he walks down the road. He boasts that he's considerate towards women, taking their feelings into account at all times. He once told Rodney that a woman is guaranteed four things from him: a well dressed man, a steak meal, care and consideration.

His so-called charm sees him entertain a string of girlfriends, although some of his partners left a lot to be desired: while lying in a hospital bed in a reflective mood during 'Sickness and Wealth', he

sums up his choice of girlfriends by admitting to Rodney that 'some of 'em have been round the track more times than a lurcher'. Ironically, he meets the love of his life via the Technomatch Matrimonial Agency. When the name Raquel Turner pops out of the computer, he arranges to meet her at Waterloo Station, before lunching at the plush Hilton Hotel in London's Park Lane. Although it was a while before they formed a meaningful relationship, it's led to them settling down and raising a son, Damien – and all within the confines of their tiny flat in Nelson Mandela House.

Despite his shortcomings, one of Del's endearing qualities is the love he has for his family, exemplified beautifully in 'May the Force be with You'. When Detective Inspector Slater wants the name of the supplier in stolen microwaves, Del won't cooperate. But when Slater discovers that Rodney's got a police record he mentions that he might frame him; Del protects his baby brother by concocting a scheme to get his family out of their current mess. And in 'Christmas Crackers', when Rodney is bored with life and tries persuading Del to go clubbing, Del reminds his little brother that it's Christmas and they couldn't leave Grandad alone.

There's a 13-year gap between Del – who was described by Detective Inspector Slater as a man 'who could talk himself out of a room with no doors' – and Rodney. When their mother died, and their father ran off, Del – just 16 – was left to fend for his younger brother, whom he classes as '42-carat gold'.

As Del is always quick to point out, he sacrificed a lot to take care of Rodney. While all the other Mods were having punch-ups at Southend, and attending The Who concerts, Del was home

DEL'S MEANINGLESS PHRASES

What was the idea behind giving Del a bank of French phrases which he consistently got muddled?

'I gave Del his first French phrase in "Big Brother". By then we were part of the European Community and I noticed all the products you bought, whether they were British or foreign goods, had ingredients and other bits of information written in different languages. I regarded Del as an entrepreneur, also someone who thought of himself as worldly-wise, yet he was living within his own personal society with people who weren't. I thought he'd most probably read, for example, a foreign statement on the back of a pair of tights and use it to try and impress people, not realising what it actually meant, and the fact that he was impressing no one.' JOHN SULLIVAN

babysitting; and if that wasn't bad enough, he also found rusks in his Hush-puppies and oyster milk stains on his Ben Sherman's.

Raising his kid brother also affected his love life. At Rodney's wedding reception, Del confides in Marlene about why he's never tied the knot himself, claiming that most of the girls he met didn't want to bring up a younger brother, so he gave them the elbow because family is the most important thing.

When Del did attend school, it was the Arthur Murray School, Lewisham, and later the Martin Luther King Comprehensive, in the notorious Class 4C. He left in 1962 without any qualifications, but possessed a get-up-and-go approach to life, even if it didn't get him any further than the streets of Peckham. He began his working life at a young age, delivering cigarettes around Lewisham for a cigarette company. In the 1960s, he launched Eels on Wheels with his chum Jumbo Mills, selling seafood outside The Nag's Head. But when the local health inspector submitted a slating report, the end was in sight for Del's fishy venture.

After briefly experiencing life as a millionaire, Del's now back in Peckham. Although he's banned from running a company, he has plans for Rodney to front TITCO, but, as ever, he intends pulling all the strings himself.

Trotterex

In the opening scenes of 'Heroes and Villains', we see a billboard advertising 'Trotterex – family planning', with the slogan, 'Go Equipped'. It's all part of Rodney's nightmare.

Trotter, George

George is mentioned by Grandad in 'The Russians are Coming', but is never seen. He is Grandad's brother, who fought at Passchendale during World War One. It seems that he survived the battle, because Grandad describes the horrific scenes George saw when the soldiers returned home. We don't hear anything more about him, except that he tried lying to the authorities about his age, claim-ing he was 14 instead of 18: he failed and was enlisted anyway.

Trotter, Gran

We learn little about Del and Rodney's Gran, but in 'Yesterday Never Comes', Del tells the devious Miranda Davenport that she worked as a charlady to an art dealer, stealing a valuable painting in the process. It has hung in the Trotters' flat for years until Del gives it to Miranda as a birthday present. She then sells it at auction for £17,600, only to be flabbergasted by Del's news that the picture, a piece of work by the late 19th-century artist, Joshua Blythe, is hot.

Trotter, Grandad

Played by Lennard Pearce

The trilby-wearing, scruffily attired Grandad liked nothing more than slouching in front of his TV sets and detaching himself from the frenetic life inside Nelson Mandela House.

Although dearly loved by Del and Rodney, Grandad's moments of senility drove them around the bend. In 'May the Force be with You', for instance, he misunderstood Del's simple instruction to put some wine in the fridge and ice cream in the freezer. Later, when Del tried to impress a girl from Canning Town, all he could offer her was a 'bowl of gunge and a Beaujolais ice lolly!'.

The whiny-voiced widower was content to live out the last few years of his life in the company of his grandchildren, although, at times, he needed to

à la Del

★ ★ ★ ★ ★ ★

'"Marque de Fabrique", as they say'
('It's Only Rock and Roll')

escape the mundanities of his existence, even if it was just an occasional visit to his overgrown allot-ment. His twilight years were barren; even Del once remarked that his primary purpose in life was to cook the Christmas dinner, a tradition which irked Rodney because it always meant the festive meal was burnt to a cinder. But as Del pointed out to his younger brother: 'All year he sits in that chair watching the tellies like an unoiled redundant cog, but he knows that come Christmas he can whirl into action. It's his role within the family circle.'

We learnt little about his wife, except that their marriage wasn't based on a deep-rooted romance. In 'Go West Young Man' he told Del about his

WHY DID GRANDAD WATCH TWO TVS?

Initially it wasn't the fact that he was watching two sets but that the Trotters had a load of televisions. Everything in the flat was for sale, and their home was basically a kind of warehouse; that's why we kept constantly changing the furniture. At first, I intended to have two sets, one waiting for repair, but when we got into reherarsals it became obvious that it would be funnier if Grandad watched both – with different channels on. It just caught on.

'Grandad was a great character: an old man who'd never really worked much in his time, and hadn't done much with his life. He always plays the politics between the two boys: one moment he is on Del's side because he seems to be up a gear and bringing more money in, but when Del's in trouble and Rodney's on the up, he'll swap sides. He's always there to offer advice from the past, although we often struggle to understand its relevance!'   JOHN SULLIVAN

Trotter International Star Agency, The

Del forms this entertainment agency in 'Stage Fright' when his old mate, Eric, is in desperate need of a singer for a function at The Starlight Rooms. Eric turns to Del because he knows that Raquel used to be an entertainer.

Trotter, Jack

Not seen in the sitcom, Del and Rodney's Great Uncle Jack is mentioned by Albert in 'A Royal Flush'. Whilst talking to Mrs Miles, who works at the Duke of Maylebury's country home in Berkshire, Albert tells her that the nearest Del and Rodney have got to nobility is Jack, a tobacco baron.

wedding night. Whilst consummating the marriage, his wife suddenly turned to him, and instead of whispering sweet nothings in his ear, asked: 'What d'you fancy for dinner tomorrow?' Grandad replied: 'Steak and kidney pudding'. However, there were moments of passion and they raised one son, the unreliable Reg, who fathered Del and Rodney.

If genuine romance was missing from his marriage it could have been due to profound shyness. He always claimed he found it difficult attracting girlfriends, though, paradoxically, he wasn't slow in finding solace in the arms of Trigger's grandmother, Alice, when his wife died. Although he insisted they were just two lonely people enjoying each other's company, he was the reason Alice and her husband, Arthur, didn't speak to each other for 15 years. Fortunately for Grandad, Arthur never discovered that he was the other man in his wife's life.

Family was important to Grandad, and he was particularly fond of his grandfather, who fought in the Boer War. Grandad treasured an old silver cigarette case that he kept as a reminder of his relative, who died whilst fighting the Zulus at the Battle of Rorke's Drift. A severe dent in the case reveals how, on that frightful day, a bullet ricocheted off the metal, narrowly missing his grandfather's heart; not that it made much difference, because the bullet went up his nose instead and blew his brains out.

Grandad's chequered work history saw him move from job to job usually not of his own volition. Before the Second World War, he worked as a security officer at a large warehouse near Kilburn, but he was sacked when his fingerprints were plastered all over 348 stolen attaché cases. He moved on to be a decorator for the council, travelling to work on a horse, until he was given the boot after just two days for wallpapering over a serving hatch.

Down on his luck, he ventured abroad with his mate Nobby Clarke, and tried joining the Foreign Legion; after being rejected they found themselves stuck in Tangiers with no money to pay for their fares home. Fortuitously they bumped into an Arab who offered them a job: taking his motor launch to Spain to deliver some cargo. Later, they discovered the cargo was a pile of guns; not that it made any difference because they were to complete seven further trips before being arrested and imprisoned outside a town called Tarifa. Grandad faced torture

until he decided to spill the beans and answer all the questions asked by the police.

We last saw Grandad in 'Thicker Than Water' before his untimely death after a short spell in hospital. His funeral took place in 'Strained Relations'.

Trotter, Joan Mavis
(known as Joannie)

Never seen in the programme, Rodney and Del's mother – who was married to Reg – died on 12 March 1964. To commemorate the anniversary of her death, Del and Rodney spend the day at her graveside, tending the grass and cleaning the headstone.

The boys were very close to their mother, who had a significant influence on their lives. Del even inherited his penchant for useless phrases from her: in 'A Slow Bus to Chingford', while contemplating the collapse of his venture into coach tours around ethnic London, he recalls her well worn saying, 'It's better to know you've lost than not to know you've won'. She became particularly vocal during the final moments of her life and Del often recalls that on her deathbed she spouted: 'Never stop believing because if you stop believing you've got nothing left to hope for,' before adding: 'You've got to have a dream; if you don't have a dream then how are you going to have a dream come true?'

Joannie was working at the town hall for a while in the early sixties when Rodney was born. It was a difficult pregnancy, especially as she was mistakenly treated for an ulcer during the first three months. She died when Rodney was a small child, so he has little recollection of his mother, and relies on Del to paint the picture of an alcohol-guzzling, peroxide blonde whose taste for garishly coloured clothes and menthol cigarettes – she was the first woman in Peckham to smoke them – meant she was a well known character in the locale. In 'The Yellow Peril', Del shares some more memories of their mother, explaining that most nights she was found propping up The Nag's Head bar, wearing her simulated beaver skin, with a rum and pep in one hand and 20 cigarettes in the other. She used to take Del, who was only a youngster at the time, along to the pub with her and stand him several pints of light and bitter, or whisky if she was in the money. At ten o'clock when it was time for his bed, she'd shout across to where he was sitting, ordering him home. Rodney, meanwhile, remained outside in the pram, and although Del maintains that she was always concerned about their welfare, Rodney isn't so sure.

The cause of Joan's death was never established in the series.

Trotter, Reg
Played by Peter Woodthorpe

Reg is Del and Rodney's father. Months after his wife, Joannie, died, he packed his bags and left, leaving the boys to fend for themselves. To make matters worse, he took Del's savings and even raided Rodney's piggy bank in search of money. It was Del's 16th birthday at the time, and he even swiped the cake.

'Episode Title'

'Thicker Than Water'

In his mid-fifties, Reg – who's Grandad's son – cuts a dishevelled, pathetic figure, a far cry from his days of flashy gear and jewellery, when he returns temporarily to Peckham in 'Thicker Than Water'. But no sooner has he wormed his way back into the Trotters' home than he's puffing Del's cigars, borrowing his clothes and ruling the roost.

For the last year or so he's been living in Newcastle and was recently admitted to the local infirmary and diagnosed as suffering from a hereditary blood disorder. He's back in Peckham to warn his children, dampening the festive spirit. But it turns out that the Newcastle Infirmary hasn't treated a patient called Trotter: they employed a Trotter, however, until he left two years previously with 57 blankets, 133 pairs of rubber gloves and the Chief Gynaecologist's Lambretta! When the truth is revealed, Reg packs his bags once again.

Trotter, Rodney

Played by Nicholas Lyndhurst

Rodney – who has a fetish for women in uniform, especially policewomen – is the archetypal plodder, who drifts aimlessly through life. It's clear that the lack of parental guidance – his mother died when he was very young and his father abandoned him shortly afterwards – has influenced him greatly. The occasional doubt about the identity of his father doesn't help his self-confidence, either. A predilection for the bugle during his days with the Boys' Brigade is explained by the suggestion that his father could have been the trumpeter or saxophonist from The Lacarno. The antithesis of his brother, Rodney is an indecisive, introspective pessimist, whose fecklessness and lack of foresight sees him struggle to emerge from Del Boy's shadow. Although he eventually shows signs of forging his own way in life and marries Cassandra, these frailties in his general demeanour don't bode well for his future happiness and his married life is far from smooth.

Excepting brief spells working for Alan Parry – as head of the computer section – and in partnership with Mickey Pearce, all of Rodney's working life has been spent employed as Del's runaround, rather than a genuine partner in the Trotter empire. This is highlighted in 'A Slow Bus to Chingford' when he ends up working not only as a night-watchman, but as a bus driver herding tourists around the ethnic reaches of London – or that was the intention until the venture collapsed before it had a chance to get off the ground.

Rodney's past is blighted by occasional brushes with the law, like the times he was fined £300 for smoking pot and £5 for riding a scooter without a crash helmet. Each time, Del – who's always quick to remind his kid brother of the fact – had to bail him out; although Rodney is grateful for such help, he feels Del is forever trying to run his life, which, perhaps, explains his rebellious streak. Despite his frustrations, he has a deep-rooted sense of loyalty to his older brother, exemplified by his actions in 'The Long Legs of the Law'. When his then girlfriend, Sandra, asks who's responsible for all the stolen goods in the flat, Rodney claims full responsibility, even though all the shady deals are orchestrated by Del.

In business, Rodney – whose middle name is Charlton (his mother was a Charlton Athletic fan) – is naïve and an apprentice of the tricks of the trade, but arguably more level-headed than his mercurial brother. Frequently frustrated with his lot, he's always assessing his life, yet lacks the courage or aptitude to go it alone successfully, as illustrated perfectly by his disastrous partnership with Mickey Pearce. However, Del could have, on occasions, encouraged his younger brother a little more, like the time Rodney had ambitions to establish his own window-cleaning business only to be talked out of it by Del, who wanted him to remain with TITCO, albeit for his own benefit. To make matters worse, Rodney realises his CV will never win him a job because during all the years he was supposedly Del's partner, he never registered for Income Tax or National Insurance, which means it looks as if he left school at 16 and vanished off the face of the earth. He regrets not securing a 'proper' job instead of humping Del's old suitcase around London. Even as a youth, Rodney's life was heavily influenced by Del, who called a halt to his service with the army cadets. He heard that Rodney was sharing a tent with a boy whose parents were big in showbusiness, and had the crazy idea that Rodney was going to become a child star. He therefore removed him from the cadets and enrolled him on a tap-dancing class instead.

Until he opted for married life, Rodney's time away from work was spent swigging beer at The Nag's Head or attending an endless round of evening classes, including art under the tutorship of Mr Stevens, and a computer diploma course. When Uncle Albert points out that Rodney has been enrolled on a three-month course for two years, Rodney claims that it's a difficult exam.

Married life does inject a degree of maturity into Rodney. Although Del still has him in his pocket, Cassandra instils a touch of inner strength into her husband. Wedlock isn't a bed of roses: they split up three times in 18 months and suffer the trauma of a miscarriage, but they're eager to make their marriage work.

Trotter Towers

During the opening scenes of 'Heroes and Villains', we see that TITCO has gone global and is now based in the opulent Trotter Towers, where Damien is head of the Trotter empire. Of course, it's all part of Rodney's nightmare.

Trotter Watch

Del forms this security firm during 'A Slow Bus to Chingford'. Believing crime is a growth area, he wants to get into the world of security while the going's good. He employs Rodney as an NSO (Nocturnal Security Officer), dresses him up in an old traffic warden's uniform, and sends him off to patrol a bus and coach garage in Tyler Street.

Trotters' Ethnic Tours

Another hairbrained, ill thought-out scheme, Trotters' Ethnic Tours is designed to fill what Del perceives as a gap in the tourist market. The bus tour of ethnic London will transport tourists to 'all those romantic places that you've heard of in fairy tales… the Lee Valley viaduct, the glow of Lower Edmonton at dusk, the excitement of a walkabout in Croydon'. In 'A Slow Bus to Chingford', Del explains that it's a family enterprise: while Grandad sells the programmes, he'll be the courier and Rodney – who's already working as a night watchman at the bus and coach garage in Tyler Street – will drive the bus.

But Trotters' Tours never gets off the ground, because no punters turn up for the inaugural trip, which isn't surprising when Del discovers that Grandad, who was official brochure distributor, decided to throw them all down a dust chute.

The Trotters' flat

Trotters' home décor

If you want to be a yuppy, you need to have your own pad, which is why Del applies to buy his council flat in 'Yuppy Love'. By the time the transfer of ownership is completed in 'Mother Nature's Son', however, he's been struggling to afford the rent, let alone mortgage payments that will be double the amount. In his pre-millionaire days there was little spare cash to spend on sprucing the flat up, or a total renovation considering Del's taste in décor.

Taking a tour around the Trotters' abode is like visiting a downmarket reject shop. Clashing, garish colours; patterns that have no chance of matching and furniture, much of which has seen better days, fill the flat. From the '4U2P' sign on the bathroom door to the mock tiger skin bedcover in Del's bedroom, the flat oozes tackiness.

Popping through to Del's bedroom, your attention is drawn to the swirling brass headboard on his bed, with side tables built in at each end. One table contains built-in controls for his radio, while the other has controls for his hidden lighting – the trouble is, none of it works. The bed is covered in black satin sheets, and the tiger skin bedcover, styles more suited to a bachelor.

Trotters' Independent Trading Company (TITCO)

According to the sign on the side of the company's Reliant van, TITCO operates as far afield as New York and Paris – but Del is renowned for fantasising about the big time. Even when he's a millionaire he's

dreaming of becoming a billionaire. One thing is for sure: TITCO will never make the Trotter brothers rich men. In fact, the business is more likely to land them in court for failure to pay income tax, VAT and National Insurance: Del's philosophy is that they can't claim social security or dole money, so why should they give the government anything.

The deep-rooted mistrust between the brothers isn't conducive to forming a sleek, prosperous company. While Del thinks he brings business acumen, contacts and money to the partnership, he feels Rodney's only skill lies in his ability to drive the three-wheeled van – badly. Rodney, meanwhile, starts to keep accounts in 'Big Brother' as he's sure that Del is cheating him, especially as Del has three or four changes of clothes a day while he has to make do with one suit purchased from an 'Almost New' shop. Del points out, however, that he's creating evidence that could be used against them by the tax office – and could result in three years behind bars.

Despite branching out in all directions, TITCO never has a rosy future, and it is put out of its misery when the Trotters become millionaires and close the company down. It is re-established – with Rodney in charge – when they lose their fortunes.

Trotters' Meat Fingers

In the opening scene of 'Heroes and Villains', we see a billboard advertising the fingers, with the statement: 'Guaranteed to contain no natural ingredients'. It's all part of Rodney's dream. Incidentally the model in the poster is John Sullivan's daughter, Amy.

Trotters' pre-blessed wine

In 'Miami Twice', Del discusses a business opportunity with the vicar who's just christened Damien. Del's describes the pre-blessed wine as the holy version of sliced bread. His ludicrous idea involves the vicar blessing crates of wine by the lorry-load, before it's shipped out across Europe. As Del can secure the wine for £1.39 a bottle, and suggests selling it for £2.50, there's a decent profit in it for everyone. But, as usual, no scheme runs smoothly with the fingerprints of Del Trotter all over it and in this case white wine is delivered, not the red that is essential for Holy Communion.

Trudy

Played by Helen Blizard

The 38-year-old peroxide blonde is seen in The Nag's Head during 'The Chance of a Lunchtime'. Her raucous laughter can be heard throughout the pub. She's so drunk that one of the men who's been drinking with her asks Mike, the landlord, to hire a cab to take her home to Battersea. It turns out she was engaged to Del back in 1970, but they split up after Rodney's pet vole nested in one of her wigs.

Trudy

Played by Lusha Kellgren

Seen initially at the airport in Mallorca, the bespectacled 13-year-old fancies Rodney – who's supposed to be 14 – and asks if he likes Bros. Trudy is also known as 'Little girl' in the episode, 'The Unlucky Winner is…'.

Tuddenham, Peter

Role: Charles

Appeared in 'A Royal Flush'

Peter, who was born in Felixstowe, performed as an amateur stand-up comedian whilst still at school, so it was no surprise that when he completed his education he worked as compère in a seaside show for a season. He was then accepted as a student actor in repertory theatre, working with Harry Hanson's Court Players on Hastings Pier.

His theatrical career was interrupted by the Second World War, during which he served in the army and was posted to work with Stars in Battledress, where he became friends with Terry-Thomas and Charlie Chester. Peter took part in the first show performed on the Normandy beaches, just seven days after D-Day.

Whilst appearing in a show for the troops in Brussels, Peter was asked to introduce Ivor Novello; and after the show, Novello offered Peter the second male lead in a tour of *Dancing Years*, with which he resumed his acting career back on civvy street.

Peter has worked in all mediums, including long spells with the BBC Radio Drama Company, and plenty of TV work, such as 52 episodes of the cult programme *Blake's 7* (he did the voices of three computers), *The Bill*, *Bergerac*, *Campion*, *Lovejoy*, *Nearest and Dearest* and *A Mind to Murder*.

Nowadays Peter is still busy in the profession; he's also a dialect coach for radio and television. In 2002 he spent four months working for Sir Peter Hall at Glyndebourne in this capacity.

Turner, Audrey

Played by Ann Lynn

Raquel's parents turn up at the Trotters' flat for an evening meal in 'Time On Our Hands'; things don't go to plan, especially when Albert gets confused in the kitchen and mixes up the gravy and the coffee!

Turner, Deanne

Make-up designer on four episodes: 'Heroes and Villains', 'Modern Men', 'Time On Our Hands' and 'If They Could See Us Now…!'

Deanne – who was born in London – studied Fine Art at West Sussex College of Art in Brighton before returning to the capital and joining the BBC in 1965. After graduating from the Beeb's make-up school she progressed and became a make-up designer working on period dramas and comedies, including *It Ain't Half Hot, Mum* and the pilot of *Are You Being Served?*

Other productions she worked on during her 30-year career with the Beeb include the feature film *Enchanted April* in 1992, *The Trial* the following year, *Middlemarch*, which won a BAFTA, in 1994 and *A Royal Scandal*, for which she won an RTS Award, in 1995. Deanne now works freelance.

Turner, James

Played by Michael Jayston

Raquel's father, who's in the antiques trade, arrives with his wife, Audrey, for an evening meal in 'Time On Our Hands'. They stay overnight, and when James walks to his car in the morning he notices the valuable 18th-century watch in the Trotters' garage.

Turner, Maisie

Unseen in the sitcom, Maisie is mentioned by Grandad in 'Thicker Than Water'. She had two sons: one by Bernie, who worked at the local market, and another by a guy she met on a chara-banc trip to see the lights.

Turner, Raquel

Played by Tessa Peake-Jones

Raquel is a frustrated actress who has not been fortunate enough to receive the big break for which she has strived for so long.

Entertainment is in her blood: she attended

tap-dancing lessons as a child, and at 17 formed a pop group, 'Double Cream', with a friend. More recently, her life as a thespian has seen her pick up the occasional bit part in inconsequential stage shows, save for her role as a flower-seller in an east coast American tour of *My Fair Lady*, and a review in the Middle East. At the time when she meets Del, she is having to supplement her meagre actress' salary (her last TV appearance was over ten years ago, a one-liner as a lizard person in an episode of *Doctor Who*) by teaching drama on Friday and Saturday evenings and working as a stripagram a further two evenings a week.

Raquel has resigned herself to the fact that she's never going to reach the top of her profession, but she clings on to the faint hope that one day a dream part will come her way – so long as it doesn't involve singing! Her sole appearance as a solo singer was at Reading's The Talk of the Town. The evening turned into a nightmare when she forgot her lines and the tune, resulting in the crowds

> ## à la Del
> ★ ★ ★ ★ ★ ★
> ## 'Potage bonne femme!'
> ('From Prussia with Love')

cheering when 'last orders' was called. All things considered, one can understand her nervousness when she's called out of retirement for a special one-off singing performance at The Starlight Rooms with the farcical Tony Angelino.

Del and Raquel first meet on a blind date, thanks to the Technomatch Matrimonial Agency. She moves into Nelson Mandela House and they go on to have a son, Damien. Although their relation-ship hits stormy waters when Del starts frequenting the gambling clubs, the problems are short-lived. There are further problems, however, when Del discovers that Raquel was once married to Roy Slater. When they separated nearly ten years ago, she reverted to her maiden name, Turner, and replaced her Christian name, Rachel, with her stage name, Raquel.

Raquel's parents failed to support her in her choice of a career on the stage and she didn't speak to them for years. She tries making up for lost time during 'Heroes and Villains' when she receives a call from her mother.

Turpin, Renee

(See 'Renee, Aunt')

Turpin, Ted

Lighting gaffer on one episode: 'The Jolly Boys' Outing'

TV announcer

Played by Patrick Lunt

While Albert sleeps in the armchair, the TV announcer on the six o'clock news reads the head-lines during 'Rodney Come Home'.

TV presenter

(See, 'Edwards, David')

Tyler, Baby

(See 'Boyce, Tyler')

Tyler Street

The bus and coach garage – which Rodney patrols in his role as security officer – is situated in Tyler Street. It's mentioned in 'A Slow Bus to Chingford'.

Tyrrell, Katie

Production secretary on four episodes: S7, episodes 5 & 6; 'Miami Twice' (Parts 1 & 2)

Katie, who was born in London in 1967, worked as a secretary for the chief executive at *The Evening Standard*, then for the deputy editor of the *Daily Mail* before applying for a job at the BBC in 1989. Initially she was employed as secretary for the Secretarial Reserve but moved into production and worked on shows such as *EastEnders; You Rang, M'Lord?; The Real McCoy; Keeping Up Appearances; May to December* and *The Brittas Empire*. Favourite shows she's worked on include *The League of Gentlemen, Fun at the Funeral Parlour, Goodness Gracious Me, People Like Us* and *Chambers*. Katie now works in radio entertainment.

Uditis, Udanne

2nd assistant director on two episodes: 'Miami Twice' (Parts 1 & 2)

Ugandan Morris

Not seen in the sitcom, Ugandan Morris – who's an ex-porter – is mentioned by Del in The Nag's Head during 'Heroes and Villains'. It seems Morris has been deported, together with all the nine-carat gold bracelets that Del had asked him to look after.

Uncle George

(See 'Trotter, George')

'Unlucky Winner is . . . , The'

Original transmission: Sunday 29 January 1989, 7.15 pm

Production dates: Saturday 21 and Sunday 22 January 1989

Original viewing figures: 17 million

Duration: 50 minutes

First repeat: Friday 29 September 1989, 7.30 pm

Subsequent repeats: 5/2/92, 28/1/94, 28/7/99, 23/2/01

CAST

Del Trotter	David Jason
Rodney Trotter	Nicholas Lyndhurst
Uncle Albert	Buster Merryfield
Cassandra	Gwyneth Strong
Mike	Kenneth MacDonald
Mr Perkins	Michael Fenton Stevens
Carmen	Gina Bellman
Trudy	Lusha Kellgren
Walk-ons:	Angie Alaimo and Yvonne Stroud

PRODUCTION TEAM

Written by John Sullivan

Title music arranged and conducted by Ronnie Hazlehurst composed and sung by John Sullivan

Make-up Designer:	Sylvia Thornton
Costume Designer:	Richard Winter
Properties Buyer:	Malcolm Rougvie
Camera Supervisor:	Ken Major
Studio Lighting Director:	Don Babbage
Studio Sound:	Alan Machin
Technical Coordinator:	Reg Poulter
Videotape Editor:	Chris Wadsworth
Production Assistant:	Amita Lochab
Assistant Floor Managers:	Kerry Waddell and Gary Sparks

'The Unlucky Winner is…'

Graphic Designer: . . . . .Iain Greenway
Vision Mixer: . . . . .Heather Gilder
Production Manager: . . . . .Adrian Pegg
Designer: . . . . .Graham Lough
Directed by Tony Dow
Produced by Gareth Gwenlan

> ### à la Del
> ★ ★ ★ ★ ★ ★
> ## 'It's "rienne va plus" as the French would say'
> ('The Miracle of Peckham')

Dels' going through a new phase: he's entering every competition around, especially those advertised on food packets. One competition, organised by Mega Flakes, requests a drawing or painting of a famous landmark, so, unbeknown to Rodney, Del sends off a painting that Rodney did as a schoolboy, entitled 'Marble Arch at Dawn'. When a letter addressed to Rodney drops through the letterbox, Del opens it and discovers his brother has won a Mallorcan holiday, staying in a 5-star hotel and with a week's spending money for the winner and their guest. Del's desperate for a bit of sun, so when Rodney wants to take Cassandra, Del makes out that the competition allows two people to tag along with the winner.

Del doesn't divulge the entire story until the trio arrive at Palma airport: Rodney's painting won first prize in the under-15 category, so he's supposed to be travelling with his parents, with Del acting as his father and Cassandra his common-law stepmother. While Cassandra finds the situation hilarious, Rodney can't believe what's going on; when he

becomes a lifelong member of The Groovy Gang, is given a metal badge to denote the fact and is taken to the hotel on the Fun Bus with all the other children, he has never been so embarrassed in all his life. But Del's devious plan to ensure Rodney passes as a teenager, which involves tampering with his passport, backfires when Rodney has the winning ticket for the Spanish lottery and is too young to claim the prize.

Vahey, Robert

Role: Harry and Dosser
Appeared as Harry in S3, episode 4 and as Dosser in 'A Royal Flush'

Actor and writer Robert Vahey was born in the Wirral in 1932. He trained at RADA before making his professional debut with the Liverpool Repertory Company in a 1954 production of *The Beaux Stratem.*

After spells at several rep companies in the north west of England, he began to receive offers for television, the first being 1957's *Angel Pavement* for the BBC, playing George Smeeth. Since then, he's become a regular face on television, with his favourite roles being Mr Cox in Granada's *The Brothers McGregor* and Bill Sayers in BBC's *Howards' Way.*

Robert, who's a founder member of Brighton Actors' Theatre, continues to work in all mediums, and has recently toured in a new play, *The Farm*, appeared in *The Bill* and recorded a corporate video for Age Concern.

His film work includes appearances in *The Key*, directed by Carol Reed, and *Honest.*

Valentine, Peter

Technical coordinator on one episode: 'Thicker Than Water'

Van Kleefe, Henry

Played by Philip Bond

Seen in 'To Hull and Back', Mr Van Kleefe originates from Amsterdam and is the man that Abdul and Boycie buy diamonds from. They try interesting Del in the deal by asking him to deliver the money (fifty grand) to Van Kleefe in Amsterdam.

Vehicles

For many people, the Trotters' grubby, oil-stained Reliant Regal van – the flagship of TITCO – is an integral part of the show, encapsulating the ambitions and realities of its owners' lives. Del constantly strives, unsuccessfully, to get ahead in life and has delusions of grandeur, signified by the 'New York, Paris, Peckham' motto emblazoned across the side of the clapped-out van which, paradoxically acts as a sharp reminder of just how little he's achieved in the business world.

One could argue that the van has become a star

'Episode Title'

in its own right, with fans here and abroad owning their own models, resplendent in TITCO's yellow livery as they bounce along the highways and byways. It's reputed that over ten vans have been used since the show's inception, but it's more likely to be around half a dozen, although it's difficult to verify, especially as continuity requirements have led to the same registration plates being used on more than one vehicle.

The van makes its debut in 'Big Brother', but it's not until 'The Russians are Coming', when the Trotters are testing their ability to react to the four-minute warning by speeding away from Nelson Mandela House, that we notice the van's registration plate, APL 911H; it's during this episode that we also get our first glimpse of the interior.

By the time 'The Yellow Peril', from the second series, is transmitted, the van is sporting the same plates but has a white bonnet, suggesting a change in vehicle. Such changes were inevitable given that different BBC prop buyers, who were responsible for securing the vehicle for the series, worked on the show over the years. Often the prop buyers had established their own contacts when it came to car hire, and at least three different vehicle hire companies were used for *Only Fools.*

Chris Ferriday was the prop buyer for Series 1, and he turned to Action Cars, based in Harrow, Middlesex. 'During the time I worked on the show, they supplied about three vans because the chassis used to give out and they weren't worth repairing,' recalls Chris. 'The BBC rarely bought a vehicle so Action Cars owned them and the Beeb paid a daily rental charge.'

The specifications handed to Action Cars, who were also used for Series 2, were fairly specific. 'We didn't want a van which was falling apart, nor did we want one which looked too new. Even the signwriting had to look right,' Chris says.

Steven Royffe runs Action Cars nowadays, and can remember the first day he became involved in the series, whilst 'A Touch of Glass' was being filmed. 'Someone else liaised with the property buyer before me, but to my knowledge we supplied about three cars,' he says. 'We got the cars via trade magazines, the *Exchange and Mart*, the *Thames Valley Trader* or by putting the word out to friends to keep their eyes open.

'We got through a few Reliants because they were old vehicles and usually it cost more money to get them up to scratch at MOT time than simply to buy another.' For continuity purposes, certain items were retained whenever a vehicle was scrapped. 'We'd keep the original seats, steering wheel and items like that. We'd also transfer the side panel, which had the signwriting on it, between vehicles,' explains Steven, who also supplied one of Boycie's Mercedes, which, at the time, belonged to Doug Sandford, a company director.

By the third series, a Reliant with a different registration is seen, although it was still supplied by Action Cars. DHV 938D makes its debut in 'Healthy Competition', and the registration plates are used to the current day. The final car (officially registered as NJB 33L) that Action Cars supplied to the BBC was sold in 1987 to Robert Hughes, a car dealer in Weybridge, but is now housed in Peter Nelson's 'Cars of the Stars' motor museum at Keswick. As well as owning the Reliant Regal Supervan 3, the museum boasts a collection of 24 vehicles (with another 36 in storage), all previously used in television shows and films, including the car from *Chitty Chitty Bang Bang*, Kitt from *Knight Rider*, *The A-Team* van, Emma Peel's Lotus from *The Avengers*, the car from *The Flintstones*, the Batmobiles, the Thunderbirds' Rolls Royce, Fab1, and *The Saint*'s original Volvo. Peter has travelled the world trying to track down the vehicles. For more information view the museum's website www.carsofthestars.com or phone 017687 73757.

Peter was scanning the pages of *Classic Car* magazine when he noticed an advert for the Trotters' yellow Reliant van, which Robert Hughes was selling for £995. 'I bought it over the phone and simply told Robert to send it up; I wasn't even bothered what condition it was in, it was just a vehicle I wanted.' When the car arrived at Keswick, Peter was pleased with the state of the van. 'It wasn't too bad; it was certainly a runner.'

Robert Hughes had acquired the Reliant Regal from Action Cars, who'd been leasing it to the BBC whenever they required it for filming. He was due to attend a 21st birthday party and wanted to make an impression by arriving in a more unusual form of transport. 'Part of my business is involved in hiring cars to production companies direct, or leasing them out to firms who source vehicles for the TV companies. I was dropping a car off to Action Cars at Harrow when I suddenly saw the Reliant van. First of all, I asked if I could borrow it for the party, but soon got the impression that it was no longer needed by the BBC and ended up buying the vehicle for £350.' Robert had big plans for the car. 'It was a very smart party I was attending, marquee and all,' he explains. 'I had a bright idea of driving across the lawn to the marquee with all the smoke pouring out!'

When 'Dates' and Series 6 were commissioned, Malcolm Rougvie was allocated to the sitcom. In need of another Reliant, with the previous vehicle having been sold, he visited Keswick and photographed Peter Nelson's van for reference pur-

used it with David Jason for a couple of charity events. They both still run, and the one I have on display (NJB 33L) has about 60,000 miles on the clock.'

For latter episodes, including the 1996 Christmas Trilogy in 1996, and recent instalments, MGM Cars supplied the vehicles. Marvin George was the prop buyer with responsibility for the vehicles on the three recent episodes: 'The main cars I had to get were the Capri and the Reliant. I normally use Action Cars, but as MGM were used for the Christmas Trilogy, back in 1996, it seemed logical to go back to them.'

Tom Dillon, who'd worked with Bob Randall at TeleFilm Cars before branching out on his own, runs MGM Cars from offices in Elstree and Burnley, but he still remembers the day Malcolm Rougvie asked TeleFilm to supply the first lime green Capri. 'After we'd sprayed it green we looked around for accessories to suit the style they were trying to create, so we put a vinyl roof on it and other little touches, like the arm hanging out the back of the boot; we were like kids, really, spending all our money on tacky stuff, which fitted the image at the time.'

The first Capri fell into disrepair, and a gap between series meant it wasn't feasible or worthwhile financially to bring the car up to MOT standard. 'Parts of the car, such as the wings, were rusted through, so we didn't bother,' recalls Tom, who had to find another model when a further series was commissioned. 'We kept hold of all the tacky items from the first car, all the added extras, and put them on the new vehicle.'

During the years, Tom has been supplying the vehicles to the production, he hasn't experienced any particular difficulties, but does recall an incident involving the Capri. 'I remember when a lot of spotlights were first fixed on the car; we had plenty of problems with that because the battery started to cook! There were about a dozen lights and when they were on, the battery was quickly drained, so much so that the wires started to melt because they couldn't take the amps.

'If the director sees the bonnet up on a car, especially if he's not car-minded, he'll think the vehicle has broken down, which doesn't seem good from our point of view. So we bought a new battery at lunchtime and it got us through the day's filming, leaving us the evening to rewire it with heavier wire which could take the load.'

Of course, no one will forget the Trotters' stretch limo-style van, which was used in the trailers for the 2001 Christmas Special, 'If They Could See Us Now…!'. Perry Aghajanoff, the Appreciation Society's president, received a call from the BBC, asking if they could borrow a Reliant van and take

it to Monte Carlo. Society member John Mansfield duly obliged.

Digital effects artist Aron Baxtor, from Condor Post Production, got to work and mapped digital images of the side of the van on to film to create the body of the limo. Richard Heeley, the BBC producer behind the trailer, told The *Evening Standard*: 'It's quite a good double joke. First of all you see the apparently normal Regal shot from behind but juxtaposed with a Porsche and a Ferrari in a glamorous Monte Carlo setting. Then you see it from the front. Those shots in themselves look funny but the punchline comes when you see the shot from the side and it turns out to be a limo.'

The other main vehicles used in the series:

OXL825E Ford Cortina (Mark II)

This black convertible with a white bonnet appeared briefly in 'Go West Young Man'. Del bought it from Boycie for the knock-down price of £25, though it was a rust bucket with bald tyres and defective brakes. Its mileage had been scaled down to 98,000, and it ended up at Boycie's because he'd taken it in part-exchange for a Vanden Plas. After pegging the milometer back to 23,000, Del sells it on to an Australian, complete with two weeks' MOT, for a tidy profit.

à la Del

★ ★ ★ ★ ★

'Chamboussiz nouvelle'

('The Longest Night')

---

poses. Then he purchased another van, which was dark red, for £100 and arranged for Bob Randall at TeleFim Cars, based in Burnley, to spray it yellow and bring it up to roadworthy condition. Bob recalls the vehicle being used in a humpbacked bridge scene in 'Dates'. 'When the van landed it virtually fell to bits, so it's just as well we had a standby vehicle to use for the rest of the filming.'

At one point in Series 6, it looked as if the car was heading for the scrapyard in the sky when John Sullivan considered blowing it up during 'Danger UXD'; however, he had second thoughts when he realised they wouldn't have been able to use the van again in subsequent series.

One of the vehicles (officially registered as WTF 946L) used during the sixth series is also now owned by Peter Nelson, who bought it in January 1989. 'The BBC used one of the vehicles not so long ago to photograph for publicity purposes, and I've

By the time the Christmas Trilogy was being recorded, with the Trotters becoming millionaires, Tom didn't think the Capri would be needed any further so sold the car. It's now owned by *Only Fools* fan Ian Nixon, who loans the vehicle to the Beeb whenever they need it.

The latest Reliant had been presented to John Sullivan after filming had been completed for 'Time On Our Hands', so Marvin had to arrange for it to be collected from John's garage, where it had been sitting for five years. 'It hadn't been used at all, so I got it delivered to MGM Cars, who restored it and put it through its MOT.'

'It needed a bit of welding,' says Tom, 'and the bodywork needed patching up a little because it had been bashed about. But that's the one which has been used since the mid-1980s. Whereas early models didn't last long, I thought it was best we picked a van in good condition which would last.'

UYP694M E-Type Jag

Seen initially at Boycie's garage, this white convertible is a present for his 'bit on the side'. Del ends up looking after it for a while and prangs it.

DJH921B Vauxhall Velox (Mark III)

Another rust bucket, sporting a new Playboy bunny motif on the chrome grill, this bottle-green car is driven by Del to the Peckham and Camberwell Chamber of Trade Dinner/Dance in 'Cash and Curry'. He later sells the motor in an attempt to raise the two grand that he needs in order to profit from the Kuvera statuette affair.

OLD190P Ford Escort (Mark II)

Eric the policeman is driving this police car in 'The Russians are Coming' when he pulls the Trotters over for speeding.

UYD177R Ford Capri Ghia

Referred to as the green prat mobile, the Capri Ghia is first seen in 'He Ain't Heavy, He's My

Uncle'. With Raquel pregnant, Del acquires the vehicle for £400 from Boycie so that she never has to venture out on foot in the vicinity, which is rife with crime. What he doesn't realise is that she may be in more danger driving the Capri, especially as it was heading for the scrap yard. Originally light green, the passage of time – and neglect – has left the paintwork dull and uninspiring, just like its performance. It's seen from time to time throughout the sitcom, including scenes at the allotments in 'Mother Nature's Son', during 'Fatal Extraction' and in the earlier special, 'Miami Twice'. More recently it's seen being driven along the esplanade at Weston-super-Mare in 'If They Could See Us Now…!', although by this point the registration plates have changed to CCR 412W.

CCR412W Ford Capri Ghia

(See above entry)

OLO77W Ford Cortina (Mark IV)

This gold-coloured car is used by Mr Ram in 'Cash and Curry'.

KCH106 Leyland Bus (Type PD2/12)

This double-decker which Del borrows to run his tours of ethnic London was built in 1956. It was originally owned by Trent Motor Traction of Derby, who operated the vehicle until 1968. It was bought by Grey-Green, who originally planned to use it as a publicity vehicle, hence the open-top. It came back into service in 1979 and was used for tours and private hire. It was also used by football clubs for their tours when parading a newly acquired trophy. In 1991 the bus was bought by a part-time driver, who later sold it on to a sightseeing firm, Big Bus Company, who re-registered it as XMD 47A.

ULR981X Council roadsweeper

The yellow council-owned roadsweeper is seen in 'Ashes to Ashes', sucking up the ashes of Trigger's late grandfather.

ROY673W Volvo

The blue Volvo is towed back to Ridgemere Hall by the Trotters in 'A Touch of Glass'. It belongs to Lady Ridgemere.

MY CAPRI GHIA

Ian Nixon, a lifelong fan of *Only Fools and Horses*, currently owns the green Capri (CCR 412W) which has been used in later episodes of the show. Here he answers some questions about being the owner of the vehicle.

When did you buy the vehicle?
June 1998.

Where did you get it?
Elstree Film Studios.

How much did you pay?
£500.

When you bought the vehicle, did you know it was the one used in *Only Fools*?
Yes. There were three Capris used in *Only Fools* over the years. As each one was scrapped, parts were moved on to the next car. My Capri has the interior from the first one and the tailgate from the second. I'm quite lucky because it's the only one left. That's why I'm going to look after it and keep it on the road, although there will probably be more welding needed underneath fairly soon!

How did you come to own the car?
My Father had gone to Elstree to hire film props and was offered the car by an employee there. I advised him to buy it, and so did his friends who'd seen it on TV. He made the deal and I went to Elstree to pick the car up. As soon as I saw the car I knew that I could do something with it, so I bought it from him.

Ian Nixon with his Capri

Have you changed the registration or does it still have the original plates?
Yes, it's the original registration number.

Do you know the ownership history of the car?
Yes. Before it was used for filming it was owned by someone from Westcliff-on-Sea, Essex.

Did you have to carry out any essential repairs when you acquired the Capri?
Quite a lot, but it's now pretty reliable.

Do you get people asking about it in the street?
All the time, and you can see that some people don't believe it's the one from the telly, which makes me laugh to myself.

NLD702V Ford Transit

Brendan O'Shaughnessy's blue transit van is seen outside The Nag's Head in 'Who's a Pretty Boy?'.

UVH643V Ford Escort (Mark II)

Seen in Boycie's salesroom, the gold-coloured Escort is on sale for £2195. Boycie is trying to sell it to Mr and Mrs Biggastaff when Del phones in 'To Hull and Back'.

G831YWL Leyland Daf Van

The blue Leyland Daf is the van that Denzil uses for his courier service, Transworld Express.

TJT705 Jaguar XJ6

Arnie's Jag is seen in 'Chain Gang'.

F805XBV Jaguar

The ice blue Jag is owned by Alan Parry and seen in 'The Chance of a Lunchtime'.

Do you use the car as a local run-around or do you only bring it out on special occasions?
Now it is back on the road I use it most days.

I notice the car appeared in the Christmas 2001 episode, 'If They Could See Us Now…!', but has it been used by the BBC on other occasions since you've owned it?
No.

How were you approached for the 'If They Could…' episode?
MGM Cars, the former owners, got in contact with me shortly before the filming started.

Did you go along to the filming?
No, but I would like a photo of David Jason with the car; so if you read this David I *would* be grateful.

Have you received lots of offers from people wanting to purchase the car?
Yes, all the time.

Would you ever part with it?
Maybe.

What do you most like about it?
The furry gear knob.

What annoys you the most about it?
The car's handling.

Are there any other interesting stories concerning the car?
One night I went out with my cousin and we drove

around Central London. As we went around Belgrave Square, passing an embassy on the way with a policeman on duty outside, I decided to try out the car's smoke-screen facility. This works by pressing a button in the car, which in turn sprays oil into the engine, causing the exhaust to smoke.

We rounded the Square again to the sound of Del's musical horn, while my cousin enthusiastically pressed the button. Clouds and clouds of smoke belched from the car's exhaust creating a smog; in fact, so much oil was used that the car stopped running! After some time turning the engine over, while London cabs backed up the road to avoid the smoke, we got the car started and proceeded on our journey, pleased with our results. Unfortunately we were not aware of the oncoming police car, which had been notified of our whereabouts and pulled us over. The policeman said: 'All I could see was this green Capri coming out of this ball of smoke.' Luckily, they didn't seem too upset and with a bit of persuasion allowed us to go on our way.'

130SKN Rolls Royce Phantom 6

The hearse is seen in 'The Frog's Legacy', when Rodney has been fooled into taking a job as chief mourner. At the time the vehicle was owned by Saul Hunnaball, whose company, Hunnaball Funeral Services, helped the BBC during the making of the 1987 Christmas Special. He sold the hearse about eight years ago to someone in Kent. The vehicle, which was worth approximately £40,000, was classed as a restricted heavy goods vehicle.

C192MCW Mark VI Granada Grosvenor

The car following the hearse (above) was also owned by the Hunnaballs.

E870KJD VW Golf

Cassandra drives this maroon VW away from the church where Damien's christening has taken place in 'Miami Twice'.

A3 TWR Jaguar XK8

Rodney's Jag is seen in 'Time On Our Hands' and was originally supplied by a Jaguar dealer in Oxford.

Ventham, Wanda

Role: Pamela Parry

Appeared in S6, episode 6; 'The Jolly Boys' Outing'; 'Miami Twice' (Part 1) and 'Mother Nature's Son'

Wanda studied stage design at art school before enrolling at the Central School of Drama in London. She made her professional debut in 1958, and repertory theatre dominated the early days of her career, at venues including Bath and Cardiff.

On stage, she's been seen in shows such as *Watch it Sailor* at London's Apollo Theatre, and *Two into One* at the capital's Shaftesbury Theatre.

Her film work includes productions like *The Knock, Mister Ten Per Cent, Doctor Kronos* and *Mrs Caldicot's Cabbage War*, while her host of television roles extend from two series as Sylvia in *Executive Stress*, Alexandra in *Out of the Shadows,* and Mrs Ridge in *All Creatures Great and Small*, to Marion Kershaw in *Boon*, three series as Rosie in *Next of Kin*, and Fiona in *Heartbeat*. Her favourite television role, meanwhile, was Ann Shepherd in *The Lotus Eaters* for the BBC.

Recent jobs have seen her appear in the film *Affair of the Necklace*, and *Coupling* for TV.

Veronique

During 'Fatal Extraction', when Del is sat in Sid's Café trying to remember the name of one of his old girlfriends, Rodney suggests Veronique from Woolworths. She is not seen in the sitcom.

Vet

Played by John D Collins

Mr Collis, the bespectacled vet, examines Duke, the Great Dane, in 'Sleeping Dogs Lie'.

LOANING MY HEARSE TO THE BBC

★ ★ ★ ★ ★ ★

'The Frog's Legacy'

Saul Hunnaball was 18 when the family business (a firm of undertakers) helped the BBC during the making of 'The Frog's Legacy'.

'An agent for the BBC was asked to source a limousine, empty coffin and some flowers, and he ended up on our doorstep. At the time, we were able to spare a couple of vehicles, which was very exciting.

'I thoroughly enjoyed *Only Fools and Horses*, so it was quite an experience to actually appear in one of the episodes. One thing that amazed me was that for the 30 seconds or so that we were seen on the screen, it took about three days to get right. Something else that was intriguing was being around people you felt you knew because you'd seen them countless times on the television.

'I was seen driving the hearse, which was worth about £40,000. Sat next to me was Adam Hussein, playing a character called Mr Jahan, who was boosted up on some cushions so that he looked more prominent than me; I just sat there with a red face!

'One of the most difficult things was when the production team needed a shot of Mr Jahan talking to me. Although it was a narrow street, they decided to lay a kind of track for the cameras to roll on so that they could shoot Mr Jahan through the window. But as there was a heavy camber on the road, and we were driving uphill slightly, it was almost impossible to get the shot they wanted, especially as we had to be parallel to the camera and so on. In the end, they opened the door of the hearse and the cameraman was basically hanging on to the door-frame with a camera on his shoulder, whilst we drove up the road.

'I think we spent the best part of a day just going up and down the road; you felt a tremendous pressure to get it right for the production team. The lengths they go to to get everything right are amazing. There were houses for sale in the street we were filming in and someone had to go along and take off all the addresses and phone numbers from the "For Sale" signs; they even put tape over our company's name on the side of the hearse. Overall, it was a very exciting occasion.' **SAUL HUNNABALL**

Vi

Played by Lyn Langridge

Vi is one of Del's neighbours who lives on his estate. Del wakes her up one night when he returns home drunk after yet another visit to the local casino.

Vic

Not seen in the sitcom, Vic is the subject of much conversation during 'Diamonds are for Heather'. He's married to Heather, whom Del falls in love with, but even though Vic walked out on his wife and kid 18 months ago, perhaps as a result of depression caused by his long-term unemployment, the fact that Heather keeps his photo on the mantelpiece shows she still feels for her husband. Unfortunately, Del failed to spot these tell-tale signs, so is dumbfounded when Heather announces that she's going to move to Southampton to live with Vic, who claims to have his life back in order. He has a decent flat and a few weeks employment as an in-store Santa, which he feels is enough to offer Heather and Darren security.

Vicar

Played by Angus Mackay

In 'The Frog's Legacy', the vicar of St Mary's in Hampshire is in charge of the wedding of Trigger's niece, Lisa, and Andrew. He also accepts one of Del's Rajah computers for a trial period, but soon realises that he has no need for it. Del is reluctant to take it back, however, and suggests he puts it in a jumble sale.

Vicar

Played by John Pennington

Seen in 'Strained Relations', the vicar oversees the service at Grandad's funeral. He is also seen in the short Christmas sketch, 'Christmas Trees', where he's overjoyed at Rodney's generosity at donating a Christmas tree to the local church.

Vicar

Played by Rex Robinson

The vicar, who married Boycie and Marlene 20 years ago, is invited to their anniversary do in 'Video Nasty'.

Vicar

Played by Treva Etienne

The vicar conducts the christening of Baby Damien at the beginning of 'Miami Twice'. He later finds himself dragged in to a business deal with Del, which involves blessing Romanian wine and distributing it throughout the country for other churches to use during Holy Communion. As usual, the project doesn't run to plan.

Vicky

Played by Kim Clifford

Vicky is the barmaid at The Nag's Head in 'To Hull and Back'.

Vicky

Played by Sarah Duncan

Seen in 'A Royal Flush', the pretty Vicky – who grew up in Berkshire – has been living in London for three months. She has a stall at the market selling her own art masterpieces.

After completing her education at a Swiss finishing school, Vicky studied at the Milan School of Art for two years before enjoying a spell at the Sorbonne. She is following in the footsteps of her mother, an artist whose work was exhibited at the Royal Academy before her untimely death on an Austrian skiing holiday, when Vicky was just 12. Vicky's full name is Lady Victoria Marsham-Hales and her father is none other than the Duke of Maylebury.

Vicky – who drives a blue Mercedes, which was a birthday present – starts chatting to Rodney at the market, but when he finds out what prices she's charging for her paintings, he tells her she's probably at the wrong market and should try Portobello Road. Due to attend the New York School of Art for a year, Vicky becomes friendly with Rodney and invites him along to her Hampshire home for the weekend. But when Del tags along, the weekend turns into a nightmare for his brother, and his brush with royalty is short-lived.

Videos

All the videos listed are produced by BBC Worldwide unless otherwise stated.

'A ROYAL FLUSH'
Catalogue No   BBCV6370
Duration   76 mins
Release date   2/2/98
Episode included   The 1986 Christmas Special

'BIG BROTHER'
Catalogue No   BBCV4678
Duration   91 mins
Release date   7/10/91
Episodes included   'Big Brother', 'Cash and Curry',
                    'Go West Young Man'

'CHAIN GANG'
Catalogue No   BBCV5296
Duration   149 mins
Release date   6/6/94
Episodes included   Two episodes from Series 6 and one
                    from Series 7: 'Chain Gang', 'Little
                    Problems' and 'Stage Fright'

ONLY FOOLS AND HORSES – COMPLETE SERIES (BOX SET)
Catalogue No   BBCV7082
Release date   30/10/00
Episodes included   A seven-episode video: the complete
                    first series and the 1981 Christmas
                    Special, 'Christmas Crackers
Description   A WHSmith exclusive

'BIG BROTHER' – COLLECTORS' EDITION (VOLUME 1)
Catalogue No   BBCV6215
Duration   90 mins
Release date   22/9/97
Episodes included   'Big Brother', 'Go West Young Man'
                    and 'Cash and Curry'
Description   Released via the Book Club and
                    retailed at £10.99

'THE SECOND TIME AROUND' – COLLECTORS' EDITION (VOLUME 2)
Catalogue No   BBCV6216
Duration   90 mins
Release date   22/9/97
Episodes included   'The Second Time Around', 'A Slow
                    Bus to Chingford' and 'The Russians
                    are Coming'
Description   Released via the Book Club and
                    retailed at £10.99

'A LOSING STREAK' – COLLECTORS' EDITION (VOLUME 3)
Catalogue No   BBCV6217
Duration   91 mins
Release date   22/9/97
Episodes included   'A Losing Streak', 'No Greater Love…'
                    and 'The Yellow Peril'
Description   Released via the Book Club and
                    retailed at £10.99

'CHRISTMAS CRACKERS' – COLLECTORS' EDITION (VOLUME 4)
Catalogue No   BBCV6218
Duration   88 mins
Release date   22/9/97
Episodes included   'Christmas Crackers', 'The Long Legs
                    of the Law' and 'Ashes to Ashes'
Description   Released via the Book Club and
                    retailed at £10.99

'DATES'
Catalogue No   BBCV5909
Duration   80 mins
Release date   2/9/96
Episode included   The 1988 Christmas Special

'FATAL EXTRACTION'
Catalogue No   BBCV6716
Duration   83 mins
Release date   7/6/99
Episode included   The 1993 Christmas Special

'HEROES AND VILLAINS'
Catalogue No   BBCV6363
Duration   59 mins
Release date   6/10/97
Episode included   The first part of the
                    1996 Christmas Trilogy

'HOMESICK'
Catalogue No   BBCV4747
Duration   118 mins
Release date   1992
Episodes included   The first four episodes from
                    Series 3: 'Homesick',
                    'Healthy Competition',
                    'Friday the 14th' and
                    'Yesterday Never Comes'

'MAY THE FORCE BE WITH YOU'
Catalogue No   BBCV4748
Duration   118 mins
Release date   1/4/92
Episodes included   Three episodes taken from
                    the Series 3: 'May the Force
                    be with You', 'Wanted' and
                    'Who's a Pretty Boy?' and
                    the 1993 Christmas Special:
                    'Thicker Than Water'

'MIAMI TWICE – THE MOVIE'
Catalogue No   BBCV6598
Duration   140 mins
Release date   12/10/98
Episodes included   The two-part 1991 movie

'MODERN MEN'
Catalogue No   BBCV6364
Duration   58 mins
Release date   20/10/97
Episode included   The second part of
                    the 1996 Christmas Trilogy

'MOTHER NATURE'S SON'
Catalogue No   BBCV6792
Duration   65 mins
Release date   1/11/99
Episode included   The 1992 Christmas Special

'RODNEY COME HOME'
Catalogue No   BBCV6707
Duration   123 mins
Release date   1/2/99
Episodes included   The 1990 Christmas Special
                    was rather oddly issued with
                    'The Sky's the Limit', episode 1
                    of Series 7

SERIES 1 BOX SET
Catalogue No   BBCV6909
Duration   214 mins
Release date   1/11/99
Deletion Date   6/4/01 (in UK)
Description   Videos and playing cards in a
                    Reliant tin box, later a cardboard box

THE COMPLETE ONLY FOOLS AND HORSES – SERIES 1
Catalogue No   BBCV4933
Duration   214 mins
Release date   6/10/96
Episodes included   Series 1 and 'Christmas Crackers' –
                    released on two cassettes

THE COMPLETE *ONLY FOOLS AND HORSES* – SERIES 2
Catalogue No	BBCV5137
Duration	231 mins
Release date	7/10/96
Episodes included	Series 2 and 'Diamonds are for Heather' – released on two cassettes

THE COMPLETE *ONLY FOOLS AND HORSES* – SERIES 3
Catalogue No	BBCV5388
Duration	236 mins
Release date	19/9/94
Episodes included	Series 3 and 'Thicker Than Water' – released on two cassettes

***ONLY FOOLS AND HORSES* (SLIP CASE) – CHRISTMAS SPECIAL**
Catalogue No	BBCV6367
Duration	174 mins
Release date	3/11/97
Episodes Included	The 1996 Christmas Trilogy: 'Heroes and Villains', 'Modern Men' and 'Time On Our Hands'
Description	One episode per video in a 'Trotter van' box

SPECIAL LIMITED EDITION BOX SET (CHRISTMAS SPECIAL 1996)
Catalogue No	BBCV6366
Duration	174 mins
Release date	6/10/97
Deletion Date	10/2/98
Episodes Included	The 1996 Christmas Trilogy
Description	Sold in a suitcase-styled box set with a t-shirt

'STRAINED RELATIONS'
Catalogue No	BBCV6104
Duration	87 mins
Release date	2/6/97
Episodes included	Three episodes from Series 4: 'Strained Relations', 'Hole in One' and 'It's Only Rock and Roll'

'THE CHANCE OF A LUNCHTIME'
Catalogue No	BBCV5570
Duration	100 mins
Release date	6/3/95
Episodes included	Two episodes from Series 7: 'The Chance of a Lunchtime' and 'He Ain't Heavy, He's My Uncle'.

THE COMPLETE *ONLY FOOLS AND HORSES* – SERIES 4
Catalogue No	BBCV7026
Duration	180 mins
Release date	5/3/01
Episodes included:	All of Series 4

THE COMPLETE *ONLY FOOLS AND HORSES* – SERIES 5
Catalogue No	BBCV6997
Duration	175 mins
Release date	2/5/00
Episodes included:	All of Series 5

THE COMPLETE *ONLY FOOLS AND HORSES* – SERIES 6
Catalogue No	BBCV6817
Duration	300 mins
Release date	4/10/99
Episodes included:	All of Series 6

THE COMPLETE *ONLY FOOLS AND HORSES* – SERIES 7
Catalogue No	BBCV7015
Duration	300 mins
Release date	30/10/00
Episodes included:	All of Series 7

'THE FROG'S LEGACY'
Catalogue No	BBCV5799
Duration	59 mins
Release date	4/3/96
Episode included	The 1987 Christmas Special

'THE JOLLY BOYS' OUTING'
Catalogue No	BBCV5421
Duration	80 mins
Release date	7/11/94
Episode included	The 1989 Christmas Special

'THE LONG LEGS OF THE LAW'
Catalogue No	BBCV4702
Duration	118 mins
Release date	4/11/91
Episodes included	The first four episodes of Series 2: 'The Long Legs of the Law', 'Ashes to Ashes', 'A Losing Streak' and 'No Greater Love…'

'THE SECOND TIME AROUND'
Catalogue No	BBCV4679
Duration	125 mins
Release date	7/10/91
Episodes included	Three episodes from Series 1: 'The Second Time Around', 'A Slow Bus to Chingford' and 'The Russians are Coming', plus the 1981 Christmas Special, 'Christmas Crackers'

THE VERY BEST OF *ONLY FOOLS AND HORSES* – 'DANGER UXD'
Catalogue No	BBCV5150
Duration	154 mins.
Release date	1/11/93
Episodes included	Three episodes from Series 6 and 7: 'Danger UXD', 'Sickness and Wealth' and 'The Class of '62

THE VERY BEST OF *ONLY FOOLS AND HORSES* – 'TEA FOR THREE'
Catalogue No	BBCV4849
Duration	148 mins
Release date	5/10/92
Episodes included	Five episodes from Series 4 and 5: 'Tea for Three', 'Happy Returns', 'The Longest Night', 'Sleeping Dogs Lie' and 'From Prussia with Love'

THE VERY BEST OF *ONLY FOOLS AND HORSES* – 'YUPPY LOVE'
Catalogue No	BBCV4855
Duration	147 mins
Release date	5/10/92
Episodes included	Three episodes from Series 6 and 7: 'Yuppy Love', 'The Unlucky Winner is…' and 'Three Men, a Woman and a Baby'

'THE YELLOW PERIL'
Catalogue No	BBCV4703
Duration	115 mins
Release date	4/11/91
Episodes included	Three episodes from the closing stages of Series 2: 'The Yellow Peril', 'It Never Rains…' and 'A Touch of Glass' plus the 1982 Christmas Special: 'Diamonds are for Heather'

'TIME ON OUR HANDS'
Catalogue No	BBCV6365
Duration	58 mins
Release date	3/11/97
Episode included	The final episode from the 1996 Christmas Trilogy

'TO HULL AND BACK'
Catalogue No	BBCV5697
Duration	90 mins
Release date	2/4/95
Episode included	The 1985 Christmas Special

'WATCHING THE GIRLS GO BY'
Catalogue No	BBCV6252
Duration	147 mins
Release date	1/6/98
Episodes included	Two episodes from Series 4: 'Watching the Girls Go By' and 'As One Door Closes'; three episodes from Series 5: 'The Miracle of Peckham', 'Video Nasty' and 'Who Wants to be a Millionaire'

***ONLY FOOLS AND HORSES* – SELECTION BOX**
Catalogue No	BBCV7051
Duration	29 mins
Release date	26/3/01
Description	All-time favourite clips chosen and introduced by celebrities for a 1997 tribute show.

'IF THEY COULD SEE US NOW…!'
Catalogue No	BBCV7289
Duration	70 mins
Release date	28/10/02
Episode included	The 2001 Christmas Special

***ONLY FOOLS AND HORSES* – THE COLLECTORS' EDITION**
Description
The complete set of episodes are presented in chronological order via 30 videos. Only available from Britannia. When you order the first video, at a cost of £10.99 (plus £3.28 p&p), the next three in the series are free. Videos thereafter cost £10.99 (plus £1.47 p&p). Enquiries: call Britannia on 08701 223311.

The satellite shopping channel, QVC, has also recently sold the entire seven series in specially designed packaging in the form of a suitcase, price £140.

A WHSMITH EXCLUSIVE
Catalogue No	(BBCV6370),(BBCV5799) and (BBCV5697)
Release date	26/10/98
Episodes included	'A Royal Flush', 'The Frog's Legacy' and 'To Hull and Back'
Description	Three videos in a beige slip case, price £24.99

A WOOLWORTH'S BOX-SET
Catalogue Nos	(BBCV5909), (BBCV6104) and (BBCV6252)
Release date	2/11/98
Episode included	'Dates', 'Strained Relations' and 'Watching the Girls Go By'
Description	Three videos in a box-set, price £24.99

A 14-VIDEO BOX-SET
Release date	28/10/02
Episodes included	The first seven series together with 'Christmas Crackers'
Description	Issued by HEC (Home Entertainment Corporation, a mail order company), price £139.99

DAILY MIRROR PROMOTION
In 1996, readers of the *Daily Mirror* and the *Sunday Mirror* were able to take part in a special promotion. The correct number of tokens entitled readers to claim two separate videos: video one (BBCM 6804) offered the episode, 'Second Time Around', while the second video (BBCM 6566) contained 'A Touch of Glass'.

★ ★ ★ CUT SCENE! CUT SCENE! ★ ★ ★

CUT FROM 'THE 1997 TRIBUTE SHOW'

John Sullivan says: 'This is Boycie's full speech for the 1997 tribute show; it was cut to pieces before recording and then cut even more after recording.'

BOYCIE'S DRAWING ROOM. NIGHT
ALL WE NEED IS A CORNER SET – FLOCK WALLPAPER – A HIGH-BACK LEATHER REPRODUCTION ANTIQUE SIDE TABLE UPON WHICH STANDS A GLASS OF COGNAC AND A CIGAR IN AN ASHTRAY.
BOYCIE IS SEATED IN CHAIR WEARING A SILK DRESSSING GOWN, CRAVAT, ETC, HAVING ANOTHER OF HIS PONCEY EVENINGS. HE IS READING THE LATEST *AUTO-TRADER* MAGAZINE. HE BECOMES AWARE OF OUR PRESENCE.
BOYCIE Oh, good evening and welcome to Boyce House. It's not often one gets the chance to pay tribute to two men of outstanding talent and achievement, and tonight is no exception, because I want to talk to you about the Trotter brothers. I've known Del Boy all my life. From those early days when I'd pop round his flat when father was out late-night shoplifting, right up

until recently – when he became a millionaire! And in many ways he's been like a brother to me: unreliable, argumentative and ungrateful. Del could be outspoken – although I've never actually seen anyone manage it. Rodney also spoke his mind, which tended to limit the conversation somewhat. Rodney was something of a character. He was the kind of man who could brighten up a party just by leaving. But, he was a lot smarter than he looked – but then again, he would have to be, wouldn't he? Derek was always very concerned with image. I think he got it from his late mother who, if my memory serves me well, used to look like Cruela de Ville on bingo night. Imagine a Tom Jones fan with attitude. I like to think that God put the Trotters on this earth to teach us that not everything in life has a purpose.
INTO FILM

OUT OF FILM AND INTO: BOYCIE'S DRAWING ROOM. NIGHT
BOYCIE Well, there you have it. That was the Trotters. (THIS FOLLOWING SEQUENCE IS ONE OF INCREASING TEETH-GRINDING JEALOUSY) And now, of course, they're

stinking rich and doing all the things other people can only dream of: holidays in Barbados, private boxes at Ascot, Ferraris – and I say – good luck to 'em.
(HIS CIGAR BREAKS IN HIS TEETH AND HE HAS TO SPIT THE TOBACCO OUT) Money hasn't changed Del Boy – he's still the same sarky git he always used to be. His attitude to money is the same as it is to fashion – it means nothing to him! I can imagine the old dog now, sitting in some plush New York restaurant proving that bad taste is all in the mind – usually in the mind of the people around him. And Rodney? He's most probably skulking around some Parisian art gallery, because he's into art. I remember him once showing me an abstract picture in a magazine and telling me what it all symbolised. It turned out to be an advert for a pizza. (LAUGHS) But I think the Trotters should be an inspiration to us all – if they can make it, anyone can! And now I hope that their millions will bring them a happy and fruitful life. Good night.
BOYCIE CLEARS FRAME.
BOYCIE (CALLS) Marlene! Where's the Prozac?

'Video Nasty'

Original transmission: Sunday 28 September 1986, 8.35 pm
Production date: Sunday 29 June 1986
Original viewing figures: 17.5 million
Duration: 30 minutes
First repeat: Thursday 8 October 1987, 8.30 pm
Subsequent repeat: 16/7/89, 12/3/98, 13/12/00

CAST
Del Trotter . . . . .David Jason
Rodney Trotter . . . . .Nicholas Lyndhurst
Uncle Albert . . . . .Buster Merryfield
Trigger .Roger Lloyd Pack
Mike . . . . .Kenneth MacDonald
Boycie .John Challis
Marlene . . . . .Sue Holderness
Mickey Pearce . . . . .Patrick Murray
Amanda . . . . .Dawn Perllman
Vicar . . . . .Rex Robinson
Tony (Chinese takeaway owner) Chua Kahjoo
Walk-ons: . . . . .Desmond Williams, Jane Linter, Robin Squire, Michael Hizer, Seamus Fox, Bob Appleby, Geoffrey Cole, Avril Kay, Errol Shaker and Diane Gurney.

PRODUCTION TEAM
Written by John Sullivan
Title music arranged and conducted by Ronnie Hazlehurst composed and sung by John Sullivan
Audience Warm-up: . . . . .Felix Bowness
Make-up Designer: . . . . .Elaine Smith
Costume Designer: . . . . .Robin Stubbs
Properties Buyer: . . . . .Maura Laverty

Camera Supervisor: . . . . .Ken Major
Studio Lighting Director: . . . . .Henry Barber
Studio Sound: . . . . .Anthony Philpot
Technical Coordinator: . . . . . .Nick Moore
Videotape Editor: . . . . .Chris Wadsworth
Production Assistants: . . . . . . .Rowena Painter
   and Alexandra Todd
Assistant Floor Manager: . . . .Adrian Pegg
Graphic Designer: . . . . .Andrew Smee
Vision Mixer: . . . . .Heather Gilder
Production Manager: . . . . .Sue Longstaff
Designer: . . . . .Mark Sevant
Produced and directed by Ray Butt

When the art class that Rodney attends is given a £10,000 grant to make a local community film, he's placed in charge of the project. While he writes the script, he hires the services of Mickey Pearce to direct the picture. But when Rodney struggles to put pen to paper, Del – who buys his brother an ancient typewriter to help prepare the screenplay – throws in a suggestion. His plot involves an escaped rhino rampaging through the streets of London, but is quickly dismissed by Rodney.

Spotting a business opportunity, Del teams up with Mickey Pearce – and an unwilling Rodney – to use the film camera for recording weddings, christenings, and even Marlene and Boycie's 20th anniversary do. Mickey also tries his hand at his own blue movie, with Amanda – dressed in a small nurse's uniform, stockings and suspenders – the star of the show. But proceedings soon get out of hand.

Villa Bella guest house

Del, Rodney and Uncle Albert have no option but to stay at this delapidated guest house in Margate during 'The Jolly Boys' Outing'. The proprietor is the greasy-haired Mrs Creswell, who is assisted by the bad-mannered Inga.

'The Jolly Boys' Outing'

Vimmal

(See 'Malik, Vimmal')

Voice

The woman's voice is heard when Del enters The Nag's Head for the first time in 'Big Brother'. She greets Del, and then confirms that she's fine when he enquires as to her well-being. The woman is never seen.

Waddell, Kerry

Assistant floor manager on six episodes: S6, episodes 1, 3–6 and 'Dates'

Kerry, who was born in the Hampshire town of Fareham, graduated from art college with a degree in theatre design. After five years in the art industry, she moved into fringe theatre, working as an assistant stage manager at various venues, including the Edinburgh Festival and Manchester Rep.

After three years in theatre, she joined the BBC as a floor assistant in 1985 and was promoted to assistant floor manager four years later. In this capacity she worked on a host of variety

and comedy shows, including *The Two Ronnies*, *Colin's Sandwich* and *The Stanley Baxter Show*.

Kerry left the Beeb in 1989 and apart from a three-year gap, during which time she moved to Portugal and raised her family, she has worked freelance ever since for companies such as Noel Gay Television, Celador Productions, Grant Naylor Productions and Disney. She's now employed as Head of Production for Steve Coogan's company, Baby Cow Productions.

Wade, Johnny

Role: Teddy
Appeared in 'To Hull and Back'
Born in Bethnal Green, Johnny started his working life as a singer after winning several talent contests. During the day he ran a market stall selling sweets,

while in the evening he was busy working, initially in cabaret, then with a band. He earned his television break as a singer in *Compact*, the sixties' soap drama, before moving on to hit musicals including *Guys and Dolls* and *South Pacific*, touring the world for over three years. He's also worked at the Royal Court.

Johnny has remained busy on the box, appearing in *Z Cars*, *Coronation Street* (playing a lorry driver), *United*, *Porridge*, *The Two Ronnies* and four series as Roger in Yorkshire TV's *You're Only Young Twice*. Recent work has seen him appear in *EastEnders* as a drunken chauffeur, and in the second series of *Sunburn*, filmed in Portugal.

Wadsworth, Chris

Videotape editor on 42 episodes: S1, episodes 2, 3, 4 & 6; S2, episodes 1, 2, 5 & 7; S3, episodes 2, 4 & 6; S4, episodes 1, 2, 5 & 7; S5, episodes 1, 3, 4 & 5; S6, episodes 1, 3–6; S7; 'Thicker Than Water'; 'Dates'; 'The Jolly Boys' Outing'; 'Rodney Come Home'; 'Miami Twice' (Parts 1 & 2); 'Mother Nature's Son'; 'Fatal Extraction'; 'Heroes and Villains'; 'Modern Men'; 'Time On Our Hands' and 'If They Could See Us Now…!'
London-born Chris Wadsworth took up editing at a young age. At school he was responsible for editing sound effects for the annual play, an interest he nurtured at King's College, London, where he obtained an engineering degree.

He developed an interest in television technology and was offered a place on an engineering voca-

tional training course at the BBC in 1975. During the course he spent three weeks working in the videotape department and three weeks in telecine.

After completing the course he applied for a permanent job with the Beeb and was offered a position in the videotape department in 1976. By 1979 he had become a senior engineer and, a year later, editor. *Only Fools and Horses* was the first comedy show he edited, but among the numerous others he's worked on are *The Generation Game*, *Sportsnight*, *Newsnight*, *Triangle* and *Jackanory*. Apart from *Only Fools*, his favourites jobs have been *Absolutely Fabulous* and an early series of *One Foot in the Grave*.

Chris left the BBC in 1998 to work freelance, although many of his assignments since leaving have been for the Corporation, including the new episodes of *Only Fools*.

MEMORIES OF ONLY FOOLS

★ ★ ★ ★ ★ ★

'I remember enjoying so many laughs while rehearsing. One particular memory that sticks in my mind relates to the episode, "Sickness and Wealth", during which Del ends up in hospital.

'One of my responsibilities was to arrange all the props and I noticed on the script the words "Fredge Fish". I assumed it was a misprint and should have read "Fresh Fish", but when I mentioned it to the rest of the team, everyone was adamant: it was no mistake – there really was a dish called fredge fish. I knew it was a wind-

up but decided to see the joke through, so told everyone that I'd do a bit of research and find out about this dish.

'When it came to presenting the fish for a hospital scene with David Jason, I put the plate in front of him – it looked like nothing on earth. When everyone asked what it was, I explained it was the fredge fish they had gone on about. Everyone cracked up because I presented a fish, sprinkled with grass to resemble herbs, and covered with flowers from the *Blue Peter* garden!'

KERRY WADDELL – Assistant floor manager

Chris Wadsworth

'Only Fools and Horses started, as far as I was concerned, on Tuesday 16 June 1981 with an edit in VT 39 at Television Centre. My BBC department, television recording, had made me an editor the previous December.

'With all the time that has passed since those days it's interesting to compare the way we produced a programme of this type then and how we do it now. The process has always started with a script and three to five weeks of location filming, covering the outside scenes for the whole series. Almost on a daily basis, John Jarvis, who edited the filmed location material in those days, would receive the rushes from the previous day. He would check for any faults with the film and then assemble the shots for each scene. He would send back regular progress reports to the production team bringing any problems to their attention.

'Back at base the editing process would continue up to and beyond the end of the location shoot. If the director was lucky he would get a clear week to continue with the editing before studio rehearsals started. The schedule would then turn into a weekly cycle of read-throughs, rehearsal, blocking, camera script, recording and editing. Add to this sound dubbing and title graphics and you can see that the workload was considerable.

'So to the day of the first studio recording. The set would have been put up the previous night, and the lighting set up. The set elements (the flat, The Nag's Head, etc.) were usually arranged in a line across the studio and facing the audience rostra.

'The day began at 10 in the morning with a stagger through the scenes. This was the first chance for the actors to perform in the set and the director to discover whether the camera script actually worked with the real lit set. Throughout the day modifications were made to the camera script to get the best picture on the screen at any one time, while considering the practical considerations imposed by lighting and sound. It is here that John Sullivan would have had his last chance to change any lines before the recording.

'At around 4.30 in the afternoon a dress rehearsal would start. Here the show would be attempted from start to finish with any film sequences run-in off a telecine machine. This film, now edited and dubbed, would have been leadered to separate the scenes for easy insertion into the studio. Telecine (TK) machines required a eight-second run-up if a neat join between the film and live action was to be achieved. Therefore, a point in the script eight seconds back from the desired start of the film would be worked out and adjusted in the dress rehearsal.

'After a dinner break, the actual recording would start at 7.30 pm. An audience would have assembled, and have been entertained by one of the regular warm-up personnel. This would also happen during recording breaks when scene changes demanded a costume or make-up change, let alone the physical problem of moving five cameras, two boom microphones and other auxiliary equipment around the sets. By now two recording machines in the basement of Television Centre, lined up by my colleagues and loaded with two new two-inch, 90-minute videotapes would be connected to the studio output. Lining up these machines and being in charge of the recording were some of my earlier responsibilities until I became an editor. Every time these machines were required to record a scene the studio technical manager (TM) would phone the VT engineer and ask him to go into record. Fifteen seconds were allowed for the machine to settle and to record a leader that I would use when the programme was edited.

'So we got going. The titles would roll. "Run TK" "8, 7, 6, 5, 4, 3, 2, 1", "On TK for 30 seconds", "Coming to camera 2", "Shot 1 on 2" the programme assistant Penny Thompson would announce on the talkback system to everyone plugged into the studios output. Complete scenes or bits of scenes were recorded and retaken until a faultless version of every line was obtained.

'I mentioned that there were two recordings made in parallel with each other. This was mainly on the grounds of safety. Because the video head wrote the information from top to bottom of the two-inch tape, any damage to this top edge would be found by the slightly protruding rotating head and you could end up with a severed tape and a ruined recording. Also, while in record, you had no idea whether the machine was committing anything to tape at all. Head clogs were the bane of anyone's life who worked near a VT machine. On replay this was easy to spot, but in record all you could monitor were the pictures and sound that were passing through the machine. So, after the call from the studio to stop recording, the VT engineer would spin both tapes back by 30 seconds or so and play the tail of the scene just recorded to check the recording. Once he was happy the studio would be told that they were "Clear so far", and that they could continue.

'It's worth mentioning a trick used in those days that would now be regarded as risky. To explain this I have to point out that the edit session of a comedy show didn't usually take place in one of the few three-machine edit suites, where you could mix from picture A to picture B and record the result on C – hence three machines. Instead, we were allocated just two machines, a player and a recorder. Mixing or any other transition other than a cut was impossible. So if a mix was required from one scene to another it would have to be arranged in the studio during that night's recording using a technique we called "roll back and mix". Being that we had two parallel

recordings, we'd roll back one, play the end of the previous scene, cue the actors off the end of the recording and then record the result on the other machine.

'After the mix was performed, the machine providing the replay was returned to record again. This is where it was risky because for a time you only had one recording of the show. After the next recording break, this master tape was fully checked to ensure every frame was fine before the studio recording could proceed. This put considerable responsibility on the shoulders of the recording engineer. Because the mix was recorded on tape I would, when it came to editing the show, only have to dub this across to the edit tape with a cut either side and thus we were able to get more out of our limited resources.

'Recording complete, a final check of the tapes was made and a technical clear given. We would then adjourn to the 4th floor "rest room" at the end of a 12-hour day.

'Editing usually followed the studio recording by a couple of days, giving the director a second look at the VHS recording of the show. On the day of the edit, I would prepare a new tape by recording the necessary test signals on the first two minutes and recording a clock that counted down the last 30 seconds before the start of the programme, which would be identified by programme title, episode title and recording number. The studio master would be loaded on my other machine and again lined up so that the test signals recorded on the night would replay perfectly and the machine would give the best replay of the recording possible. In those days engineering went hand in hand with creative decisions. At last, with most of the engineering out of the way, the editing started. Very often this would be my first look at the show if I hadn't attended the actual recording. This had its advantages, as I could be objective about the various takes and not aware of any agony in obtaining the performances. With the director, we would then choose the best takes of any section. With comedy, the audience will really only laugh well the first time they see the joke, so we always tried to save the first take.

'Vision mixing was out of the question with two machines, so was sound mixing because to change anything on tape, the tape machine has to go into full record, which obliterates any old material. To get over the problem and allow audio mixing, I had an audio tape recorder in the suite which was used to record a second copy of the outgoing sound from the recorder. If this was running in sync, I had the two copies of the same out-going sound, enabling me to enter audio record early at any time in the run up before the vision edit point and to perform an audio mix independent of the vision. I was then able to blend one laugh into another and hide my work.

'Every edit was treated in the same way whether it was the removal of lines for time, going between takes or simply joining scenes together. Timings were crucial because we had to get the programme as near as possible to 30 minutes. In those days the presentation department was more lenient on durations, realising that editing was difficult and that doing another pass would affect the quality of both audio and video. We were years away from digital recording and it was always a shame to see the programme sharpen up in pace and flow while at the same time watch the pictures lose that first generation sparkle.

'Captions were added using a CAT (Caption Apparatus Trolley) – a camera pointing at black cards with white writing. Timing of this was trial and error. Again caption machines were several years away.

'Climb on board the time machine and we will return to the present day. Assistant Floor Manager Anthony Dow is now Tony Dow – Director; Gareth Gwenlan is Producer following the retirement of Ray Butt. I am still an editor. Not that I mind this in any way. It's still a joy to work with such great material. Today with the huge improvements in technology the editor's role has become more vital. Digital recording is now used so no longer do I suffer a reduction in quality while editing from one tape to another.

'Today we have also said goodbye to editing on film and tape, as now, after the recording, the pictures and sound are digitised on to a computer hard drive. Software is then used to assemble a sequence of this material. The huge advantage is the fact that the sequence does not physically exist; it can be pulled apart or shortened at will until perfection or exhaustion is reached. Vision mixing is on the touch of a key so a mix sequence is no longer constructed in front of the audience, all you have to make sure of, on the night of recording, is that you have a perfect performance of each scene. Film machines are no longer used to insert the location scenes even if they are shot on film, as they are now transferred to tape and run in from a tape machine. Recording machines are now in the studio gallery and under the control of the studio resource manager. The computer editing system is also used to edit the location sequences shown to the live studio audience.

'The one process that is extra and has to follow the final edit of a programme is a "conform" where the studio tapes are again used to replace the quality reduced computer pictures used during the assembly of the programme.

'After the programme is back on tape the show is given its polish of a final audio dub in which any sounds to which I don't have access are used to rebalance sections; any extra music is also added. A final check is then made to ensure everything is audible and perfect.

'We still strive to produce an entertaining show which, once recorded and edited, will allow millions to laugh at Del, Rodders and the rest of the gang. The most important part of any production remains the script. That was as true in 1981 as it is today. Without the words it's not only the actors who would be silent. Much as he would loath me to say it, all praise to John Sullivan for his creation and the succession of brilliant scripts that have made this programme the most popular situation comedy of all time.

'The first series of *Only Fools and Horses* went out in the autumn of 1981 to a moderate reaction, not bad but by no means an instant success. The great thing about the BBC in those days is that it gave programmes a chance of finding an audience. Today, I think the BBC has entered a ratings battle along with all its rivals and wants instant success. I really do believe that if we were to start *Only Fools and Horses* today it wouldn't get further than the first series. There's a sobering thought!' **CHRIS WADSWORTH**

Wagland, George

Vision supervisor on location video in 'Diamonds are for Heather'

Wainwright, Mr

Mr Wainwright, who immigrated with his family from the West Indies in 1956, is not seen in the sitcom. He employs Anna, the German language student, in 'From Prussia with Love', for a time. When their son, Spencer, gets her pregnant and doesn't want to face up to his responsibilities, Anna tells Mr Wainwright, but he thinks she's lying and is a bad influence on his son so throws her out. Mrs Wainwright is not seen in the sitcom.

Wainwright, Spencer

Anna, the German language student, mentions Spencer in 'From Prussia with Love'. Not seen in the sitcom, Spencer is a university student. He returned home one day, plied Anna with champagne and they ended up in bed. He's the father of her baby, although he doesn't want to face the fact.

Waiter, The

Played by Barry Wilmore
Appeared in S1, episode 2
The effeminate waiter serves Rodney and Del at the gay nightclub in 'Go West Young Man'. The Club's extortionate prices see the brothers forking out £7 for two drinks. The waiter's dress sense leaves much to be desired – he wears a black shirt open to the navel, and white trousers.

Waiter, The (in the Indian restaurant)

(See 'Tony')

Waiter, The

Played by Paul Cooper
Seen in 'Danger UXD', the waiter serves Rodney and Cassandra at the upmarket hamburger restaurant.

Waiter, The

Seen in 'Chain Gang', the waiter supplies Arnie with a glass of water at the upmarket Italian restaurant in Chelsea.

Waiter

In 'The Chance of a Lunchtime', the waiter – who works at the restaurant where Rodney and Cassandra try patching up their differences – waits on the married couple.

Walker, Fatty

An old school friend of Del, Trigger and Roy Slater, Fatty is mentioned by Del at the police station during 'May the Force be with You'. He recalls the time Slater was dragged to the ground and while Walker sat on his face, Trigger put itching powder in his belly button.

Walker, John

Film cameraman on eight episodes: S2, episodes 1, 2, 4–7 and 'Miami Twice' (Parts 1 & 2)
London-born John Walker joined a small documentary film unit – which made promotional films for drug companies, and adverts and training films for the health service – straight from school, gaining experience in everything from sound recording to library work.

After spells with two other companies in the same field, he applied to the BBC in 1965 for the post of trainee assistant cameraman; he was offered a job in '66 and after a year's training became an assistant cameraman. For the next nine years he worked in the drama department, during which time he was promoted to cameraman. His drama career started with five years on *The Onedin Line* before moving on to numerous other productions, including over 40 episodes of *Bergerac*. In light entertainment he worked on shows such as *Solo* and *One Foot in the Grave*.

John left the BBC in 1995 after 30 years' service. He now lives on the edge of Exmoor and occasionally works freelance.

Wall, Kim

Role: Justin
Appeared in 'If They Could See Us Now…!'
Kim had already worked on a John Sullivan series, playing Baker in *Heartburn Hotel*, when he appeared as Justin in the 2001 Christmas Special. He's also been seen in plenty of dramas over the years, including *Dempsey and Makepeace*, *Boon*, *Murder Most Horrid* and *Casualty*. More recently, though, he's played various roles in *The People's Harry Enfield* and been in three series of S4C's *Barry Welsh Is Coming*.

A busy stage actor: Kim's various roles include Mercutio in *Romeo and Juliet*, Lucky Eric in *Bouncers*, Alec D'Urbeville in *Tess* and Doug Bradshaw in *Scissor Happy*.

Wallace (the butler)

Played by Donald Bisset
Seen in 'A Touch of Glass', Wallace is Lord and Lady Ridgemere's aged butler at Ridgemere Hall. A true snob, he takes an instant dislike to the Trotters and isn't afraid to show his feelings throughout the episode.

Wallace, Mike

Played by Conrad Nelson
Mike, who's a financial adviser from Merseyside, is one of the *Goldrush* contestants in 'If They Could See Us Now…!'.

Walmsley, Eric

Designer on seven episodes: S4
After attending London's Central School of Art and Design, where he studied Theatre and Television Design, Eric – who was born in Eton, Berkshire, in 1940 – applied to the BBC for a job as holiday relief assistant director in 1962. He was given a three-month contract and his first assignment on the

'**D**esigners were always allocated shows by the design manager, according to their experience. At the time, I had already worked on several comedy series, so during an interview with Harry Smith (design manager at the time) I asked if I could work on a drama production for a change. So he gave me *Only Fools and Horses* just to keep me on my toes!

'The pace of work was certainly equal to a drama series but the great bonus was that we all had a lot of laughs along the way! We had a six-week run-up to the start of filming and then went straight into the studios for seven weekly shows in front of a live audience. The most important thing was to have the scripts up front for all the episodes so that we could plan ahead, but this wasn't always possible. An unforeseen event, like the death of Lennard Pearce, threw the whole series into confusion, and John Sullivan must have had a few nightmares thinking up ways to rewrite the scripts. He very cleverly, though, came up with the idea of bringing Grandad's funeral into the storyline, so I was suddenly asked to arrange for a grave to be dug in Hammersmith Cemetery complete with the (empty) coffin and floral tributes. And so, out of a sad occasion, John Sullivan came shining through to find the funny side of things, getting a great laugh right on cue when Del finds that his hat has been buried six feet under, along with the coffin!

'In another episode, "As One Door Closes", Del and Rodney chase a rare, exotic butterfly around a park, in order to claim a large financial reward. We filmed the scene in Ravenscourt Park and needed some waterlilies in flower for the butterfly to land on. As it was the middle of November, we thought there was no chance of this happening, so after a lot of hunting, our properties buyer, Maura Laverty, came up with some artificial waterlilies, which sank as soon as we tried them out on water; so we

mounted them all on cork floats and tied them down with nylon line to stage-weights at the bottom of the lake.

'Another scene called for Del and Rodney to pay a visit to their mum's grave. Designed by Andy Dimond for a much earlier episode, the original sculptures for the huge monu-

mental memorial had gone literally "under the hammer", (all unwanted scenery was chopped up after the show, thus ensuring continued employment for all concerned) and all Andy could offer was a rather blurred and crumpled Polaroid photo of his creation. This induced a mild state of panic in the design office until, under threat of serious harassment, Andy eventually remembered the name of the book he had used for the sculptures of angels and cherubs. Armed with a copy of *Nineteenth Century American Monumental Masonry*, we went straight off to see our 20th-century polystyrene sculptor, Dick Budden, whose first words were: "Well, when do you want it by? Could it be next year?" As next year was not an option, we finally persuaded him to knock it together in three weeks, just in time for us to erect it on an unknown grave in the middle of Highgate Cemetery! All credit to Dick, the angels and cherubs were beautifully carved and gilded, and it looked resplendent in the setting sun with a laurel bush strategically placed to hide the stage-weight and brace holding it all up from the back. It all reminded me of the favourite quotation of Murray Pearcey (my tutor at art college): "Little drops of water, little blobs of paint, make things look exactly what they ain't!"

'Setting up the film locations and designing the sets for the studio shows was really intensive, but also very enjoyable. All of us working on the show were committed to getting the best results from the scripts, and a friendly team spirit quickly

developed. It was great fun to have a laugh with David Jason and Nicholas Lyndhurst between shots on location: they were friendly, relaxed and very amusing, but always professional as soon as they heard the word: "Action!"'

ERIC WALMSLEY

twice-weekly magazine programme *Compact*, followed by *Moonstrike* and a play, *Birth of a Private Man*, about a daring escape over the Berlin Wall.

Eric has worked in the television and film industry for 35 years. In 1964, however, he took a break for a couple of years and managed a family art business in Poole, Dorset, during which time he opened an art gallery to exhibit the paintings and sculptures of Dorset artists.

Eric accepted voluntary redundancy from the BBC in 1995, and now works as a freelance production designer, with a recent assignment being Art Director on Trevor Nunn's production of *The Merchant of Venice*, filmed for BBC Television at Pinewood Studios in 2000. His favourite jobs included *Winter Dreams*, a ballet by Sir Kenneth MacMillan, and George Gershwin's *Porgy and Bess*, for which Eric was awarded an Emmy by the Academy of Television Arts and Sciences in Los Angeles for his outstanding achievement as Art Director. Other television credits include *Warship*, *Wings*, *Secret Army*, *Top of the Pops*, *Don't Wait Up*, *Bergerac* and *Young Musician of the Year*.

'Wanted'

Original transmission: Thursday 15 December 1983, 8.30 pm

Production date: Sunday 6 November 1983

Original viewing figures: 11.2 million

Duration: 30 minutes

First repeat: Monday 20 August 1984, 7.35 pm

Subsequent repeats: 5/10/91, 19/3/95, 15/7/98, 5/5/00

CAST

Del Trotter . . . . .David Jason
Rodney Trotter . . . . .Nicholas Lyndhurst
Grandad Trotter . . . . .Lennard Pearce
Mickey Pearce . . . . .Patrick Murray
Blossom . . . . .Toni Palmer
Trigger . . . . .Roger Lloyd Pack
Boycie . . . . .John Challis
Karen (the barmaid) . . . . .Michèle Winstanley
Walk-on: . . . .(People in pub) Alan Forbes and 15 extras

PRODUCTION TEAM

Written by John Sullivan
Title music arranged and conducted by Ronnie Hazlehurst composed and sung by John Sullivan
Audience Warm-up: . . . . .Felix Bowness
Make-up Designer: . . . . .Denise Baron
Costume Designer: . . . . .Dinah Collin
Properties Buyer: . . . . .Penny Rollinson
Film Cameraman: . . . . .Ian Hilton
Film Sound: . . . . .Clive Derbyshire
Film Editor: . . . . .Mike Jackson
Camera Supervisor: . . . . .Ron Peverall
Studio Lighting Director: . . . . .Don Babbage
Studio Sound: . . . . .Dave Thompson
Technical Coordinator: . . . . . .Bob Warman
Videotape Editor: . . . . .Chris Wadsworth
Production Assistant: . . . . .Penny Thompson
Assistant Floor Manager: . . . .Tony Dow

'Wanted'

Graphic Designer: . . . . .Mic Rolph
Vision Mixer: . . . . .Angela Beveridge
Production Manager: . . . . .Andy Smith
Designer: . . . . .Bryan Ellis
Produced and directed by Ray Butt

Rodney plays the good Samaritan and tries helping a drunken woman in the street. He soon wishes he hadn't, however, when she starts shouting 'Rape!' at the top of her voice and accusing him of molesting her. Worried to death, Rodney rushes from the scene. When Del finds out about the incident, he hides the fact that the woman was Blossom, a demented character who's let out of a nearby mental home at weekends and has a record of accusing people of such crimes. For a laugh, Del decides to string Rodney along, claiming the police were out in force last night, looking for someone they've termed the 'Peckham Pouncer'.

Believing the police are after him, Rodney goes into hiding, although he should have picked a better place than the tank room inside Nelson Mandela House's ventilation system, because when he lights up one of his 'funny fags', and the aroma wafts out through the air vents, it doesn't take long for Del to know where he is.

Ward, Bill

Role: Tom Witton (the gamekeeper)
Appeared in S3, episode 3
Bill, who died in 1984, was a busy character actor whose other credits include playing a caretaker in

an episode of *Dear John*, as well as appearing in *Shoulder to Shoulder* and the big screen version of *Till Death Us Do Part*.

Ward, Gaynor

Role: Janice
Appeared in S1, episode 5
Gaynor no longer works in the acting profession.

Warman, Bob

Technical coordinator on one episode: S3, episode 6

Warm-up artist

The role of the warm-up artist in preparing the studio audience for the situation comedy about to be recorded is often underestimated. Bobby Bragg's services were often called upon to 'warm-up' the audience before *Only Fools* and here he explains about his role in the overall production of an episode.

'When people arrive in a television studio for the first time, they can feel uncomfortable and a little uneasy when confronted by massive lighting rigs, sound booms, cameras, and a myriad of people wandering about. The job of the warm-up man, 20 minutes before recording begins, is to relax, inform, and explain in a humorous way what the heck is going on!

'A job well done is when you have transformed three hundred individual people into one single laughing unit, ready to greet the cast with enthusiasm and to give generous reactions to the performance.

'Once the show is under way there are many stops: costume and make-up changes, set changes, moving cameras and sound from one set to the next, and then the dreaded technical breakdown, which is when the warm-up comes into his own, keeping the audience bubbling along, and most importantly, keeping the level of enthusiasm going for the next scene, which could be 15 or 20 minutes away.

'There is one unwritten law for the warm-up man: not to be funnier than the show; that is why it was always great to work on *Only Fools* because

Warm-up artist Bobby Bragg

once the comedic brilliance of David, Nick and the team brought John's words to life, there was nothing I could do to top it.

'There were so many great moments over the years on *Fools*. One that springs to mind is the legendary scene where Del falls through the flap of the open bar. Ray Butt was producing and directing in those days, and when everything was set to record the scene, he told the crew: "Get this right, lads, we only have one go at it, we'll never be able to recreate the spontaneity by doing it again – good luck." The scene was shot in one take and the rest is history.

'I think that everyone knew in the early days that we were taking part in something special and were proud to be a part of it; as time went on the whole *Fools* team became like a very close knit family.

'I think that working on a show like *Only Fools and Horses* is rather like having a baby: you're there at the birth, you grow up together, you experience the highs and lows over the years and you are there at the end.

'The end came, or so we thought, in 1996, with the final Christmas show. Having worked on over five thousand television shows in my career, I have never experienced an atmosphere like the one that night in Studio One at Television Centre.

'There was excitement and great anticipation. Everyone knew that they were witnessing a piece of broadcasting history and they wouldn't be disappointed: an inspired script and brilliant perfor-

mances from David and Nick gave us the final classic episode.

'At the end of the recording, I thanked David and Nick, not only for a great evening, but for all the years of laughter they'd given us. At that moment the audience stood as one and cheered. David wanted to say a few words, but as I went to hand him the mike, Nick put his arms around him; as they hugged each other the cheering grew louder and both were unable to speak. As the tears flowed, I thanked John Sullivan – who had now arrived on the floor, followed by producer Gareth Gwenlen and director Tony Dow. Still the audience cheered and the emotion overwhelmed everyone on the floor – even I was filling up. And still the people cheered.

'No words could describe those moments, and nor should they, the audience had said it all. If I never work again, I will always be able to tell my kids that I was there.'

BOBBY BRAGG – Warm-up artist

Warnecke, Gordon

Role: Henry
Appeared in S7, episode 1

Gordon's career as an actor has seen him employed on both stage and screen. His theatre assignments include appearing in *Julius Caesar*, *Bite of the Night*, *The Will* and *Blood*, while his television appearances include Hanif in *Boon*, Ranjith in *Birds of a Feather*, Jabbaar in *EastEnders*, Dil Palmer in *Brookside* and Mr Kapur in *The Bill*.

On the big screen, he's appeared in films such as *The Dream Child*, *A Nice Arrangement*, *The Pleasure Principle* and *My Beautiful Launderette*.

Warren, Albert

By the time his name is mentioned in 'If They Could See Us Now…!', Albert is already dead. Nicknamed Bunny, Albert served with the RAF at Biggin Hill from 1939 to '42. His funeral takes place during the Christmas 2001 episode.

Warren, Jean

Role: Sonia
Appeared in 'Dates'

Jean, who was born in Feltham, Middlesex, in 1950, trained at the Bristol Old Vic Theatre School before making her professional debut playing Atahualipa's wife in *The Royal Hunt of the Sun* at Salisbury Playhouse, where she'd worked prior to drama school. Her first experience of television was in a Greek play for BBC's education department, although other credits in this medium include Julie in *Sink or Swim*, Lottie in *Olympian Way*, Rosie in *Minder*, Elaine in *Soldier, Soldier* and her favourite roles, Maureen in *Boys from the Blackstuff*, Denise Cropper in *As Time Goes By*, Michelle – Granville's girlfriend – in *Open All Hours* as well as her part in *Only Fools*.

On the stage, her many appearances include playing Parker in *Engaged* at the Royal National Theatre, Sheila in *A Worthy Guest* at the Royal Court, and Olivia in *Twelfth Night*.

Jean remains busy in the profession and has recently finished filming a cameo for a BBC film, *I Capture the Castle*.

Warwick, David

Role: TV presenter
Appeared in S6, episode 2

David, who was born in Crewe, originally trained as a teacher before joining the local rep as an assistant stage manager. During the early part of his career he supplemented his income by working as a drain layer's labourer, driving a van, reading the weather, taxiing and working at IBM.

He made his television debut as a walk-on in *Z Cars* and went on to appear regularly on television, including one series of *The Fall and Rise of Reginald Perrin*, playing Reggie's son, Mark, the would-be actor. The 1970s was a busy decade for David, but when he left the sitcom he returned to rep for three years.

Between 1980 and 1983 he lived in New Zealand where he acted and started directing, something he

MEMORIES OF PLAYING SONIA

★ ★ ★ ★ ★

'Playing Sonia meant I found myself working with Tony Dow again. When I was younger I appeared in the West End in various plays. One of them was a slightly risqué production (produced by the legendary Kenneth Tynan) called *Carte Blanche*, which now seems very tame! One of our stagehands was an innocent and sweet-natured young lad, and as we all streamed past in various exotic costumes he would always help us with props, open the door, etc.

'Tony and I always got on and had a laugh; we become good friends for the run of the show. Never has the phrase, "Be nice to people on the way up", been more meaningful because that curly-haired lad has certainly gone on to great things. He's employed me often over the years and he always laughs at my little comic offerings – bless him!

'Working with David Jason was also a happy experience, and anyone who has, knows he doesn't put on airs and graces. When I turned up at Waterloo Station for my scene under the famous clock, I immediately went to get a bacon butty from the food wagon. There was David, pre make-up and wardrobe, queuing like everyone else.

'When he had his Del Boy kit on, he clowned with the crowds that gathered around us, showing a genuine kindness for all. Later, at lunch, I expressed disappointment in the pudding I'd chosen, and without a moment's hesitation, David picked it up, queued patiently at the food wagon, and brought me back a better pudding – that's the sort of bloke he is.'

JEAN WARREN

has continued since returning to England after failing to qualify for permanent residency.

David, who declined the chance to join *Coronation Street* early on in his career, has appeared in many television shows, including *Peak Practice*, *EastEnders* and *Keeping Up Appearances*.

Wat Schuift Het?

The title of the Dutch version of *Only Fools and Horses* translates as *What's It Worth?*. The adaptation was made by Endemol Entertainments, shown on RTL4, and starred Johnny Kraaykamp Jnr as Stef (based on Del), Sacco Van der Made as Granpa (based on Grandad) and Kasper Van Kooten as Robbie (based on Rodney).

The family name was Aarsman, but unlike their British predecessors, they owned a dog.

'Watching the Girls Go By'

Original transmission: Thursday 28 March 1985, 8.00 pm

Production date: 24 February 1985

Original viewing figures: 14.4 million

Duration: 30 minutes

First repeat: Saturday 14 December 1985, 8.05 pm

Subsequent repeats: 23/11/91, 24/5/96, 29/5/98, 27/9/00

CAST

Del Trotter . . . . .David Jason
Rodney Trotter . . . . .Nicholas Lyndhurst
Uncle Albert . . . . .Buster Merryfield
Trigger . . . . .Roger Lloyd Pack
Mike .Kenneth MacDonald
Maureen . . . . .Nula Conwell
Mickey Pearce . . . . .Patrick Murray
Yvonne . . . . .Carolyn Allen
Boycie . . . . .John Challis
Tommy . . . . .Ricky Kennedy
Walk-ons: . . . .(In pub) Sam Smart, David Doyle, Kerry-Ann White, Kim Benson, Catherine Clarke. (In club) Monica Ramone and Lawrence Ferdinand

PRODUCTION TEAM

Written by John Sullivan
Title music arranged and conducted by Ronnie Hazlehurst composed and sung by John Sullivan
Make-up Designer: . . . . .Linda McInnes
Costume Designer: . . . . .Richard Winter
Properties Buyer: . . . . .Chris Ferriday
Camera Supervisor: . . . . .Stuart Lindley
Studio Lighting Director: . . . .Don Babbage
Studio Sound: . . . . .Dave Thompson
Technical Coordinator: . . . . . .Tony Mutimer
Videotape Editor: . . . . .Chris Booth
Production Assistant: . . . . . . .Lesley Bywater
Assistant Floor Manager: . . . .Gavin Clarke
Vision Mixer: . . . . .Heather Gilder
Production Manager: . . . . . . .Andy Smith
Designer: . . . . .Eric Walmsley
Directed by Susan Belbin
Produced by Ray Butt

There's a do at The Nag's Head on Saturday night and Mickey Pearce has bet Rodney £50 that he won't bring a girl; egged along by pride, Rodney accepts the bet, even though he hasn't anyone to ask. When Del suggests Big Brenda, the Southern Area shot-put champion, Rodney is determined to find his own partner. Donning a new white jacket, black shirt and white tie, Rodney sets off to catch his girl but, with Del remarking that he looks like a liquorice allsort, his chances of success are slim.

To ease the pressure on Rodney, Del buys the bet off his brother: he'll fork out if he loses but will pocket the £50 if he wins. In search of a girl, they head for a seedy nightclub full of shady characters and tarty women. It seems their luck is out when Del admits the only thing he's pulled is a ligament in his back trying to break dance. But then Del spots an old flame, Yvonne, an exotic dancer, and pays her to escort Rodney to the do.

Saturday night is a wash-out for Rodney, especially as Yvonne – introduced as his girlfriend – stands up on the counter and strips. And the smile

A serious accident in 1990 restricted his work as a stunt artist and he now concentrates on coordinating. His extensive list of credits include doubling for Brian Wilde in *Last of the Summer Wine* for eight years, *Coronation Street*, *EastEnders*, *Cracker* and the movie *A Fish Called Wanda*.

Wei, Rex

Role: Mr Chin

Appeared in S2, episode 5

Rex's other screen credits include two appearances in *The Professionals* and playing a Korean ship's captain in *Night Watch*. He's also worked on several films, such as 1974's *The Bunny Caper* and *Ping Pong* in 1986.

Welcome, Josephine

Role: Dr Shaheed

Appeared in S6, episode 5

à la Del

★ ★ ★ ★ ★ ★

'Au contraire, au contraire'

('Stage Fright')

is soon wiped off Del's face when he discovers the £50 bet was actually for 50p!

Watts, Chris

Technical coordinator on five episodes: S3, episodes 1– 4 & 7

Wayne

Played by Kelly Garfield

Appeared in S1, episode 6

Seen but not heard in 'The Russians are Coming', Wayne is a young, enthusiastic policeman whose partner, Eric, pulls the Trotters over for speeding along at 60 in a built-up area. Eric says Wayne is on the hunt for his first 'nick'.

Wayne

In 'Miami Twice', the non-speaking Wayne drives Boycie, Marlene and Young Tyler around the Everglades during their Miami holiday. He's also with the Boyce family when they notice Del and Rodney stranded in alligator country.

Webb, Chris

Stunt artist on one episode: 'Dates'

Chris, who is seen jumping out of the way of Rodney's car in 'Dates', worked in various jobs before becoming a stuntman. As well as being employed by an insurance company, he served in the army and tried his luck as a salesman.

Upon taking a friend's advice, he took up working as an extra, whilst attending the City Lit, a London drama school. Stunt work soon came his way, too, and he opted to specialise in the profession when the stunt register was established.

Wendy

Played by Jilli Foot

Also referred to as 'English girl', Wendy meets Del and Rodney on their holiday in Benidorm. Together with her friend, they flee the Trotters' apartment upon seeing Grandad's false teeth in a glass while he's sprawled out asleep on the bed.

Wesley

When Raquel and Del plan to go out celebrating the relaunch of TITCO during 'If They Could See Us Now…!', Raquel tells Damien to pop over to Wesley's flat and she'll pick him up later. He's not seen in the sitcom.

West, Hilary

Vision mixer on seven episodes: S1 and 'Christmas Crackers'

Hilary began her BBC career in the finance department back in 1968, before moving into TV production as a secretary. After working as a production assistant on all genres of programme, she eventually transferred to light entertainment, initially working with Harold Snoad on *Seven of One* in 1973. Hilary now works as a freelance vision mixer, and for some time has worked on *EastEnders*.

Weston, Steve

Role: Kenny Malcolm

Appeared in 'Heroes and Villains'

Born in London in 1962, Steve worked as a layout artist before being bitten by the acting bug and training at the East 15 Acting School. He made his first professional appearance as John Worthing in a

production of Oscar Wilde's The Importance of Being Earnest, before spending some time in theatre up and down the country.

His first taste of television came as Glen Tempany in London's Burning, but his favourite roles are playing John Valekue in EastEnders and Colin Adcroft in Holby City. Other small-screen credits include Burnside, Masie Raine, The Bill and The Knock.

As well as stage and television, Steve is busy in the film world, having just completed a picture in Kenya, where he played Mr Morrison in Nowhere in Africa.

Whaley, Charles

Assistant floor manager on two episodes: 'Miami Twice' (Parts 1 & 2)

Zimbabwean-born Charles Whaley was an actor in South Africa before arriving in the UK in 1980. Wanting a more secure career, he decided to work behind the scenes in television and joined the BBC in 1984, initially as an assistant floor manager. By the time he took voluntary redundancy from the Beeb he was a production manager, a job he now does on a freelance basis. Recent assignments include The Vault, a quiz show for Carlton Television.

White, Bay

Role: Old lady
Appeared in 'Heroes and Villains'

Bay, who was born in Boreham, Essex, in 1918, trained at the London Theatre Studio for two years (1936–38) and made her debut on the stage soon after drama school, in Chekhov's The Wood Demon. A lengthy spell in repertory theatres and various tours followed before she made her small-screen debut in Kaleidoscope in 1948.

Other television credits include New Scotland Yard, Dixon of Dock Green, Whatever Happened to the Likely Lads?, The Citadel, Crossroads, Troubleshooters, Angels, Brookside, League of Gentlemen and, in 1981,

her favourite role, Gran in Thames TV's Stig of the Dump. On the big screen she's been seen in productions such as A Night to Remember, A Town Like Alice and, recently, A Kind of Hush.

Although she no longer works in theatre, she has over the years appeared in numerous West End shows, including two years with the Old Vic, working with Ralph Richardson and Laurence Olivier.

Whitmore, Richard

Role: Newsreader
Appeared in S7, episode 1 and 'Mother Nature's Son' (voice only)

Richard, who was born in Hitchin in 1933, was a mainstay in BBC newsreading during the 1970s and '80s. His career in journalism and broadcasting started with the Hertford Express in 1951, before he left to launch his own freelance agency.

His first job at the Beeb was for television and radio in the south-east, and he progressed to reading the national news on BBC1. He has also written a number of books, and although he no longer reads the news for the BBC, he appears occasionally on television: he's played himself in a 1987 episode of The New Statesman and in Gobble in 1996, while he played a newsreader in 1991's King Ralph and a Radio 4 presenter in In the Red. Recently, he's been working in the theatre, playing Baron Hardup in Cinderella and Peter Quince in A Midsummer Night's Dream.

'Who Wants to be a Millionaire'

Original transmission: Sunday 5 October 1986, 8.35 pm
Production date: Sunday 13 July 1986
Original viewing figures: 18.8 million
Duration: 30 minutes
First repeat: Thursday 15 October 1987, 8.30 pm
Subsequent repeats: 23/7/89, 3/4/98

CAST

Del Trotter . . . . .David Jason
Rodney Trotter . . . . .Nicholas Lyndhurst
Uncle Albert . . . . .Buster Merryfield
Mike .Kenneth MacDonald
Boycie . . . . .John Challis
Jumbo Mills . . . . .Nick Stringer
Walk-on: . . . . .Judd Solo

PRODUCTION TEAM

Written by John Sullivan
Title music arranged and conducted by Ronnie Hazlehurst composed and sung by John Sullivan
Audience Warm-up: . . . . .Felix Bowness
Make-up Designer: . . . . .Elaine Smith
Costume Designer: . . . . .Robin Stubbs
Properties Buyer: . . . . .Maura Laverty
Camera Supervisor: . . . . .Ken Major
Studio Lighting Director: . . . . . .Henry Barber
Studio Sound: . . . . .Anthony Philpot
Technical Coordinator: . . . . . . .Nick Moore
Videotape Editor: . . . . .Graham Taylor
Production Assistants: . . . . .Rowena Painter
and Alexandra Todd
Assistant Floor Manager: . . . . .Adrian Pegg
Graphic Designer: . . . . .Andrew Smee
Vision Mixer: . . . . .Heather Gilder
Production Manager: . . . . .Sue Longstaff
Designer: . . . . .Mark Sevant
Produced and directed by Ray Butt

Del's old partner from the '60s, Jumbo Mills – who emigrated to Australia in 1967 – is back in town, and his loud mouth and arrogant behaviour is rubbing everyone up the wrong way. But there is a deep friendship between Del and Jumbo, exemplified by the fact that Jumbo (who's made a fortune during his time Down Under) asks Del to reform their partnership, with Del

'Who's a Pretty Boy?'

fronting his Australian business, importing prestigious European cars from Boycie.

After plenty of thought, Del decides to accept Jumbo's offer and secures a position for Rodney, too. Even though Uncle Albert isn't interested in going with the Trotter boys, Del and Rodney send their applications to Australia House. While Del rejoices when his application is approved, Rodney is declined due to his criminal record. It's a hard decision to make, but Del believes this opportunity – which could make him a millionaire – is too good to turn down. But when he picks up the phone to tell Jumbo his decision, family ties play on his mind and he declines a new life.

'Who's a Pretty Boy?'

Original transmission: Thursday 22 December 1983, 8.30 pm

Production date: Sunday 30 October 1983

Original viewing figures: 11.9 million

Duration: 30 minutes

First repeat: Monday 27 August 1984, 8.15 pm

Subsequent repeats: 12/10/91, 26/3/95, 27/10/97, 12/5/00

CAST

Del Trotter	David Jason
Rodney Trotter	Nicholas Lyndhurst
Grandad Trotter	Lennard Pearce
Brendan O'Shaughnessy	David Jackson
Karen (the barmaid)	Michèle Winstanley
Denzil	Paul Barber
Corinne	Eva Mottley
Louis (the pet shop owner)	Anthony Morton
Mike Fisher	
(The Nag's Head landlord)	Kenneth MacDonald
Walk-ons:	(Indian in pub) Ali Baba.
	(In pub) Derek Holt and 12 extras

PRODUCTION TEAM

Written by John Sullivan

Title music arranged and conducted by Ronnie Hazlehurst composed and sung by John Sullivan

Audience warm-up:	Felix Bowness
Make-up Designer:	Denise Baron
Costume Designer:	Dinah Collin
Properties Buyer:	Penny Rollinson
Film Cameraman:	Ian Hilton
Film Sound:	Clive Derbyshire
Film Editor:	Mike Jackson
Camera Supervisor:	Ron Peverall
Studio Lighting Director:	Don Babbage
Studio Sound:	Dave Thompson
Technical Coordinator:	Chris Watts
Videotape Editor:	Mike Taylor
Production Assistant:	Penny Thompson
Assistant Floor Manager:	Tony Dow
Graphic Designer:	Mic Rolph
Vision Mixer:	Angela Beveridge
Production Manager:	Andy Smith
Designer:	Bryan Ellis

Produced and directed by Ray Butt

Del's annoyed with Brendan O'Shaughnessy, a painter and decorator, for supplying him with the incorrect paint, so when he finds out that the Irishman is planning to paint Denzil's lounge for £200, he takes revenge by pitching an offer himself.

He pops around to Denzil's flat, tells blatant lies about Brendan burning down a house in Kings' Avenue because he was drunk and in charge of a blow torch, and claims he himself used to be in the decorating business until the demand became so great he had to pack it in. Denzil is soon pleading with Del to paint his lounge, even

though his wife Corinne isn't amused because she hates the sight of Del.

Problems begin when Rodney leaves the kettle on the gas, filling the room with condensation and burning the kettle in the process; then to top it all, Corinne's beloved canary is killed by the paint fumes. To try and cover things up, Grandad is despatched to Louis Lombardi's pet store to buy a replacement canary. Although he hasn't any in stock, Lombardi agrees to sell his own pet bird for £45. This appears to do the trick because when Corinne arrives home she doesn't notice any difference in the look of the bird – except that when she left earlier that day, her canary was dead! The Trotters should have taken notice of the message left on the kitchen door, asking them to keep out.

After being thrown out of the flat, they head for The Nag's Head, but it's not long before Brendan is rubbing the salt into the wound by announcing he's been given the decorating job again. But Del has just one more plan to wipe the smile off his smug face.

Why do only fools and horses work?

The etymology of the phrase 'Why do only fools and horses work?' is uncertain, but the truncated 'Why do only fools work?' seems to date back to 19th-century America, although its origin is obscured.

Wickham, Peter

Role: Australian reporter

Appeared in S5, episode 2

Peter's work encompasses all strands of the acting profession. On stage he's recently played The Resident in *Indian Ink* and Richard Wyndham in *The Holly and the Ivy*, while on television he was seen as a policeman in an episode of *Some Mothers Do 'Ave 'Em*, as Ken Jones in *A Sense of Guilt* and as McIntosh in *To Be the Best*.

Widow Manky

A non-speaking member of the Over-Sixties' Club, Widow Manky is seen at The Nag's Head in 'He Ain't Heavy, He's My Uncle'. Mike, the barman, refers to her when he asks Del who the woman is that Albert keeps eyeing up.

Wilkinson, Geoffrey

Role: Eric

Appeared in 'A Royal Flush'

After leaving school in his home town of Nottingham, Geoffrey enlisted in the army. Upon returning to civvy street a few years later, he moved into engineering for two years before enrolling at the Guildhall School of Music and Drama. He graduated in 1964 and spent the next year touring schools as part of Caryl Jenner's Children's Theatre. Rep work followed, beginning at Sidmouth in Devon, and the occasional bit part on television.

Between 1969 and 1977 he took a break from

acting and worked for the National Coal Board, but returned to the stage with a spell at Sheffield's Crucible Theatre. Television work came his way, including appearances in *Emmerdale Farm, Strangers, The Mallens, Juliet Bravo* and *Bergerac*.

More recent appearances include a couple of roles in *Heartbeat*, Mr Hobbs in *Where the Heart Is*, Mr Grieves in *My Wonderful Life*, the desk sergeant in *Dalziel and Pascoe* and a doctor in *Crossroads*.

Wilkinson, Graham

Studio sound supervisor on one episode: 'Rodney Come Home'

London-born Graham Wilkinson wanted to forge a career in electronics, but when he failed his maths A-level he worked in military research for a year instead. He joined the BBC in 1968 and worked as a technical operator at Bristol, gaining experience in shows like *Wild World, Going for a Song* and *Tom, Tom*, a children's programme.

He joined television sound at London in 1969 and went on to work on numerous shows, *Jackanory; Softly, Softly; 'Allo 'Allo!; Are You Being Served?; In Sickness and In Health; No Place Like Home* and *The Brittas Empire* among them.

By the time he went freelance in 1996, Graham was working as a sound supervisor and had clocked up 28 years' service. Recent projects have included *Time Gentlemen, Please* for Sky One, *Heartburn Hotel* and *Open House* for Channel 5.

Wilkinson, John

Film editor on one episode: 'A Royal Flush'

Wilkinson, Katie

Production secretary on three episodes: 'Heroes and Villains', 'Modern Men' and 'Time On Our Hands'

Katie – who was born in Weybridge, Surrey, in 1970 – joined the BBC in 1988 straight from sixth form. Early programmes she worked on include *Ben Elton – Man From Auntie, May to December, So Haunt Me, KYTV* and *Last of the Summer Wine*. After 13 years in the industry she now works as a production assistant and recent assignments have included *The Stand Up Show, Chambers* and *People Like Us*. Her favourite programmes to work on to date are *Over Here, Only Fools* and *Ain't Misbehavin*.

Willcocks, Jessica

Role: Janice Scott
Appeared in 'If They Could See Us Now…!'

Jessica's other television appearances include various roles in shows like *Harry Enfield's Yule Log Chums, People Like Us, Le Show, This Is Pop* and playing Minge in *Absolutely Fabulous*. On stage she's appeared as Viola in *Twelfth Night*, Delyth in *Tom and the Magical Flower* and Jodie in *Can't Stand Up for Falling Down*.

Williams, Kate

Role: Mrs Miles
Appeared in 'A Royal Flush'

Kate trained at East 15's Acting School between 1962 and '65, before establishing a successful career

on screen and stage. On television she had a leading role as Joan Booth in the ITV sitcom *Love Thy Neighbour*, while other credits include Molly in *Hot Money*, Brigitte in *Best of Both Worlds*, Mrs Coles in *Randall and Hopkirk (Deceased)*, Mrs McClusky in *Berkeley Square*, two series of *Time After Time* and four series of *May to December*.

On the big screen she played a mother in *Quadrophenia* and was seen in *Return to the Secret Garden, The Table, Poor Cow* and *No Hard Feelings*, while in the theatre her many credits include *She Stoops to Conquer, Chorus Girls* and *Liza of Lambeth*.

Williams, Roger

Properties buyer on eight episodes: S2 and 'A Royal Flush'

Willson, Jane

Production assistant on one episode: 'The Frog's Legacy'

Wilmore, Barry

Role: Waiter
Appeared in S1, episode 2

Wilmot Road

In 'The Frog's Legacy', Del mentions Wilmot Road while explaining the location of a job he may have secured for Rodney. The place of employment is down an alley, opposite a flashy office block and between an undertaker's and the Light of Nepal restaurant.

Winser, Mike

Cameraman on location video in 'Diamonds are for Heather'

Winstanley, Michèle

Role: Karen (the barmaid)
Appeared in S3, episodes 5, 6 & 7 and 'Thicker Than Water'

Michèle, who was born in Eindhoven, Holland, in 1964, was six months old when her British parents settled in Islington.

She began her acting career at the Anna Scher Children's Theatre Club, attending after-school classes between 1974 and 1982; her first professional assignment came in 1978, aged 14, playing Blanche, a schoolgirl, in an instalment of *Armchair Theatre* titled *Quiet as a Nun*, with Patsy Kensit. Her next TV job came at the age of 16 in the teenagers' series *Going Out*, written by *Brookside* creator, Phil Redmond.

Her early days were largely spent on the big and small screen, including *Shine on Harvey Moon, The Comic Strip Presents, Staggered Walker, Straight to Hell* and *Remembrance*. Nowadays, as well as acting, she's working as a playwright and director. The first play she penned, *Keepers*, premièred at the Hampstead Theatre in October 2000, and she's currently writing her second commission for the Soho Theatre.

Winston

Not seen in the sitcom, Winston talks to Del on the phone in 'A Losing Steak'. Del tries persuading him to buy a dodgy mink coat for £50, which could

easily be cat's fur, but Del should have saved his breath because Winston isn't interested.

Winter, Richard

Costume designer on 13 episodes: S4; S6, episodes 1, 3–6 and 'Dates'

Born in Malvern, Richard worked in costume and set design in the theatre before joining the BBC in 1970. After five years as a costume assistant, he was promoted to designer and over 26 years worked on a multitude of shows, including *The Explorers*, filmed in Africa, *Tenko, Alas Smith and Jones, Mike Yarwood in Persons* and *One Foot in the Grave*.

Richard was made redundant from the Beeb in 1996 and now runs his own business buying and selling property in the Bournemouth area.

Wirtz, Aad

Dubbing mixer on one episode: 'Mother Nature's Son'

Aad arrived from Holland in 1975 and worked with Cine-Lingual Sound Studios for nearly ten years, concentrating on post-production sound. After a spell at Ladbroke Films in London, consolidating the skills he'd mastered in the industry, he established Interact Sound Limited with three partners in 1990.

Aad's extensive list of film and television credits include *Mike Barrett: England Manager, Snakes and Ladders, Darkness Falls, Fever Pitch, Love in a Cold Climate, Cold Enough for Snow, Memento Mori* and *Lorna Doone*.

Witton, Tom

Played by Bill Ward

The unfortunate gamekeeper (Tom Witton) is gagged and bundled into the Trotters' van in 'Friday the 14th'. Believing he's the escapee from the local institute for the criminally insane, the Trotters – who are taking a weekend break to do a spot of fishing – find him prowling around Boycie's weekend cottage in Cornwall, overpower him and take him to the local police station. Unfortunately for Witton, the gagging does little good for his asthma, which explains the wheezing when the gag is removed.

Woman at opera

Played by Richenda Carey

Seen at the Theatre Royal, Drury Lane, in 'A Royal Flush', the opera-goer is continually disturbed by Del and June, and tersely exchanges a few words.

Woman at window

Played by Christina Michaels

A member of the Peckham Bowling Club, the woman is seen in the clubhouse during 'Ashes to Ashes'. When the Trotters try scattering Arthur's ashes over the bowling green, they scarper when they realise people are in the clubhouse, leaving the urn in the middle of the green. A woman spots the urn and calls the club captain over, but by the time he arrives at the window, the urn has been retrieved and the captain thinks she's been drinking too much.

Woman in club

Played by Jean Harrington

The woman is seated on a stool in a nightclub during 'Rodney Come Home'. Classing her as a 'mature type', Mickey Pearce and Chris attempt striking up a conversation but get nowhere.

Woman in crowd

Played by Marie Lorraine

The woman is a diner at the upmarket Italian restaurant at Chelsea, where Arnie is supposed to be meeting Mr Stavros to discuss selling his gold chains. She's seen in 'Chain Gang' accusing Boycie of mugging Arnie – who's collapsed on the floor. Boycie is trying to get his hands on Arnie's briefcase which contains the gold chains and thousands of pounds, the lion's share (£7,500) of which belongs to him.

Woman in crowd

Played by Blanche Coleman

Seen briefly at the market in 'To Hull and Back', the woman corrects Del on the price he's quoted whilst trying to sell his Japanese watches.

Woman in kiosk

Played by Jeanne Mockford

In 'The Longest Night', the woman is working at the tobacco kiosk when Lennox Gilbey enters the Top-Buy supermarket. He wants some cigarettes and cheekily asks the woman to put them on his account.

Woman in market (Gwen)

Played by Angela Moran

Seen in 'A Royal Flush', the woman watches Del carry out his sales pitch at the local market.

Wood, Jake

Role: Trainee
Appeared in 'The Jolly Boys' Outing'

Jake's busy acting career has already included a host of television appearances, such as Jimmy in *Inspector Morse*, a yob in *One Foot in the Grave*, Danny in *Casualty*, Private Kemp in *A Touch of Frost*, Kill Crazy in several instalments of *Red Dwarf*, a policeman in *Bramwell* and Pete Ainsworth in *Tough Love*. He's also worked on the stage and appeared in several films, including *Truth or Dare* and *Dad Savage*.

Woodcock, Steven

Role: Jevon
Appeared in S6, episodes 1, 5 & 6; 'Dates' and 'The Jolly Boys' Outing'

Steven, who was born in Hackney, London, in 1964,

made his professional acting debut in 1980, appearing in a Black Lion's film, *Walcott*, but his career has been largely spent working in television, where his credits include playing Glenroy in *Grange Hill*, Dennis in *Girls on Top*, a van driver in *Paradise Postponed*, Raschid in *Casualty*, Winston in *A Very Peculiar Practice* and, one of his favourite roles, Clyde Tavernier in *EastEnders*. Nowadays, Steven is concentrating on his work as a musician and screen writer.

Wooden, Ed

Videotape editor on two episodes: 'A Royal Flush' and 'The Frog's Legacy'

Born in Kingston-upon-Thames, Ed joined the BBC as a trainee engineer in 1963. Early assignments as an editor include *Juke Box Jury* and *The Morecambe and Wise Show*. Other shows he's worked on during the 29 years spent with the Beeb range from *The Young Ones* and *Bottom* to *Three Of A Kind* and *Comic Relief*.

Ed left the BBC in the early 1990s and worked freelance for a while, but he's now enjoying his retirement.

Woodford, Nigel

Film sound recordist on four episodes: S2, episodes 2, 4, 5 & 7

Born in London in 1944, Nigel joined the BBC as a

Nigel Woodford (wearing glasses) on location

technical operator in 1962 and began working on shows such as *Dr Finlay's Casebook*, *Maigret*, *Tonight* and *The Newcomers*. Nigel, who's worked in the television and film industry for 39 years, left the Beeb in 1983 and now runs Richmond Film Services, hiring out sound equipment to production companies.

Woodley, Peter

Camera supervisor on four episodes: 'Heroes and Villains', 'Modern Men', 'Time On Our Hands' and 'If They Could See Us Now…!'

Woods, Donal

Designer on five episodes: 'Mother Nature's Son', 'Fatal Extraction', 'Heroes and Villains', 'Modern Men' and 'Time On Our Hands'

à la Del

★ ★ ★ ★ ★ ★

'Revenons à nos moutons!'

('The Sky's the Limit')

Woodthorpe, Peter

Role: Reg Trotter

Appeared in 'Thicker Than Water'

Peter was born in York in 1931. He studied bio-chemistry at Cambridge for two years before leaving to appear in the original production of *Waiting for Godot*, a West End engagement which lasted 40 weeks.

One of Britain's best known character actors, he made his name in theatre while still in his twenties, winning many plaudits for leading performances in productions like *The Caretaker* and *Poor Bitos*.

In recent years, he has concentrated on films and television. On the big screen he has appeared in productions such as *Hysteria*, *Charge of the Light Brigade*, *To Catch a King*, *A Christmas Carol*, *The Red Monarch*, *The Hunchback of Notre Dame* and *Merlin*.

His more recent television work includes playing Max, the pathologist, in the first two series of *Inspector Morse*, but he's been seen in many shows, like *Minder*, *Singles*, *Chance in a Million*, *Coronation Street* and *Three Of A Kind*.

Woolley, James

Role: Mr Frazer

Appeared in S4, episode 3

Born in the Somerset town of Taunton in 1945, James graduated from the Central School of Speech and Drama in 1968 and began working in repertory theatre, intitially at Frinton on Sea. He continues working on the stage and recent credits include *Fallen Angels* at London's Apollo Theatre, and *The Deep Blue Sea* at Nottingham Playhouse.

He's also worked extensively on the big and small screen, including *Coupling* and *The Colour of Justice*, both for the BBC. Other television credits range from *Upstairs, Downstairs; The Duchess of Duke Street* and *Trial and Retribution* to *Green Fingers*, *The Firm* and *The Politician's Wife*. Among the films he's worked on are *Intimate Contact*, *Spys*, *Maurice* and *Poor Little Rich Girl*.

'Yellow Peril, The'

Original transmission: Thursday 18 November 1982, 8.30 pm

Production date: Sunday 6 June 1982

Original viewing figures: 8.2 million

Duration: 30 minutes

First repeat: Tuesday 2 August 1983, 8.30 pm

Subsequent repeats: 16/11/90, 6/1/95, 20/8/98, 11/2/00

CAST

Del Trotter	David Jason
Rodney Trotter	Nicholas Lyndhurst
Grandad Trotter	Lennard Pearce
Trigger	Roger Lloyd Pack
Mr Chin (the Chinese takeaway owner)	Rex Wei
Walk-ons:	(Chinese kitchen hands)

Free Lee Own and Arnold Lee

PRODUCTION TEAM

Written by John Sullivan

Title music arranged and conducted by Ronnie Hazlehurst

Composed and sung by John Sullivan

Make-up designer:	Shaunna Harrison
Costume Designer:	Anushia Nieradzik
Properties Buyer:	Roger Williams
Film Cameraman:	John Walker
Film Sound:	Dennis Panchen and Nigel Woodford
Film Editor:	Mike Jackson
Camera Supervisor:	Ron Peverall
Studio Lighting Director:	Henry Barber
Studio Sound:	Dave Thompson
Technical Coordinator:	Robert Hignett
Videotape Editor:	Chris Wadsworth
Production Assistant:	Penny Thompson
Assistant Floor Manager:	Tony Dow
Graphic Designer:	Peter Clayton and Fen Symonds
Vision Mixer:	Angela Beveridge
Production Managers:	Janet Bone and Sue Bysh
Designer:	Andy Dimond

Produced by Ray Butt

'Yesterday Never Comes'

Original transmission: Thursday 1 December 1983, 8.30 pm

Production date: Sunday 23 October 1983

Original viewing figures: 10.6 million

Duration: 30 minutes

First repeat: Monday 6 August 1984, 8.00 pm

Subsequent repeats: 21/9/91, 5/3/95, 14/4/00

CAST

Del Trotter	David Jason
Rodney Trotter	Nicholas Lyndhurst
Grandad Trotter	Lennard Pearce

MEMORIES OF 'THE YELLOW PERIL'

★ ★ ★ ★ ★ ★

'The tombstone was actually made of carved jabo-lite and painted with luminous yellow paint. It was lit with ultra violet or black light. When I received the script, it was obvious from the way John Sullivan had described it in the script that the tombstone wasn't tiny; by the time I'd finished with it, it was about eight feet tall.

'When it came to designing it, my assistant and I spent some time researching monuments in the library. We found out about all different sorts of figures that people had had carved, stuck them all together by putting tracings on top of tracings until we came up with the actual design. We took our ideas to Ray Butt and John Sullivan who liked them, then passed it onto a scenic artist at the BBC who carved it.'

ANDY DIMOND – Designer

Mrs Murphy . . . . .Lucita Lijertwood
Miranda Davenport . . . . .Juliet Hammond
Harry (the furniture restorer) . . .Robert Vahey
Auctioneer . . . . .Garard Green
Walk-ons: . . . .(Pretty girl outside café)
Anne Colver. (Gallery rep. at auction) Peter Whitaker. (People in café) Liz D'Esterre and Darrell Brook. (Rolls Royce chauffeur) Jay Roberts. (People at auction room) Victor Reynolds, Lionel Stevens, Gwynne Sullivan, Derek Suthern and 16 extras.
Audience warm-up: . . . . .Felix Bowness

PRODUCTION TEAM
Written by John Sullivan
Title music arranged and conducted by Ronnie Hazlehurst
Composed and sung by John Sullivan
Make-up designer: . . . . .Denise Baron
Costume Designer: . . . . .Dinah Collin
Properties Buyer: . . . . .Penny Rollinson
Film Cameraman: . . . . .Ian Hilton
Film Sound: . . . . .Clive Derbyshire
Film Editor: . . . . .Mike Jackson
Camera Supervisor: . . . . .Chris Glass
Studio Lighting Director: . . . . .Don Babbage
Studio Sound: . . . . .Dave Thompson
Technical Coordinator: . . . . . .Chris Watts
Videotape Editor: . . . . .Chris Wadsworth
Production Assistant: . . . . .Penny Thompson
Assistant Floor Manager: . . . .Tony Dow
Graphic Designer: . . . . .Mic Rolph
Vision Mixer: . . . . .Angela Beveridge
Production Manager: . . . . .Andy Smith
Designer: . . . . .Anthony Thorpe
Produced and directed by Ray Butt

Del's making a mug of himself again, this time taken in by a so-called reputable antiques' dealer, Miranda Davenport, who owns a shop in Chelsea. When he tries passing off a woodworm-infested cabinet, made out of old banana boxes, as a genuine Queen Anne antique, Miranda isn't hoodwinked when she turns up at the Trotters' flat in response to an advert in the local rag. Before she leaves, she spots a painting on the wall; she doesn't let on about its value, claims it's worthless, then befriends Del in order to get her hands on the painting. In the end, Del is easily led and gives the painting to Miranda as a gift.

Later, when Del arrives at her shop to ask Miranda out to lunch, Harry – the furniture restorer – redirects him to the local auction rooms, where Miranda is bidding on various lots. Not expecting his arrival, she's keen to get rid of Del, but just as she's about to achieve her goal, Lot 24 is called: a recently discovered piece of work by the late 19th-century artist, Joshua Blythe. Del recognizes the picture as none other than the one that used to hang in his flat. Realising he's been made a fool of by Miranda, he has great joy in having the last laugh by informing her that the picture is, in fact, stolen property.

Young Towser
(See 'Towser, Young')

'Yesterday Never Comes'

'Yuppy Love'
Original transmission: Sunday 8 January 1989, 7.15 pm
Production date: Sunday 18 December 1989
Original viewing figures: 13.9 million
Duration: 50 minutes
First repeat: Friday 8 September 1989, 7.15 pm
Subsequent repeats: 8/1/92, 25/10/93, 2/6/95, 18/7/97, 23/6/99, 13/1/01, 19/6/02

CAST
Del Trotter . . . . .David Jason
Rodney Trotter . . . . .Nicholas Lyndhurst
Uncle Albert . . . . .Buster Merryfield
Trigger . . . . .Roger Lloyd Pack
Cassandra . . . . .Gwyneth Strong
Mickey Pearce . . . . .Patrick Murray
Jevon . . . . .Steven Woodcock
Emma . . . . .Francesca Brill
Marsha . . . . .Laura Jackson
Dale .Diana Katis
Snobby girl . . . . .Hazel McBride
Barman . . . . .William Thomas
Girl in disco . . . . .Tracy Clarke
Walk-ons: . . . . .Laney Ashton,
Adrian Fletcher, Georgie Price, Richard Davis, Don Paul, Heather Downham, Shalima Bowers, Beverley Knock, Doreen Chanter, Jazzy Northover, Debbie Knight and Dadina Sagger.

PRODUCTION TEAM
Written by John Sullivan
Title music arranged and conducted by Ronnie Hazlehurst
Composed and sung by John Sullivan
Make-up designer: . . . . .Jean Steward
Costume Designer: . . . . .Richard Winter
Properties Buyer: . . . . .Malcolm Rougvie
Film Cameraman: . . . . .Alec Curtis
Film Sound: . . . . .Michael Spencer
Film Editor: . . . . .John Jarvis
Camera Supervisor: . . . . .Ron Green
Studio Lighting Director: . . . . .Don Babbage
Studio Sound: . . . . .Alan Machin
Technical Coordinator: . . . . . .Reg Poulter
Videotape Editor: . . . . .Chris Wadsworth
Production Assistants: . . . . . . .Amita Lochab and Faith Harris
Assistant Floor Manager: . . . .Kerry Waddell
Vision Mixer: . . . . .Heather Gilder
Production Managers: . . . . . . .Adrian Pegg and Gill Anderson
Designer: . . . . .Graham Lough
Directed by Tony Dow
Produced by Gareth Gwenlan

'Yuppy Love'

Since watching the movie, *Wall Street*, Del sees himself as some high-flying executive; his new filofax, red braces and tortoiseshell cigar holder all support his new image. He's even submitted an application to buy his council flat so that he can sell it on for a quick profit. Del is adamant: he wants to become a yuppy.

He ditches The Nag's Head for plusher surroundings but his attempts to move up in the world – financially as well as socially – are dreams that are out of his reach. Sadly, Del's the only one who fails to see that.

Rodney, meanwhile, is still trying to better himself academically, even though it's taking him an inordinate amount of time to complete his computer diploma at the local Adult Education Centre.

But, at long last, Rodney's love life takes a turn for the better when he meets Cassandra, who's also studying at evening class. A subsequent meeting at a disco leads to the first kiss and the first date.

Yvonne

Played by Carolyn Allen

Del meets Yvonne – who's 'all body and no brains' – at a seedy nightclub during 'Watching the Girls Go By'. She's an exotic dancer but Del refers to her as a stripper. She's been sacked from most of the clubs she's worked at because she's hitting the bottle too hard. Keen to break into singing, Del promises her a chance to sing at The Nag's Head if she helps him win a bet by accompanying Rodney to a do.

Zimbabwe House

This tower block is on the Nyrere housing estate. The only resident we get to meet is June Snell, who used to date Del.

Zoe

Played by Lisa Price

Zoe, who appears in the closing scene of 'No Greater Love…', is Rodney's next girlfriend after the more mature, Irene Mackay. The shapely Zoe met Rodney at a roller-disco and is 18.

'Yuppy Love'

The Return of the Trotters

When the Trotters struck gold in 'Time On Our Hands', it looked as if the lights were being switched off for good at Nelson Mandela House. As the boys headed off to live the life of Riley, fans wondered if they would ever see them again, or had the last orders really been called at The Nag's Head?

Although no one had any intention of making another full series of *Only Fools and Horses*, the door was kept slightly ajar for a possible return of John Sullivan's much-loved sitcom. After all, surely Del would never settle for putting his feet up in front of a log fire and puffing on his oversized cigars while frittering away his new-found wealth on the money market?

However, if Tony Dow had acted on Sullivan's initial suggestion as to how to close 'Time On Our Hands', the Trotters' return would have been much more difficult. 'In the script I wanted them to turn into cartoon characters as they walked off into the sunset,' admits John. 'I felt that once they were cartoons they were no longer real and couldn't return, but Tony didn't pick up on it, I don't know why.'

Tony answers the question by explaining that it wasn't a conscious decision. 'We did make it look a little like a cartoon setting, but I just felt we had to be careful with the characters themselves.'

The final instalment of the Christmas Trilogy was watched by a record-breaking 24.3 million viewers and brought overwhelming praise from all corners of the media world, with many people clamouring for more. 'It came to an end initially because David was looking to go on to a new role,' explains Gareth Gwenlan, 'so we all agreed to finish it with the Trilogy. But the response was *so* extraordinary; we all met afterwards and although we didn't want to do any more in terms of a series, we agreed in principle to try and do one for the Millennium.'

John Sullivan, meanwhile, believes it was a comment Gareth made during an interview that sparked off the excitement concerning a new story for the Millennium. 'There was certainly a lot of press interest, that's for sure. Then Gareth, off his own bat, said: "Maybe we'll do a special for the Millennium." Although it was three or four years off we started receiving more and more interest,' recalls John. 'Then David Jason was misquoted at a press conference for *Frost*. A reporter asked why he wasn't doing any more *Fools and Horses*,

and he was reported as saying something like: "Oh, I haven't been asked." Of course, that kicked it off like crazy. The phone kept ringing, and my agent said: "Don't let it be you who killed the series off." So the process started there, really, although, of course, we all had other work to finish.' Deep down, though, John still didn't think he'd ever revisit *Only Fools*, and assumed that all the interest would fade away. 'But it didn't, which I'm pleased about.'

The main challenge for Gareth Gwenlan was always going to be arranging a period of time when both David Jason and Nicholas Lyndhurst would be available. 'David was under contract with Yorkshire Television for a long time, so the Millennium passed and we hadn't done anything,' recalls Gareth. With everyone having agreed that it would be best to coincide with a special occasion, the prospect of a return to Trotterland seemed bleak, that was until John Sullivan had a conversation with Gareth, some 18 months ago. 'John had all these ideas, so I suggested that we just go ahead and do one more anyway.'

Gareth contacted David Jason and Nicholas Lyndhurst, and together with John Sullivan, they met for dinner and discussed the proposal. 'As soon as John explained the ideas he had, David got excited and became Del Boy. He'd come in looking like Frost, which he was working on at the time, and within five minutes was animated and looking just like Del, it was remarkable. David told us that he was available between November 2001 and March 2002, and Nick said he'd make himself available, so it looked as if we finally had a chance.'

Next step in the complex process saw Gareth presenting the idea to the BBC hierarchy. During discussions with the actors, it became evident that there was too much material for just one programme, so Gareth floated the idea of three new shows. 'Of course they were interested, although they swallowed a bit hard when I told them what the budget was going to be, but then David, Nick and John don't come cheap and we've always made it with very high production levels, which has helped to distinguish it from other shows.'

Fortunately the BBC gave the nod and dates were blocked out in the actors' diaries, while John Sullivan settled down to write the first script. But within days the tragic events in America on 11 September shocked the world. The catastrophe shook John so much that he didn't know whether he could continue. 'Things

that happen in your life can affect your ability to write scripts, such as the illness or even death of a loved one, but you still try and struggle through. I hadn't got very far into the 'If They Could See Us Now…!' script when 11 September arrived; for some while after that I found it impossible to go into my office and be funny – like everyone else, I was deeply shocked. Then someone said to me how the country needed a laugh, and he was so right; I thought that, perhaps, through *Fools* I could do my bit to help: maybe I could put a smile back on people's faces. That simple statement inspired me to carry on with the script.'

When it came to deciding on the story-line for 'If They Could See Us Now…!', John was sure about one thing: wealth wouldn't change the habits of Del and Rodney. 'Whilst the Trotters had their millions, and lived a life of luxury for a time, jetting off to all the best places in the world, they still did all the things they had done back in Peckham; it's just that they were three miles further up the ladder. They were still gambling, still eyeing up long-legged women and they continued to enjoy their Friday night curries, although it became the finest cuisine from Asia and not a mutton vindaloo, and three pints of lager at The Star of Bengal. The guys just wouldn't change and would always return to Peckham some day because it's where their roots are.'

Their days living in the lap of luxury were short-lived however, and the Trotters were back to where they had started much sooner than expected, thanks to Del who gambled their fortunes on the Central American money market, only to see the financial markets collapse and them lose their millions in the process. To make matters worse, Del and Rodney had an endless list of creditors.

'I did a lot of research into bankruptcy before writing "If They Could See Us Now…!",' John points out. 'The Trotters' main creditor turned out to be the Inland Revenue because I was looking for an organisation which would have little sympathy. I found out that, apparently, they give you a year's grace to pay the money back, with interest, and if you don't, they sell everything you own, including property. I thought the story-line would work out nicely because at the end of Christmas Night, Del would be given a year to pay off his debts, leaving us 12 months in which to show the next two instalments.'

Keenly anticipated by fans of the sitcom, the first episode was transmitted on Christmas Day

2001, attracting 20.3 million viewers, the festive period's biggest audience. Not surprisingly, John Sullivan was pleased, particularly as he faced several challenges when revisiting the lives of the Trotter family. 'Even though it's a show that's 21 years old, it was almost like starting afresh. They were set in an alien environment, being in the south of France, and I wanted to get them back to Peckham as quickly as possible because it doesn't work taking characters out of their normal environment for too long, especially as they'd become millionaires and being rich just isn't funny in comedy. The audience numbers grew by one million during the show. It was almost as if the audience grew just as the Trotters returned home.'

After an interval of five years, there was a degree of re-establishing evident in John Sullivan's script; he had also been rocked by the deaths of Buster Merryfield and Ken MacDonald since 'Time On Our Hands'. 'They were terrible problems to have to cope with,' John admits. 'But I thought the end result was a professional job all round. Some newspapers rubbished it a bit, but I don't think they're professional enough to take in what it's all about. It's not easy covering two deaths and treating the actors with respect whilst still trying to make people laugh.'

Producer Gareth Gwenlan, however, wasn't convinced that any re-establishment was necessary in the script. 'It was a class programme and I'm very proud of it, but, quite honestly, the first 15 to 20 minutes weren't needed. Nevertheless, when it's repeated it will be one of those episodes that people like more and more. Take "Miami Twice", which initially wasn't everybody's favourite episode but is now one of the highest rated.'

'It was a hard time for John, bearing in mind all he had to cover in the episode,' explains Tony Dow, who once again directed the show. 'I think it was a cracking episode, and episode two is an absolutely splendid, traditional show, while episode three is almost like signing off again.'

When asked what he likes most about John Sullivan's writing, Gareth focuses on one of many aspects he admires in his work. 'He's always walking that narrow line between tragedy and comedy. John is a firm believer, as I am, that comedy should be firmly rooted in reality first of all. Life isn't a series of laughs, and you often get a much heightened sense of emotion if you have been laughing before, or a heightened sense of fun if you have been very serious. John is the master of writing real dialogue in real situations, and then – depending on how it's going to be played – getting the most wonderful warm laughter, or even tears in your eyes before something outrageously funny happens. It's this clever, rich, textured writing which works so well – it's not just a series of funny gags, it's all about character development.'

As far as the actors were concerned, they were

Designing the costumes

Initially, Tony Dow and Gareth Gwenlan wanted to assemble the personnel who had worked on the Christmas Trilogy, back in 1996, but for various reasons this wasn't possible. When costume designer Robin Stubbs wasn't available, Jacky Levy was recruited on to the team. After studying fashion design at Harrow School of Art, she worked in the fashion industry before opting for a change of direction. Within a few years of joining the BBC as an assistant costume designer, she was promoted to designer and built up an impressive list of credits, including *Grange Hill*; *Bergerac*; *EastEnders*; *The Mary Whitehouse Experience*; *One Foot in the Grave*; *Roger, Roger* and *Heartburn Hotel*, before leaving to work freelance.

Jacky, who'd worked with Tony Dow and Gareth Gwenlan on previous productions, looked forward to joining the *Only Fools* team. 'I enjoyed it very much and, to be honest, it's a shame when the third episode was completed. It can be difficult coming in on something which is already established, but that wasn't the case with *Only Fools*.'

When it came to kitting out the characters after more than five years, Jacky virtually started from scratch. 'There was a rail of costumes kept at the BBC costume store, but the only item I used was a pair of lime green satin pyjamas which had been made for Del Boy.' As the Trotters had briefly enjoyed the lifestyle of millionaires, Jacky could dress everyone up in more expensive attire. When their money was lost on the stock exchange, they retained their clothes. 'Obviously you don't lose your clothes,' explains Jacky, 'but we did bring the styles down a little bit, although we didn't return to the old fashions.'

Jacky certainly had her work cut out considering the number of main characters she had to dress. Each character has their own unique style, which has to be considered, such as Sid, who'd become a more prominent character. 'He's a scruffy character and I hired his outfits from the BBC costume store, along with those for Trigger and Denzil, because they all wear fairly old clothes. Roy Heather is such a nice man, and he had an idea of how he wanted to look behind the bar.'

Jacky stresses the importance of accepting the performer's input. 'One wants them to feel comfortable in what they're wearing. When I first fitted David I took a lot of outfits over to his house and then returned what we didn't use; ensuring David was happy with his outfits was probably the first major challenge.'

But there were challenges throughout the three episodes, some of which can't be disclosed at this stage, prior to the shows being transmitted, but arranging for a gladiator's outfit to be made for 'If They Could See Us Now…!' can be discussed. 'It was made specially by the same maker who made all of Russell Crowe's armour for *Gladiator*. The brief from John Sullivan and Tony Dow was that they wanted it to be fairly authentic while also appearing slightly jokey, but not to the point where people would think he'd hired it from the local joke shop. When it comes to designing special outfits like that, I always try and get Tony Dow, the director, to see it early on in the fitting process, so he's got a good idea of what the end product will be.'

When deciding upon outfits for the other main characters, Jacky would meet them to share ideas. Such meetings often took place at nearby coffee bars once Jacky had completed her preparatory work. 'Normally I read the script, break it down and ensure I know what the actors require for the show, such as nightwear, evening wear, casual clothes, whatever. I also need to know how many days' worth of story they're appearing in. Then I ring them up and have a chat; after that we meet up and discuss the style of the outfits before we go shopping. But, as I said, for people like Roger Lloyd Pack and Paul Barber, they came to the costume store and I did the fitting there; Roger, actually, likes to go along the rails of old clothes and pick things out himself. So it's slightly different for each character.'

Another character Jacky had to dress was Damien Trotter, played by Ben Smith. 'He was a great kid, very enthusiastic. We had to buy a lot of oversized clothes to make him look like his character. I'd worked with kids a lot before on *Grange Hill* and you find many of them are into certain labels and have to look a certain way, but Benjamin was great. He was prepared to wear anything the character needed, which I thought was a very mature attitude for someone his age.'

On most productions there is the occasional item of clothing that the costume designer is unable to acquire, such as a special jacket that David Jason wanted to wear for the Monaco scenes in 'If They Could See Us Now…!'. 'I got very close to finding the style of blazer he wanted, but certain jackets are only in fashion for a couple of years, after which time you just cannot get them for love or money. There are always particular things you're asked for, but sometimes you have to come to a compromise.'

Jacky found recording the last episode, 'Sleepless in Peckham', which is likely to be transmitted during Christmas 2002, an emotional time. 'It was partly because of the storylines, with the Trotters experiencing more than their fair share of good and bad luck, which always plays on the emotional side. John's work is all about the ups and downs of life, which is why it works so well. Quite a few of the audience were shedding a tear – I was certainly quite choked.'

Designing the sets

During the 23 years David Hitchcock spent as a staff production designer at the BBC, he worked on a number of successful shows, including John Sullivan's *Just Good Friends*, which he regards as his first major success in terms of production design. Over the years he's worked with John Sullivan, Ray Butt, Gareth Gwenlan and Tony Dow, but designing the sets for 'If They Could See Us Now…!' was his first taste of *Only Fools*. Previously, other commitments had prevented him making his debut as a designer on the show and he was delighted to join the team this time around.

David, who's a Geordie, studied at the Hornsey College of Art before moving on to complete a degree in architecture. Upon graduating he worked for Lloyds Bank as an architect for nearly two years; although he enjoyed his days with the bank, he had always harboured a dream of working in film or television and finally decided to try his luck in the television industry. In the early 1970s he was offered a short-term contract as a design relief assistant at the Beeb, covering for designers on vacation. The first programme he worked on in this capacity was *Dixon of Dock Green,* while he cut his teeth as an acting designer on *Happy Ever After* and *Not the Nine O'Clock News,* the show he believes placed his name on the map. As a fully fledged designer, David's extensive list of credits includes setting up *Lovejoy* and *Casualty.*

Over the years, David's worked several times with *Only Fools'* incumbent director, Tony Dow. 'I'm comfortable working with Tony, and he's comfortable having me as the designer – and I'm quite good at controlling the budget, which is always very important,' he says with a smile.

Having to resurrect the feel and look of all the sets last used five years previously was a task that David relished. 'The previous designer, Donal, had kept hold of a few elevations and a couple of files, which were useful, but I had to do a lot of fishing around as well. If you remember at the end of "Time On Our Hands", the Trotters leave the flat with the old curtains hanging, carpet on the floor and that reed and bamboo paper on the walls. We decided to change the carpet for the new episodes, but the one thing that everybody remembers is the wallpaper, so I tried to keep it the same. I searched and searched for some rolls of that design, which hasn't been made for years.'

David turned to Roy Bell Wallcoverings, a company that specialises in supplying wallpapers and fabrics to television and film companies, who supplied the paper when it was first used. The 1970s design, Nairn Flock, was made by Nairn Williamson, a company that no longer exists. Initially it didn't look hopeful. 'We found out it would cost thousands to try and reprint the paper,' explains David, 'so I had to think of other alternatives. As we had photos we were going to cut a stencil and hand paint the pattern on to white paper.'

Then David had a bit of good fortune when he decided to phone his contact at Eastdales, near Slough, who'd helped supply items during the making of the 1996 Christmas Trilogy. 'Fortunately they found half a dozen rolls in their warehouse. They were probably the last six rolls in the entire universe!'

The previous curtains were still in stock, so the overall look of the flat was established,

although David did inject some subtle touches of his own, such as net curtains. 'I always maintained that Raquel would have done something about that.' When he told the rest of the production team what he was planning to do, there was a huge sigh of relief from certain quarters. 'The lighting guy almost sank to his knees to thank me,' laughs David. 'Lighting is much more sensitive now in comedy and having the windows of the flat where they were caused him a constant headache. And, anyway, I thought it looked more natural to have the nets.

'It was a very old fashioned set and only designed for two or three people. Nowadays it would have been designed in a totally different way because when you have six or seven people in there you can't move! It's a nightmare because firstly you can't push cameras upstage because there are no natural traps. And, of course, I would alter the position of the window; I'd never have it upstage like that because it makes the lighting difficult. Out of interest, if you watch very carefully during "Time On Our Hands", you'll spot a camera track past on the back of the balcony – it looks like a pigeon.'

Another feature David has tried to influence is the use of the flat's balcony. 'I commented that there had never been anything on the balcony. Tony Dow reminded me of the satellite dish the Trotters had installed for one episode, but I pointed out that people use balconies for all sorts of things. You look around a council estate nowadays and see a range of items on the balconies: bikes, washing, even sofas sometimes. So come the next episode there will be a bit of that.

'It's very difficult stamping your own authority on a set like the Trotters' flat; in fact, you can't because it's established and people are comfortable with it. But you can add a few extras to it, such as the stereo system we saw in 'If They Could See Us Now…!'. All right, it only cost about £30 and is a cheap and nasty old thing, but it adds an extra element to the flat.'

Some of the furniture has also been updated. 'Something as simple as a sofa can cause a lot of problems,' explains David. 'The sofa seems to have grown and grown to such an extent that it's now too big. And when you put in the dining table and have all the characters there, including Cassandra, Raquel and Damien, it's very difficult to work with, partly because, as I said earlier, there's nowhere for a camera to go.'

Although he's proud to have finally worked on *Only Fools,* the experience wasn't without its pressures. 'Timescales were incredibly tight at times,' admits David. 'Take the set for the quiz show in 'If They Could See Us Now…!' for example: I went in and looked around the studio we were using at Pinewood at midday on Friday; we were heading off to Monte Carlo on the Monday to start shooting over there, so I was left with four hours to draw a design and get a model made up – normally you get six weeks!'

David's job also entails helping to find the right locations for particular shots. 'I would say that I've found the majority of locations I've worked on during my career. As a designer I can look at somewhere and say: "I can do this to that which will then enable you to use that location over there as well." Basically, it can save a lot of time.'

Only Fools was no exception and David recalls scouring the French countryside for locations in the second instalment of the current trilogy. 'We had to find a French village and I recalled a drama series I'd worked on, which we'd shot in Normandy. So we went to this village I remembered but it had changed so much. It used to be very quiet with cafés everywhere, but now was simply a route for lorries. When you have six pages of dialogue you need somewhere that is very controlled. So after driving about a thousand miles, we pitched up at this little village on the Cherbourg peninsula.'

That region of France provided the team with a port, a wine warehouse and a village, all requirements for the particular episode. 'It was a quiet little place on the coast – almost like a ghost town, which was great for us. A lot of the scenes were set around cafés and I ended up turning the town hall into one.'

The nature of David's job has its frustrations,

"ONLY FOOLS" JAN 2002

FACIA.
BLINDS.

FALSE
WALL

sale warehouses and spotted lots of bits and pieces, like these naff, mock marble carvings, which I thought would be ideal for the mausoleum. I was also able to use some little cherubs I'd seen a few months back. On the original script, John Sullivan had also written a few instructions, indicating that he wanted some trumpeting angels and a plaque dedicated to God, all of which he's got. It's certainly very Trotteresque.'

Another set David has had to redesign is Del's bedroom. 'This is a scene which is cut in between another scene using a different location, which happens to be very red in colour. When you switch between scenes one of the things you try to do is change the colours; as a result, I can't do Del's old red bed. Also, the bed head doesn't exist anymore, nor does the wallpaper, so it's going to be a totally different look.'

as he explains. 'We had locals coming up to us saying: "How long has this café been here?" Occasionally the establishing shots, the wide-angle shots, where you'll quite often see a lot of my work, get the elbow because the director needs to tighten up the time.'

Another task for David has been designing a mausoleum that contains the grave of Del and Rodney's mother. 'I trundled up to a cemetery in Kensal Green, London, took some snaps and pinched a few ideas. Then I visited various whole-

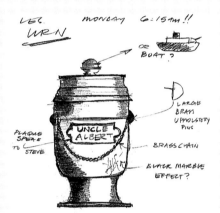

David Hitchcock (above left) outside a café in France. Also shown are some of the sketches he drew whilst carrying out his research.

pleased to be reunited after a five-year gap. John Challis said: 'It's so good to have the gang back together. The show is a phenomenon.'

Paul Barber was equally pleased to be stepping into Denzil's shoes again, although he also reflected on the sadness surrounding the loss of his friend, Ken MacDonald. 'It's strange without Ken because he'd always be there, telling a few gags on set, making everybody laugh.'

The loss of both Buster Merryfield and Ken MacDonald affected the entire cast, as David Jason explained during an interview for the official BBC press information. He said: 'It changes the balance in the show – they're missed. Certainly Ken MacDonald was a tremendous funster. He never, never stopped laughing and playing practical jokes. He was just wonderful.'

David was pleased to be back, though. 'I didn't expect to be back but it's a very pleasant experience. There's been tremendous pressure – from the general public, mainly – to ask us to come back, so, after much deliberation, we said: "Why not?" We're delighted to be able to give people a laugh.'

Working with Nicholas Lyndhurst again was a major draw. 'Nick and I get on so well; we respect each other and it's a joy to work with him. He's extremely talented and he makes it fun, so because of that we're still here.'

It wasn't just in front of the camera that the regular faces returned: many of those involved behind the scenes had worked on previous shows, including Gail Evans, who was production assistant on 'Miami Twice' and 'Mother Nature's Son', but this time had risen to the position of associate producer. Gail thoroughly enjoyed working on the current trilogy of episodes. Having just finished filming the last scene, she says: 'It's a shot of the Trotters' van driving away into the distance; this was the vehicle John Sullivan owned, but I think after using it for these three episodes, it's finally bitten the dust. The poor thing was leaking oil and I don't think it would be reparable again.'

Gail has been working on the latest instalments since September 2001, and is looking forward to taking a month's holiday to help recharge her batteries after what has been a fraught, but exhilarating time. 'Whatever project I work on next, I'm sure it won't be as much fun as *Only Fools*. Obviously there has been so much to organise, as is always the way when John is writing as we go along, because scenes change constantly, and it's been one of the most complicated and challenging shows I've worked on, partly because I've been helping to coordinate a multi-million pound programme which has also involved filming abroad.'

One of her duties included employing and liaising with the French fixers, who helped set up the location shooting in Monte Carlo, Cherbourg and Paris. 'That can be difficult,' admits Gail. 'When we were filming the location scenes for "If They Could See Us Now…!",

Dominique Combe didn't know the series, so we had to explain to him why lines were funny. It was only when we showed him an episode, he met the characters and watched the filming that he realised how funny the programme was; so that was difficult, asking someone else to be your representative in a foreign country and help sell the programme on your behalf.'

One new face, however, was production designer David Hitchcock, for whom it was a pleasure to be working on the show. If circumstances had been different, though, he would probably have become a regular himself by now. 'I was quite often asked to be the designer on the show but I was always tied up with something else and the dates never worked out – that is until now,' explains David, who was a BBC staff designer for 23 years before turning freelance six years ago. 'The previous designer, Donal Woods, who worked on the Christmas Trilogy in 1996 was occupied on another project so these three episodes fell my way. It's always a pleasure to work on a classic, and this is certainly a classic.'

When Ray Butt, the show's former producer/director, first heard about the return of the sitcom for another three episodes, he wasn't convinced it was a good idea. 'I intially thought it was a mistake, although I hoped I would be proved wrong,' he stresses. 'I probably will be because Sullivan writes brilliant material. He's the best comedy writer for years, if not the best of all time. But, yes, I was surprised. I didn't think David Jason would do it anymore because he's always so busy; I also wondered if they were both a bit long in the tooth for it now. Nick, for example, was 19 when we started, so now he'd be about 39 and he's still supposed to be the young, innocent brother, which doesn't really ring true. But I'm sure I'll be wrong and will watch all three episode and have a good old laugh.'

As for the next two instalments, due to be transmitted this autumn, John Sullivan is understandably reluctant to disclose much detail. In the second instalment, we'll be catching up with the Trotters as the 12-month period in which they have to clear their debts comes to a close. But the million-dollar question is will there be any further episodes? 'I think that's it,' says Gareth Gwenlan, shaking his head. 'Some of them are too rich to do it any longer,' he adds with a smile, 'while some of us have got other work to go on and do.'

John Sullivan agrees. 'We've haven't got Buster or Ken now, so you start wondering if you'll be pushing your luck if we considered going on. And there comes a point when the actors start wondering if they're just too old to play the characters anymore. So I think these current episodes will be the end.'

Recording those final scenes was a tear-jerking experience for all those involved in the show, actors and crew alike. Gail Evans was no exception, finding the last studio day one of mixed emotions. 'First of all there was a lovely end-of-

term feeling, but as the day wore on, with everybody emotionally charged, it became very sad realising we wouldn't be getting back together. Even though I'd been on the filming and read the scripts, I still couldn't help shedding a tear whilst sitting at the back of the gallery. Part of that is due to the story-line, but it's also because one knows that's the end.

'It's definitely my favourite show I've worked on. The lovely thing about *Only Fools* is the family atmosphere which exists between the cast and crew – it's like old friends reuniting whenever we get back together – although, sadly, it seems as if this was the last time.'

If the only time we see the Trotters again is in the endless string of repeats which will undoubtedly follow, you can feel sure that the show will still give many of its modern contemporaries a run for their money in the ratings war. There is much criticism aimed at the new crop of sitcoms, many of which don't survive beyond the first series. So what's wrong with the state of comedy shows today? 'A lot of the trouble is current comedy seems geared towards a much younger audience than comedy was traditionally made for,' says Gareth Gwenlan. 'Although there are people watching comedy programmes for the first time, there are many millions of others who aren't watching because there isn't very much for them. In television nowadays, there does appear to be a thrust to capture an audience that isn't yet part of the television ethos. I'm all for trying to find something for the younger people, but it seems at the moment to be done at the expense of the core comedy years, which is 30 plus. The pendulum has swung too far. But, like most things, fashions in television go in cycles, so there's always hope.'

INSTALMENT ONE

'If They Could See Us Now…!'

Transmitted 25 December 2001
Original Viewing Figures: 20.3 million

Sadly for the Trotters, living the life of Riley is short-lived: they invested their millions into Central American funds, just before the bottom fell out of the money markets, wiping billions off stocks and shares. Losing every penny has forced them to swap sunny Monte Carlo and a jet-set lifestyle for their old pad back in Nelson Mandela House. To make matters worse, Rodney is still experiencing problems in the 'bedroom department'.

Just when it looks as if things couldn't get any worse, Cassandra takes a phone call informing them that Uncle Albert – who'd retired to the seaside and the arms of Elsie Partridge – has died. At the funeral, all the regular faces turn up, but a moment of confusion finds Del, Rodney, Cassandra, Raquel and

The New Damian

An important new role to be cast was that of Damien Trotter. Finding the right person to play an infant or junior is never easy, as Gareth Gwenlan points out. 'Babies are okay because they just lie there in the pram and if they cry it doesn't matter, but young kids between about three and seven can be very difficult. At that age you can't really rely on them. But Ben Smith is excellent: he's very bright and can handle the scenes well.'

Ben enjoyed playing Damien immensely and was happy to answer the following questions.

Were you a fan of *Only Fools and Horses* before you started playing Damien?
Yes, my mum has a lot of the videos – she loves David Jason!

How did you get the part of Damien?
I went along for an audition and had to read a script in a different accent.

What do you remember about the audition?
When I met the producer, director and writer I felt really at ease with them. I remember we all laughed and joked about.

How did you feel when you were offered the part?
I was nearly crying, I couldn't believe it.

What did your friends and family say?
Everyone thought it was fantastic and was a great experience for me to work with famous actors and actresses.

Who's your favourite character?
Paul, who plays Denzil. He's a lovely man and was so kind to me.

Tell me what it was like on your first day with the *Only Fools* team?
I was nervous at first, but then everyone came and introduced themselves and I felt much better. My nerves quickly disappeared.

Who looked after you on the set?
Anna Brabbins, she's great!

What do you think of the character?
Brilliant! It was a really cool part to play.

Do you have any particular memories/anecdotes concerning the role in *Only Fools*?
The whole experience of filming and meeting great people will always be in my thoughts. I have great memories.

Damien arriving at the wrong funeral, and missing Albert's service altogether.

Later, the Trotters' financial plight is highlighted when Del's declared bankrupt, with debts of £48,754, plus interest, to clear, with the Inland Revenue giving them a year to pay up. There seems little option but to re-establish TITCO, but as Del is banned from running a company, it's Rodney who takes up the challenge of controlling the family firm – even if it's only a superficial change in Del's eyes as he's still intending to pull all the strings.

With Cassandra applying for her old job at the bank, and Rodney back in business, the couple are trying – albeit slowly – to re-adjust to life back in Peckham; they're even talking about getting their own pad and starting a family, once they've unloaded their 'memory baggage', which won't be easy, especially as Rodney has to persuade his wife to try Fantasy Therapy, a new-fangled idea from America, which sees Rodney dressing up as a Roman soldier and Cassandra as a policewoman!

Del, meanwhile, devises a plan to help pay off their debts. He appears as a contestant on the game show *Goldrush*, and is enjoying a run of luck until he gets stuck on the £50,000 question. One of the rules allows him to make an SOS call, so he chooses Rodney to help him, but when his younger brother's answer is deemed to be incorrect, Del is out of the game. It hits him hard and he takes off into the night, leaving Raquel and Damien stranded at the television studio. Finally, he returns to the flat, upset and drunk; but then the Trotters receive an unexpected call from the show's producer informing them that a mistake had been made

and Del can collect his £50,000; thinking the caller is none other than the mischievous Mickey Pearce playing a prank, Del tells them to donate the money to charity!

CAST

Del Trotter	David Jason
Rodney Trotter	Nicholas Lyndhurst
Raquel	Tessa Peake-Jones
Cassandra	Gwyneth Strong
Boycie	John Challis
Trigger	Roger Lloyd Pack
Marlene	Sue Holderness
Denzil	Paul Barber
Sid	Roy Heather
Mickey Pearce	Patrick Murray
Justin	Kim Wall
Roland	Colum Convey
Marion	Joan Hodges
Damien	Benjamin Smith
Concierge	Dominique Combe

and
Paul Strike, Jessica Willcocks, Conrad Nelson, Richard Braine, Jonathan Ross

PRODUCTION TEAM

Written by John Sullivan
Title music composed and sung by John Sullivan

Music:	Graham Jarvis
French Fixer:	Dominique Combe
Costume Designer:	Jacky Levy and Pam Maddox
Make-up Designer:	Deanne Turner and Lori Misselbrook
Production Buyer:	Marvin George
Art Director:	Les McCallum
Casting Adviser:	Tracey Gillham
Programme Finance Associate:	Honor Newton

Location Manager:	Peter Chadwick
Unit Manager:	Caroline McCarthy
1st Assistant Director:	Marcus Catlin
2nd Assistant Director:	Anna Brabbins
3rd Assistant Director:	Scott Bunce
Grip:	Dave Holliday
Lighting Gaffer:	Pat Deveney
Sound Recordist:	Reg Mills
Boom Operator:	John Lewis
Camera Operator:	John Hembrough
Studio Resource Manager:	Kim Jowitt
Vision Mixer:	John Barclay
Floor Manager:	Vivien Ackland-Snow
Camera Supervisor:	Peter Woodley
Sound Supervisor:	Laurie Taylor and Nick Roast
Lighting Director:	Martin Kempton
Production Coordinator:	Claudia Cuffy
Assistant Production Manager:	Jo Alloway
Stage Manager:	Anna Brabbins
Production Assistant:	Caroline Gardener
Associate Producer:	Gail Evans
Editor:	Chris Wadsworth
Director of Photography:	John Rhodes
Production Designer:	David Hitchcock
Executive Producer:	John Sullivan
Producer:	Gareth Gwenlan
Director:	Tony Dow

The programme was dedicated
to the memory of Buster Merryfield (1920–1999)
and Kenneth MacDonald (1951–2001)

TITCO's Sales Ledger

September 1981 — *One-legged turkeys*

Swapped a gross of disposable lighters, a space invaders game, two facial saunas, five water-damaged sleeping bags and a moon-roof for a Peugeot for a van-load of these birds. Told Rodney, 'You know it makes sense!' He didn't believe me.

September 1981 — *Briefcases*

Bought 25 from Trigg. Olde English vinyl, good quality, too. Only trouble is they're rejects. The bleedin' combinations are locked inside so can't open them — and they're too hot! I've decided to cut my losses and dump the lot in the river.

October 1982 — *Watches*

Répondez s'il vous plaît, these are! Bought from Trigg at £4 a throw, they'll pass for Longines or Cartiers any day. Have to be careful, though: they're so hot you need oven gloves before winding them up!

October 1982 — *French nylon tights*

Really authentic these, the crème de la menthe of the hosiery world. As worn by Sacha Distel's mum and Charles Aznavour's sister — they're run-proof and fun-proof.

November 1982 — *Perfume*

Yves Saint Dior – Parfum de Toilette. Complete waste of time. Didn't sell any. When I did find a punter to buy one, she returned it claiming she hadn't smelt anything so bad since the cat sanctuary was bombed during the war! Bloody cheek — what does she expect when they're filled up via the bath tub!

November 1982 — *Camel-hair overcoats*

Selling them for £20 each, a real bargain, or £25 if your name is Ahmed. Even flogged one to Rodders.

November 1982 — *Georgian digital clocks*

These sell well. Managed to clear the lot.

November 1982 — *Underwater watches*

Tell the time in cities all around the world, except London. Still, they're ideal for deep-sea divers — well, perhaps that's not such a good idea, especially as you can't take them underwater.

December 1982 — *China cats*

Bought for £1.25 each from auction. Neat little revolving musical boxes. Rodney, the dipstick that he is, thinks they're a waste of dosh because all they play is 'How Much is that Doggy in the Window?' — I can't see what difference it makes.

December 1982 — *Telescopic Christmas trees*

Great idea: flexible, telescopic trees with all the trimmings, baubles, etc. Some might say they're tacky, I think they're lovely jubbly.

November 1983 — *Oranges*

Fresh 'uns from Seville, selling three for 25p. They're so fresh they were playing castanets earlier.

November 1983 — *Battery-operated barking dogs*

Prince William had one of these in his nursery. Made in Burma, retailing for £14.65. I'm flogging them for £6. Must remember the main part of my sales spiel: 'I don't care whether your nipper has got measles, mumps or a scabby eye, beause these are guaranteed to bring a smile right back on to his face.'

December 1984 — *Cricket bats*

We had some comeback on these, and just because I said they were signed by Viv Richards. In fact, they were signed by Viv Richards, it's just that instead of the famous cricketer, Davey Richards' oldest sister, Viv, signed them. What's wrong with that?

March 1985 — *Suntan lotion*

That dipstick of a brother! He's only landed us with £500 worth of suntan oil just when the second ice-age is coming!

March 1985 — *Kandy Dolls*

These near-perfect dolls seemed a good deal until I heard them talk. Uttering Bugs Bunny's 'What's Up Doc?' ain't no good, but good old Rodders will still try flogging them down the Arndale Centre.

April 1985 — *Louvre doors*

Just when I managed to arrange the finance — thanks to my good old mate Denzil — and bought 165 of these blasted doors from Teddy Cummings, Brendan O'Shaughnessy, the Irish git, tells me his contract to refit a housing estate at Nunhead has been cancelled.

August 1986 — *Cordless phones*

These Nomad cordless telephones are faulty stock, but they're worth a gamble.

September 1986 — *Sunbed*

Tried dumping this one off on Mike at The Nag's Head. Retailing at £375, I thought £120 was a bargain. I even promised to throw in a super deluxe plug-in telephone, but he wouldn't have any of it.

December 1986 — *Cutlery*

Canteens of cutlery. Handmade from Indonesian steel, with ivory-effect handles, and packaged nicely in synthetic leather cases. An exclusive line, they're only available from Harrods, Liberty's, Patel's Multi-Mart and TITCO, of course. Tried selling these 36-piece sets for £3.50. They sold so badly I'd rather have shingles than these knives and forks!

December 1987 — *Portable computers*

Rajah computers from Mauritius. Bought 30, sold five. It didn't help when the local Office of Fair Trading announced to the local press that they were useless.

December 1987 — *Inframax massagers*

Infra-red massagers, which cure rheumatics and other such ailments. Had Rodders hobbling through the market pretending to have a serious bout of lumbago. Later had Albert playing the scene — he seemed to overdo it, though, and put the punters right off.

December 1988 — *Ladies' electric razors*

These went like hot cakes! We sold over 400, making us over £2000 in a month. Lovely jubbly!

December 1988 — *Dolls*

These were a dead loss because the eyes had been inserted incorrectly, leaving them cross-eyed. The kids seemed to snap them up, anyway; although we did have problems with one kid — who I think was a bit funny anyhow — because the doll gave her nightmares.

January 1989 — *Video recorders*

Taiwanese recorders bought from Ronnie Nelson. You can tell by all the flashing lights that they're top-of-the-range machines. Rodney's a cheeky git! He remarked that Taiwan is the only country that doesn't have rubbish tips — they send everything to me instead. The only problem with these machines is that the wrong operating instructions are included; it's all right if you can speak a foreign lingo though because they're not printed in English.

January 1989 — *Tomatoes*

Bought 25 ten-kilo boxes of fresh Jersey tomatoes at Folkestone — they were straight off the ferry. Flogging them for £2.50 a box, a great bargain. Managed to sell three boxes to Mike at The Nag's Head.

January 1989 — *Dolls*

These weren't any old dolls, these turned out to be sex dolls in all shapes, sizes and colours! And to think I was doing Denzil a favour by taking them off his hands. We had to get rid of Lusty Linda, Erotic Estelle and the rest of their friends pretty sharp.

January 1989 — *La Dolce Vita Italian shirts*

Italian shirts, but made in Malaya — you know it makes sense . . . I think. Had a go at selling them on to Monkey Harris.

February 1989 — *Executive mobile phones*

Bought 100 from Mickey Pearce and Jevon, who've set up a partnership — can't see that lasting long. They normally retail for £199.99, but I got them for 25 nicker each. They're real state of the art, and I've got them on a sale-or-return basis, so can't be bad. Pity they play havoc with the TV channels, though; must be something to do with the satellites.

December 1989 — *Radio/cassettes*

Albanian-made car stereos. I tried selling them for £10.99, with a Kylie Minogue LP thrown in for good measure, and ended up reducing the price to £10 and forgetting the album. The punters weren't convinced.

December 1990 — *Dolls*

Tried getting rid of these in the Arndale Centre. They're great little things; they even sing lullabies. The trouble is, they sing in Korean!

January 1991 — *Antha chimes*

Door chimes that play 36 different national anthems. Made in Macau. Retail at £36.50, but I'm selling for £13, inclusive of batteries and fitting. Trigger bought one, but Mike wasn't too impressed, he thought they were cheap and tacky. I told him, do you think I'd have one on my door if that was the case?

January 1991 — *Fax machines*

Futafax: the fax machines of tomorrow, today. Reject stock. Unreliable, but all the flashing lights are pretty impressive. Managed to sell one to Mike at the pub.

February 1991 — *Wigs*

'Crowning Glory — wigs of distinction'. Managed to buy a batch from Mustapha's nephew, who works at a top West End wigmaker. They're seconds but no-one would know. I'd secured plenty of orders from all the old tarts down the pub; trouble is, they turned out to be blokes' wigs.

December 1991 — *Wine*

Managed to get my hands on some Romanian wine. Got a vicar to bless it so we could sell it on around the country as Trotters' pre-blessed wine. Not a bad idea, until I find out I've been supplied with white wine, and it's supposed to be red.

December 1992 — *Spring Water*

Clearing up Grandad's old allotment and discovered a hidden spring. Companies seem to be making a mint these days selling bottled water so decided it was about time we jumped on the bandwagon. Brings in a lot of money.

December 1993 — *Skiing equipment*

Some great stuff. The jacket is padded in fibreglass and quilted in natural nylon. It would normally set you back about £120, but I'm selling it for £35 — I must be a mug. All made in Fiji.

December 1993 — *Camcorders*

Russian ex-military cameras. They're not rejects, either. Designed for tank warfare. Temporary set back is that the video cassettes don't fit British TVs, which is why I've asked Ronnie Nelson to order some Russian video recorders.

December 1996 — *Radio alarm clocks*

Bought 150 Lativan radio alarm clocks, but they seem to have a mind of their own because they go off whenever they bloody well feel like it.

December 1996 — *Cycling helmets*

Managed to get my hands on 200 aerodynamic cycling helmets, although they're really horseriders' crash hats sprayed red.

December 1996 — *Hairdryers*

Radically designed hairdryers. Normally selling for £69.99, I'm getting rid of them for £15.

Filming Schedule

READY FOR THE START OF EACH SERIES, A PRODUCTION

SCHEDULE WAS COMPILED FOR EVERYONE INVOLVED

IN THE LOCATION FILMING (CAST AND CREW).

THE FOLLOWING EXTRACTS REVEAL THE TYPE OF INFORMATION COLLATED.

ONLY FOOLS & HORSES

SERIES 'F'

FILM SCHEDULE   Prog.No: 1/LLC K751X

Filming dates: 6th-28th November 1988

Producer	GARETH GWENLAN
Director	TONY DOW
Production Manager	ADRIAN PEGG
Production Assistant	AMITA LOCHAB
Assistant Floor Managers	KERRY WADDELL
	PAUL DALE
Cameraman	ALEC CURTIS
Assistant Cameraman	ADRIAN SMITH
Sound Recordist	MICHAEL SPENCER
Assistant Sound Recordist	ROSS FARNCOMBE
Gaffer	PETE ROBINSON
Grips	ALFIE WILLIAMS
Designer	GRAHAM LOUGH
Design Assistant	ALISON POPKIEWICZ
Properties Buyer	MALCOLM ROUGVIE
Visual Effects	GRAHAM BROWN
Costume Designer	RICHARD WINTER
Costume Assistant	ANDREW DUCKETT
Dressers	COLIN MAY
	MARTIN TAYLOR
	NATALIE HARRIS
	JEAN STEWARD
Make-Up Designer	HELEN WARREN
Make-Up Assistant	
	RAY JOBLING
Production Ops. Supervisor	BERNIE O'BRIEN
Production Operatives	PAT O'CONNELL
	MARTIN O'LOUGHLIN
	JO MORLEY (ext. 1587)
P.S.M.	JOHN JARVIS
Film Editor	
	MANGE TOUT
Caterers	

Welcome to the mayhem everyone!

Yes, it's that time again - when all thoughts of sleeping disappear and you realise that NO-ONE is going to get a Christmas present from you!

Still, we ARE going to have a good time - even though it might not seem like it at the moment. Rumour has it that our Director might even buy us all a drink, but I'm sure it's just hot air.

Anyway, have fun - any problems just call me (or Kerry or Paul) and we'll do our best.

Adrian

"ONLY FOOLS & HORSES"   Series 'F'   FILM DIARY (2)

SATURDAY	SUNDAY	MONDAY	TUESDAY	WEDNESDAY	THURSDAY	FRIDAY
26th Nov DAY OFF	27th Nov Ext.Police Station 1/36 'Kings Ave' 2/2 2/15 Int/Ext.Car 2/13 2/14	28th Nov Hilton Hotel 1/14 1/16	29th Nov Readthru Ep.1.	30th Nov Rehearsals	1st Dec Rehearsals	2nd Dec Rehearsals
3rd Dec Rehearsals	4th Dec DAY OFF	5th Dec Rehearsals	6th Dec Rehearsals	7th Dec Rehearsals	8th Dec 1100 Tech.(1) 1145 Planning Mtg.Ep.2	9th Dec Rehearsals
10th Dec PRE-REC STUDIO 1.	11th Dec 0900 Edit Pre-Rec 1 STUDIO 1.	12th Dec 1500-2330 Edit Ep.1.	13th Dec Readthru Ep.2.	14th Dec Rehearsals	15th Dec 1100 Tech.(2) 1145 Planning Mtg.Ep.3	16th Dec Rehearsals
17th Dec PRE-REC STUDIO 2.	18th Dec 0900 Edit Pre-Rec 2 STUDIO 2.	19th Dec	20th Dec 1000-1700 Sypher Ep.1.	21st Dec	22nd Dec 1500-2330 Edit Ep.2.	23rd Dec 1430-1730 Sypher Ep.2.
24th Dec	25th Dec TX EP.1.	26th Dec	27th Dec Poss. filming Filming tba	28th Dec Poss. filming Filming tba	29th Dec Poss. filming Filming tba	30th Dec Poss. filming

"ONLY FOOLS & HORSES"   Series 'F'   FILM DIARY (1)

SATURDAY	SUNDAY	MONDAY	TUESDAY	WEDNESDAY	THURSDAY	FRIDAY
5th Nov	6th Nov Waterloo Station 1/8 1/10 1/12 1/35 Travel to Bristol	7th Nov Int.Disco 2/9 2/11	8th Nov Int.Disco 2/9 2/11 Int.Restaurant 3/8 3/12	9th Nov Car chase 1/9 1/11 1/13 1/15 1/18	10th Nov Car crash 1/9 1/11 1/13 1/15 1/17 1/18	11th Nov Ext.Datadate Agency 1/5 Car crash 1/17
12th Nov DAY OFF	13th Nov Ext.Estate 3/7 3/13 Ext.Dirty Barry's 3/9 3/11	14th Nov Ext. One Eleven Club 4/1 4/4	15th Nov Education Centre 2/3 2/5 2/6 2/7	16th Nov Ext.Nags Head Pub 1/29 1/32 1/34 1/24	17th Nov Ext.Italian Restaurant 1/3	18th Nov Filming tba
19th Nov DAY OFF	20th Nov Int/Ext Italian Restaurant 4/6 4/7	21st Nov Int/Ext Italian Restaurant 4/6 4/7	22nd Nov Filming tba	23rd Nov Filming tba Travel to London	24th Nov Filming tba	25th Nov Ext.Raquel's Flat 1/27 1/31 1/33 Ext.Wasteland 3/14

- iii -

WORK & TRAVEL

NAME	Su 6	M 7	T 8	W 9	Th 10	F 11	Sa 12	Su 13	M 14	Tu 15	16	17	18	19	Su 20	M 21	Tu 22	W 23	Th 24	F 25	Sa 26	Su 27	M 28
											NOVEMBER 1988												
DAVID JASON	W						T/W	W	W	W	W	W	TBC	DO	W	W	TBC	TBC	TBC	W		W	W
NICHOLAS LYNDHURST		T	W	W	W	W	DO	W	W	W	W	TBC	TBC	DO	W	W	TBC	TBC	TBC	W		W	
BUSTER MERRYFIELD							T/W	T					T	T	W	T							
PATRICK MURRAY		T	W	W	T																	W	
STEVEN WOODCOCK		T	W	W	T																		
GWYNNETH STRONG		T	W	W	T			T/W	W	T												W	
FRANCESCA BRILL		T	W	W	T																	W	
TRACY CLARKE		T	W	W	T																		
ANDREE BERNARD			T	W	W	W	T																
ROGER LLOYD-PACK			T	W	W	W	T			T	W	T	T	W	W	T							
PAUL BERINGER			T	W	T					T/W	T									W			
MARGARET NORRIS			T	W	T					T/W	T									W			
PAUL BARBER								T/W	T														
TOMMY BUSON								T/W	T														
TESSA PEAKE-JONES	W									T/W	T								W				W
(Stunt Driver)			T	W	W	W	T																
(Nerys Double)			T	W	W	W	T																
PAUL COOPER		T/W	T																				
(Policeman Double)			T	W	T																		

W-Filming   T-Travel   DO-Day Off on Location   TBC-to be confirmed

---

UNIT HOTEL:

                    The Holiday Inn
                    Old Market,
                    Lower Castle Street,
                    BRISTOL BS1 3AD

Tel: 0272-294281
Fax: 0272-225838
Tlx: 449720

Hotels in Bristol are, generally, extremely expensive. The BBC rate for the above hotel is £35.00 per night inclusive of VAT but exclusive of breakfast.

Please remember that you are all responsible for paying your own hotel bills from your personal expenses.

Exceptions will be made when the unit hotel cannot accommodate artists who have been booked at short notice, and the BBC has to find alternative accommodation on an actuality basis. In these cases, I will refund the money on presentation of an invoice, (see note below), in lieu of expenses.

The BBC will NOT pay for room service, drinks, telephone calls, or the dirty movie channel!

The following BBC members of staff are booked into the hotel from Sunday 6th-Tuesday 22nd November, inclusive.

GARETH GWENLAN
TONY DOW
ADRIAN PEGG
AMITA LOCHAB
KERRY WADDELL
PAUL DALE
JEAN STEWARD
ALISON POPKIEWICZ
MICHAEL SPENCER
ROSS FARNCOMBE
PETER ROBINSON

Directions: Take the M4 out of London turning off at Junction 19 onto the M32 for Bristol. Turn left at the end onto the Inner Circuit Road. The next slip road will take you to a roundabout where you turn right, then follow the road and you'll see the Holiday Inn on the right.

Parking is in the NCP - residents can get their tickets stamped at Reception.

Sunday 6th November 1988
Sunrise: 0702   Sunset : 1625

UNIT CALL/RENDEZVOUS:	0830 having had breakfast
	(To turn over at 0845)
LOCATION:	Waterloo Station, Waterloo Road, London SE1
CONTACT:	

TO SHOOT:
1/8	(D2)	Del waits for Raquel - CLOCK @ 1230	[0:15]
1/10	(D2)	Del approached by Sonia - CLOCK @ 1235	[0:35]
1/12	(D2)	Del & Raquel meet - CLOCK @ 1245	[0:52]
1/35	(D6)	Raquel walks towards trains - 1225	[0:10]

TRANSPORT: Coach to leave TC @ 0815
Artists dressed & made-up & having had breakfast at TC if required please.

DIRECTIONS: Map 1   Cross Waterloo Bridge to the south side roundabout and continue straight on down Waterloo Road. Turn right at Bayliss Road and right again into the Waterloo Station entrance road. Please park where available here.
(& Parking)

COSTUME & MAKE-UP   Domino 5 to travel direct to Bristol

PROPS & PROP VEHICLES: Huge bouquet of flowers
Heavy suitcase for Raquel

CATERERS: **NOT REQUIRED AT THIS LOCATION**

ESTIMATED WRAP: 1300

Following WRAP at this location we will travel to BRISTOL
(The coach will leave Television Centre for Bristol at 1530 - please advise Kerry if you wish to travel on it)

Thursday 10th November 1988
Sunrise: 0718   Sunset : 1629

UNIT CALL/RENDEZVOUS:	0730 for breakfast (to turn over at 0830)

Filton Sports Centre (as Wednesday)

TO COMPLETE: (if required)	1/9 (D2) Rodney picks up Nerys in the van	[1:00]
	1/11 (D2) Yobs in American car cut him up	[0:25]
	1/13 (D2) Rodney tells Nerys how tough he is	[0:55]
	1/15 (D2) The chase zooms past Trigger	[0:08]
TO SHOOT:	1/17 (part 2) Van caushes crash at lights	[1:05]
	1/18 (D2) Van stops after chase	

PROPS & PROP VEHICLES:	Trotters van
	Police metro
	Car to crash into metro
	3 other cars
	Yobs American car
	Low-Loader or A-Frame & towing vehicle
	Traffic lights
DESIGN:	Set road works
CATERERS:	0730 Breakfast
	Coffee, lunch, tea for approx. 50
TECHNICAL EQUIPMENT ETC:	Bonnet & Side mounts
ESTIMATED WRAP:	1630

Sunday 6th November 1988 – Continued

ARTISTS	CALLS
David Jason	Del
Jean Warren	Sonia
Tessa Peake-Jones	Raquel

Supporting Artists	Calls
	Policeman WO1 (own uniform)
	Traveller 1
	Traveller 2
	Traveller 3
	Traveller 4
	Traveller 5
	Traveller 6

Thursday 10th November 1988 – Continued

ARTISTS	CALLS
Nicholas Lyndhurst	Rodney
Andree Bernard	Nerys
Roger Lloyd-Pack	Trigger
Colin Skeaping (Stunt co-ord)	Rods double
	Yob stunt driver
Paul Beringer	P.C.
Margaret Norris	W.P.C.
	Nerys' double
	Police driver double

Supporting Artists	Calls
	Yob 1
	Yob 2
	Yob 3
	Old Man
	Workman 1
	Workman 2

CRASH

Friday 11th November 1988 - continued

UNIT CALL: 1045

LOCATION 2: Fishpool Hill,
Brentry,
Bristol

CONTACT:

JUMP

TO SHOOT: 1/17 (part 1) Van jumps over hump

TRANSPORT: Coach to leave hotel at 1015, artists made-up and dressed please.

DIRECTIONS Map Take the A38 out of town. TURN LEFT
(& Parking): onto MONKS PARK AVENUE. STRAIGHT ON
into PEN PARK ROAD and LEFT at the end
into KNOLE LANE. TURN RIGHT into
BRENTRY LANE - drive to the junction
with FISHPOOL LANE and park as
directed.

PROPS & PROP VEHICLES: Trotters van
Yobs American car
Stunt ramp

CATERERS: Coffee on arrival.
Lunch, tea for approx. 50

TECHNICAL EQUIPMENT ETC:

ESTIMATED WRAP: 1600

ALSO PICK-UP DAY AS REQUIRED

ARTISTS	CALLS
Nicholas Lyndhurst	Rodney
Andree Bernard	Nerys
	Rodney's Double
	Nerys' Double
	Yob Stunt Driver
	Other Stuntmen

Supporting Artists	Calls

15

Monday 28th November 1988
Sunrise: 0739   Sunset : 1557

UNIT CALL/RENDEZVOUS: 0900 to light & dress
(To turn over outside at 0930 - for establishing shot - (no artists), inside at 1000)

Sorry but there will be NO CATERING today due to police restrictions - the lunch break will be longer to allow for finding your own lunch. Parking for ALL private cars including camera and sound cars MUST be in the NCP at the rear of the HILTON, only vehicles over 6'3 with a prior arrangement may park in the street as directed. NO COSTUME/MAKE-UP vehicles or Glendale today please. Coach to drop off and return as instructed.

LOCATION: The London Hilton,
Park Lane,
London,
W1

CONTACT: Ms. Alex Spratt, Press & PR.
01-493 8000

TO SHOOT: 1/14 (D2) Establishing shot exterior Hilton then
Del & Raquel begin their meal   [3:20]
1/16 (D2) Del pays, they arrange another date   [2:05]

TRANSPORT: Coach to leave TC at 0900
Artists made-up and dressed please, havin
had breakfast at TC.

DIRECTIONS: Map 7
& Parking)
Holland Park Avenue / Bayswater
Road / Marble Arch. Turn right into
Park Lane. The London Hilton is on the
left.

PROPS & PROP VEHICLES: Food etc.
Money for Del
Restaurant bill
Raquel's bouquet

CATERERS: NOT TODAY.

TECHNICAL EQUIPMENT ETC:

43

Monday 28th November 1988 - Continued

ESTIMATED WRAP: 1800

ARTISTS	CALLS
David Jason	Del
Tessa Peake-Jones	Raquel
Nicholas Courtney	Charles

Supporting Artists	Calls
Waiter 1	
Waiter 2	
Female Diner 1	
Female Diner 2	
Female Diner 3	
Female Diner 4	
Female Diner 5	
Female Diner 6	
Female Diner 7	
Female Diner 8	
Male Diner 1	
Male Diner 2	
Male Diner 3	
Male Diner 4	
Male Diner 5	
Male Diner 6	
Male Diner 7	
Male Diner 8	

Selected Scripts

THIS SECTION OF THE BOOK CONTAINS THREE SEPARATE SCRIPTS, TWO OF WHICH

ARE BEING PUBLISHED FOR THE FIRST TIME. 'NO GREATER LOVE...' WAS FIRST

TRANSMITTED ON BRITISH SCREENS ON 11 NOVEMBER 1982. WHEN JOHN SULLIVAN

HELD DISCUSSIONS WITH TELEVISION EXECUTIVES IN THE STATES REGARDING AN AMERICAN

VERSION OF ONLY FOOLS, HE ADAPTED THIS SCRIPT AS A POTENTIAL PILOT EPISODE; SADLY,

THE PILOT WAS NEVER RECORDED. THIS SCRIPT IS BEING PUBLISHED TO SHOW HOW THE EPISODE

WAS ADAPTED TO BECOME 'THIS TIME NEXT YEAR'. THIS PIECE OF ONLY FOOLS HISTORY

HAS NEVER BEEN SEEN BY ANY FAN, SO IT'S A WELCOME ADDITION TO THE BOOK.

FINALLY, I AM VERY GRATEFUL TO JOHN FOR ALLOWING ME TO PUBLISH THE SCRIPT

FOR THE CHRISTMAS 2001 EPISODE, 'IF THEY COULD SEE US NOW...!'.

'No Greater Love'
Recording 13 June 1982

SCENE 1
WE SEE THE VAN PARKED AT KERB. DEL IS WEARING A BRAND NEW AND FINELY TAILORED CAMEL HAIR OVERCOAT. RODNEY IS ALSO WEARING A SIMILAR CAMEL HAIR OVERCOAT WHICH IS FAR TOO BIG FOR HIM. DEL IS BUTTONING UP THE COAT FOR ROD.

ROD Look, I don't like camelhair, Del!

DEL (OFFENDED) This is not camel hair, this is genuine polyester!...There you go. Have a look in the mirror (DEL ADJUSTS THE VAN'S WING MIRROR) It's 'andsome, innit?

ROD What d'you mean 'andsome? It's miles too big for me!

DEL Course it's not, that's the fashion!

ROD Well how come your one fits like was made to measure?

DEL It's small on me. I saved the best one for you, Rodney!

ROD But it's horrible!

DEL (HURT) You could at least wear it for a while, to see if you get used to it. I mean, it's a gift, Rodney, a gift. (MOVES TO BACK OF VAN AND OPENS THE DOOR) RODNEY CLOSES HIS EYES AND SILENTLY CURSES HIMSELF FOR HIS THOUGHTLESSNESS. DEL HAS THE SUITCASE OPEN IN THE BACK OF THE VAN. HE IS FILLING IT WITH VARIOUS ITEMS OF WOMEN'S CLOTHING (SKIRTS, BLOUSES, BRAS AND SEXY UNDERWEAR) WHICH HE TAKES FROM A LARGE CARDBOARD BOX. THE REPENTANT RODNEY APPEARS AT BACK OF VAN.

ROD You're right, Del. Once you've had it on for a while it really grows on you, don't it!

DEL D'you like it then?

ROD Like it? I love it, Del! I think it's really, really smart! Cheers!

DEL I'm glad you like it. That's a score you owe me.

ROD A score? But you said it was a gift!

DEL At 20 nicker it is a gift! That'd come to hundred and eighty up Bond Street!

ROD Yeah, but....

DEL Don't worry about the money, Rodders, I'll take it out of yer wages!... You said you liked it!

ROD I know… Yeah, I know. Cheers, Del.

DEL (NOW PREOCCUPIED WITH HIS LITTLE BLACK BOOK) That's all right, Rodders. What are brothers for? I want you to pop down and see Mrs Singh. According to the book, she had a dinner service and two Persian rugs off us a month ago, and she ain't paid a penny off 'em since! See if she's interested in any of that gear while you're at it. (INDICATES SUITCASE)

ROD But Mrs Singh is a Hindu! Hindus don't wear peek-a-boo bras and nifty knickers!

DEL What are you, some kind of Swami or something? You don't know what goes on under them saris! Go on, I'll see you later.

THEY PART AND MOVE OFF IN OPPOSITE DIRECTIONS. WE PAN WITH RODNEY WHO IS BECOMING INCREASINGLY SELF-CONCIOUS ABOUT HIS OVER-GROWN OVERCOAT. HE ARRIVES AT THE HOUSE WHERE

MRS SINGH LIVES. A WOMAN IS JUST OPENING THE FRONT DOOR AND IS ABOUT TO ENTER. THIS IS IRENE, SHE IS IN HER LATER THIRTIES, SPEAKS WITH A LONDON ACCENT BUT IS NOT A 'COR BLIMEY' TYPE. IRENE HAS KEPT HER LOOKS AND HER FIGURE. EVERY MALE VIEWER SHOULD UNDERSTAND WHY RODNEY FEELS AN INSTANT SEXUAL ATTRACTION.

ROD (REACTS) Er, excuse me, d'you know if Mrs Singh's in?

IRENE Mrs Singh doesn't live here anymore! She left about three weeks ago. I've got her flat.

ROD Great! Did she say where she was moving to?

IRENE Bangladesh!

ROD Oh good, for a moment there I thought we'd lost her!

IRENE Can I do anything for you?

ROD (REACTS) Not really. Mrs Singh bought a few items off us. She was supposed to be paying for them on the weekly.

IRENE I see. What are you, a tallyman?

ROD No, no I'm not a tallyman. (INDICATING SUITCASE) It's just that every so often I manage to lay me hands on a few... bargains!

IRENE What are you selling today?

ROD Women's clothing, skirts, blouses, under... under... lingerie, that sort of thing.

IRENE Really? Well bring them in, I might be interested. (SHE STEPS INTO HALL)

ROD (NOW BECOMING NERVOUS) Er... right! (LOOKS DOWN THE ROAD FOR DEL)

IRENE Well, are you coming in or not?

ROD Yeah... okay! (WITH AS MUCH CONFIDENCE AS HE CAN MUSTER, RODNEY ENTERS)

SCENE 2

IT IS A REASONABLY BRIGHT AND PLEASANT FLAT. THE FURNISHING IS EARLY MFI. SOMEWHERE IN THE ROOM SHOULD BE A BLACK AND WHITE WEDDING PHOTO. RODNEY IS ALONE IN THE ROOM. HE SITS NERVOUSLY ON EDGE OF SOFA DRINKING A SCOTCH AND SOMETHING. HE LIES BACK, FORCING HIMSELF TO RELAX. HE SURVEYS THE ROOM WITH A WRY SMILE – MAYBE CONSIDERING ALL THE POSSIBILITIES. HE DOES A DOUBLE TAKE ON THE WEDDING PHOTO, SITS BACK IN NERVOUS POSITION.

ROD Bloody hell, he's a big bloke!

IRENE Sorry, I can't hear you!

ROD No, no, it's nothing!

IRENE ENTERS FROM THE BEDROOM, SHE IS WEARING A VERY TIGHT SKIRT WITH A THIGH-LENGTH SPLIT UP THE SIDE, AND A LOW-CUT BLOUSE. SHE DOES A TWIRL. RODNEY REACTS.

IRENE What do you think?

ROD (WEAK VOICE) T'rrific!

IRENE You don't think this split is too revealing?

ROD No! It's just right!

IRENE (INDICATING ZIP, WHICH IS AT BACK OF SKIRT) I can't quite reach this zip. Could you help me?

ROD, OBVIOUSLY RELISHING THE THOUGHT OF PHYSICAL CONTACT WITHIN SUCH A SHORT SPACE OF TIME, MOVES TOWARDS HER. HE NOW HESITATES AS HE REMEMBERS THE WEDDING PHOTO.

ROD Er, what – what time does your husband get home?

IRENE He doesn't. My husband is... away!

ROD Oh! (NOW WITH RENEWED CONFIDENCE, HE PLACES HIS LEFT HAND FIRMLY ON IRENE'S BACKSIDE AND PULLS THE ZIP UP WITH HIS RIGHT HAND)

IRENE Ooh, you've got a strong grip!

ROD It's all that free school milk they kept giving us! You on your own then?

IRENE No.

ROD Oh!

IRENE There's my son, Marcus.

ROD (ASSUMING MARCUS TO BE A CHILD, LOWERS HIS VOICE) Is he asleep in the bedroom?

IRENE No, he's down the snooker hall! He's 16. I hope you don't mind me asking, but have you been ill recently – or lost a lot of weight?

ROD Eh? (NOW REALISES SHE MEANS THE EXTRA LARGE COAT) Oh this? No, it's the fashion.

IRENE Is it really? I'm so out of touch these days. I seem to spend every hour of the day in this flat.

ROD Don't you know many people round this area?

IRENE No, I only moved here last month. I come from East London you see.

ROD It must get pretty gutty being all on your own of an evening.

IRENE Hmm, specially for someone who's been used to going out and enjoying herself! Are there any nice places around here?

ROD (THINKS ABOUT IT) Na! There's a dinner 'n' dance place in Streatham that's supposed to be really good, I er, I was thinking of giving it a try Saturday night.

IRENE Well I hope you and your girlfriend enjoy it.

ROD No, I haven't got a girlfriend! Well, when I say I haven't got a girlfriend, I mean I haven't got a regular one!

IRENE Hundreds of casuals though, I bet!

ROD Oh yeah, all over the place! The thing is, they're all busy Saturday night.... I was wondering... er,... what I mean is, would you - if you're not busy – I suppose you are, but if you're not – would you like to go with me?

IRENE Well that's very nice of you... but you se...

ROD No, no that's OK. You've made other arrangements, I understand!

IRENE I haven't made other arrangements!

ROD You're washing your hair!

IRENE No!

ROD You're mending your bike?

IRENE No, I did that last Tuesday.

ROD So, what is it?

IRENE How old are you?

ROD I'm not a kid, if that's what you mean! I'm 23 and a half!

IRENE That's what I mean! You're 23 and a half and I'm... I'm older than you.

ROD So?

IRENE It doesn't bother you?

ROD No! Does it bother you?

IRENE Well... No!

ROD So where's the problem?

IRENE There isn't one! Thank you for the invitation, I'd love to go out with you! See you Saturday night.

ROD About eight thirty, I'll pick you up in the va... in a mini cab.

IRENE There's just one thing... Do you mind telling me your name? It could get embarrassing if I sit there all night and call you thingy!

ROD Sorry. I'm Rodney.

IRENE Irene.

ROD No – Rodney.

IRENE REACTS.

ROD Nice to meet you, Irene (DOESN'T KNOW WHETHER TO KISS HER ON THE CHEEK OR SHAKE HANDS. FINALLY DECIDES ON A GENTLE HANDSHAKE. HE MOVES)

ROD Well, I'd better get my suit down the cleaners.

IRENE Rodney, you are sure aren't you? People might stare.

ROD Let them stare! That kind of thing doesn't bother me, Irene. I went out with a Chinese girl once! (EXITS) IRENE REACTS TO HIS UNINTENTIONAL PUT-DOWN.

SCENE 3

NIGHT, THE TROTTERS' LOUNGE. GRANDAD IS WATCHING THE TVs, WHICH ARE EACH SHOWING DIFFERENT PROGRAMMES. DEL IS AT THE TABLE AND HAS JUST FINISHED HIS TEA. RODNEY'S TEA OF EGG AND CHIPS REMAINS UNTOUCHED. RODNEY IS ON THE PHONE TALKING TO IRENE. HE SPEAKS IN A HUSHED, ROMANTIC TONE.

ROD (ON PHONE) of course I missed you today. I missed you yesterday, and the day before that, and the day before that, and the day before that. I'm thinking about you all the time.

DEL Are you?

GRANDAD Really? Ah...

GRANDAD AND DEL LOOK AT EACH OTHER AND REACT.

DEL Oi!

ROD (TO DEL. STILL IN SAME GOOEY VOICE) Yeah? (REACTS) (MASCULINE) I mean, yeah?

DEL (INDICATING TO RODNEY'S MEAL) Can I dip me bread in your egg?

ROD Help yourself.

DEL REACTS.

ROD (ON PHONE) Oh, that was my brother. Yeah, I'll see you later. Of course I do! I can't. There are people here, See you soon. Bye. (REPLACES RECEIVER)

GRANDAD Who was that, Rodney?

ROD Eh? Oh, er Mickey Pearce.

DEL AND GRANDAD REACT.

DEL Mickey Pearce?

RODNEY SITS AT THE TABLE

ROD Del, I want some advice. I've got a problem.

DEL (HORRIFIED) I don't wanna hear it, Rodney! I'd rather die in ignorance! I mean there's never been anything like that in our family – wait a minute – Mickey Pearce is on holiday in Spain.

ROD Oh yeah. Well, that wasn't him on the phone – it was a girl.

DEL (GREAT SIGH OF RELIEF) Don't ever do that to me again, Rodney. I'll be up all night with heartburn. So, you've got a bird have you? That explains it!

ROD Explains what?

DEL It explains why you've been acting lollopy for the last week or so! You wanna pull your socks up; it's beginning to affect business!

ROD How can it affect business?

DEL (INDICATING HIS LITTLE BLACK BOOK) Look at this! There's some tart in here called – Irene Mackay – who bought 17 quidsworth of clothes off you. And you're letting her pay it back at 25 pence a week!

RODNEY REACTS.

DEL That means you've got to go to her flat every week for a year.

ROD (LICENTIOUS GRIN) Yeah, I know!

DEL PUTS TWO AND TWO TOGETHER. INDICATES PHONE THEN BLACK BOOK.

DEL Oh! I gettit, Rodney's got a mystery.

ROD Irene's not a mystery! We've been seeing quite a lot of each other. In fact we've become very close! Promise me you won't laugh.

DEL Course I won't!

ROD I think I'm in love.

DEL BURSTS OUT LAUGHING.

GRANDAD Do us a favour, Rodney. It was only a month ago you were in love with that skinny bird from the dry-cleaners. Now along comes some other little girl and you're away again.

ROD Marguerite from the dry cleaners was just infatuation! This is the real thing! And Irene's not a little girl – she's a woman.

DEL How old is she? Twenty?

ROD No, she's about 30.

DEL What'd you mean *about* 30? How old is she exactly?

ROD Forty.

DEL AND GRANDAD Forty?

DEL You're not serious, are you?

ROD What's wrong with going out with a woman of 40?

DEL Nothing, if you happen to be 50! I mean, she's too old for me!

GRANDAD I'd have to think twice!

ROD Why don't you wrap up, Grandad?

DEL He's right, Rodney. I mean, when Irene was drinking frothy coffee with some Ted up the Lyceum, you were still struggling to keep your gripe water down… No, bruv, this is one problem you're gonna have to solve on your own.

ROD But that's not the problem!

DEL You mean there's something else?

ROD Yeah. Her husband!

DEL She's married as well!

ROD He's not living with her. He's away.

GRANDAD Where?

ROD Parkhurst.

DEL I don't believe you! I just don't believe you! You're going case-o with the wife of a convict?

ROD You don't 'arf jump to conclusions, don't you, Del? Just cause he's in Parkhurst doesn't automatically mean he's a convict! He could be a warder, or even the governor!

DEL And is he?

ROD Is he what?

DEL Is he the warder or the governor?

ROD No, he's a convict - but you weren't sure, were you?

GRANDAD What's he in for, Rodney?

ROD Well, this and that.

DEL Like what?

ROD Er… wounding with intent, GBH and attempted murder.

DEL Got a bit of a temper, has he?

ROD Well this is why poor Irene's had such an unhappy life with him. He used to beat her up, Del! She's moved over this way from the East End to get away from him.

DEL Wait a minute! What d'you mean, 'to get away from him'? He's on the bloody Isle of Wight, Rodders!

ROD Yeah… He's being released soon… And that's the problem. That's why I wanted your advice, Del. When he's released, do you think I should go and see him, explain to him about me and Irene, man to man?

DEL Well let me put it this way, if one day you find that you're really fed up with having knees in the middle of yer legs, then go and see him. If on the other hand you've grown attached to them, immigrate to Vietnam – you stupid little plonker, what do you think this is, *Jackanory*? This bloke's a killer!

GRANDAD He only got done for attempted murder.

DEL Maybe that was a bit of practice! Rodney could be his first big success!

ROD You're just like the rest of modern society – frightened!

DEL Frightened? What, of the nutters out there in the shadows? Yeah, they really frighten me, Rodney!

ROD Well, I've got a life to live and I'm not havin' a mindless thug like her old man, Tommy Mackay, telling me what I can and can't do! This is a battle I'm gonna have to win.

DEL What are you gonna do, carry tins of spinach round with you? You wanted my advice, Rodney. Steer clear of Irene or learn to sleep with one eye open.

ROD I'll think about it, Del. I'll see you later, I'm going round to Irene's! (EXITS)

DEL (CALLS) When we pay our last respects to you, you will be in a concrete overcoat supporting the M26. SOUND OF FRONT DOOR SLAMMING.

GRANDAD What are you gonna do, Del Boy?

DEL Nothing! You know what he's like with birds,

falls in and out of love more times than Starsky and Hutch. Anyway, most of them give him the elbow within a fortnight.

GRANDAD In case she don't?

DEL I'll put his name down for BUPA!

SCENE 4

DAY, THE NAG'S HEAD. THE BAR IS SPARSELY CROWDED. A FEW YOUNG PUNKS ARE PLAYING THE SPACE INVADER. RODNEY SITS ALONE AT A TABLE SIPPING A SCOTCH. HE IS DEPRESSED – LIFE HAS KICKED HIM IN THE STOMACH.

DEL Morning, my little pot pourri. Giss a Tia Maria and pineapple juice, and 'arf of lager for lover boy.

JULIE He's on scotch, that's his fourth!

DEL Is it? Well, give him one more, then that's his lot! DEL JOINS RODNEY AT TABLE.

DEL I've had a good day, Rodders. I've knocked all of then Georgian digital clocks out.

ROD Yeah? T'rrific!

DEL Look after this coat. Don't let anybody sit on it. Now, what's wrong with you?

ROD Nuffing!

DEL Don't give me that, Rodney! What's happened?

ROD It's Irene!

DEL She's been turned down for her free bus pass?

ROD She's finished with me!

DEL Oh well, all's well that ends well, I suppose.

ROD What do you mean 'all's well that end's well'? It hasn't ended well for me, has it?

DEL Oh, come on now. Look at it like this. You've had a good time, a few drinks, a little bit of Humpty Dumpty and now it's finished!

ROD Yer a pig, ain't yer? That is the pinnacle of your aesthetic appreciation innit – a few drinks and a bit of Humpty Dumpty!

DEL Yeah… I'm just trying to put it into perspective, Rodney. You didn't honestly think anything was gonna come of it, did you?

ROD I loved her, Del!

DEL Oh come on, Rodney, believe me, bruv, it's all for the best in the long run. I know what would have happened. One day you'd have gone down the roller disco and met some blinding 18-year-old sort who'd have knocked your eyes out. And she'd go head over heels for you, wouldn't she?

ROD (ALLOWS HIMSELF A LITTLE SMILE AND A SHRUG) Well…

DEL Then you would have had to break the news to Irene! How do you think a 40-year-old woman would feel, losing in love to a younger woman? And she wouldn't just be losing any man, she'd be losing *you*.

ROD I've never thought of it like that.

DEL That scar would never heal!

ROD No… poor chick!

DEL Exactly! Che sara, sara, as the French say. Anyway, her old man was released yesterday, so it's saved you from all that!

ROD Yeah! Sorry if I've bin a bit of a pain lately.

DEL Of course you ain't!

ROD Leave off! I mean, I've been acting like a right wally!

DEL Now I don't want you talking like that, Rodney! The emotions that you have been experiencing are what separate you from them morons. (INDICATES THE PUNKS) THE PUNKS REACT.

DEL You have proved that you are a human being, in the fullest sense of the word. You have a heart, Rodney, and those feeling deserve respect and dignity. Don't feel ashamed of them – feel proud!

ROD Yeah! Thanks, Del!

DEL I'll fetch our drinks.

MOVES TO THE COUNTER WHERE JULIE HAS PLACED THE DRINKS.

JULIE What's up with him?

DEL Oh, some old tart's given him the sack. You know what he's like! (RETURNS TO THE TABLE) RODNEY IS JUST DOWNING HIS ORIGINAL SCOTCH.

DEL And oi, if you're looking for answers, you won't find any in the bottom of a glass!

ROD I just fancied a drink, that's all!

DEL That's all right then, you just stay off the bottle. MARCUS ENTERS. HE'S ANOTHER PUNK WITH PARTICULARY SPIKEY HAIR. HE IS WEARING ONE OF THE OVER-COATS.

MARCUS Hello, Rodney.

ROD Oh, hello, Marcus. (TO DEL) This is Irene's son. This is my brother.

MARCUS Watchyer, Del.

DEL Hello, son. MARCUS JOINS THE OTHER PUNKS.

DEL Smart looking kid, ain't he? I bet he could pick up BBC2 with that hair. RODNEY IS NOW PUZZLING OVER SOMETHING.

DEL What's up with you now?

ROD Nothing really. How did you know Irene's husband was released yesterday?

DEL You said!

ROD Did I? But I didn't know!

DEL You must have – how else would I have known?

ROD Yeah. I s'pose I must have! DEL IS NOW GETTING EDGY.

DEL Right, let's drink up, see if we can do a bit this afternoon.

ROD Ready when you are. (STANDS) How did Marcus know your name?

DEL What? You introduced me!

ROD But I just said you were my brother, I didn't say your name!

DEL Well, perhaps he's heard me name before!

ROD He's never met you before!

DEL (INDICATES HIS INITIAL MEDALLION) Well, look, I'm wearing a big 'D' ain't I, it's obvious me name's Del!

ROD But that could stand for Daniel, David, Douglas… He's wearing one of your coats.

DEL Yeah, they're the fashion, ain't they? Come on, let's go!

ROD (CALLS) Oi, Marcus! How do you know his name?

MARCUS I met him last Thursday when he took mum out for a drink! RODNEY REACTS. DEL REACTS.

ROD You took Irene out?

DEL It's not what you think, Rodney! I had to talk to her about you.

ROD Me? What did you tell her about me?

DEL I didn't tell her anything about you, I just told her a few home truths, that's all. I told her that if she really thought anything of you, she'd leave you alone! PAUSE.

ROD (SPITS THE WORDS) Thanks, Del! Where would I be without you? Happy maybe!

DEL I did it for you, Rodney! I mean, do you wanna end up dead?

ROD No! But it's nice to have the choice! (POINTS A THEATENING FINGER) One of these days, Del Boy – one of these days… (EXITS)

DEL (CALLS) I only did it for you, Rodney! EVERYONE IN THE PUB IS STARING AT DEL.

DEL (TO JULIE) That's the thanks I get! JULIE, WITH A LOOK OF CONTEMPT TURNS AWAY FROM DEL AND MOVES TO OTHER END OF BAR. DEL REACTS.

SCENE 5

NIGHT, LONDON BACK STREET. WE SEE THE VAN PARKED AT KERB. DEL, WEARING HIS NEW COAT, IS AT ONE OF THE DOORS TALKING TO A YOUNG INDIAN (AHMED).

AHMED IS ALSO WEARING ONE OF THE COATS, WHICH IS TOO BIG FOR HIM.

DEL Oh yes, it was made for you, Ahmed, my son.

AHMED (EXAMINING COAT) It's too big, man!

DEL No, it's not. That's the fashion, innit? It's beautiful at the back here.

AHMED But yours isn't too big!

DEL It's small on me! I reserved the best one for you. You can't go wrong for 25 nicker, can yer?

AHMED All right, man, I'll take it.

DEL That's it. You know it makes sense! D'you want to pay now or have it on the weekly?

AHMED I'll pay you two pounds a week, Del.

DEL All right, my son, I'll see you next week. You won't catch cold in that.

DEL MOVES OFF DOWN THE STREET.

SCENE 6

NIGHT, SMALL ALLEYWAY.

WE SEE DEL PASSING A SMALL ALLEYWAY. AS HE SOES SO, A WEST INDIAN (LEROY) LEAPS UP FORM THE ALLEY AND DRAGS THE STRUGGLING DEL BACK INTO THE ALLEY. CUT TO THE ALLEY. THE MAN THROWS DEL AGAINST THE WALL.

DEL What's your game?

LEROY Take it easy, man, you might hurt yourself! There's someone here who's been dying to meet you.

DEL Oh yeah - who's that then?

TOMMY MACKAY – 40ISH – AND WITH A FACE THAT MAKES McVICAR'S SEEM ANGELIC – STEPS FROM THE SHADOWS.

TOMMY Me! The name's Mackay. Tommy Mackay. Ring a bell, does it?

DEL REACTS. FOR THE FIRST TIME, WE SHOULD SENSE DEL'S FEAR.

DEL I think I've heard it before.

TOMMY You bet your life you've heard it before, sunshine! You were seen out with my wife, Trotter. Guilty or not guilty?

DEL It was just a friendly drink!

TOMMY But I'm not a friendly geezer. That kind of thing makes me very 'angry'. I'm gonna teach you a lesson that you'll remember for the rest of your life, Rodney, my old son!

DEL Look, let's not be hasty about (REACTS) Rodney? Did you say Rodney?

TOMMY That's right. Rodney Trotter, that's you, annit?

DEL SIGHS, A MIXTURE OF RELIEF AND LAUGHTER.

DEL Rodney Trotter!! (HIS EXPRESSION CHANGES AS HE SCANS THE THUGS' FACES)

DEL Yeah, I'm Rodney Trotter!

TOMMY Good! Right – let me have him!

TOMMY AND LEROY REMOVE THEIR JACKETS. DEL REMOVES HIS OVERCOAT. TOMMY AND LEROY THROW THEIR JACKETS TO THE GROUND. DEL THROWS HIS OVERCOAT INTO THE DARKNESS BEHIND HIM. SLIGHT PAUSE – DEL REACTS. HE TURNS TO SEE THAT HIS BRAND-NEW OVERCOAT HAS LANDED IN A PUDDLE. DEL TURNS BACK, NOW SNARLING AND SEETHING WITH ANGER. THE CHANGE SHOULD BE REMINISCENT OF DAVID BANNER'S TRANSFORMATION FROM THE MILD-MANNERED DOCTOR INTO THE INCREDIBLE HULK.

DEL Now look what you've made me do! That's a brand new coat! Right! I'm gonna get you for that!

CUT TO ALLEY. WE CAN HEAR THE THUDS AND THUMPS, MOANS AND GROANS OF A VICIOUS FIGHT. WE CAN SEE SHADOWS FLICKERING ACROSS THE ALLEY WALL.

TOMMY Hold him, Leroy, hold him!

WE HEAR A DUSTBIN CLATTERING AS IT IS KNOCKED OVER IN THE STRUGGLE. THE DUSTBIN LID ROLLS OUT OF THE ALLEY, ACROSS THE PAVEMENT AND CRASHES TO A HALT IN THE KERB. THE FIGHT CONTINUES.

LEROY (PLEADING VOICE) No, no, let go, man! Don't sneeze! Aaaaarrrgggghhhhh!

WE SEE A POLICE CONSTABLE CROSSING AT THE TOP OF THE STREET. HIS ATTENTION IS DRAWN TO THE ALLEY BY THE SOUND OF THE SCREAM. HE RUSHES DOWN THE ROAD AND ARRIVES AT ALLEY. HE OBSERVES THE BLOOD-LETTING GOING ON INSIDE, TURNS AND RUNS BACK UP THE ROAD OUT OF SIGHT. EVENTUALLY THE SOUND OF FIGHTING SUBSIDES INTO JUST THE OCCASIONAL THUD. NOW THERE IS SILENCE SAVE FOR THE SOUND OF EXHAUSTED LUNGS GULPING FOR AIR. DEL, DRAGGING HIS OVERCOAT BEHIND HIM, STAGGERS FROM THE ALLEY. DEL'S FACE IS SWOLLEN AND BRUISED, BLOOD RUNS FROM HIS LIPS. ONE SLEEVE OF HIS SUIT JACKET HAS BEEN RIPPED FROM THE SHOULDER. HIS WHITE SHIRT IS SPECKLED WITH BLOOD AND IS HANGING OUT, HIS TIE HAS BEEN RIPPED. HE LEANS AGAINST THE WALL AND TAKES GREAT GULPS OF COLD AIR. HE LOOKS DOWN AND STUDIES THE STATE OF HIS CLOTHING. HE PUTS HIS OVERCOAT ON, WINCING AT HIS DAMAGED SHOULDER. WE SEE THE GREAT MUDDY, DAMP PATCH DOWN ONE SIDE OF HIS OVERCOAT. AS HE STAGGERS AWAY FROM THE CAMERA AND DOWN THE ROAD TOWARDS THE VAN WE SEE THAT THE SOLE OF ONE SHOE IS HANGING OFF.

SCENE 7

NIGHT, THE NAG'S HEAD.

THE BAR IS CROWDED – SOMEWHERE A POP RECORD PLAYS, MINGLING WITH THE DRONE OF CONVERSATIONS AND GENERAL PUB SOUNDS. RODNEY, NOW IN A SUIT, SITS ALONE AT THE BAR CLUTCHING AN ALMOST FINISHED LAGER. DEL, IN THE SAME CONDITION AS THE PREVIOUS SCENE AND STILL SLIGHTLY UNSTEADY, PUSHES HIS WAY THROUGH THE CROWD. OTHER CUSTOMERS REACT TO HIS CONDITION.

DEL Rodney!

RODNEY, WITHOUT TURNING TO LOOK AT HIM, REACTS TO THE SOUND OF DEL'S VOICE.

DEL Guess what I've done for you, Rodders

ROD If it's another example of your so-called brotherly love, forget it. As far as I'm concerned you are no longer my broth… (REACTS AS HE SEES DEL'S CONDITION. NOW WITH DEEP BROTHERLY CONCERN) What the bloody hell's happened to you?

DEL Eh? Oh this! It's nothing, I er, I walked into a door.

ROD And did all that?

DEL Yeah, it was a revolving door! (LAUGHS THEN WINCES AND HOLDS HIS BRUSIED CHEEK) Now, listen, I had a bit of luck tonight, Rodney. I bumped into Tommy Mackay. That was lucky, wasn't it?

ROD And he did that?

DEL No, no – I had one too many and fell down the stairs in Monkey Harris's house.

ROD He lives in a bungalow.

DEL What? He's moved. Just shut up and listen, will you? Look – I had a chat with Tommy. And guess what? I have done what all the psychiatrists and social workers couldn't do! I've rehabilitated him, Rodders. He's seen the error of his way! He won't give you any more problems. I've cleared the path for you and Irene!

ROD Me and Irene? Oh no, that's all over, Del!

DEL What?

ROD We had a long talk about it, we both realised it would never work.

DEL It will work, Rodney! There's a box of Black Magic in the van; I've only had one out of 'em. Whip 'em round to her a bit lively!

ROD It's no good, Del! It was just circumstances that threw us together. She was lonely and in a strange part of town, and I was just looking for a mother figure. You were right, Del.

DEL No, I wasn't, Rodney!

ROD I don't mean about me and Irene!

DEL What d'you mean then?

ROD Well, I went down the roller-disco this afternoon! I met this bird, Zoe.

DEL Zoe?

ROD Eighteen, with a body that makes Bo Derek look like a cert for plastic surgery! Irene was just infatuation, but this is love! Here she comes!

ZOE PUSHES HER WAY THROUGH THE CROWD.

ROD All right, babe? This is my brother; he fell down some stairs.

ZOE Nice to meet you.

DEL (TOTALLY STUNNED BY TURN OF EVENTS) 'lo!

ZOE (TO RODNEY) We going then?

ROD (FINISHES HIS DRINK) See yer later, Del Boy.

DEL Yeah! See ya, Rodders, Zoe.

RODNEY CALLS FROM DOOR.

ROD Hey, Del! I'd get that head looked at if I was you! (EXIT)

DEL Yeah! Truest bloody words you've said for ages, Rodney!

JULIE What happened to you?

DEL Me? Nothing happened to me, Julie! But Rodney got a bloody good hiding tonight!

JULIE AND DEL REACT.

ONLY FOOLS AND HORSES – THE AMERICAN VERSION

'THE AMERICAN VERSION WAS RETITLED *THIS TIME NEXT YEAR* AND THE CHARACTER OF RODNEY

WAS RENAMED MARLON BY THE THEN PRODUCER, ED WEINBERGER, WHO THOUGHT RODNEY WAS NOT

A VERY AMERICAN NAME. THE FAMILY WAS ALSO RENAMED THE FLANNAGANS AS ED BELIEVED THEY

WOULD WORK BEST AS EITHER A BLACK FAMILY OR IRISH-AMERICANS.

'IT WAS PLANNED TO BE MADE AS A 45-MINUTE SHOW, THEREFORE AN AMERICAN HOUR WHEN YOU

INCLUDE THE NUMEROUS COMMERCIAL BREAKS. THE PROGRAMME – WHICH WOULD HAVE BASICALLY BEEN

AN ADAPTATION OF THE EPISODE, "NO GREATER LOVE…" – WAS NEVER RECORDED ALTHOUGH THE RIGHTS

TO THE SERIES ARE PRESENTLY WITH ANOTHER AMERICAN COMPANY WHO HAVE A TEAM OF WRITERS

WORKING ON IT – BUT I HAVE LEARNED NOT TO HOLD MY BREATH.'   JOHN SULLIVAN

'This Time Next Year…'
by John Sullivan

INTERIOR. THE FLANNAGANS' APARTMENT/LIVING ROOM. DAY. ALTHOUGH WE ARE IN THE FLANNAGANS' APARTMENT, OUR FIRST IMPRESSION IS THAT WE ARE IN A VIDEO STUDIO. DEL FLANNAGAN'S RUGGED AND HANDSOME FACE ALMOST FILLS THE SCREEN AS HE TALKS DIRECTLY TO CAMERA. DEL IS 35 AND IS WEARING A SMART SUIT AND NECKTIE, BUT THE IMAGE OF SOPHISTICATION IS RUINED BY A SLIGHTLY-TOO-THICK GOLD CHAIN THAT HANGS OUTSIDE OF HIS SHIRT. ON WALL BEHIND HIM WE SEE A SIGN WHICH READS: "HIGH HOPES VIDEO DATING AGENCY".

DEL (SEDUCTIVELY) Hi, my name's Del Flannagan and if you'd allow me just a few minutes of your life, I'd like to tell you a little about myself.
AS WE ZOOM OUT WE FIND WE ARE IN THE FLANNAGANS' APARTMENT AND THE "HIGH HOPES" SIGN IS PINNED ROUGHLY TO THE LIVING ROOM WALL. AS WE ZOOM BACK FURTHER WE FIND DEL'S 23-YEAR-OLD BROTHER, MARLON WHO LOOKS EMBARRASSED BY THE WHOLE PROCEEDINGS. MARLON IS OPERATING A CAMCORDER ON A TRIPOD. IN BACKGROUND WE WILL FIND GRAMPS, 70-SOMETHING AND ASLEEP IN ARMCHAIR. DEL CONTINUES OVER:
DEL I am the Chairman of a chain of department stores right here in Philadelphia. We specialise in the supply of quality goods ranging from hi-tech electronic equipment to fine antiques and objet d'art.
WE SEE MARLON'S INCREDULOUS REACTION TO THIS AND THEN CUT TO HIS MENTAL PICTURE.
CUT TO MARLON'S MIND: THE REAL PICTURE.
EXTERIOR. DOWNMARKET STREET. DAY
WE SEE A STORE THAT SELLS SECOND-HAND AND FIRE-AND-WATER-DAMAGED GOODS (REAL CRAP). A SIGN ABOVE STORE TELLS US THIS IS: "JUNK & FUNK" "TOP QUALITY SECOND-HAND AND SLIGHTLY DAMAGED GOODS".
CUT BACK TO FLANNAGANS' APARTMENT.
DEL My late-mother, God bless the woman's spirit… (CROSSES HIMSELF. MARLON CROSSES HIMSELF. GRAMPS, IN HIS SLEEP, CROSSES HIMSELF) always told me, 'Never put all your eggs in one basket' and that's been my motto

ever since. Diversity and profit – and it's held me in good stead. You've most probably seen my trucks out on the streets without ever realising who owned them.
CUT TO MARLON'S MIND: THE REAL PICTURE.
THE FLANNAGANS' OLD VAN WITH ITS HAND PAINTED LOGO: "THE FLANNAGAN CORPORATION. PARIS – ROME – PHILADELPHIA". IT IS PARKED AT A KERB WITH HOOD UP AND SMOKE IS BELCHING FROM THE ENGINE. MARLON IS JUST LOOKING AT IT IN PHILOSOPHICAL MODE, DEL IS RANTING AND RAGING AT VEHICLE AND THEN KICKS ONE OF THE HEADLAMPS.
CUT BACK TO THE FLANNAGANS' APARTMENT.
DEL I was also the innovator of the Flannagans' now famous Personalised Executive Home-Marketing Division.
CUT TO MARLON'S MIND: THE REAL PICTURE.
EXTERIOR. DOWN-MARKET STREET. NIGHT
WE SEE DEL AND MARLON, LIKE A COUPLE OF TYPICAL DOOR-TO-DOOR SALESMEN (OPEN SUITCASE FILLED WITH MEN'S SHIRTS AND SWEATERS) STANDING AT DOORWAY TRYING TO SELL TO A SLOBBY, MIDDLE-AGED MAN IN VEST AND PANTS WHO LOOKS AS IF HE'S JUST WOKEN UP.
MAN I don't want nothing. Just get outa here.
DEL But just feel the quality.
MARLON (NO ENTHUSIASM) It's very you, sir.
MAN (CALLS BACK INTO HOUSE) Vera, call the police.
DEL You don't even know the price.
MAN Get off my door.
MARLON (NO ENTHUSIASM) It's very you, sir
CUT BACK TO THE FLANNAGAN APARTMENT.
DEL I'm 30 years old… (A GUILTY EYE MOVEMENT AT THIS)
MARLON (OUT OF VISION. A STIFLED LAUGH)
DEL … and I live in an 18-room penthouse condominium on Society Hill.
MARLON SURVEYS THE APARTMENT.
DEL I'm unmarried and I live with my biological family, which consists of my younger brother, Marlon, who's a real smart kid and is more than *just* a brother to me – (CLENCHED TEETH) he's my best friend as well.
CUT TO MARLON'S MIND: THE REAL PICTURE.
INTERIOR. THE STAIRWELL/FLANNAGANS' APARTMENT BLOCK. DAY
MARLON IS RUNNING DOWN THE STAIRS IN FEAR OF HIS LIFE. DEL IS CHASING HIM, ANGRY AS THUNDER.

MARLON IS SCREAMING IN A MONOTONOUS TONE A LA MCAULEY CAULKIN IN *HOME ALONE*.
MARLON Aaaaghhhhh!
DEL I'll kill you, Marlon, you stupid little dipstick!
CUT BACK TO THE FLANNAGANS' APARTMENT.
DEL Also living with us is our beloved Grandfather. He was a naval hero in the Second World War but is still extremely active within the community.
WE SEE GRAMPS START TO SNORE.
DEL My interests in life are manifold.
MARLON REACTS TO DEL USING SUCH A WORD.
MARLON (QUIETLY) Manifold?
GRAMPS (HAS WOKEN) What?
DEL (REACTS TO THE NOISE) I enjoy the ordinary and the opulent. A baseball game – the opera – a barbecue or haute cuisine – particularly if it's French. You may be wondering why a high-profile person like me should need the services of a video dating agency. A man once said, 'It's lonely at the top'. Well, let me tell you, it's true. I know – I was that man!
MARLON (QUIETLY) Oh God!
DEL I'm looking for – *someone*. Who knows? It could be you. And if you're looking for someone, who knows? It could be me. So, come on, don't be shy. I'm just a human being – a very warm human being with a *lot* to give and no one to give it to!
IN BACKGROUND WE HEAR THE SOUND OF MARLON EFFECTING A VOMIT.
DEL So, why not give me a call at the High Hopes Video Dating Agency. I'll be waiting… Cut!
Hey, Marlon, don't bring your attitude into the studio with you! Just because you're my kid brother doesn't give you the right to voice your personal opinions on my tape. Can you edit that sniggering out?
MARLON Yeah. The vomit sound could prove a problem.
DEL I'm not too worried about that. Gramps, when the calls come through, stagger the chicks – I don't want 'em queuing or nothing, it looks untidy.
GRAMPS I'll supply tickets.
MARLON I suppose there must be *somebody* out there with an IQ compatible with that video.
DEL Well, of course there is!
MARLON Doesn't that frighten you?
DEL Not in the least. Tell me the truth.
MARLON Who opened the door and let the truth back in? Del, you founded the High Hopes Dating Agency over a year ago and so far you've only managed to match two people, and look at the problems that caused!
DEL How was I to know he was an escaped serial killer? He lied on the application form.
MARLON (IRONICALLY) No!!
GRAMPS Still makes me shiver just thinking about that poor woman. Sitting in her apartment watching TV and playing footsie with The Surf City Scalper. God knows what would have happened if his picture hadn't come up on *America's Most Wanted*.
DEL I tried to counsellor her. I was round at her place for a whole week.
MARLON You were tryna get the film rights!
DEL She wanted *half*! God, I hate greedy women! I gotta good feeling, Marlon. Our luck's about to change. This time next year we'll be millionaires!
MARLON You said that this time last year.
DEL So my crystal ball needs checking! Don't worry, we are blessed. Come on, business calls.

INTERIOR. JUNK & FUNK. DAY.
WE HAVE PILES OF BOXES DISPLAYING LOGOS FOR ALL MANNER OF ITEMS – AUTO PARTS, VIDEO GAMES, BEAUTY AIDS – SOME ARE MARKED 'REJECT' OR 'FIRE DAMAGED'. MARLON IS MOVING BOXES AROUND, ETC, AND GENERALLY BUSYING HIMSELF WHILST KEEPING

AN EAR ON GRAMPS WHO IS AT COUNTER TALKING TO A COMPLAINING CUSTOMER. THE CUSTOMER IS A MAN OF 40, DEFINITELY NOT AN INTELLIGENT MAN, BUT STREET WISE. HE IS ASSERTIVE IN HIS OBJECTIONS BUT NEVER RAISES HIS VOICE. THE OBJECT OF COMPLAINT IS A MINI-MUSIC CENTRE WHICH IS ON COUNTER.

GRAMPS So what's the problem with it?

CUSTOMER Well, to cut a long story short and not wishing to mince words, basically speaking, it doesn't work.

GRAMPS What makes you think that?

CUSTOMER It's little things, like it doesn't work. No lights come on and no sound comes from it which, seeing as it's a music centre, suggests to me it doesn't work.

GRAMPS Have you switched the volume up?

CUSTOMER Thank you, I didn't think of that. Yes, I switched the volume up and it doesn't work.

GRAMPS Well, my grandson, who owns the store, has gone out on business. He's the only one who can make a decision.

MARLON Gramps, Del doesn't *own* the store. Del and I are *partners* in the store!

GRAMPS Yes. (TO CUSTOMER) Del's the only one who can make a decision.

WE SEE MARLON'S REACTION TO THIS PUT-DOWN.

DEL ENTERS FROM BACK OF STORE.

DEL I'm back. What's the problem?

GRAMPS This guy complaining about this music centre. No lights come on and no sound comes out.

CUSTOMER It doesn't work.

DEL That's a sweeping statement, sir. When did you buy it?

CUSTOMER Just over a week ago.

DEL Damn, the guarantee's run out! I think you're looking at this beautiful item from the wrong angle, sir. This is not just a CD player.

MARLON No, it's a radio as well and that doesn't work either.

CUSTOMER He's right.

MARLON EXITS TO FRONT OF STORE WITH A BOX.

DEL What I mean is: this is a conversation piece! People come into your house and go, 'Hey, what a charming music centre.' It's something for you and them to discuss.

CUSTOMER Yeah, you're right. I've had friends round and we have discussed it – like how it doesn't work.

DEL You call them *friends*!! They come into your house and criticise your property! What did they want you to do, play music on it?

CUSTOMER It was suggested.

DEL They're not friends! They're free-loaders! They come into your place and expect you to use *your* electricity for their enjoyment. And I bet they expected coffee and food.

CUSTOMER Well, it was a party.

DEL I've met 'em and I've dumped 'em! *True* friends would look at this and say, 'Hey, neat machine' but not expect you to end up out of pocket for their pleasure! How long are you gonna continue to bank-roll these leeches?

CUSTOMER (IS ABOUT TO PROTEST – THEN CONSIDERS DEL'S WORDS) One of my friends ran off with my missus!

DEL Was that good or bad?

CUSTOMER Bad! I mean, she wasn't beautiful, but I'm just an ordinary-looking guy myself, know what I mean?

DEL Not really.

CUSTOMER She was mine and I loved her. Friends, uh?

DEL Unload 'em, tell 'em to move on down the road a'piece! Get a new circle of friends, people who'll love you for yourself and not just for your music centre.

CUSTOMER You could be right! But how'd you do that at my age?

GRAMPS Marlon doesn't socialise much.

DEL Yeah, and he's an intelligent kid, got diplomas in maths and art. Maybe the two of you could go out one evening. Watch a game. Discuss art and… maths.

CUSTOMER I don't know. I don't make friends easy.

MARLON ENTERS FROM FRONT OF STORE.

CUSTOMER You wanna go out for a beer one night?

MARLON What?

CUSTOMER You and me. Have a beer and a pizza. Discuss maths and art.

MARLON No.

MARLON EXITS TO BACK OF STORE.

DEL (TO CUSTOMER) He's just playing hard to get. In the meantime, why not take a look at this pamphlet from the High Hopes Dating Agency. I went to them and I've got friends coming outa my ears.

CUSTOMER Can I come out with you and your friends?

DEL No. Read the pamphlet and give 'em a call.

CUSTOMER Okay, will do.

THE CUSTOMER WANDERS TOWARDS EXIT DOOR READING THE PAMPHLET.

DEL You forgot your music centre.

CUSTOMER That's okay. (EXITS)

DEL (TO GRAMPS) That's customer satisfaction.

INT. JUNK & FUNK. SAME DAY

GRAMPS IS EATING A SANDWICH AS HE WATCHES A TV.

DEL ENTERS FROM BACK ROOM WEARING A SMART CASHMERE OVERCOAT, WHICH FITS HIM NEATLY. HE CALLS BACK INTO ROOM.

DEL Come on, Marlon, take a look at yourself in the mirror.

MARLON (OUT OF VISION) It doesn't suit me!

DEL Let me be the judge of that. Come on in.

MARLON ENTERS. HE TOO IS WEARING A CASHMERE OVERCOAT, BUT HIS IS THREE SIZES TOO BIG FOR HIM. HE MOVES TO MIRROR.

GRAMPS Very smart, Marlon. Very smart. You're not going out in it, are you?

MARLON (CHECKING IT IN MIRROR) No I'm not!

DEL Come on – you look like a businessman!

MARLON I look like a businessman who's picked up the wrong coat! Look, it's way too big for me!

DEL No, that's the fashion!

MARLON So how comes yours fits like it was tailor made?

DEL This is too small on me. I saved the best one for you. D'you see *GQ* this month? Wesley Snipes is on the cover in a coat just like that. People might mistake you for him.

MARLON Very likely!

GRAMPS During the war…

DEL & MARLON (LOW GROANS) Oh no!

GRAMPS During the war I was sailing the Pacific on a destroyer, and one of my shipmates was called Snipes.

MARLON (GENUINE INTEREST) Yeah? You think he coulda been Wesley's grandfather?

GRAMPS You never know.

DEL Hey, wouldn't that be something? You sailed with Wesley Snipes' grandpa.

GRAMPS Thata be something! I don't think it was him, though, he was a short, blonde guy. One day we were attacked by a kamikaze pilot. Came diving towards us, straight outa the sun. I remember saying to Snipes, 'Look at that son of a bitch, the way he's carrying on he's gonna kill himself.'

MARLON TRIES TO REMOVE COAT.

DEL Don't take it off, Marlon – it might grow on you.

MARLON I don't like it! I mean, I… I don't like it!

DEL You could try wearing it for a while. I mean, it is a gift, Marlon. It is a gift. (DEL MOVES TOWARDS BACK ROOM) You know what's wrong with you – you got a gratitude problem. (EXITS)

MARLON SILENTLY CURSES HIMSELF FOR HIS BAD MANNERS.

MARLON (TO GRAMPS) I didn't know it was a *gift*! (CALLS) Hey, you were right, Del, it is kinda growing on me. Yeah, I like it now.

DEL ENTERS, PULLING BEHIND HIM A METAL CLOTHES RACK ON WHEELS UPON WHICH HANGS TWENTY OR SO CASHMERE OVERCOATS.

DEL You're not just saying that?

MARLON No, I *really* like it.

DEL Good. That's 20 bucks you owe me.

MARLON Twenty b… But you said it was a gift!

DEL At 20 bucks it is a gift! You'd pay a thousand for that in Paris. This is the finest French merchandising.

MARLON CHECKS THE LABEL ON ONE OF THE COATS ON RACK.

MARLON This says 'Made in Taiwan'.

DEL (TO GRAMPS) You missed a label! Come on, Marlon, wear the coat. You'll be a walking advertisement for our business.

MARLON What'd you mean, 'our business'? We haven't got a 'business'! All that crap in the video recording! 'I'm the chairman of an international corporation.' All we do is buy and sell damaged goods. Water damaged, fire damaged, damage damaged, if they're not damaged we don't buy 'em!

DEL That's why we can buy cheap and sell cheap. Look, someone's TV is broken – they need a replacement and cheap. That's where we come in.

MARLON But ours are broken *before* we sell 'em!

GRAMPS Saves time!

DEL Look, Marlon, so business hasn't been too hot recently. A temporary set-back. But can't you feel the thrill of what we do? It's exciting, unpredictable. We can go out in the morning with 20 cents in our pocket…

MARLON And come home at night broke.

DEL This time next year we'll be millionaires.

MARLON You said that this time last year.

DEL So, what am I, a clairvoyant?

GRAMPS Your uncle Charlie is a medium.

DEL TAKES A COAT FROM RACK.

DEL Yeah? Well, take that round to him, should fit him like a glove! Okay, Marlon, concentrate, we got business to attend to. (HANDS MARLON A VALISE) I want you to go and see Mrs Singh. She bought a 35-piece dinner service and three Persian-type rugs off us. She was paying us back at 15 dollars a week but hasn't made a payment for the last two months. And while you're there, see if she's interested in any of this.

DEL OPENS VALISE WHICH IS FILLED WITH WOMEN'S CLOTHES, INCLUDING UNDERGARMENTS.

MARLON Del, Mrs Singh is a Hindu! Hindu's do not go around in peek-a-boo bras and crotchless panties!

DEL What are you, a Swami or something? You don't know what goes on under them saris! I'll meet you down at Crystal's Bar in a couple of hours – I gotta meeting there.

MARLON Have I *gotta* wear the coat?

DEL It's creative selling, Marlon. Winter's approaching – it gets pretty cold here in Philadelphia.

GRAMPS Cold! You kids don't know what cold is! During the war – (WE HEAR A LOW GROAN FROM DEL AND MARLON AS GRAMPS IS ABOUT TO GO INTO YET *ANOTHER* WAR SAGA)

GRAMPS During the war I sailed on the Russian convoys. One night it was so cold the flame on my lighter froze.

DEL I'm outa here!

MARLON Right behind you!

DEL AND MARLON, CARRYING VALISE, EXIT STREET DOOR.

INTERIOR. IRENE'S LIVING ROOM. DAY

THE APARTMENT IS BRIGHT AND CLEAN, THE FURNITURE, HOWEVER, HAS SEEN BETTER DAYS. IRENE,

A SLIM, ATTRACTIVE 40 YEAR OLD, IS STANDING LOOKING FRUSTRATED AT HER TV SCREEN WHICH IS A MESS OF FUZZY LINES. SHE EJECTS VIDEO CASSETTE FROM VCR AND THEN PUSHES IT BACK INTO MACHINE. PRESSES PLAY – BUT THE SCREEN IS STILL A MESS. WE HEAR FRONT DOOR BELL. IRENE OPENS DOOR TO MARLON AND THE VALISE.

MARLON Oh, good morning.

IRENE Hi. Come in.

IRENE LEAVES A SLIGHTLY BEMUSED MARLON AT DOOR. MARLON ENTERS CAUTIOUSLY.

IRENE (RE TV) Look at that. Have you ever seen anything like it?

MARLON No, that's bad.

IRENE It happens when I switch the video channel on.

MARLON Any idea what's wrong with it?

IRENE Aren't you supposed to tell me? You're the TV repairman.

MARLON *Me*? I'm not a TV repairman.

IRENE (A STEP BACK IN FEAR) Then who the hell are you?

MARLON I'm here to see Mrs Singh.

IRENE Mrs Singh moved. I've taken over the lease.

MARLON She moved? D'you know where she's gone?

IRENE India.

MARLON Oh, thank God for that, for a moment I thought we'd lost her.

IRENE You could call the landlord and get her forwarding address.

MARLON No, that's okay. We can't go pursuing the poor woman right across Asia-Minor for 34 dollars.

IRENE Are you a debt-collector?

MARLON No, no! I'm a salesman. My brother and I run the Flannagan Import Export Corporation.

IRENE I'm sorry, I've never heard of it, but then I've only moved here recently. The only time I've seen the name Flannagan was on a beat-up old van being stopped by the police.

MARLON Really? Our firm specialises in the acquisition of quality merchandise – antiques, objet d'art, digital clocks – that kind of thing. And then one of our representatives – such as myself – will call and offer the aforementioned merchandise to valued and trusted customers.

IRENE (SMILES AT THE IRONY) Like Mrs Singh?

MARLON (RETURNS THE SMILE) Yeah.

IRENE So, what are you selling today?

MARLON Women's clothing. Skirts, blouses, panti… pan… linge… more blouses.

IRENE Mind if I take a look?

MARLON Sure.

MARLON OPENS SUITCASE AND THE FIRST THING HE BRINGS OUT IS A PEEK-A-BOO BRA. HE QUICKLY HIDES BENEATH THE OTHER CLOTHES.

INTERIOR. CRYSTAL'S BAR. DAY

WE FIND DEL AT BAR WITH A BEER (OR EXOTIC COCKTAIL) AND A HAMBURGER. HE IS STUDYING A USED-CAR SALES MAGAZINE. CRYSTAL APPROACHES BEHIND BAR, SHE IS CARRYING A PHONE. WE WILL SOON DISCOVER THAT CRYSTAL HAS A SOFT SPOT FOR DEL.

CRYSTAL (A SWEET SMILE) Del, there's a call for you.

DEL Thanks, Crystal honey. It's most probably my Wall Street broker.

CRYSTAL No, it's Marlon.

DEL Oh. (TAKES PHONE) Marlon, where are you? Mrs Singh's moved? What d'you mean, she's moved? Yeah, I know what 'moved' means! It's that thing Grampa rarely does! So, where's she gone? India! Oh good, we got her cornered. No, we'll have to write the debt off. So, what are you doing now? Yeah! Well try'n sell her something,

don't make it a wasted journey. I'll see you. (TO CRYSTAL) Never trust a woman!

CRYSTAL Sweet of you to warn me!

INTERIOR. IRENE'S LIVING ROOM. DAY

MARLON IS ALONE IN ROOM. HE REPLACES TELEPHONE RECEIVER AND THEN SWITCHES TV ON – AGAIN FUZZY LINES. HE STARTS TWIDDLING WITH THE VCR. HE PRESSES PLAY AND WE NOW SEE DEL'S VIDEO ON TV SCREEN.

DEL (ON TV) 'Hi, my name's Del and if you'd allow me just a few minutes of your life, I'd like to tell you a little about mys…

MARLON QUICKLY SWITCHES TV OFF. IRENE ENTERS WEARING A TIGHT-FITTING SKIRT WITH A SPLIT UP SIDE AND A LOW-CUT BLOUSE. MARLON REACTS.

IRENE Well, what d'you think? Be honest.

MARLON (WEAKLY) S'perfect.

IRENE You don't think this split's too revealing?

MARLON No, just right. So, are you on your own here?

IRENE No. There's my son, Zack.

MARLON (ASSUMING ZACK TO BE A CHILD HE LOWERS HIS VOICE) Oh. Is he asleep in the bedroom?

IRENE Last time I looked he was. How much is this skirt and blouse?

MARLON I think it could be a special offer.

IRENE I don't have a lot of money.

MARLON Don't worry. You can pay so much a week.

IRENE I thought you only did that for 'trusted' customers.

MARLON I trust you.

IRENE You don't know me.

MARLON Call it intuition.

IRENE Thank you. (IRENE CANNOT REACH ZIP AT BACK OF SKIRT) Could you help with this zip?

MARLON Sure.

MARLON BEGINS TO WORK ON ZIP. AT THIS POINT ZACK ENTERS. HE IS 21, A TALL AND LARGE YOUNG MAN WHO LOOKS OLDER. MARLON REELS AWAY FROM IRENE IN FEAR.

ZACK (TO IRENE) Why'd you let me sleep late? I'm supposed to meet the guys. Who are you?

MARLON I'm no one!

IRENE He's a salesman.

ZACK Oh. I'll see you later, Mom.

ZACK EXITS STREET DOOR.

MARLON That's your son? For a moment I thought it was your husband.

IRENE Husband? That's Zack, he's 21. Bruce, my husband, and I… we're not together. (QUICKLY CHANGES SUBJECT. RE: MARLON'S OVER-SIZED OVERCOAT) I hope you don't mind me asking, but have you been ill recently?

MARLON What? Oh, the coat? No, this is the fashion. Wesley Snipes wears one.

IRENE Does he really? Well, I'm so out of touch these days, I seem to spend every day and night in this apartment. I moved from upstate about a month ago so I don't know many people.

MARLON Must get pretty boring sitting in night after night.

IRENE Yeah, specially as I'm used to going out and enjoying myself. Are there any nice places round here?

MARLON (THINKS ABOUT IT) Na… D'you like blues music?

IRENE Love it.

MARLON There's a new club opened downtown, everyone's talking about it. A live band every weekend. I was thinking of trying it tonight.

IRENE Well, I hope you and your girlfriend have a great time.

MARLON I haven't got a girlfriend. (QUICKLY TRIES TO

CORRECT THE IMPRESSION) Well, when I say I haven't got a girlfriend, I mean not a regular one.

IRENE Hundreds of casuals though, I bet.

MARLON Yeah, all over town. The thing is, they're all busy tonight, so I was wondering if… er… what I mean is, if you're not doing anything – I expect you are – but if you're not – would you like to come with me?

IRENE That's very nice of you. The thing is…

MARLON You've made other arrangements.

IRENE No.

MARLON You're washing your hair.

IRENE No.

MARLON You're unblocking the toilet.

IRENE I did that yesterday.

MARLON So what is it?

IRENE How old are you?

MARLON I'm not a kid, if that's what you mean. I'm 23 and a half.

IRENE That's what I mean. I'm old enough to be your… elder sister.

MARLON So?

IRENE Doesn't that bother you?

MARLON No. Does it bother you?

IRENE Well… I s'ppose not.

MARLON So, where's the problem?

IRENE Well, I guess there isn't one. Thank you, I'd love to go out with you tonight.

MARLON Eight thirty?

IRENE I'll be ready. There's just one thing. D'you mind telling me your name? It could get a bit awkward if I have to keep saying 'Hey, you'.

MARLON Oh, sorry. Marlon.

IRENE Irene.

MARLON No, Marlon! Oh, excuse me. I thought… Nice to meet you, Irene.

IRENE Same here.

THEY SHAKE HANDS AWKWARDLY AND HOLD HANDS A LITTLE LONGER THAN USUAL. MARLON PICKS UP HIS SUITCASE AND MOVES TO DOOR.

IRENE Marlon, you're are sure about this, aren't you. People might look.

MARLON Let 'em look. That kind of thing doesn't bother me. Last Christmas I danced with my friend's grandmother!

IRENE REACTS. NOT QUITE THE COMPLIMENT SHE WAS LOOKING FOR. MARLON EXITS.

INTERIOR. THE FLANNAGANS' APARTMENT. NIGHT

THIS IS A WEEK LATER. DEL AND GRAMPS ARE AT TABLE EATING DINNER. MARLON'S DINNER IS UNTOUCHED. THE RACK OF COATS IS IN BACKGROUND. MARLON IS ON PHONE, SPEAKING IN ROMANTIC, HUSHED TONES TO IRENE.

MARLON (ON PHONE) Of course I missed you today. I missed you yesterday as well.

DEL AND GRAMPS SMILE AT EACH OTHER.

MARLON I miss you every hour we're not together.

DEL Hey, Marlon. Can I dunk my bread in your egg?

MARLON (TAKEN ABACK) Help yourself.

DEL DUNKS HIS BREAD IN MARLON'S EGG.

MARLON (ON PHONE) Yeah, okay, I'll see you soon. What? You know I do! I can't, there are people here! No, *you* put the phone down first… Okay, bye.

MARLON HANGS UP, MOVES TOWARDS BEDROOM DOOR.

DEL Who was that?

MARLON (NOT WISHING TO GET INTO EXPLANATIONS) Eh? Oh, just a pal.

MARLON EXITS. DEL AND GRAMPS HAVE STOPPED EATING.

DEL A pal! You don't tell a pal to hang up first! You don't tell a pal you're thinking of him all the time – not unless he owes you money! Is Marlon gay?

GRAMPS (CASUALLY) Could be. He likes paintings… Maybe it's something hereditary.

DEL But it's never happened in our family before.

GRAMPS It's gotta start somewhere.

MARLON ENTERS FROM BEDROOM.

DEL Marlon, would you like to talk?

MARLON About what?

DEL Anything! I want you to know that if there's anything worrying you – anything at all – I'm here.

MARLON Yeah… I have got a little problem. That phone call…

DEL It wasn't that guy with the music centre, was it?

MARLON It wasn't a guy. It was a girl.

DEL (TRIES TO HIDE HIS GREAT RELIEF) Okay. Well, that explains a lot.

MARLON Explains what?

DEL Well, for the last week or so you've been walking round with a goofy grin on your face. So, you got yourself a new broad, uh?

MARLON She's not a broad!

DEL Well, whatever she is – it's starting to affect business. (PRODUCES HIS LITTLE RED BOOK) Look at this. There's some dame called Irene Mackay. She bought a hundred dollarsworth of clothes from us and you're letting her pay back at two dollars a week! That means you've gotta go round her house every week for the next year!

MARLON (LOVE-SICK GRIN) Yeah, I know!

DEL Oh, I geddit! She's the mystery chick?

MARLON Yeah. We've been seeing a lot of each other – well, for the last week or so. Promise you won't laugh.

DEL Of course not.

MARLON I think I'm in love.

DEL AND GRAMPS BURST OUT LAUGHING.

GRAMPS Last month you were in love with the girl from the dry-cleaners.

MARLON Margarita was infatuation! This is different. And Irene's not a girl – she's a woman.

DEL He's fallen in love with someone who can vote this time! So how old is she – 20?

MARLON No. About 30.

DEL What'd you mean *about* 30? How old exactly?

MARLON Forty.

DEL AND GRAMPS Forty!

MARLON What's wrong with going out with a woman of 40?

DEL Nothing! If you happen to be 50! Gee, she's too old for me!

GRAMPS I'd have to think twice!

MARLON Lots of younger guys go out with older women these days. You read it in the papers.

THE PHONE BEGINS RINGING.

DEL No, lots of younger guys go out with *rich* older women! Has this Tom Jones fan got any money?

MARLON Yeah, she's related to the Rockafellers, that's why she's paying us two dollars a week for a bunch of cheap clothes!

DEL (ANSWERS PHONE) Toy Boys R Us. Oh, hi, Mick – the new shipment of Korean umbrellas has arrived? I'm very excited, Mick, call me back when I've calmed down. (DEL HANGS UP)

GRAMPS This Irene dame – it's never gonna work, Marlon.

DEL Be fair, we've sold antiques younger than her.

MARLON Our age difference isn't the problem.

DEL There's something else?

MARLON Her husband!

DEL Holy shhhe's married? I don't believe I'm hearing this! What's her old man like? Is he a big guy?

MARLON Yeah! (AN ALARMED THOUGHT) I'm not taking one of them coats round!

GRAMPS How's her husband feel about all this then, Marlon?

MARLON He doesn't know. He's away.

DEL Where?

MARLON New Jersey State Penitentiary.

DEL New Jersey…! You're having an affair with the wife of a convict?

MARLON Boy, you really jump to conclusions! Just coz he's in the State Pen doesn't automatically mean he's a convict! He could be a warden or even the governor.

GRAMPS And is he?

MARLON What?

DEL A warden or the governor?

MARLON No – he's a convict – but you weren't sure!

GRAMPS What's he in for?

MARLON Oh – this'n'that.

GRAMPS Like?

MARLON Armed robbery, aggravated assault and attempted murder.

DEL He's got a bit of a temper, uh?

MARLON That's why poor Irene's had such an unhappy life. He used to beat up on her and the kid. That's why she moved here, to get away from him.

DEL What do you mean, get away from him? He's in the joint.

MARLON But he's being released soon. That's why I need your advice. When he gets out, d'you think I should go see him and explain about me and Irene, man to man?

DEL …! Lemme put it this way. If you suddenly find you're really fed up with having knees in the middle of your legs, then go 'n' see him! But if you've grown quite attached to 'em, then emigrate to Iceland, you dipstick! This guy's a killer!

GRAMPS No, he's only in for *attempted* murder.

DEL Maybe that was just a bit of practice for when Marlon come along! Marlon, I'm your big brother – I've looked after you since you were a little kid, ever since Mom died – God bless the woman's spirit. (CROSSES HIMSELF. MARLON AND GRAMPS CROSS THEMSELVES) I brought you up and I fought your battles for you. Have I ever given you wrong advice?

MARLON …Yes.

DEL So I'm not Doctor Ruth. But I'm telling you now, get outa this situation – and quick.

GRAMPS Okay if I eat your fries?

MARLON Please do. Look, Del, I know you're my big brother and I know what you did to me – for me! But I'm not three years old anymore. I'm a full-grown man and I got my own life to lead. And I think that's what I oughta be doing. (GRABS COAT)

DEL Where you going?

MARLON Irene's. She said I could move in with her if I wanted to. And now seems a good a time as any.

GRAMPS What are you gonna do if her old man comes looking for you?

MARLON I don't know. But I'll tell you something I *won't* do – I won't hide! If he wants a piece of me he won't have to look too far… I'll see you around.

DEL Yeah, but how will I recognise you?

MARLON I'll be the guy in the outsize cashmere coat.

MARLON EXITS FRONT DOOR.

GRAMPS What are you gonna do, Del?

DEL The stupid little jerk! I gotta think of a way outa this before her old man gets sprung.

GRAMPS What happens if you can't think of anything?

DEL Dunno. I'll find out what Marlon's favourite hymns are.

INTERIOR. CRYSTAL'S BAR. NIGHT

A WEEK LATER. A FEW TOUGH-LOOKING YOUNG MEN (EARLY 20S) AND ALL WEARING CASHMERE OVERCOATS, ARE PLAYING POOL. AMONGST THE PEOPLE AT BAR WE SEE ANOTHER COUPLE OF MEN ARE ALSO WEARING THE SAME OVERCOATS. A FEW BIRTHDAY CARDS ARE DISPLAYED BEHIND BAR. DEL ENTERS WEARING HIS COAT.

MAN AT BAR Hey, Crystal, same again.

CRYSTAL (SNARLS) I only got one pair of hands! Wait! (SEES DEL – NOW SWEET SMILES) Hi, Del, what can I get you?

DEL Just my usual, Crystal, s'il vous plait.

CRYSTAL What's wrong with Marlon?

DEL I don't know. He moved out a week ago.

CRYSTAL Well, he's come home. He's over at the table.

WE SEE MARLON AT TABLE, LOOKING DEPRESSED AND DRINKING MORE THAN IS GOOD FOR HIM.

CRYSTAL It's none of my business, and I shouldn't be complaining, but he's drinking Scotch and that's his fifth.

DEL Okay, Crystal, thanks, leave it to me… Hey, who's birthday is it?

CRYSTAL Mine.

DEL Congratulations. How old are you?

CRYSTAL Another year! I was hopin' to go out tonight and celebrate. You know, nightclub, supper. But – no one to go with.

DEL Well, maybe I could be of assistance.

CRYSTAL Really?

DEL (TAKES AN APPLICATION FORM FROM INSIDE OVERCOAT) Fill in this application form – I'll find you someone in no time.

CRYSTAL (STONEY FACED) Thank you.

DEL Hey! Will you bring the drinks to the table?

CRYSTAL (SNARLS) Can't you see I'm busy?

DEL Whoa! (TO A CUSTOMER) Who put a hedgehog in her pants?

DEL JOINS MARLON AT TABLE.

DEL Mind if I sit down?

MARLON It's a free country.

DEL I've had a real good week. Unloaded all but two of the cashmere overcoats, a shipment of Korean umbrellas and two crates of Victorian digital clocks.

MARLON (BITTER) I couldn't be more pleased.

DEL Okay, what's wrong?

MARLON Irene. She's dumped me. No explanation – just said she thought it best if we quit.

DEL Well, you gotta try 'n' be philosophical about it. All's well that ends well.

MARLON What do you mean, all's well that ends well? It hasn't ended well for me, has it?

DEL Come on, be positive about it. You and Irene had some good times together. You had a few laughs, you got your rocks off. And now it's over.

MARLON You're a real pig, you know that?

DEL I'm just tryna put it in perspective for you.

MARLON I loved her, Del.

DEL Okay, but it's best in the long run. At your age, love can be a fickle thing. I know exactly what would have happened: one day you'd walk into the sports gym and see some beautiful 19-year-old bombshell with a figure that'd knock your eyes out – and she'd fall head over heels in love with you, wouldn't she?

MARLON (A MODEST SHRUG) Well…

DEL Then you'd have to break the news to Irene. How's that gonna make a 40-year-old woman feel? Losing in love to a younger girl. And she wouldn't be losing just *any* man – she'd be losing *you*!

MARLON I never thought of it like that.

DEL That scar would never heal.

MARLON No… Poor chick!

DEL Exactly. Besides, her husband was released from prison yesterday, so you're saved from all that.

MARLON Yeah, you're most probably right. Look, I'm sorry if I've been a pain in the butt.

DEL Hey, I don't wanna hear you talking like that. You've proved that you are a human being in the fullest sense of the word. You have a heart. You love. You give, honestly.

And those feelings deserve respect. Don't feel ashamed – feel *proud*. I'll get our drinks.

DEL MOVES TO BAR WHERE CRYSTAL HAS PLACED A COUPLE OF DRINKS.

CRYSTAL What's wrong with him?

DEL Oh, some old broad's given him the sack.

DEL RETURNS TO TABLE WITH DRINKS.

MARLON I'm glad you're my brother.

DEL Hey, don't go getting girlie on me. And remember, no one's ever found an answer at the bottom of a glass.

MARLON I know. Last one. (TOASTS DEL) To my big brother, who's always been there for me.

DEL (CLINKS GLASSES) And always will be.

ZACK ENTERS AND PASSES DEL AND THE TABLE. ZACK IS ALSO WEARING ONE OF THE CASHMERE COATS.

ZACK Yo, Marlon. Hiya, Del.

MARLON Hi, Zack.

DEL Hello, son.

ZACK JOINS THE OTHER GUYS AT POOL TABLE.

MARLON'S FACE IS SCREWED UP IN CONCENTRATION.

DEL What's wrong now? You wanna go somewhere?

MARLON No… How did you know Irene's husband was being released yesterday?

DEL Musta heard… Come on, let's get outa here.

MARLON How did Irene's son know your name?

DEL (NOW FURTIVELY) Erm… I'm wearing a signet-ring with 'D' on it – obvious my name's Del.

MARLON No. It could stand for Darryl, Dennis, David… Zack's wearing one of your coats!

DEL We're all wearing 'em, it's the fashion. Come on.

MARLON Hey, Zack. How did you know his name?

ZACK I met him yesterday when he called round to see Mom.

DEL REACTS TO THIS.

MARLON You went to see Irene?

DEL Now look, Marlon, it's *not* what you think! I just went round to *talk* to her. I told her a few home truths.

MARLON Like?

DEL I said; if she *really* cared about you she oughta finish the affair – before someone got hurt.

MARLON Where would I be without you, eh? Happy maybe!

DEL You *wanna* get killed?

MARLON No! But it's nice to have the choice!

DEL Where you going?

MARLON I'm gonna work out! I'm gonna punch the bag till it bleeds and pretend it's you!

MARLON STORMS OUT OF BAR.

DEL (TO CRYSTAL) That wasn't a very nice thing to say, was it?

CRYSTAL STARES AT HIM HARD IN DISBELIEF.

CRYSTAL You'd do that to your own brother? You're disgusting!

DEL Hey, don't call me disgusting till you know me better!

CRYSTAL SHAKES HER HEAD SADLY AT HIM AND MOVES AWAY.

EXTERIOR. ALLEY OUTSIDE OF CRYSTAL'S BAR. NIGHT THE ALLEY IS POORLY LIT. DEL EXITS CRYSTAL'S BAR AND STARTS TO WALK DOWN ALLEY. NOW KARL, A TOUGH-LOOKING 30-YEAR-OLD HOOD, JUMPS OUT OF THE SHADOWS, GRABS DEL AND SLAMS HIM FACE FIRST AGAINST WALL. DEL HIDES HIS FEAR. HE KNOWS HE CAN TALK HIS WAY OUT OF MOST SITUATIONS, FAILING THAT HE CAN FIGHT.

DEL If you're a client of my video-dating agency I can always introduce you to someone else!

KARL I'm the only one making the introductions tonight, pal. There's someone here who's been dying to meet you.

DEL Oh, come on, you haven't brought your sister along?

KARL Shuddup! (HE SPINS DEL ROUND)

NOW A MAN APPEARS OUT OF THE SHADOWS AND WALKS MENACINGLY TOWARDS DEL. THIS IS BRUCE MACKAY (IRENE'S HUSBAND). HE IS HARD-BITTEN, ROCK-FACED AND POWERFULLY BUILT.

BRUCE Bruce Mackay's the name – loving husband of Irene. Any bells ringing?

DEL Ooh, like Santa's sleigh!

BRUCE Yeah, you bet your life you've heard of me, pal. A friend tells me you've been seen with my wife!

DEL It was nothing – just a friendly chat.

BRUCE That's nice. Trouble is, I'm not as friendly as you, ole pal. Somebody messes with what's mine and I tend to get – what's the word, Karl?

KARL Petulant.

BRUCE Yeah. Now I'm about to teach you some real good manners, Marlon.

DEL Come on, can't we just talk about this… Marlon? Did you say *Marlon*?

BRUCE Yeah. That's you, isn't it? Marlon Flannagan.

DEL SIGHS WITH A MIXTURE OF RELIEF AND LAUGHTER.

DEL Yeah – that's me. I'm Marlon.

BRUCE Good! Give him some air, Karl. Let the man breathe.

KARL RELEASES DEL AND NOW DEL STANDS A FEW YARDS APART FROM THE TWO GRINNING MEN. DEL NOW GESTURES BEHIND THEM, AS IF SOMEONE HAS ENTERED THE ALLEY.

DEL Hey, just stay outa this!

BRUCE AND KARL TURN TO SEE WHO HAS ENTERED. DEL TAKES HIS CHANCE AND FLIES AT THEM FISTS FLAYING THE AIR. WE CUT TO A NEW ANGLE WHERE WE CAN NO LONGER SEE THE COMBATANTS, ONLY THEIR SHADOWS ON THE WALL AND THE SOUND OF A VICIOUS FIGHT.

INTERIOR. THE FLANNAGANS' APARTMENT. NIGHT GRAMPS IS WATCHING THE TV. THE FRONT DOOR OPENS AND DEL AND CRYSTAL ENTER TOGETHER. CRYSTAL IS SUPPORTING DEL WHOSE FACE IS BLOODY. HIS COAT AND SHIRT ARE RIPPED AND BLOODSTAINED.

CRYSTAL Don't panic, Gramps. Everything's gonna be okay.

GRAMPS Something's happened! Who did this to you, Del?

DEL Nothing happened to *me* – but Marlon got the chili kicked out of him!

GRAMPS Marlon?

DEL MOVES AWAY WEAKLY.

CRYSTAL I think he's delirious. One minute he's in my bar tryna sell his overcoats, the next he was being beat up in the alley outside.

GRAMPS That's what's wrong with modern America. We've lost the art of complaining.

DEL (CHECKING HIMSELF IN MIRROR) Look at my beautiful face! It's hard to believe that I actually *won*! (TAKES COMB AND STRAIGHTENS HIS HAIR)

CRYSTAL I tried to get him to go to hospital.

DEL It's only cuts and bruises.

CRYSTAL You may have internal injuries.

DEL Yeah, but they don't show…

CRYSTAL Okay, your life. I'll see you around.

DEL Thanks for everything, Crystal. And, hey, happy birthday.

CRYSTAL *Thanks*! (CRYSTAL AND GRAMPS MOVE TO HALL – OR OUT OF EARSHOT OF DEL) He should get himself to hospital.

GRAMPS He won't go to hospital – they frighten him. I remember when he was about 19 and he got stabbed in the shoulder outside some nightclub. He wouldn't go to hospital then. Cured himself – Germolene and a monogrammed handkerchief.

CRYSTAL Did he know the person who did it?

GRAMPS Oh sure, he knew 'em.

CRYSTAL And I bet he didn't go to the police either.

GRAMPS No. Well he couldn't really, he was engaged to her at the time.

CRYSTAL Nite, Gramps.

GRAMPS See you, Crystal.

CRYSTAL EXITS.

GRAMPS I'll get a brandy. (MOVES TO KITCHEN DOOR) Would you like one?

DEL Thanks, Gramps.

GRAMPS EXITS TO KITCHEN. DEL IS IN FRONT OF MIRROR DABBING HIS CUTS WITH A TISSUE. MARLON ENTERS FROM FRONT DOOR. HE SEES ONLY THE BACK OF DEL. HE TURNS HIS BACK AS DEL TURNS TOWARDS HIM.

DEL Marlon.

MARLON Don't talk to me! I'm never gonna talk to you again for the rest of my life – or for a very long time, whichever comes first! I've been doing a lot of thinking tonight, and I've come to one conclusion – I don't care about you any more! As far as I'm concerned you are no longer my broth… (TURNS AND SEES DEL. NOW DEEP CONCERN) Oh, my God, what happened to you?

DEL I fell down some stairs… About seven flights! I bumped into Bruce Mackay, that's what happened!

MARLON And he did this?

DEL No, a passer-by attacked me for no reason as Brucie and me were having a little chinwag! Yes, he did it! He thought I was you.

MARLON He thought you were…! God, how must Irene have described me! Del, when are you ever gonna let me grow up? You won't even let me take my own beatings now!

DEL No. What a dirty-rat! You just listen to me, Marlon. Tonight, on your behalf, I succeeded where all the prison psychiatrists and social workers failed. I got him to see the error of his ways. He's out of your life forever. I've cleared the path of true love for you and what's-her-face.

MARLON Irene? That's all over, Del.

DEL What'd you mean 'all over'? It's not all over, Marlon! I've got a box of Belgian chocolates in the van – I've only had one out of it – take 'em round to her now.

MARLON I was thinking about what you said tonight at Crystal's, so I called Irene. We talked it over and figured it all out. She was just lonely in a new city – and I was just looking for a mother figure. We came to our senses. You were right, Del.

DEL No I wasn't! Older women are great! They got experience – they have wisdom – they take naps in the evening, you can get out and be back and they never know!

MARLON I mean you were right about me meeting someone else. I was at the sports gym and this girl came in. Zoe.

DEL (THROUGH PAINED LIPS) Zoe?

MARLON Man, she is great! Eighteen, with a figure that makes Alicia Silverstone look a cert for plastic surgery. I've just come back to change, I'm going to a party with her.

MARLON MOVES TOWARDS BEDROOM.

MARLON Hey, if I was you I'd have that head looked at. (EXITS)

DEL They're the truest damn words you've spoken for years, Marlon!

CHRISTMAS SPECIAL 2001

'If They Could See Us Now...!'

EXERTIOR. UP-MARKET, LONDON. DAY
PRESENT TIME. WE SEE A BLACK CAB DRIVING
THROUGH THE HEAVY LONDON TRAFFIC TOWARDS US.
CUT TO INTERIOR. THE CAB/LONDON. DAY
(OR VOICE OFF)
DEL AND RODNEY ARE BOTH DRESSED IN THEIR BEST
SUITS AND LOOK BUSINESSLIKE AND AFFLUENT –
ALTHOUGH DEL'S TIE RUINS THE IMAGE SLIGHTLY.
RODNEY IS LOOKING SOMEWHAT EDGY.

DEL What's up with you, Rodney?

ROD I'm nervous, that's all. I mean, this bloke we're
going to see – Justin. He's not gonna be asking me about
my private life and that sorta thing, is he?

DEL Of course not! Well, not *that* private! I mean, he don't
wanna know about you and Cassandra's little problems.

ROD Oh good… (QUICKLY AND DEFENSIVELY BECAUSE
OF THE DRIVER) What problems? Me and Cassandra
haven't got any problems!

DEL That's not what you were saying the other night.

ROD All right, so there's been a few minor hiccups in the
bedroom department, that's all – but they're personal
and I told you in confidence.

DEL Look, I'm not gonna go telling Justin about thongs
and things (fongs and fings)… I'm not gonna tell him
what Cassandra wears either. (LAUGHS)

CUT TO INTERIOR JUSTIN'S OFFICE. DAY
AT THIS POINT WE HAVE NO IDEA OF GEOGRAPHY. IT IS
A SMALL, BASIC AND PRACTICAL OFFICE, WITH FEW
LUXURIES. THE DECOR, FURNISHING, ETC, SHOULD
OFFER NO CLUE AS TO THE BUSINESS THAT TAKES PLACE
HERE. RODNEY AND DEL SIT IN FRONT OF AN OLD DESK
UPON WHICH SITS A FEW FILES AND A LAPTOP. JUSTIN IS
SEATED BEHIND DESK. JUSTIN IS TRENDY BUT FRIENDLY.
WE SHOULD GET THE IMPRESSION THAT HE MAY BE A
JOURNALIST OR A WRITER OF SOME KIND.

JUSTIN Sorry, it's been particularly busy today. Okay,
we are in a 'go' situation. You don't mind if I record this?

DEL Oh mai oui, mai oui, you carry on, Justin.
JUSTIN PRODUCES A DICTAPHONE.

JUSTIN Thanks. Now, I've got all the basic detail about
your business careers, etcetera. But, what I'd like to do is
to get an insight into the real *you*.
RODNEY GULPS AT WHAT MIGHT BE COMING.

JUSTIN How you started, how you became so successful,
but more importantly – your lives and your (HEAVY
FRENCH ACCENT) *raison d'etre*.

DEL Oh, *Laboratoires Garnier* (Laboratwa Garny).

JUSTIN (PUZZLED) Quite. So, in your own time and in
your own words. (JUSTIN SWITCHES DICTAPHONE ON
AND BEGINS TAKING NOTES)

DEL Where do I start, Justin? Up until a few years ago
we were *very* ordinary people, leading *very* ordinary lives,
weren't we, Rodney?
RODNEY JUST STARES, ALMOST AT CAMERA, AS WE GO
INTO HIS MIND.
A VERY FAST SEQUENCE OF FLASHBACKS FROM THEIR
'VERY ORDINARY LIVES'.
1. FROM 'DANGER UXD'
WE SEE THE SECOND DOLL POP UP BEHIND BAR IN
TROTTERS' FLAT. DEL, RODNEY AND ALBERT RUSH TO
DOOR IN FEAR.
2. FROM 'THE JOLLY BOYS' OUTING'
THE COACH EXPLODES. WE SEE RODNEY OBSERVING IT
FROM INSIDE TELEPHONE KIOSK. WE SEE DEL, STANDING
ALONGSIDE THE OTHER JOLLY BOYS, WATCHING THE
FLAMES.

3. FROM 'A TOUCH OF GLASS!'
WE SEE DEL AND RODNEY UP STEP LADDER HOLDING
LARGE, CANVAS SACK BENEATH CHANDELIER. WE SEE
SECOND CHANDELIER IN BACKGROUND CRASH TO THE
FLOOR.
4. FROM 'MIAMI TWICE', PART TWO 'OH TO BE IN
ENGLAND'
WE SEE THE ALLIGATOR ROAR AND DEL AND RODNEY
RUN FROM THE EVERGLADE.
5. FROM 'HEROES AND VILLAINS'
WE SEE DEL AND RODNEY RUNNING THROUGH THE
URBAN MIST DRESSED AS BATMAN AND ROBIN.

BACK TO INTERIOR JUSTIN'S OFFICE. DAY
PRESENT TIME.

ROD Yeah.

DEL But then, as you know, one day I discovered an
almost priceless and historic artefact. Well, to begin with
we didn't know what to do with it.

ROD That's right. At first we thought about donating it
to the British Museum as a national treasure.

DEL But in the end we decided to flog it. So, before you
know it, me and Rodders have got nigh on six and 'arf
million quid. So, we divide out the dosh and gave our
old Uncle Albert a nice little drink.
SOUND OVER: THE 'PWUFF' OF A CAMERA FLASHLIGHT.
A STILL PHOTOGRAPH.

INTERIOR, HOSPITAL LOBBY. DAY
IN BACKGROUND IS THE DOORS TO A HOSPITAL WARD.
A SIGN ABOVE DOORS READS 'PECKHAM GENERAL
HOSPITAL, THE TROTTER WING'. OVER THIS WE HEAR:

DEL (VOICE OVER) But then, as is our nature, Justin,
we thought of others first and gave generously to charity.
BENEATH SIGN WE FIND A SMILING BUT EMBARRASSED
RODNEY, IN HIS BEST SUIT AND NAVY BLUE TIE,
STANDING NEXT A SMILING PRINCE PHILIP. ON THE
OTHER SIDE WE FIND THE QUEEN, IN A TOPCOAT AND
HAT, STANDING NEXT TO DEL WHO IS GRINNING
BROADLY. HE IS WEARING A SILVER MOHAIR SUIT, A RED
SHIRT AND A MULTI-COLOURED TIE. DEL'S RIGHT ARM IS
TIGHT ROUND THE QUEEN'S WAIST AND HIS LEFT HAND
AND INDEX FINGER IS POINTING UP TO THE 'TROTTER
WING' SIGN. (ALTHOUGH THE TROTTERS HAVE MADE A
WONDERFULLY CHARITABLE DONATION TO THE LOCAL
COMMUNITY, RATHER THAN THE SOMBRE APPROACH
BEING DEMONSTRATED BY THE OTHERS, DEL'S STYLE
REFLECTS THE OPENING OF A NEW BETTING SHOP.)

INTERIOR. JUSTIN'S OFFICE. DAY.

DEL But eventually we started thinking about the future.
So we got in touch with this City stockbroker who advised
us to put our money in a new and 'vibrant' venture.

ROD It was the Central American Market. It was
attracting massive funds from all over the world.

DEL We were making money quicker than the royal
mint. That old Central American market just couldn't
go wrong – all our investments turned to gold.

ROD But we weren't flash.

DEL Oh no, we weren't flash.
FLASHBACK.
EXTERIOR. SKY. DAY
A CLEAR BLUE SKY. A BRITISH AIRWAYS CONCORDE
GLIDES INTO FRAME.
THIS WOULD BE MAY/EARLY JUNE 2000.

INTERIOR. CONCORDE. DAY

ROD (VOICE OVER) I mean, even when we went away
on business, we always took the family with us.

DEL (VOICE OVER) We've always been very family
orientated. There'd be me and Raquel, my significant
other.

WE FIND DEL AND RAQUEL SEATED TOGETHER. DEL IS IN
A VERY BRIGHT SHIRT.
THEY ARE OBVIOUSLY A HAPPY COUPLE AS THEY RAISE
THEIR CHAMPAGNE GLASSES TO EACH OTHER. THEY
NOW TURN AND SMILE TO THE PEOPLE SITTING
OPPOSITE.

DEL (VOICE OVER) And Rodney and Cassandra.
WE FIND RODNEY AND CASSANDRA ARE SEATED
OPPOSITE (CASSANDRA IN WINDOW SEAT, RODNEY IN
AISLE SEAT. RODNEY AND CASSANDRA RETURN THE
SMILES.

DEL (VOICE OVER) And, of course, my young son,
Damien.
NOW WE SEE, SEATED BEHIND RODNEY, IS THE 11-YEAR-
OLD DAMIEN. HIS HAIR IS STYLED IN THAT GELLED,
SPIKY URBAN FASHION. DAMIEN HAS A THICK ELASTIC
BAND. HE QUICKLY PULLS THE BAND BACK AND THEN
TWANGS IT AT THE UNSEEN EAR OF UNCLE RODNEY.
SOUND OVER: A TWANG AND A SMACK.

ROD (OUT OF VISION) Aaarggh!
WE CUT TO DEL WHO ACTUALLY LAUGHS AT THIS –
HE LAUGHS TO THE PAINED RODNEY IN THAT 'HE'S
A LITTLE RASCAL' WAY.

FLASHBACK.
EXTERIOR. MAIN FACADE LUXURIOUS HOTEL. MONTE
CARLO. NIGHT

DEL (VOICE OVER) And we just went about our business
in our own quiet little way.
WE NOW SEE A WHITE STRETCH LIMO, WITH TINTED
GLASS WINDOWS, PULL UP AT HOTEL DOORS. THE CAR
DOORS OPEN AND THE TROTTERS ARE DISGORGED.
DEL IS WEARING A PARTICULARLY BRIGHT AND GAUDY
BLAZER.

INTERIOR. THE HOTEL FRONT LOBBY. NIGHT
THE WEALTHY AND CHOSEN ARE ALL AROUND
CHATTING, ETC. THE TROTTERS WALK TO THE
RECEPTION DESK.

DEL (VOICE OVER) And although it wasn't a world we were
brought up in, even if I say so myself, we just blended in.
OTHER GUESTS TURN AND LOOK AT DEL. THE
CONCIERGE APPROACHES.

CONCIERGE Good evening, Monsieur Trotter. It is a
pleasure to see you once again.

DEL Bonnet de douche, Dominique.
DEL HANDS DOMINIQUE A FEW NOTES.

INTERIOR. THE HOTEL CONSERVATORY OR VERANDAH
ANOTHER DAY. GENTEEL GUESTS ARE SIPPING
AFTERNOON TEA. DEL, RODNEY AND RAQUEL ARE AT A
TABLE FOR FOUR. A WORRIED CASSANDRA APPROACHES.

CASS Del, you've got to have a word with Damien.
People are complaining.

RAQ (SLIGHTLY TOO POSH) Oh no, what's he done now?

CASS He's just weed in the swimming pool.
SOME OTHER GUESTS LOOK ACROSS.

DEL (CHUCKLES IN EMBARRASSMENT. POSH) Oh leave it
out, Cassandra. (SMILING TO OTHER GUESTS) All young
boys have a Johnny Cash in the swimming pool, don't
they?

CASS Yes, but not from the top of the four-metre diving
board.
DEL AND RODNEY BOTH CHOKE ON THEIR TEA (OR
REACT IN SOME WAY TO THE VISION). RAQUEL STANDS
AND SMILES TO OTHER GUESTS. NOW RAQUEL AND
CASSANDRA RUSH AWAY TO MAIN HOTEL.

DEL Little git!

EXTERIOR. THE CASINO/GARDENS. NIGHT
THE EVENING-SUITED DEL AND RODNEY WANDER
INTO SHOT. DEL PAUSES TO LIGHT A CIGAR.

DEL This is the bizzo, annit, Rodders?

ROD It's not too bad, is it?

DEL BREATHES IN THE SCENTED NIGHT AIR.

DEL Uncle Albert would have loved all this.

ROD Yeah, but you can bet your life he's been here before. He's happy down there on the coast. Right next door to the sea *and* he's living in sin with old Elsie Partridge – his, er, (SMILING AS HE QUOTES ALBERT) 'girlfriend'.

DEL (LAUGHS) Girlfriend! I heard she cut the ribbon at the opening of Stonehenge.

THEY BOTH LAUGH.

ROD And at least we aint gotta go through the Battle of the Baltic every night. During the war.

ROD During the war.

DEL During the war.

THEY LAUGH WARMLY AT ALBERT AND HIS SAGAS.

DEL (INDICATES CASINO) Come on, Rodney, I feel lucky.

ROD I can't. I promised Cassandra – no gambling, no discos, no women, no boozing.

DEL But she meant not to excess. I mean, you're not on probation, are you?

ROD Well, a little roll of the dice aint gonna hurt anyone, is it?

DEL Course not. And they've got a disco in there. It's good for your health, Rodney, coz jiving is aerobic… Come on, I'll order a few bottles of champagne before we get started… During the war.

THEY WANDER AWAY TOWARDS CASINO, ASCEND THE STEPS AND DISAPPEAR INTO CASINO, MIMICKING ALBERT.

ROD During the war.

DEL During the war.

NOW WE HEAR DEL'S VOICE FROM PRESENT TIME .

DEL (VOICE OVER) (CAN BARELY SPEAK THE AWFUL TRUTH) But then, just as everything was going so well, something… something terrible happened.

FLASHBACK

EXTERIOR. THE HOTEL/MONTE CARLO. DAY

THE LIMO WAITS AS DEL DESCENDS STEPS. DEL IS DRESSED IN A SMART SUIT, SUNGLASSES, ETC. HE CLIMBS IN BACK OF LIMO AND IT PULLS AWAY.

INTERIOR. THE LIMO. DAY

DEL SETTLES IN BACK OF CAR. HE HAS A CIGAR BETWEEN HIS LIPS. HE PICKS UP NEWSPAPER FROM SEAT: *NEW YORK HERALD TRIBUNE*. NOW HIS FACE FREEZES IN TERROR AS HE READS THE HEADLINES. HE REMOVES SUNGLASSES AND THE CIGAR DROPS FROM HIS LIPS AS THE EVER-GROWING HORROR IMPACTS. WE SEE THE FRONT PAGE OF NEWSPAPER: 'CENTRAL AMERICAN MARKET CRASHES', 'BILLIONS WIPED OFF STOCK-MARKETS', 'THOUSANDS RUINED'.

DEL (CHILLED/HORRIFIED) Chateauneuf du Pape!

PRESENT TIME

INTERIOR. JUSTIN'S OFFICE. DAY

JUSTIN IS STANDING IN FRONT OF THE LOCKER WITH ITS DOOR OPEN.

ROD It turned out that the negotiations between the Central American countries had collapsed.

DEL We were wiped out, nicht a coin. We'd even paid for the hotel on a credit card – a credit card which had now been withdrawn.

ROD But Derek is, if nothing else, a creative businessman, and he came up with a solution to our dilemma.

EXTERIOR. THE HOTEL/MONTE CARLO. DAY OR NIGHT

IMMEDIATELY WE SEE THE TROTTERS, LED BY DEL, RUNNING OUT OF THE HOTEL WITH THEIR LUGGAGE IN HAND AS THEY EXECUTE AN EN-MASSE RUNNER.

DEL (ENCOURAGING HIS TROOPS) Come on, let's go… Don't look back! Don't look back!

THE FIVE OF THEM RUN AWAY DOWN THE HILL. WE NOW SEE THE CONCIERGE, DOMINIQUE, RUNNING AFTER THEM BRANDISHING THE BILL.

CONCIERGE Monsieur Trotter! Please wait, sir. Monsieur Trotter.

INTERIOR JUSTIN'S OFFICE. DAY

WE COME UP ON THE DEVASTATED TROTTERS. WE HEAR JUSTIN.

JUSTIN (OUT OF VISION) It's time to go.

WE NOW SEE JUSTIN. HIS LOCKER DOOR IS OPEN AND, DURING THE FLASHBACKS, HE HAS DONNED A CLOAK AND WIG. WE NOW REALISE HE IS A BARRISTER. JUSTIN OPENS HIS OFFICE DOOR. OUTSIDE WE SEE A CORRIDOR AND A SIGN UPON A WALL WHICH READS 'SOUTH LONDON BANKRUPTCY COURT'. WE NOW REALISE JUSTIN'S OFFICE IS ACTUALLY IN THE COURT BUILDING.

INTERIOR. THE COURTHOUSE. CORRIDOR. DAY

DEL, RODNEY AND JUSTIN EXIT FROM OFFICE AND BEGIN WALKING DOWN CORRIDOR.

JUSTIN And how long did it take for the news to hit the UK?

ROD About as long as it took someone to press a button on the Internet. Suddenly all our so-called business associates wouldn't return our calls. We were cast into the financial wilderness.

DEL But fortunately we were born into a strong community, and when all our old friends back in Peckham heard the news they were just as devastated as us.

FLASHBACK

INTERIOR. THE NAGS HEAD. DAY

WE COME UP ON THE FRONT PAGE OF THE *PECKHAM ECHO*, WHICH WE SHALL DISCOVER IS BEING HELD BY BOYCIE. THE HEADLINE, ACCOMPANIED BY A PHOTO OF DEL AND RODNEY IN CHAMPAGNE/CELEBRATORY MOOD, READS 'LOCAL MILLIONAIRES GO BUST'. SOUND OVER: WE HEAR UPROARIOUS LAUGHTER. WE DISCOVER THE LAUGHTER COMES FROM; BOYCIE, MARLENE, DENZIL, SID AND MICKEY PEARCE. TRIGGER, WHO HASN'T GOT THE FULL PICTURE YET, SIMPLY SMILES VAGUELY.

PRESENT TIME

INTERIOR. COURTROOM. DAY

THE COURT IS EMPTY EXCEPT FOR DEL, RODNEY AND JUSTIN WHO ARE SEATED AT TABLE.

JUSTIN There's a name that crops up every now and then. (CHECKS PAPERWORK) Michael Fisher – a landlord of a public house – The Nags Head, Peckham. What part did he play in the proceedings?

DEL Mike invested his life savings in our venture.

ROD He actually remortgaged the pub.

JUSTIN I see. Will Mr Fisher be giving evidence?

DEL No, he's in prison.

JUSTIN IS HORRIFIED.

DEL The Fraud Squad claimed he tried to recoup his losses by embezzling the brewery. Never has a man been more innocent.

JUSTIN I take it he's pleading not guilty?

ROD No, he confessed to everything.

INTERIOR. COURT LOBBY. DAY

HERE WE FIND BOYCIE, MARLENE, DENZIL, SID AND TRIGGER STANDING/SITTING AROUND DRINKING COFFEE. DENZIL IS NERVOUS, PACING AND CONTINUALLY CHECKING HIS WATCH.

BOYCIE For God's sake, Denzil, will you sit down? You're wearing the marble out!

DENZIL I can't help it, I've never been a character witness before.

SID And d'you think *we* have?

MARLENE I'm worried. I think Del's made a terrible mistake.

BOYCIE Well, of course, he'd made a terrible mistake, that's why he's in court.

MARLENE No, I mean having you four as character witnesses! It's like inviting the Manson Family to dinner.

BOYCIE We met Del and Rodney earlier and they seemed quietly confident. They've arranged to meet Raquel and Cassandra for a celebration lunch. So I'd avoid Pizza Hut if I was you. (LAUGHS)

MARLENE Del wasn't confident, he was deeply worried. I mean, he didn't even touch me up.

BOYCIE REACTS.

TRIGGER There's nothing to be nervous about, Denzil. All you've gotta do is go in there and tell the truth.

DENZIL Trigger, if I go in there and tell the truth, Del and Rodney'll spend the next five years sharpening Jeffrey Archer's pencils.

SID I'm the one who's got most to worry about.

MARLENE Why?

SID Coz I'm managing The Nags Head until Mike is released. But how do I know exactly what he got up to?

DENZIL Yeah. I mean, how does Sid know Mike didn't post-date some of his fiddles. So the police'll think it's *Sid's* fiddles?

SID What are you gonna do in there, Trig?

TRIGGER I'm gonna tell 'em I hear voices.

DENZIL No, Trig, you're not on trial, you're a character witness.

TRIGGER I know, but I hear voices.

BOYCIE Oh, God, it's gonna be one of them days!

INTERIOR. THE COURTROOM. DAY

THE CLERK OF THE COURT AND A COUPLE OF OTHER OFFICIALS ARE NOW ALSO IN ROOM. DEL, RODNEY AND JUSTIN ARE AT THEIR BENCH DEEP IN DISCUSSION. JUSTIN IS STUDYING A FILE.

JUSTIN I notice that your respective properties were company-owned. So you both lost your homes?

ROD (ANGER AIMED AT DEL) Yes! (TO JUSTIN) I had a lovely place right on the river.

DEL (AT RODNEY) And I had an *estate*! (TO JUSTIN) Peacocks everywhere! But we were not homeless. Thanks to my foresight, some years previously, I had bought another property where we could all live.

ROD Yeah, it's called our old flat at Nelson Mandela House. That just shows you how our fortunes altered. Suddenly everything changed. All our good luck turned to bad. Every day was just more rows and more bad news. We thought things couldn't get worse – oh boy, how wrong could we be?

FLASHBACK

INTERIOR. THE TROTTERS' LOUNGE/NELSON MANDELA HOUSE. NIGHT

WE COME UP FULL ON THE TV SCREEN WHICH IS SHOWING THE OPENING OF THE GAME SHOW *GOLDRUSH*. THIS IS MERELY THE INTRODUCTION TO THE GAME SO WE WILL KNOW IT LATER. WE HAVE HI-TECH FLASHING LIGHTS, AS PER ALL MODERN GAME SHOWS: *THE WEAKEST LINK, WHO WANTS TO BE A MILLIONAIRE, SHAFTED, THE PEOPLE VERSUS*, ETC. AS OUR SHOW'S BASIS IS *THE RAINBOW ROAD*, WHEREBY THE PRIZE MONEY INCREASES AS THE CONTESTANT ADVANCES ALONG THE RAINBOW, OUR LIGHTS CONSIST OF THE SEVEN COLOURS OF THE RAINBOW, PLUS GOLD.

THREE CONTESTANTS ARE STOOD BEHIND HI-TECH PODIUMS. JONATHAN ROSS INTRODUCES THE SHOW.

JR Good evening and welcome to the quiz show *everyone* is talking about. Well, I don't know for sure if *everyone* is talking about it! I don't know if they're talking about it in Tristan da Cuna or Rotherham, but in general terms, well at least in my house, *everyone* is talking about it! This is the show where you can win anything from one pound to one hundred thousand pounds! This is the fastest game show on TV. This is Monday, this is live, this is Jonathan Ross and this is *Goldrush*!

MUSICAL THEME (PERHAPS SPANDAU BALLET'S 'GOLD') ACCOMPANIED BY UNCONTROLLED APPLAUSE.

WE PULL OUT FROM TV AND INTO LOUNGE. BUT TV CONTINUES IN BACKGROUND.

JR So, let's start as always by meeting our three lucky contestants.

EACH CONTESTANT WAVES TO CAMERA AS THEY ARE INTRODUCED BY JR.

JR Number one, we have Melanie Jones from Cardiff. Melanie is a housewife and the mother of two sons, Gareth and Anthony. Melanie's hobbies include cooking, the theatre and ballroom dancing. Number two is Dave Simmons from Somerset.

BY NOW THE TV WILL HAVE BEEN SWITCHED OFF. AN ANGRY DEL IS WANDERING ROUND WITH THE PHONE TO HIS EAR AS HE WAITS FOR HIS CALL TO BE ANSWERED. RODNEY IS SLUMPED IN AN ARMCHAIR READING A NEWSPAPER THE HEADLINES OF WHICH CONCERN EURO 2000. CASSANDRA IS SEATED AND TRYING TO HOLD BACK THE TEARS. RAQUEL ENTERS FROM KITCHEN AND SLAMS A COUPLE OF PLATES OF FISH FINGERS AND CHIPS DOWN ON TABLE. RAQUEL GIVES DEL A DAMNING LOOK.

DEL Don't look at me with that Ann Robinson face!

RAQ I'll look at you any way I like!

DEL (REF TO RODNEY LOUNGING ABOUT) At least *I'm* tryna do something about it!

CASS And what exactly are you doing?

DEL I'm after a stockbroker!

ROD You've already got a stockbroker!

DEL Yes, *that's* the one I'm after! Why didn't he call me and tell me the market was about to crash?

RAQ He phoned you at least *six* times. He phoned on the Monday and said he needed to talk to you urgently! But you were too busy to speak to him!

DEL I was water skiing!

ROD You just wasted our bloody birthright!

RAQ And then Trotters Independent Traders hired a helicopter to fly to Nice to collect some magazines.

ROD Unbelievable!

CASS That was you!

ROD Eh? Oh yeah.

DEL All right, listen up! I'm a strong man, I've got big shoulders. The buck stops here! I take full responsibility! Even though it was Rodney's fault.

ROD Me? How the hell was it my fault?

DEL You were the company's Director of Administration.

CASS That just meant Rodney arranged the Christmas parties!

DEL Yeah, and they were about as exciting as a Buddhists' hen night!

CASS *You* were the Managing Director, *you* were the Chairman, *you* were the Chief Executive *and* you were the President.

DEL Oh, so it's *my* fault now, is it?

ROD It's either you or this is the Chinese year of the dodo!

RAQ Wait a minute. You can't lay *all* the blame at Derek's door. I know it's tempting, but…

ROD But why is it whenever we've got something good going, *anything* that remotely resembles a *future*, he nauses it up!

RAQ (DEFIANTLY) That's just the way he is!

DEL (TAKING IT AS A VOTE OF CONFIDENCE) Thank you!

CASS (TO DEL) And it's unfair of you to blame Rodney for all of this! After all, he is your brother!

DEL Yes, and just like a brother, he's let me down all his life.

ROD Oh, is that right? And if I've been such a let down, why did you insist on having me around.

DEL To keep my promise to Mum.

RODNEY IS ABOUT TO SAY SOMETHING.

DEL *And* you never know when you might need some bone marrow!

THE PHONE RINGS.

DEL Cassandra, answer that please.

CASS (SNARLS ANGRILY) Yes, sir, straight away.

CASSANDRA ANSWER THE PHONE.

DEL Look, don't worry, this time next year we'll be millionaires.

ROD This time last *week* we were millionaires.

CASS (ON PHONE) Sorry, I can't hear you very well. Hold on.

CASSANDRA EXITS TO KITCHEN.

DEL I'm being serious. I've thought of a way to make us some serious spondula. A hundred thousand pounds! Invest it wisely…

ROD & RAQ (LAUGHING) Invest it wisely!

DEL Invest it wisely and we'll have enough to buy us both a nice little gaff each.

ROD All right, what's the plan?

DEL I wasn't gonna say anything, but… Ready? I'm gonna apply to go on that new quiz show, *Goldrush*!

RODNEY AND RAQUEL BURST OUT LAUGHING.

DEL Did I say something?

RAQ Derek, last night one of the questions was, ' Who introduced the potato to England?' And you said King Edward.

RODNEY AND RAQUEL LAUGH UPROARIOUSLY AGAIN.

DEL I didn't hear the question properly.

ROD Del, if you wanna appear on telly why don't you try for something more simple – like go on *Stars in their Eyes* as Barry White.

RODNEY AND RAQUEL BURST OUT LAUGHING AGAIN.

CASSANDRA ENTERS FROM KITCHEN WITH TELEPHONE.

CASS Del, it's Elsie Partridge's son.

DEL What's he want?

CASS (HOLDING BACK THE TEARS) It's Uncle Albert… I'm sorry. So sorry.

THE ARGUING HAS GIVEN WAY TO A COLD SILENCE.

EXTERIOR. URBAN STREET/COASTAL TOWN. DAY

WE SEE STREET NAME 'WATERSIDE ROAD'.

IT IS A LONG ROAD WITH CARS PARKED EITHER SIDE. BUT OUTSIDE ONE HOUSE CONES HAVE BEEN PLACED TO PROTECT A LARGE SPACE FOR THE HEARSE AND FUNERAL CARS. WE SEE PEOPLE, ALL DRESSED FOR A FUNERAL, SOME CARRYING WREATHS, APPROACHING AND ENTERING HOUSE. COMING OFF ROAD, AND CLOSE TO HOUSE, IS A SIDE ROAD. WE NOW SEE THE GREEN CAPRI APPROACHING. THERE ARE RIBBONS GOING FROM THE TOP AND EITHER SIDE OF THE WINDSCREEN AND DOOR ARCHES AND DOVETAILING DOWN TO THE FRONT GRILL (LIKE A BRIDAL CAR), BUT THESE RIBBONS ARE BLACK.

DEL IS DRIVING, RODNEY IS IN FRONT PASSENGER SEAT. RAQUEL, CASSANDRA AND DAMIEN ARE IN BACK SEAT. UPON SEEING THE CONES AND MOURNERS, WE HEAR RODNEY.

ROD Here we are.

DEL PULLS THE CAPRI TO A HALT IN THE SIDE ROAD AND THE TROTTERS BEGIN TO ALIGHT. DEL STRAIGHTENS HIS ARMS AND STEELS HIS BODY AS IF READY FOR COMBAT.

DEL Right, we ready?

ROD (INDICATES CAR BOOT) Shall I bring the wreath?

CASS Best leave it till the hearse arrives.

THE TROTTERS ALL WALK OFF TOWARDS WATERSIDE ROAD AND THE HOUSE.

INTERIOR. THE FUNERAL HOUSE/LIVING ROOM. DAY

IT IS A CLEAN HOUSE, BUT THE DECOR SUGGESTS THAT OF AN ELDERLY PERSON. THE FEMININE TOUCH IS EVERYWHERE. FURNITURE HAS BEEN PUSHED BACK TO GIVE THE MOURNERS MORE ROOM. IT IS REASONABLY CROWDED WITH MOURNERS OF VARIOUS AGES. A WOMAN (MARION) STANDS AT DOOR HOLDING A TRAY OF SHERRY. THE TROTTERS ENTER.

DEL Oh hello. We're Albert's nephews, Derek and Rodney from Peckham.

MARION Hello, I'm Marion. I did a bit of cleaning for Albert. Lovely old man – went on a bit.

DEL Yeah… This is Rodney's wife Cassandra, my son Damien, and Raquel, my significant other.

RAQUEL REACTS TO 'SIGNIFICANT OTHER'.

MARION Nice to meet you all. Please, come in and have a drink.

THE TROTTERS TAKE A SHERRY AND MOVE FURTHER INTO ROOM. (WE SHOULDN'T NOTICE, BUT DAMIEN, WHO IS BEHIND THEM, HAS ALSO TAKEN A SHERRY.) RAQUEL, WITHOUT EVEN SEEING THIS, OR EVEN TURNING ROUND, *KNOWS* WHAT HE'S DONE.

RAQ Damien, put it back.

NOW WE SEE DAMIEN WITH THE SHERRY. HE PUTS IT BACK ON TRAY. THERE IS AN OLD PIANO IN ROOM. DEL TOUCHES IT WARMLY AS HE IMAGINES ALBERT SEATED THERE MURDERING SOME SONG OR ANOTHER.

ROD You can almost hear him, can't you? Doing grievous bodily harm to 'Red Sails in the Sunset' or something.

DEL NOW HAS A TEAR IN HIS EYE.

DEL I feel bad, you know. Leaving him down here on his own while we went off globe-trotting.

RAQ He wasn't on his own. He was with Elsie.

DEL But Elsie's been in a rest home for the last six months.

CASS But he had all her family around him – and all his old mates at the British Legion.

RAQ And he used to come up and stay with us.

ROD He was having a good time, Del. And we provided well for him, didn't we? Don't beat yourself up.

DEL I still wish we'd have taken him with us to Barbados and all the other places.

ROD We used to ask him. But, if you remember, the Ancient Mariner, who'd be around the world more times than a Russian satellite, had *never* had a passport.

DEL (FORCES A SMILE/LAUGH) Caw, if Hitler had found out, Albert would have been in right trouble.

THEY ALL LAUGH/SMILE AT THIS. ON MANTLEPIECE, OR SIDEBOARD, DEL HAS FOUND A BRANDY GLASS BEARING THE GOLD ETCHING OF 'ALBERT'.

DEL Look at that. The old sod had his own mono-grammed brandy glass.

A MAN CLOSE BY TURNS UPON HEARING THIS. THE MAN (ROLAND) IS IN HIS FIFTIES, FIT-LOOKING AND COCKNEY.

ROLAND Yeah, he loved his Cognac, didn't he?

THE TROTTERS ALL AGREE.

ROLAND (MIMICKING AN OLD MAN) 'Just to keep the colds at bay.' Remember? (INTRODUCES HIMSELF) Oh, excuse me, Roland. I was married to Albert's niece Eileen.

DEL Nice to meet you. My brother, Rodney, and his wife, Cassandra, my son, Damien, and…

RAQ (GETS IN QUICK) Raquel, and this is Derek – my significant other!

DURING THE NEXT FEW EXCHANGES DEL BECOMES MORE AGITATED AND ANGRY.

ROLAND Nice to meet you all. I suppose we'll all miss him in our way.

ROD Yeah, we're missing him already.

ROLAND I tell you something we won't miss. All them bloody wartime sagas.

RAQUEL AND CASSANDRA ARE NOW DESPERATELY TRYING TO KEEP THE PEACE.

RAQ Oh, we used to love hearing about his past.

ROD That's right! We couldn't get enough of it!

ROLAND Yeah, but he could go on though, couldn't he? He never stopped!

DEL You'll have to blame me for that – Roland! Coz I loved his stories so much, when he said 'And then Germany surrendered', I used to say, 'Tell us about the day war was declared' and he'd take us right the way through it again. We'd sit up all night!

ROLAND Well, more fool you. I used to tell him straight, you can cut all that John Wayne crap out. The way he spoke, you'd think he won it on his own!

ROD Well, in many ways that's true. Everyone involved was fighting their own individual wars!

DEL Yeah. And they were risking their lives for our liberty – so that 50 years later prats like you would have the freedom to knock 'em!

RAQ Derek!

CASS Take it easy, Del!

DEL They gotta garden here, Roland, coz maybe me and you could go outside and have a more detailed chat!

ROD Del, that's enough, mate!

DAMIEN Go'n Dad, deck 'im!

ROLAND Woh, woh, hold on, I'm sorry. I didn't mean to upset anyone.

DEL (FLEXING THE SHOULDERS, ETC) That's all right then! S'all right, no problem.

RAQ Calm down.

DEL S'all right. Yeah, all right.

ROLAND MOVES AWAY.

MARION (CALLS) The hearse is here.

ROD I'll get our wreath.

RODNEY EXITS.

RAQ (TO DEL) Have you calmed down?

DEL (NICE AND CALM) Yeah, yeah, don't you worry about me, I'm fine, sweetheart. (NOW LOSES HIS RAG AGAIN) I'll tell you another thing! You'll notice none of the others bothered to turn up! Boycie and Marlene! Denzil and Trigger! 'Oh, yes, well be there to show our respect, Del Boy!' And where are they? You'd think Sid might have put an appearance in, he was in the war – na, too busy making money at the pub.

RAQ Well, maybe they had problems! It is a bit of a journey.

DEL I bet good old Mike made a bigger effort to get here than them, and he's in nick!

RAQ Come on, you, outside.

RAQUEL, DEL AND DAMIEN EXIT. ROLAND APPROACHES CASSANDRA.

ROLAND I didn't mean to offend anyone.

CASS It's okay. Emotions running a bit high, that's all.

ROLAND Yeah. I bet old Bunny's up there having a right laugh at us, eh?

CASS Yeah, I bet he is… Bunny?

ROLAND Yeah, Albert.

CASS Why'd you call him Bunny?

ROLAND That's what they called him in the RAF, coz his surname was Warren.

EXTERIOR. WATERSIDE ROAD/COASTAL TOWN. DAY
COME UP ON HEARSE PARKED IN KERB. ON TOP OF THE HEARSE IS A LARGE FLORAL SPITFIRE. THE UNDERTAKER IS PLACING A LARGE FLORAL PROPELLER AGAINST COFFIN. WE SEE RAQUEL LOOKING AT A LARGE FLORAL AND GOLDEN BELL WHICH IS INSIDE HEARSE. (THIS IS

MEANT TO REPRESENT THE FIGHTER SQUADRONS' 'SCRAMBLE' BELL. WE SEE A SIGN HAS BEEN ATTACHED TO BELL WHICH READS: 'BIGGIN HILL. 1939–1942'. WE SEE DEL'S FACE AS HE STARES AT THE APPARITION. DAMIEN IS STARING IN AWE AT THE FLORAL SPITFIRE.

DAMIEN Is that a Spitfire, Dad?

DEL, UNABLE TO SPEAK, JUST NODS. CASSANDRA JOINS DEL AND RAQUEL.

CASS (QUIETLY) We're at the wrong funeral.

DEL NODS.

RAQ We know.

AS DEL TURNS ROUND HE SPOTS SOMETHING IN THE DISTANCE. A LONG WAY UP ROAD WE SEE ANOTHER FUNERAL IS TAKING PLACE. WE CUT TO SECOND FUNERAL.

EXTERIOR. WATERSIDE ROAD/ SECOND HOUSE. DAY
A SECOND HEARSE STANDS IN KERB. INSIDE HEARSE WE HAVE A FLORAL 'ALBERT', ALONG WITH MANY OTHER WREATHS. THE ONLY WREATH WITH A NAUTICAL THEME IS A FLORAL OLD-FASHIONED SHIP'S WHEEL. WALKING OUT OF THE HOUSE, AND ALL DRESSED IN BLACK, WE SEE BOYCIE AND MARLENE, TRIGGER AND DENZIL, SID AND MICKEY PEARCE. THEY NOW LOOK UP ROAD AND SEE THE TROTTERS (MINUS RODNEY) STANDING AT FIRST FUNERAL.
GREAT CONFUSION AND CONSTERNATION FALLS OVER THEIR FACES. DEL, RAQUEL AND CASSANDRA, LOOK UP TOWARDS THE REAL FUNERAL AND SHRUG AND GESTURE WITH GREAT EMBARRASSMENT. NOW WE HEAR RODNEY'S VOICE.

ROD (VOICE OVER) Hold on.

WE CUT TO FIND RODNEY RUNNING ROUND FROM SIDEROAD CARRYING A LARGE, GOLDEN FLORAL ANCHOR. HE STOPS AS HE SPOTS THE FIRST HEARSE – SPITFIRE AND PROPELLER, ETC. HE LOOKS TO DEL FOR AN EXPLANATION. DEL JUST SHRUGS.

INTERIOR. THE COURTROOM. DAY
JUSTIN Gentlemen, you have my deepest sympathies for your loss. But I have to bring you back to the business in hand. Are there any mitigating circumstances you'd like me to inform the court of.

DEL Yes, there is. You must remember, we were always slaves to detail, weren't we, Rodney?

ROD Absolutely. We made certain that we *always* got our cheques off to the Inland Revenue on time…

DEL *Always.*

CLERK OF THE COURT Be upstanding. The Inland Revenue versus Trotters Independent Traders.

DEL Fair do's they *bounced* – but they were *always* on time.

PRESENT TIME (FROM NOW ON)
INTERIOR. THE TROTTERS' LOUNGE. DAY
WE HAVE BOXES OF ELECTRONIC GAMES ('ACTION STATION' MADE IN BELARUS, NINTENDO/GAMEBOY SORT OF THING) PILED IN ROOM. DAMIEN IS PLAYING ON ONE OF THE 'ACTION STATIONS'. HE MOVES THE JOY-STICK AROUND AND IS VERY INVOLVED WITH THE GAME, WHEN WE HEAR A COUPLE OF BEEPS AND THEN A FARTY SQUEAK AND THE MACHINE DIES. DAMIEN SHAKES IT, WHACKS IT AND THEN GIVES UP THE GHOST.

DAMIEN I don't believe it! Where's he get all this crap from?

WE HEAR FRONT DOOR OPEN AND THEN RODNEY AND CASSANDRA ENTER. THEY HAVE JUST RETURNED FROM COURT. RODNEY APPEARS ASHEN AND SHAKEN BY THE EXPERIENCE. HE IS CARRYING FIVE BOXES FROM 'PIZZA HUT'.

DAMIEN (DISAPPOINTED) Ah, I thought they were gonna bang you up.

ROD Well, you were wrong, weren't you, Rat Boy. I was exonerated of all responsibility.

DAMIEN So you both got off?

CASS Not quite.

NOW A STUNNED DEL ENTERS FOLLOWED BY RAQUEL. DEL APPEARS TO BE IN A STATE OF SHOCK.

RAQ You sit down, I'll make you a cup of tea.

DEL I need something stronger than tea, Raquel.

DEL GOES TO BAR AND POURS HIMSELF A DRINK.

DAMIEN What happened, Dad?

DEL The court declared me bankrupt.

DAMIEN (EXCITED) Does that mean you're going to prison?

RAQ No! Well, not yet.

CASS (TO RODNEY – REF TO DAMIEN) Why does he keep on about prison?

ROD Well, all his mates' Dads are doing time and he feels left out.

RAQ Damien, go to your room and tidy it.

DAMIEN I tidied it this morning.

RAQ (SHOUTS) Well go 'n' tidy it again!

DAMIEN RELUCTANTLY EXITS TO BEDROOMS AREA.

RAQ So what exactly does it mean?

DEL The Inland Revenue gives you one year to pay the debt off.

CASS Then they come in and take all your goods… well, anything of any value.

RAQ (LOOKS AT ALL THE FURNITURE) So it won't affect us then.

DEL There is something of value here, sweetheart, you're standing in it – this flat. They'll sell our home. They'll steal the roof from over our heads.

ROD (A GRITTY DETERMINATION) Take it from me, that is not going to happen, Derek!

DEL (HOPEFULLY) No? Why, you thought of something?

ROD No, I mean, you've had it on the market for five years and no one's even looked at it.

DEL That's because I had it up for it's true value. They'll auction it for a third of its price!

ROD What are we gonna do then?

CASS I suppose you could always look for a job.

THIS STARTLES DEL AND ROD.

RAQ Trigger said they're recruiting down at his depot. The pay's not too bad either. I know it's road-sweeping, but…

ROD (TO DEL) She's right.

DEL I suppose so.

ROD I'll help you with your application if you like.

DEL Me?

RAQ You can't expect Del to go out sweeping the roads!

DEL PUFFS UP PROUDLY AT RAQUEL'S SUPPORT.

RAQ Not at his age! I was talking about you.

ROD Me?

CASS Oh, come on, could you honestly see Rodney pushing a broom around?

DEL They give training!

RAQ And how much do you actually owe the taxman?

DEL Forty eight thousand, seven hundred and fifty.

ROD Four.

DEL Eh?

ROD Forty eight thousand, seven hundred and fifty four.

CASS Plus interest.

RAQUEL LOOKS AROUND THE LOUNGE.

RAQ (FIGHTING BACK THE TEARS) Oh well, I never really liked this place anyway.

RAQUEL EXITS TO KITCHEN WIPING TEARS AWAY.

DEL There are, see, you've upset her.

ROD What, by adding four quid?

DEL (INDICATES CASS) No, it's dopey there mentioning interest – it's worried her.

CASS (LOSES HER TEMPER WITH DEL) Oh, I don't want to talk to you any more! I'm going to have a shower.

CASSANDRA EXITS TO BEDROOMS AREA.

DEL Don't use all the hot water.

DEL EXITS TO KITCHEN.

THE KITCHEN

RAQUEL WIPES A TEAR AWAY AS SHE DISHES UP THE PIZZA. DEL JOINS HER.

DEL Hey, come on, sweetheart. We'll be back on our feet in a little while.

RAQ How? You owe nearly forty nine thousand pounds *plus* interest!

DEL Yeah, I admit it's not the best start. But I've got it all worked out. See, I'm a trader, bin doing it since I was 12. I could sell rice to the Chinese. So, I'm gonna start trading again. I'm gonna work for a little local firm.

RAQ Yeah? Like who?

DEL It's called Trotters Independent Traders.

RAQ What are you talking about? The firm's been liquidised or liquidated or whatever the stupid word is.

DEL No, the firm can carry on. I've just been banned from *running* it. There's nothing to stop me from *working* for it. All we need is a new managing director.

RAQ Oh, God, I actually got excited then! Derek, who is gonna be stupid enough to take over Trotters Independent Traders?

DEL JUST SMILES AT HER.

THE LOUNGE.

RODNEY IS SEATED, HEAD IN HANDS, FRETTING ABOUT THEIR PREDICAMENT. DEL ENTERS FROM KITCHEN.

DEL Well, I don't know what we're gonna do, Rodney.

ROD No, me neither.

DEL I mean, I'm disqualified from running my *own* company – if I ask for a loan the taxman'll nick me – and if I deal in cash Customs and Excise will nick me. I mean, my credit rating is so low I can't even pay with money! If only there was another firm of traders I could work for.

ROD Yeah.

DEL Oh it's no good you tryna make me feel better, Rodney. Trotters Independent Traders is no more. It's kaput. It's as dead as an Emu… Although I suppose that's not strictly true. The company can continue operating, but I can't run it.

ROD I know.

DEL If only there was *someone* out there who could take it over. Someone young and energetic. Someone with ideas and drive. But, the question is, who?

ROD Yeah.

DEL REACTS WITH A 'OH COME ON, DOPEY, TAKE THE BAIT'.

ROD Hang on a minute.

DEL (EAGER) Yeah, what is it, Rodney?

ROD Oh no, he emigrated, didn't he?

DEL SHAKES HIS HEAD IN PURE FRUSTRATION. NOW, FINALLY, THE PENNY DROPS FOR RODNEY.

ROD There might be one person, Del.

DEL Whom?

ROD Me!

DEL You? How'd you mean, Rodney?

ROD Well, look. You've been made bankrupt and therefore are not allowed to run a company. But I haven't!

DEL No, you've got me all confused now.

ROD (SIGHS) Let me explain it in simple terms. Legally there is nothing to stop me from taking over Trotters Independent Traders.

DEL Let me see if I understand this. You're saying that you will run the firm?

ROD By George, I think he's got it.

DEL That is *brilliant*, Rodney! 'Argent comptant' as they say in Cannes. We'll go see our lawyer tomorrow, and have your name registered at Company House. Managing Director – Rodney Trotter.

RAQUEL ENTERS FROM KITCHEN CARRYING A PLATE OF PIZZA FOR DAMIEN.

DEL Raquel, you'll never guess. Rodney's come up with an idea to save the family. He's gonna be the new managing director and I'm gonna be in charge of sales and purchasing and finance.

RAQUEL OPENS DOOR TO BEDROOMS AREA. WE CAN HEAR THE SOUND OF A SHOWER RUNNING. RODNEY IS ABOUT TO PROTEST AT DEL ELECTING HIS OWN ROLE.

RAQ Congratulations, Rodney. I'm surprised you didn't think of that, Del.

DEL That's just what I was thinking!

NOW WE HEAR CASSANDRA SCREAM.

CASS (OUT O F SIGHT) Aauuuhh!

RAQUEL NOW SEES SOMETHING FURTHER DOWN INNER HALL.

RAQ (SHOUTS) Damien, get away from that keyhole!

RAQUEL EXITS TO BEDROOMS AREA. AGAIN DEL LAUGHS TO RODNEY IN THAT 'HE'S A LITTLE SCALLYWAG, AIN'T HE?' WAY. RODNEY JUST STARES ANGRILY AHEAD AND CONTROLS HIS BOILING ANGER.

INTERIOR. THE NAGS HEAD. NIGHT

A WEEK LATER. SID IS BEHIND BAR WITH HIS EVER-BURNING CIGARETTE BETWEEN HIS LIPS. BOYCIE, MARLENE AND DENZIL ARE AT BAR. MICKEY PEARCE IS SEATED AND READING THE *PECKHAM ECHO*.

SID The world's full of surprises, annit? Look at that, Mickey Pearce has learnt to read.

THEY LAUGH. MICKEY IS READING A SMALL AD, WHICH READS: (PERHAPS MICKEY READS IT OUT TO A COUPLE OF MATES)

'TROTTERS INDEPENDENT TRADERS. NOW UNDER NEW MANAGEMENT. MANAGING DIRECTOR: RODNEY TROTTER. BESIDES CONTINUING TO SUPPLY OUR VALUED CLIENTELE WITH OUR TRADITIONAL SERVICES OF INTERNATIONAL BARGAIN PRICED GOODS, WE NOW OFFER THE NEW FACILITIES OF; PARTY PLANNING, HOSPITALITY AND DEDICATED CONSULTANCY SUPPORT'. MICKEY MOVES TO BAR WITH THE NEWSPAPER.

MICKEY You seen this in the local paper? Rodney Trotter's a managing director.

BOYCIE Yeah, and Cliff Richard's on 40 Silk Cut a day. (LAUGHS)

MICKEY No, it's true. Have a look.

MARLENE (READS) Hospitality and party-planning.

BOYCIE D'you remember their last do? Depressing, weren't it?

DENZIL That was Albert's funeral.

BOYCIE No, I was talking about Rodney's wedding.

MICKEY (READING AD) Consultancy Support!

BOYCIE The only support the Trotters have ever had was their Grandad's old truss.

MICKEY Rodney's having a laugh, ain't he? I'm gonna give him a call, wind him right up.

MARLENE Oh, leave him alone, he's doing his best.

DENZIL Yeah, and they've just suffered a setback, losing all their money and Del being made bankrupt.

BOYCIE Yes. Don't you think it would be a rather insensitive act on your part, Mickey?

MICKEY (A SENSE OF GUILT) Yeah, I suppose you're right.

BOYCIE (HANDS MICKEY A MOBILE PHONE) Here are, use my phone. (LAUGHS)

INTERIOR. THE TROTTERS' LOUNGE. NIGHT

SAME TIME. DAMIEN IS LAID OUT ON SETTEE LISTENING TO HIS WALKMAN. RODNEY IS DRESSED TO GO OUT. HE IS SEATED AND READING A MAGAZINE. WE CUT TO ROD'S MAGAZINE WHICH IS FOLDED TO A PAGE THE HEADLINES OF WHICH READ 'THE POWER OF FANTASY', BY PROFESSOR MICHAEL BYRNE, 'THE SEXUAL

MINEFIELD OF MODERN RELATIONSHIPS'. RAQUEL ENTERS FROM KITCHEN AND RODNEY QUICKLY CLOSES MAGAZINE. RAQUEL IS IN THE PROCESS OF DOING HER MAKE-UP, ETC.

RAQ Damien. We're going out in a minute to celebrate Daddy's new job with Uncle Rodney. Get yourself ready and go over to Wesley's flat. We'll pick you up on our way home tonight.

DURING RAQUEL'S LINES, DEL ENTERS FROM BEDROOMS AREA. DAMIEN NOW SPEAKS IN STRONG JAMAICAN ACCENT AND DOES GANG SIGN WITH HIS FINGERS.

DAMIEN Yeah, yeah, don't fuzz me, bitch, me gun is hungry.

DEL & RAQ Oi!

DEL (REMOVES CASSETTE FROM WALKMAN) If you don't stop listening to Gangsta Rap, you'll get a rap yourself, right round yer lug'ole. Now go 'n' get ready.

RODNEY SMILES AT DAMIEN.

DAMIEN Honkey.

ROD Rat Boy.

DAMIEN EXITS FOLLOWED BY RAQUEL.

DEL You ready then, Rodders?

ROD IS LIGHTING A ROLL-UP.

ROD I'm waiting for Cassandra. She's just getting… (LIGHTS CIGARETTE)

DEL OPENS THE BEDROOM DOOR AND LOOKS IN.

DEL Hurry up, darling.

ROD (FINISHES HIS LINE) dressed.

DEL (MIMES A PAIR OF KNICKERS)(QUIETLY) They're nice.

ROD I don't believe you did that! Bloody 'ell, and we're not even going out with you.

DEL Why not?

ROD Because we're going out on our own… (PROUD OF HIMSELF) Cassandra suggested it… I think me becoming managing director has made a difference. They say that power is an aphrodisiac.

DEL She must be bubbling then.

ROD Yeah well… I'm taking her out to a club. See, when we met, the first thing we did together was dance. So I thought it might rekindle those old memories.

DEL Na, best take her to dinner. There's a little place just opened down Joma Kenyata Grove. She'll love it.

ROD No, you don't understand. See, dancing is the human form of the mating ritual, annit?

DEL Yeah, but that's if you're a *good* dancer!

ROD I am a good dancer.

DEL You're not, Rodney. I remember you in that disco in Monte Carlo. You looked like Billy Elliott with worms. (INDICATES BEDROOM) But if what I saw in there just now is anything go by, you're on a winner already.

ROD (FURIOUS) Look, will you stop talking about my wife and her… Really?

DEL Oh yeah! G-String! More like dental floss.

DOORBELL RINGS. DEL EXITS TO HALL AND OPENS DOOR TO TRIGGER. DEL ENTERS FROM HALL, FOLLOWED BY TRIGGER.

TRIGGER All right, Dave?

ROD Yeah, fine, Trig.

DEL I'm just gonna hurry Raquel up. (OPENS DOOR TO BEDROOMS AREA) (CALLS) Hurry up, Raquel, I'm gonna need another shave in a minute!

DEL EXITS TO BEDROOMS AREA. TRIG IS SEATED AT DINING TABLE. RODNEY SELECTS A CD. RODNEY NOW BECOMES PUZZLED BY TRIGGER'S PRESENCE.

ROD So, what you doing here, Trig?

TRIGGER Del said he'd give me a lift to the pub.

ROD Oh right…

RODNEY PLACES CD IN MUSIC CENTRE. NOW SOMETHING OCCURS TO HIM.

ROD But you live closer to the pub than us.

TRIGGER I know.

ROD In fact, you have to walk *past* the pub to get to our flat.

TRIGGER Yeah, but Del said he'd give me a lift.

ROD Right.

BY NOW MUSIC IS PLAYING – SOMETHING CLASSICAL. RODNEY LISTENS TO THE MUSIC AND ALLOWS IT TO SOOTHE HIS FEVERED BROW.

TRIGGER You put a bit of music on, Dave?

ROD Yeah. It's Mozart's Concerto in D Major. I find it helps me unwind… eases my executive stress.

TRIGGER Ain't there no words to this, Dave?

ROD Words? No… no words. Sorta instrumental.

DEL ENTERS FROM BEDROOMS AREA.

DEL (REACTS TO THE MUSIC) What's this?

TRIGGER It's Mozart's Concerto in D Major. It's the karaoke version?

ROD I'm gonna switch it off now.

RODNEY SWITCHES CD OFF. RAQUEL ENTERS FROM BEDROOMS AREA.

RAQ I've just got to take something out of the freezer, then I'm ready.

CASSANDRA ENTERS FROM BEDROOMS AREA AS PHONE BEGINS RINGING.

DEL (TO CASS) Get that, darling, will yer?

CASS (ANGRILY) Yes, sir. I'll organise your bloody appointment book in a minute. (ANSWERS PHONE) Trotters Independent Traders. How may I help you?

DEL That is one moody mare, annit?

ROD Can you blame her? You're treating her like she's your personal secretary *and* you've just had a butchers at her drawers.

DEL Look, the only reason I like her to answer the phone is coz she's got a nice voice. And, anyway, if you and Cassandra weren't so proud you could be living at her Mum and Dad's house.

ROD We've been all through that before. We're happy here – well, we're here anyway. I'm running the firm now and Cass has applied for her old job back at the bank, so eventually we might have enough money to get our own place.

CASS (HAND OVER MOUTHPIECE) I don't know who it is, he sounds foreign. He wants to speak to the boss.

CASSANDRA HANDS THE PHONE TO DEL.

ROD Excuse me! I'm the boss now!!

CASS Oh sorry, I keep forgetting.

RODNEY SNATCHES PHONE.

ROD Bloody 'ell! I knew it was lonely at the top but I didn't think it'd be this quick!

DEL (FED UP) I'm gonna get a drink.

DEL EXITS TO KITCHEN.

ROD (ON PHONE) Trotters Independent Traders. How may we help you?

INTERIOR. THE NAGS HEAD. NIGHT
MICKEY PEARCE HAS THE MOBILE PHONE TO HIS EAR. BOYCIE, DENZIL AND MARLENE ARE CLOSE BY WAITING TO HEAR THE FUN.

WE NOW INTERCUT BETWEEN THE NAGS HEAD AND THE TROTTERS' LOUNGE

MICKEY (ON PHONE, A COD ASIAN-ACCENT) 'allo? I am weeshing to speak with managing director.

ROD (ON PHONE) Yes, this is he. My name is Rodney Trotter, I am the managing director.

CASS I'll pour us some wine.

CASSANDRA EXITS TO KITCHEN.

MICKEY (ON PHONE) Good evening, sir. I am representative of Sultan of Brunei.

THE OTHERS STIFLE THEIR LAUGHTER.

ROD (BELIEVING IT) Oh wow! (TO RAQUEL) You'll never guess who's on the phone. The Sultan of Brunei.

RAQ (TOTALLY UNIMPRESSED) Yeah, right!

MICKEY (ON PHONE) My name is Asif Hassan.

ROD (ON PHONE) It's very nice to speak to you, sir.

DEL ENTERS FROM KITCHEN.

DEL Who's he talking to?

RAQ The Sultan of Brunei.

DEL (TOTALLY UNIMPRESSED) Yeah, right!

ROD (ON PHONE) And how may I be of assistance, sir?

MICKEY (ON PHONE) You have advertisement in newspaper and His Highness he would like to talk with you.

ROD (TO DEL) He's seen my advert.

DEL What, the Sultan of Brunei reads the *Peckham Echo*? (QUIETLY) What a Moby.

MICKEY (ON PHONE) His Highness would like you to fly to Brunei and be his consultant.

ROD (ON PHONE) No problem. And what exactly would he like to consult with me about?

MICKEY (ON PHONE) Recently His Highness bought a crappy old three-wheeled van (NOW IN HIS OWN VOICE) and wants to know how to start it on cold mornings. (LAUGHS)

NOW BOYCIE, DENZIL, SID AND MARLENE BURST INTO LAUGHTER.

RODNEY HEARS THE PEELS OF LAUGHTER FROM THE PHONES EARPIECE AND KNOWS HE'S BEEN HAD. RODNEY STARTS LAUGHING AS IF HE WAS THE ONE PLAYING THE JOKE.

ROD (ON PHONE) I had you going there, didn't I? I knew it was you all the time. I was just winding you up!

MORE LAUGHTER FROM EARPIECE.

ROD (ON PHONE) Shove it, will you? Just shove it!

RODNEY SLAMS PHONE DOWN. RODNEY STORMS OUT TO HALL AND OUT OF FRONT DOOR. WE HEAR FRONT DOOR SLAM.

RAQ (SMILES) When the going gets tough, the tough get going.

DEL Yeah. Rodney's got going straight out the front door!

CASSANDRA, WHO HAS HEARD THE SLAMMING AND SHOUTING, ENTERS FROM KITCHEN WITH GLASSES OF WINE.

CASS What's happened?

TRIGGER Dave's just had a big row with the Sultan of Brunei.

CASS Yeah, right!

CASSANDRA EXITS TO HALL AND PURSUES RODNEY.

INTERIOR. BISTRO. NIGHT
SAME NIGHT. RODNEY AND CASSANDRA SEATED AT TABLE AWAY FROM OTHER DINERS – ISOLATED JUST ENOUGH SO THAT THEY CAN HAVE AN INTIMATE CONVERSATION. THEY HAVE FINISHED THE MEAL, AND COFFEE AND LIQUEURS ARE JUST BEING SERVED.

ROD (TO WAITER) Thank you very much. (RAISES THE GLASS OF BRANDY) To… the future.

CASS Yeah, the future.

THEY CLINK GLASSES.

BEAT.

ROD Cass, I'd like us to try for a baby.

IT'S SO OUT OF THE BLUE THAT CASSANDRA ALMOST SPITS THE BRANDY BACK INTO GLASS. SHE CHECKS TO SEE NO ONE HAS HEARD.

CASS Rodney, some restaurants don't like that sort of thing.

ROD What? (INDICATES TABLE) No, not here… I mean, in the future – soon.

CASS We weren't very successful at it last time, were we?

ROD It'll be different next time. Take it from me, I know about these things.

CASS And what about… you know, the way things are?

ROD Yes, I'm glad you brought that up. Recently I, erm, I bought this magazine.

CASS I hate it when you buy those magazines.

ROD (CHECKS ROUND THE ROOM) Not that sort of magazine!

CASS You always end up making comparisons and that sort of thing.

ROD Look, it is a man's magazine – but not that sort. It's serious. And there's a fella writing in there who's an expert on marital problems. He's developed a sort of psychological healing process… I'd like us to try it. You never know, do you?

CASS No. So, who is he?

ROD He's American, West Coast, and he says that most couples problems stem from by-gone days – all those – you know – things from the past…

CASS Like the childish way you used to behave?

ROD (CHEERFULLY) Yeah, that sort of thing… He calls that 'memory baggage'.

CASS And how do we unload our memory baggage?

ROD We become different people.

CASS Different people?

ROD Yeah. I mean, we don't have to go to a plastic surgeon or nothing. It's simply 'remembering to forget'. To forget who you were and becoming reborn. His clinic is called 'fantasy therapy'.

CASS Wait a moment. Does this involve dressing up?

ROD No, no, it doesn't! It's all based on a theory known as iconoclastic auto-suggestion.

CASS Sorry?

ROD It's 'the subconscious rejecting reality' and something else. Basically, each person writes down their fantasy figure, and the other person, for a little while, becomes that figure.

CASS And it doesn't involve dressing up?

ROD Absolutely not. It's all up here… We, sorta, suspend reality and create our own make believe world. What do you think? You willing to give it a try?

CASS All right then.

ROD (EXCITED LIKE ON A PROMISE) Yeah? (NOW TRIES TO BE SERIOUS AND PROFESSIONAL) Well, that's good – very healthy.

CASS It does involve dressing up, doesn't it?

ROD Yes…

CASS (SHE IS BEGIN TO TURN ON) Okay, let's go for it.

ROD (CAN'T BELIEVE HIS LUCK) Cosmic! (RODNEY PRODUCES A SMALL NOTEBOOK AND PEN) Go'n then, you write down yours and I'll write down mine.

THEY BOTH WRITE SOMETHING ON PAGES. THEY NOW EXCHANGE SLIPS OF PAPER.

CASS (READS HER PAGE) I never watch *The Bill*.

RODNEY LOOKS ROUND, HOPING NO ONE HAS HEARD.

ROD I recorded a few of the shows. I'll, erm, let you have a look.

CASS All right… Your turn.

RODNEY OPENS HIS PIECE OF PAPER AND READS IT.

ROD I didn't know you fancied him!

CASS (MORE AND MORE TURNED ON) Yeah – a little bit.

ROD Oh bloody 'ell, Cass! How am I s'pposed to be him?

CASS (NOW IN A LATHER) I don't know and I don't care. Rodney, to hell with putting clothes on, let's go home and take some off!

ROD Yeah? Right! (SHOUTS TO WAITER) The bill, please. And hurry!

INTERIOR. THE TROTTERS' LOUNGE. NIGHT
THE ROOM IS IN DARKNESS. THE FRONT DOOR AND THEN HALL DOOR ARE FLUNG OPEN AND RODNEY AND CASSANDRA RUSH IN, KISSING AND DESPERATE NOT TO LOSE THE MOMENT. THEY MOVES TO THEIR BEDROOM AND SWITCH LIGHT ON. THEY SMILE AT EACH OTHER. SUDDENLY THE LIGHTS IN LOUNGE ARE SWITCHED ON. WE SEE DEL HAS ENTERED FROM BEDROOMS AREA. HE IS IN PYJAMAS AND DRESSING GOWN.

DEL All right? I thought you two'd be in bed.

ROD Yeah, we're just going. Nite.

DEL I couldn't sleep.

ROD No? Oh well, nite.

DEL I was laying in there thinking about the family and all that's happened. Mum, Albert.

ROD Yeah? Well, goodnight.

INTERIOR. RODNEY AND CASSANDRA'S BEDROOM (ALBERT'S OLD ROOM)

IT HASN'T BEEN REDECORATED OR REFURNISHED. RODNEY AND CASSANDRA ARE EITHER SIDE OF BED. DEL ENTERS (OR HOVERS IN DOORWAY)

DEL (SMILING WARMLY AND NOSTALGICALLY) Look at that, eh? Caw, if that old bed could speak it could tell a few tales. Just think, Grandad had his first fit in that bed. Albert slept in it for years – laying there, snoring, tossing 'n' turning, scratching his old beard… It's a piece of history… Oh well. Goodnight.

DEL, UNAWARE OF THE TIME-BOMB HE HAS LEFT, EXITS AND CLOSES DOOR. RODNEY AND CASSANDRA LOOK AT THE CLOSING DOOR, THEN BACK AT THE BED AND THEN AT EACH OTHER.

INTERIOR. A BAR. DAY

RODNEY IS SEATED AT BAR WHERE HE HAS A GLASS HALF-FILLED WITH WATER. DEL IS SEATED NEXT TO HIM WITH A SCOTCH AND SODA. RODNEY IS NOW MORE CONCILIATORY.

ROD It's not just you! It's Raquel, it's Damien and all his friends, and Trigger and everyone else who calls in the flat at any time of day or night. The flat is overcrowded, Del!

DEL The flat's *always* been overcrowded! I complained to the council once and they said it was *designed* for overcrowding.

ROD But Cassie and I sleep in Albert's old room which comes *directly* off the lounge! I mean, tryna imagine what it's like. We lay in bed and all we can hear is you watching the telly.

DEL I thought you liked the telly.

ROD But me and Cass can't help thinking that; if *we* can hear *you*, then you can hear *us*.

DEL Nope, we've never heard a sound from your room.

ROD *Exactly!*

RODNEY KNOCKS BACK HIS DRINK.

THIS IS THAT CLICHE SCENE OF SOMEONE DRINKING TOO MUCH AND A FRIEND POINTING IT OUT – IT'S ALMOST: 'YOU'LL FIND NO ANSWERS AT THE BOTTOM OF A GLASS'.

DEL All right, calm down. And listen to me… (TAPS RODNEY'S GLASS) That's gonna solve nothing.

ROD I know, I know! It's just sometimes – sometimes I get so, sort of… It's water!

DEL That's what I mean. Why don't you have a proper drink?

ROD No! Years ago I used to give in to that sort of temptation. I'm a different man now, much stronger… just a small one.

DEL You know it makes sense. (CALLS TO WAITRESS) Two large scotch darling. (TO RODNEY) So, what can I do to help you?

ROD Go out! All of you. Leave me and Cass on our own for once.

DEL (SMILES) This must be your lucky day, Rodney. Listen, I wasn't gonna say anything yet coz it's a big surprise – a sorta secret,

DEL'S FOLLOWING LINE TRAILS OVER INTO INCOMING SCENE.

EXTERIOR. NELSON MANDELA HOUSE. DAY

A CHAUFFEUR-DRIVEN MERCEDES/JAGUAR IS PARKED CLOSE BY. DEL, RAQUEL AND DAMIEN, IN THEIR BEST SUITS, ETC, EXIT NELSON MANDELA HOUSE. RAQUEL AND DAMIEN ARE EXCITED AND PREPARED FOR A GREAT NIGHT OUT. RAQUEL SEES THE LIMOUSINE AND IS IMPRESSED BY DEL'S STYLE.

DEL (VOICE OVER)…but I'm taking Raquel and Damien out next Thursday.

ROD Really?

DEL And we'll be leaving nice and early, so you'll have the entire evening to yourselves.

THEY CLIMB INTO BACK OF CAR.

DEL (TO DRIVER) Ready when you are.

RAQ At least give us a clue.

DEL All right. (SINGLE OF DEL) This is gonna be a night you'll never forget. Other than that I'm saying nothing. Sit back in comfort and enjoy the evening. What did Monkey Harris say when you phoned him?

RAQ How'd you mean?

DEL I asked you to phone Monkey and say 'yes'.

RAQ Oh, I forgot, Del. I'm sorry. I was busy getting ready and… sorry! Was it important?

DEL Was it important? He's got a consignment of electronic personal organisers and they've been selling like crazy. Monkey's got another 200 which I want me name on. They'll be gone by tomorrow. You've let me down, Raquel.

DAMIEN (JAMAICAN ACCENT AND PATOIS – DAMIEN IS ACTUALLY SAYING: 'YOU DISRESPECT YOUR MAN, WOMAN. YOU CAN'T DO THE SIMPLEST THING'.) You dis you man, woman, you can't do simple ting.

RAQ Shut up! (SLAPS DAMIEN ROUND HEAD)

INTERIOR. TROTTERS' LOUNGE. NIGHT

CURTAINS ARE PULLED, SIDELIGHTS ARE GLOWING SEDUCTIVELY. A ROMANTIC SONG IS PLAYING ON THE MUSIC CENTRE AND A GLASS OF RED WINE STANDS ON BAR. AT THIS MOMENT NOBODY IS IN LOUNGE. WE NOW HEAR THE FRONT DOOR CLOSE AND DEL ENTERS IN A HURRY. HE REACTS TO THE SUBDUED LIGHTING. HE PICKS UP PHONE AND DIALS A NUMBER. THE KITCHEN DOOR IS OPEN AND DEL NOW HOVERS BETWEEN KITCHEN AND LOUNGE.

DEL (TO PHONE) Come on, Monkey, I'm in a hurry.

NOW THE DOOR TO BEDROOMS AREA OPENS AND CASSANDRA ENTERS DRESSED AS A POLICEWOMAN (MINUS THE HAT). SHE IS WEARING A BRUNETTE WIG. THIS IS THE BEGINNING OF HERS AND ROD'S FANTASY THERAPY. SHE NOW BECOMES AWARE HER COSTUME IS NOT COMPLETE. SHE TOUCHES HER HEAD AND REALISES SHE HAS FORGOTTEN THE HAT. SHE LOOKS AROUND THE ROOM FOR THE MISSING ITEM AND THEN EXITS BACK TO BEDROOMS AREA. DEL SPOTS HER AND, BELIEVING IT TO BE A REAL POLICEWOMAN, HIDES IN KITCHEN. THE MOMENT CASSANDRA EXITS, DEL BEGINS COLLECTING UP THE 'ACTION STATIONS' GAMES AND HIDING THEM BEHIND CURTAINS. NOW THE PHONE CRACKLES AND DEL ANSWERS IT.

DEL (ON PHONE) Hello, Monk'? I'll have to call you back, we're being raided!

DEL SWITCHES PHONE OFF. HE NOW HAS NO MORE ROOM BEHIND CURTAINS AND SO EXITS TO KITCHEN CARRYING THE REMAINING GAMES. CASSANDRA NOW ENTERS FROM BEDROOMS AREA, HER UNIFORM NOW COMPLETE WITH HAT. SHE MOVES TO BAR AND KNOCKS BACK THE GLASS OF RED WINE IN ONE GULP. NOW THE DOOR TO ALBERT'S BEDROOM OPENS AND RODNEY ENTERS, DRESSED AS A GLADIATOR – LEATHER-TONGED BOOT UP HIS CALVES, METAL BODY ARMOUR, ONE OF THOSE METAL-COVERED SKIRTS, A SWORD IN SCABBARD, AND A HELMET WITH EAR PROTECTORS AND LARGE BUSHY BRUSH. HE SMILES TO CASSANDRA AS HE MOVES TO BAR. AT THIS POINT, AND UNSEEN BY RODNEY AND CASSANDRA, DEL ENTERS FROM KITCHEN AND REACTS TO THE APPARITION BEFORE HIM. DEL'S JAW DROPS EVEN FURTHER AS RODNEY PUTS HIS ARMS AROUND THE POLICEWOMAN. (CASSANDRA HAS HER BACK TO DEL SO HE STILL DOESN'T KNOW IT IS HER. RODNEY IS NOW FACING DEL AND NODS TO HIM. DEL, JUST RETURNS A WEAK NOD. RODNEY CLOSES HIS EYES AND KISSES CASSANDRA. NOW RODNEY'S EYES OPEN AS HE REALISES WHAT HE HAS JUST SEEN. RODNEY LOOKS AT DEL AGAIN.

DEL All right?

RODNEY AND CASSANDRA PANIC AS THEY FIND DEL IN THEIR MIDST.

CASS Oh my God!

DEL (RELIEVED) Oh it's you, Cassandra! I thought you was a real policewoman! You almost gave me a connory!

ROD You said you were going out!

DEL I went out.

ROD What you doing here then?

DEL I come back. Why you dressed like that?

ROD Like what?

DEL Like a couple of Mobies.

RODNEY AND CASSANDRA ARE STUCK IN THIS SITUATION AND CANNOT FIND ANYWAY OUT. THEY PLAY FOR TIME.

ROD What, like *this*? Oh, don't be so naive, Derek. (TO CASS) Can you believe him?

CASS (FALSE LAUGHTER) Isn't it obvious?

DEL It might be to some people, darling, but I'm not from the planet Dippy.

ROD Derek… Cassie and I are…

CASS (NERVOUSLY SEARCHING FOR AN ANSWER) We're going to a fancy-dress party.

DEL Oh right! (TO CASS) So who you supposed to be?

CASS That one from *The Bill*.

DEL Who, Reg Hollis?

CASS *No!* (TO RODNEY) What's her name?

ROD (INNOCENTLY AND DEFENSIVELY) I don't know!

DEL Well, whoever it is, you look very nice, darling… A bit scary, but…

DEL NOW DOES A DELIBERATELY SLOW TURN TO RODNEY. HE WEARS A WRY SMILE AND IS OBVIOUSLY GOING TO ENJOY THIS NEXT MOMENT.

DEL And what about you, Rodders?

ROD (DEFENSIVELY) What about me?

DEL Who are you going as?

ROD Russell Crowe.

DEL BURSTS OUT LAUGHING.

DEL Russell Crowe!. You look like Spartacus with piles!

ROD Look, it's just a fancy-dress party, that's all.

DEL It's a bit early for a fancy-dress party, annit? Arf past five!

ROD Yeah, it is a bit early, that's coz it's a… It's a… an early fancy-dress party.

CASS My ex-boss at the bank invited us. He can't have late parties – people have to be up for work in the morning.

CASSANDRA MOVES TO BAR.

DEL (QUIETLY TO ROD) That's a bit of a choker, annit? You were hoping for a bit of fun and games tonight, weren't yer?

ROD Yeah. Never mind, eh.

DEL Bad luck, bruv… Well, go'n then.

ROD Go'n then, what?

DEL Off you go. I'll lock up.

RODNEY AND CASSANDRA ARE STUMPED.

CASS Erm…

ROD No, we're in no hurry.

DEL HANDS RODNEY HIS WHITE TRENCH COAT WHICH IS HANGING IN HALL.

DEL Listen, Rodney, Cassandra is trying to get her job

back at the bank. So the last thing she wants to do is turn up late for her boss's party. What's that gonna look like! (TO CASS) What you've gotta do is make a big impression.
DEL THROWS RODNEY A SET OF CAR KEYS.
DEL Here you go. Take the Capri.
ROD Right.
CASS Thanks, Del.
DEL Oi, oi, you're family. Now off you go and have a good time. (DEL PLACES RODNEY'S RAINCOAT OVER HIS SHOULDERS) There are, don't want you getting rusty, do we?
NOW, LIKE TWO PEOPLE WHO HAVE JUST BEEN HYPNOTISED, RODNEY AND CASSANDRA STEP OUT INTO OUTER HALLWAY AND AWAIT THEIR FATE. THE DOOR SLOWLY CLOSES ON THEM.

LOUNGE
DEL ENTERS AND PRESSES REDIAL ON PHONE. WE HEAR THE RAPID BEEPS AND THEN RINGING TONE.
DEL Come on, Monk, I've gotta be there by six.

INTERIOR. HALLWAY (EXTERIOR TROTTERS' FLAT). NIGHT
RODNEY AND CASSANDRA ARE STILL STANDING JUST OUTSIDE FRONT DOOR.
ROD What in God's name are we gonna do? I mean, people might see us!
CASS Well, there's nothing strange in a policewoman walking on the estate.
ROD But what about me? I look like Ben Hur in a mac!
CASS Well, I can say I've just arrested you.
ROD What for?
CASS There must be a law against going round dressed like that.
THE LIFT DOOR OPENS AND DAMIEN ALIGHTS.
ROD Oh no!
DAMIEN DOESN'T REACT. HE OPENS DOOR WITH HIS KEY.
DAMIEN (CALLS INTO FLAT) Hurry up, Dad, the driver's got another job to go to. (TO RODNEY) Pervert.
RODNEY CANNOT ANSWER. DAMIEN EXITS TO THE STILL OPEN LIFT. NOW A CONCERNED DEL APPEARS AT FRONT DOOR.
DEL Oh thank Gawd you're still here. I've just remembered something! Look, I know you were both looking forward to this party, and I don't mean to spoil your fun, but d'you mind not going?
RODNEY AND CASSANDRA BOTH GRAB THE CHANCE WILLING.
ROD No, no problem at all.
CASS Anything for you, Del.
THEY ARE PAST DEL AND BACK INTO THE FLAT IN A FLASH THAT TAKES DEL BY SURPRISE.

INTERIOR. THE TROTTERS' LOUNGE.
A RELIEVED RODNEY AND CASSANDRA ARE BACK IN THEIR SANCTUARY. DEL ENTERS.
DEL It's just that there might be a *very* important call coming through later. You'll be in all evening, won't you?
ROD Absolutely. And no worries, we'll go to the bank's next party.
DEL You're 42 carat, Rodney. I'll see you about midnight. Russell Crowe! More like Daffy Duck.
DEL LAUGHS AND EXITS. ROD AND CASSANDRA LAUGH WITH RELIEF AND FALL INTO EACH OTHERS ARMS.
INTERIOR. THE NAGS HEAD. NIGHT
SAME NIGHT. DENZIL, TRIGGER, MICKEY PEARCE, BOYCIE AND MARLENE ARE SEATED AROUND BAR – THE MEN PLAYING CARDS, MARLENE APPLYING LIPSTICK. SID IS BEHIND BAR. THE TV IS ON AND WE SEE AND HEAR

THE OPENING OF *GOLDRUSH*. AT THIS MOMENT NONE OF THE REGULARS ARE PAYING TOO MUCH ATTENTION TO THE TV. JONATHAN ROSS IS ON SCREEN.
JR (ON TV) Welcome to another edition of the quiz show that is taking the country by storm. Not *this* country – but we're big in Bosnia…

INTERIOR. THE TROTTERS' LOUNGE. NIGHT
THE ROOM IS EMPTY BUT THE TV IS ON AND SHOWING *GOLDRUSH*. FROM INSIDE ALBERT'S OLD ROOM WE CAN HEAR THE SOUNDS OF LOVE.
JR (ON TV) (CONTINUES) and we're massive in Macedonia. This is the show where you can win anything from one pound to one hundred thousand pounds! This is the fastest game show on TV, this is Thursday, this is Live, this is Jonathan Ross and this is *Goldrush*!
THEME MUSIC, WILD APPLAUSE.
CASS (OUT OF SIGHT) Oooh, Rodney!
ROD (OUT OF SIGHT) Oh, Cass!
JR (ON TV) So let's start as always by meeting our three lucky contestants.
WE NOW HAVE SINGLE SHOTS OF EACH CONTESTANT WHO WILL WAVE TO CAMERA AS JR INTRODUCES THEM. MIKE IS 55, MIDDLE-CLASS AND SELF ASSURED. JANICE IS 30, WORKING CLASS AND NERVY.
JR We have Mike Wallis from Merseyside. Mike is a financial adviser, married with two horses and his pastimes include golf, real ale and dressage. (TO MIKE) I've seen dressage on Olympic show-jumping. It's sort of rodeo on prozac. Mike Wallis.
APPLAUSE.

INTERIOR. NAGS HEAD. NIGHT
THE TV CONTINUES SHOWING GOLDRUSH.
JR (ON TV) Next we have Janice Scott from Newquay. Janice is married to Ian and has a three-year-old daughter Meryl. Her hobbies are rock climbing and amateur opera. (TO JANICE) And she's only three?
A 'OH NO' FROM AUDIENCE.
JR (SHOUTS AT AUDIENCE) This is *class*! And finally we have Derek Trotter from Peckham.
AT THIS ALL HEADS TURN TO TV SCREEN. THERE, ON THE SCREEN, WE SEE DEL SMILING AND WAVING TO CAMERA. AS JR CONTINUES OVER, BOYCIE'S JAW DROPS AND HIS CARDS FALL FROM HIS HANDS. DENZIL AND MICKEY P JUST STARE AT SCREEN INCREDULOUSLY.
JR Derek is a businessman who lives with Raquel…
WE SEE RAQUEL AND DAMIEN IN AUDIENCE. RAQUEL IS SMILING NERVOUSLY.
JR (CONTINUES)…his significant other.
RAQUEL'S SMILE DIES.

THE NAGS HEAD
SID'S CIGARETTE FALLS FROM HIS LIPS. MARLENE HAS A LIPSTICK SMUDGE GOING TWO INCHES UP HER FACE AS JR CONTINUES ON SCREEN OVER DEL'S FACE.
JR (ON TV) He has an eleven-year-old son, Damien, and his pastimes include fine wines, the theatre and sixteenth-century Italian Renaissance art. (NOW WITH REF TO DEL'S SUIT AND TIE) Yeah, right!
TRIGGER SMILES.

INTERIOR. THE TROTTERS' LOUNGE. NIGHT
THE TV CONTINUES.
JR (ON TV) As always, we start with the timed round. So let's see who's got the fastest finger.
CASS (OUT OF SIGHT) (FROM BEDROOM) Oooh, Rodney.
INTERIOR . THE *GOLDRUSH* STUDIO. NIGHT
JR (TO CONTESTANTS) Whose famous diary recorded the Plague and the Great Fire of London?
DEL HITS HIS BUTTON FIRST AND CAMERA ZOOMS IN.
DEL Mrs Dale's.

JR IS QUITE STUNNED BY THIS ANSWER. HE TRIES TO TAKE IT IN IN A POLITE A WAY AS POSSIBLE.
JR Good try, Del, but I'm afraid you're wrong. You're frozen at the back of the queue.
JANICE PRESSES HER BUTTON AND CAMERA ZOOMS IN.
JANICE Is it Bridget Jones, Jonathan?
JR Again, so close, Janice, but *so* far! You go to the back, Del you move up one place. Mike, get this right and you'll be the first challenger on the Rainbow Road. (TO AUDIENCE) And what's at the end of the rainbow?
JR, CONTESTANTS AND AUDIENCE A pot of gold!
APPLAUSE.
MIKE I think I know it, Jonathan. It's Adrian Mole's.
JR Oh bad luck, Mike! It was Samuel Pepys. You go to the back of the queue, everyone else moves forward, which means Derek is the first challenger on the Rainbow Road. Del, come and join me.
APPLAUSE, APPLAUSE AS A DELIGHTED DEL WALKS ACROSS AND JOINS JR.

INTERIOR. THE NAGS HEAD. NIGHT
ON SCREEN WE SEE DEL WALKING UP TO JOIN JR. THE FACES OF THE REGULARS GATHERED AROUND THE TV SET ARE NOW FROZEN IN SHOCK.

INTERIOR. THE *GOLDRUSH* STUDIO. NIGHT
WE COME UP ON RAQUEL WHO IS OPEN-MOUTHED IN AMAZEMENT. DAMIEN IS APPLAUDING HIS DAD. DEL IS NOW STANDING WITH JR.
JR First things first, Del, there's your pound. What ever happens that's yours – and welcome to the BBC.
DEL (CHECKS COIN) Make sure it ain't Irish.
JR The rules are simple, which is just as well. You'll be given a series of questions each one having a multiple choice of three answers. With each correct answer you move to another colour of the rainbow and the prize money increases, right the way up to the gold question which is worth one hundred thousand pounds.
DEL Lovely jubbly!
JR But you also have a number of options to help you on your way. You have a Shot in the Dark, you have an SOS or you can Drop One.
LAUGHTER FROM AUDIENCE.
JR (SHOUTS AT AUDIENCE) This is *class*! But be warned, Janice and Mike can play their Aces at any time and challenge you. So, if you're ready, let's play *Goldrush*!
THE LIGHTING IN STUDIO NOW TURNS BLUE AS THE FIRST COLOUR OF THE RAINBOW.

INTERIOR. THE NAGS HEAD. NIGHT
A SHORT TIME LEAP.
THERE IS AN AIR OF ELECTRIC TENSION IN THE PUB. EVERYONE IS NOW DRINKING SPIRITS AND THERE IS A FUG OF SMOKE ALL AROUND. WE CAN SEE DEL ON SCREEN AND HE IS OBVIOUSLY STRUGGLING. THE STUDIO LIGHTING IS NOW YELLOW TO INDICATE DEL'S PROGRESS ALONG THE RAINBOW ROAD.
JR (ON TV) You have 20 seconds left. Which is the highest mountain in Africa – Kilimanjaro or Fuji?
DENZIL (SHOUTS AT SCREEN) It's Kilimanjaro! Any idiot knows that!
TRIGGER I didn't.
BOYCIE Denzil, anyone who has come home from Ibiza with a duty-free brain cell knows it's Kilimanjaro. But this is Derek Trotter.

INTERIOR. THE *GOLDRUSH* STUDIO
DEL IS A STUDY IN PERSPIRATION AS HE PONDERS THE QUESTION.
DEL I'm gonna go with Kilimanjaro.
WE SEE RAQUEL'S RELIEF AT THIS DECISION.
JR Derek, that is the right answer!

A RELIEVED DEL SHAKES HANDS WITH JR AND THEN WIPES THE PERSPIRATION FROM HIS FOREHEAD.

DEL I thought it was, Jonathan, coz Fuji make cameras, don't they?

THE STUDIO LIGHTS TURN INDIGO.

JR Well done. Now let's move up to the next colour and take a look at the two thousand pound question.

INTERIOR. THE *GOLDRUSH* STUDIO
LIGHTING IS NOW RED.

JR Del, you're doing really well. Janice has just challenged you, got it wrong and doubled your money to ten thousand. (THE LIGHTING CHANGES TO GREEN) The next question is worth twenty-five thousand pounds. You've still got a Shot in the Dark and an SOS. Let's look at the question. In which state was President Kennedy when he was assassinated in 1963?

BEFORE JR CAN GIVE THE THREE ANSWERS

DEL Well he was in a terrible state, he died!

SEE RAQUEL'S REACTION TO THIS. JR LOOKS AT DEL AND SHAKES HIS HEAD SLOWLY.

JR You were a little bit too quick there, Del. Let me give you the answers. Was it Texas, Florida or California?

DEL Oh, I see. Sorry… Erm… I think I'll play my Shot in the Dark, Jonathan.

INTERIOR. THE NAGS HEAD. NIGHT
NOW THE BAR IS EVEN MORE CROWDED. THE ATMOSPHERE IS EVEN MORE TENSE AS DEL IS ON THE VERGE OF AN IMPORTANT MILESTONE.

DEL I'll go for Florida.

EVERYONE IN PUB No!

TWO SECONDS LATER.

TRIGGER No!

INTERIOR. THE *GOLDRUSH* STUDIO

JR Del, I'm afraid Florida is wrong. It was Texas. But you played your Shot in the Dark, which means you're still in the game. But you have to answer a penalty question. Get this wrong, you lose the money and you're frozen out of the game. Okay, here's the penalty question. How many wheels does a Reliant Robin have? Is it three, four or two?

DEL IS JUST ONE GREAT BIG SMILE.

INTERIOR. THE *GOLDRUSH* STUDIO
WE SEE THE TENSION ON RAQUEL'S FACE – THIS IS NOW SERIOUS. THE STUDIO LIGHTING IS NOW **VIOLET**.

JR This question is worth fifty thousand pounds. If you're correct these lights will turn to gold – and you'll be answering the one hundred thousand pound question.

DEL IS EXCITED AND VERY EAGER – AS WE WILL SEE, TOO EAGER.

JR For fifty thousand pounds. Which classical guitarist wrote the opera *The Child and the Enchantment*? Was it Ravel, Sergovia or Rodrigo?

DEL I think I know it, Jonathan.

AS HE REPEATS THE ANSWERS DEL GIVES JR THE EYE AND LITTLE NODS OF THE HEAD IN A 'HELP ME OUT' MANNER.

DEL I think it's Ravel… (A LOOK AND A MOVEMENT OF THE EYES TO JR)

JR IS UNMOVED.

DEL Then again I keep thinking it's Sergovia.
(A TINY NOD OF THE HEAD TOWARDS JR. NOTHING IN RETURN)

DEL Of course, it could be Rodrigo?
(ANOTHER EYE-QUESTION. JR GIVES NOTHING)

JR You're right, Del. It's definitely one of those three.

DEL I think I'll try my SOS, Jonathan.

JR I think you're wise. Who would you like to be your saviour?

DEL My brother, Rodney.

INTERIOR. THE TROTTERS' LOUNGE. NIGHT
SILENCE EXCEPT FOR JR AND DEL ON TV

JR (ON TV) And where's Rodney tonight?

DEL (ON TV) He's back at the flat, taking care of business.

FROM THE BEDROOM.

ROD (OUT OF SIGHT) (TOTAL PLEASURE) Aaahhh.

THE PHONE BEGINS RINGING IN LOUNGE.

ROD (OUT OF SIGHT) No! No! No!

CASS (OUT OF SIGHT) You'd better answer it, Roddy.

ROD (OUT OF SIGHT) No, not *now! Leave* it.

CASS (OUT OF SIGHT) But Del said he was expecting a very important call.

ROD (OUT OF SIGHT) Oh bloody hell!

THE BEDROOM DOOR OPENS AND A FURIOUS RODNEY APPEARS. HE IS NOW DOWN TO BOXER SHORTS BUT IS STILL WEARING THE BREASTPLATE AND ONE ARMOURED BOOT AS HE STORMS ACROSS TO PHONE.

INTERIOR. *GOLDRUSH* STUDIO. NIGHT
WE CAN HEAR RINGING TONE IN STUDIO. THE PHONE IS NOW ANSWERED.

ROD (OUT OF SIGHT) (ANGRY) Hello?

JR Is that Rodney?

ROD (OUT OF SIGHT) Yeah.

JR Rodney, this is Jonathan Ross at the Goldrush studio.

ROD (OUT OF SIGHT) Oh piss off, Mickey, I'm getting angry!

JR REACTS. DEL CLOSES HIS EYES AND COVERS HIS FACE WITH HIS HANDS. RAQUEL REACTS. DAMIEN GRINS AT THIS.

THE NAGS HEAD
EVERYONE JUST STARES AT SCREEN IN DEEP SHOCK AT WHAT THEY HAVE JUST HEARD. MICKEY PEARCE AND BOYCIE ARE GRINNING. TRIGGER SMILES.

THE TROTTERS' LOUNGE
RODNEY IS STANDING WITH PHONE IN HAND BUT WITH BACK TO TV SET. CASSANDRA, WHO ALSO IN A STATE OF UNDRESS, LIKE JULIET BRAVO COMING HOME FROM AN ORGY, HAS ENTERED FROM BEDROOM.

ROD (HAND OVER MOUTHPIECE) It's Mickey Pearce pretending to be Jonathan Ross.

CASS Roddy.

CASSANDRA POINTS TO TV WHERE WE SEE DEL AND JR.

ROD Oh my God… (NOW REALLY SUCKING UP) Oh hi, Jonathan, how are you?

THE *GOLDRUSH* STUDIO

DEL (MIMES RODNEY'S TOADYING) Oh hi, Jonathan, how are you?

JR I'm fine. I've got Derek here and he's on twenty five thousand pounds.

ROD (PHONE DISTORT) (INCREDULOUSLY) *You're kidding!*

DEL REACTS – HE'D LIKE TO SMACK RODNEY STRAIGHT IN THE EYE.

JR No, I'm deadly serious. But he's got a problem with the fifty thousand pound question and he's chosen you as his saviour. So listen carefully, you'll have 20 seconds to answer.

DEL Right, listen carefully, Rodney.

ROD (PHONE DISTORT) Hang on, what's in it for me?

WE NOW INTERCUT BETWEEN THE STUDIO AND THE LOUNGE.

DEL I'll give you a drink! Now, listen. Which classical guitarist wrote the opera *The Child and the Enchantment*? Was it Ravel, Sergovia or Rodrigo?

ROD (ON PHONE)…Ravel.

DEL How sure are you?

ROD (ON PHONE) One hundred percent, Derek.

DEL Good boy, Rodders.

PHONE GOES DEAD.

ROD Take it away, Derek!

RODNEY AND CASSANDRA NOW WATCH TV.

ROD (TO CASSANDRA) I know my classics.

DEL It's Ravel, Jonathan.

JR You don't have to take his answer.

DEL No, he knows what he's talking about… It's Ravel.

JR Del… It's wrong. It was Sergovia.

SEE RODNEY'S TERRIFIED FACE. DEL IS BEMUSED AND CONFUSED.

DEL But Rodney said it was Ravel.

JR Bad luck, Del.

DEL But he's got GCEs in Maths and Art.

JR Del, you've used all your options, you've lost all your money, you're frozen out. Janice, join me on the Rainbow Road.

WE SEE RAQUEL'S DEEP DISAPPOINTMENT. AS JANICE JOINS JR WE SEE DEL IN THE BACKGROUND WALKING AWAY DEFEATED. HE TURNS BACK JUST HOPING SOMETHING MIGHT HAPPEN TO SAVE HIM, AND THEN CONTINUES HIS WALK INTO OBLIVION.

INTERIOR. TROTTERS' LOUNGE. NIGHT.
FOUR HOURS LATER. RODNEY AND CASSANDRA, BOTH NOW IN NORMAL CLOTHES, PACE THE ROOM AWAITING THE VENGEANCE.

ROD I was… I was… I was so certain it was Ravel…

CASS Roddy, you did your best.

ROD Yeah, I did… Del seemed to be okay, didn't he?

CASS No. He kicked the podium over as he left the set.

ROD No, I think that was an accident.

CASS No, he kicked it – it fell over! Jonathan Ross picked it up.

WE HEAR THE FRONT DOOR SLAM. THE HALL DOOR OPENS AND DAMIEN ENTERS. HE GIVES RODNEY A CONDEMNING SNEER. NOW RAQUEL ENTERS. SHE SIMPLY STARES AT RODNEY.

ROD (A SIMPERING SMILE) All right?

RAQ (A VINEGARY SMILE) Yeah! You?

ROD Where's Del?

RAQ I haven't a clue, Rodney. At the end of the show he disappeared. He just went off into the night and abandoned his child and his wi… his significant other – in an area of London we've never been in before.

ROD (RELIEVED) Oh, thank Christ!

RAQ Thankfully the studio paid for a cab home. I'm gonna make a coffee.

CASS (SHE WANTS TO DISCUSS) Raquel…

RAQ (TOO UPSET TO SPEAK) *Don't!* We're friends.

RAQUEL EXITS TO KITCHEN.

DAMIEN I don't know why my Dad didn't have Trigger as his SOS.

CASS Because Trigger wouldn't have had a clue!

DAMIEN Yeah, (REF TO RODNEY) And he was spot on, weren't he?

DAMIEN EXITS TO BEDROOMS AREA. WE NOW HEAR FRONT DOOR SLAM. RODNEY STANDS ERECT LIKE A GUARDSMAN – A GUARDSMAN WHO'S ABOUT TO FACE NAPOLEON'S CAVALRY. DEL ENTERS FROM HALL. HE HAS OBVIOUSLY HAD TOO MUCH TO DRINK. RAQUEL ENTERS FROM KITCHEN.

RAQ What the hell happened to you?

DEL (A BIT BELLIGERENT) I went out!

RAQ (EQUALLY BELLIGERENT) Oh good. Long as I know!

DEL All right, Rodney? And what sorta evening you had?

ROD Not very good, to be honest.

DEL No? Well, bloody snap! You Moby!

ROD Del, I honestly believed it was Ravel. So did Cassandra, didn't yer?

RODNEY NODS TO CASSANDRA 'PLEASE HELP ME'.

CASS Yeah, I did as well.

DEL Well you're both dipsticks then! I'll tell you another thing, you're never borrowing my Capri again.

ROD Yeah. Well, that bone marrow – you can forget it!

DEL Everyone knows Ravel makes shoes!

CASS *What*?

ROD Shoes? Oh, the shoes shops in the… yeah, right!

DEL It was a trick question and you fell for it!

ROD I'm sorry. Still, at least you won a… a pound.

DEL That didn't even pay for me bus fare home. Anyway, after the show I went out to a few clubs to drown me sorrow. (MOMENTARILY FORGETS RAQUEL IS THERE AND ALMOST ADMITS TO CHATTING UP A LAP DANCER) I was in one club and I was talking this lap… this lap… lap… lap… lap… laptop salesman. And even he knew it wasn't Ravel! (TO RAQ) Fancy a drink, sweetheart?

RAQ No!

RAQUEL EXITS TO KITCHEN.

DEL I'm gonna go and have a word with my beloved Raquel. Don't go away!

DEL EXITS TO KITCHEN

ROD (TO CASS) For the rest of my entire life, getting that question wrong – in front of my family, and friends, and the entire British nation, is gonna be the most embarrassing thing that's ever happened to me.

NOW FROM KITCHEN WE HEAR.

RAQ (OUT OF SIGHT) (LAUGHING) *Russell Crowe*?

WE HEAR DEL AND RAQUEL LAUGHING.

ROD Or maybe not!

THE PHONE STARTS RINGING. RODNEY PICKS THE PHONE UP AS DEL AND RAQUEL ENTER FROM KITCHEN.

ROD (ANSWERS PHONE) Yeah, who is it? Who shall I says calling? (NOW WORRIED) Yes, hold on a moment! (HAND OVER MOUTHPIECE)(TO DEL) It's the producer of *Goldrush*. He wants to talk to you.

DEL What's he want? It's that poxy podium, annit? I bet someone's damaged it! (TAKES PHONE) Hello? Yes, this is me. Now, about your podium…

DEL'S FACE NOW CHANGES TO ONE OF AMAZEMENT – TOTAL AMAZEMENT – AS THE NEWS IS RELATED TO HIM.

DEL (ON PHONE) No!… No!… (LEAVES MOUTHPIECE FREE SO CALLER CAN HEAR) You won't believe this! They made a *mistake*! It *was* Ravel all along!

ROD, RAQ, CASS No!

ROD I *knew* I was right!

DEL He says I can keep the fifty grand *and* go back on the show!

ROD, RAQ, CASS (INSTANT CELEBRATION) *Yes!*

DEL PLACES HIS HAND OVER MOUTHPIECE.

DEL Have a day off you lot, will yer? Who'd you think this *really* is?

WE HEAR MOANS OF DISAPPOINTMENT AS THE TERRIBLE TRUTH DAWNS.

ROD Bloody Mickey Pearce! I'm gonna murder him.

DEL Leave it to me. (ON PHONE) We'd like you to give all the money to charity. And if you phone this flat once more I'll come down there and turn your arse into shredded duck.

REPLACES THE RECEIVER WITH CHEERS FROM THE OTHERS.

INTERIOR. THE *GOLDRUSH* STUDIOS. NIGHT

THE PRODUCER REPLACES HIS TELEPHONE RECEIVER.

PRODUCER (STUNNED) Jonathan. He said give the fifty grand to charity.

WE FIND JONATHAN ROSS SEATED ON STAGE.

JR You're kidding! Oh, what a nice guy.

INTERIOR. THE TROTTERS' LOUNGE. NIGHT

DESPITE HAVING JUST LOST FIFTY GRAND THERE IS AN AIR OF CELEBRATION HAVING, AS THEY BELIEVE, JUST PISSED MICKEY PEARCE OFF.

DEL When are people gonna learn? We're the Trotters – and we're *back*!

ROD Yes!

DEL AND RODNEY HIGH FIVE (OR EVERYONE). FREEZE.

Peckham
Photo,
Gallery

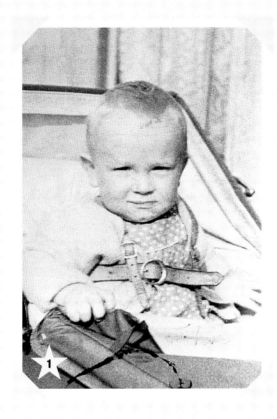

1. Aged seven months

2. John as a 15 year old

3. A serious-looking John Sullivan, aged 23

4. Present day

1. David Jason (back row, 2nd from right) with the rest of the company appearing at Bournemouth Pier in 1967

2. An early publicity shot

3. David Jason (far left) appears in *Honeymoon Bedlam* at Bournemouth Pier in 1967

4. A promotional poster for the Bournemouth production

5. David Jason whilst on location in Bristol for *Only Fools and Horses*

SUMMER ENTERTAINMENT AT THE PIER THEATRE

PIER Theatre

BY ARRANGEMENT
IN ASSOCIATION WITH
BERNARD DELFONT

The BRIAN RIX
Theatre of Laughter
presents

A SEASON OF TWO FARCES

DICK EMERY

NORMAN BORCE

PAULINE BARKER

DAVID BROWNING

GEORGE MOON

JOHN NEWBURY

'Honeymoon Bedlam!'
'Chase Me, Comrade!'

DAVID JASON

DOROTHY VERNON

1. Aged 14, Nicholas played the lead in BBC's *The Prince and the Pauper*

2. Nicholas takes time out to go fishing whilst away on location filming 'The Jolly Boys' Outing'

3. Playing Rodney

4. Nicholas played two roles in *The Prince and the Pauper*

1. Posing for a publicity shot

2. Donning uniform in *The Island*

3. Lennard making an early stage appearance at Cambridge

4. During school days

5. Lennard (far right) was best man at the wedding of Stephen Ward in India in 1943. He was serving with the Bengal Entertainments Services Association

1. Buster (left) holidaying with his parents

2. He became Southern Command boxing champion in 1945

3. In April 1942, Buster married his

4. He turned to acting professionally upon retiring from his position as a bank manager in Thames Ditton

1. Tessa during her drama-school days

2. Posing for a publicity shot

3. Appearing in *Charley's Aunt*, her first professional stage play

4. A present day portrait

1. Enjoying a day
on the beach

2. Gwyneth
played Jan in the
children's series
The Flocton Flyer

3. Playing
Cassandra in
one of Gwyneth's
favourite jobs of
all time'

4. A present day
portrait

1. John, aged two

2. Enjoying a day-trip to Weston-super-Mare in 1950

3. John in 1972, aged 30

4. A 1995 portrait

5. John in 1986, aged 44

1. Donning a beret at seven months

2. Sue, aged ten, in her acrobatic dancing days

3. Competing as a horse-mad teenager

4. Soon after leaving drama school, Sue appeared as Sally Bowles in *Cabaret*

5. With her children, Harriet and Freddie, in 1987

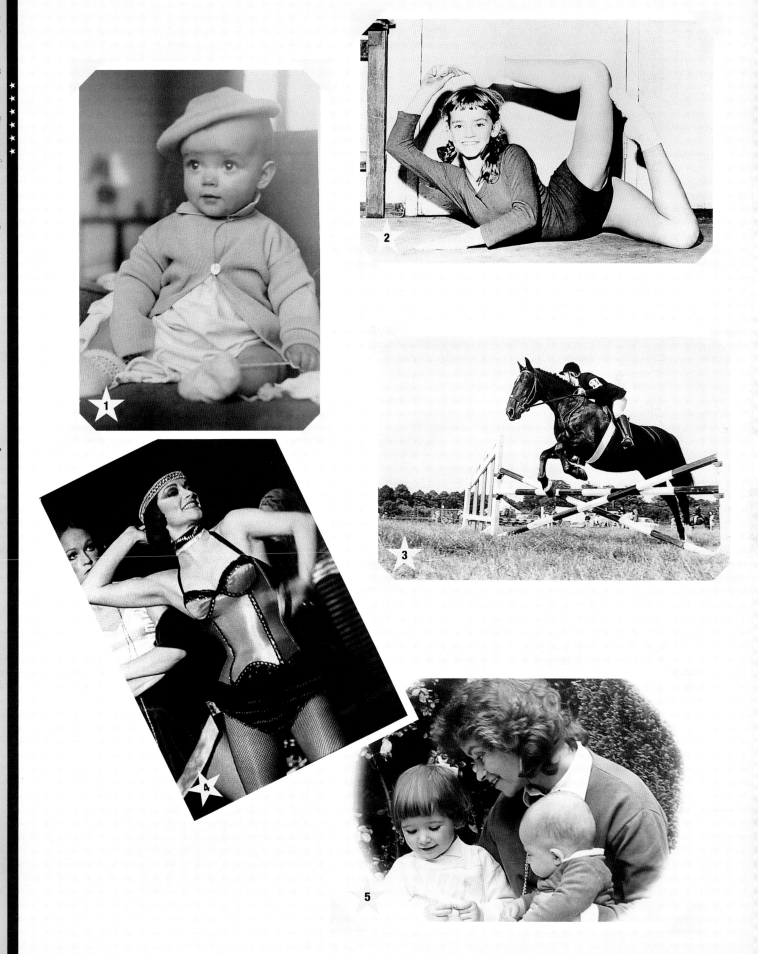

1

2

1. Roger as a toddler in 1946, with his parents in the background

2. Smartly dressed in 1947

3. A 1966 portrait

4. Enjoying a paddle with his brother, Chris (right), at Herne Bay, 1953

5. Donning a flat cap in 1963

4

3

5

1 Playing a
[den]tist in a 1976
[pro]duction of
[Pla]za Suite with
[the] Woodley
[Pla]yers

2 Roy in his
[on]e-man show
[Aft]er Agincourt
[in 1]977

3 Roy (far right)
[ap]pearing in The
[Am]orous Prawn

4 An early
[19]70s
[ap]pearance for
[the] Woodley
[Pla]yers in Say
[Wh]o You Are

5 Another scene
[fro]m The
[Am]orous Prawn

1. As a baby in 1950

2. First communion, with his parents, in 1958

3. In 1970 Ken appeared in *Spring Head Jack* at the National Youth Theatre

4. Ken, in 1955, aged four

5. At home with his family (wife Sheila, son William and daughter Charlotte) in 1990

1

2

3

1 A teenager
in Liverpool

2 An early
portrait

3 Paul made
his stage debut
in Hair

4 A recent shot

5 A scene from
BBC's crime
series Gangsters
with Paul playing
Aileson

4

5

Bibliography

The following publications have proved useful sources of information whilst writing this book.

BEASLEY, JOHN D, *The Story of Peckham – London Borough of Southwark, Neighbourhood Histories No.3,* second edition, Council of the London Borough of Southwark, 1983, ISBN 0905849051

CLARK, STEVE, *The Only Fools and Horses Story,* BBC, 1998, ISBN 056338445X

HAYWARD, ANTHONY, *Who's Who on Television,* Boxtree, 1996, ISBN 075221067X

LEWISOHN, MARK, *Guide to TV Comedy,* BBC, 1998, ISBN 0563369779

MERRYFIELD, BUSTER, *During the War and other encounters,* Summersdale, 1996, ISBN 1873475543

Quarterly newsletter produced by Perry and the team running the Only Fools and Horses Appreciation Society

The extensive internet database www.imdb.com